Praise for

Internet Measurement:

Infrastructure, Traffic, and Applications

This extraordinary book is a change in the way of viewing the Internet. By providing useful and ready-to-apply measurement techniques, it allows a shift from qualitative perception toward quantificational perception of a complex system such as the Internet. Measurement is one foundational approach critical to the advance of both science and engineering. Though the book focuses on the field of Internet measurement, its comprehensive treatment of both theoretical and practical issues applies to many other fields of computer science and engineering as well. Highly recommended!

> — Virgílio Almeida
> Professor of Computer Science, Federal University of Minas Gerais

The area of Internet Measurement has made significant progress over the last ten years, providing us with new ways to understand, operate and improve the Internet. This book brings together the major methods, discoveries and applications of Internet measurement in a coherent textbook that will be equally useful to students, researchers, and practitioners.

> — Constantine Dovrolis
> Assistant Professor, Georgia Institute of Technology

This book is a gem! Written by two of the leading researchers/practitioners in the field of Internet measurement this book provides readable, thorough and insightful coverage of both the principles and the practice of network measurement. It's a "must read" for everyone interested in the field.

> — James Kurose
> Distinguished University Professor, University of Massachusetts, Amherst

"Internet Measurement," by Crovella and Krishnamurthy, lives up to the promise of its title. People with no experience in the area will find a discussion both broad – covering the range of internet measurement – and deep – exploring many issues in great detail – helping them locate those parts of the field most relevant to them. People well versed in the area will appreciate having so much information organized in one volume. And, researchers working in the area of Internet measurement will undoubtedly learn from this book, and will have lots to say about the points made by the authors.

> — Greg Minshall

A comprehensive reference source for Internet traffic measurement. Highly recommended for the next generation of networking researchers.

> — Carey Williamson
> iCORE Chair, University of Calgary

Internet Measurement

Internet Measurement

Infrastructure, Traffic, and Applications

Mark Crovella
Balachander Krishnamurthy

John Wiley & Sons, Ltd

Other Wiley Editorial Offices

John Wiley & Sons Inc., 111 River Street, Hoboken, NJ 07030, USA

Jossey-Bass, 989 Market Street, San Francisco, CA 94103-1741, USA

Wiley-VCH Verlag GmbH, Boschstr. 12, D-69469 Weinheim, Germany

John Wiley & Sons Australia Ltd, 33 Park Road, Milton, Queensland 4064, Australia

John Wiley & Sons (Asia) Pte Ltd, 2 Clementi Loop #02-01, Jin Xing Distripark, Singapore 129809

John Wiley & Sons Canada Ltd, 22 Worcester Road, Etobicoke, Ontario, Canada M9W 1L1

Wiley also publishes its books in a variety of electronic formats. Some content that appears in print may not be
available in electronic books.

Library of Congress Cataloging-in-Publication Data
Crovella, Mark.
  Internet measurement : infrastructure, traffic, and applications / Mark
Crovella, Balachander Krishnamurthy.
      p. cm.
  Includes bibliographical references and index.
  ISBN 13 978-0-470-01461-5 (cloth)
   ISBN 10 0-470-01461-X (cloth)

1. Internet--Statistical methods.
2. Telecommunication--Traffic--Management. I. Krishnamurthy,
Balachander,
1961-
II. Title.
 TK5105.875.I57C774 2006
 004.67'8--dc22
                              2006007168
British Library Cataloguing in Publication Data

A catalogue record for this book is available from the British Library

ISBN 13: 978-0-470-01461-5
ISBN 10: 0-470-01461-X

Printed and bound in Great Britain by Antony Rowe Ltd, Chippenham.
This book is printed on acid-free paper responsibly manufactured from sustainable forestry
in which at least two trees are planted for each one used for paper production.

To my wonderful children: Benjamin, Emily, Ian, and Colin

—Mark Crovella

Dedicated with affection, gratitude, and respect to the memories of

மஹாலிங்கம் பஞ்ஜாபகேசன்

ஜானகிராமன் கௌரிகாந்தன்

—Balachander Krishnamurthy

Under France's Ancien Regime, the foot had varying lengths depending on where one lived; furthermore it could divided into a variable number of inches. The Convention, which had proclaimed the (first) French Republic in 1792, introduced the meter in 1795 as the ten-millionth part of the meridian circle between the North Pole and the Equator. To acquaint the public with the new unit of measure, 16 marble standard meters were installed in the busiest parts of Paris in 1796 and 1797. This is the only example still in its original position; it is at 36, rue de Vaugirard, Paris 6eme.

Contents

List of Tables

List of Figures

Acknowledgments

We would like to thank many people for their time, interest, and willingness to help us with the book. The reviewers are not responsible for any errors in the book. We thank them for answering questions, reading draft versions of the chapters, and giving valuable feedback.

We thank Carey Williamson for his review of the entire book and numerous thoughtful comments. Our thanks to Greg Minshall for his complete read and for providing valuable feedback on a number of topics.

We also thank Paul Barford and Dina Papagiannaki for their reviews of several chapters and useful suggestions. We also thank the various reviewers who reviewed on behalf of the publisher including Constantine Dovrolis, Chen-Nee Chuah, Russell Clark, Yan Chen, and Anat Bremler Barr.

The comments of David Poole (Chapter 3), Supratik Bhattacharyya (Chapter 4), Constantine Dovrolis (Chapters 5, 6, and 10), Walter Willinger and Matthew Roughan (Chapter 6), Anees Shaikh, Michael Rabinovich, and Craig Wills (Chapter 7), Duane Wessels (Chapter 7, on DNS), Yatin Chawathe (Chapter 7, on P2P), Jacobus van der Merwe (Chapter 7, on multimedia), Mark Claypool (Chapter 7, on networked games), Greg Minshall, Lorrie Cranor, Martin Arlitt, and Jeffrey Mogul (Chapter 8), Mark Allman and Henk Uijterwaal (Chapter 10) were very helpful. They took time off their busy schedules to give detailed feedback electronically and in many cases face to face. We thank them for the same.

We thank Jay Borkenhagen for his insights on a variety of topics related to evolution of ISPs and their internal engineering and Kavé Salamatian for discussions concerning the nature of Internet modeling. Wu-Chang Feng's detailed comments on the networked games section were very helpful. Duane Wessels provided valuable help on DNS and answered several questions.

We also thank Roy Arends, Martin Arlitt, Grenville Armitage, Steven Bellovin, Andre Broido, Nevil Brownlee, Benoit Claise, Edith Cohen, Michalis Faloutsos, Chris Frazier, Emden Gansner, Tristan Henderson, Sugih Jamin, Leonard Kleinrock, Eric Kolaczyk, George Kollios, Anukool Lakhina, Carsten Lund, David Meyer, Jörg Micheel, Mikhail Mikhailov, Michael Mitzenmacher, Mark Nottingham,

Andrew Odlyzko, Jitendra Padhye, Dave Plonka, Jürgen Quittek, Sylvia Ratnasamy, Matthew Roughan, Henning Schulzrinne, Aman Shaikh, Oliver Spatscheck, Paul Vixie, Jim Xu, and Artur Ziviani for answering various questions.

We would like to thank Jonathan Shipley at Wiley for shepherding our book through the editorial process. We also thank Vivian Ward, Deborah Egleton, Sam Crowe, Claire Jardine, David Barnard, and Sarah Lewis for their help in processing the book. Our thanks also to Gaynor Redvers-Mutton who assisted us early on.

Mark wrote portions of this book at Boston University with support from Sprint, Intel, and the National Science Foundation (NSF), and portions while he was on sabbatical at the Laboratoire d'Informatique de Paris 6 (LIP6) with support from Centre National de la Recherche Scientifique (CNRS). Both institutions are exciting intellectual environments and wonderful places to work; I thank my colleagues on both sides of the Atlantic for their support and encouragement. Most importantly, I have depended on my family and friends at many times and in many ways as I wrote this book and I want to thank them (you know who you are!) from the bottom of my heart.

Balachander would like to thank AT&T Labs–Research management, especially David Belanger, for his encouragement. Thanks to tnn for keeping me supplied with my drugs of choice: r adams, j farrar, and rare bruce juice. Thanks to Karthik L for the carnatica cornucopia. It was a pleasure to partner with Wendy on the cover design. Thanks to mjs for being an able attorney and a better friend, albeit one suffering from a pollyannish optimism of ever surpassing me in the ranks of bumhood. Balachander wrote this book on an IBM Thinkpad T-41P running Linux, in several places around the world; the hosts in various places deserve thanks including Chris and Mary Malley, Rob Mason; special thanks to Cristina Ruggieri for the extended use of her mother's house south of Il colle Aventino.

Part I

Background

1

Introduction

The Internet is a communication network connecting digital devices. It is remarkably versatile, moving information among a vast diversity of desktop computers, super-computers, personal digital assistants, satellites, spacecraft, cellular phones, sensors, wireless devices, embedded systems, and other systems. Indeed, almost any form of digital electronics can be provided with an Internet connection.

As a result, the Internet has become a globally pervasive 'nervous system' for electronic information processing. It connects devices and networks in all continents and in virtually every country, and it permeates many walks of life. The Internet is used for personal communication, for commercial enterprise, for public dissemination of information, and for transmission of secret data. Information on the Internet is exchanged in multiple languages and alphabets. Digital media is distributed through the Internet in text, audio and video formats. Electronic commerce is used daily in many countries to sell virtually any product.

Accordingly, the Internet is a huge system. The first Internet node was installed in 1969 as part of a research project; at the current time (2006) there are hundreds of millions of devices connected to the Internet. The Internet is no longer a research project; current traffic estimates on the Internet range up to several petabytes a day, and the Internet is still growing rapidly. In the near future it will undoubtedly continue to expand in both size and functionality.

One might presume that a system as important as the Internet – with as much impact on society and as much future potential – would be well understood. In fact, while the building blocks of the Internet (its protocols and individual components) are the subject of intensive study and design effort, the immense global entity that is the Internet today has not been precisely characterized. Many quantitative measures of the Internet are simply absent.

There are a number of reasons for this state of affairs. First of all, the physical structure of the Internet is not the result of any centralized design or plan. The Internet has been built by a large set of independent organizations, often having somewhat different goals. In addition, its construction has taken place (relatively speaking) quite quickly – the vast majority of Internet infrastructure has been installed since the early 1990s.

Another reason for our limited knowledge about the Internet is that the network is dynamic. It is constantly changing in size, configuration, traffic, and application mix. Traffic and application mix vary dramatically in different parts of the network. Devices are moved about, and are frequently connected and disconnected from the network. Even when good measures of some Internet properties are known at one time or in one location, these measures may not apply elsewhere or in the future.

Technical and social factors also affect our ability to quantify the Internet's properties. Internet devices do not always provide the kind of measurements that are most useful for understanding the network. Many useful measures of Internet behavior are hidden from view, in some cases because the architecture of the Internet itself interferes. Collecting measurements of the Internet can result in huge datasets that are difficult to store, transfer, process, and analyze. Commercial service providers often do not share information about the internal details of their networks. Some forms of Internet measurement can violate privacy and raise security concerns.

Finally, the Internet shows a number of unusual statistical properties that complicate measurement attempts. These impose the need for extra care in taking and analyzing Internet measurements, and require the use of nonstandard statistical methods.

All of these factors complicate and impede Internet measurement, and have led to a scarcity of quantitative characterizations of the Internet. Unanswered Internet measurement questions span a diverse range. Some are very general and basic questions, such as "How big is the Internet?" and "How much traffic flows over the Internet?" However, many more practical and immediately useful facts are also unknown: "What is the structure of the Internet? What are the statistical properties of network traffic? What demands do different applications place on the network?" At lower levels of detail, network users and engineers often lack answers to even more specific questions about network properties, such as "What is the capacity of the path to my server?" and "How much peer-to-peer traffic is flowing on my network?"

However, all hope is not lost. There has been an immense amount of effort expended in recent years on various aspects of Internet measurement. Significant progress has been made on many fronts. Important aspects of the Internet's structure have been measured, at least in part, and some general understanding of how the network is organized is starting to emerge. Network traffic has been studied and many aspects of its statistics have been clarified. Applications such as the Web have been characterized and their properties have been documented.

More importantly, there have been considerable achievements in understanding the specific challenges presented by Internet measurement, and in developing tools and methods to overcome those challenges. Tools are available for a wide range of Internet measurement tasks, and general methods have been developed to overcome many of the challenges presented in Internet measurement. As result, ongoing measurement of the Internet is becoming easier, and our ability to quantify and characterize the Internet is improving.

This book is about the field of Internet measurement. It covers the goals of various kinds of Internet measurements, the challenges that are presented by Internet measurement, the methods and tools that have been developed to facilitate Internet measurement, and the results that have been obtained to date in measuring the Internet.

1.1   Why Measure the Internet?

Why are Internet measurements important? The answer varies; many different people and organizations have an interest in measuring the network or in obtaining Internet measurements. But broadly speaking, interest in Internet measurements arises for three kinds of reasons: commercial, social, and technical.

Commercially, the ability to sell a product or provide information about a product to a large number of people requires a variety of Internet measurements. For example, demographic information is important: what is the reach of the Internet? How many individuals are connected in a given area? What fraction of users have high-speed connectivity and how many are dependent on dial-up connectivity? Where should network access points be placed? Will users with wireless connectivity be able to access the Internet?

Effective commerce on the Internet also requires an understanding of the network's performance properties. How long do Web pages take to download from a vendor's site? What is the capacity of the path from a customer to a vendor's Web server? How often do network problems prevent efficient transfer of information through the network? In fact these questions are so important that a number of companies have been created to provide answers, via services or products.

Socially, the need for statistics is clear: understanding the amount of network activity involving various sites and protocols gives considerable insight into social issues. Governments, scientists, and corporations may desire to have information about social implications of Internet use.

For example, popular Web sites attract a considerable amount of traffic. Given the millions of sites from which information may be available, it is important to have characterizations of popularity and content. In another example, emerging protocols are indicators of popularity of a new application. This is shown by the sudden appearance of Napster and later KaZaa, which pointed to the imminent explosion in file sharing.

Finally, there are many technical reasons for Internet measurement. The design of network components and protocols is strongly driven by the nature of Internet workloads. For example, router designs depend strongly on the statistical properties of network traffic and packet size distribution. The statistical properties of Web pages influence the performance and design of Web servers and browsers. Understanding the topology of the network helps identify the places where performance problems may arise and how applications may choose to adapt to the network. The popularity of new applications (such as network games) leads to efforts to build variants (new games). The popularity of new applications can also drive improvements to associated protocols – as in the case of the explosion of Web traffic, which motivated the improvement of the basic HTTP/1.0 protocol to yield HTTP/1.1.

1.2   How to Read this Book

Thus, the growing interest in Internet measurement is not surprising. In general, a need for metrics often signals the emergence of a discipline. The ability to measure is crucial to systematically capture a body of knowledge. The goal of this book is to present what is known about the emerging field of Internet measurement.

Although the field of Internet measurement is relatively new, there are already a vast set of results in the area. It is a considerable challenge to organize a body of work as large as that in this book. We have adopted an approach based on a number of principles.

First, we have divided the 'things being measured' into three areas:

Infrastructure. This includes things like links and routers, and their interconnection patterns and various properties. It also includes properties that arise due to the interaction of traffic with the network, such as delay, loss, and throughput.
Traffic. This covers traffic measurement of all kinds, including traffic volume and higher-level characterizations.
Applications. This looks at the most important applications: DNS, Web, peer-to-peer, and online games.

Within each of these three areas, we have organized the topics into four parts:

Properties. This reviews the properties and metrics that are important to measure in this area. For example, in the case of traffic one may seek to measure bytes or packets per unit time, among other metrics.
Challenges. This discusses the various difficulties that arise when trying to mea-

sure the above properties. Example challenges include the inability to determine network topology due to lack of accurate measurement methods.

Tools. This covers the methods and tools that have been developed to measure properties and overcome the above challenges, where possible. Example tools are path capacity measurement methods, or inference techniques to supply missing data.

State of the Art. This summarizes what is known about the properties of interest in today's (2006) Internet. For example, the known statistical properties of Internet traffic are covered.

Here we must note a caveat: the Internet changes at a fast pace. Any attempt to present 'State of the Art' in Internet measurements is certain to be quickly outdated, at least in some aspects. In state of the art discussions we have tried to emphasize the properties that seem to be relatively invariant (or slowly changing) in time. However, material in these sections is likely to have a shorter shelf life than the rest of the book.

Organization of the Book. Having discussed the structuring principles we have used, we can now review the organization of the book. The general organization of the book is shown in Figure 1.1.

In the figure, dotted arrows represent various options for reasonable starting points (we discuss these options later). Solid arrows represent how chapters depend on each other. An arrow from Chapter A to Chapter B means that Chapter B assumes familiarity with concepts or topics introduced in Chapter A (and all Chapter A's predecessors).

Part I consists of Chapters 1 through 4. These chapters provide background material that is necessary to understand before the body of the book can begin. The first chapter after this one, **Chapter 2**, provides an introduction to the architecture of the Internet. It covers the organizational principles of the Internet at an introductory level, providing the reader who has little previous knowledge of the Internet enough background to understand what follows in the rest of the book. **Chapter 3** covers the analytic tools needed to discuss Internet measurements in a formal way, covering basics in linear algebra, probability models, statistics, and graph theory. As with Chapter 2, the coverage is not thorough, but provides sufficient foundation for topics later in the book. Note however that the sections on probability, statistics, and graph theory each include subsections entitled "Special Issues in the Internet." These cover topics that arise particularly in Internet measurement and should be read even if one is already familiar with the basics in this chapter. **Chapter 4** covers the pragmatics of Internet measurement: where and how measurements can be taken, how time is measured, what existing sources of data already exist, and how measurements are taken at different layers.

Part II represents the body of the book, which is organized according to the principles mentioned above. It consists of Chapters 5 to 7. **Chapter 5** covers infras-

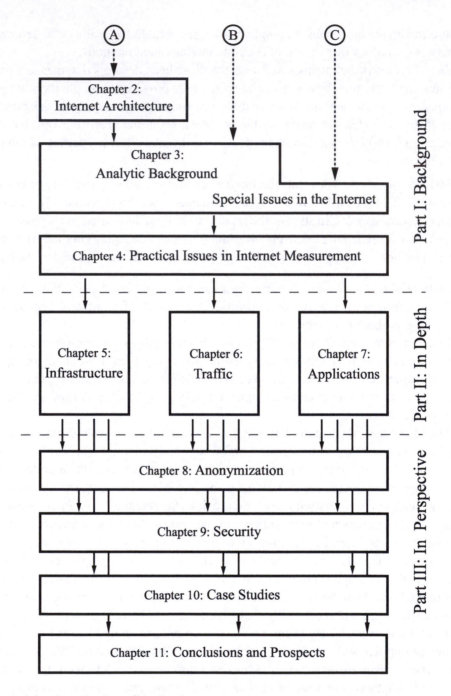

Figure 1.1   Organization of the Book.

tructure, **Chapter 6** covers traffic, and **Chapter 7** covers applications. Within each of these chapters subject matter is organized according to Properties, Challenges, Tools, and State of the Art.

Part III covers material that spans multiple areas. It consists of Chapters 8 to 11. **Chapter 8** covers methods for removing sensitive information from measured data: anonymization. Anonymization can be needed when any kind of measurements are shared – infrastructure, traffic, or application measurements. **Chapter 9** covers ways in which Internet measurements can be used in the area of security. The need for security oriented analysis of Internet measurements has grown as the importance of the Internet has increased, and as the volume and variety of attacks has grown. Next, **Chapter 10** looks at some examples of Internet measurement in practice. It looks at some specific software tools that have been developed for Internet measurement, and some specific large-scale projects that are focused on Internet measurement. Finally, **Chapter 11** concludes with an attempt to review where the field of Internet measurement has come from, and (to the extent possible) where it is going.

Paths Through the Book. This book can be read in different ways depending on the reader's background and goals. We expect this book to be useful to networking practitioners, to new and seasoned researchers in Internet measurement, and to outside experts such as statisticians and physicists with an interest in the field.

First of all, readers coming from outside the field of networking can start at **A** in Figure 1.1. This provides the necessary background in networking for the non-specialist.

Readers with a basic understanding of networking (equivalent to an undergraduate course in computer networks) can start at **B** in Figure 1.1, i.e., skip Chapter 2 and begin at Chapter 3.

Furthermore, if the reader is grounded in the analytic methods covered in Chapter 3, most of the chapter can be skipped; however, the three subsections entitled "Special Issues in the Internet" should be read regardless. This is entry point **C**. Graduate students in computer science will probably want to start here.

Leaving the "Background" chapters, the "In Depth" chapters are relatively independent of each other. Readers having a special interest in one topic (for example, a reader looking for a review of Internet traffic measurement) can move directly to the chapter of interest. Furthermore, readers already having a background in Internet measurement can turn directly to the sections of interest in Chapters 5 through 11.

Finally the "In Perspective" chapters cover topics that relate to multiple areas. Anonymization and security connect in various ways to infrastructure, traffic, and applications. The case studies involve tools and projects addressing multiple areas as well. These chapters are best read after most or all of Part II.

1.3   Resources for More Information

At many places throughout this book we note texts and references to the research literature that provide more information about topics at hand. As already mentioned, this literature is extensive; we have attempted to restrict citations to key papers in each area, but nonetheless our bibliography runs to around 900 entries. This large set of references is needed because almost all of the literature in this area is in the form of RFCs and research papers in journals, conferences, and workshops. There are few or no prior books that extensively cover our topics. As such, there are many topics in the book which can only be covered completely by combining information from a large number of papers or other publications.

Where possible we have tried to cite journal papers rather than conference papers, and conference papers rather than workshop papers. This is in the expectation that journal papers represent the most polished results in an area, and that they should have the longest shelf life. Likewise, conference papers are often more rigorously reviewed than workshop papers. We also reference many RFCs, which represent relatively durable sources of information and are often needed for in-depth understanding of certain protocols.

It is clear that Internet measurement is a rapidly advancing field. New developments on most of the topics in this book are appearing regularly. Here we note where to look for ongoing and future work in the field.

The *Internet Measurement Conference* (IMC) has a purview most closely related to the focus of this book. It began as a small workshop in 2001 and 2002, became a larger conference in 2003, and has taken place annually since then. This is a high-quality conference; in recent years it has selected its program of about 35 papers from about 150 submissions. The conference has grown dramatically in submissions and attendance since its inception; the growth of IMC is indicative of the increasing level of research interest in Internet measurement.

Another venue that has this topic as its primary focus is the *Passive and Active Measurement* (PAM) workshop. The focus of PAM is to present up-and-coming work and serve as an early testbed to discuss ideas. There has been considerable work relating to measurement infrastructure hardware that has primarily been presented in this venue. There has been significant growth in submissions and attendance in PAM as well.

Internet measurement topics have been addressed in the broader networking literature as well. The Infocom conference is broad and generally has a more analytic bent than other networking conferences. It has featured measurement-related research work in several areas of link-level, flow-level, and bandwidth measurements, as well as topology modeling. The ACM SIGMETRICS conference has a focus on measurement issues in computer systems in general, and as such covers topics in Internet measurement (as well as a number of topics outside the scope of this book). Finally, ACM SIGCOMM focuses on all aspects related to network communication and protocols, and has presented papers that include an Internet measurement component.

The flagship journal in computer networking is *IEEE/ACM Transactions on Networking*, which has published many significant papers on Internet measurement. Other journals sometimes carrying results in Internet measurement are *Computer Communication Review* and *Computer Networks*.

2

Internet Architecture

To measure the Internet properly and to correctly interpret the results of Internet measurement, it is essential to understand the Internet's architecture. The design of the Internet affects our ability to measure it, and determines many of the questions that we seek to answer via measurement. Furthermore, measurement results cannot be interpreted accurately unless we keep in mind the details of how the Internet actually works.

In this chapter we lay the groundwork for a solid understanding of Internet measurement. We first cover the Internet architecture at the level of basic organizational principles. Next we dive into a more detailed view of how the Internet operates. We then turn to the major protocols used in the Internet and describe their features, with particular attention to aspects that bear on measurement. Finally, we survey some of the main applications used in the Internet.

A complete description of the Internet's organization involves many details that cannot be covered here; instead we provide only a set of simplified essentials that are necessary for effective Internet measurement. For more details on the topics in this chapter, there are a number of sources: for a detailed overview of the Internet's design, see [KR00]; the design of TCP (a key protocol) is presented in [Ste93]; more information on routing is in [Hui95]; more details on network devices are in [Per99]; and a discussion of Internet design principles is presented in [Cla88].

2.1   The Internet's Architecture

To start we will first look at the basic architectural principles of the Internet.

2.1.1   The History of the Internet

To place the architectural principles of the Internet in context it is helpful to review the history of the Internet's development.

Beginnings.   The current Internet has evolved from a set of experiments begun in the late 1960s. At the time, electronic computers were scarce resources, and scientists needed physical access to a computer in order to use it. The Advanced Research Projects Agency (ARPA) within the US government sought a means to allow scientists and researchers to share each others' computers remotely. To enable this, ARPA sponsored research on computer networking. In 1969 the first nodes on the ARPANET were brought online at the University of California, Los Angeles (UCLA), the Stanford Research Institute (SRI), the University of Utah, and the University of California, Santa Barbara (UCSB).

The key design decision made at the outset of ARPANET development was to base the network architecture on *packet switching*. In packet switching, data moves through the network in discrete units called packets. Each packet contains addressing information allowing network nodes to forward the packet toward its destination. Packets are moved through the network independently of each other, and the network infrastructure is shared among all its users as packets from different users are transmitted and stored concurrently in network devices. The inspiration for packet switching came from studies begun in the 1950s (as described in [Bar64]).

The ARPANET was quite useful and successful; it grew to about 100 nodes by 1975. At that time, ARPA concluded that it was stable and handed it over to the US Defense Communication Agency for operational management. Meanwhile, at about the same time ARPA began research on using packet switching over radio and satellite communication links. By the late 1970s there were successful efforts to link wired, satellite, and radio packet switched networks allowing packets to move from one kind of network to another.

The 1970s also saw the emergence of *local area networks* (LANs). These are networks that can cheaply connect many devices within a relatively small geographic area, such as a single building or a single campus. Many LANs were connected to the growing ARPANET via *gateways*. The ability to move packets between the many LAN-connected hosts and the ARPANET dramatically increased the number of systems and users on the network.

Reorganization.   ARPA's efforts to make connections among separate kinds of networks led to a redesign of the network's software into the form used today, known as TCP/IP. TCP and IP are the most important protocols used in the Internet; we describe them in more detail later. The ARPANET was converted over to TCP/IP in January 1983.

A further change to the ARPANET in the early 1980s concerned its internal organization. As we will see later in this chapter, the services provided by the Internet are implemented using switching devices called *routers* that are interconnected by transmission media called *links*. Routers and links are owned and managed by many different organizations; for example, a university might own and manage the routers on its campus. At the same time, the protocols used in the ARPANET required each router to be able to communicate with all other routers using compatible software. This led to stresses as the network grew. For example, if router software needed to be upgraded, many people in separate organizations needed to coordinate their actions.

For this reason, in the early 1980s the decision was made to split the network into a set of *autonomous systems* (ASes). Each AS is a set of routers and links under the same administration; such a structure allows the routers in separate ASes to be managed somewhat independently (more details on this come in Section 2.2.2). One of the ASes was formed from the ARPANET routers and played a central role in the network. Such an AS is called a *backbone* – a central portion of the network that serves to interconnect the other networks and tends to carry traffic over the longest distances. Thus by the mid-1980s the architecture of the network had become that of a backbone (ARPANET) connecting a set of enterprise networks (ASes run by separate universities and companies). Around this time the idea of the system as an *Internet* – a 'network of networks' – began to take hold.

Transition to Commercial Operation.   In the late 1980s the US National Science Foundation took a role in augmenting the backbone, leading to the NSFNET. The NSFNET became the network backbone when the ARPANET was retired in 1990. NSF also encouraged the development of intermediate regional networks, each serving to connect many enterprise networks to the backbone. This led to a three-tiered organization (backbone, regional networks, enterprise networks) by the early 1990s.

NSF's charter prohibited commercial organizations from using networks paid for by NSF. However, by the late 1980s many companies were using TCP/IP and were seeking to connect their networks so as to exchange email and transfer files. In 1987 the first commercial Internet Service Provider (ISP) was founded; many other commercial ISPs soon sprung up. This began the transition of the network to commercial operation. In 1990 NSF turned over NSFNET to a nonprofit corporation to operate it and make improvements (such as upgrade link speeds). By 1995 the NSFNET backbone was retired – it was no longer needed because there were so many commercial ISPs. At this point the Internet no longer had a single default backbone; many different ISPs were running backbone networks in competition with each other.

A further significant event driving commercialization was the emergence of the World Wide Web in the mid-1990s. The invention of the Web in 1990 made the Internet dramatically easier to use. The release of the first graphical Web browser

(Mosaic) in 1994 led to an explosion of interest in the Internet. While the pre-Web Internet was largely used by academic, government, and industrial researchers, the Web brought millions of non-academic users to the Internet. Internet connectivity became a service widely sold directly to private individuals, similar to telephone service or electricity.

Today, the organization of the commercial Internet is somewhat complex. First of all, it consists of many large ISPs running backbone networks. These ISPs are in competition but generally form agreements to carry each others' traffic. Large ISPs typically connect to other large ISPs in multiple locations. Beyond the largest ISPs, there are many other ISPs that vary in size from those serving large regions (many cities hundreds of miles apart) to those that provide service only within a single city or an even smaller area. These mid-size ISPs buy service from larger ISPs (sometimes backbone ISPs) and sell service to smaller ISPs or individual customers. Many companies and other institutions run large networks to provide network connectivity to their employees and constituents; these enterprise networks also buy service from one or more larger ISPs. Finally, so-called 'last mile' providers sell Internet access to private individuals using connection technologies like telephone dial-up, cable modem, or digital subscriber line (DSL).

Internet Measurement Capabilities. Internet measurement has taken different forms during different phases of the Internet's growth. From its inception in 1969, the original ARPANET was designed and built with integrated self-measurement capabilities. This capability supported its early roles as both a utility for sharing scarce computational resources, and an experimental network used to explore packet-switching principles as described in [KN74]. The built-in measurement capabilities of the ARPANET were extensive, including the ability to trace the passage of a single packet through the network, directly measure the traffic flowing between any two nodes, and query routers for their instantaneous workload statistics.

As the ARPANET grew, it lost most of its built-in measurement capabilities.[1] Comprehensive measurement of the ARPANET ended in 1975. By the mid-1980s it was clear that new network measurement capabilities needed to be defined. In 1987 the groundwork for SNMP was begun, and in 1988 the first version of `traceroute` was written. (Both SNMP and `traceroute` are discussed in detail later.)

Starting in the late 1980s, the NSFNET provided a single Internet backbone with accessible measurement points. NSFNET freely provided a variety of traffic count statistics, collected via SNMP and custom tools (for details see [NSF]). By September 1991 the growth of traffic had made it necessary to employ sampling in collecting some traffic statistics.

---

[1]Other than ICMP, which will be described shortly.

However, since the transition of the Internet to a commercially operated, fully decentralized network, there is no longer any single top-level ISP. Thus there is no single point in the Internet where global traffic statistics or measurements may be collected. Furthermore, as already mentioned, a collection of commercial providers now serve as top-level or backbone providers. As commercial entities, most ISPs do not make traffic statistics or other network measurements generally available. For both of these reasons, comprehensive Internet measurements are no longer available (more on this issue is in [Fra95, TMW97]).

The Internet Design Process.   Finally, one of ARPA's important early decisions was to make all the results of their networking research open and freely available. As a result, from the outset the technical development of the Internet adopted a style more similar to research collaboration than to traditional hierarchical project management. This is captured in the maxim that Internet design decisions are based on "rough consensus and running code." Accordingly all Internet design documents, including technical specifications as well as a wide variety of related information, are freely distributed in a format known as *Requests for Comments* (RFCs).

By 1992 the large community of engineers and researchers involved in Internet development had organized into the Internet Engineering Task Force (IETF). Nowadays, the IETF is the forum where Internet standards are developed and RFCs are adopted. It is an entirely open organization in which anyone is free to participate. Most IETF activity is conducted using public email lists and via documents placed in publicly accessible archives. The IETF holds meetings three times per year.

The ultimate authority on the interoperability specifications of the Internet are the RFCs. In the rest of the book we will frequently touch on technical details of the Internet; most of these can be explored in more detail by reading the relevant RFCs. The RFCs that govern the most important protocols can be found by consulting *Internet Official Protocol Standards* [Inta].

2.1.2   The Organization of the Internet

We now turn to the design of the Internet itself; in this section we introduce the organization of the Internet at a high level.

Packet Switching.   As already mentioned, the Internet is a *packet switched* network. The idea of packet-switching is in contrast to *circuit switching*. In circuit-switched networks (such as the telephone system), users communicate by establishing a physical circuit through the network. A physical circuit is a temporarily reserved path through the network between communicating systems. In a circuit-switched network each device along the path is notified before communication begins, and reserves

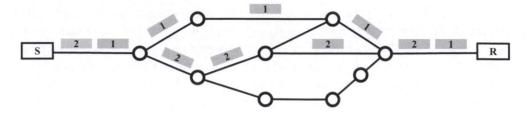

Figure 2.1   A packet-switched network. Data is flowing from S (sender) to R (receiver). Circles are routers and connecting lines are links.

resources such as buffer space or processing time to be used in supporting the new circuit.

Packet switching is simpler than circuit switching. In a packet-switched network, data to be moved from one system to another is first broken up into packets – pieces with a maximum allowed size. Each packet carries the necessary information for intermediate devices to move the packet towards its destination. The network does not reserve resources in advance of the communication. Instead each packet is handled separately as it arrives at each network device. Packets that are part of a single data transfer may follow different paths through the network.

To accomplish this, the network is constructed as a collection of interconnected *routers* and *links*. Links physically move packets from place to place. Routers receive packets from incoming links and place them on outgoing links so as to direct them towards their destination. The sending and receiving systems (PCs, servers, and other devices) are called *endsystems*. This process is illustrated in Figure 2.1. In this figure, data is flowing from left to right. The sending endsystem (S) breaks the data object up into packets, which are sent through the network over links and routers. The receiving endsystem (R) then reassembles the data object from its component packets.

Protocols and Layers.   Using packet switching to provide reliable, efficient communication is a complex task. The complexity is managed by defining *protocols* – communication standards – for various subtasks, and by organizing those protocols into *layers*.

The protocols used in the Internet are usually considered to be organized into four layers. Each layer has a particular responsibility, and provides a service to the layer above it. An upper-level protocol performs its tasks by making use of the services provided by protocols in the layer below it. The four Internet layers are shown in Figure 2.2. Here we give an overview of the layers and examples of the protocols used at each layer; later in the chapter we discuss certain protocols in more detail.

Starting at the lowest layer, the *link* layer is responsible for physically interfacing with the underlying communication medium. The link layer's job is to actually

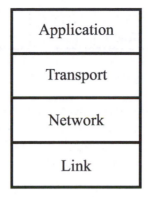

Figure 2.2 Protocol layers in the Internet.

move a packet from one location to another, and each link layer protocol is closely connected to the properties of the particular communication medium. Example link layer protocols are Ethernet and WiFi (IEEE 802.11).

The *network* layer is responsible for moving packets over sequences of links toward their intended destinations. The functions provided by this layer are largely provided by routers as they perform *packet forwarding* – the selection of the proper outgoing link for each incoming packet. The key protocol at this layer is IP, the *Internet Protocol*.

The *transport* layer is concerned with providing a message service to applications that allows a flow of data between hosts. In principle, the application need not be concerned with the fact that communication actually takes place in the form of packets; the transport layer can hide this fact from the application. The functions provided by this layer are mainly implemented in endsystems.

There are two key protocols at the transport layer, which differ in the kind of service that they provide to the application layer. TCP, the *Transmission Control Protocol*, provides a reliable flow of data between two hosts. The TCP sender divides the data passed to it from the application into packets and ensures that those packets are correctly delivered to the receiving system. The TCP receiver reconstructs the original data from its component packets and delivers the result to the receiving application.

The other key transport protocol is UDP, the *User Datagram Protocol*. UDP provides a simpler service than TCP. UDP merely sends *datagrams* – small chunks of data that can fit into a single packet. It does not ensure that datagrams are correctly received, and there is no provision for sending data objects that are larger than what can fit into a single packet.

Finally, the *application* layer is concerned with implementing each particular application. Currently, some of the most important applications used in the Internet

Ethernet	IP	TCP	HTTP	Application Data
Header	Header	Header	Header	(Web page)

Figure 2.3   Nested headers, using the Web as example.

are email, the World Wide Web (Web), peer-to-peer (P2P) programs, online games, streaming multimedia, file transfer, and the Domain Name System (DNS). Example protocols at this level include the DNS protocol, HTTP (HyperText Transfer Protocol) for the Web, and SMTP (Simple Mail Transfer Protocol) for email.

The application and transport layer protocols are *end-to-end* protocols, which means that they are only implemented in endsystems, and that intermediate nodes (routers) do not participate in them. On the other hand, the network and link layer protocols are *hop-by-hop* protocols, meaning that they are implemented in routers as well as endsystems.

Headers.   Each protocol needs to transmit control data to achieve its purpose. The layering of protocols naturally leads to the prepending of this control data in the form of headers.

The basic idea is that when constructing a packet, each protocol takes what is provided by the higher layer, prepends its control information to the front of the packet (and occasionally to the end of the packet), and passes the result to the next lower layer protocol. The result is that packet headers are nested. When a packet is received, the lowest layer inspects and removes its header, and passes the resulting packet up to the next higher layer.

As an example application consider the Web. When a Web server sends a page to a user, protocols at each level are involved, each of which adds a header. All of the headers contained in a typical packet used to deliver a Web page are shown in Figure 2.3. First the Web server prepends to the Web page its control information (such as the media type of the page, the length of the page in bytes, and so on) which comprises the HTTP Header. The Web server application then passes the resulting data to the TCP layer. TCP prepends its header (needed to ensure reliable delivery of the entire Web page) and passes the result to the IP layer. IP prepends its header (information required to deliver the packet to its eventual destination) and then passes the result to the link layer. Finally the link layer (assumed in this case to be Ethernet) prepends the header it needs to move the packet over the physical medium.

One implication this has for network measurement is that the data being sent by the application is only a portion of the bytes that are passing over the network. Thus, when capturing packets or measuring traffic, one must be careful to specify exactly what is being measured: in some cases this will be just application data, and in other cases it will include some or all packet headers.

Internet Protocol – IP.   The most important protocol in the Internet is IP. This is the primary network layer protocol.

IP provides an unreliable service. It does the best job it can to deliver a packet to its final destination, but there are no guarantees. For that reason, IP is called *best-effort* service. This does not mean that reliable data transfer does not take place in the Internet; it merely means that ensuring reliable transfer (when needed) is the job of another protocol (e.g., TCP) acting at a higher layer.

Each connection between a host and the network is called an *interface*. Each interface must have an address that is used to identify the source and destination of each packet. The IP protocol defines the format of addresses. These so-called *IP addresses* are 32-bit numbers.[2] IP addresses are expressed as four decimal numbers, each representing 8 bits of the address (e.g., `128.197.13.20`).

IP addresses are often grouped by their *prefixes*. A prefix is an initial set of bits that all the addresses in the group have in common. For example, `128.197.0.0/16` specifies all the IP addresses that have their first 16 bits equal to `128.197`.

IP addresses are assigned to interfaces in a manner that reflects network organization. Each IP address contains two distinct pieces of information: the *network ID* and the *host ID*. Internet terminology often uses the term *network* for logically contiguous portions of the Internet such as local area networks (LANs). The network ID uniquely specifies the particular LAN or other network to which the interface is connected, while the host ID specifies the particular interface within that network. The network ID occupies high-order bits in the IP address, while the host ID uses the remaining low-order bits. The number of bits assigned to the network ID varies from network to network and is specified as a prefix length; e.g., one can speak of a '/24 network.' The total number of interfaces that can be connected to a network is determined by the number of bits in the network's host ID.

Transmission Control Protocol – TCP.   Since IP does not guarantee the delivery of any given packet, it is the job of a higher layer to ensure reliable data delivery. That function is provided by TCP.

In addition to ensuring reliable data delivery, TCP is also designed to adapt to properties of the network and to be robust in the face of many kinds of failures. One of the main network properties to which TCP adapts is the presence of network congestion. TCP is designed to reduce its transmission rate in the presence of congestion, in an attempt to reduce the degree of congestion in the network.

The basic service model provided by TCP is that of a *connection*. A connection is a reliable communication channel between applications on two hosts. The TCP

---

[2]For simplicity in this section we discuss only IPv4, the current version of the Internet Protocol. IPv6, the next version of the protocol, differs from IPv4 in a number of ways, including the size of addresses.

protocol specifies how connections are initiated, used, and released. An application
on one host opens the connection by sending an initiating packet to the receiver,
which then responds with an acknowledgment packet. When the sender then confirms
the acknowledgment by sending a third packet, the connection is open.

TCP's connection service is provided to the application by having both the connection initiator and receiver create end points called *sockets*. Applications read and
write data to and from sockets. Each socket has a socket number consisting of the IP
address of the host and a 16-bit number local to that host, called a *port*.

Port numbers below 1024 are called *well-known ports*. These ports are reserved
for standard services. For example, the World Wide Web service uses port 80. To
contact a Web server on a given host, one opens a connection to port 80 on that host.
At the other end of the connection, the particular port used by the client can vary (but
is above 1024 for unprivileged users).

The general approach that TCP uses to ensure reliability is *acknowledgments*.
TCP breaks data up into *segments*, which usually correspond to IP packets; each
segment has an associated sequence number. When a sender transmits a segment, it
sets a timer. When the segment is received at the destination, the receiver sends back
an acknowledgment that specifies the next sequence number it expects to receive. If
the sender's timer expires before the acknowledgment for the outstanding segment is
received, the sender retransmits the segment.

Congestion avoidance is implemented by varying the number of unacknowledged
packets that the sender allows at any given time, which is called the *window size*.
Window size is an indirect measure of the rate at which the sender is placing packets
into the network. When a sender infers that packets are lost (because acknowledgments do not arrive or arrive out of order), then it decreases its window size to reduce
its sending rate. Subsequently, if packet loss abates, the sender will begin to increase
its window size. The particular way in which the window size is adjusted is called
TCP's *congestion control algorithm*.

2.1.3   Design Principles of the Internet

To meet the functional goals for the Internet, network architects and engineers have
made many specific design decisions. Looking at the entire set of Internet design
decisions, a number of general principles can be identified.

Decentralized Design and Operation.   The Internet is a loose interconnection of
networks, belonging to many owners. Thus it is not really 'one network,' as there
is no single authority or organization that is solely responsible for the construction,
configuration, or operation of the Internet.

Connecting a host to the Internet does not require the consent of any global au-

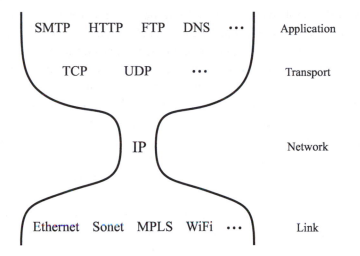

Figure 2.4 The IP hourglass.

thority. To connect a host to the Internet it is only necessary to obtain permission from the local service provider. The local service provider is the organization that operates the particular network to which one wishes to connect. Likewise, a service provider may obtain Internet connectivity simply by arranging to be a customer of another provider.

The decentralized nature of the Internet has been a significant factor in its rapid growth. The fact that anyone can connect to the Internet merely by finding someone else willing to provide service has made it very easy to expand the Internet. However, it also means that knowledge about the current configuration of the Internet can be hard to obtain, as we will discuss in Chapter 5.

The IP Hourglass. The overarching goal of Internet technology development has been to provide *connectivity*. One of the most significant accomplishments of the Internet's design has been achieving connectivity among a wide variety of computing devices that use a wide variety of communication technologies.

An important factor in achieving this goal has been the development and pervasive use of IP. One of the key design principles made possible by IP is the *IP hourglass*, sometimes referred to as "IP over everything."

This design principle is illustrated in Figure 2.4. The figure shows that there are many different protocols used at the application and transport layers, and there are many different communication technologies used at the link layer.[3] However, there is only one protocol that is used at the network layer: IP.

---

[3]The particular protocols and link technologies in this figure are only for illustration purposes; many of these will be described later in the book.

This design principle has allowed the Internet to easily extend to encompass both new applications and new communication media. In the case of new applications, it is only necessary to find a way to implement necessary communication via IP (generally, by using an existing transport protocol). In the case of new communication media, it is only necessary to find a way for the medium to transport IP packets. The simplicity of this approach has made it possible to extend the Internet to include very diverse communication media, such as satellites, wireless local area networks, cellular telephony, electrical wiring, and optical fiber. However, this design principle also contributes to the difficulty of measuring the Internet since it hides details of the particular physical medium in use from measurements made at the network level.

Stateless Switching.   Another one of the principles behind Internet design is that switching elements (routers) are generally expected to be *stateless* with respect to the connections passing through them. That is, routers do not maintain any local state (such as entries in tables or data structures) on a per-connection basis. This is in contrast to circuit switching, in which local storage is allocated to each circuit.

When a packet arrives at a router, the router inspects the packet's IP header to determine how to forward the packet. Routers maintain tables that specify which outgoing link is to be used for each destination network. The router chooses the outgoing link based on the network specified in the packet's destination IP address. This process does not involve any examination of any higher-level protocol headers that may be contained within the IP packet. Thus, even if the packet is part of a TCP connection, the router does not use that fact in forwarding the packet.

This design principle has allowed Internet routers to be very simple, at least as compared to telephony switches. However, the simplicity of Internet routers has also contributed to difficulty in measuring the Internet, since routers do not capture or track many important aspects of the traffic passing through them.

The End-to-end Argument.   The simplicity of switching elements is related to the *end-to-end* argument [SRC84]. The end-to-end argument starts from the realization that many network functions require cooperation from endsystems for correct and complete operation. It concludes that one should not attempt to provide such functions within the network (except for performance reasons) since doing so would not simplify the endsystem. In the case of routers, the argument is applied to the management of connections. For example, reliable transfer of a connection's data through the network will always need to be checked at the endsystems, regardless of how much effort is expended in intermediate devices to ensure reliability. This argues against placing complexity in routers to ensure reliable delivery or otherwise manage connections.

The end-to-end argument has been used successfully to guide many design decisions in the Internet. However, this same principle leads to a lack of instrumentation at many points in the network, since it tends to encourage the design of network elements with minimal functionality.

2.2 Details of Internet Operation

Having reviewed the high-level principles behind the Internet's design, we now turn to a more detailed look at how the Internet is organized.

2.2.1 Endsystems, Links, and Routers

As mentioned above, the basic components of the Internet can be classified as either endsystems, links, or routers. Endsystems are also called *hosts* because they host applications. We will use the term *network elements* to encompass endsystems, links, and routers.

Endsystems often take on the roles of either *client* or *server.* In the client–server model, an application running on the client host makes requests to an application running on the server host. The server then responds with information to satisfy the request. A typical example is the organization of the Web; a user running a browser application has the role of client, making requests for and receiving Web pages from a remote server. In other cases, neither endsystem may be solely a server or a client; rather, the endsystems have the roles of *peers.* For example, in a file-sharing system a node may sometimes generate requests for data from a peer, and other times satisfy requests for data from a peer. Hosts may vary from relatively small devices such as PDAs or cell phones to large, powerful systems such as supercomputers.

Routers are the intermediaries that direct packet traffic through the network. Routers can be connected by a wide variety of transmission media, but from the perspective of the IP protocol a packet moving from router to router traverses a single logical link, called a 'hop.' Generally routers connect to multiple logical links, and a router's prime function is to choose an outgoing link for each incoming packet. Routers range in size from small devices used in homes or offices that connect relatively low-speed links to very powerful devices used in network backbones that connect very high capacity links.

Links are the media that physically move packets from one place to another. Links can be implemented via wireless media (radio or infrared) or a wide range of wired media (electrical or optical). Link speeds vary considerably, with lower capacity links more often used at network access points and the highest capacity links mainly used in network backbones.

Table 2.1 shows examples of technologies used in network links. It illustrates the diversity of network link types and the range of capacities present in network links. Link speeds are measured in bits per second (bps); one thousand bits per second is 1 Kbps, one million bits per second is 1 Mbps, and one billion bits per second is 1 Gbps. Note that the "Speed" listed in the table is maximum possible capacity under ideal conditions.

2.2.2 Autonomous Systems

Although the Internet is conceptually simply a collection of endsystems, links, and routers, in practice the Internet has considerable additional structure. In reality the Internet is comprised of a collection of separately managed networks. Some of these networks are operated as for-profit services (e.g., commercial Internet Service Providers); these entities are often in competition with each other. Other networks are operated by nonprofit organizations, companies interested in providing service for their employees, educational institutions, and even private individuals.

A principal challenge in organizing the Internet is to allow this heterogeneous collection of network operators to collaborate so as to ensure connectivity among all parts of the Internet, while at the same time allowing independent organizations to retain control over their own resources (network elements).

For this reason, the individual network elements comprising the Internet are organized into *Autonomous Systems* (ASes). An autonomous system is a collection of network elements under the control of a single organization. A single ISP may operate multiple autonomous systems, but no AS is operated by more than one ISP. ASes range in size from very large (comprising tens of thousands of endsystems and routers) to quite small (only one or two routers).

Autonomous systems exchange traffic at connection points, sometimes called *peering* points or *exchange* points. These connections are formed by establishing a link between routers in each AS, called *gateway* routers. Almost all autonomous systems have at least two connections with other ASes. In some cases, for example among large ISPs, two ASes may even connect to each other at multiple points.

Thus the Internet can be thought of as a collection of connected ASes. This is a higher-level view of the Internet than the router level, and reflects the Internet's administrative boundaries.

2.2.3 Routing

Once a packet is placed into the network by an endsystem, it must be forwarded to its eventual destination as specified by the packet's destination IP address. As packets move from router to router, the key decision made by each router is the selection of the proper outgoing interface for the packet. Placing a packet on an outgoing interface

Table 2.1 Common link technologies and speeds. OC stands for 'Optical Carrier' level, in 51.84 Mbps increments.

Technology	Speed	Physical Medium	Example Application
GSM Mobile Telephone Service	9.6 to 14.4 Kbps	RF in space (wireless)	Mobile telephone for business and personal use
Regular Telephone Service (POTS)	Up to 56 Kbps	Twisted-pair (copper wiring)	Home and small business access
General Packet Radio Service (GPRS)	56 to 114 Kbps	RF in space (wireless)	Mobile telephone for business and personal use
ISDN (Home/BRI)	64 Kbps to 128 Kbps	Twisted-pair	Home and small business access
Satellite (e.g., DirecPC)	400 Kbps	RF in space (wireless)	Home and small business access
T-1	1.544 Mbps	Twisted-pair, coaxial cable, or optical fiber	Connecting enterprise networks to ISP, or ISP to ISP
Bluetooth	Up to 2 Mbps	RF in space 2.4 GHz band	Connecting low power devices (PDAs, etc.) over short range (10 m)
Digital Subscriber Line (DSL)	512 Kbps to 8 Mbps	Twisted-pair	Home, small business, and enterprise access using existing copper lines
Ethernet	10 Mbps	Twisted-pair, coaxial cable, or optical fiber	Most popular business or home local area network (LAN)
802.11b (WiFi)	up to 11 Mbps	RF, 2.4 GHz band	Wireless LAN
802.11g (WiFi)	up to 54 Mbps	RF, 2.4 GHz band	Wireless LAN
802.11a (WiFi)	up to 54 Mbps	RF, 5 GHz band	Wireless LAN
Cable Modem	512 Kbps to 52 Mbps	Coaxial cable	Connecting home, business, or school to ISP
DS3 / T-3	44.736 Mbps	Coaxial cable	Local ISP to backbone ISP, or smaller links within backbone ISP
OC-1	51.84 Mbps	Optical fiber	Local ISP to backbone ISP, or smaller links within backbone ISP
Fast Ethernet	100 Mbps	Copper wiring	Local area network
Fiber Distributed-Data Interface (FDDI)	100 Mbps	Optical fiber	Local area network
OC-3 / SDH	155.52 Mbps	Optical fiber	Backbone ISP
OC-12 / STM-4	622.08 Mbps	Optical fiber	Backbone ISP
Gigabit Ethernet	1 Gbps	Optical fiber or copper wiring	High-speed local area network
OC-24	1.244 Gbps	Optical fiber	Backbone ISP
OC-48 / STM-16	2.488 Gbps	Optical fiber	Backbone ISP
OC-192 / STM-64	10 Gbps	Optical fiber	Backbone ISP
OC-256	13.271 Gbps	Optical fiber	Backbone ISP

is called *forwarding;* the decision of which interface to use, and the method by which this decision is reached, is called *routing.* The sequence of links taken by a packet from its source to destination is called the packet's *path.*

In the Internet, the routing function is distributed, meaning that there is no single host or manager that is responsible for determining how all packets should be routed. Instead, each router is responsible for exchanging necessary information with other routers and independently determining how to forward the packets that it receives.

To perform the routing function, routers must exchange information about the configuration and state of the network. There are many changes in network state that may affect how packets should be routed – such as when a new network is added, or a new link is added, or an existing link or router fails. In each of these cases, some routers will need to change their packet forwarding decisions to respond to changes in the network configuration. Furthermore, operators may wish to change how packets are forwarded, for example, to favor certain links over others. The information exchanged by routers to accomplish these tasks is governed by routing protocols. There are a variety of routing protocols, which differ in the kind of information that is exchanged and in the associated ways in which packet forwarding decisions are made.

In the Internet, routing is hierarchical. Specifically, routing is organized into two levels: *intra-AS* routing and *inter-AS* routing (also called *intra-domain* and *inter-domain* routing). Within an AS, it is most often the case that all routers use the same routing protocol. However, different ASes may use different routing protocols. Between ASes there is a single routing protocol that is always used. We will describe routing protocols in more detail shortly.

There are two basic reasons for the use of hierarchical routing in the Internet. The first is a matter of scale. The Internet is too large for a single routing database to be used for all its routers. The cost of exchanging routing information among all Internet routers for each change in network state would be prohibitive. By organizing routing hierarchically, changes in network state only need to affect a limited number of routers.

The second reason for hierarchical routing is to allow engineering independence among autonomous systems. The separate entities that operate autonomous systems naturally want to manage their networks and control their internal routing in a way that is as independent as possible from decisions made by other operators.

Figure 2.5 shows an example of how routers are organized into ASes. In this example there are three ASes, each with multiple routers and multiple connections to other ASes. In this figure, gateway routers are white and internal routers are gray. The figure shows that AS 1 and AS 2 connect at two different points.

The path that packets take from the sender (S) to the receiver (R) in this example is determined as follows. The inter-domain routing algorithm determines that at the

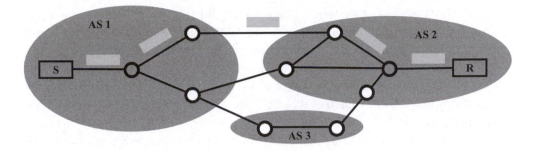

Figure 2.5 Hierarchical organization and routing. Light circles are inter-domain gateways; dark circles are internal routers. Packets are flowing from S to R over both intra-domain and inter-domain links.

AS level, the path to the receiver should be directly from AS 1 to AS 2 (rather than, for example, passing through AS 3). This decision is passed to the routers within AS 1. The intra-domain routing algorithm within AS 1 determines that the router level path to the receiver should consist of the first three hops as shown. Finally, the intra-domain routing algorithm within AS 2 determines that the remainder of the router level path to the receiver should be as shown.

Intra-domain Routing. The purpose of an intra-domain routing protocol is to exchange information among the routers in a domain so that each router knows how to forward packets to any network. Forwarding should occur in a way that avoids *routing loops* – the endless cycling of packets – and takes the 'best' path to each destination. The precise specification of the best path to each destination should be under the control of network managers.

There are two intra-domain routing protocols relevant to Internet measurement: IS–IS and OSPF. Within each AS only one of these protocols is used. The details of their operation differ; for brevity we only describe OSPF here.

OSPF is a *link state* protocol. In such protocols, all routers maintain a 'map' of the network that is updated whenever a link is added or removed. For example, when a router crashes, all of the links connected to it are considered failed, and every other router in the network must be informed of this fact. The network map includes information specifying what other networks are directly connected to each router.

Since all routers maintain a complete copy of the network map, each router can compute the best path to each destination. If the network is not too large, this computation does not require much time. All routers use the same rules for computing best paths, and so the forwarding decisions made by routers are consistent. In particular, routing loops do not occur when each router has the same view of the network.

To ensure that each router has the same map of the network, each router continually monitors the links to which it is connected. When a router detects that a link state has changed (i.e., a link is newly available or newly unavailable), it initiates a *flooding* protocol whose goal is to inform each other router of the link state change. The messages exchanged by OSPF to do this are called *link state advertisements* or LSAs. The details of the flooding protocol are involved, but each router potentially sends a copy of the LSA to each of its neighbors until every router in the network has been informed.

Network managers can affect the choice of best path through the network by the assignment of *link weights*. Each link is assigned a numerical weight. The algorithm used by OSPF for computing the path to a particular destination selects the path over which the sum of link weights is minimized. This is the meaning of 'Open Shortest Path First,' which is the full name of OSPF.

Finally, it is often the case that the destination network is not within the current autonomous system. To handle this, the intra-domain routing protocol must include a means to inform each router of the proper external gateway to use for each external network. In OSPF, external gateways that learn about outside networks inform the other routers in their own network using *exterior link state advertisements*.

Inter-domain Routing.   The job of inter-domain routing is more challenging than intra-domain routing. Inter-domain routing affects the exchange of traffic between ISPs, which has economic implications. When ISP A connects to two or more other ISPs, say ISP B and ISP C, each of which can carry traffic toward a particular destination, the choice of whether to use ISP B or ISP C can depend on business agreements. In this case ISP A will want to employ *policy routing*, that is, the preference of certain routes for organization-specific reasons.

The *Border Gateway Protocol* (BGP) is the protocol used for inter-domain routing, and it has features that allow efficient inter-domain routing, while preserving the ability of individual organizations to employ policy routing. The basic function of BGP is to allow an AS to notify its neighbors what networks it can reach. This is done through the exchange of BGP messages between external gateways.

If AS 1 advertises that Network A is reachable via one of AS 1's external gateways, this implicitly signifies that AS 1 is willing to carry traffic destined for Network A. Again, this is in part an economic decision; adding traffic to AS 1's network can degrade its performance or require an upgrade to its link or router capacities.

Meeting the twin goals of efficient and organization-specific routing is made possible because BGP is based on the exchange of *path vectors*. A path vector is a particular network ID (or collection of network IDs) along with the sequence of ASes along the path to that network. Thus a path vector is a specification of a particular AS path that can be taken to get to the given network. The basic way that BGP works is that when AS 1 receives a path vector from AS 2, it adds its own AS number to the beginning of the path and then potentially advertises the new path vector to some or all of its neighbors.

As already noted, the decision of whether to advertise reachability (i.e., a particular path vector) and who to advertise it to, is an involved one. First of all, if AS 1 finds its own AS number is already on the path somewhere, it must not advertise the new path vector because doing so would create a routing loop. Beyond this consideration, the operators of AS 1 may wish to impose some policies on which neighbors, if any, should receive the new path vector.

When an AS receives more than one path advertisement for a particular external network, the BGP protocol specifies how the best path is chosen. The full process is rather involved, but in general BGP will tend to prefer short paths (measured in terms of the number of ASes on the path) while respecting the policy routing decisions of the AS operator. For example, in Figure 2.5, both AS 2 and AS 3 will advertise reachability to R's network. However, the path vector advertised by AS 2 will be shorter than that coming from AS 3, and so (if there are no policy routing constraints) AS 1 will choose to send packets destined for R directly to AS 2, as shown in the figure.

2.3 Protocols

Having seen a high-level view of how the Internet operates, we now turn to details of its various protocols.

As already noted, the Internet is organized around protocols, which are standardized in various RFCs. In this section we review the most important protocols that are relevant to Internet measurements. We do not provide a complete description of each protocol, but instead just give an overview of the aspects that are relevant to Internet measurement. For detailed description of each protocol, the reader is referred to the relevant RFCs. As already mentioned, the RFC or RFCs that govern the most important protocols can be found by consulting [Inta].

Previous sections have already described five important protocols: IP, TCP, UDP, OSPF, and BGP. Here we will not repeat the description of their operation; in this section we will only include additional details relevant to measurement.

The protocols that we are concerned with can be grouped into five categories: network layer, transport layer, routing, network management, and application layer. In the following subsections we will treat the relevant protocols in that order.

2.3.1   IP

IP is the Internet's primary network layer protocol. The primary role of IP was discussed in Section 2.1.2. Here we provide additional low-level details.

First of all, there are actually two versions of IP currently in use in the Internet. The vast majority of packets currently use IP version 4 (IPv4). This is the version that has been in use since 1983. The new version of IP is IPv6. The principal difference between IPv4 and IPv6 is that in IPv6, addresses have been increased in size from 32 to 128 bits.

Since IPv6 is still not in widespread use, there are few mature measurement methods or results that are specific to IPv6. As a result in this book when we refer to IP we mean IPv4, and we will explicitly note whenever we are referring to IPv6.

The IP header consists of a fixed part and a variable part. The fixed part is 20 bytes in length, and the variable part can be up to 40 bytes in length. The fixed part includes, among other fields:

- the 32-bit Source address;
- the 32-bit Destination address;
- a Protocol field;
- a Version field;
- an Identification field (also called IP ID);
- a Fragmentation Offset field; and
- a Time-to-live (TTL) field.

The purpose and format of the source and destination addresses have already been discussed. The protocol field specifies what higher-level protocol (e.g., TCP, UDP, etc.) is being carried in the packet. The version field distinguishes between IPv4 and IPv6.

The identification and fragmentation offset fields have to do with *fragmentation.* The need for fragmentation arises because link types can vary in terms of the maximum size packet they can handle. When a packet is too big for a particular link along its path, the packet can be broken into multiple smaller IP packets called fragments.

The identification field and fragmentation offset field are used to reassemble the fragments when they arrive at the destination. The identification field is used to recognize fragments that belong to the same original packet. Each packet created by an endsystem is given an identification that is supposed to be unique for the address–destination pair and protocol over the time that the packet may be in transit. In practice, many endsystems generate identification values simply by incrementing a counter.

The fragmentation offset field is used to specify the part of the original packet to which this fragment corresponds. Together, the identification and fragmentation offset fields allow a receiving endsystem to reassemble the original IP packet before passing it to the next upper layer protocol. The identification field can sometimes be useful in Internet measurement, as we will see in Chapter 5.

The TTL field is used to limit packet lifetimes. When the packet is first placed in the network, its value is set to a nonzero integer (a typical default value is 64 or 255). Each time the packet passes through a router this value is decremented by one. If the value ever reaches zero, the router discards the packet. The purpose of the TTL field is to prevent packets from cycling endlessly in the network, which could happen in the event of routing loops.

With respect to Internet measurement, the TTL field has a particularly useful function. When a router discards a packet whose TTL has reached zero, it is required to send a TIME EXCEEDED message back to the packet's source address.[4] This means that if the original packet is sent with its TTL set to some value, say 5, then the sender will subsequently receive a TIME EXCEEDED message containing the address of the router that is 5 hops along the path to the packet's destination. This is the mechanism used in network topology discovery tools like `traceroute`, as will be discussed in Chapter 5 (Section 5.3.1).

Apart from the fixed part of the IP header, it is possible to have up to 40 additional bytes of optional header information. Options are not expected to be present in most IP packets, and in fact many routers do not provide support for them. In relation to Internet measurement, one option deserves mention: *Record Route*.

The Record Route option, when present, instructs each router to add its IP address to the options part of the packet's IP header. In principle, this is a very useful feature for network measurement. However, two factors limit its utility in practice: first, as already mentioned, not all routers support options processing and so some routers along the path may not appear in the header. Second, the fact that the options field can be at most 40 bytes limits the number of addresses that can be held in the options field to 9.[5] Thus, at most 9 routers along a packet's path can be discovered using this approach. In the early days of the Internet packets did not pass through more than 9 routers, but in today's Internet the paths between hosts are often much longer.

2.3.2 TCP

As discussed in Section 2.1.2, TCP is the principal transport protocol used for reliable data delivery in the Internet. The role and basic functioning of TCP have already been described. Here we cover additional details related to measurement.

---

[4]The TIME EXCEEDED message is part of the ICMP protocol, which will be discussed in Section 2.3.5.

[5]Three bytes are required to specify the option itself (Record Route).

Like the IP header, the TCP header consists of a fixed part and an optional part. Only the fixed part contains fields relevant to Internet measurement. Those fields are:

- the 16-bit Source port;
- the 16-bit Destination port;
- a Sequence number;
- an Acknowledgment number;
- various 1-bit flags, including SYN, ACK, and FIN.

The source port and destination port are used to specify which application's data is contained in the packet. The endsystem uses the destination port to determine what higher-level application should receive the packet's contents. The sequence and acknowledgment numbers are used in ensuring reliable delivery of data.

The TCP SYN flag is used in initiating a connection. As already mentioned, connection initiation involves the exchange of three segments (i.e., packets). First, the connection initiator sends the other endsystem a packet that has the SYN flag set. This is referred to as a *SYN packet* or *SYN segment*. The responding endsystem then sends a packet in response with both the SYN and ACK flags set (called a *SYN-ACK* packet). Finally, the initiator sends a third packet with only the ACK flag set, at which point the connection is open. This sequence (called the *three-way handshake*) is necessary to ensure that both endsystems are ready to receive data before data transmission actually begins.

The FIN flag is used when the connection is being terminated. Either endsystem can be the first to send the other a packet with the FIN flag set. However, the complete process of closing a connection requires each endsystem to eventually send a FIN packet, and for each endsystem to send an acknowledgment of the other's FIN packet.

TCP flags can have a role in Internet measurement. For example, when logging packet traffic, counting SYN packets is a simple way to count the number of distinct connections that are represented in the captured traffic.

2.3.3   UDP

The purpose of UDP is to provide a simple unreliable datagram service to applications. A datagram is a message that occupies only a single packet.

Many client–server applications that have one request and one response use UDP for transport. This can be practical because, although UDP is itself unreliable, applications can themselves enforce reliability by setting timeouts for replies and retransmitting when necessary. For example, conventional queries in DNS are made using UDP.[6]

---

[6]DNS will be described in Section 2.3.8.

Since the service provided by UDP is so similar to that provided by IP, the UDP header is quite simple. It provides little more than just source and destination ports, used to identify which application is associated with the data. For example, when a DNS query is made, the destination port will be 53, which is the well-known port assigned to DNS.

2.3.4 Routing Protocols

The principal routing protocols used in the Internet are the intra-domain routing protocols OSPF and IS–IS, and the inter-domain routing protocol BGP. The purposes and principles of these protocols have been described in Section 2.2.3.

Of these protocols, BGP is the most important for Internet measurement. BGP seeks to publish information about the reachability of each network to all BGP routers in the Internet. It does this by advertising paths (at the AS level) to networks. As a result, it is possible to obtain information about the AS-level organization of the Internet by capturing BGP messages. This will be discussed in detail in Chapter 5.

2.3.5 ICMP

The Internet Control Message Protocol (ICMP) was the first protocol developed for network monitoring and management. It only provides a limited set of services, but has the advantage that all routers must support it.

The ICMP protocol consists of 11 kinds of messages, each of which is sent in a single IP packet. ICMP messages fall into two categories: messages allowing routers to report errors in packet processing, and messages allowing routers to respond to requests for information. Of these, the most significant for Internet measurement are:

- TIME EXCEEDED;
- ECHO and ECHO REPLY; and
- TIMESTAMP and TIMESTAMP REPLY.

The purpose of the TIME EXCEEDED message was discussed in Section 2.3.1. The ECHO message is used to see if a particular destination is reachable and responding. When a host receives an ECHO message it is required to send an ECHO REPLY message back. This protocol is frequently used in Internet measurement; for example, it is the mechanism used by the `ping` program (discussed in Chapter 5, Section 5.3.1).

Finally, the TIMESTAMP message is used to ask a router to report its current time. It is not required that all routers implement the TIMESTAMP REPLY message, but any router that does must maintain a local clock. On receiving a TIMESTAMP message, the router sends back a TIMESTAMP REPLY containing the number of milliseconds since midnight UTC, according to its local clock. Note however that there is no formal requirement on the accuracy of a router's local clock. More discussion on time measurement is in Chapter 4 (Section 4.2).

2.3.6 SNMP

While ICMP has the advantage of wide availability, its capabilities are rather limited. Hence most network monitoring and management tasks make use of another protocol – the Simple Network Management Protocol (SNMP).

SNMP is the most widely used protocol for managing network elements (including servers, workstations, routers, hubs, and other network-attached devices). SNMP is used for network performance measurement, debugging, and capacity planning [Sta99].

SNMP uses UDP for transport. Currently there are three versions of SNMP: v1, v2, and v3. SNMP v2 offers a number of additional protocol operations as well as other enhancements over SNMP v1. SNMP v3 adds security and remote configuration capabilities.

To be managed by SNMP, a device must run an SNMP management process, called an *SNMP agent.* The SNMP agent responds to requests for information about the device. The available information is specified in a particular form called a *management information base* (MIB) [RM90]. The SNMP agent has local knowledge of device information and translates that information into an SNMP MIB. Each managed device has one or more MIBs that detail the exact format and nature of the management data that it can provide.

The SNMP protocol specifies how a *management station* (a host used to manage other devices) interacts with SNMP agents. This includes specifying the format of the messages used to query an SNMP agent for the values of particular entries in its MIB.

MIBs can include information about device status (e.g., whether the device is operating normally) and information about the device's activity and workload. For example, an SNMP MIB in a router can provide a count of how many packets the router has processed since its last reboot.

A wide variety of MIBs have been defined; most are not standardized. However, all current routers support the MIB-II Management Information Base which is the only MIB that has reached IETF standard status [MR]. The MIB-II MIB is the primary source of device management information within backbone networks. In an Ethernet, similar information can be obtained via the RMON Management Information Base [Wal00].

More details about SNMP, including its use in traffic measurement, can be found in Chapter 6 (Section 6.3.3).

2.3.7 IP Multicast

So far, our description of packet movement through the network has assumed one sender and one receiver. However, Internet protocols also support *multicast*, in which packets are sent to multiple receivers.

A set of network addresses have been set aside for use in IP multicast. Each network address corresponds to a group of hosts, which is called a *multicast group*. When a packet is sent to a multicast address, routers attempt to deliver copies of that packet to each host in the corresponding multicast group.

In IP multicast, a sender who wishes to transmit a packet to a group only sends a *single* packet. This packet is then replicated in routers along the way to each receiver. Routers make copies of the packet whenever it must be forwarded on multiple outgoing links in order to reach the receivers. The result is that the set of paths from the sender to the receivers forms a tree. This scheme is efficient, since each link in the tree only carries one copy of the packet.

However, the efficiency of IP multicast comes at a cost, namely increased state in routers. Unlike regular IP packet forwarding, IP multicast is *not* a connectionless service. Each participant in a multicast group must register with a router, which then maintains local state regarding the members of the multicast group.

The mechanics of multicast group management and routing can be complicated and do not concern us here. However, it is important to note that these complications add some complexity to the task of network management. For this reason as well as others, many network operators do not enable multicast capabilities in the routers that they manage.

Nonetheless, in networks where IP multicast is enabled, it can be a very useful tool for measurement. The properties of IP multicast make it particularly useful for network probing. Consequently a number of Internet measurement techniques are based on IP multicast, as will we see in Chapter 5 (Section 5.3.7).

2.3.8 DNS

Having covered lower-layer protocols, we now turn to application-layer protocols. The first application-layer protocol that concerns us is the protocol used in the Domain Name System (DNS).

DNS was formalized by Paul Mockapetris in 1983 to move beyond the single `Host.txt` file that was being maintained by hand. It became increasingly harder to maintain consistency in host names and a hierarchical system was born. At its base, DNS is just a mechanism for translating an object into other objects. While general, DNS is an application-layer protocol used almost exclusively for bidirectional translation between hostnames and IP addresses. Most applications use string versions of IP addresses (such as `www.balthazar.com`) and these string versions are looked up in a database and converted into `a.b.c.d` IP addresses (such as `194.255.14.124` for this example). A wide variety of applications use DNS for mapping strings to address form and vice versa. DNS is often the first step in many Internet transactions that use names of servers (such as URLs in the Web). Over the years this application has grown in importance and in traffic volume due to its use for applications beyond just name translation.

There are a dozen professional organizations using heterogeneous hardware and software, who run the 13 root DNS server installations. These are Verisign, USC-ISI, Cogent, UMD, NASA-ARC, ISC, DOD-NIC, ARL, Autonomica, RIPE, ICANN, and WIDE [DNSe]. The engineering groups at these organizations cooperate with each other and the Internet community at large to ensure that the DNS system is robust and reliably accessible to all users. They participate in technical discussions regarding provisioning, evolving DNS, and coordinating reactions to any DNS-related crises.

DNS is thus a database distributed across servers that handles name and address resolution on a hierarchical basis. The DNS naming scheme consists of a collection of top-level domains below the *root* of a hierarchy, organized into separately administered *zones*. The top-level domains (TLD) include the well-known (and limited in number) `.com`, `.edu`, `.org` domains, as well as all the country domains such as `.in` (for India) and `.nz` for New Zealand. There are 264 top-level domains [TLD] as of February 2006, indicating the penetration of the Internet to virtually every country in the world. The various zones have a set of *authoritative* DNS servers who have the official mapping for names and addresses within their zones. There are primary and secondary authoritative servers, with the secondary ones updating their copy when zone information changes on primary servers. The names and IP addresses for the authoritative DNS servers of zones are registered with the root servers. In turn, a local DNS server (often with a cache associated with it) can contact the authoritative DNS server for translations and reply to clients behind it. The *local* DNS server is local to many of the clients in the sense that it is typically placed close to these clients, often on the same local area network. Authoritative DNS servers can be placed far from the clients.

Clients use a resolver library to communicate with the local DNS server. Typical resolver libraries include functions like `gethostbyaddr()` to convert address to string form, and `gethostbyname()` for the reverse. The local DNS server can cache successful and unsuccessful replies in order to use the information later. A typical DNS transaction consists of a client's lookup request sent using UDP to a DNS server running on a well-known port – 53. Most DNS requests and responses fit in a single datagram. However, there are DNS transactions that involve TCP – often as a backup if UDP fails or if the information requested will not fit in a single datagram.

TCP is also used if multiple queries need to be sent or during *zone transfers* – secondary authoritative servers transferring information reliably from primary authoritative servers. A DNS query follows one of two paths: an *iterative* mode in which the query is successively forwarded until it is answered or *recursively*, where the queried server takes it upon itself to fetch the answer before returning the response to the requesting client. Cached responses have a time to live associated with them, allowing them to safely hand back the cached responses for future queries for the same name/address. There can be a significant difference in response times between a cached DNS response and a non-cached one. This is one reason for the *negative* caching; i.e., caching unsuccessful replies. Note that caching of DNS mappings can also take place in application-level components, such as Web browsers.

There are various RFCs that cover DNS. Chief among them are RFC 1034 [Moc87a], RFC 1035 [Moc87b], and RFC 1591 [Pos94].

2.3.9 HTTP

The next application-layer protocol of interest is the HyperText Transfer Protocol (HTTP). HTTP is the protocol used in the World Wide Web.

HTTP was proposed as a protocol for exchanging requests between clients and servers on the World Wide Web in the early 1990s. The HTTP protocol formalizes the way in which Web browsers send HTTP requests and receive responses from Web sites all over the world. The details of the HTTP protocol are quite complex; at least one book [KR01] covers it in detail. Chapters 6 and 7 of [KR01] provide detailed explanations of the HTTP/1.0 and HTTP/1.1 versions of the protocol, respectively. For the purposes of this book, the requisite protocol details will be sketched here and later in Chapter 7 (Section 7.3).

HTTP relies on the Uniform Resource Identifier (URI [BLFM98]) naming mechanism to identify resources (object, service, or a collection of entities clearly identified and located anywhere on the network) on the World Wide Web. An HTTP request is sent by a client to a server and the response is sent back from the server. Note that all HTTP transactions are initiated by the client; the server cannot respond before receiving a request. Clients and servers do not maintain state across requests and thus each request–response pair is an independent message exchange. The request message consists of a method, a URI, a protocol version identifier, optional request header fields, and an optional entity – a representation of data sent with the request. The method is one of a set of extensible request *methods* that are specified by the client to perform operations such as requesting, creating, or deleting a *resource*. The response includes a response code (indicating success, failure, etc.), meta-information about the resource as well (the last time the resource was modified, its content length, etc.), and an optional body (the contents of the resource).

Note that the server responding to the HTTP request may not be the *origin server* (where resources reside or are generated) but can be an intermediary such as a proxy.

HTTP is an application-layer protocol like the File Transfer Protocol (FTP) or Simple Mail Transfer Protocol (SMTP). Although HTTP can make use of any underlying transport protocol to transmit HTTP messages between clients and servers, practically all known implementations use the Transmission Control Protocol (TCP) as their transport-level protocol.

HTTP has several RFCs associated with it. The original version, HTTP/0.9 [BL92], was proposed in January 1992 and the first official version, HTTP/1.0, was described in the Informational RFC 1945 [BLFF96] in 1996. The Proposed Standard version of HTTP/1.1 was described in RFC 2616 [FGM+99] in 1996. It is expected to be finally standardized soon.

2.3.10   P2P

Our last application-layer protocol topic concerns the set of protocols used in peer-to-peer (P2P) applications.

Peer-to-peer networks and associated protocols began in the late 1990s with the advent of Napster [Nap] in 1999. Napster introduced a way to create a centralized index of files that users on the network want to share openly with others. This was a departure from the FTP model (discussed later in Section 2.4) where users needed to know the location of the FTP server and the name of the file to download, and without a searching or indexing mechanism. Although mechanisms like Gopher and Archie had introduced rudimentary search mechanisms on the Internet earlier, the key departure in P2P was the facility for each client to be also a server. By creating an index and allowing it to grow, Napster allowed arbitrary sets of users (peers) to download arbitrary files from anyone willing to share. Initially the set of resources exchanged were primarily audio (music) files, although this changed quickly to encompass a wide variety of resources. There is still a question about the legality of most P2P exchanges since the shared resources are often copyrighted material.

In a P2P network, the peers organize themselves into networks with a set of often transient members (peers join and leave the network at any time) and upload files to and download files from each other. In HTTP there is a client and a server in every transaction; in general there are many more clients than servers. In P2P, every client is a potential server and vice versa. Since the nodes that participate in P2P networks also devote some computing resources, such systems scale with the number of hosts in terms of hardware, bandwidth, and disk space. As additional peers join a P2P network they add to the download capacity of all nodes. Currently P2P traffic constitutes the largest share of Internet traffic.

There are numerous P2P networks with their corresponding protocols. The protocols have to locate content and route query requests and query responses. All of the P2P protocols share the following steps:

1. Locate the content by issuing a search.
2. Choose the server(s) from which to download based on the responses received.
3. Issue download request(s) and receive the response.

Multiple network protocols are always used within a single P2P transaction. A key thing to note is that the different steps of the transaction have varying bandwidth requirements. Queries may be sent in UDP and the resources downloaded using TCP.

P2P protocols can be broadly categorized into three groups:

1. Protocols that depend on a central index to query, such as Napster.
2. Protocols that flood their queries through their neighbors and select from the responses, such as Gnutella.
3. Protocols that use a hierarchical model by using 'super-peers' as intermediaries to send queries.

P2P protocols such as Napster receive information about files available on various peers and maintain a centralized search facility. As keyword queries come to this centralized facility the response about matching servers with the content is returned to the client node.

The second group consists of protocols like Gnutella, which unlike Napster, use a decentralized searching and downloading algorithm. An *overlay* of the various peers is dynamically constructed and queries are distributed (flooded) over portions of the overlay by neighbors forwarding the queries to others up to a certain radius. However, this leads to linear growth of the load on the node as the number of queries increase and thus systems like Gnutella do not scale well. To handle the scaling problem, the research community came up with numerous distributed hash table (DHT) based solutions, where the peers are organized in a structured overlay easing the query routing problem. Due to P2P nodes joining and leaving the network, the hash table data structure has to be updated. Such maintenance work is left to all the nodes in the system. However, none of the various research-based protocols have become popular. There is one DHT-based P2P search network called OverNet that has been incorporated into the popular eDonkey2000 P2P network.

The third group relying on a hierarchical model uses supernodes as intermediaries. Supernodes retain information (pointers) about the data in the peers and queries are sent to the supernodes. A key distinction of KaZaa like P2P protocols that rely on supernodes is their recognition that all peers do not have the same bandwidth. The list of popular file sharing P2P networks is quite large [ORe, Sly].

There is a significant churn in the popularity of the protocols; the original version of Napster, for example, has been shut down due to legal troubles associated with concerns of violating copyright of resources shared. Currently, the popular protocols include BitTorrent [Bit], KaZaa [Kaz], eDonkey [HB02], DirectConnect [Dir], and Limewire [Lim]. Given the nature of the application and its connection to sharing resources of suspicious ownership, no significant attempts have been made to standardize any of the protocols using the IETF process.

2.4   Applications

The previous section examined the various key protocols on the Internet. While some of the protocols are popular in terms of volume of traffic (packets and bytes) due to the current set of popular applications, many of the lower-layer protocols will be popular for the foreseeable future. The probability of a replacement or even a significant competitor to the transport protocols TCP and to a lesser extent UDP is fairly low. Likewise, DNS will probably remain the only naming-related (and thus key) protocol. However, the higher-layer protocols will almost certainly shift in popularity. For example, HTTP used to be the most popular protocol until quite recently. Within the set of P2P protocols BitTorrent has largely surpassed all others in popularity. Similar shifts are quite likely to occur in the future.

Although the manner in which applications use protocols tends to change less frequently, periodically novel and disruptive technologies do cause perturbation. The popularity of the World Wide Web and the HTTP's protocol dependence on TCP for transport led to poor use of TCP. Downloading embedded images in HTML files led to the setting up of numerous short-lived TCP connections. Another example of this effect concerns the advent of Content Distribution Networks in the mid- to late 1990s, which increased traffic in DNS for the first time in decades. This was due to the novel use of DNS as a way to balance load on CDN servers.

In this section we will examine a variety of applications that have shifted in popularity over the years and how they use the underlying protocols. The key applications we examine are email, FTP, Web, multimedia, file sharing, and network games. A measurement-oriented discussion of the set of popular applications is the focus of Chapter 7.

File Transfer Protocol (FTP).   FTP allows users to copy files to and from machines. The protocol was standardized [BBC+71, PR85] in 1971 to facilitate transfers of files in any format and encourage the indirect use of remote machines. The user establishes an authenticated connection to the FTP server by supplying a user identifier and a password. It is also possible to establish an anonymous connection, bypassing the need for a real password. Until the early 1990s, FTP was the primary means for exchanging large files; as a result over half of the traffic on the Internet was due to

FTP. The underlying transport-level protocol for FTP is TCP. The control channel allows a variety of user-level FTP commands and responses to be exchanged. A control connection from machine A can enable machine B to send data to machine C, once the control connections are set up. It is thus possible to remotely FTP files between two different machines via a FTP client on a third machine.

Email. Electronic mail was first delivered in 1972 over the ARPANET. Within a year, three-quarters of the traffic on the ARPANET consisted of email. Email has been popular for more than three decades. Within the last few years, the rapid growth of unwanted mail ('spam') has led to the first serious dip in the popularity and usefulness of this application. Email currently runs on top of SMTP (Simple Mail Transfer Protocol); previously, FTP was used to transfer mail files. SMTP connections use TCP as their transport protocol. A SMTP server on the sending side sets up a connection with the receiving SMTP server on the well-known port 25. It exchanges identification information first about itself, and then the intended recipient of the mail. If the second step does not result in an error, the content of the email is then sent. Note that email may be relayed by an intermediate SMTP server to the final destination and the sending server may thus not communicate directly with the intended recipient's server.

Web. The World Wide Web exploded into prominence in the early to mid-1990s and remained a dominant application for a decade. While it has recently lost ground in terms of number of bytes due to the dramatic increase in peer-to-peer traffic, Web remains one of the most widely used applications in terms of number of users. A typical Web connection between a client (which is usually a browser but can be a program like a spider) and Web server is over TCP on the well-known port 80. Connections are initiated by the client and the server parses the client's request and sends the response. In the early version of the HTTP protocol (HTTP/1.0), the request for each resource including embedded images in a Web page required setting up a new HTTP, and thus a new TCP, connection. Since most of the resources on the Web were fairly small and so fitted in a packet, the overhead of setting up a new TCP connection for each resource was very high. The HTTP/1.1 version of the protocol introduced persistent connections, whereby the underlying TCP connection remained open for multiple requests. Persistent connections helped to reduce the problem of numerous separate connections. By sending multiple requests on the persistent connection without waiting for responses to the earlier requests, faster turnaround was enabled. This technique, called *pipelining*, allows for better use of the connection between the client and the server. Although there have been a few research proposals on using UDP for short Web response transfers, TCP remains the only transport protocol used on the Web today.

Real-time Applications: Multimedia.   Concurrent with the popularity of the World Wide Web, the delivery of multimedia documents began to increase. Web pages that initially consisted of just text and static images, now often include short audio and later video clips. Bandwidth to the end user was often the limiting factor and the popularity of multimedia objects has grown steadily.

Networked Games.   The networked games application is one of the newest application gaining in popularity in terms of number of users if not traffic volume. Moving from single-user games on a personal computer, to large-scale games on thousands of networked machines, scores of networked games involving millions of users have become popular. Massively multiplayer interactive games involving users playing roles have attracted widespread following in several countries. Large-scale infrastructure to host such games has sprung up. Some of the games require very low latencies and extraordinary levels of robustness when it comes to packet loss and link failures.

3

Analytic Background

To study the Internet in a quantitative fashion, we will need a variety of tools. Some tools are mathematical: linear algebra, probability, statistics, and graph theory. Others are definitions: specifying the metrics we use in measuring the Internet. In this chapter, we provide a review of these sets of tools.

In some parts we will spend extra time on special topics that relate specifically to studying the Internet. These special Internet-related discussions arise in the sections on probability, statistics, and graph theory.

In what follows we do not provide complete introductions to linear algebra, probability, statistics, or graph theory. Instead we concentrate on introducing just the necessary concepts – those that are used later in the book. For additional depth in linear algebra the reader may refer to [Str88], for more depth in probability [All90, Ros02], and for additional depth in graph theory [Bol77].

This chapter also defines the notation used in the book; each section covers notation used for that topic. As a convenience all of the most important notation is collected in Table 3.1.[1]

3.1   Linear Algebra

Collections of measurements or other values are often conveniently expressed as *vectors*. A vector, denoted $\vec{v}$, is a named and ordered collection of values called *components*. For example, $\vec{v} = [17, 3, 0, -10]$. We denote the ith component of $\vec{v}$ as $\vec{v}_i$, so in the last example $\vec{v}_2 = 3$. When we write $\vec{v} \in \mathbb{R}^n$ we mean that $\vec{v}$ has n components. To contrast with a vector, a single value is often called a *scalar*.

---

[1]There is some overlap of notation: for example, capital letters are used both for matrices and random variables, and $\rightarrow$ is used for limits and paths. When these notations are used in the book, the meaning will be clear from the context.

Table 3.1 Notation.

General	
$\{\ldots\}$	A set
$\{X \mid \text{condition}\}$	Set of X's meeting the condition
$\#\{\ldots\}$	Number of elements in the set
$A \rightarrow B$	Path from A to B
$a \ll b$	a is much smaller than b
$\exp(a)$	e^a
$a(x) \sim b(x)$	$\lim_{x \rightarrow \infty} a(x)/b(x) \rightarrow c$ for some constant c
Linear Algebra	
$\vec{x}, \vec{y}$, etc.	Vectors
$\|\vec{x}\|_2$	Euclidean (l_2) norm of the vector $\vec{x}$
$[a, b, \ldots]$	Vector having components $a, b, \ldots$
A, B, etc.	Matrices
A^T	Transpose of A
A^{-1}	Inverse of A
Probability	
$P[\ldots]$	Probability of an event
X, Y, etc.	Random variables
$p_X(x)$	PDF or distribution function of X
$p_{X,Y}(x, y)$	Joint PDF or distribution function of X and Y
$F_X(x)$	Cumulative distribution of X, $P[X \leq x]$
$E[X]$	Expected value of X
μ_X	Mean of X
$\text{Var}(X), \sigma_X^2$	Variance of X
$\text{Cov}(X, Y)$	Covariance of X and Y
$\hat{a}$	An estimate or an estimator of a
$\mathcal{N}(\mu, \sigma^2)$	The Normal (Gaussian) distribution, mean μ and variance σ^2

Addition and subtraction of vectors is done component-by-component. So if

$$\vec{a} = \vec{x} + \vec{y},$$

then

$$\vec{a}_i = \vec{x}_i + \vec{y}_i \qquad \text{for } i = 1, ..., n$$

for $\vec{a} \in \mathbb{R}^n$, $\vec{x} \in \mathbb{R}^n$, and $\vec{y} \in \mathbb{R}^n$. Addition and subtraction of vectors is only defined if the vectors have the same number of components. Multiplication of a vector by a scalar is also component-by-component:

$$c \cdot \vec{x} = [cx_1, cx_2, ..., cx_n].$$

A *norm* of a vector is a measure of its magnitude. The l_p norm of a vector $\vec{v}$ having n elements is denoted $\|\vec{v}\|_p$ and is defined as:

$$\|\vec{v}\|_p \equiv \left(\sum_{i=1,...,n} |\vec{v}_i|^p \right)^{1/p}.$$

We will generally use the l_2 norm:

$$\|\vec{v}\|_2 \equiv \sqrt{\sum_{i=1,...,n} (\vec{v}_i)^2}.$$

If $\vec{v}$ is interpreted as a point in n-dimensional Euclidean space, then $\|\vec{v}\|_2$ is the distance of the point from the origin. Likewise:

$$\|\vec{x} - \vec{y}\|_2$$

is the Euclidean distance between points $\vec{x}$ and $\vec{y}$.

Two nonzero vectors $\vec{x} \in \mathbb{R}^n$ and $\vec{y} \in \mathbb{R}^n$ are *orthogonal* if:

$$\sum_{i=1,...,n} \vec{x}_i \cdot \vec{y}_i = 0.$$

If two vectors are orthogonal then they can be thought of as perpendicular: the lines from the origin to each point are perpendicular in Euclidean space.

A *matrix A* is a rectangular array of values. We denote the value in the ith row and the jth column as A_{ij}. Each matrix A has a *transpose*, denoted A^T, which consists of interchanging the rows and columns of A; that is, $A_{ji}^T = A_{ij}$.

A linear function applied to a vector can be expressed as a *matrix–vector multiplication*. When we write:

$$\vec{y} = A\vec{x} \tag{3.1}$$

we mean that $\vec{y}$ is a linear function of $\vec{x}$ defined as:

$$\vec{y}_i = \sum_{j=1,...,n} A_{ij} \cdot \vec{x}_j \qquad \text{for } i = 1, ..., m \tag{3.2}$$

when $\vec{y} \in \mathbb{R}^m$, $\vec{x} \in \mathbb{R}^n$, and A is an $m \times n$ matrix (having m rows and n columns).

Associated with any square matrix is a set of vectors known as *eigenvectors* and a set of numbers known as *eigenvalues*. Given an $n \times n$ matrix A, if there is a vector $\vec{x} \in \mathbb{R}^n$ (which is not all zeros) such that:

$$A\vec{x} = \lambda\vec{x}$$

for some scalar λ then $\vec{x}$ is an eigenvector of A with corresponding eigenvalue λ. This means that the effect of multiplying $\vec{x}$ by A is the same as if each component of $\vec{x}$ had been multiplied by the single value λ; that is, the length of $\vec{x}$ has changed, but not its direction. An $n \times n$ matrix can have up to n distinct eigenvalues and up to n orthogonal eigenvectors. For more details see [Str88].

Finally, it is sometimes the case that we will use *alternate algebras* in connection with matrices and vectors. So far we have been discussing the $(+, \times)$ algebra, in which matrix–vector multiplication is defined as the sum of products. One can define algebras using other operators instead.

One algebra that arises in connection with Internet modeling is the $(\min, \times)$ algebra. In this case, Equation (3.1) is interpreted to mean

$$\vec{y}_i = \min_{j=1,...,n} A_{ij} \cdot \vec{x}_j \qquad \text{for } i = 1, ..., m. \tag{3.3}$$

Another case is that of Boolean algebra in which values are either true or false, and the operations involved are 'and,' denoted $\wedge$, and 'or,' denoted $\vee$. Then we can construct an $(\vee, \wedge)$ algebra in which Equation (3.1) is interpreted to mean

$$\vec{y}_i = \bigvee_{j=1,...,n} A_{ij} \wedge \vec{x}_j \qquad \text{for } i = 1, ..., m. \tag{3.4}$$

3.2   Probability

We often treat some kinds of Internet measurements as if they arose from random processes. The tools of probability allow us to speak quantitatively about random objects. In this section we first cover general background in probability, and then special topics that arise in Internet measurement.

3.2.1 Background

Random Variables. A *random variable* is the outcome of a random event or experiment that yields a numeric value.[2] We assume that for any particular value x there is a fixed probability that the random variable will not exceed this value. For a random variable X this is written $P[X \le x]$. This probability is a function of x, called the *cumulative distribution function* (CDF), and is written $F_X(x)$. Sometimes the subscript X will be omitted if it does not introduce ambiguity, e.g., $F(x)$. On occasion we will also work with the complementary cumulative distribution function (CCDF), which is $\bar{F}(x) = 1 - F(x)$ or $P[X > x]$.

A random variable that takes on only a finite set of values or a countably infinite set of values is a *discrete* random variable. Alternatively, if a random variable can take on an uncountably infinite set of values it is *continuous*.

A continuous random variable has a *probability density function* (PDF) which is defined as:

$$p_X(x) \equiv \frac{dF(x)}{dx}.$$

Again, the subscript X can be omitted if unambiguous. The probability that a continuous random variable happens to take on a value in the range $(x_1, x_2]$ is:

$$P[x_1 < X \le x_2] = F(x_2) - F(x_1) = \int_{x_1}^{x_2} p(u)\, du.$$

For a discrete random variable, we can talk about the probability that the random variable takes on a particular value. In this case the random variable has a discrete *distribution function* defined by

$$p_X(x) \equiv P[X = x].$$

In this case, $p_X(x)$ is only defined for the values that X can take. Note that we use the same notation for both distribution functions and probability density functions; the distinction is inferred from context.

The *expected value* of a continuous random variable X is defined as

$$E[X] \equiv \int_{-\infty}^{\infty} u\, p(u)\, du.$$

Note that this value may be infinite (undefined) if the integral is not convergent. The *mean* of a random variable X is its expected value and is denoted μ_X. The *nth moment* of X is:

$$E[X^n] \equiv \int_{-\infty}^{\infty} u^n\, p(u)\, du.$$

---

[2]One can also define a random variable that takes on symbolic values (e.g., the outcome of a coin flip: either 'heads' or 'tails'). We will generally work with numeric random variables, unless otherwise noted.

We will often be concerned with *variability*, that is, the tendency of a random variable to take on a wide range of values. Our principal metric in this regard is *variance*:

$$\text{Var}(X) \equiv E[(X - \mu)^2] = \int_{-\infty}^{\infty} (u - \mu)^2 \, p(u) \, du.$$

The variance of X is also denoted σ_X^2. As can be seen from the definition, variance is heavily influenced by values far from the mean. Note that variance may also be infinite if the above integral does not converge. Variance is measured in units that are the square of the units of X; to obtain a quantity in the same units as X one takes the *standard deviation*:

$$\sigma_X \equiv \sqrt{\sigma_X^2}.$$

When dealing with more than one random variable, we can consider *joint probability*. The joint CDF of X and Y is

$$F_{X,Y}(x, y) \equiv P[X \leq x, Y \leq y].$$

This is the probability of the compound event that $X \leq x$ and $Y \leq y$. The joint PDF is

$$p_{X,Y}(x, y) \equiv \frac{d^2 F_{X,Y}(x, y)}{dx \, dy}.$$

The *covariance* of X and Y is defined as:

$$\text{Cov}(X, Y) \equiv E[(X - \mu_X)(Y - \mu_Y)] = \int_{-\infty}^{\infty} \int_{-\infty}^{\infty} (x - \mu_X)(y - \mu_Y) \, p_{X,Y}(x, y) \, dx \, dy.$$

Covariance is also denoted $\sigma_{X,Y}^2$. If covariance is positive, then X and Y tend to be above or below their means at the same time, while if it is negative then X tends to be below its mean when Y is above its mean, or vice versa.

Two random variables X and Y are *independent* if knowledge of the value of X does not provide any information about the value of Y. Formally we define independence between X and Y as the condition that:

$$p_{X,Y}(x, y) = p_X(x) \cdot p_Y(y) \quad \forall x, y.$$

When X and Y are not independent, we say they are *dependent*. When X and Y are independent, then their covariance is zero; however, the converse is not necessarily true.

We will also be concerned with *conditional* probability. For events A and B, conditional probability $P[A \mid B]$ is defined as

$$P[A \mid B] \equiv \frac{P[A, B]}{P[B]}.$$

The *conditional distribution of X* given an event is the distribution of X given that we know that the event has occurred, and is denoted

$$p(x \,|\, \text{event}).$$

For example, given discrete random variables X and Y, we would write

$$p(x \,|\, Y = y)$$

to denote the distribution function of X given that we happen to know that Y has taken on the value y. This is defined as:

$$p(x \,|\, Y = y) = \frac{p_{X,Y}(x, y)}{p_Y(y)}.$$

Likewise one can define the *conditional expectation* of X given an event:

$$E[X \,|\, \text{event}] \equiv \int_{-\infty}^{\infty} u \, p(u \,|\, \text{event}) \, du.$$

The Central Limit Theorem. At times we will work with sums of random variables. The resulting sum is random and has a distribution.

The most important fact in this regard is the *Central Limit Theorem*. Consider a set of independent random variables $X_1, X_2, ..., X_N$ each having an arbitrary probability distribution such that each distribution has mean μ and variance σ^2.

Then the Central Limit Theorem states that as $N \to \infty$, the distribution of the normalized sum $\frac{1}{\sqrt{N}} \sum_{i=1,...,N} X_i - \mu$ converges to the Normal distribution with zero mean and standard deviation σ^2. This can be written:

$$\frac{1}{\sqrt{N}} \sum_{i=1,...,N} X_i - \mu \xrightarrow{d} \mathcal{N}(0, \sigma^2).$$

There are a few things to note about the Central Limit Theorem. First, the random variables involved must have finite mean and variance; the Central Limit Theorem does not apply in the case when the mean or variance of the X_i's is infinite. Second, note that the standard deviation of the sum $\sum_{i=1,...,N} X_i$ grows in proportion to $\sqrt{N}$ while the mean of the sum grows in proportion to N. Thus, summing random variables (at least, those having finite variance) tends to decrease *relative* variability: the ratio of the standard deviation to the mean shrinks according to $1/\sqrt{N}$. Third, the Central Limit Theorem does not state the *rate* at which the distribution of the sum converges to the Normal, i.e., how big N must be before the distribution is close to the Normal. The actual rate depends on the particular distributions of the X_i's. In general, when the distributions of the X_i's are highly skewed, the convergence will occur more slowly. Finally, we note that the Central Limit Theorem can apply in some cases where the X_i's are dependent; in such cases, dependence among the X_i's also affects the rate at which the distribution of the sum converges to the Normal.

Table 3.2   Distributions commonly encountered in Internet modeling. $p(x)$ is the probability density function; $F(x)$ is the cumulative distribution function; Γ is the standard gamma function.

Distribution	Definition	Domain
Exponential	$p(x) = \lambda\, e^{-\lambda x}$	$x > 0$
Normal	$p(x) = \frac{1}{\sigma\sqrt{2\pi}}\,\exp\left[-\frac{1}{2}\left(\frac{x-\mu}{\sigma}\right)^2\right]$	$-\infty < x < \infty$
Gamma	$p(x) = \frac{(x-\gamma)^{\alpha-1}\exp[-(x-\gamma)/\beta]}{\beta^\alpha\,\Gamma(\alpha)}$	$x > \gamma$
Extreme	$F(x) = \exp\left[-\exp\left(-\frac{(x-\alpha)}{\beta}\right)\right]$	$-\infty < x < \infty$
Lognormal	$p(x) = \frac{1}{x\,\sigma\sqrt{2\pi}}\,\exp\left[-\frac{1}{2}\left(\frac{\log x-\mu}{\sigma}\right)^2\right]$	$x > 0$
Pareto	$p(x) = \alpha\, k^\alpha\, x^{-\alpha-1}$	$x > k$
Weibull	$p(x) = \frac{b x^{b-1}}{a^b}\,\exp\left[-\left(\frac{x}{a}\right)^b\right]$	$x > 0$

Commonly Encountered Distributions.   Certain distributions tend to be frequently employed when working with Internet measurements. Table 3.2 shows some of these distributions. Some distributions are specified in terms of their PDF and others in terms of their CDF. In many cases only one of these has a closed-form expression. For example, the CDF of the Normal distribution does not have a closed form. The table also shows the *domain* of the distribution, i.e., the set of values x for which the distribution has nonzero probability. A comprehensive survey of standard distribution functions appears in the series of references [JKB94a, JKB94b, JKK94].

Stochastic Processes.   One often encounters a situation in which measurements are presented in some order; typically such measurements arrive over time. To use the tools of probability in this setting we need to define a *sequence* of random variables. Such a sequence is called a *stochastic process*. For additional background on stochastic processes, see [BD81, BJR94, Ros02].

A stochastic process is a collection of random variables indexed on a set; usually the index denotes time. There are two common cases: a continuous-time stochastic process:

$$\{X_t,\ t \geq 0\}$$

and a discrete-time stochastic process:

$$\{X_n, \ n = 1, 2, ...\}.$$

Usually we will be concerned with discrete-time stochastic processes.

A simple stochastic process is one in which all random variables are independent. Such a stochastic process could be fully specified by stating the distribution of each X_n. Unfortunately this is not always the case. Frequently there is some dependence among the random variables. This is the situation in modeling many sequential measurements in the Internet, since the previous measurement often gives some indication as to what the next measurement might be.

One useful measure of dependence among X_i's is the autocovariance, which is a *second-order* property (i.e., involving two random variables):

$$\sigma_{X_i, X_j} = \text{Cov}(X_i, X_j) \equiv E[(X_i - \mu_{X_i})(X_j - \mu_{X_j})].$$

Given a discrete-time stochastic process with some arbitrary dependence among the X_i's, a complete characterization would consist of specifying all *first-order* distributions:

$$p_{X_1}(\cdot), \ p_{X_2}(\cdot), \ ...$$

as well as all *second-order* distributions:

$$p_{X_1, X_2}(\cdot), \ p_{X_1, X_3}(\cdot), \ ..., \ p_{X_2, X_3}(\cdot), \ p_{X_2, X_4}(\cdot), \ ...$$

as well as all third-order, fourth-order, and higher-order distributions. Clearly, to make this manageable we have to simplify the description somewhat.

One condition that can simplify the specification of a stochastic process is *stationarity*. A process is *strictly stationary* if all of its distribution functions are invariant under time shifts, e.g., for a discrete-time process:

$$p_{X_n, X_{n+1}, ..., X_{n+N-1}}(\cdot) = p_{X_{n+k}, X_{n+k+1}, ..., X_{n+k+N-1}}(\cdot)$$

for all n, k, and N. This simplifies things, but is still restrictive. A simpler condition is *second-order* stationarity. A process is second-order stationary if its first- and second-order distributions are invariant under time shifts:

$$p_{X_i, X_j}(\cdot) = p_{X_{i+k}, X_{j+k}}(\cdot)$$

for any i, j, and k. Even simpler, a process is *wide-sense* or *weakly* stationary if just its mean and autocovariance are invariant with time, i.e.,

$$
\begin{aligned}
E[X_n] &= E[X_1] \\
\text{Cov}(X_n, X_{n+k}) &= \text{Cov}(X_1, X_{k+1})
\end{aligned}
$$

for all n and k. Finally, a process is *first-order* stationary if its first-order distributions do not change with time, i.e.,

$$p_{X_i}(\cdot) = p_{X_{i+k}}(\cdot)$$

for all i and k. The *marginal* distribution of a first-order or higher-order stationary process is the distribution of X_n for any n, i.e., $F_{X_n}(x)$. When we use the term *stationary* in subsequent chapters we mean wide-sense stationary.

If a process is at least wide-sense stationary, then useful properties can be specified without regard to the particular time instant n. In particular, we will be concerned with two measures of dependence between the X_i's: *autocorrelation* and *entropy rate*.

The autocovariance of a wide-sense stationary process depends only on the distance k between random variables X_i and X_{i+k}, which is called the *lag*. Autocovariance at lag k is denoted $\gamma(k)$. The *autocorrelation $r(k)$* of a process is its normalized autocovariance, defined as

$$r(k) \equiv \gamma(k)/\gamma(0) = \gamma(k)/\sigma_X^2.$$

Autocorrelation varies between -1 and 1. Values of $r(k)$ that are different from zero indicate dependence among random variables separated by lag k.

Autocorrelation applies only to random variables that take on numeric values. Another measure of dependence is *entropy rate*, which applies to either numeric or symbolic (non-numeric) random variables. The notions of entropy and entropy rate come from the field of information theory, which is concerned with the predictability of symbol sequences. For more background on the following topics see [CT91].

Given a discrete random variable X which takes on values from a symbol set $\mathcal{H}$, its entropy is defined as:

$$H(X) \equiv \sum_{x \in \mathcal{H}} p(x) \log 1/p(x)$$

where the log is taken to the base 2. Entropy can be thought of as the average number of bits required to encode one realization of the random variable; this is based on the observation that the optimal encoding of the value x requires $\log 1/p(x)$ bits.

The *joint entropy $H(X_1, X_2)$* of a pair of discrete random variables X_1, X_2 with joint distribution $p(x_1, x_2)$ is

$$H(X_1, X_2) \equiv \sum_{x_1 \in \mathcal{H}} \sum_{x_2 \in \mathcal{H}} p(x_1, x_2) \log 1/p(x_1, x_2).$$

Again, this can be thought of as the average number of bits required to encode a *pair* of symbols. Note that if there is dependence between X_1 and X_2, then $H(X_1, X_2) < H(X_1) + H(X_2)$.

For a stochastic process $\{X_i\}$ the entropy per symbol in a sequence of n symbols is defined as:

$$H_n(\mathcal{H}) = \frac{1}{n} H(X_1, X_2, ..., X_n).$$

Finally, the *entropy rate* of the process is defined as:

$$H(\mathcal{H}) = \lim_{n \to \infty} H_n(\mathcal{H}).$$

This limit exists if the process is strictly stationary and $H(X_1)$ is finite.

Entropy rate describes the amount of information required to predict the next symbol in a sequence given knowledge of all of the previous symbols seen so far. As such, a value of entropy rate $H(\mathcal{H})$ that is less than the entropy of a single random variable $H(X_1)$ indicates dependence among the random variables in the stochastic process.

3.2.2 Special Issues in the Internet

A number of particular issues arise when using probabilistic methods in connection with Internet measurement. In this section we review those issues.

Relevant Stochastic Processes. There are particular kinds of stochastic processes that often arise in connection with modeling network traffic and user activity. Often one is concerned with events occurring at specific points in time, which we can generically call *arrivals*. An *arrival process* is a stochastic process in which successive random variables correspond to time instants of arrivals: $\{A_n, n = 0, 1, ...\}$.

The arrival process has the property that it is nondecreasing, and so it is not stationary. Thus it is often more convenient to work with interarrivals, which may or may not be stationary. These can be modeled as an *interarrival process*, i.e., $\{I_n, n = 1, 2, ...\}$ where $I_n \equiv A_n - A_{n-1}$. As with any stochastic process, one simple summarization of an interarrival process consists of a characterization of the distribution and perhaps the second-order properties of interarrivals.

Another useful model for a sequence of events is the *time series of counts*. In this view, one establishes fixed-size time intervals and counts how many arrivals occur in each time interval. For a fixed time interval T, this yields $\{C_n, n = 0, 1, ...\}$ where $C_n \equiv \#\{A_m \mid nT < A_m \leq (n+1)T\}$. The particular value of T chosen is called the *timescale* of the time series of counts. The time series of counts is the most common form in which network traffic is reported.

The time series of counts contains less information than the arrival process view, because precise arrival times are lost. In general, it is not possible to reconstruct the sequence of arrivals from the counts – although one may choose to construct an approximation to the arrival process by making additional assumptions (such as assuming Poisson arrivals within a time interval). The resulting approximation can be useful if the assumption agrees with the data, or does not affect the answer to the problem at hand.

The time series of counts will generally be a more compact description of data than the arrival process view (at least as long as the average arrival rate is greater than $1/T$). The presence of correlations in interarrival times will generally result in correlations in the time series of counts – although for any particular arrival process $\{A_n\}$, the strength of the correlations in the counts will vary with T. In fact, even when interarrivals are independent, it is possible that the time series of counts may show correlations.

Short Tails and Long Tails.   A particularly important part of a distribution is its upper tail – the portion of the distribution that describes the probability of large values. In the case of network measurements, large values can dominate system performance, so a precise understanding of the probability of large values is often a prime concern. As a result, considerable attention is paid to the *shape* of the distribution's upper tail, meaning the particular way in which the upper tail approaches zero.

For a random variable X having distribution $F(x)$, we are concerned with the shape of $1 - F(x) = P[X > x]$ for large x. We will say that the distribution's tail declines *exponentially* if there exists a $\lambda > 0$ such that

$$1 - F(x) \sim e^{-\lambda x}$$

where $a(x) \sim b(x)$ means that $lim_{x \to \infty} a(x)/b(x) \to c$ for some constant c. This means that as x grows large, the probability of observing values greater than x becomes vanishingly small. Other terms for distributions with this property are *short-tailed* or *light-tailed*. Many of the most commonly used distributions have tails which decline exponentially or faster. The Normal distribution, the exponential distribution, and the uniform distribution all decline exponentially or faster. For such distributions, the probability of an extremely large observation (e.g., many standard deviations above the mean) is negligible or zero.

In contrast, a distribution whose upper tail declines more slowly than any exponential is referred to as a *subexponential* distribution [GK98]. Formally we define a subexponential distribution as one for which

$$(1 - F(x))e^{\lambda x} \to \infty \text{ as } x \to \infty \text{ for all } \lambda > 0.$$

Such a distribution is said to have a *long tail*. These distributions have very high, or

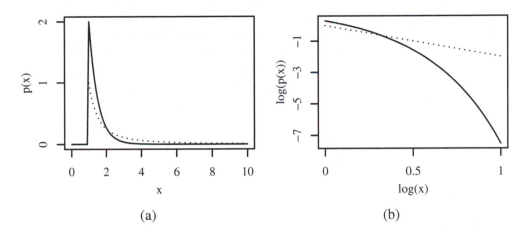

Figure 3.1 Comparison of short- and long-tailed distributions: (a) linear scale (b) log–log scale. Dotted line: heavy-tailed Pareto distribution; solid line: light-tailed exponential distribution.

even infinite, variance. The practical result is that samples from such distributions show extremely large observations with non-negligible frequency.

A special case of the subexponential distribution is the *heavy-tailed* distribution. Such distributions have tails that asymptotically approach a hyperbolic (power-law) shape. Formally these are distributions for which

$$1 - F(x) \sim x^{-\alpha} \quad 0 < \alpha \le 2.$$

Such a distribution will have a PDF that also follows a power-law:

$$p(x) \sim x^{-\alpha-1}.$$

A random variable following this distribution will show extremely high variability; in fact, the variance of this distribution is infinite, and when $\alpha \le 1$ this distribution has infinite mean.

The distributions shown in the upper part of Table 3.2 are short-tailed, while those in the lower part of the table are long-tailed distributions (among the latter, the Pareto is heavy-tailed). Note that the fact that a distribution is short-tailed, long-tailed, or heavy-tailed depends only on the shape of the upper tail and not on the body of the distribution.

A comparison of a short-tailed and a long-tailed distribution is shown in Figure 3.1. In the figure, the solid line corresponds to a (light-tailed) exponential distribution, $p(x) = 2e^{-2(x-1)}$. The dotted line corresponds to a (heavy-tailed) Pareto distribution, $p(x) = x^{-2}$. In both cases the domain of the distribution is $x > 1$. Figure 3.1(a) plots the two distributions on linear axes. Plotted this way, it is hard to visually distinguish the different tail shapes. However, if the two distributions are plotted on log–log axes, the tail shapes are quite distinct, as shown in Figure 3.1(b). The figure also shows that by the time x reaches 10, the PDF of the light-tailed distribution has declined to a very small value – about 10^{-7}. In contrast, for the same value of x, the PDF of the heavy-tailed distribution has only declined to about 10^{-2}.

We will discuss long-tailed distributions in more detail when studying network traffic in Chapter 6 (Section 6.3.3). In addition, subexponential distributions and heavy tails are reviewed in [AFT98].

3.3   Statistics

Statistics encompasses many different techniques, but in this section we will be mainly concerned with *descriptive* statistics – characterizations of data. In this section we first cover general issues, and then specific topics in statistics that arise in working with Internet measurements.

3.3.1   Background

Terms used in describing data can be confused with similar terms used to describe probability models. For example, we may speak about the "mean of a dataset" or the "mean of a random variable." The sense of the word 'mean' is entirely different in the two cases. In the first case we are talking about an objectively measurable quantity which is the average of a set of known values. In the second case we are talking about a property of an abstract mathematical construct. Many other terms can be subject to this confusion, including 'variance,' 'probability,' 'cumulative distribution,' and 'autocorrelation.' When there is potential for ambiguity, or to emphasize the distinction, we will tag terms describing data with the adjective 'empirical.' Thus we will often use phrases like 'empirical mean' for a description of data while reserving the simple term 'mean' for a property of a random variable.[3]

Measured data can be either *numerical* (i.e., numbers) or *categorical* (e.g., symbols, names, tokens, etc.). Of course, many datasets consist of a mixture of the two kinds.

---

[3]Sometimes the adjective 'sample' is used for this purpose, as in 'sample mean.' However, this term is better used to distinguish between a sample taken from a fixed population, and the entire population. In some settings involving Internet measurement, there is no well-defined population that is being sampled, so we will not generally use this term.

Describing a Set of Measurements. The simplest descriptions of numerical data are measures of central tendency and dispersion. Given a dataset $\{x_i, i = 1, ..., N\}$ central tendency tells us where on the number line the values tend to be located. Empirical *mean* (average) is the most widely used measure of central tendency:

$$\bar{x} = \frac{1}{N} \sum_{i=1,...,N} x_i.$$

Other measures are the *mode* (most common value) and *median* (value which divides the sorted dataset into two equal parts).

Dispersion is generally measured by (empirical) *variance*:

$$s^2 = \frac{1}{N} \sum_{i=1,...,N} (x_i - \bar{x})^2.$$

Variance is measured in squared units; the square root of variance is standard deviation, which is expressed in the same units as the data. A simple dimensionless measure of the dispersion of a dataset is its *coefficient of variation:* $s/\bar{x}$.

A more detailed description of a dataset is in terms of *quantiles*. The *pth* quantile is the value below which the fraction p of the values lie. The median is the 0.5-quantile. This can also be expressed as a *percentile*, e.g., the *90th* percentile is the value that is larger than 90% of the data.

Even more detailed is a *histogram*. The histogram is defined in terms of a set of *bins* that are a partition of the observed values. For example, one might define a set of bins as $\{[\infty, -10), [-10, 0), [0, 10), [10, \infty]\}$. The histogram then counts how many values fall in each bin. The histogram is a natural empirical analog of a random variable's probability density function or distribution function. To make the connection closer, one can normalize the histogram by dividing each count by the total number of observations. An example histogram is shown in Figure 3.2(a).

A considerable problem in creating histograms is determining the bin boundaries. The usual purpose of the histogram is to estimate the *density* of points over the given ranges of the number line. If bins are too large, the density may be changing too much within the bin. If bins are too small, there may be too few observations to accurately estimate density, and the space required to store the histogram grows large. Generally one must experiment with a range of different bin sizes or boundaries before good results are obtained.

The most detailed view of a dataset is its empirical cumulative distribution function. All of the previous methods involve summarization of data in which some detail is lost. In contrast, the CDF potentially provides information about each value in the dataset.

The CDF is formed by plotting, for each unique value in the data set, the fraction

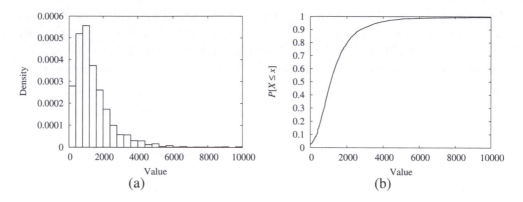

Figure 3.2   Example (a) histogram and (b) empirical CDF of a dataset.

of data items that are smaller than that value. In other words, one plots the quantile corresponding to each unique value in the dataset. An example empirical CDF is shown in Figure 3.2(b). As can be seen from the figure, large values in the histogram correspond to steep slopes in the CDF. However, it is important to note that the CDF involves no binning or averaging of data values and so provides more information to the viewer than does the histogram.

Most of these descriptions do not apply to categorical (symbolic) data. However, the concept of probability distribution does apply to categorical data. One can measure the empirical probability of each symbol in the dataset. This means that an analog of the histogram can be constructed for categorical data, in which the empirical probability of each symbol is plotted. Since there is usually no natural ordering over sets of symbols, the histogram is often plotted simply in order of decreasing empirical probability. Such a categorical-data histogram is shown in Figure 3.3.

Describing Memory and Stability.   As already mentioned, in many settings measurements arrive over time or in some particular order – *time series* data. An important question in this case is whether successive measurements tend to have any relation to each other. When the value of a measurement tends to give some information about the likely values of future measurements, we say the system has *memory*.

To measure memory in numeric data, one can compute the empirical autocorrelation function (ACF). This is defined as:

$$\hat{r}(k) = \frac{\frac{1}{N-k}\sum_{i=1,\dots,N-k}(x_i - \bar{x})(x_{i+k} - \bar{x})}{s^2}.$$

Note that the autocorrelation function *of a stochastic process* is only defined when that process is stationary. However, the empirical ACF can be computed for any dataset. Thus care should be taken in interpreting the empirical ACF, since the dataset

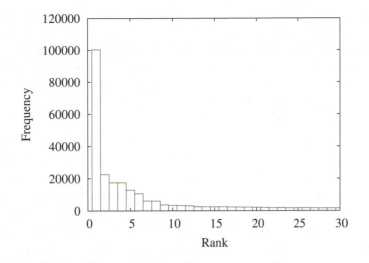

Figure 3.3 Distribution of categorical data: frequency vs. rank.

may actually exhibit predictable changes over time. For example, periodic behavior in the dataset will result in peaks in the ACF at values related to the underlying periodicity. In Chapter 6 (Section 6.2.2) we discuss issues that arise in parameter estimation when data show effects of system memory.

Another issue in describing time series data is *stability*. Data is stable if its empirical statistics do not seem to be changing over time. This concept is subjective; to use it in practice one must define some objective measures that can be tested. A typical approach is to break the dataset into *windows*. For example, given a dataset of 1000 observations, one might divide it up into 10 windows consisting of the first 100 observations, the second 100 observations, and so on. The empirical statistics for each window are then computed, e.g., the empirical mean and variance. If the resulting set of statistics do not seem to show any consistent or predictable variation (such as a trend or a sudden shift) then one may choose to accept the characterization of the dataset as exhibiting stability.

3.3.2   Special Issues in the Internet

Internet data frequently presents unusual properties that bear on statistical characterization.

High Variability.   As mentioned above, a central concern when analyzing measurement data is the magnitude of variation present in the data. Traditional statistical methods have focused on situations in which data shows low or moderate variability. For example, traditional statistical methods frequently make the assumption that measured data approximately follows a Normal distribution. This assumption is often warranted, in particular because the Central Limit Theorem shows that the sum of many sources of variation will generally show a Normal distribution.

When data follows a Normal distribution, almost all observations will lie within three standard deviations of the mean. As already noted, the tails of the Normal distribution decline exponentially and so the probability of observations far from the mean is negligible.

In contrast, Internet measurements are often quite different. In many cases Internet data shows *high variability*. High variability is the property that data values vary over orders of magnitude, with most observations taking small values, but with appreciable numbers of observations taking larger values, including some that are extremely large. In most cases of high variability, data values range over three or more orders of magnitude. The empirical distribution is said to be highly *skewed*.

Often a given dataset may be well modeled with a subexponential or heavy-tailed distribution, meaning that for practical purposes we get good answers to engineering questions if we use such distributions as a model for the data. This can be taken as another definition of high variability.

Data showing high variability consists of many small values mixed with a few large values. Even though most observations are small, the few large observations will dominate the empirical statistics of the dataset, such as the dataset's mean and variance. The chance occurrence of a single large value can dramatically change those statistics. As a result, mean and variance are unreliable metrics to use when working with highly variable data. A better approach is to focus either on dataset quantiles (which are not strongly affected by unusually large values) or on the entire empirical distribution.

However, the usual methods of examining empirical distributions (histogram and empirical CDF) do not focus on the key characteristics of highly variable data. The histogram and CDF do not emphasize the shape of the distributional tail. Rather, as can be seen in Figure 3.1, the key characteristic of long-tailed distributions is best seen when plotting the CCDF on log–log axes. The same is true when working with empirical CDFs. Thus an important way of characterizing highly variable data is to plot the empirical CCDF on log–log axes.

We treat the statistical implications of high variability in more detail in Chapter 6, Section 6.2.2.

Zipf's Law.   High variability is a property of numeric data. However, distributions of categorical (symbolic) data can also be highly skewed. Skewed distributions of categorical data show up frequently in Internet measurements.

The most commonly used description for this kind of data is termed *Zipf's law*.

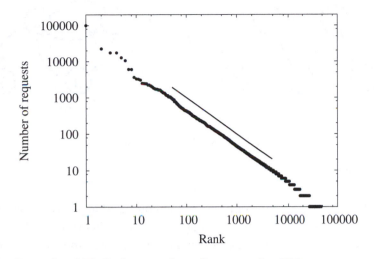

Figure 3.4 Example of Zipf's law: number of requests for Web page vs. rank of page (from [CBC95]). Reference line has slope -1.

Zipf's law is a model for the shape of a categorical distribution when data values are ordered by decreasing empirical probability (frequency) as in Figure 3.3.

Consider a set of categorical data items (such as names of Web servers or URLs of Web pages) to which repeated references are made. Over some time interval, count the number of references made to each item, denoted by R. Now sort the items in order of decreasing number of references made and let an item's place on this list be denoted by n. Then Zipf's law refers to the situation where

$$R = cn^{-\beta}$$

for some positive constants c and β.

In its original formulation, Zipf's law set $\beta = 1$ so that popularity (R) and rank (n) are inversely proportional [Zip49]. In practice, various values of β are found, with values often near to or less than 1. In addition, Zipf's law may not hold exactly for all values of n; however, even when it only approximately holds, it is a useful way to describe high variability in the distribution of references to symbolic data.

An example of Zipf's law is shown in Figure 3.4. The data used in this figure is a set of references to Web objects (URLs). The empirical distribution is plotted on log–log axes so that Zipf's law is manifested as a straight line. The reference line plotted above the data has slope -1, showing that for this dataset Zipf's law holds well for more than three orders of magnitude with β very close to 1.

Evidence for Zipf's law in computing systems (particularly the Internet) is widespread [ABCdO96, CBC95, Gla94, NHM+98]; an overview of Zipf's law in Internet data is presented in [BCF+99].

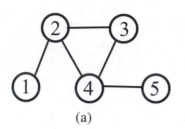
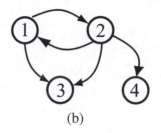

(a)   (b)

Figure 3.5   Example graphs: (a) undirected; (b) directed.

3.4   Graphs

Many kinds of Internet measurements are topological, that is, concerned with inter-connection patterns. We will use concepts from graph theory to analyze such data. In this section we first cover general background in graph theory, and then special topics that arise in Internet measurement.

3.4.1   Background

A *graph* is a pair $\mathcal{G} = (V, E)$ in which V is a set of *vertices* (also called *nodes*) and E is a set of *edges*. An edge $e \in E$ represents a connection between two vertices; it is denoted (v_1, v_2) where $v_1, v_2 \in V$. Two vertices connected by an edge are said to be *neighbors*.

A graph can be *directed* or *undirected*. In a directed graph, edges have direction; (v_1, v_2) represents a connection in the direction from v_1 to v_2. In an undirected graph there is no difference between (v_1, v_2) and (v_2, v_1). Figure 3.5(a) shows an undirected graph with five vertices and five edges; Figure 3.5(b) shows a directed graph with four vertices and five edges.

In a *weighted* graph each edge from vertex i to vertex j has an associated weight $w_{ij} \in \mathbb{R}$. Otherwise the graph is *unweighted*.

Given some graph $\mathcal{G}$, we can define a *subgraph* $\mathcal{G}'$ as follows. The vertices in $\mathcal{G}'$ are a subset of the vertices in $\mathcal{G}$, and the edges in $\mathcal{G}'$ are only those edges from $\mathcal{G}$ that connect vertices in $\mathcal{G}'$. That is, $\mathcal{G}' = (V', E')$ with $V' \subset V$ and $(v_1, v_2) \in E'$ if and only if $(v_1, v_2) \in E$ and $v_1, v_2 \in V'$.

A *clique* is a graph or subgraph in which each vertex has an edge to each other vertex. Thus in an undirected clique consisting of n vertices there are $(n^2 - n)/2$ edges. The graph in Figure 3.5(a) contains a clique consisting of vertices 2, 3, and 4.

A sequence of vertices $v_1, v_2, ..., v_n$ is a *path* if there is an edge from each vertex to the next vertex in the sequence. If the graph is directed, then each edge must be in the direction from the current vertex to the next vertex in sequence. Two vertices v_i and v_j are *connected* if there is a path that starts with v_i and ends with v_j. A *connected graph* is an undirected graph with a path between each pair of vertices, and a *strongly connected graph* is a directed graph that has a path from each vertex to every other vertex. A *strongly connected component* S of a directed graph $\mathcal{G}$ is a strongly connected subgraph of $\mathcal{G}$ such that no other vertex from $\mathcal{G}$ may be added to S keeping S still strongly connected. The graph in Figure 3.5(b) contains a strongly connected component consisting of vertices 1 and 2.

Characterizing Graph Structure. There are a number of metrics that can be useful in understanding the structure of a graph.

The *degree* of a vertex is the number of edges incident to it. In a directed graph, the *indegree* of a vertex is the number of incident edges that are directed toward the vertex, and the *outdegree* is the number directed away from the vertex.

The *shortest path length* between two vertices i and j is the number of edges comprising the shortest path (or a shortest path) between i and j. The diameter of a connected graph is the longest such path between any two vertices.

Characteristic path length is a measure of how long 'typical' paths are in a graph. If we denote the shortest path length between vertices i and j as $d(i,j)$, then any particular vertex i has an average shortest path length given by

$$d(i) = \frac{\sum_{v \in V \setminus \{i\}} d(i,v)}{|V| - 1}.$$

Then the characteristic path length L is the median value of $d(i)$ over all $i \in V$.

Clustering refers to the tendency for neighbors of a node to themselves be neighbors. A highly clustered graph contains many subgraphs that are cliques or nearly cliques. The tendency for a graph to be clustered can be captured in its *clustering coefficient*, defined as follows. Suppose that in an undirected graph, a vertex i has k_i neighbors. Then at most $k_i(k_i - 1)/2$ edges can exist between those neighbors. Let $C(i)$ denote the fraction of those allowable edges that actually exist. Then the clustering coefficient C is the average of $C(i)$ over all vertices $i \in V$.

Betweenness measures the centrality of a vertex. Given the set of shortest paths between all pairs of vertices in a graph, the betweenness b_i of a vertex i is the total number of those paths that pass through that vertex.

Finally, a useful way to represent an entire graph is as an *incidence* matrix. Given a graph $\mathcal{G} = (V, E)$ having $|V| = n$ vertices, one forms the $n \times n$ incidence matrix M as follows. Each vertex in V corresponds to one row and one column of M. If the graph $\mathcal{G}$ is weighted then the entries M_{ij} are equal to w_{ij} when there is an edge from vertex i to vertex j, and zero otherwise. If $\mathcal{G}$ is unweighted then the entries M_{ij} are 1 when there is an edge from i to j, and zero otherwise. If $\mathcal{G}$ is undirected, then the matrix M is symmetric, i.e., $M_{ij} = M_{ji}$. For example, for the graph in Figure 3.5(a) the corresponding matrix is:

$$M = \begin{bmatrix} 0 & 1 & 0 & 0 & 0 \\ 1 & 0 & 1 & 1 & 0 \\ 0 & 1 & 0 & 1 & 0 \\ 0 & 1 & 1 & 0 & 1 \\ 0 & 0 & 0 & 1 & 0 \end{bmatrix}$$

3.4.2   Special Issues in the Internet

In this section we cover topics in graph theory that arise specifically in the context of Internet measurements. More detail on graphs related to the Internet, primarily from a statistical physics perspective, is in [DM03] and [BS03].

Paths and Edges.   Often we will be concerned with a set of paths defined over a graph. In particular, given a connected graph $\mathcal{G} = (V, E)$, we will define a set of *all-pairs* paths. The set of all-pairs paths defines a unique path (not necessarily the shortest path) between each pair of vertices $i, j \in V$ where $i \neq j$.

Given a graph $\mathcal{G} = (V, E)$ with n vertices and m edges, we define the *routing matrix A* as follows. The matrix A is $m \times k$; the rows of A correspond to edges in E and the columns of A correspond to pairs of vertices in V. Hence A has

$$k = (n^2 - n)/2$$

columns. The path between the pair of vertices corresponding to column k is specified by setting $A_{j,k} = 1$ if edge j is part of path k, and zero otherwise. Note that in general this matrix has many more columns than rows.

The routing matrix arises in the *tomography equation*. The tomography equation relates measurements corresponding to paths to measurements corresponding to edges. We start with a vector of measurements on paths $\vec{x} \in \mathbb{R}^k$. Then the tomography equation is:

$$\vec{y} = A\vec{x}, \tag{3.5}$$

yielding a set of measurements on edges $\vec{y} \in \mathbb{R}^m$ (with $k > m$).

The equation applies whenever measurements on an edge are the sum of measurements of all the paths that pass over the edge. For example, in measuring traffic in a network, nodes correspond to network ingress and egress points and edges correspond to network links. One may start with measurements of the traffic volume in a given time interval that flows from each source (ingress) to each destination (egress). This is termed an origin–destination (OD) flow. The tomography equation then specifies the relationship between OD flow traffic, and the traffic flowing over each link in the network.

In addition, we will also work with the transpose of the routing matrix:

$$G \equiv A^T.$$

The matrix G is useful in relating edge and path measurements as well. It is used in the following equation:

$$\vec{z} = G\vec{w}. \tag{3.6}$$

In this case $\vec{z} \in \mathbb{R}^k$ represents a set of measurements over paths and $\vec{w} \in \mathbb{R}^m$ represents corresponding measurements over links.

Equation (3.6) describes the situation in which link metrics are additive over paths. For example, the packet delay along a path is the sum of the delays on each link of the path. In this case, there are more components in $\vec{z}$ than $\vec{w}$.

Another setting in which Equation (3.6) arises is in bandwidth (capacity) measurement. In this case, the bandwidth of a path is equal to the minimum of the bandwidths of the links in the path. As a result, we can use Equation (3.6) if we interpret it in terms of $(\min, \times)$ algebra.

Finally, Equation (3.6) also applies to fault detection. When a link fails, each path containing that link is unavailable. If we interpret $\vec{w}$ as signifying link failures (where a 1 indicates a failed link) then $\vec{z}$ specifies the resulting set of path failures. To apply the equation to this situation we interpret it in terms of $(\vee, \wedge)$ algebra. This is discussed in more detail in Chapter 5 (Section 5.3.7).

Commonly Encountered Graph Models.   A number of kinds of random graphs have important roles in Internet modeling. In this section we cover three important models: the *Erdös–Rényi* random graph, the *generalized* random graph, and the *preferential attachment* graph.

The first random graph model was proposed by Erdös and Rényi [ER59] and is denoted $G_{n,p}$. This graph consists of n vertices. Each of the $(n^2 - n)/2$ possible edges is present with probability p and occurs independently of all other edges.

The statistical properties of the Erdös–Rényi random graph are well understood (a good review is [Bol01]). The expected number of edges in such a graph is

$$\mu_M = \frac{(n^2 - n)p}{2}.$$

Since each edge contributes to the degree of two vertices, the expected degree of a vertex is

$$\mu_D = \frac{2\,\mu_M}{n} = np - p.$$

Thus, for large graphs with small average degree, p is a very small value.

The degree D of a vertex in the $G_{n,p}$ graph is a random variable that approximately follows a Poisson distribution:

$$p_D(d) = e^{-\mu_D} \frac{(\mu_D)^d}{d!}.$$

This is a light-tailed distribution; the probability of extremely high degree nodes in such a graph is negligible.

In the Erdös–Rényi random graph, the degree of each node d_i is determined by the random process that creates the graph. In contrast one can define a *generalized random graph* with any fixed degree sequence $\{d_i, i = 1, ..., n\}$. In this model, each degree d_i is assigned to one of the n vertices so that each vertex has an associated degree. Edges are then constructed randomly between vertices to satisfy the given degree of each vertex. In this case the graph may not be connected and may contain self-loops and duplicate links.

Since the degree sequence of the generalized random graph is arbitrary, it can exhibit properties that are very different from the Erdös–Rényi random graph. In particular it can be used to model graphs with long-tailed or heavy-tailed degree distributions. The property of highly variable degree distributions has been seen in a number of graphs associated with Internet measurements, which will be discussed in Chapter 5 (Section 5.4.2). More details on the generalized random graph model are in [ACL00, CHK$^+$01].

A third kind of random graph is the *preferential attachment* model. This model is based on two ideas: the graph is constructed through the incremental addition of both vertices and edges (i.e., it is a *growing network* model); and the addition of edges to the graph is influenced by the degree distribution at the time the edge is added.

Specifically, the graph starts with a small set of m_0 connected vertices. At each step of graph construction, one adds a new vertex with m edges ($m < m_0$) that connect the new vertex to already existing vertices. For each added edge, the choice of which vertex to connect is made randomly with probability proportional to d_i, where d_i is the degree of vertex i [BA99].

This model generates connected graphs with average degree $\mu_D = 2m$. The most salient property of such graphs is that the degree distribution tends to follow a power law:

$$p_D(d) \sim d^{-3}.$$

The resulting graph has been called a *scale-free* graph. Slightly more elaborate models can be used to generate graphs whose degree distributions follow power laws with exponents other than -3. This style of graph generation has been called a 'rich get richer' approach since new vertices attach preferentially to existing vertices with high degree. The general way that this process leads to power laws was first explored in [Sim55].

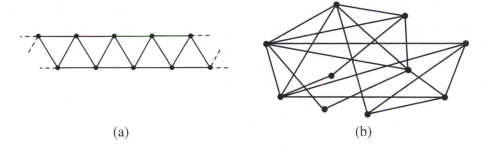

(a)   (b)

Figure 3.6   Example graphs: (a) regular; (b) random.

Small World Graphs.   Two important properties of graphs that can vary in different ways are characteristic path length (L) and clustering coefficient (C).

Consider first a highly regular graph such as shown in Figure 3.6(a) (dotted edges wrap around). In such a graph, characteristic path length grows approximately linearly in the number of vertices n, meaning that a typical path between vertices is long, and passes through a large fraction of all vertices in the graph. In addition, a regular graph such as this shows high clustering; many neighbors of a given vertex are themselves neighbors.

In contrast, the graph shown in Figure 3.6(b) has the same number of vertices and edges as the regular graph, but the vertices are randomly connected; it is a $G_{n,p}$ graph. In random graphs, the characteristic path length grows slowly in the number of vertices n. In fact it can be shown that the characteristic path length grows proportionally to $\log(n)$. Thus most paths in the random graph are short. On the other hand, large random graphs show very small amounts of clustering; the probability that two neighbors of a given vertex are themselves neighbors is p, which for large random graphs with small average degree is a very small value.

These two graph models thus occupy opposite ends of a spectrum: from the regular graph that is highly clustered with long paths, to the random graph that exhibits short paths and a low degree of clustering. An important class of graphs lies 'in between' these two: so-called *small world* graphs. A small world graph is one with a high degree of clustering, but a short characteristic path length. The term 'small world' comes from social science research that has noted the typically short chain of acquaintances needed to connect randomly chosen individuals – also known as 'six degrees of separation.' This phenomenon was first described in [TM69]. Subsequently, small world graphs have been observed in a variety of settings, including the neural network of the worm *C. elegans*, the collaboration graph of film actors, the power grid of the western United States, and graphs associated with the Internet [WS98, BT02].

Small world graphs have some properties of regular graphs (high clustering) and some properties of random graphs (short paths). In fact, to construct a small world graph it is sufficient to start with a regular graph and randomly rewire some edges. Rewiring consists of selecting one vertex of that edge, disconnecting the edge from that vertex, and reconnecting it to another vertex chosen uniformly at random. Starting with a graph like that in Figure 3.6(a), one way to construct a small world graph is as follows. Start by choosing some rewiring probability $p \in [0, 1]$. Next, visit each edge once and rewire it with probability p.

The surprising result is that very little random rewiring is necessary to dramatically shorten characteristic path length. Values of p as low as 0.01 can yield graphs with characteristic path length very close to the corresponding random graph, but with clustering coefficients very close to the original regular graph [WS98].

3.5   Metrics

The previous sections have defined mathematical concepts that are useful in building models for Internet measurement. Another set of important concepts are the definitions used to precisely specify how measurements are made and reported. More detailed discussion of these topics is in [PAMM98].

A *metric* is a quantity that can in principle be objectively measured. Usually we expect that there is at least one clearly specified procedure for obtaining the metric.

While most metrics have relatively simple specifications, some metrics are implicitly defined by their associated measurement methodology. For example, measurement of the Bulk Transfer Capacity of a path is implicitly defined by the measurement process used, and does not have a simpler specification (see Chapter 5, Section 5.3.4).

There are many kinds of procedures one may use for obtaining a metric. It may be possible to measure the metric directly. The metric may be constructed as a function (e.g., sum) of other metrics. The metric may be estimated using the results of a particular procedure. In each of these cases, it is important to separate the clear definition of the metric from the particular procedure used to obtain the metric.

Each procedure or methodology for obtaining a metric is subject to error. The fact that error is possible means that each reported metric has an associated level of uncertainty. It is important in obtaining and reporting metrics to strive to minimize the error and uncertainty in measurements, to understand and document sources of uncertainty and error, and to quantify to the extent possible the amount of uncertainty and error in a set of measurements.

Sampling.   Sampling refers to the process of collecting a subset of possible measurements or carrying out only a subset of measurements. For example, one may sample the router graph of the Internet by collecting a set of `traceroute` measurements, or one may sample packets from a link by capturing one out of each set of N packets that passes the measurement point. Sampling arises in connection with both infrastructure measurement (Chapter 5, Section 5.4.2) and traffic measurement (covered in Chapter 6, Section 6.3.3).

Sampling is used when statistical characterizations of measurements are needed, but not every measurement is required. So, for example, one would not use sampled traffic to reconstruct the state of a TCP connection, because it is necessary to examine each packet to do so. However, one could use sampled traffic to characterize the average packet size in the traffic on a particular link.

Since sampling is used to form statistical characterizations, it is important to ensure that the sampling procedure does not itself affect the characterizations obtained. When the procedure used does not affect the characterizations obtained, it is referred to as *unbiased* sampling.

Biased sampling can arise in a number of ways. First, the sampling process may inadvertently share some common characteristics with the measurements. For example, if one takes measurements of a periodic process at fixed intervals having the same frequency, the resulting measurements can show aliasing; an accurate distribution of process values will not be observed.

Second, the procedure used may introduce bias by its very nature. For example, if one performs a set of `traceroute` measurements from one source to a set of destinations, the resulting view of topology will appear to be approximately tree-like regardless of the true interconnection pattern of the measured routers. This procedure thus gives a biased view of network topology.

Third, the conditions under which the measurements are taken may not be *representative*. The question of what constitutes a representative set of measurements does not have a formal or precise answer. It is rather a heuristic notion that relates a set of measurements to a particular research or engineering question. When we say that a set of measurements is representative, we mean that the biases introduced by the sampling process do not affect the answers to the engineering or research questions at hand. For example, measurements of network traffic in an edge network (campus or enterprise) may not be representative when asking engineering questions concerning backbone (large ISP) networks.

Time Averages and Event Averages. Related to the notion of biased sampling is the distinction between *time average* and *event average* views of a system.

Consider a system operating in a stationary regime, meaning that its statistical properties are not changing over time (for example, a network operating under a stable workload). A natural way to characterize the system's statistical properties is via their time averages, meaning their average over a given time interval. More precisely, imagine that some system metric $X(t)$ can be measured at arbitrarily closely spaced intervals, so that it is possible to estimate

$$\mu_X = \frac{1}{\tau} \int_{t_0}^{t_0+\tau} X(t)\, dt$$

as accurately as desired. Then the value of μ_X obtained represents the time average value of the metric $X(t)$.

In reality, no metric can be measured at arbitrarily closely spaced intervals, nor would it be desirable to do so because of the volume of data produced. In practical settings, one measures a system at particular time points $\{t_0, t_1, ..., t_N\}$. This is a kind of sampling, and holds the potential for sampling bias.

Sometimes the timepoints chosen for sampling are related to changes in system state. Such changes in system state are events, and the average obtained is called an event average. This is:

$$\frac{1}{N+1} \sum_{t \in \{t_0, t_1, ..., t_N\}} X(t).$$

For example, consider a setting in which one is using probe packets to measure the queue length in a router. The time taken for the packet to pass through the router is treated as a measure of the router's queue length, $X(t)$. The event in this case is the arrival of a packet at the router. However, the arrival of probe packets at the router may not be independent of the state of the queue. This could happen in many ways; to take one example, it may be the case that probe packets are more likely to arrive at the router when the upstream link is lightly loaded. In this case, probes tend to arrive when the router's queue is unusually small. Then the event average of $X(t)$ will tend to be smaller than the time average of $X(t)$.

The way to avoid this kind of sampling bias is to measure at time points that are independent of system state. One way to do this is *random additive sampling*, in which the sampling times $\{t_0, t_1, ...\}$ are separated by independent, random intervals $T = t_{n+1} - t_n$ having a common distribution $p_T(t)$. The quality of the sampling depends on the distribution of inter-sampling times $p_T(t)$ [BM92].

In general, random additive sampling avoids bias due to synchronization between the sampling process and the process being measured, and it ensures that event averages (resulting from sampling) are equal to time averages.

The most commonly encountered form of random additive sampling is *Poisson sampling*, in which inter-sampling intervals are distributed exponentially with some rate $\lambda > 0$. That is,

$$p_T(t) = \lambda e^{-\lambda t}.$$

The advantage of Poisson sampling is that the probability of a sample occurring in any time interval is not changed when conditioned on knowledge of previous sampling times. That is, knowledge of previous sampling times gives no information about future sampling times.

Finally, we note that even when the sampling process used does yield biased event averages, if one has additional knowledge about the sampling process and the process being measured it can be possible to recover time averages (i.e., remove the sampling bias) using the tools of *Palm calculus*. Palm calculus is a set of analytic results that relate time average and event average views of a system. For more on Palm calculus applied to networking see [Bou04].

3.6 Measurement and Modeling

Measuring the Internet is frequently intertwined with the process of *modeling*. Measurements and models are very different things, but each provides helpful – often indispensable – underpinning for the other. As a result, in this book we will frequently move between discussions of measurements and discussions of related models. So before we begin to use models it is very helpful to understand exactly what models are, why we use them, and how they relate to measurements. More detail on the topics in this section can be found in [SF03].

3.6.1 Models in General

In computing, the models used are often simplified descriptions of computer systems – a *system model*. For example, a network researcher may build a model of a network, consisting of simplified representations of links and routers with a particular connection pattern. This model can be used to construct a simulation that answers questions about network performance under varying workloads. A general overview of issues in system modeling for the Internet is presented in [FK02].

In contrast, in this book the primary focus is on measured data. We will use models to help us understand Internet measurements. As a result, the models we will use are simplified descriptions of measurements – *data models*.

What is a Data Model? Data models can take a variety of forms. The two that are most common are *descriptive* data models and *constructive* data models.

A descriptive data model is a compact summary of a set of measurements. For example, one may summarize the variation of traffic on a particular network as "a sinusoid with period 24 hours" or one may summarize the distribution of round trip times in a network as "Gaussian with mean 100 ms and standard deviation 10 ms." The key feature of such a model is an underlying *idealized* representation: e.g., a sine wave, or a Normal distribution. Furthermore, the model contains *parameters* whose values are based on the measured data: in this case a 24-hour period, or a mean of 100 ms and standard deviation of 10 ms.

In contrast to descriptive models, a constructive data model is a succinct description of a *process* that gives rise to an output (i.e., a dataset) of interest. For example, one may build a constructive model of network traffic as "the superposition of a set of flows arriving independently, each consisting of a random number of packets." Or one may model a network topology as "the result of an incremental growth process involving preferential attachment."[4] In either case, there is an idealized mechanism or process at work that could have generated the dataset in question.

In the constructive approach to data modeling, one may start with a real system and simplify it, as in system modeling. However, the primary purpose is not to represent or simulate the real system, but rather to characterize a dataset concisely.

In each case, the model is only approximate. Real data will not match the idealized representation exactly. This is proper and entirely to be expected; all models omit details of the data by their very nature. This fact introduces a fundamental tension between the simplicity and utility of a model. This was summarized by the statistician George Box as "All models are wrong, but some models are useful" [Box79].

Often the model involves a random process or component. In such cases we can speak quantitatively about whether the model *could have* generated the observed data, by considering the probability that the random process would produce as output the data at hand. We can compare models by asking "Under which model is the observed data more likely?"

To build a data model, one starts with a collection of real data and perhaps a system description. Regardless of whether one takes the descriptive or constructive approach, there are three key steps involved: first, one chooses the underlying idealization (e.g., the sinusoid or the Normal distribution). This is called the *model selection* problem. Then one selects values for the model parameters that are appropriate given the data at hand; this is the *parameter estimation* problem. When one is done, the idea is that the model 'could have' generated the observed data. The third step is *validating* the model – confirming that the observed data is a (relatively) likely output of the model.

In the model selection step, one tends to prefer models with fewer parameters over those with more parameters. That is, one prefers models that are *parsimonious*. There are many reasons for this. First of all, a model with more parameters will tend to fit data better. In that case, the improvement in fit may be a result of the additional degrees of freedom rather than due to a better model choice. Related to this idea is the

---

[4]These descriptions, owing to their brevity, are somewhat imprecise. In reality, a proper model definition needs to be precise and unambiguous.

problem of *over-fitting;* a model with many parameters may fit a particular dataset well but may not be a good fit for a different dataset. Another virtue of parsimony is that models with a small set of parameters can often be more easily interpreted than more complex models. Finally, in cases where the parameters have physical significance, then a smaller set of parameters means fewer phenomena are at work in generating the observed data. In this case, Occam's razor[5] suggests that the model with fewer parameters is to be preferred; in some sense it is 'more likely' to have generated the observed data.

Unfortunately, each modeling approach has certain drawbacks. The descriptive approach does not shed much light on questions like: "Why is the data like this?" and "What will happen if the system changes?" The descriptive modeling approach may not use all available information; e.g., one may know something about how the data was generated that is not reflected in the model.

On the other hand, the constructive approach yields models that can be difficult to generalize – such models may have many parameters. The nature of the output of such a model may not be obvious without simulation or analysis. Furthermore, it may be impossible for the model to match the data in every aspect.

Why Build Models?   Although they are difficult to build well, data models are very useful. There are a variety of motivations for building data models.

First, a data model provides a compact summary of a set of measurements. In the example above, many measurements were summarized as "Gaussian with mean 100 ms and standard deviation 10 ms." Clearly, a data model can be a very efficient way to represent a huge dataset. As a result, one can manipulate, publish, or disseminate a data model in ways not possible for the underlying dataset (e.g., they can be published in research papers).

Another role for a data model is to expose properties of measurements that are important for particular engineering problems. This can happen when parameters are *interpretable.* Interpretable here means that the parameter value has a relationship to an underlying cause or engineering question. As interpretable parameters change, we understand how something in the real system changes – like system performance. In the example involving round trip times, both mean (100 ms) and standard deviation (10 ms) are interpretable in terms of network performance.

Finally, in simulations one often needs the ability to generate random but 'realistic' data as input. The starting point is usually a data model. Using a data model, one can generate large amounts of new data that agree in key properties with empirical measurements. Furthermore, in cases where parameters are interpretable, data mod-

---

[5]"Entities are not to be multiplied without necessity." In other words, given two equally predictive theories, choose the simpler.

els allow asking 'what if' questions. One can generate simulation inputs that span a range of realistic values and explore the resulting consequences.

Both descriptive and constructive models are useful in simulation. For example, a simulation may incorporate a descriptive model for the packet loss processes at a wireless link. On the other hand, to simulate traffic on a link, a simulation may use a constructive model consisting of the superposition of many file transfers.

3.6.2   The Use of Probability Models

It is often the case that the models we use are probabilistic – that is, they contain random variables or stochastic processes. Probabilistic models are very common, and yet their use involves some subtleties.

Like all models, probabilistic models are abstractions. What distinguishes a probabilistic model is that it involves objects that have random behavior, meaning behavior that cannot be predicted in advance. In our context this may seem odd – computer systems are rigorously designed to avoid random behavior at all costs. A computer system that exhibits random behavior is usually considered broken.

So why use random models in the context of the Internet? The answer is not that the processes involved are fundamentally random. Rather, it is that some factors determining the processes are unknown or unimportant. Generally we use randomness to capture system or data properties that we don't want to specify, or don't know how to specify. Thus we may treat the delay experienced by a packet in the Internet as random (with some distribution). This is not because the value is really random – hopefully it is deterministic. Rather it is because the value is the result of an immense number of particular system properties that are far too tedious to specify.

It is important therefore to distinguish sharply between the properties of a probabilistic model and the properties of real (empirically measured) data. The distinction is this: data properties are observable quantities by definition. However, *a probabilistic model may well contain assumptions that are not operationally testable or directly observable, and therefore cannot actually be said to apply to real data.* For example, the notions of 'stationarity,' 'independence,' and even 'probability,' 'mean,' and 'variance'[6] are properties of models, but not of data. More discussion of this issue is in [Mat89].

Making a clear distinction between properties of models and properties of data can help avoid confusion. For example, the distinction makes clear that it is meaningless to ask whether a particular dataset "is stationary." Rather, a meaningful statement would be "a stationary model is useful for describing this data" or "this data is consistent with a stationary model for the problem at hand." To highlight this distinction

---

[6]Excluding the 'empirical' senses of those terms as discussed in Section 3.3.1.

Table 3.3 Model properties and data properties.

Model Properties		
Autocorrelation	$E[(X_i - \mu_{X_i})(X_j - \mu_{X_j})] \neq 0, \quad i \neq j$	(Sec. 3.2.1)
Stationarity	$E[X_n] = E[X_1] \quad \forall n$, etc.	(Sec. 3.2.1)
Long Tail	$\bar{F}(x)\,e^{\lambda x} \to \infty$ as $x \to \infty$ for all $\lambda > 0$	(Sec. 3.2.2)
Data Properties		
System Memory	Tendency for nearby observations to be similar	
Stability	Tendency for empirical statistic to not vary with time	
High Variability	Highly skewed histogram that may be well modeled by a long-tailed distribution	

some examples are given in Table 3.3. The upper portion of the table shows some commonly used properties of models; the lower portion of the table shows properties associated with data.

In fact, as pointed out in [PAMM98], it can be misleading to use probabilistic terms in *defining* metrics. This is because when definitions are made in terms of probabilities, they can include hidden assumptions that derive from an implicitly assumed stochastic model.

Finally, this view makes clear that we use probabilistic models because they help us answer questions. In fact, there is not much use for a probabilistic model apart from a set of questions that it can help to answer. So we will not ask whether a model is the 'correct' one for a set of data. We cannot answer this question as posed. A better approach is to ask: "Does this model give useful answers to the questions for which it is employed?"

4

Practical Issues in Internet Measurement

Thus far in the book we have presented motivation for Internet measurements built around the basic measurement concepts outlined in Chapter 3. These concepts rely on the Internet architecture outlined in Chapter 2. We now examine the nuts and bolts of Internet measurement. Among them are the various practical issues to be considered in designing and carrying them out, the different databases that are involved in basic Internet operation, such as routing and their role in measurement, and the differences in measurements across the various protocol layers.

The first practical issue is enumerating all the places where Internet measurements are carried out. Increasingly, even measurements for a single application are rarely done in a single location. Depending on the nature of applications and the complexity of the measurements involved, there might be sophisticated hardware and software requirements. While software is generally mobile, measurement hardware is typically co-located next to the links and routers being measured. The cost of hardware and their configuration complexities may limit the places where measurements are done. In the first section we will examine a variety of issues related to the measurement location problem.

One of the key components of measurement is the notion of time. Time is a basic entity with strong implications on precision of measurements, synchronizing across various locations where measurements may be carried out simultaneously, time of day when measurements are carried out to ensure representativeness, etc. Time plays an important role in virtually all inferences drawn from measurements. A detailed examination of the various practical issues involved in dealing with this key ingredient of measurements is presented in the second section.

An introduction to the various databases and registries and their role in mea-

surements is discussed next. A variety of databases related to various Internet infrastructure issues have been created over the years since the inception of the Internet. They play an important role in all Internet activities, including measurement.
The databases range from the Domain Name System (DNS) to various address registries created to handle the allocation of address spaces to different geographical
demographics. The typical information registered with the registries includes address range specifics (prefixes and Autonomous Systems), contact information about
the administrative entity, etc. The registries are queried to obtain a range of information useful for inferring about location, configuration, distribution, inter-domain
connections, routing specifics, etc. Many measurement applications depend on the
information present in these databases.

   Moving from measurement location and role of databases, we finally examine
how measurements differ across the different protocol layers. We discuss the issues
involved in capturing data at different levels of granularities across the layers and the
need for tailored instrumentation. Considerable research has been carried out in this
arena, resulting in advancements in hardware and software necessary to keep up with
the growth in volume and speed of traffic. Finally, overlays – logical abstractions over
the physical network – have been playing an important role in the Internet. Overlays
have primarily been a good vehicle to try out new Internet routing techniques and
applications built on top of them. The proliferation of projects and measurement
techniques that take advantage of overlays is examined.

4.1   Where can Measurements be Made?

Measurements are made virtually at every point on the Internet spectrum: at or near
the router, at the links connecting routers, in local area networks, at network ingress
and egress points at small and large administrative infrastructures, inside network
backbones, and in the wide area. In this section we will examine in depth the issues
surrounding measurement at each of these locations.

   Figure 4.1 shows the various locations where measurements are done in and
around an Internet Service Provider (ISP). The various components shown are typical
in a large ISP but also found in large networking organizations that do not provide
commercial connectivity services. The backbone routers, access routers, and gateway routers all communicate with each other using an intra-Autonomous System
protocol. An ISP is free to choose its routing protocol for communication inside its
boundaries. The set of gateway routers are responsible for routing traffic between
the ISP and other Autonomous Systems. These routers exchange large Internet routing tables and communicate using inter-Autonomous System routing protocols. The
primary inter-AS routing protocol is Border Gateway Protocol [RL95]; BGP speak-

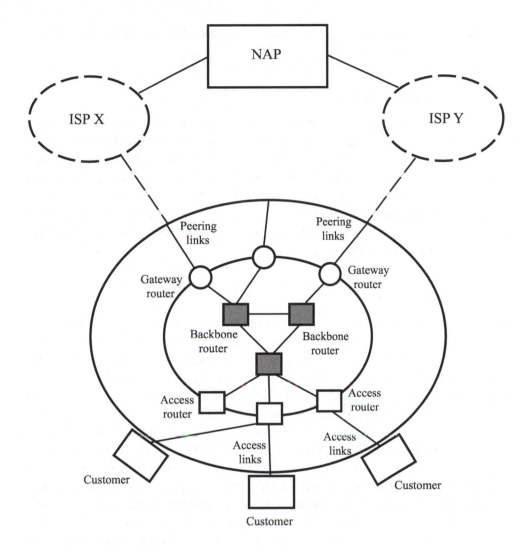

Figure 4.1 Measurement locations in an ISP.

ing routers that communicate with each other to exchange routes are called *peering routers*. Gateway routers control the location and amount of traffic exchanged with other ASes (ISP-X and ISP-Y in Figure 4.1). The access routers provide connectivity to a set of customer networks over access links. In many cases multiple customers are connected over the same link. Access links vary in capacity based on the ISP and the customer needs; they can provide dial-up access through a bank of modems or dedicated higher-speed connection. A network access point (NAP) is an exchange point of multiple ISPs that can exchange traffic. In the rest of the section we will examine each of these entities and connections in more detail from the viewpoint of measurement locations.

4.1.1   Local Area Network

Measurement at the local area network is generally carried out for local testbeds and is typically not of significant interest in the 'Internet' measurement sense. However, measurements of local latency and hardware-related measurements are typically done on a LAN. There is complete control on what is being measured and unbiased and precise measurements can be carried out at this level. Performance-related measurements at higher layers are also done on LANs. A key area of growing interest in the LAN context, however, is Wireless LAN – there have been increasing measurements related to wireless done here.

4.1.2   Inside a Backbone

Measurements are routinely carried out inside the backbone, although the data is not always made available. ISPs and other large administrative entities constantly monitor the network for a variety of purposes: ensuring availability, scanning for outages or attacks, topology changes, compliance with service level agreements, traffic trends such as diurnal, weekday activities, and other periodicities. Typically measurements inside the backbone are done from an intra-organizational point of view: such measurements help in proper provisioning of resources, and indicate when router and link upgrades may be warranted. Feedback can be provided to an ISP's customers about performance characteristics. For large-scale shifts, such as significant upgrades at the protocol level (e.g., migrating to MPLS), measurements may be a key driving factor.

A key objective of backbone measurements is capacity planning, to see if additional points of presence (PoPs, often a metropolitan area) are needed or if existing PoPs in a network need additional capacity [PTZD03]. If a network is peering with other large providers and there is a significant shift in traffic on the peering link, it may have to be upgraded. The most common technique is to use the Simple Network Management Protocol (SNMP) polling mechanism to gather traffic characteristics. The widely used SNMP data provide the basic information needed to measure packet loss, delay, and throughput. SNMP data can be gathered from virtually everywhere within the network.

Although SNMP is ubiquitous, the aggregate nature of its traffic data and lack of information about source and destination requires additional work to be done on top of SNMP. Packet tracing is the next alternative which provides time stamps at high precision. With an ever-changing set of applications dominating the traffic, periodic monitoring of backbone traffic at small timescales (below one second) can help identify bursts and traffic aggregation potential. Such an analysis [ZRMD03] can be done via short packet traces gathered on high-speed links inside a backbone.

Allocating bandwidth to various links inside an ISP (provisioning) is a key activity carried out by ISPs [FTD03]. Different applications have varying degrees of sensitivity to latency, utilization at links need to be set based on meeting requirements such as delay, and overall end-to-end queuing delay needs to be bounded. The actual traffic mix has to be measured inside the network for proper provisioning. Typically ISPs over-provision the network, but the appropriate degree of over-provisioning has to be computed. Packet-level traces have been gathered [FML+03] on various links inside a backbone to examine changes in traffic patterns.

A backbone can use long-term information on link utilization, for example, to help identify PoPs that need more capacity. Several high-speed monitors, ranging from OC12MON (622 megabits/sec), OC48MON (2.4 gigabits/sec), all the way to OC192MON (9.6 gigabits/sec) have been built to carry out measurements inside the backbone. Measurements inside the backbone provide an in-depth view of all the traffic associated with a set of customers that an organization could use to provide tailored service to them. It is also important to ensure that the various service level agreements (SLAs) that have been signed by the ISP with various customers in terms are met; this requires packet delay measurements.

Not all applications are equally sensitive to latency: email for example can be delayed by several milliseconds to a second without significant impact. With aggressive spam filtering in modern email systems, the delay can be even larger. However, interactive applications such as streaming multimedia may be much more sensitive to latencies. By provisioning bandwidth, it may be possible to ensure that stringent latency requirements are met. Since the origin and destination of latency-sensitive traffic may be between any pair of PoPs, traffic across all pairs needs to be monitored. Measurement-based modeling has aided in proper provisioning of bandwidth.

Another advantage of backbone measurements is the ability to monitor various links inside a backbone along with the current routing information to get a detailed view. At a macro level, traffic shifts, such as sudden growth in a particular protocol, can be gleaned by sampled measurements inside the backbone. Various traffic matrices are created to capture traffic between arbitrary prefixes, cities, and customers. At a micro level, backbone measurements allow setting of proper weights in interior gateway protocols to balance traffic across the various links. Backbone measurements have significant storage requirements and have to contend with a network that is constantly changing. There is ongoing work in combining traffic matrix and routing data [RGM+04].

Due to the increase in attacks on the Internet, monitoring the backbone for sudden increases can help in identifying potential attacks within the network. Anomaly detection techniques can be strengthened by watching for significant changes in traffic patterns between points of presences. One way of examining presence of attacks is to examine link utilizations periodically and notice significant increases. Gathering link-based statistics on all the links can be prohibitive in large ISPs and thus smarter techniques (such as examining counts of links [LCD04b]) would be needed.

There may also be failures inside the network that are not related to attacks that may need to be periodically monitored to ensure availability. Path failures trigger rerouting while equipment failures are often reflected at the transport layer. Although a customer may be multi-homed at the IP layer, failures at shared links at layer-1 will not provide the expected degree of protection [RGH$^+$04]. Links between various routers within a backbone may fail. The link between an access router and a backbone router may fail, or two backbone routers may become disconnected. Depending on the nature of interconnection between these routers it may be possible to restore connectivity quickly [ICBD04]. Routes could be recovered quickly if precomputed alternate shortest paths are available. Routing update messages could be given higher priority to enable faster recovery.

4.1.3   Entry Points into a Network

Measurements at the entry points of a network are common: they are done typically at gateway routers, peering routers, BGP endpoints (iBGP and eBGP), and access routers. We examine each of these locations now.

Gateway Router.   At the gateway router and border firewalls a variety of measurements are carried out primarily having to do with access control and overall statistics. As the entry point to the network such routers and firewalls are the first line of defense and the best place to filter out unwanted traffic. The Internet gateway routers export per-flow summaries of traffic (via the ubiquitous *netflow* tool) which includes information about start and ending time of flows, duration, source and destination IP addresses and ports, and autonomous systems, etc. The information available from the dumped flow records is enough to construct traffic aggregate reports on a per-customer basis. It is also possible to learn the fraction of the traffic destined to customers inside the network and the portion of traffic that is transiting through the network.

Peering Router.   Earlier we introduced peering routers as ones that speak BGP to exchange routing information. Peering can be *public* or *private*. Two ASes that exchange routing information can do it at multiple locations that are known only to them and thus *private*. An AS can peer at publicly known places with other peers as well.

The recent trend in North America has been to gradually move away from a public peering model to private peering for a variety of commercial and competition reasons. In earlier days Network Access Points were based on switch technology (FDDI, Ethernet, or ATM) but they could not keep up with the explosive growth in Internet traffic. The larger ISPs began to exchange traffic directly with each other using fiber connections (such as OC-12s and OC-48s) at neutral sites and are able to expand by increasing peering capacity at such central locations.

The goal of measurements at the peering level has to do with inter-domain connectivity. From a business/economic point of view and to ensure balanced exchange, private peers ensure that traffic volumes exchanged between them are approximately equal. Deviations from expectation can trigger policy decisions: peering at other locations instead of the current ones or peering with other ASes. Note that such deviations from balanced levels would require the exceeding peer to pay for the surplus traffic. Aggregated netflow data is often a source for generating data needed for such purposes.

The reasons for measurements of the various exterior gateway protocols (such as BGP) include examining convergence of routing, better use of inter-domain protocol attributes to improve the set of AS paths to be chosen, fixing problems with incorrect or repeated route-related announcements, locating routing loops, etc. BGP policy changes are done to achieve a better balance of load on the different peering links. Routing loops in BGP, be they transient or persistent, are caused by incorrect announcements or withdrawals from external ASes. The affected ASes may have to protect themselves, and one way for this is to examine packet traces and see if the same packet crosses the same monitored point with identical payload, differing only in the TTL field. The particular BGP update that caused the loop has to be close to the occurrence of the loop in a temporal sense for it to be the source of the error. This has implications on where such monitoring has to be carried out [SMD03]. Since traffic is exchanged at multiple peering points simultaneously, the advertisements of routes may not be consistent and may need to be checked. This may require monitoring of the internal (iBGP) routes by an AS.

Faults can be deliberately injected to examine their impact, such as how long before the route is repaired, a better path is discovered, or to examine the difference between the reaction of various ISPs. By participating in remote BGP peering sessions, active measurements can be done to examine failure rates of peering routers and the frequency with which such failures occur. Routing instability is often a result of a few network paths in the Internet.

Access router. Access routers connect the backbone to the set of customers either via dialup lines for smaller residential customers or via higher bandwidth connections for business customers. They are also the routers used to connect to the larger servers such as those providing Web access and email access. For customers, the availability is key and measurements are routinely done to ensure that the failure rate is low to non-existent. Next, service level agreements with larger business customers need to be ensured. If a customer is responsible for providing a latency-sensitive application such as live streaming multimedia or voice over IP (VOIP), the SLA may be quite stringent. Service level agreements go beyond simple high availability, low delay, and low packet loss. Some customers may require packet filtering to be done on their behalf to ensure only packets from a set of sources and packets to a set of destinations are delivered. The filtering may also include limitations on the number of packets in a certain interval. If quality of service is provided then packets may have to be marked to ensure the same. Many customers require that they be provided with periodic statistics ranging from volume to application-specific partition or communication patterns between selected customers. Busier Web servers and email servers require constant performance monitoring and ensure that anomalous events are kept to a minimum. Many customers that provide busy servers expect the access provider to look for attacks and sudden fluctuations in network traffic in a pro-active manner.

4.1.4   Mirror Sites/Network Exchange Points

An Internet Exchange Point [InX] permits various ISPs to exchange traffic at designated peering points. Such exchange points often serve as a redundancy mechanism for ISPs while reducing dependency on upstream providers. Based on the amount of traffic exchanged in each direction the costs can be distributed between the exchange points, although peers typically have roughly similar amounts of traffic in either direction. An exchange point is an interesting location to carry out measurements as it gives a focused view on the actual traffic traversing between ISPs at these points. Traffic monitors that are capable of monitoring bidirectional traffic permit analysis of differences in traffic patterns from a directional viewpoint; for example, if there is more request traffic on one ISP and more response traffic on the other, this might indicate data sources of interest being located in the other ISP.

By purchasing a connection to an exchange point, participants can exchange traffic with all others connected to it; this is similar to hub airports like Heathrow in London, where different airlines exchange passengers [Bak00]. There are numerous exchange points around the world ranging from government-run entities to not-for-profit to industry cooperative ventures. Among the big ones in the United States are MAE-East in Washington D.C. and MAE-West in San Jose and Mountain View, California (MAE is an acronym for Metropolitan Area Ethernet). The Commercial Internet Exchange (CIX) is situated in Palo Alto while the first large free exchange was set up in Hong Kong. The research and education Asia Pacific Advanced Network (APAN) has set up exchange points in Tokyo, Seoul, Chicago, etc. that are connected to each other. The Asia-Pacific Region Internet Exchange spans Novosibirsk to Wellington.

One of the primary purposes of a network exchange point is to keep traffic local; i.e., move traffic between two participants without having to route it through long distance routes. Measurements are needed to ensure that most of the traffic is thus local. One advantage of measuring in exchange points is that it is possible to get a broader idea of shifts in traffic patterns. For example, the longitudinal study [Mkc00] of an exchange point showed traffic shifts between applications with increases in brand new applications.

4.1.5 Wide Area Network

The various measurement sites we have examined thus far are restricted to a single location or point of presence. The amount of traffic at each of these places may differ significantly. We now examine measurements on a wide area network: across the Internet on multiple locations be they co-ordinated and carried out simultaneously or separately over a period of time. Almost any Internet topology related measurement such as distance estimation has to be carried out in the wide area. By their very nature such measurements access numerous autonomous systems and administrative entities. Modeling the Internet as a geometric space with coordinates, properly locating landmarks to carry out measurements, multi-site measurement platforms are some of the interesting issues in wide area measurements. Representativeness of measurements requires that user populations, choices of clients, servers, etc. are reasonably well represented so that proper inferences can be made

Various places in the network. Measurements in more than one place in the network are typically done by researchers as well as measurement companies as a service to companies interested in performance characteristics. The typical locations where measurements are carried out include all the ones listed above but across a wider area; i.e., at multiple points of presence on the Internet.

Multi-site measurements. Often a collection of nodes are used for the purpose of carrying out co-operative measurements. Certain network characteristics and certain applications require that measurements be carried out *simultaneously* from multiple places on the Internet. For example, to obtain a measure of how typical users might experience a Web site, measurements might be carried out on several locations on the Internet corresponding to different user populations.

Carrying out multi-site measurements in a co-ordinated fashion may require clock synchronization, execution serialization, and a command and control mechanism capable of handling access and resource control. The potential for problems are thus magnified as a result of having to deal with diverse problems on different sites, each of which may require some tailoring of the measurement experiment. Beyond technical issues, there are several administrative issues that are unique to multi-site measurements. Concerns about security and resource constraints may result in limited access to local data, processor, and the network. Thus there could be significant variance in measurement capabilities within a single multi-site platform; inferences drawn from such measurements have to be tempered by the potential impact of such constraints.

There have been numerous platforms constructed explicitly to carry out simultaneous measurements from multiple locations. Chief among them are NIMI [AMMP96] and PlanetLab [Plab]. Later in Chapter 10, in examining various case studies, we will examine the range of problems faced during multi-site measurements, the tools and testbeds created to handle this scenario, and the typical applications for which such experiments are essential. More recent work in the AT-MEN [KMS05] project examines how measurements in multiple sites under different administrative entities can be triggered and coordinated. The combination of triggering new measurements exploiting the capabilities of multiple data sites and using existing historical measurements allows for measurement reuse. This is primarily due to the fact that the same parameter is often measured by multiple applications and many measured parameters exhibit varying degrees of stationarity across time and space. For example, many applications on the Internet interested in performance may measure a DNS component which may be reusable across applications if there is not considerable variance in the timescale of interest. Measurements may also be reused across applications.

Representativeness.   Key concerns in carrying out measurements in the wide area network include ensuring representativeness of the entities being measured, the sites/clients from which measurements are carried out, and the paths the measurements might traverse.

With effort it is possible to send probes, say, to a very large number of entities being measured using diverse paths. The entities could be authoritative DNS servers (in a survey of server software, for example), Web sites (to study a wide variety of Web-related measurements, such as end-to-end latency or protocol compliance), or a particular kind of peer-to-peer resource from numerous nodes in diverse P2P networks. Sending probes to a large number of entities, while clearly feasible, risks incurring delays. However, it is virtually impossible to carry out Internet measurements in the wide area from a very large number of nodes at tens of thousands of sites without access to a very large infrastructure. Few research organizations have that kind of access. Companies that have been set up with this aim are often reluctant to provide significant details about their methodologies. Most organizations have to rely on a few dozen to a few hundred client sites from which measurements could be carried out. This could be done by using measurement platforms such as NIMI or PlanetLab, as discussed earlier. The client set has to be representative of the larger Internet and it should be possible to glean some broad inferences from the union of the measurement nodes chosen.

Although attempts to find representative user populations are difficult, attempts are made to map the measurement locales into at least a reasonable subset of the diverse characteristics represented by the various user classes that access a particular application. Among the difficulties are the reluctance on the part of network administrators to share data with others due to privacy and competitive issues.

Given the millions of Web clients on the Internet, including browsers with users behind them and client programs such as crawlers and indexers, it is important to be able to somehow come up with a notion of *representative* collections of clients. This is inherently difficult given the diversity of clients and the user populations behind them. It is somewhat feasible to obtain a cross-section of Web sites, especially due to statistical properties such as skewed access popularity of a few sites and a few resources within such sites. We discuss this in more detail later in Section 7.3.4. But it is much harder to get a handle on client populations given the advent of wireless users and other mobile clients. Demographic information about number of clients using different access technologies (dial-up, cable, DSL, etc.) can be used to get some notion of representativeness. However, the actual fraction of users in each of these categories accessing a particular Web site would have to be factored in as well. As stated earlier, measuring along the path between the clients and the servers is significantly harder. The later version of the HTTP protocol (HTTP/1.1) does have capabilities to target intermediaries but the compliance to the protocol specification is spotty at best. Also, redirection driven either by using Content Distribution Networks or server-farm configurations makes it harder to locate and precisely measure the effect of intermediaries. Some of these difficulties have been faced by companies (such as Keynote [Keya]) that have created commercial performance measurement services for Internet content providers.

4.2   Role of Time

A frequent requirement arising in Internet measurement is the capture of time information. Many of the measurement tasks described in Chapters 5 through 7 require accurate time measurement – for example: measuring round trip times of packets; measuring the delays incurred as packets pass through routers and over links; producing a time-ordered view of measurements taken at different places in the network;

and measuring the performance (response time and throughput) of Internet components.

The Internet is a distributed system with components that are often separated by considerable distances; as a result obtaining accurate time information in the Internet can be challenging. In the case where an accurate clock exists, the distance between components induces communication latency which can make clock readings stale by the time they arrive. Furthermore, many applications (such as packet capture) can require exceptionally precise time information that exceeds the limitations of commonly used clocks.

4.2.1   Background

We start with some terminology for discussing clocks, based on [Mil92, PV02b]. We will denote the true time at any instant as t, and the apparent time reported by a clock at time t as $C(t)$.

Offset. The offset $\theta(t)$ of a clock is the difference between the time it reports and true time, i.e., $\theta(t) = C(t) - t$. An *accurate* clock is one for which $\theta(t)$ is always near zero.

Rate and Skew. The rate of a clock is the first derivative of its apparent time with respect to true time, i.e., $\gamma(t) = dC(t)/dt$. Clearly, an accurate clock will have $\gamma(t)$ always close to 1, or at least the average value of $\gamma(t)$ over relevant timescales will be close to 1. This quantity is often treated as constant, so that the t index is dropped. However, more detailed models of clocks take into account the variability of rate over different timescales. The *skew* of a clock is the difference between its rate and the correct rate, i.e., skew = $\gamma - 1$. This dimensionless quantity is often measured in parts per million (PPM).

Resolution. The resolution of a clock is the smallest amount by which its reported time $C(t)$ can change. Resolution gives a lower bound on the clock's uncertainty.

Note that accuracy is a more stringent requirement than zero skew and so is harder to obtain. A clock that has large offset (and so is inaccurate) but has zero skew is still useful for certain types of measurements. For example, packet round trip times, packet interarrival times, or measurements of server response time only require a clock with zero skew. On the other hand, measurements of one-way packet delay, or time-ordering of events occurring in different places, requires clocks with zero offsets.

Furthermore, the purposes for taking measurements strongly affect the requirements for the associated clocks. For example, one-way packet delays in the Internet will often have magnitudes on the scale of tens or hundreds of milliseconds. Thus, although the clocks involved must be synchronized, it may be acceptable to have resolution and offsets on the order of milliseconds, and even a slight skew. On the other hand, packet interarrival times on a high-speed link may be on the scale of microseconds. For such measurements, the clocks can have any offset, but their resolution must be on the order of nanoseconds, and their skew must be close to zero.

A related factor is that the resolution requirements placed on time measurement typically diminish as one goes up the protocol stack. Response times of a quarter second for DNS, or a few seconds for HTTP, or a few minutes for a P2P application are all within the typical range. As a result, logging done at higher layers is often at a lower resolution; for example, Web logs are generally recorded at 1 s resolution and good Web performance is often described only as 'sub-second' response time.

4.2.2 Sources of Time Information

These considerations suggest that different kinds of clocks are appropriate for different sorts of Internet measurement tasks. There are a number of classes of time sources typically used in Internet measurement, and each is suited to slightly different purposes.

External Time Sources

High-quality reference time is available from a number of sources. The US National Institute of Standards and Technology (NIST) operates three radio services that disseminate time information. Radio clocks are available which make use of these services and provide accuracies on the order of milliseconds to tens of milliseconds [Mil92].

Even more accurate is the Global Positioning System (GPS) which is operated by the US Department of Defense. GPS consists of a constellation of 32 satellites in 12-hour orbits, and is available worldwide. By fusing information from multiple satellites, GPS receivers can achieve accuracy on the order of hundreds of nanoseconds to microseconds. Unfortunately, GPS technology requires relatively large antennas that have at least a partial view of the sky.

Another time source is the CDMA cellular phone system. This timing source is guaranteed to have offset of less than 10 microseconds (which is a requirement for correct operation of CDMA technology). In practice, CDMA base stations take their time from GPS receivers, so it is in essence an alternative source of GPS timing. It has the distinct advantage over GPS of being available indoors, and just uses a small antenna; however, it is only available in areas having CDMA telephony providers.

Such providers are common in the USA, Australia, China, Korea, and Japan, but are virtually absent in Europe.

For both GPS and CDMA time sources, a variety of commercial providers make devices that act as clocks and can be read by PC hardware or accessed via NTP (which is described below). Some specialized network monitoring cards are also capable of reading CDMA and GPS receivers [EMG].

PC-based Clocks

Most commonly, Internet measurements are performed using standard PC hardware. There are a number of ways that time information can be obtained on a PC.

Standard PCs have two clocks. A battery-powered *Hardware Clock* keeps track of time when the system is turned off, and is not typically used while the system is running.

A *Software Clock* is the usual source of time while the system is running. This clock is read using `gettimeofday()` on Unix systems and `GetSystemTime()` on Windows systems. The clock is implemented via a high-priority interrupt generated by a crystal oscillator. The resolution of the clock is determined by the interrupt period, and on current systems is typically 10 ms. The skew of this clock is determined by the properties of the oscillator, and can be in the range $\pm$ 50 PPM, e.g., 50 μs per second. Thus the software clock needs to be corrected on a regular basis.

A third source of time information on PCs is the Time Stamp Counter (TSC) register which has been available on Intel processors starting with the Pentium. The TSC register is incremented every processor cycle. Since the TSC measures processor cycles rather than time directly, it is necessary to calibrate the particular rate of a processor before converting its TSC values to time. The number of CPU cycles per microsecond is measured at boot time, and this constant is used to transform the value in the TSC register to time in microseconds. This clock has resolution better than 1 μs. In Linux systems the TSC is used to interpolate between the values provided by the software clock, so that the `gettimeofday()` function can have true resolution of 1 μs (which is the lower limit defined by the `gettimeofday()` interface definition).

The TSC register has very high oscillator stability; its skew can be as small as 0.1 PPM. However, standard system software can introduce a variety of errors when attempting to exploit this level of precision. To address this, a number of approaches have been developed which make it possible to calibrate and use the TSC as an exceptionally accurate time source [PV02b].

4.2.3 Synchronized Time

Many Internet measurement tasks involve measurements taken using different clocks. For example, one-way packet delay measurements involve measuring the departure time of a packet in one location, and the arrival time of the packet at another point. Accurate determination of the true delay can be obtained in one of two ways. First, one can use clocks that are synchronized, meaning that they have low offset with respect to each other. Second, it is sometimes possible after measurements are made to infer clock offsets and remove their effects.

Synchronized Clocks

Techniques for synchronizing clocks over a network have been intensively studied since the 1980s, and best practices have been incorporated into the Network Time Protocol (NTP) [Mil92, ntp]. NTP is widely deployed in hosts and routers and is universally used in the Internet for clock synchronization.

NTP is organized around the *synchronization subnets*, which are a hierarchical set of time servers and clients. A level in the hierarchy is called a *stratum*; servers at stratum 1 are synchronized to national standards by radio, satellite, or modem. To provide accurate and reliable service, clients typically make use of multiple redundant servers, over different network paths.

At designated intervals, a client sends a request to each configured server and obtains a response. The request and response are both timestamped on departure and arrival, resulting in four timestamps. Using these timestamps, the client calculates an estimate of the clock offset and round trip delay for each server. The general approach taken is that an upper bound on the offset error is half of the round trip time.

Offset estimates are filtered to discard outliers. In the process the algorithm builds up estimates of the accuracy of each server (called *dispersion*), which is used along with stratum level to organize the synchronization subnet into a shortest path spanning tree.

The clock offsets calculated in each round are processed to obtain a consistent subset, then weighted by dispersion and combined to produce a correction used to set the local clock. NTP then attempts to correct the local clock as gradually as possible. Corrections of less than 128 milliseconds are made through gradual changes to the clock; only adjustments of more then 128 milliseconds are made as abrupt changes [Mil98].

While the accuracy of stratum 1 NTP servers can be in the range of 10 μs, a client synchronizing to a stratum 1 server over an Ethernet can achieve clock accuracy of around 1 millisecond, while a client synchronizing over a wide area network can have from 10 to 100 ms accuracy.

Improvements to NTP have been proposed. NTP version 4 (not yet standardized) is designed to achieve microsecond accuracy. Improved clock synchronization methods have been developed based on the stability of the TSC register [VBP04], and methods have also been proposed based on non-hierarchical distribution of time information [GCS03].

In addition, custom clock synchronization approaches have been developed for specialized situations. Probabilistic methods have been developed for low-latency networks (i.e., workstation clusters) [LMC99] and methods based on periodic broadcast have been developed for wireless and sensor networks [EGE02].

Synchronizing Measured Times After the Fact

In the absence of tightly synchronized clocks, it can still be possible in some circumstances to obtain accurate measurements of quantities such as one-way packet delay. This problem was formulated and initial algorithms were proposed in [Pax98].

In the case of two clocks, we can think of the problem as one of inferring from a series of measurements the *relative* offset and *relative* skew of the two clocks involved.

In general, extremely precise measures of relative offset are often unnecessary. As already noted, one-way delay measurements are often on the order of tens or hundreds of milliseconds, which gives an approximate range of the accuracy needed in relative offset estimation. In the case where packets travel symmetric paths it is possible to estimate relative offset using minimum observed round trip times [Pax98]. Path asymmetry is frequent and strong enough that this approach may introduce some error [CPB93a], but that error may be tolerable in certain cases.

A more challenging problem is the elimination of relative skew. This is important because many performance questions involve *variation* in delays rather than magnitude of delays, and relative skew affects measured delay variation. Given some sequence of measured one-way delays, relative skew can be removed by fitting median lines to the data [Pax98], by linear programming [MST99], or by computation of convex hulls [ZLX02].

4.3   Role of Internet Directories and Databases

Although the Internet consists of a very large number of infrastructural entities and hundreds of millions of users, there are surprisingly very few Internet-wide databases. Broadly there are two key databases: address registries and the Domain Name System (DNS). Both play an important role in measurement. The databases are queried during normal Internet use but also as part of measurement efforts. DNS and some address registries are key to the day-to-day operation of the Internet. These benefit from constant maintenance and are rarely out of date. Some of the other databases discussed in this section play only a supporting role and may have information that is not current.

In this section we present an introduction to the databases and discuss typical ways in which they are used in the course of measurement. We also examine the problems faced in dealing with the databases during measurement.

4.3.1 Internet Address and Routing Registries

The Department of Defense in the USA was initially in charge of allocating address ranges to various organizations as well as assigning domain names. Jon Postel manually and largely single-handedly maintained all the assigned Internet numbers before a formal setup was created. The process of transition from a government-managed operation to a decentralized autonomous entity was begun with the creation of InterNIC [INI], leading to the creation of address registries and a distinct mechanism for domain names.

The hierarchy for address allocation and handling is as follows: IANA (Internet Assigned Numbers Authority) controls regional Internet registries some of which include national Internet registries. Below them are local registries; these are typically ISPs with end users as their primary customers. Figure 4.2 (adapted from [APN]) shows how IP addresses are distributed to end users.

An Internet Routing Registry (IRR) was created at the beginning of the commercial Internet in 1995 [IRR] with the purpose of aiding in the engineering of addressing and routing. Multiple networking organizations cooperate in this venture and have set up a clearinghouse for AS number mapping and checking correctness of interdomain routing questions. An AS uses internal routing algorithms to route traffic between components under its administrative control and uses BGP to communicate with other ASes. The mapping from an AS to a list of networks internal to the AS is registered with a routing registry. The IRR allows a network operator to verify whether the information being exchanged in a BGP session is actually correct. For example, if a peer claims to originate a prefix it can be independently verified. While this may not be a constant practice on the part of most ISPs, they can at least ensure that no one is attempting to claim origination of prefixes owned by the ISP. Information in the IRR can be out of date [WG03], and incomplete as the registry is dependent completely on voluntarily supplied information. Individual ISPs are free to register and update their information at their discretion.

Mirroring is provided so database queries can be done locally in numerous places. From a small handful in 1995 the number of interconnected databases has grown to

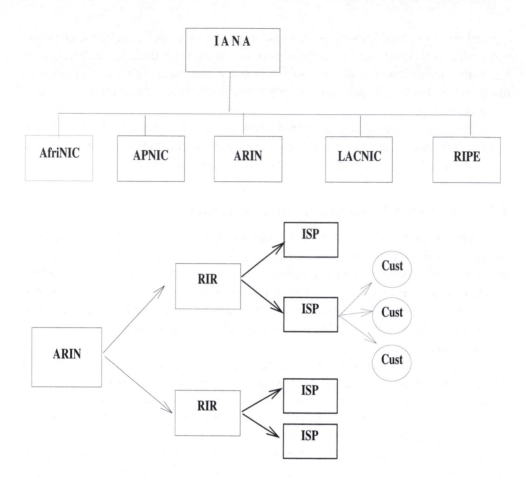

Figure 4.2   IPv4 address distribution.

over 50 covering many regions of the world: North and South America, Europe, Asia and the Far-East. All Internet Service Providers can register either locally with a regional routing registry or with the IRR. Routing registries are primarily used for filtering routing announcements at the edge of a network. A Routing Assets Database (RADb [RAD]) has been set up as a registry of routing information where policy and announcements of participating networks are present to aid in solving routing-related problems. The updating of the Routing Assets Database does not require manual intervention but the networks submitting information may not send in updates promptly. Information in the database may thus be stale. Note that the Routing Assets Database is just one of numerous databases that are part of the Internet Routing Registry with the key distinction being that RADb handles routing registration for networks that are not covered by other registries [RFQ].

Regional Internet Registries There are presently five regional registries: APNIC, ARIN, RIPE, and the two new and emerging LACNIC and AfriNIC; these represent large geographically contiguous portions of the earth. Compared to the earlier days of the Internet, where large chunks of address spaces were handed out somewhat indiscriminately, the regional address registries, such as APNIC, take a more conservative position in handling such resources. Routing tables, which are exchanged in BGP, have become bloated.

Regional registries help manage the rate of growth of tables. Since the number of ASes is currently limited, care has to be taken to limit their proliferation and a unique one is handed out only when there is a need for multihoming and an internal routing policy different from its gateway peers. The routing registries have to arbitrate between the demands of the local customers (such as ISPs and large corporate entities) and the overall needs of the Internet.

APNIC, the Asia Pacific Network Information Centre, based in Brisbane, Australia, covers over 40 countries including some that have a significant and growing fraction of Internet traffic. APNIC, like other regional registries, supports allocation and registration and has both national registries and various privately operated Internet Service Providers among its members. ARIN, the American Registry for Internet Numbers, based in Virginia, USA serves over 40 countries and has over 2000 members who are ISPs. RIPE (*Réseaux IP Européens*, is a regional registry serving (primarily) the European region, consisting of 90 countries and nearly 4000 members.

A relatively recent and rather slowly growing region in terms of Internet traffic is the Latin American and Caribbean region, handled by the emerging LACNIC regional registry. They manage the address space and autonomous systems in the region and coordinate with other regional registries. The most recent entry is the emerging African Network Information Centre or AfriNIC. While the overall fraction of Internet traffic is probably the smallest in this region, significant growth is expected given the large number of countries and fraction of population joining the Internet.

4.3.2 Domain Name System

In Chapter 2 (Section 2.3.8) we discussed the Domain Name System (DNS). DNS is both the naming system and the name of the protocol used to convert Internet names into addresses and vice versa. It is one of the key hierarchical databases on which most Internet applications depend, and also plays a significant role in Internet measurement. The Internet Routing Registries, while useful, perform an auxiliary function and are not essential for the proper functioning of the Internet. The DNS however is vital for the day-to-day operation of the Internet.

The DNS 'database' is actually not a single file or collection of files that are stored on a machine, but a large and diverse collection of databases spread throughout the Internet. Each such location where the local information about the set of machines and addresses is maintained can be tiny or arbitrarily large. Individual user applications trigger lookups and are treated as clients to the local DNS server. Recent lookups can be cached for varying duration of times at the local level to accelerate potential future lookups. The contents of a local database, its cache, and caching policies, are not visible to the external world. Likewise there is no public registry consisting of the set of authoritative servers for a domain. Domain names themselves can be thought of as a tree with branches separating lower-level domains. Administrative partitioning of a domain name space is via the notion of zones. There are various kinds of 'resource records' that DNS uses to map names to data. Among the popular ones are 'A' record (an address record), 'NS' record (name server record) indicating where information about a zone can be found, and 'MX' record used by the SMTP (Simple Mail Transfer Protocol) to find the mail server intended to handle the exchange.

In database terms, DNS provides loose coherency: it is permissible for dynamic addition to the global collection of mappings without each change triggering replications throughout the Internet. Additions of a new top-level domain name are done highly infrequently and the handful of root servers are synchronized to ensure their ability to handle queries about such changes. The hierarchical nature of DNS partitions the work done to handle a vast majority of the typical queries. Caches at the local DNS servers reduce need for communication with the authoritative servers. Since there is a timeout associated with the mapping returned, caches are obligated to refresh their copy before returning it as a response locally. The local copy of the database is often replicated to ensure there is no single point of failure. Clients are configured to serially try one of several local servers in case of failures.

It is important to note that although DNS is a database it is not easy to search it as DNS is not a directory service. DNS resolvers send queries to the DNS servers. The most popular resolver library implementation is the BIND [BIN] package which includes the name server daemon (*named*), and tools like *dig* (Domain Internet Groper). *dig* is used mostly by administrators to look up information in the global DNS database and is a significant improvement over the earlier *nslookup* tool.

4.3.3   Measurement-related Issues in Dealing with Databases

Most measurement on the Internet requires translating names to addresses or vice versa, looking up administrative information, and examining prefix allocation to administrative entities. In other words, the databases discussed above play an important role. Among the problems faced during the access of the databases is that information can be potentially out of date as many of the databases are constantly evolving.

The information may be cached at various locations and the cached information may be stale (e.g., when the time to live field is ignored in DNS mappings). Occasionally the information may be incomplete or accessible to only authorized users present in access-control lists. Inferences made from measurements as a result of these problems will naturally be suspect. The results may also not stand the test of time.

4.4 Measurements Across Various Protocol Layers

So far we have examined the various places where measurements can be carried out: at various components of the physical network. We have also seen the supporting role played by various key registries and databases. We now examine how measurements differ depending on the particular layer of the protocol stack. While some of the differences are obvious – such as scale issues in dealing with raw packets as opposed to higher-level meta-information gleaned from application logs – there are several other subtle differences. We will allude to the differences here and point to the later portions of the book where they are discussed in context and in depth. What follows is thus a high-level overview that prepares the reader for the complexities discussed in more detail in Chapters 5–7.

We examine the measurement issues along three axes:

- Differences in capturing data along the various layers.
- The necessary changes to the infrastructure and instrumentation needed at each of the layers for gathering data.
- Contrasting local, remote, and distributed data gathering.

We conclude with a brief look at measurements on overlays.

4.4.1 Issues in Capturing Data

As hinted earlier, capturing data for measurement varies in technique, complexity, volume, and difficulty among other things, depending on the layer of the protocol stack. We will divide the layers into three broad groups:

- Lower-level protocol data, consisting primarily of router- and link-level data.
- Packet traces and flow-level data involving challenges in terms of detail and representing a larger unit of data.
- Application-level data, gathered at the application layer via wide variety of tools.

Lower-level Protocol Data

When data is gathered at the router or other infrastructural entities, often the key issue is the amount of data that has to be examined. At lower levels large amounts of data are processed quickly. The primary task of the entities is to facilitate quick movement of traffic, and thus any additional tasks may have a performance impact. Worse yet, if any of the resources such as computing or redirecting are impacted, it may lead to packet delay or loss. Depending on the higher-level protocol, such a loss may or may not be fixed. Since traffic flow can be bursty it is hard to predict the amount of resources needed by line cards on a router to ensure its various tasks such as looking up routes, filtering, and handling other constraints. If a fixed fraction of router resources have to be spent in aiding measurements, then it might limit its ability to handle sudden fluctuations in traffic. Even if it were possible to have hardware that can keep up with the flow of a reasonable portion of the traffic traversing the router or a link, gathering simple metrics about them such as counts can consume significant resources. Not all routers and links are constantly busy. Peering routers may be able to provide topology information more easily for example and keep up with the volume of traffic traversing them. In Chapter 5 we will examine the various problems at routers, links, switches, and other Internet infrastructural components.

A typical recourse is to periodically poll for the data or to aggregate the data and export information periodically. Polling technique is reflected in the popular Simple Network Management Protocol (SNMP) which we introduced in Chapter 2. Aggregation is carried out by grouping sets of communication into flows and periodically publishing a record consisting of information about the key characteristics of the exchange such as participating IP addresses, number of packets, etc. The primary observation is that often it is only possible to gather meta-information and statistics at the lower levels.

One advantage of data at this level is its uniformity: given the kind of measurement-related information gathered at lower levels it is possible to agree on a format. This has a cascading effect: tools constructed to process the data can be readily shared and in fact the data can be anonymized for sharing with others in a similar fashion across sites. We will see how divergence at the data level can cause problems for sharing later in Chapter 8.

Obviously to gather information at points close to infrastructural entities access to them is necessary. While not impossible, it is generally harder to gather information about router-level properties remotely.

Issues in Gathering Packet Traces and Flows

As we move up from router-level data to packet-level data there are some similarities and differences in gathering data. The volume remains large and the ability to process any reasonable fraction of data in real time is difficult. Hardware monitors are constantly updated to handle high-speed links (e.g., OC-192mon [Mic05]). Even storing the data passively in real time is a challenge.

Often the gathering of packet-level traces is done without complete knowledge of what fields might be needed. If the data is transient, it is impossible to compensate for any fields that were not gathered in the first place. Typically, more data is gathered and filtered to process the desired fields.

Beyond packet traces, routers often participate in gathering aggregate information about flow of packets between a pair of endpoints. A unidirectional flow connection is often defined by a source and destination IP address and port number, protocol, source router interface, and type of service. The router gathers *meta-information* about the flow in the form of number of packets and bytes used in the exchange, and periodically exports, i.e., outputs, flow records. Cisco's *netflow* [Netc] provides summarization flow records with around 30 fields. The most widely used fields are the source and destination IP addresses and port numbers, the protocol, the start and end time of the flow, source and destination prefixes and Autonomous Systems. Cisco netflow records are dumped when the two endpoints have had a quiescent period of 30 seconds (a configurable parameter, called inactive timeout), or the remote side has closed the connection, or if the flow has exceeded a fairly long activity period (often 30 minutes), or if the router needs to flush its memory cache. Although flow records are aggregated meta-information, simply keeping track of the large number of ongoing flows and being able to output all the records can overwhelm a router. Memory and computation constraints combined with the fact that the primary role of a router is to route packets, leads to sampling the packets before augmenting corresponding flow records being maintained in memory.

The combination of volume and lack of awareness of the precise fields has led to the use of *sampling* in capturing packet traces and in flow construction at the router. Rather than capture every packet, often 1 in every n packets are recorded. Variations on this simple technique include random sampling, count or time based sampling, or flow-state based sampling. The flow collector, which is often an external piece of hardware and software, likewise may have its own bandwidth, memory, and computation constraints in simply draining the packet sampled flows made available by the router. The flow collector may thus resort to its own sampling.

It is possible to correct for errors in sampling via statistical techniques. Sampled data might be considered safe to share with others but the semantic content of each record may be higher. A sampled subset may represent the whole data stream and thus sampling may inhibit sharing! The sheer volume of data at the packet level has led to considerable work on sampling which we examine in depth in Chapter 6 (Section 6.3.3)

A key issue in dealing with packet traces is the tailored software required to reconstruct the traces after the capture. Since packets may be lost or retransmitted, the software needs to be able to compensate for this to recreate the actual pattern of exchange. Information about the directionality of the packet traversal may be required depending on where the packets are gathered and whether additional information about the location is available. With changes in protocol the software has to be updated. While the traditional protocols such as TCP and DNS tend not to change, many of the protocols associated with newer applications (such as networked games and some P2P applications) change the protocol periodically.

Application-level Data Gathering

In general, gathering data at the application level is easier than at the lower levels. Often the time constraints are more relaxed as many applications operate at human awareness timeframe rather than at microsecond rates. Logging is a fairly common operation in most applications and is available as default in several applications. Given the wide range of configuration potential there can be significant diversity in data. Data logging and processing software may have to be tailored to the various configurations.

For interactions across the Internet, application-level data can be captured at the client (originator of requests), server (where the application resides), or at a variety of places in between. For example, Web proxies routinely capture data that includes information about client requests and server responses. Depending on where the proxies reside, they can gather data without significant overhead visible to the clients or servers.

There are several generic tools available to process application-level data via high-level software such as scripts and programs. Anonymization is generally easier, enabling sharing of data more widely at this level.

4.4.2   Changes to Infrastructure/Instrumentation

Gathering data at the various levels often requires changes to the infrastructure. As we mentioned at the outset of the book, measurement is at best an afterthought when it comes to the infrastructural entities in the Internet. Especially at the lower levels, there are typically few choices in how measurements can be done. Periodic sampling, such as SNMP, does require instrumentation but no real change to the infrastructure.

As we move to the packet level, specific devices have to be constructed to keep up with the volume. Significant hardware-level customization such as faster linecards are needed to keep up with the traffic rate and naturally have to be customized to the router variant. Special cards make modification hard and have to be adapted for the same router family with each new generation of routers. To ensure that gathering packet traces does not interfere with the functioning of the router, taps and passive monitoring or packet mirroring devices need to be added.

At the application layer, it is generally easier to change the software to adapt to alternate protocols or protocol variants. Such tools are also more publicly available for interested parties to adapt to their local configuration. In fact, at the application layer, collaborative construction of processing tools is feasible along with an ability to agree on a generic output format. Most of the Web server and proxy logs for example are in one of two formats: Common Log or Extended Common Log. XML formats have been created to unify and simplify exchange of log information across numerous sites [Xml].

4.4.3   Local vs. Remote vs. Distributed Data Gathering

Low-level data gathering is typically only done locally – in a local area network or within a campus under the same administrative control. It is virtually impossible to trigger remote data gathering about routers and links since they are often under strict administrative controls that do not allow remote measurements. While it is possible to target a link or a router remotely to try and obtain round trip time and other traffic-related information, there is a significant amount of guesswork involved. For example, it may not be possible to know which of the interfaces of a router is configured to respond at any given time. Distributed data gathering at lower levels is even less likely given the lack of access.

Packet traces can be obtained at various points in the network: at endsystems they require access to the host or link. They cannot likewise be remotely triggered as typical programs like *tcpdump* used to capture packet streams require local administrator-level access to the monitored link. When gathered locally it is possible to have an idea of expected packets at the destination network. In the middle of the network it may be possible to sniff links but significant work would be needed to separate out unrelated packet streams and reconstruct the exchanges of interest. The problem is further compounded if the traces have to be captured simultaneously as a variety of clock skew issues have to be handled to coordinate the multiple streams.

The generally better and more widespread facilities for gathering data at the application level make for better remote and distributed gathering as well. Application-level data is often gathered locally, remotely, and simultaneously at distributed locations. The availability of higher-layer software, such as scripts and short programs that log application-level data allow for easier installation in various locations. A command and control structure is more easily constructed to start and suspend remote data gatherings. The difficulties with clock skew and monitoring simultaneous gatherings are still present but they are not insurmountable. A key factor is that most application-level data is considered to be innocuous from the viewpoint of impact to users and applications at the various locations. In lower-level data gathering there is often a requirement to construct explicit and tailored hardware to ensure that there is no possible impact due to data gathering. At the application layer, while it is possible for data gathering to cause a visible load on the system, it often has an impact that is not visible when compared to the timescales of interest to users. An added delay of a few microseconds as a result of logging is invisible in a Web response that is of the order of a second or more. The same delay at a router would be unacceptable.

4.4.4 Measurement on Overlays

An overlay is a logical abstraction introduced over the physical network substrate for a variety of purposes. Overlays have been around for a long time and have been used to introduce and experiment with new services on the Internet. Autonomous Systems follow BGP routes and they would not necessarily be able to locate congested links and avoid them. Services can be introduced using the overlay abstraction in a way that circumvents performance problems in the physical counterpart. One way to do this is to use probes in different ASes that compute the best links and if such a path was better than the one selected by BGP, it would be chosen [Ove02]. The cooperating set of intermediate nodes serve as routing helpers in the overlay network. Overlays can be used to study alternate routing technologies, finding routes between arbitrary pairs of hosts, measure packet loss and delays between hosts. Measurements regarding effectiveness of reactive routing and comparing loss and latency reduction to the direct Internet path between pairs of nodes, and impact on path selection have been made. Among the metrics of interest are how often overlay nodes have to probe each other to efficiently compute good paths and detect network outages.

The rapidly growing set of peer-to-peer networks are simply overlay networks used at the application layer. Query messages and responses are sent between nodes over the overlay before selecting appropriate node(s) from which files are downloaded. There have even been proposals to use a set of cooperating nodes in a peer-to-peer network to function as a cooperative measurement overlay to help answer queries related to network performance characteristics.

Part II

In Depth

5

Infrastructure

As discussed in Chapter 1, the physical Internet is in many ways a poorly understood object. In this chapter we survey the physical properties of the Internet, how they can be measured, and what is known at present about the Internet's infrastructure.

5.1 Properties

To begin with, we review the important properties of the Internet's infrastructure. Our approach is bottom-up: we start with physical properties of the component devices that make up the Internet. Then we turn to topology, i.e., how the component devices are interconnected. Next we survey properties of Internet paths – routes taken through the network. Finally we look at how traffic interacts with and is affected by physical infrastructure. In this chapter our discussion of traffic will focus only on those properties such as packet delay and loss which are strongly affected by physical infrastructure. There are many additional properties of traffic that are the subject of more detailed discussion in Chapter 6.

5.1.1 Physical Device Properties

As described in Section 2.2.1, the basic building blocks of the Internet are endsystems, links, and routers. Of these, the infrastructure that concerns us here consists of the Internet's links and routers.

Links

Viewed at the IP layer, the progress of a packet through the network consists of passing from node to node over a sequence of hops. Each hop can be thought of as traversing a link.

A link may be a single point-to-point transmission medium (such as a direct link or leased telephone line), a sequence of connections that are switched below the IP layer (such as multiple Ethernet segments), or a broadcast medium (such as an Ethernet or a WiFi network). Common link technologies and their properties are listed in Chapter 2, Table 2.1.

Each link has a number of properties that can be of interest. *Propagation delay* is the time required for a signal to traverse the link. *Capacity* is the maximum data rate that can be achieved by the link. Furthermore, a number of performance properties can be associated with a link, including packet delay, packet loss, and jitter. These will be discussed in more detail in Section 5.1.3.

Routers

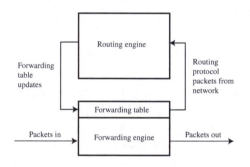

Figure 5.1 Typical router organization.

Routers move packets from one link to another. The internal architecture of routers varies, but a typical organization is shown in Figure 5.1. The key function of the router is to inspect each incoming packet and to select the proper outgoing interface based on the packet's destination address and the router's forwarding table. In high-performance routers this function is separated architecturally from the more involved logic required to participate in the routing protocol – analyzing incoming routing messages, updating the forwarding table, and generating outgoing routing messages. This allows the 'fast path' of packet forwarding to be insulated from the processing demands of protocol processing.

A typical organization for a forwarding engine is shown in Figure 5.2. Packets arriving on each interface are inspected and placed on the proper outgoing interface. The rate at which an outgoing interface moves packets away is the outgoing link's capacity. Since packets may arrive faster than the outgoing interface can take them away, internal buffers are required to hold packets awaiting transmission on each outgoing interface. Usually these buffers are organized as FIFO queues. Packets arriving at a full buffer are simply discarded with no further processing, which is known as

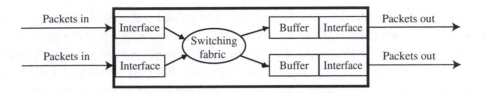

Figure 5.2 Internals of the forwarding engine.

the *drop-tail* service discipline. However, some routers can be configured to perform *active queue management* in which the decision regarding which packets to discard, and when packets should be discarded, is under the control of a more sophisticated algorithm such as RED [FJ93].

Many network measurement techniques rely on eliciting responses from routers, and the details of router internal architectures can affect the time taken to generate responses. In particular, the time required by a router to respond to a protocol message such as an ICMP packet can differ substantially from the time it takes to forward a packet [GP02].

A number of properties of routers are important to measure. From a static standpoint, one may be interested in the set of IP addresses used on the router's interfaces, the geographic location of the router, and the particular type of router or protocol variants it supports. From a dynamic standpoint, one may be concerned with the time a router requires to respond to an ICMP message as well as the time it requires to forward a packet.

Wireless

The use of wireless Internet connectivity has been steadily growing over the last several years. The ubiquitous need to be connected to the Internet has led to the untethering of users from their work and home environments. It is now possible for users to connect to the Internet from many public places such as airports, coffee shops, and even from some 'wilderness' locations. The common wireless media used is radio frequencies, although infrared is also feasible. Note that the primary goal of wireless connections is to link users to wired infrastructures rather than provide end-to-end wireless access. The wireless payload is affixed to radio signals and the modulated signal is transmitted at a specific frequency to a receiver that is tuned to that frequency. The radio waves travel between the wireless adapter on a laptop and a wireless access point which is connected to the Internet using cables. The adapter can be a card or, as is more typical in modern laptops and PCs, is built-in.

The choice of wireless technology dictates the distance at which one can receive such signals, the data rate, reliability, potential interference, and the number of concurrent users. The interference stems from the fact that there is no real regulation covering the radio spectrum and several home appliances and other wireless networks can interfere in the proper functioning. There are general issues of how easy it would be to configure wireless LANs, but lately these have been reduced to 'plug and play'. However, the very open nature of wireless LANs allows for unauthenticated users to try and access the frequencies leading to a host of security measures ranging from passwords, to filtering based on MAC addresses, to encryption. The open nature of wireless LANs remains a fairly serious security problem, although many explicitly enable open networks to allow others to use their Internet connectivity.

There is a wide range of technologies to choose from for wireless networking. Narrowband technology, as the name suggests, has a very narrow signal range and the receiver tunes into that narrow range avoiding communication on other frequency ranges. Wideband technology (also known as spread-spectrum) allows for a signal that can be more easily detected by a receiver. Infrared technology, using a high frequency range, is also used but is nowhere as popular as wideband.

The principal choices for local area wireless networking are the 802.x family of standards that have been instituted by the Institute of Electrical and Electronics Engineers (IEEE) over the last 15 years. 802.11a, 802.11b, and the more recent 802.11g are three versions of the standard and vary in throughput, data rate, the number of non-overlapping channels and range. Wireless transmission can be impeded by several physical objects such as walls. The 802.11b standard is better known as 'Wi-Fi' (wireless fidelity). The different 802.11 standards support the ability of the link to switch between different data rates [LPP04] leading to significant shifts in the available bandwidth between the laptop and the access point.

Bluetooth [SG03] offers connectivity over shorter distances: between 30 and 300 feet without a line of sight requirement. Bluetooth devices consume a lot less power than 802.x devices and are cheaper. Bluetooth falls under the category of Personal Area Networking and allows actions such as connecting to the Internet via a cell phone that may be a few feet away. Bluetooth allows a wide range of devices to communicate with each other once appropriate modules are installed in them. Technically Bluetooth competes with 802.11 standard devices. Bluetooth can handle voice and data simultaneously and thus a popular use is triggering a cell phone to dial a number by voice command. Bluetooth is capable of supporting synchronous and asynchronous network services.

On the other extreme is WiMAX which is a broadband fixed wireless technology covered by the 802.16 Wireless Metropolitan Area Network standards. WiMAX is in its initial stages of development and deployment. Once widely deployed, it may turn out to be more popular than WiFi due to its wider reach.

Measurements involving wireless communication typically deal with signal strength, the amount of power consumed, data bit rates, degree of coverage, session-related information (duration, set-up time, list of applications used, handoffs between access points if any), and error rates. Other measurements include traditional metrics such as link capacity, available and effective bandwidth, identifying bottleneck links, etc. Measurements tend to be complicated due to the combination of wired and wireless networks with varying cross-traffic. Typical single-access networks' link capacity is defined by fixed physical characteristics of the link. In 802.11b networks the capacity changes over time [Joh05] due to user mobility, physical obstructions, cross-traffic on the same frequency (which also leads to packet loss), etc.

5.1.2 Topology Properties

The interconnection patterns of Internet components can be visualized at four levels: *autonomous system, point of presence, router*, and *interface.*

As described in Chapter 2, the Internet is a collection of independently operated and managed networks, organized into autonomous systems (also called routing domains). An autonomous system (AS) may consist of a single network or multiple networks; and a single organization may operate one or more autonomous systems. The routing protocol within an AS is determined by the domain administrator; routing between ASes uses the BGP protocol.

The interconnection pattern of ASes forms a graph called the *AS graph.* In this graph, vertices are ASes and edges connect ASes that directly exchange traffic. This is the coarsest view of the Internet's topology.

The AS graph may be annotated in various ways. Edges between ASes can be categorized according to the commercial relationship of the ASes (e.g., peer–peer or customer–provider) [Hus99a, Hus99b]. Additionally, some pairs of ASes may have multiple connection points; the AS graph can be extended to a multigraph to capture this property.

Within an AS, routers are often collected into identifiable physical locations called *points of presence* (PoPs). A PoP consists of one or more routers in a single location. The PoP-level graph of an ISP is often the most detailed view that an ISP makes publicly available.

An even more detailed view of topology is the *router graph.* In this graph, vertices are routers and edges are one-hop connections between routers. In interpreting the router graph, it is important to distinguish a one-hop connection from a single point-to-point physical link. For example, when a number of routers are connected to broadcast media (such as a FDDI ring or an Ethernet) the resulting router graph will be a complete graph with edges between all router pairs. Further, a single IP hop may be implemented via a sequence of layer-2 devices such as Ethernet switches.

The router graph may be annotated in a number of ways. Each edge can be annotated with its propagation delay and capacity, and vertices can be labeled with their physical location and owning AS. It can also be useful to label routers as belonging to PoPs, so that the PoP-level graph can be obtained from the router graph.

Finally the finest-grain view is given by the *interface graph*. In this graph, vertices are router interfaces and edges are one-hop connections. This graph is important because it is what is directly measured by the `traceroute` tool (which is described in Section 5.3.1). The router graph can be obtained from the interface graph by merging the interface vertices associated with each router as described later.

5.1.3   Interaction of Traffic and Network

Certain aspects of network structure constrain traffic properties: in particular these are minimum possible delay and maximum possible throughput. These are physical limits imposed by infrastructure.

Within these limits, the conditions actually experienced by a packet or set of packets will vary. There are many important properties of traffic that are influenced by network conditions. These traffic properties can be thought of as being determined by the interaction between traffic and the network infrastructure. Definitions of terms used here are in Section 3.5.

Packet Delay

The delay experienced by a packet as it passes through the network is the sum of contributions from various phenomena:

1. *Routing delay.* Routing delay (also called *forwarding delay*) is the time a packet spends inside a router – the time between the arrival of the trailing bit at the router, and the moment the first bit of the packet is placed on the output link. This delay can be broken down into three parts:

   (a) *Packet processing delay.* After a packet arrives, the router looks up its destination address in the forwarding table to determine the appropriate output port. The packet is then moved to the output port through the router's internal switching system. These operations impose various delays on a packet, some of which can be proportional to packet size.

   (b) *Queuing delay.* Queuing delay is the time spent waiting in queues inside routers. In most routers the significant queues are at the output ports. Thus, queuing delay can be thought of as a measure of congestion on the output link.

   (c) *Additional delay.* Routers may occasionally show non-work-conserving behavior (failure to place waiting packets on output links that are in fact idle). In this case, routers can add additional delays to packet forwarding that are not due to either queuing delay or packet processing delay.

2. *Transmission delay.* Transmission delay is the time required to place a packet onto a link. It can be thought of as the time between when a packet's leading bit and trailing bit are placed on a link. For a packet of size s and a link with capacity t, transmission delay can be modeled as s/t.

3. *Propagation delay.* Propagation delay is the time required for a packet to pass from one end of a link to the other end. It can be thought of as the time between when the leading bit of the packet leaves the first router and arrives at the second router. For a link with physical length d in which signals propagate with speed v, propagation delay can be modeled as d/v.

Packet delay is an additive metric. Each of the delay phenomena listed above can potentially occur at each hop along a path, and per-hop delays are additive along a path. Thus, given a set of per-hop delays $\vec{d}_{(h)}$ and a routing matrix $G = A^T$, we can express the set of per-path delays $\vec{d}_{(p)}$ by $\vec{d}_{(p)} = G\vec{d}_{(h)}$.

Packet Loss

Packet loss occurs when a packet is explicitly dropped by a network element, or when it becomes corrupted and subsequently rejected by error-checking (e.g., based on Ethernet, IP, or TCP checksums). The most significant source of packet loss is generally due to congestion. When the output link of a router is busy, the router may explicitly drop packets destined for that output link. This effect leads to correlated patterns of packet loss, so packet loss models involving a distinction between packet-dropping and non-dropping states are commonly used [Gil60, JS00, SCK00].

Conceptually, explicit packet drops in a router could be fully characterized as an arrival process of 'drop' events. However, precise information regarding the instants at which packets are lost is usually difficult to obtain. Instead, packet losses can be characterized as a time series of counts. In this case, counts per unit time can be interpreted as estimates of a time-varying rate of loss. The most commonly used measure is the relative rate of packet loss, which is the fraction of packets lost in a time period. If C_n is the number of packets entering a network element in time period n, and L_n is the number of packets lost during that time period, the relative packet loss rate can be estimated as $\ell_n = L_n/C_n$.

Relative packet loss rate along a path is a multiplicative function of relative loss rates in individual network elements, as long as losses occur independently. That is, if network element i has relative loss rate $\ell_{n,i}$ in time period n, then the aggregate loss rate along that path is

$$\ell_n = 1 - \prod_i (1 - \ell_{n,i}).$$

As long as all $\ell_{n,i} < 1$, this can be converted to a linear relationship by taking logarithms. Thus for a vector of per-hop log complementary loss rates $\vec{l}_{(h)} = \log(1 - \vec{\ell}_{(h)})$, we can estimate path loss rates $\vec{\ell}_{(p)}$ as

$$\log(1 - \vec{\ell}_{(p)}) = \vec{l}_{(p)} = G\vec{l}_{(h)}.$$

Throughput

The combination of capacity limits on network elements and traffic-induced congestion places limits on throughput – the rate at which traffic can flow through the network. If the time interval T is large compared to the time required to traverse a network path, the throughput of the path during time period n can be estimated as C_n/T. Here C_n counts the number of packets that pass over the entire path without loss. The reciprocal of throughput T/C_n is the average packet interarrival time during time interval n. Since most network elements are limited by per-byte processing rather than per-packet processing, another important measure of throughput is bytes per unit time, B_n/T.

Throughput over a sequence of hops is determined by the element(s) with minimum available capacity. The bottleneck may be an endsystem (whose capacity is affected by transport protocols) or a network-internal element. When attention is restricted to network-internal elements, throughput on a set of paths $\vec{t}_{(p)}$ is determined by per-hop capacities $\vec{t}_{(h)}$ by $\vec{t}_{(p)} = G\vec{t}_{(h)}$, where matrix multiplication is performed in $(\min, \times)$ algebra as discussed in Section 3.4.2.

Packet Jitter

Jitter is a measure of the smoothness of a packet arrival process, and can be expressed as the variability of packet interarrival times. Jitter can occur due to time-varying queuing delays in routers along a path. Packet arrivals with low jitter are more predictable and often lead to more reliable application-level performance. For example, media streams with high jitter will show uneven play-out rates.

Characterizing packet jitter requires measurements of packet interarrivals. Complete characterization of packet jitter is given by the interarrival process $\{I_n\}$. More parsimonious and commonly used measures of packet jitter are the moments of the distribution of $\{I_n\}$, e.g., the variance of interarrivals.

Connections

Measurements of packet loss rate, packet delay, and throughput for individual connections can be important for questions involving TCP. Since the average rate at which TCP sends packets is determined by its window size and the current round trip time (RTT) in the network, measures of network RTT within connections can be valuable. The rate at which TCP sends packets is the load it places on the network per unit time; however, packets being sent may be retransmissions. Thus bytes are not necessarily delivered to the application at the rate that the connection sends them. The term *goodput* is used for the rate at which the application endpoint successfully receives data.

One reason for measuring connection-specific RTT and loss rate is that the behavior of common TCP variants has been analyzed, and it is possible to use these quantities to predict a connection's throughput, goodput, and duration [PFTK98, CSA00]. This can lead to models that predict the performance of a potential TCP connection based on passively observed network metrics [GGR02].

5.2 Challenges

Having described the infrastructure properties that are important to measure, we now turn to the challenges that are encountered when measuring those properties.

The challenges to infrastructure measurement take a variety of forms: first, the core elements of the network are deliberately very simple and so do not always support detailed measurement; second, the layered IP model tends to impede visibility of lower layers; third, measurement of some network components can be hampered by specialized network devices; and last, operators avoid providing information about their networks for competitive reasons.

As can be seen, each of these challenges to measurement of Internet infrastructure is a kind of 'poor observability.' As is the case with traffic (Chapter 6), measurement is severely hampered because observability is not built into the design of Internet protocols and components.

5.2.1 Core Simplicity

In contrast to circuit-switched networks such as the telephone network, switching elements in the Internet are designed to be *stateless* with respect to the connections or flows passing through them. Switching elements (routers) are not required to keep track of the connections passing through them or otherwise maintain per-flow state. This stateless approach to the design of switching infrastructure has been called the "stupid network" [Ise97]. This design principle has allowed Internet routers to be very simple, at least as compared to telephony switches.

In fact most forms of instrumentation, even simple per-packet or per-byte counters, add economic cost and complexity of design that can be significant.

The simplicity of routers has undoubtedly been a factor enabling the explosive growth of the Internet. However, the same principle leads to a lack of observability at many points in the network.

Since network elements do not track packets individually, the interaction of traffic with the network is hard to observe. Measurements of packet delay, loss, and through-put are provided on an aggregated basis through SNMP (Chapter 6, Section 6.3.3) but detailed measurement of these properties requires packet capture.

5.2.2 Hidden Layers

The IP hourglass, discussed in Section 2.1.3, has implications for observability as well. Below the IP level, packet transmission can be implemented in many ways that are often very different. These details are hidden at the IP level; even detailed measurements such as packet capture cannot detect these differences. For example, packets passing over one IP hop may pass over a wireless link with complex sig-naling and link-layer retransmission. In another case, packets passing over a single IP hop may actually traverse a label-switched path through many layer-2 switching elements. The abstraction provided by the IP hourglass encourages this phenomenon and its effect may become more pronounced with the advent of all-optical networks.

5.2.3 Hidden Pieces

The end-to-end argument points out that certain functions can only be correctly per-formed by endsystems. The implications of this architecture principle are that in-termediate elements in the data path should forward IP packets without regard to connection-level semantics, and that TCP connections should terminate in endsys-tems rather than at points intermediate along the data path.

A number of devices deviate from the end-to-end architecture principle. Such devices, collectively called 'middleboxes,' are in increasingly common use in the Internet. Middleboxes include firewalls, address translators, and proxies [All03].

There are a number of reasons for the use of middleboxes:

1. Security. Firewalls are used to block unwanted packets from entering or leaving a network. They rely on inspecting the connection-level semantics of packets (e.g., port numbers) to determine whether packets should be blocked, i.e., discarded.
2. Management. Traffic shapers discard packets selectively based on the type of traf-fic they represent. For example, a traffic shaper may be used to ensure that no more than 10% of a network's traffic is devoted to peer-to-peer applications.
3. Performance. Proxies are middleboxes that terminate TCP connections inside the network. For example, a caching proxy will intercept a request for a Web page and

serve it out of the local cache to avoid the performance penalty of retrieving the object from the origin server.

4. Address translation. Network address translators (NATs) change the network layer addresses and the transport layer port addresses in passing traffic from one network to another. This allows addresses inside one network to be reused (by mapping them to port numbers outside the network). This can be attractive when IP addresses are scarce, or when one desires to keep true IP addresses hidden.

Each of these types of middlebox impedes visibility of network components in some way. For example, firewalls may block UDP or ICMP packets being used by `traceroute`; NATs can prevent the discovery of endsystems via `ping`.

5.2.4 Administrative Barriers

Finally, there are a number of administrative reasons why Internet infrastructure can be challenging to measure.

Internet service providers frequently seek to hide internal details of their networks from outside knowledge. The configuration details of individual routers, their interconnection patterns, and the amount of traffic carried over network links are all considered competition-sensitive. This may be because a competitor can gain an advantage in negotiation or pricing if these details are known.

As a result, ISPs frequently block traffic that may be used to measure infrastructure. For example, ICMP ECHO packets (as used by `ping`) may be blocked at an ISP's ingress routers. Likewise, attempts to make SNMP connections to routers from outside the ISP's network are generally blocked. Information that an ISP does provide, such as network topologies, is often simplified; e.g., rather than publishing router-level topologies, ISPs often publish PoP-level topologies.

Thus, it can be difficult to obtain a detailed picture of portions of the Internet infrastructure simply because ISPs actively seek to hide such details from outside discovery.

5.3 Tools

In this section we discuss tools for measuring infrastructure properties. We first cover general active and passive methods for discovery of infrastructure properties. We then review analysis methods that combine results from different kinds of measurements. Next we look at two special cases that have been the focus of considerable effort: bandwidth measurement and latency measurement. We conclude with a review of the use of inference to supply missing data in infrastructure measurement.

5.3.1   Active Measurement

Active measurement refers to methods that involve adding traffic to the network for the purposes of measurement.

Ping

`Ping` sends an ICMP ECHO packet to a target, and captures the ECHO REPLY packet. `Ping` is useful for checking connectivity to the target, and for measuring the instantaneous RTT between the sender and the target. It has the advantage that only the sender need be under experimental control; the target merely responds in normal fashion (i.e., according to rules of the IP protocol). `Ping` is one of the oldest, and most commonly used tools for infrastructure measurement.

The RTT measured by `ping` consists of the total instantaneous delay along the path from sender to target, and the path from the target back to the sender. However, with such measurements, it can be difficult to determine the direction in which congestion is experienced. If the delay in one direction only is desired, then the usual approach is for both endsystems to be under experimental control. In this case accurate measurement of one-way delays requires synchronized clocks, or a method to remove clock offset and skew from measurements (as described in Chapter 4, Section 4.2). An example tool that measures one-way delay is OWAMP [owa]. OWAMP requires a demon process to run on the target, which listens for and records probe packets sent by the sender.

When using probes such as `ping` to measure RTT, it is important to consider whether periodicities in the RTTs being measured have the potential to affect the results. For this reason, the `zing` tool allows probes to be sent at random, exponentially distributed intervals, to allow unbiased sampling of RTT [ZDPS01].

Traceroute

As pointed out in [VE03], the lack of observability in the Internet service model often leads to users distorting network features to obtain desired data. A good example is found in `traceroute`, which uses the TTL field in a clever but unintended way.

As discussed in Chapter 2 (Section 2.3.1) the IP header contains a *time to live* (TTL) field that is initialized by the sending host and decremented by one each time the packet passes through a router. If the field ever reaches zero, the IP protocol requires that the packet be discarded and an error indication be sent back to the original sender. The error indication is an ICMP TIME EXCEEDED packet.

The source address of the ICMP TIME EXCEEDED packet is an interface of the router that discarded the original packet (in particular, it is the interface that is used

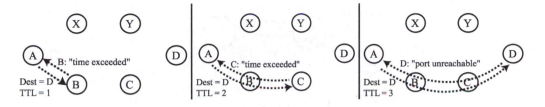

Figure 5.3 `Traceroute` in operation.

to transmit the returning ICMP packet [Bak]). So if a packet having a TTL set to n is sent towards a particular destination, the router that is n hops along the path can be identified from the resulting ICMP TIME EXCEEDED packet, as long as the path to the destination is more than n hops.

The usual operation of `traceroute` is shown in Figure 5.3. In this figure, node A is trying to discover the path to node D. It sends a sequence of UDP probe packets with increasing TTL to an "unlikely" port on destination D. The destination host can be identified since it will respond with an ICMP *port unreachable* packet. From the responses received, A can infer that the path to D is

$$A \rightarrow B \rightarrow C \rightarrow D.$$

A large-scale measurement system that uses `traceroute` to discover network topology is the `skitter` project, which is described in Chapter 10.

This method of discovering network paths has a number of caveats relating to the asymmetry of paths, the instability of paths and resulting false edges, the problem of IP alias resolution, and the problem of measurement load. We treat each of these in turn.

Path Asymmetry. The nodes visited by `traceroute` are those in the *forward* path from the source to the destination. This is not necessarily the same as the set of nodes in the *reverse* path. That is, if D were sending packets to A, those packets are *not* guaranteed to follow the path

$$D \rightarrow C \rightarrow B \rightarrow A.$$

Instead, they may pass through other nodes (such as X or Y). Path asymmetry is common in the Internet, and so the output of `traceroute` must be interpreted only in terms of a directed path from source to destination.

Unstable Paths and False Edges. Strictly speaking, `traceroute` only reports the nodes visited by successive probe packets with increasing TTL. It is only valid to

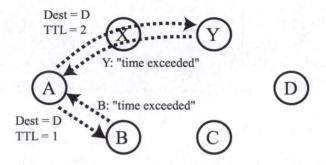

Figure 5.4   `Traceroute` behavior with unstable paths.

interpret this sequence as an IP path if the path being measured does not change during the measurement process.

If IP paths are not stable over the measurement period, then successive probes may follow different paths. An example of this is shown in Figure 5.4. In this case, when sending to node D, node A alternates between using B and X as the next hop. When sending to D, node X uses Y as the next hop.

In the example the first probe packet takes the path toward B, and the second probe packet takes the path toward X. This yields the inferred path segment

$$A \rightarrow B \rightarrow Y.$$

This incorrectly inferred path seems to show a direct (one-hop) connection between nodes B and Y, where none need necessarily exist. The inferred connection between B and Y is a *false edge*.

In fact, there are many possible sequences of probe responses that may be observed:

$$A \rightarrow B \rightarrow C \rightarrow D$$
$$A \rightarrow B \rightarrow Y \rightarrow D$$
$$A \rightarrow X \rightarrow C \rightarrow D$$
$$A \rightarrow X \rightarrow Y \rightarrow D$$

Of these four sequences, only the first and last are in fact valid paths in this example. A typical method for avoiding false edges and invalid paths is to eliminate from consideration any `traceroute` output that shows path instability (multiple observed paths over a short measurement period). There is further discussion of these issues in [HBkC03, HPMkc02].

Alias Resolution.   It is important to note that `traceroute` discovers *interfaces* rather than *routers*. Nodes along the path (routers) will generally have multiple network interfaces. Each network interface has a different IP address. The source IP address in the ICMP TIME EXCEEDED response packet is the address of the interface that the router uses when sending packets to the source.[1] In the example shown in Figure 5.3, assume that node B has three interfaces; it connects to A via interface 200.0.0.1, it connects to C via interface 200.0.0.2, and it connects to X via interface 200.0.0.3. Then the IP address in the source field of the TIME EXCEEDED response will be 200.0.0.1. This is the address that A is able to discover.

This is important because one generally does not know *a priori* which interfaces belong to the same router. For example, if X were to use traceroute to discover the path to D, and if the path passed through node B, the interface discovered by X would be 200.0.0.3. Given these two sets of path measurements (A to D, and X to D), it would not be clear that both paths passed through the same node (B).

This problem arises whenever one seeks to form a router-level topology map from a collection of traceroute measurements. A number of methods have been developed for *alias resolution* – discovering whether two interfaces belong to the same router.

A commonly used method for alias resolution is to send ICMP ECHO packets to both interfaces from the same source. If both interfaces belong to the same router, the responses will both be sent from one interface (as per the RFC1812 mandated behavior). By matching ECHO REPLY messages having the same source interface, one can infer that the original ECHO packets were sent to a common router [PG98, GT00].

Other responses that can be used to aid in alias resolution are IP identifications (IP IDs) and TTLs contained in the packets from the responding router [SMW02] (IP IDs and TTLs were discussed in Chapter 2, Section 2.3.1). Many routers generate IP IDs for outgoing packets in increasing sequence. Thus two packets from the same router will tend to have IP IDs that are close together in value. In addition, all packets from the same router arriving at a given point will have the same value in the TTL field (unless paths change during measurement). Thus, if two packets arrive at a measurement point with different TTLs, that is an indication that the packets came from different routers.

Another approach is to use the Record Route option. As described in Chapter 2 (Section 2.3.1), routers that support this option will insert the address of the interface on which the packet is sent into the header of the packet during the forwarding process [Pos81]. This interface is often different from the one which appears in an ICMP ECHO REPLY [Keyb]. This allows the two interfaces to be associated with the same router.

---

[1]RFC1812 dictates that the source address of an ICMP packet should be set to the address of the outgoing interface, rather than the address of the interface on which the triggering packet was received [Bak].

Finally, it is also possible at times to 'guess' addresses that correspond to adjacent routers. For example, for ease of management links between two routers are often given addresses that only differ by 1; e.g., `200.0.0.1` and `200.0.0.2`.

Measurement Load.   An additional concern in `traceroute`-style measurements can be seen in Figure 5.3: the link from A to B is traversed three times. In general, `traceroute`-style measurements can place considerable load on individual network links, especially in experiments attempting large-scale topology discovery.

There are two variants of the measurement load problem. In the first case, running `traceroute` from a single source to many destinations will tend to place heavy measurement load on links near the source. In the second case, running `traceroute` from multiple sources to the same destination will tend to place a heavy load on links near the destination.

Optimizations have been used to try to minimize these problems. The basic idea is to track interfaces that have been visited already, and stop probing when an interface is visited that has already been seen. These optimizations assume that routes are stable and that there is only a single path between each source and destination, so that the set of paths used by a single source forms a tree, and the set of paths converging on a single destination also forms a tree.

In the single-source case, this optimization involves performing the `traceroute` in reverse. That is, the first probe packet sent is intended to travel all the way to the destination; subsequent packets reduce TTL by one so as to report on nodes in the path in reverse order. In terms of Figure 5.3, the progression of probes is from right to left. The advantage of this scheme is that when an interface is reported that has been previously seen, the probing process can stop. This is true because earlier measurements will already have discovered the rest of the path to such a previously-seen node [GT00].

In the multiple-source case, this optimization involves exchanging information among probe sources about previously-seen nodes. In this case, probes are sent with increasing TTL. For example, assume that A has discovered the path to D to be: A → B → C → D. When X begins running `traceroute` to D (with increasing TTL), it discovers node B on the path. If it has access to the path information already discovered by A, it can stop, because it can infer that the remainder of the path (B → C → D) will be the same as already discovered by A.

In a setting where multiple sources are running `traceroute` to multiple destinations (as is typical, for example, with `skitter`), these two kinds of optimizations are both desirable. However, they imply different probing strategies; one way to obtain the benefits of both optimizations is to attempt to start in the 'middle' of the path and then probe both forward and backward until previously-visited nodes are seen [DRFC05].

Variants.   In addition to its use for discovering router-level topology, `traceroute` can be used to explore AS-level topology as well. The basic idea is to determine for each router or interface on the `traceroute` path the AS to which it belongs. Once this is known, the AS path can be formed by simply aggregating all nodes in the router path that are part of the same AS.

In practice it can be difficult to associate each interface accurately with the correct AS. Mappings of interfaces to ASes may be extracted from route registries, or from BGP tables, but these need to be used with care [CJW01, MRWK03].

We note that some aspects of the methods used in this section do not apply to IPv6 routers. IPv6 headers do not contain an IP ID field, and the IPv6 address space is so large that address guessing is not likely to be effective. These issues are discussed in more detail in [WCVY03].

Finally, while most topology discovery is concerned with the IP level, it can also be useful to discover the layer-2 topology of a large Ethernet. This can be done through inspection of the SNMP MIBs of the physical devices [BBGR03].

Other Active Methods

Another useful tool for active network measurement is multicast. Probes sent via multicast have the property that a single probe is replicated by routers along the path, so that network conditions experienced by a single upstream packet are reflected in measurable properties of multiple downstream packets. This makes it possible to correlate end-to-end measurements from a set of intersecting network paths to infer performance characteristics of the intersection [ABC+00]. These inference techniques will be discussed in more detail in Section 5.3.7.

A general idea in active probing is that packets sent at nearly the same time over the same path experience similar network conditions. One way this can be used is to infer the network conditions during packet loss. Generally, when an active probe is lost, whatever information it might provide is lost with it. However, if two packets are sent at nearly the same time, and only one packet is lost, then the other packet's delay conveys some information about the network conditions experienced by the lost packet [LC01]. A similar idea can be used to infer queue size at access routers, as described in [CKL+04].

System Support for Active Measurement

Many active measurement methods involve injecting arbitrary packets into the network, or capturing arbitrary packets from the network. Unrestricted access to the network interface raises security issues, and network administrators are often hesitant to grant such access. Furthermore, efficient packet injection and accurate measurement of packet departure and arrival times is best done at the operating system kernel level. For this reason libraries and system interfaces have been defined that are specialized for active network measurement.

`Scriptroute` [SWA03] is a tool that allows unprivileged users the ability to capture packets from the network, and inject packets into the network, within policy boundaries established by system administrators. `PeriScope` [HBB02] is a programmable library implemented inside the operating system kernel, with an application programming interface (API). Using the API, applications can define new probing structures (number, size, type, and departure timing of probing packets) and inference techniques for extracting results from the arrival pattern of probe responses.

5.3.2   Passive Measurement

Passive measurement refers to capturing traffic that is generated by other users and applications, rather than as part of the measurement process. The most common use of passive traffic measurement is to understand the properties of traffic itself, and so is covered as part of Chapter 6. In this section we focus only on passive methods for infrastructure measurement. These generally consist of capturing and analyzing control plane (routing) traffic.

BGP

The inter-domain routing system, as implemented via BGP, determines how traffic is exchanged among autonomous systems. Thus a BGP routing table provides partial information about the AS-level topology – the connections between ASes that are present to support traffic exchange.

A BGP routing table is the set of AS paths that are advertised via BGP at a particular point in the Internet. Each path represents a sequence of ASes that may be used to reach a particular range of IP addresses (specified by an address prefix, e.g., `200.20.10.0/24`). The fact that two ASes appear in sequence in an AS path is evidence that they are directly connected and is the basis for inferring AS-level topology from BGP tables.

Each AS advertises to its neighbors the routes that it knows. Hence routes are propagated in reverse direction from traffic flow. That is, if AS 1 advertises to AS 2 that it has a route to prefix `200.20.10.0/24`, then traffic toward that prefix will flow from AS 2 to AS 1. As a result, to understand how traffic flows into any particular AS, it is necessary to obtain BGP tables (sometimes called *views*) from many other ASes. This fact has led to the establishment of the `routeviews` repository, which collects BGP views from a large set of ASes [Rou]. Although `routeviews`

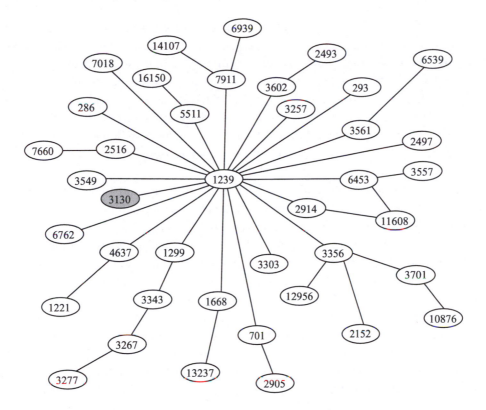

Figure 5.5 Partial AS topology from BGP. Data from `routeviews`.

was mainly intended to aid network operators in understanding the state of the BGP system, it has become a very useful data source for passive Internet topology monitoring and analysis.

A portion of the `routeviews` database is shown in Figure 5.5. This figure shows a set of paths to a particular prefix within AS 3130 (shaded in the figure); as can be seen, all paths to AS 3130 also pass through AS 1239. Numbers in the figure are ASes. Each path is the sequence of ASes taken to reach the given prefix starting from a different AS. Thus each path comes from a different BGP view stored in the `routeviews` repository.

This figure shows some of the strengths and weaknesses of passive topology discovery via BGP. The principal strength is the large set of AS–AS connections that are easily learned simply by processing BGP views. However, there are considerable drawbacks as well. First, note that the paths form a structure that is approximately tree-like, rooted at the target AS. Any cross-connections between ASes that may exist are not discovered (because such connections are not used in routing to the target prefix). This drawback may be partially addressed by fusing the information obtained by considering routes to all prefixes, i.e., by merging all available BGP tables. Nonetheless, many cross-edges will still be missing from the resulting AS graph.

A second problem is that route aggregation and filtering tends to hide certain AS–AS connections from view. If the target AS (3130 in this case) aggregates routes before advertising them, the corresponding AS edges will not be visible in the resulting AS graph. For example, if AS 3130 has customer ASes with contiguous address prefixes then AS 3130 may not issue separate advertisements for these ASes and those ASes will not appear in the AS graph.

Filtering also affects the ability to observe AS–AS edges. If two ASes peer they will not globally advertise routes that include this peering relationship. Hence the resulting AS graph will not show the peering edge.

A third problem with the AS graphs derived from BGP views is that many ASes (especially tier-1 ASes) will have multiple physical connections. Often large ISPs will peer at multiple locations for efficiency and redundancy. However, only a single edge between the two ASes will be visible in the resulting AS graph.

Besides using `routeviews` data, it is possible to obtain BGP updates directly by registering to receive them through a session with a BGP-speaking router (this is described in more detail in Chapter 6, Section 6.3.1). These updates (route announcements and withdrawals) provide a local view of how routes are changing in the network as a whole, which can shed light on the current inter-domain topology. However, there are a number of caveats: it may not be possible to obtain BGP updates at the point of interest; the local view obtained from BGP is necessarily incomplete (just as when using BGP tables); and routing anomalies and 'noise' in BGP updates can make it difficult to infer the true state of the inter-domain routing system. In particular, it is important to measure and interpret BGP update streams carefully; some guidelines for how to do this are presented in [WZP+02].

OSPF

It is also possible to obtain infrastructure measurements passively within a single autonomous system or enterprise network. This can be done by capturing control plane traffic generated by the interior gateway protocol, usually IS–IS or OSPF.

Using OSPF as an example, one can passively capture link state announcements (LSAs) within a routing domain. The particular location where announcements are captured is not as important as was the case for BGP, because OSPF is a flooding protocol designed to send all announcements to all participating nodes. Link state announcements may be the result of OSPF's soft-state refresh mechanism, or they may be the result of topology changes in the underlying network. In the case of topology changes, LSAs indicate that a particular link has become unavailable or has resumed availability. In addition, LSAs are issued when external routes (routes to prefixes outside the routing domain) change availability.

Thus passive capture of OSPF traffic can provide considerable insight into the topology of the router graph within the autonomous system, as well as into the dynamics of the external routing system. More details and examples of OSPF analysis are found in [SIG$^+$02].

5.3.3 Fused Measurements

In measuring infrastructure or discovering topology characteristics, it is often useful to fuse different kinds of measurements, including combining both active and passive measurements.

One difficulty with active measurement is the large amount of probe traffic that is required, even when the goal is simply to map a single AS. One strategy for reducing the probe traffic required to map an AS is to make use of passive topology measurements (BGP views). Using these views, one can identify a limited set of addresses that are likely to be part of the target AS. One can then limit probes to just those addresses, as described in [SMW02].

Another way to improve the quality of AS maps is to augment passively obtained BGP topologies with additional inter-AS connections inferred from active (traceroute) measurements. Likewise one can make use of the Internet Routing Registries as an additional source to augment BGP-derived topologies [CGJ$^+$02a]. In studying congestion dynamics it is possible to correlate large sets of RTT measurements with BGP-derived topology data to localize performance degradations in the Internet [BBCKM02].

5.3.4 Bandwidth Measurement

Apart from the general measurement approaches covered above, there are two specific problems that have been the focus of considerable effort in Internet measurement: bandwidth measurement and latency measurement. In this section we cover bandwidth measurement and in the next section we cover latency measurement.

The terms *bandwidth* or *throughput* are used in networking to mean the amount of data that the network can transmit per unit time. Measurement of bandwidth is important for applications that intend to adapt their behavior to the properties of the network. Examples include:

- Streaming media applications, where the goal is to adjust the transmission rate to the network bandwidth;

- Server selection, where the goal is to find a server with an appropriate bandwidth connection to the client;
- Estimating the bandwidth-delay product for use in TCP flow control;
- Overlay networks, where the goal is to route data over good-performing paths; and
- Verification of service level agreements between network customers and providers.

Generally bandwidth measurement is an active process, in which packets are injected into the network and the measurement process is based on resulting observations. Sometimes both endpoints of the measurement path are assumed to be instrumented, while in other settings only one endpoint is active and the other endpoint is simply expected to respond to an ICMP ECHO or a similar trigger. However, some passive methods of bandwidth measurement have been proposed, and applications can use their own data packets as a source of information for bandwidth estimation.

Along any Internet path there will be one link that has minimum throughput during the measurement period. This link is called the *bottleneck* link and it determines the maximum throughput of the entire path. In some settings it is sufficient merely to measure the bottleneck bandwidth, while in other settings the bandwidth of each link is desired. In the cases where a single IP hop is realized via a sequence of multiple physical links (as in a VPN or an MPLS-switched network) it can be quite challenging to infer link-by-link bandwidth.

There are three kinds of bandwidth that may be of interest to measure: capacity, available bandwidth, and bulk transfer capacity.

1. *Capacity.* The capacity of a link or path is the maximum possible throughput that a link or path can sustain. This is sometimes called 'uncongested' bandwidth. Capacity is a property of a path that does not frequently change; it only changes when the underlying infrastructure – router and/or link speeds – changes. Sometimes the term *bottleneck bandwidth* is also used, but this term can lead to confusion with respect to available bandwidth, and so we will not use it.

2. *Available bandwidth.* The available bandwidth is the portion of capacity that is not being used during a given time interval. For example, if a link's capacity is 1000 Mbit/sec and currently 600 Mbit/sec are flowing over the link, then the available bandwidth is 400 Mbit/sec. This is sometimes also called *residual capacity*.

   Available bandwidth varies on a fine timescale, and so is generally defined with respect to some averaging timescale τ. At any instant a network interface is either busy transmitting data or is idle. Average utilization during the period $(t - \tau, t]$ is defined as the fraction of time during that interval that the interface is busy sending data. That is, if $u(t) \in \{0, 1\}$ denotes the instantaneous activity of the link at time t ($u(t) = 1$ iff the interface is busy) then the average utilization of the associated link is defined as

$$\bar{u}(t - \tau, t) = \frac{1}{\tau} \int_{t-\tau}^{t} u(x) \, dx.$$

Available bandwidth of a hop with capacity C for the given time interval is then

$$(1 - \bar{u}(t - \tau, t)) \, C.$$

3. *Bulk transfer capacity.* The available bandwidth is not necessarily what would be obtained by a new connection making use of the link or path. Most reliable data transfer in the Internet makes use of TCP for flow control, and the control algorithms of TCP will interact with competing traffic in a complex manner. For example, if the available bandwidth on a given path is 400 Mbit/sec, a new connection flowing over that path may flow at 400 Mbit/sec, or 500 Mbit/sec, or even 300 Mbit/sec. Bulk transfer capacity is the rate that a new single, long-lived TCP connection would obtain over the given path. The definition assumes that the connection's rate is only limited by its congestion window and not by other factors (such as the receiver's advertised window).

The different kinds of bandwidth necessitate more precise definitions of the notion of bottleneck link. When concerned with measuring capacity, the key link is the *narrow* link – the link with minimum capacity along the path. In the case of available bandwidth, one is concerned with the *tight* link – the link with minimum available bandwidth. Note that for a given path these two links may not be the same.

Methods for measuring bandwidth are generally focused on observing how packet delay is affected by link properties. The factors that contribute to packet delay were covered in Section 5.1.3 and are important to review to understand bandwidth estimation methods. As described in that section, link bandwidth primarily affects packet transmission in two ways: *queuing delay* and *transmission delay*. These two ways are each exploited in various bandwidth measurement methods.

In the case of queuing delay, the way a link's capacity and available bandwidth affects a packet depends on the sizes of packets that are queued ahead of it for the link. In the case of transmission delay, the way a link's capacity affects a packet depends on the size of the packet itself. The first effect is the basis for *packet-pair* methods. The second effect is the basis for *size-delay* methods. A third approach is simply to send sufficient traffic to congest the network path, and a fourth method is to transfer data using TCP over the path being measured. Each of these four methods is discussed below.

Packet-Pair Methods

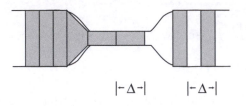

Figure 5.6   Packet-pair spacing set at narrow link.

Capacity Measurement. Packet-pair methods were the first methods developed for capacity measurement and are based on ideas set out in [Jac88, Kes91, Bol93].

The basic idea of the packet-pair method is illustrated in Figure 5.6. In this figure packets of equal size are progressing from left to right and are queuing at the narrow link. The lower capacity of the narrow link imposes a fixed delay between the leading edge of each successive packet, related to the fixed packet size. As packets leave the narrow link, this fixed delay is preserved. Downstream, this fixed delay can be measured and used to infer the bandwidth of the narrow link.

For a given packet pair, we define the inter-packet gap Δ_i as the time between when the leading edge of the first packet arrives at link i, and when the leading edge of the second packet arrives at the same point. The arrival in question of each packet occurs at the moment when the router interface begins to place the packet on the outgoing link. In the case shown in the figure, there are no intervening packets between the two packets forming the packet pair. In that case, if the first packet has size L and the capacity of link i is C_i, then

$$\Delta_{i+1} = \max\left(\Delta_i, \frac{L}{C_i}\right).$$

Note that for this effect to occur, the probe packets must queue back-to-back at the narrow link. If the capacity of the narrow link is C and the interpacket gap at the source is Δ_0, then one way to make queuing at the narrow link likely is to send probe packets with $\Delta_0 < L/C$.

The basic principle behind capacity estimation by this method is to send packet pairs over a network path consisting of H links. Then if no other packets are flowing over any links of the path, and if probe packets queue for service at the narrow link,

$$\Delta_{H+1} = \max_{i \in 0,\dots,H}\left(\Delta_i, \frac{L}{C_i}\right) = \frac{L}{\min_{i \in 0,\dots,H} C_i} = \frac{L}{C}$$

where C is the capacity of the path.[2] One then estimates C as L/Δ_{H+1}.

Two difficulties arise in applying this principle in practice. First, it is necessary to

---

[2]We define C_0 to be L/Δ_0.

Figure 5.7   The probe gap method.

ensure that packets queue for service at the bottleneck link. This means that packet sending rates must be varied to ensure that sending rate is greater than the bottleneck link. This can be accomplished by setting Δ_0 as small as possible by sending packets back-to-back on the first hop. However, sending many packets at this high rate can impose a noticeable measurement load on some links in the path.

The second and much more difficult problem is that it is likely that individual packets in the pair will experience different queuing delays along the path. This can happen due to *cross-traffic* – traffic sharing one or more links with the probe traffic. The effect of cross-traffic can be hard to predict. In general, variation in the amount of cross-traffic may cause any particular packet pair to report a bandwidth estimate that is either greater or smaller than the true value.

The problem of cross-traffic has generally been addressed by sending many packet pairs and by using various filtering methods to try to eliminate erroneous measurements; some example methods are described in [CC96, Pax97b, LB01]. A useful insight in this regard is that packet pairs that observe the minimum queuing delay are likely to give the best estimates [KCL+04]. Unfortunately, when a large number of packet pairs are sent, the correct value may not even be the most commonly obtained estimate. Algorithms for careful selection of the best estimate from a collection of packet-pair measurements are given in [DRM04].

Available Bandwidth.   A set of related techniques called *probe gap methods* have been developed for measuring available bandwidth.

Rather than measuring available bandwidth directly, probe gap methods seek to measure the amount of cross-traffic flowing over the tight link during a measurement interval. Available bandwidth is then obtained by measuring the capacity of the tight link and subtracting.

The general idea is illustrated in Figure 5.7. Probe packets are sent with some initial gap Δ_i and after passing through the tight link $i + 1$, have a new gap Δ_{i+1}. The new gap is determined by the old gap plus the size of any cross-traffic packets that arrived between the trailing edge of the first probe packet and the trailing edge of the second probe packet. The method assumes FIFO queuing within the router so that all such cross-traffic packets are emitted in between the two probe packets. It also assumes that the router queue does not empty between arrival of the first and second probe packets. Furthermore, it assumes that the initial gap Δ_i is equal to the gap Δ_0 when packets are emitted at the source.

Another assumption made in this method is that the tight link is the same as the narrow link. This assumption means that one can use a measurement of the narrow link capacity C in computing available bandwidth. Finally, one assumes that the final gap Δ_{H+1}, which is what can be measured, is the same as the gap set by the tight link Δ_{i+1}.

If these assumptions hold, then the available bandwidth A can be estimated as:

$$A = C \times \left(1 - \frac{\Delta_{H+1} - \Delta_0}{\Delta_0} \right).$$

This calculation requires an estimate of capacity C which can be obtained using packet-pair methods described above.

One key to this method is ensuring that the tight link's queue does not empty between arrival of the two packets forming the probe pair. This can be accomplished by first estimating the narrow link's capacity, and then computing the inter-packet gap that corresponds to the transmission time of the first packet in the probe pair over the narrow link, which is the approach taken in [SKK03]. Larger probe packets thus provide measures of A over larger intervals τ.

Unfortunately, to guarantee that the tight link does not empty between probe packets requires sending the two packets close together. This can lead to placing a heavy load on the tight link, which can affect the cross-traffic being measured. Hence it is useful to vary the inter-packet spacing in the probe in a manner designed to efficiently sample a wide range of timescales τ [RCR+00].

Size-Delay Methods

In a packet-pair probe, the gap Δ between two packets carries information about the capacity of a previously traversed link. However it is also possible to extract similar information from the transmission time of a single packet. The key observation is that, in the absence of any cross-traffic, the delay experienced as a packet passes over a link is affected by the packet's size and the link's capacity. By varying packet size one can observe the effect on delay and infer the link's capacity. This method was first described in [Bel92, Jac97].

At each hop, the principal delays experienced by a probe packet are queuing delay, transmission delay, and propagation delay. Propagation delay is determined by link length and signal propagation speed, and so is independent of packet size. Likewise, queuing delay is determined by packets ahead of the probe packet and is not determined by properties of the probe packet itself. Only transmission delay is affected by link capacity and probe packet size.

Thus, if there is no cross-traffic we can express the delay of a packet of size L after it has passed over i hops as

$$T_i(L) = \alpha_i + \sum_{k=1}^{i} \frac{L}{C_k} = \alpha_i + \beta_i L$$

where α_i consists of the delays up to hop i that do not depend on L. The last equality shows that we can capture all of the capacities up to hop i in a single term:

$$\beta_i = \sum_{k=1}^{i} \frac{1}{C_k}.$$

The relationship of β_i to L is what can be measured. The general approach is to send a number of packets with varying size L, and estimate α_i and β_i from the resulting measurements, e.g., by linear regression. Then the capacity at each hop can be estimated as

$$C_i = \frac{1}{\beta_i - \beta_{i-1}}$$

(letting $\beta_0 = 0$).

Implementing this method in practice requires measuring the propagation time of probe packets. In the absence of instrumentation at each point in the path, one generally uses TTL-limited packets to elicit ICMP TIME EXCEEDED responses at each hop. One then measures RTT rather than one-way delay. In the absence of any cross-traffic, the time that ICMP TIME EXCEEDED replies spend returning to the sender can be captured in the α_i term above, since all such replies are of the same size.

A significant advantage of the size-delay approach is that it yields an estimate of capacity for each link along the path. This is in contrast to the packet-pair approach which only measures the narrow link in the path.

As with packet-pair probing, a considerable complication in using size-delay methods is the need for probe packets to pass through the network without queuing behind any cross-traffic. This problem is generally addressed by sending many probes for each hop being measured, and looking for the minimum propagation time over the entire set of probes at a given hop. One assumes that the minimum propagation time found reflects the absence of queuing at any hop. As the length of the path being probed grows, this assumption becomes more suspect, as it becomes harder for a packet to pass through many hops without experiencing queuing at any one of them.

Another concern is that as the length of the path grows, the quantity $1/(\beta_i - \beta_{i-1})$ becomes harder to measure accurately. The fact that packets have a limited size range places limits on the accuracy of an estimate of β_i. As i increases, differences between successive β_i values grow smaller, and small errors in estimating β_i translate into large errors in estimating C_i. Thus, since both noise and estimation error grow with increasing path length, it can be very hard to use size-delay methods to measure long paths [Dow99].

Finally, it is important to note that this method assumes that the packet's size does not vary as the packet traverses the path. In fact, this is not always the case: layer 2 headers can have different sizes in different hops. The extent of the inaccuracy introduced depends on the size of the packet – such errors will be greater for smaller packets.

There are a number of ways that the packet-pair and size-delay methods can be combined and extended to solve specific problems. One idea is to send packet pairs of varying sizes. When a packet pair consists of a large packet followed by one or more additional smaller packets, the large packet may be more likely to queue at a given link. If the large packet is TTL-limited, then it will be discarded at the link to be measured. In this case, the remaining packet(s) will continue to the destination bearing information about the delay experienced by the larger packet up to the link where it was dropped [LB00]. This idea can be extended to measurement of arbitrary path segments using even more elaborate probing schemes, as described in [HBB03, PV02a].

Self-induced Congestion

A somewhat different approach to bandwidth measurement is *self-induced congestion*. The goal of this method is to find the *minimum probe rate* that creates congestion (queuing) on the path. Available bandwidth measurement is usually approached via self-induced congestion.

The basic idea is to send packets at a given rate R and note whether a queue appears to be building up along the path being measured. The buildup of a queue is assumed to take place at the tight link. This buildup can be inferred from an increasing trend in one-way delays of the probing packets over time. On the other hand, if the sending rate R is less than the available bandwidth at the tight link, then one-way delays should not on average increase. The packet train length used determines the timescale over which the probe interacts with the cross-traffic on the path. Thus it is directly related to the averaging timescale τ [JD05].

This method yields a 'yes' or 'no' response for each sending rate R. To efficiently find the true available bandwidth, one can adopt a binary search strategy [JD02], or an exponentially increasing rate [RRB+03].

The self-induced congestion method assumes that cross-traffic behaves like a fluid, i.e., that the amount of cross-traffic arriving in any interval is equal to a fixed mean rate times the interval duration. In reality, traffic arrivals are generally quite bursty on fine timescales (see Chapter 6, Section 6.4.1). The result is that, in practice, available bandwidth estimators can suffer from underestimation bias [LRL05]. This bias diminishes as the probe packet train length increases.

Other difficulties with self-induced congestion methods include the fact that the probing traffic is by definition large enough to affect cross-traffic, and hence may be changing the very quantity that is being measured. Queue buildup is assumed to take place at a single link; the presence of multiple links with roughly the same available bandwidth will cause underestimation. Further, the assumption is made that cross-traffic is changing slowly enough that the quantity being measured is stable long enough for methods to converge. Finally, these methods assume FIFO queuing at all routers, which is generally but not always the case in the current Internet. An empirical comparison of various available bandwidth measurement tools is given in [SMH$^+$05].

Bulk Transfer Capacity Measurement

Bulk transfer capacity (BTC) measurement is conceptually simple: one opens a TCP connection over the path to be measured and sends as much data as the path can handle. The resulting throughput is the BTC. Although this method is somewhat intrusive, it is much simpler and more robust than most other bandwidth estimation methods.

A number of issues arise with this basic approach. First, a TCP connection requires cooperation from both endpoints. The usual approach is to install software at both endpoints – a commonly used tool is `iperf` [TCD03]. To avoid instrumenting both ends of the path, the tool `TReno` emulates a TCP connection using ICMP ECHO packets [MM96]. The ECHO REPLY packets from the remote endpoint are processed as if they were TCP acknowledgments.

Beyond implementation issues, there are many factors that influence TCP throughput which must be addressed to make BTC measurements meaningful. First, the throughput obtained by a TCP transfer is affected by the transfer size – the number of bytes transferred. To provide a consistent estimate, one usually initiates a long transfer (requiring many tens of seconds). Second, the nature of the cross-traffic on the path strongly affects results: competing TCP connections will tend to back off in response to increased packet losses due to the new connection; competing UDP connections are not guaranteed to do so. Moreover, if there are many competing TCP connections their aggregate back-off behavior will be different than a single competing TCP connection. Third, TCP throughput can be limited by buffer sizes at each endpoint, and it is not the intent of BTC to be affected by these factors. Finally, variations in the specification and implementation of the TCP variant used will affect

BTC measurement. Standards for BTC measurement have been developed to avoid these issues to the extent possible [All01, MA].

Caveats in Bandwidth Measurement

A number of issues involved in bandwidth measurement have already been mentioned. However, it is worthwhile to add some additional observations.

A significant issue (that will grow more acute over time) is that for many links, speeds are so high that both single-packet and two-packet methods result in extremely short delays that are difficult or impossible to measure accurately. For example, a 1500 byte packet passing over an OC-192 link experiences on the order of 1 microsecond in transmission delay. This makes it extremely challenging to measure the capacity of such a link using either packet-pair or size-delay methods. Not only must measurement systems and their clocks be capable of sub-microsecond precision, but such measurements are highly sensitive to noise induced by cross-traffic. To some extent these issues can be addressed in the case of packet-pair methods by using long trains of packets as probes rather than just pairs of packets [JT03].

It is also the case that many of the assumptions made in bandwidth measurement methods break down when there are wireless links or cable modem links in the path. WiFi (802.11) wireless networks can change rate on the timescale of seconds. Additionally, packets may not be delivered in FIFO order in WiFi or cable modem networks. Further discussion of these issues is found in [LPP04].

Another set of issues concerns the effect of other layer-2 devices. Per-hop capacity estimation methods (size-delay methods) make the assumption that each IP (layer-3) hop consists of a point-to-point medium with a single transmission rate. However, some layer-2 devices such as Ethernet switches can cause underestimation of a hop's capacity by introducing additional transmission delays [PDM03].

Finally, we note that a review of many pitfalls in available bandwidth measurement is provided in [JD04a], and a review of many bandwidth measurement methods and tools, with additional details, is provided in [PMDkc03].

5.3.5   Latency Measurement and Estimation

Besides bandwidth measurement, a second important problem is measurement or estimation of latency over paths in the Internet.

Latency estimation is important for content delivery networks, peer-to-peer networks, multiuser games, overlay routing networks, and applications employing dynamic server selection. A common aspect of each of these applications is an element of choice among alternatives as a method for improving performance. For example, content delivery networks attempt to serve Web objects to a client from the closest available replica. Peer-to-peer networks attempt to retrieve objects from close peers, and may effectively self-organize based on proximity. Multiuser games are highly sensitive to inter-player delays and so players seek to find other players that are nearby. Dynamic server selection methods attempt to retrieve Web objects or other data objects from the closest server that possesses a replica.

In each of these cases, the notion of *network latency* is central. The general idea is that network latency is an indicator of the performance that the intervening network path may support. The most common metric for network latency is minimum RTT (minRTT). MinRTT is of particular interest because it changes on a relatively long timescale – i.e., only when topology or routing changes. Beyond minRTT, network latency may be defined in terms of instantaneous round-trip time, which dynamically varies due to congestion. In principle, network latency estimation might be concerned with one-way delays as well, although little work has been done in this direction.

In latency estimation the challenges are somewhat different from the case of bandwidth measurement: if one endpoint of the path can be instrumented, then measuring latency is fairly straightforward (via `ping`). Instead the challenges in latency estimation fall into two cases:

1. *Proxy-based methods.* In many cases neither of the path endpoints can participate in the measurement process. A challenge in this case is to estimate the instantaneous round-trip time between the endpoints. To address this problem, methods using additional *proxy* hosts have been developed. The proxies are capable of making measurements to nodes and to other proxies.
2. *Embedding-based methods.* In other cases, the hosts involved are capable of making measurements, but one does not want to measure each path of interest directly. In this setting, minRTT is often the metric of interest. It can be time-consuming to measure minRTT (requiring many RTT measurements) and it can be too expensive to measure minRTT among all pairs of nodes in a network. To address this case, embedding methods have been developed. In an embedding, each node is given a set of coordinates that are then used to estimate the latency (minRTT) between nodes.

In both cases we seek to estimate the latency between a pair of nodes in the network, without sending a probe between them.

All the methods proposed for latency estimation rely on some fixed nodes that act as proxies or landmarks. In some cases these are active nodes that perform measurements; in other cases they are passive and simply serve as reference points. In the discussion below we will use the terms *node* for a host to be located and *landmark* or *proxy* for a helper host.

In estimating distances an important question concerns the *triangle inequality*.

Given three points x, y, and z, and a function $d(\cdot, \cdot)$ that denotes the distance between two points, the triangle inequality requires that

$$d(x, y) + d(y, z) \geq d(x, z).$$

This property holds for distance measurements in metric spaces (such as Euclidean space).

When the points concerned are network nodes and the distance function is network latency, it is often the case that the triangle inequality does not hold. Instantaneous RTT measurements vary on short timescales and so $d(x, y)$, $d(y, z)$, and $d(x, z)$ can be hard to compare if measured at slightly different points in time. With respect to minRTT, the triangle inequality may not hold for more subtle reasons. Since routing in the Internet is not generally shortest-path, packets sent from x to z may not be able to make use of the routes from x to y and from y to z. As a result, the path taken by packets from $x \rightarrow z$ may be longer than the sum of the two paths $x \rightarrow y$ and $y \rightarrow z$. This can happen, e.g., as a result of inter-AS routing policies [ZLPG05].

Proxy-based Methods

Proxy-based methods are generally aimed at estimation of the current RTT between two nodes. A simple method can be formulated based on an assumption of shortest-path routing, and the consequent validity of the triangle inequality. A set of proxies $\{\ell_i\}$ is selected. For two nodes n_1 and n_2, the triangle inequality requires that $d(n_1, n_2)$ is bounded below by

$$L = \max_i |d(n_1, \ell_i) - d(n_2, \ell_i)|$$

and is bounded above by

$$U = \min_i |d(n_1, \ell_i) - d(n_2, \ell_i)|.$$

Weighted averages of L and U can be used as estimates of $d(n_1, n_2)$ [Hot94]. Unfortunately the estimates provided by L and U can be quite coarse depending on the location of the proxies. As a result, these methods can be inaccurate [GS95].

An approach that makes use of specially deployed measurement infrastructure is IDMaps [FJP+99]. IDMaps assumes the availability of particular proxies, called *tracers*. The latency between nodes n_1 and n_2 is estimated as the latency between n_1 and its nearest tracer, plus the latency between n_2 and its nearest tracer, plus the measured latency between the two tracers. The system also uses a collection of servers that respond to client queries and return network latency estimates.

The accuracy of IDMaps is limited when one or both nodes are far from the nearest tracers. Improvements have focused on choosing the number and location of tracers in an informed manner [CLKO02].

King is a tool that addresses some drawbacks of IDMaps by exploiting the DNS system [GSG02]. Rather than relying on specially deployed tracers, King uses a node's local DNS server as its measurement proxy. The method used in King is based on two observations:

1. Most nodes in the Internet are located close to their local DNS servers. The local DNS server for a node is usually within the administrative domain for the node and latency between the node and the DNS server is usually small.
2. One can trigger exchanges between arbitrary DNS servers using recursive DNS queries. For example, given two name servers in different domains, e.g., `dns.first.com` and `dns.second.com`, a recursive query to `dns.first.com` for a name like `any.second.com` will trigger a DNS request from `dns.first.com` to `dns.second.com`.

Based on these two observations, King measures the time taken by a recursive query to `dns.first.com` for `any.second.com` to estimate the latency between a host in the domain `first.com` and a host in the domain `second.com`. The details of how King works are covered in Chapter 7 (Section 7.2.5).

Embedding-based Methods

The embedding approach is generally focused on estimating minRTT. In this approach, one assigns to each node a location in an abstract, high-dimensional Euclidean space $\mathbb{R}^r$. A node's location in that space can be fixed using a set of measurements to *landmarks*. Only the landmarks need to perform all-pairs latency measurements, and a large number of landmarks is not necessary to achieve accurate estimates.

The first system to explore the embedding approach was GNP [NZ02], which works as follows. At initialization, the N landmarks $\ell_1, \ell_2, \ldots, \ell_N$ perform all-pairs latency measurements yielding the set of measured latencies $d(\ell_i, \ell_j)$. Each landmark ℓ_i is then assigned a coordinate vector $\vec{x}_i \in \mathbb{R}^r$. This assignment is obtained by minimization of the objective function:

$$f_\ell(\vec{x}_1, \ldots, \vec{x}_N) = \sum_{i,j \in 1,\ldots,N} err(d(\ell_i, \ell_j), \|\vec{x}_i - \vec{x}_j\|_2)$$

where $err(a, b)$ is typically the simple squared error

$$err(a, b) = (a - b)^2.$$

This formulation results in a nonlinear optimization problem whose solution is approximated via iterative methods. The dimension of the Euclidean space (r) is a tunable parameter.

After initialization, each landmark has a coordinate vector. Each ordinary node then measures latencies to all N landmarks. Node n_i finds its own coordinate vector $\vec{x}_i$ by minimizing a similar objective function:

$$f_n(\vec{x}_i) = \sum_{j \in 1, \ldots, N} err(d(n_i, \ell_j), \|\vec{x}_i - \vec{x}_j\|_2).$$

The benefit of this procedure is that, after each node has a coordinate vector, the latency between nodes n_i and n_j can be estimated without any additional measurement. The estimate is simply:

$$d(n_i, n_j) \approx \|\vec{x}_i - \vec{x}_j\|_2.$$

The Embedding Problem.   In fact, the problem that GNP addresses is a version of the *embedding problem*, which has been extensively studied in other fields. In what follows we describe the embedding problem formally in order to put related latency estimation methods in broader context.

The embedding problem can be cast as follows. We seek a 'good' mapping of an arbitrary *metric space* into a *Euclidean space*. A metric space is a pair (X, d) where X is a set and d is a *metric*. A metric is a distance function such that for $x, y, z \in X$, d satisfies:

1. symmetry: $d(x, y) = d(y, x)$;
2. positive definiteness: $d(x, y) \geq 0$ with equality iff $x = y$; and
3. the triangle inequality: $d(x, y) + d(x, z) \geq d(y, z)$.

A Euclidean space is a metric space in which $X = \mathbb{R}^n$ for some n, and the metric is the Euclidean or l_2 norm $d(\vec{x}, \vec{y}) = \|\vec{x} - \vec{y}\|_2$. An *embedding* of a metric space (X, d) into a Euclidean space $(\mathbb{R}^n, \delta)$ is a function that assigns a point in $\mathbb{R}^n$ to each element of X, i.e., a mapping $\phi : X \to \mathbb{R}^n$.

The *distortion* of an embedding is the smallest value of c_2/c_1 that guarantees that

$$c_1 \cdot d(x, y) \leq \delta(\phi(x), \phi(y)) \leq c_2 \cdot d(x, y)$$

for all pairs $x, y \in X$ and $c_1, c_2 > 0$. A perfect embedding has distortion equal to 1 and is called an *isometry*. Distortion is a worst-case measure of the quality of an embedding; an average-case measure is *stress*. The stress of an embedding is

$$\frac{\sum_{x,y \in X} (\delta(\phi(x), \phi(y)) - d(x, y))^2}{\sum_{x,y \in X} d(x, y)^2}.$$

Given (X, d) and $(\mathbb{R}^n, \delta)$, the *embedding problem* consists of finding a ϕ that minimizes distortion, stress, or another error metric on distances. In general, finding an exact solution is a nonlinear optimization problem, because in Euclidean space, δ is a nonlinear function of its arguments. A good review of commonly used embedding methods is [HS03].

The most commonly used term for the process of embedding an arbitrary finite metric space into a Euclidean space is *multidimensional scaling* (MDS). Multidimensional scaling is generally treated as an optimization problem in which the objective function is stress. The particular choice of optimization algorithm used can affect the quality of the solution found [YH87].

In some cases the distance data provided is derived from a configuration of objects in an actual Euclidean space, so there is an embedding which is an isometry. In the special case where an isometry exists, it can be found via the methods of *distance geometry* [Blu70]. Methods based on distance geometry generally assume complete, exact distance measurements, and are not sufficiently robust in the face of the significant distortion required for a Euclidean embedding of network latency. Applications of distance geometry to the embedding problem are often referred to as *classical metric* MDS [Tor52].

Other Embedding-based Methods. In this context, GNP can be seen as an application of MDS to the problem of embedding network latencies. The effectiveness of the MDS step in GNP has a strong influence on the resulting accuracy of the method, and so more sophisticated optimization algorithms have been proposed. For example, one can use an iterative approach based on simulating an explosion of particles under a force field [TS03].

Another issue with the basic GNP algorithm is that the measurement load on landmarks can grow quite high. The measurement traffic arriving at each landmark grows in proportion to the number of target hosts as the system scales. To address this one can use multiple landmark sets, with each target measuring distance to only one landmark set. The local coordinates obtained in this way are not directly comparable between two targets using different measurement sets, but one can compute a transformation function that maps each set of local coordinates to a canonical global coordinate system [PCW$^+$03].

Another way to diminish measurement load is to dispense with landmarks altogether. In this case, all nodes measure their latencies to subsets of other nodes and exchange coordinates at the same time. Each node adjusts its own coordinates based on the measured latencies to other nodes. Through this gradual adjustment process eventually each node obtains a set of coordinates that is consistent with all other nodes [DCKM04].

In contrast to MDS, a different way of finding a good ϕ is the *Lipschitz em-*

bedding. A Lipschitz embedding is defined in terms of a set D of subsets of X, $D = \{L_1, L_2, ..., L_n\}$. The distance function d is extended to a set $L \subset X$ as follows: let $d(x, L) = \min_{y \in L} d(x, y)$. Then the Lipschitz embedding of X with respect to D is the mapping ϕ such that

$$\phi(x) = [d(x, L_1), d(x, L_2), ..., d(x, L_n)]$$

where $\#\{D\} = n$ and the mapping is into the vector space $\mathbb{R}^n$. Thus, the Lipschitz embedding defines a coordinate space in which each axis i corresponds to the minimum distance from x to the nearest member of L_i. In embedding network distances, one generally uses Lipschitz embeddings in which each L_i is a singleton, and so each L_i is just a landmark ℓ_i. Hence the interpretation of the Lipschitz embedding is particularly simple: component i of the vector $\phi(x)$ is simply the distance from x to landmark ℓ_i.

The intuition behind the Lipschitz embedding is that in a metric space, two nearby points (say, a and b) will typically have similar distances to a third point (say, x). This is required by the triangle inequality:

$$|d(a, x) - d(b, x)| \leq d(a, b).$$

So under a Lipschitz embedding ϕ, the magnitude of the difference between any component of $\phi(a)$ and the corresponding component of $\phi(b)$ is bounded above by $d(a, b)$.

The Lipschitz embedding is the basis for a number of important theoretical results on minimum-distortion embeddings [JL84, Bou85, LLR95]. For network latency estimation, it has the advantage of being very simple to formulate and fast to compute, and shows accuracy comparable to MDS-based methods [TC03, LHC03].

Other Approaches

In some cases it may be sufficient to simply partition nodes into sets such that all nodes in a set are relatively close to each other in terms of network latency. This can be done via measurements to a fixed set of landmarks [RHKS02]. Another approach suitable for measuring router–router latencies is to use ICMP TIMESTAMP REQUEST messages, which requires removing the artifacts associated with clock skew across routers [AGR03].

5.3.6   Geolocation

It is a natural question to ask where entities comprising the Internet *physically are*. The actual location of network infrastructure sheds light on how infrastructure relates to population, social organization, and economic activity. Further, finding the geographic location of network elements can be useful for a wide variety of social, economic, and engineering purposes (as evidenced by the workshop series on location aware computing starting in 2003 [TS05]). The geolocation problem is this: given the network address of a target host, what is the host's geographic location?

It is important to recognize that many geolocation methods commonly used can be quite inaccurate. These inaccuracies arise for a number of reasons. First, the address that is being located may not be correct; a user can employ various methods to hide their true IP address from view. Second, even if the target user does not wish to hide their location, it may be impossible to take the measurements needed to correctly geolocate the target host. For example, the target host may be behind a firewall or NAT device that blocks measurement probes. Third, some commonly used methods rely on location databases that map entire networks, organizations, or address blocks to a single location. Using location databases, geolocation of a host in New Jersey may be highly inaccurate if the host is part of an organization with headquarters in Florida. Finally, users may not wish to be geolocated and may employ countermeasures intended to defeat geolocation.

Geolocation is a potentially intrusive technology. In some cases users may not want to divulge their location at all, while in other cases they may be willing to do so while placing restrictions on the precision with which their location is known, or on whether their location information may be passed on or stored. The privacy issues involved in collecting and using location information are beyond our scope, but the `geopriv` working group within the IETF has defined a set of standards for handling location information. The requirements document for authorization, security and privacy in handling location information is RFC 3693 [CMM$^+$04].

Name-based Geolocation. A particularly simple approach to geolocation is to inspect the DNS names of the target host, or of hosts topologically close to the target host. This method is based on the observation that network operators often assign geographically relevant names to router interfaces. When the target host is not a router, looking at a router that is close in terms of network topology (e.g., one IP hop away) may give useful information. This method is error-prone because it is not always the case that routers have geographically meaningful names, and it is not certain to be the case in the future, but empirical evidence shows that it can sometimes be a useful tool for today's Internet [PS01].

Since each ISP will tend to use different conventions for naming routers, tools generally maintain a database of hand-crafted regular expressions that define how to extract the location information from each ISP's domain names. One way this method can be checked for accuracy is by comparing known distances between cities with the measured propagation delay and flagging inconsistent cases, as described in [PN99].

Delay-based Geolocation.   Another approach is to exploit the relationship between measured network delay and distance. Measurements of network delay that are used in such a way must be estimates of *minimum* delay along the measured path. This is because congestion along the path can increase delay significantly and degrade the expected correlation between delay and distance. Furthermore, it is clear that since network paths are rarely geodesic great-circle paths, the measured path will be longer than what would be predicted by the true distance between endpoints.

There are two main methods for delay-based geolocation: best-landmark and constraint-based. Both methods start from a set of N *landmarks* $\{\ell_i, i = 1, ..., N\}$. Landmarks are hosts with known geographic location. We denote the measured minimum delay (or minimum RTT) between nodes n_1 and n_2 as $d(n_1, n_2)$.

The idea behind the best-landmark method is to map the target node to the location of the closest landmark [PS01]. This method starts by measuring the network delay from each landmark to all others:

$$\vec{\ell_i} = [d(\ell_i, \ell_1),\ d(\ell_i, \ell_2), ...,\ d(\ell_i, \ell_N)].$$

To locate a target node τ, one takes measurements of minimum latency to all landmarks, and constructs the corresponding measurement vector:

$$\vec{\tau} = [d(\tau, \ell_1),\ d(\tau, \ell_2), ...,\ d(\tau, \ell_N)].$$

One then chooses the best landmark to be that whose measurement vector is most similar to $\vec{\tau}$. A simple way to do this is to find the landmark that is closest by the l_2 norm:

$$m = \arg \min_{\ell_i} \|\vec{\ell_i} - \vec{\tau}\|_2.$$

Other measures of similarity between ℓ_i and τ may be used as well [ZFdRD04]. One way to look at this method is that it constructs a Lipschitz embedding of landmarks and the target, and then chooses the closest landmark to the target in the resulting Euclidean space (see Section 5.3.5).

A problem with the best-landmark approach is that the accuracy of the inferred location is limited by the spatial distribution of landmarks. If there is no landmark close to the target, then the inferred location will be inaccurate.

A technique that does not have this limitation is constraint-based geolocation. In the constraint-based approach, one exploits the known properties of signal propagation in fiber. Most long-distance network paths are optical fiber, through which light travels at very nearly two-thirds of the speed of light in a vacuum [PV03].

The basic idea is that given geographic distances from a target host to the set of landmarks, an estimation of the location of the target host would be feasible using

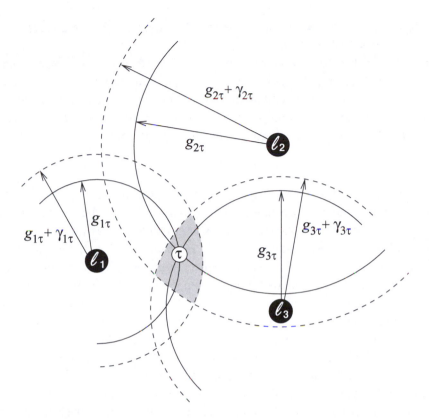

Figure 5.8 Multilateration with geographic distance constraints.

multilateration. Multilateration is the process of estimating a position using a sufficient number of distances to some fixed points, e.g., as used in the Global Positioning System (GPS).

The challenge in using multilateration is the accurate measurement of the distances between the target point to be located and the reference points. For example, GPS uses multilateration to three satellites to estimate the position of a given GPS receiver. In this case, the distance between the GPS receiver and a satellite is measured by the time taken for a signal sent from the satellite to arrive at the GPS receiver.

The key to using multilateration in the Internet is that no matter the reason, delay between a landmark and target is only distorted *additively* with respect to the time for light in fiber to pass over the great-circle path. That is, the presence of slow access links, non-great-circle paths, congestion-induced delay, and other delays due to passing through routers all *add* delay to the value obtained by dividing distance by the speed of light in fiber. So, given a measured delay between two locations, the result obtained by multiplying it by the speed of light in fiber is always an upper bound on the true distance.

Thus, for each landmark ℓ_i we can use $d(\ell_i, \tau)$ to obtain an upper bound on the distance to the target. Figure 5.8 shows this situation for a set of landmarks $\{\ell_1, \ell_2, \ell_3\}$ and a target τ. Each landmark ℓ_i computes its geographic distance constraint to a target host τ by multiplying minimum measured latency by the speed of light in fiber. The computed geographic distance constraint is

$$\hat{g}_{i\tau} = g_{i\tau} + \gamma_{i\tau},$$

i.e., it consists of a portion reflecting the true geographic distance $g_{i\tau}$ plus an additive distortion represented by $\gamma_{i\tau}$. Since $\gamma_{i\tau}$ is always nonnegative, the true location of the target host τ lies somewhere within the gray area, the *target region*.

The addition of more landmarks cannot increase the size of the target region, and may decrease the size of the target region. In general, if a sufficient number of landmarks are used, often the target region becomes small enough to yield a useful location estimate. Given a small enough target region, a reasonable guess as to the host's location is at the region's centroid.

For a given path between ℓ_i and τ, any *predictable* delays that are not propagation delays should be subtracted from $d(\ell_i, \tau)$ before converting to distance. For example, a landmark may have a fixed additive latency that is added to all delay measurements because the landmark is connected to the network via a slow local link. Eliminating these delays from consideration will improve the accuracy of the resulting estimates [GZCF04].

Location Databases.   Finally, a reasonable approach to geolocation is simply to construct manually a large database of mappings between IP addresses and their known locations. Examples of such services are [geo, neth]. If accurate location databases are available for some IP addresses, then one can leverage address clustering information (e.g., obtained from BGP) to infer sets of addresses that are likely to be in the same area [PS01]. The general approach of network aware clustering was introduced in [KW00].

Location information can be provided by network administrators. The DNS has been proposed as a repository for such information. RFC 1876 defines a new Resource Record for the DNS that captures location information [DVGD96]. However, adoption has been limited, perhaps because administrators have little incentive to register the location records.

The `whois` databases include location entries for autonomous systems and allocated address blocks. A number of tools query these databases in order to obtain the location information recorded therein to infer the geographic location of a host [MPDkc00]. This information, however, may be inaccurate or stale. Moreover, if a large and geographically dispersed block of IP addresses is allocated to a single entity, the `whois` database may contain just a single entry for the entire block.

Finally we note that in contrast to the case for the wired Internet, a large body of work has looked at wireless geolocation. The most notable is GPS; however, GPS is ineffective indoors. Some systems that have been developed for use indoors are [BP00, HH94, HHS$^+$99].

5.3.7 Inference

Hidden data in infrastructure measurement can sometimes be reconstructed via inference procedures. Methods have been developed to infer network topology, network-internal delays, and packet loss rates using only end-to-end measurements, a process called *network tomography*. In this section we review inference methods useful for infrastructure properties (inference methods for traffic are covered in Section 6.3.4).

The tomography problem arises whenever link-level or other network internal measurements are hidden. For example, this can happen because ISPs do not in general make internal measurements available outside their organizations.

The general network tomography problem is based on the relationship

$$\vec{y} = G\vec{x} \tag{5.1}$$

where $\vec{y}$ is a set of m end-to-end measurements (packet loss probabilities or network latencies), $G = A^T$ is the $m \times n$ routing matrix, and $\vec{x}$ are the n individual link measurements (as described in Section 3.4.2). Some set of measurements $\vec{y}$ are available, and correspond to particular paths that can be measured as defined by G. The goal is to infer either the per-link properties $\vec{x}$ or the routing matrix G.

Network Internal Delays and Loss Rates

There is a variety of assumptions that must be made in estimating network internal delays or loss rates from end-to-end measurements. First, links may be treated as unidirectional or bidirectional. Second, paths may be treated as symmetric or asymmetric. Third, the path measurements taken may be round-trip or one-way. And finally, the probing strategy may involve multicast probes or unicast probes.

The general framework defined by Equation (5.1) can be adopted under any of these assumptions. However, the measurement methods, and the consequent interpretation of the results, vary depending on the assumptions made. The most realistic assumptions are that links are unidirectional and paths are asymmetric. However this can make it hard to obtain useful measurements, because one-way delays are difficult to measure.

In general, Equation (5.1) can have no solutions for $\vec{x}$, a unique solution, or an infinite number of solutions. If $G^T G$ is a full rank matrix, then the equation can be solved directly for all link measurements: the solution is given by

$$\vec{x} = (G^T G)^{-1} G^T \vec{y}.$$

Otherwise, one can determine which link measurements, if any, can be computed directly by examining the routing matrix G [SSWY01].

In order to go further and make inferences on all links, one must make additional assumptions. A general strategy is to look for *maximum likelihood* solutions. Given measurements $\vec{y}$, one defines the likelihood of a particular solution $l(G, \vec{x})$ as

$$l(G, \vec{x}) = p(\vec{y} \mid G, \vec{x})$$

where $p(\vec{y} \mid G, \vec{x})$ is the probability of seeing the observations $\vec{y}$ given a particular routing matrix and set of link parameters. The additional assumptions that are added take the form of models or constraints that affect how one calculates $p(\vec{y} \mid G, \vec{x})$.

Multicast-based Methods. The first method to address the network tomography problem was the MINC approach, which is based on the use of multicast probes [CDHT99]. The general idea is illustrated in Figure 5.9.

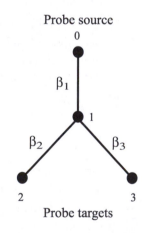

Probe source
0

β_1

1

β_2 β_3

2   3

Probe targets

Figure 5.9   The tomography setting.

The figure shows the network tomography problem in its simplest form. There are three network links, three endsystems and one internal node in the network. Each link has an associated loss rate $\beta_i, i = 1, 2, 3$. The goal is to estimate all three loss rates from loss rate measurements made only on the paths $0 \to 2$ and $0 \to 3$. Note that there are three links and only two path measurements, so the problem as stated is underdetermined (multiple solutions can be consistent with observed data).

In the MINC approach, rather than working with loss *rates*, one works with loss *events*. In particular, the method makes use of correlations in loss events arising through the use of multicast probes. The probe source (node 0) sends multicast packets toward the endsystems (nodes 2 and 3). When the multicast packet reaches the branching point 1, a copy of the packet is sent down each of the links $1 \to 2$ and $1 \to 3$. If the packet is lost on link $0 \to 1$ it will reach neither node 2 nor node 3. The general idea is that packets that are not seen at either node 2 or node 3 are assumed to be lost on link $0 \rightarrow 1$. Packets seen at one node, but not the other, are assumed to be lost on the link leading to the node where the packet is unseen. Repeating this experiment many times, one can build up an estimate of the loss rates on each of the three links.

The modeling assumption is that of multicast probes, in which losses on different links and at different times are assumed to be independent. In that case, one can form a maximum likelihood estimator of loss rates as follows. When a probe is sent, four events are possible, which can be denoted $\{00, 01, 10, 11\}$ according to whether the probe is received at an endpoint (1) or lost somewhere in the network (0). Thus, a probe lost on link $1 \rightarrow 2$ but successfully transmitted to node 3 will result in the event 01. Let $\hat{p}(x)$ denote the proportion of trials in which event x is observed. Then the maximum likelihood estimates of per-link loss rates are:

$$\hat{\beta}_1 = 1 - \frac{(\hat{p}(01) + \hat{p}(11))(\hat{p}(10) + \hat{p}(11))}{\hat{p}(11)}$$

$$\hat{\beta}_2 = 1 - \frac{\hat{p}(11)}{\hat{p}(01) + \hat{p}(11)}$$

$$\hat{\beta}_3 = 1 - \frac{\hat{p}(11)}{\hat{p}(10) + \hat{p}(11)}.$$

This general idea can be extended to trees of arbitrary topology [CDHT99]. The resulting maximum likelihood estimators are more complex, but embody the same basic principle.

The method as described applies to a single multicast probe, and measures a single tree. As such it cannot typically measure *all* links in a network (since most network topologies are not trees). To measure larger portions of the network it is possible to measure multiple trees and fuse the separately obtained data into a single view [BDPT02].

Unicast-based Methods. Although multicast-based tomography is efficient and effective, many networks do not support multicast. Moreover, multicast is not generally available on paths that span multiple ISPs in the Internet. As a result, methods have been developed to address the tomography problem using only unicast probes.

Referring to Figure 5.9, if one were to simply send unicast probes along the two paths $0 \rightarrow 2$ and $0 \rightarrow 3$, the resulting set of two average path loss rates would be insufficient to identify the set of three average network internal loss rates β_1, β_2, and β_3. That is, the internal loss rates are not *identifiable* using simple unicast-based average path measures: alternate values such as $\beta_1 x, \beta_2/x$, and β_3/x (for some x) would yield the same set of observed average path measures.

To mimic the success of multicast inference, one can start from the observation that multicast methods are effective because the loss of a probe on a link shared between two paths can be detected at both endpoints. This suggests that a unicast probing method should attempt to imitate the 'shared fate' of multicast probes.

To do this, one can use *packet pairs.* Packet pairs are unicast probes sent back-to-back. The packets may be destined for different receivers, but will generally share a common set of links in their paths. Such packet pairs will tend to exhibit a certain degree of shared fate, because when a packet pair arrives at a full queue, it is likely that both packets will be lost (rather than just one packet). Likewise, both packets are likely to experience the same delay passing over shared links. This allows using packet pairs in place of multicast probes [CN00, HBB00].

Unicast methods are generally not as accurate, but are more flexible than multicast-based methods. For example, unicast-based methods can be extended to passive measurements, in which probe-like information is gathered from normal network traffic [TCN01]. A review of tomography approaches is provided in [CHNY02].

Dominant Congested Links

General network tomography seeks to discover the loss rates or delays on each link in a network. However, in many settings there may be one link along a path that is responsible for the majority of losses or delays, which is called the *dominant* congested link. In this case it may be sufficient to determine whether a dominant congested link exists, and if so, identify that link.

An approach is to send periodic probes along the path, and observe the sequence of delay values. Lost probes will not carry delay measurements to the endpoint, but the delay experienced by a lost probe can be inferred from the delays experienced by the probes that were not lost. If a preponderance of lost probes have similar inferred delays, one can infer that there is a dominant congested link in the path [WWTK03].

To identify *which* link is the dominant congested link one can make the following assumptions. Suppose links are classified as 'good' or 'bad,' (not very lossy, or very lossy) and the incidence of bad links is rare. Further, it is assumed that a path is only bad if it contains a bad link. Under these assumptions, when bad performance is observed on two intersecting paths, the most probable explanation is that one of the links in common between the two paths is a bad link. This allows one to construct maximum likelihood methods for identifying such bad links [PQW03, Duf03].

A notion midway between general network tomography and identification of dominant congested links is identification of a *metric-induced* topology. A metric-induced topology is a weighted, directed graph in which vertices represent endpoints and routers, and edges represent a sequence of one or more network links. Only those sequences of links which collectively have a metric value (such as loss rate or delay) above a given threshold are represented by edges in the topology. Such topologies can be discovered through unicast probing [BBH05].

Efficient Measurement Designs

A related role for inference is in reducing the measurement burden required to obtain network measurements. In a network with m endpoints, there are $O(m^2)$ paths whose end-to-end properties one may wish to measure. Naive schemes that send probes along all paths can add significant traffic to the network and do not scale well as the network size grows.

Consider a network consisting of m endpoints, in which all paths are being measured. Referring back to Equation (5.1):

$$\vec{y} = G\vec{x},$$

where $\vec{y}$ is a vector of $(m^2 - m)$ path measurements. However, there are only n independent quantities: the n link measurements. Thus it is only necessary to measure enough paths (components of $\vec{y}$) to reconstruct the remaining paths.

This problem reduces to that of finding a minimal basis set of k linearly independent paths that can fully describe all the $O(m^2)$ paths. This is equivalent to selecting k rows of G that span the row space of G. In the best case, k will equal the rank of G. Algorithms for efficiently finding this basis set, and thereby determining the minimal set of paths to measure, are given in [CBSK04].

When a link is failed or unavailable, each path that contains that link is unavailable. In this case the tomography equation $\vec{y} = G\vec{x}$ can be applied somewhat differently. Let an unavailable link or path be assigned the Boolean value 'true,' and an available link or path be assigned the value 'false.' We interpret the vector $\vec{x}$ as signifying which links have failed, and the vector $\vec{y}$ as signifying which paths are unavailable as a result. In place of the 1's in G we put 'true,' and for the 0's we put 'false.' Then the tomography equation holds in this case as well, when the equation is interpreted in terms of $(\vee, \wedge)$ Boolean algebra (Equation (3.4) in Chapter 3, Section 3.1). As a result, a set of rows of G that span the row space of G in Boolean algebra define a sufficient set of paths to monitor in order to detect any link failure. An efficient method for identifying the minimal set of rows that spans the row space of G in Boolean algebra is described in [NT04].

If one wishes to further reduce the number of measured paths, one can adopt a statistical estimation approach. Typical routing matrices have been found to show low *effective* rank, meaning that a set of paths even smaller than the rank of G can be sufficient to allow inference of the *majority* of link measurements. In this case, approximate measures of path metrics can be formed from the estimated link measurements [CKC05].

Topology Identification

A final role for inference is in supplying missing topology information. For example, multicast protocols can benefit from an understanding of the topology of the distribution tree connecting a sender to a set of receivers. However, in many cases, direct topology measurement (e.g., via `traceroute`) may be too expensive or impossible.

One approach to this problem is based on multicast probes in a manner somewhat similar to MINC. In this case, the correlation of losses seen at receivers is used to group receiver nodes with 'similar' loss patterns. These nodes are assumed to be near each other in the multicast tree. Such nodes are connected together in a subtree, and then the process proceeds recursively to build an approximation of the entire distribution tree as a binary tree [RM99].

The resulting topology is cast in terms of a binary tree. This may be sufficient for some purposes, such as identifying which nodes are close to each other topologically. If a more accurate view of topology is desired, then methods must construct trees of varying degree [DHPT02].

As with loss and delay tomography, it can be useful to probe a set of trees and fuse the resulting measurements. Algorithms for fusing topology information from multiple multicast trees are given in [CRN03].

5.3.8   Other Tools

Besides those mentioned so far, methods exist for measuring a number of other infrastructure properties. One can measure rates of packet reordering in the network by observing properties of TCP connections [BS02]. Further, one can measure one-way packet loss rates to and from unmodified hosts by sending selected TCP packets to the remote host, and deducing which packets were lost in each direction from the remote host's response [Sav99].

5.4   State of the Art

Having reviewed the important features of Internet infrastructure and the tools and methods used to learn about those features, we now turn to what is known about those features.

As with all properties of the Internet, infrastructure properties change with time.

While many properties discussed in this section are large-scale properties that should change slowly, it is important to keep in mind that what we can describe at the current time is only a 'snapshot' of a system undergoing constant change.

5.4.1 Equipment Properties

At the lowest level, empirically observed properties of individual components of the Internet are of interest. The behavior of links and other communication devices is largely predictable from design and engineering considerations. However, routers are more complex, and so here we review some questions regarding routers that have been investigated experimentally.

Experimental evaluation of backbone routers shows that in many cases, the delay a packet experiences as it passes through a router is very small [PMF+02]. For some routers, the minimum delay can be as low as 20 microseconds. This occurs when the packet arrives and departs on the same interface, and there is little additional traffic at the interface. Delays can be greater if the packet enters and leaves on different interfaces, but are still on the order of tens of microseconds.

However, if a router is heavily loaded, queuing delays can be on the order of tens of milliseconds. A further source of delays (which can be in the range of milliseconds) is incurred when packets carry IP options. In addition, on rare occasion routers will delay transmitting packets even where there is no other traffic waiting for transmission on the output link (this affects less than 1% of packets). These delays can be on the order of milliseconds, and seem to occur when periodic processes running within router software are activated [PMF+02].

It is also useful to understand how routers produce and consume traffic, e.g., routing messages. Routers participating in OSPF exchanges were studied in [SG01]. Results show that link state announcements (LSAs), which are the most common message type exchanged in OSPF, require on the order of 100 microseconds to be processed. Much of the time required can be attributed to data copying within the router. The time required to process an OSPF packet tends to vary linearly with the number of LSAs contained in the packet, while delay associated with shortest-path calculation scales quadratically with the number of nodes in a fully connected topology.

Finally, another set of devices that are complex and can delay packets are middleboxes, such as NATs and firewalls. Results show that such devices can introduce delays ranging from one millisecond to hundreds of milliseconds when forwarding packets [All03].

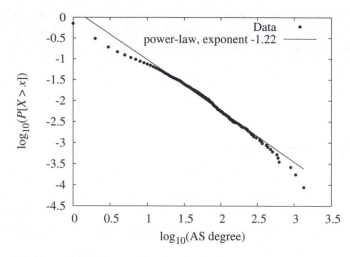

Figure 5.10   Highly variable degree distribution in the AS graph.

5.4.2   Topology Properties

At the next higher level, components are connected together into a topology. This section covers what is known about the interconnection patterns of Internet components. Background on terms and concepts relating to topology properties is found in Chapter 3 (Section 3.4.1).

Static Properties of the Autonomous System Graph

The highest-level view of Internet topology is in terms of the AS graph – the graph in which nodes are ASes and edges exist between ASes that directly exchange traffic.

High Variability in Degree Distribution.   Traditional random graphs such as Erdös–Rényi graphs show low variability in degree distribution (see Chapter 3, Section 3.4.2). This is not the case for the AS graph; the most salient property of the AS graph is its highly variable degree distribution. In fact, as first noted in [SFFF03], the degree distribution of measured AS graphs is often well approximated by a power-law.

Figure 5.10 shows data from [CCG+02], in the form analyzed in [SFFF03]. The AS graph used in this figure was generated by fusing a variety of topology measurements, including BGP-based measurements (taken from routeviews) and the contents of routing registries; as such it represents one of the most complete views of AS topology at the time of measurement (2001). The figure shows the log–log complementary distribution function (a plot of $\log(1 - F(x))$ against $\log x$) for the node degree in this AS graph. The fitted line corresponds to a power-law with exponent −1.22.

This plot is typical of AS graph measurements. It shows that AS degree follows a distribution remarkably close to a power-law. This phenomenon has been confirmed in AS topology measurements dating back to at least 1997 [SFFF03].

Note that the data in Figure 5.10 shows some distinct deviations from strict power-law behavior, as discussed in [CCG+02]. Furthermore, the AS graph used is undoubtedly incomplete; in particular, some true edges are certainly missing from the measured graph [ZM03]. As a result, the conclusion that such graphs are well modeled using power-laws is at best only an approximation. Nonetheless, node degree clearly shows high variability: most ASes have low degree (less than 5) but a few ASes have very high degree (measured in the thousands).

The property of high variability in AS degree has a number of implications. First, it represents an important invariant that should be present in any realistic models of AS topology. In fact, early methods used for generating representative network topologies did not show this property; more recently, new topology generators have been proposed to incorporate this property [MLMB01]. Outputs from topology generators that incorporate high variability tend to show other properties similar to those of empirically measured AS graphs as well [TGJ+02].

Second, this result focuses attention on the fact that some autonomous systems are *very* highly connected, while most others are much less so, which has implications for traffic patterns and inter-domain routing. More generally, it lends weight to the conclusion that different autonomous systems have dramatically different roles in the network. Indeed, node degree seems to be highly correlated with AS size (as measured by the number of routers in the AS), and AS size also shows high variability [TDG+01]. This suggests that the largest autonomous systems, i.e., tier-1 Internet service providers, are the most highly connected.

Last, the presence of high variability stimulates and informs questions about the mechanisms of Internet growth. A number of *generative* models have been proposed for Internet growth that explicitly incorporate power-law or highly variable degree distributions. These are constructive models in which graphs grow over time, through the incremental addition of nodes and edges. In particular:

- Power-law degree distributions can arise in a growing network if newly added nodes connect to existing nodes with probability proportional to the degree of the existing node [BA99]. This so-called 'rich get richer' phenomenon was originally proposed to explain power laws in social statistics [Sim55]. However, historical measurements of Internet growth do not seem to lend support to this explanatory mechanism [CCG+02].
- Power-law degree distributions can also arise in a growing network if newly added

nodes connect to existing nodes in a way that tends to minimize both the physical length of the new connection, as well as the average number of hops to other nodes in the network [FKP02].

- Finally, power-law *size* distributions can arise if new autonomous systems appear at an exponentially increasing rate, and each AS grows exponentially as well. If the size of an AS is correlated with its degree then highly variable degree distributions may result [FKB$^+$03].

Small World Properties. As discussed in Chapter 3 (Section 3.4.1), the 'small world phenomenon' concerns the interplay of two graph properties: *diameter* and *clustering*. Diameter is a measure of typical distance between two vertices in the graph, and clustering refers to the tendency for two neighbors of a node to be neighbors themselves. Highly structured graphs (e.g., lattices) tend to have a high degree of clustering along with high diameter, while classical random graphs tend to have low diameter and a low degree of clustering. Small world graphs lie in between: such graphs have a high degree of clustering but low diameter [WS98].

In fact, the AS graph is a small world graph. Evidence presented in [BT02] shows measurements of the AS graph taken in January 2002 containing 12,709 ASes and 27,384 edges. For this AS graph, the average path length is 3.6 and the clustering coefficient (a measure of clustering) is 0.46. Random graphs with the same number of nodes and similar average path length have clustering coefficients around 0.0014. Thus the clustering coefficient in the AS graph is more than 300 times larger than would be the case for a corresponding random graph.

Most pairs of ASes are separated by a relatively small number of intervening ASes (on average, in the range of 3 to 4). Further, there is a high degree of clustering among ASes. It appears that individual clusters (subgraphs showing especially dense interconnection) can contain ASes with similar geographic location or business interests [GMZ03]. More discussion of small world properties of the AS graph is in [PSV04].

AS Relationships. So far, we have considered *unlabeled* AS graphs. In addition, there are useful ways to annotate AS graph nodes and edges.

A common question concerns identifying 'hierarchy' within the AS graph. The inter-domain routing system does not define a hierarchy among ASes. However, inspecting the AS graph clearly shows that ASes play different roles within the network.

One way to identify the most significant ASes is by their degree in the AS graph. As already seen, degree is strongly correlated with AS size. Hence ASes of high degree are likely to be 'top-tier' ASes; further 'tiers' can be defined by degree ranges [GR97].

The exchange of traffic between two ASes is determined by routing policies (implemented via BGP). Each AS's routing policies are designed to enforce its commercial agreements. The commercial relationship between two ASes can be classified as customer–provider, peering, mutual transit, or mutual backup [Hus99a, Hus99b]. Of these, the most common are customer–provider and peering. In a customer–provider relationship, the provider AS agrees to carry *transit* traffic from the customer. Transit traffic is traffic that is not destined for a customer of the provider. Thus, the provider is acting as a gateway for the customer to access the rest of the Internet. In a peering relationship, the two ASes agree to exchange only non-transit traffic; that is, only traffic that is destined for a customer of one of the two ASes. This type of arrangement is more common between large ASes, both having many customers.

These relationships are enforced by the choice of which routes are advertised via BGP, and to whom they are advertised. As such, the nature of the relationship can be hard to determine without direct access to BGP traffic between the ASes of interest. Hence methods have been developed to infer the nature of AS–AS relationships, yielding an AS graph with annotated edges [Gao00, SARK02].

The resulting annotated AS graphs can also be used as another method for placing ASes into a hierarchy. Conceptually, ASes that only act as peers or providers are 'top-tier' ASes. Likewise, ASes that only act as customers comprise the lowest tier. More sophisticated AS ranking methods combine information from the annotated AS graph with the number of prefixes and address blocks advertised by the AS [Huf].

Static Properties of Router Graphs

Another important view of Internet topology is in terms of the router graph – the graph in which nodes are routers and edges denote direct (one IP hop) connections between routers.

Some example router graphs are shown in Figures 5.11 and 5.12. (More examples of router graphs in the form of network maps are in [CK90].) Figure 5.11 shows the router graph of the ARPANET, precursor to the Internet, in 1972 (based on [Nei]). Shaded squares in the figure are routers (IMPs and TIPs) and ovals are attached computers (endsystems). At the time, the complete router graph was fully known and could fit in a single drawing.

In the case of the modern Internet, obtaining such a complete view of the router graph is impossible. However, portions of the router graph may be available. One way to decompose the router graph into smaller pieces for measurement is to focus on the subgraph corresponding to a single AS or network (e.g., as was done in [SMW02]). An example of the router graph for a single network is shown in Figure 5.12. This is a diagram of the Abilene network, which is the US national research and education

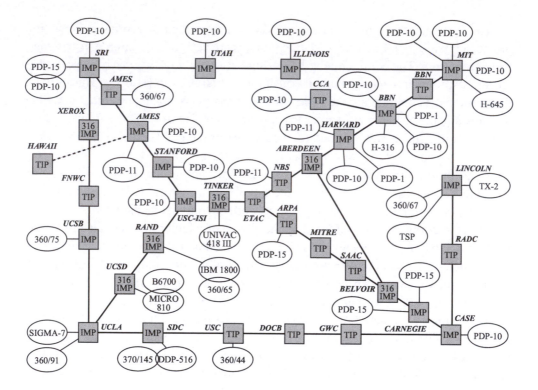

Figure 5.11   Map of the ARPANET as of December 30, 1972.

backbone. In this figure, routers and links within the Abilene network are shown; links to routers in external networks are not shown.

High Variability in Degree Distribution.   Like the AS graph, measurements of the router graph show that it too exhibits high variability in degree distribution [FFF99]. Measured router graphs show a range of node degrees; most nodes have degree less than 5 but some can have degrees greater than 100 [GT00].

It is important to note that current topology measurement methods tend to introduce a form of *sampling bias*. In studies that use traceroute to discover topology, traceroute targets are passive and plentiful, while traceroute sources require deployment of dedicated measurement infrastructure, and are therefore scarce. As such, when traces are run from a relatively small set of sources to a much larger set of destinations, those nodes and links closest to the sources are explored much more thoroughly than those that are distant from the sources and destinations. This effect tends to artificially increase the proportion of low-degree nodes in the sampled graph, because the majority of edges are far from traceroute sources and are thus undersampled. The resulting sampling bias can be strong enough to dramat-

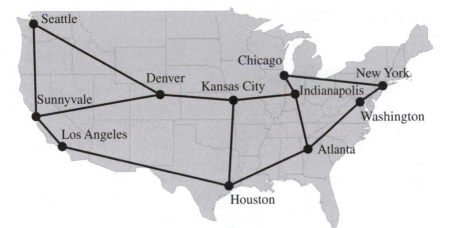

Figure 5.12 Map of the Abilene network as of 2005.

ically change the nature of the degree distribution in the sampled graph [LBCX03, CM05a].

In addition it is clear that unlike the case of the AS graph, measured portions of the Internet's router graph comprise only a tiny fraction of the total graph. While the AS graph can be measured passively (by obtaining BGP tables and traffic), the router graph requires active measurement (via `traceroute`), and the rate at which network elements are explored can be slow in practice [BBBC01].

These considerations suggest caution in interpreting measurements made to date of the router graph. Nonetheless, they do not invalidate the empirically observed property that node degree in the router graph can be highly variable. This fact is somewhat surprising in light of known network maps such as Figures 5.11 and 5.12 which often show mesh-like interconnection of routers with relatively narrow bounds on node degree.

One possible explanation is that high degree nodes in the router graph may tend to appear close to the network edge, e.g., at access points, rather than in the core of the network [LAWD04]. This conclusion comes from considering the technological constraints imposed on router and link bandwidth and connectivity. The total bandwidth of a router generally declines as the number of links connected (i.e., its degree) increases. Thus, in the core of a network where high bandwidth is essential, routers will tend to low degree. On the other hand, at network edges the need to serve many users with relatively low bandwidth connections leads to routers with higher degree. In addition, the goals of network robustness suggest that core networks are likely to show mesh-like interconnection patterns similar to Figures 5.11 and 5.12. Figure 5.13 shows a graph exhibiting both high variability in node degree and a mesh-like core;

this graph was generated from a model that incorporates practical technological constraints.

Figure 5.13   Example synthetic graph meeting technological constraints for routers.

We note that many studies have failed to distinguish sharply between graph models appropriate for the AS graph, and those appropriate for router graphs. This has led to confusion for a number of reasons. First, the quality of data is much better for the AS graph than for router graphs; currently, a reliable characterization of node degree in router-level graphs is not available. Second, the structures of the two graphs are very different. In the AS graph, highly connected nodes tend to be top-tier ASes – 'central' nodes. In the router graph, it is more likely that highly connected nodes tend to be at the 'edges' of the network.

Path Properties.   As in the case of the AS graph, typical paths through the router graph tend to be short. Measures of the number of IP hops between nodes in the Internet show average values around 16; paths of more than 30 hops are rare [BM01].

Despite the fact that path lengths in the Internet are relatively short, measurements show that they are often longer than necessary. The paths taken by packets through the Internet can be longer than the shortest possible paths in terms of number of IP hops, leading to *path inflation* [SCH+99]. This effect seems to be due mainly to AS–AS peering policies and inter-domain routing [SMA03].

Dynamic Aspects of Topology

Apart from static properties of the current Internet, the manner in which the Internet's infrastructure changes over time is also of considerable interest.

Growth and Change.   Since its inception as the ARPANET in 1969, the Internet has grown steadily and rapidly. At the present (2006) the Internet is still growing at a very rapid pace, both at the AS and the router level.

The size of the AS graph can be measured by the number of distinct autonomous

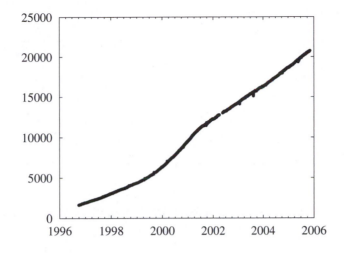

Figure 5.14 Number of unique AS numbers advertised within the BGP system [Hus05].

systems advertised in the inter-domain routing space of the public Internet. This quantity has been measured on a regular basis since 1997 [Hus05]; the data is shown in Figure 5.14. As the figure shows, more than 20,000 AS numbers are currently advertised. The figure also shows that the growth rate of AS advertisements was largest during the Internet boom period of 1999–2001, but that the addition of new ASes has occurred more slowly since then.

Note that the figures shown here are in fact net growth; in practice the evolution of the AS graph involves both the addition of new autonomous systems and the disappearance of existing autonomous systems. Furthermore, the evolution of the AS graph involves addition and deletion of edges between ASes over time [PSVV01, CCG+02].

Measuring the growth of the Internet at the router and endsystem level is much more difficult. Before the DNS was established, almost all hosts on the Internet were registered with the Network Information Center so that their entries could be placed in a centralized host table. In contrast, in the modern Internet there is no single centralized host registry.

An additional difficulty is that the router-level graph is huge, and changes rapidly as equipment comes online, fails, and is reconfigured. For these and other reasons, no comprehensive studies of the number of routers active in the Internet exist.

There are a number of ways that one might try to measure the number of hosts (endsystems and routers) connected to the network:

- One might count the number of addresses that have been allocated by the Regional Internet Registries. This is a very serious overestimate; it is known that a large fraction of allocated addresses are not in use. For example, in the early days

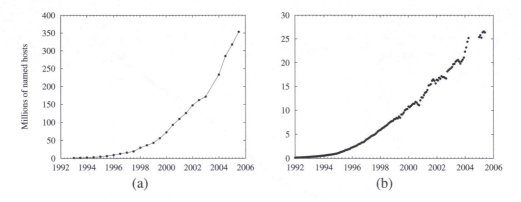

Figure 5.15   Number of hosts registered in DNS, in millions: (a) total hosts [Con05]; (b) hosts in European top level domains only [Cen05a].

of the Internet large blocks of address space were allocated to relatively small organizations.

- One might count the number of addresses that are announced in the BGP system. The BGP system propagates announcements for address ranges (prefixes) within which at least some addresses are in use. This is not as bad as the last method, since it avoids counting many address ranges that have been allocated but are not in use. However, it is still an overestimate because the prefixes contained in BGP announcements may still contain many addresses that are not in use.

- One could simply try to probe all announced addresses using `ping`. However, many hosts are only intermittently connected to the network, through dialup or wireless connections. Many other hosts connect to the network through firewalls that block probes, or through Network Address Translation (NAT) devices which hide their IP addresses from visibility in the public Internet. Hence this method is an underestimate.

- Finally, one can query the DNS to find the set of all IP addresses that have been allocated a DNS name. However, a host need not be assigned a DNS name to connect to the Internet, so the number of named hosts is another underestimate of the size of the Internet. Details on how DNS is organized are in Chapter 4, Section 4.3.

While none of these methods is perfect, to get some idea of Internet change and growth we will look at results based on the last method: counting the number of host names registered in the DNS. Figure 5.15 shows measurements of the number of hosts (in millions) registered in the DNS starting from 1992. Figure 5.15(a) shows results for the entire DNS [Con05]; Figure 5.15(b) shows results restricted only to hosts registered in European Top Level Domains (e.g., `.fr`, `.uk`, etc.) [Cen05a].

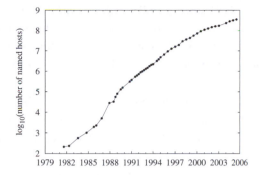

Figure 5.16 Semi-log plot of hosts registered in DNS [Con05].

These data were collected in slightly different ways and some noise in the data is due to imperfections in the collection process.

The figure documents the explosion in size of the Internet that began in the mid-1990s (coincident with the large-scale adoption of the World Wide Web). This growth appears to follow the same general pattern whether one looks at the global system or a regional system (Europe). The figure shows that rapid growth in the size of the network continued through 2006. The quick pace of change in the network underlines the difficulty of capturing representative views of the router graph.

New technological infrastructure often follows a path of early exponential growth, followed by a gradual slowing in deployment [AH88]. During the 1990s many claims were made that the physical infrastructure of the Internet was growing exponentially.[3] To assess this claim we can examine size data on a semi-log plot, on which exponential growth would appear as a straight line. Figure 5.16 shows a semi-log plot of the data from Figure 5.15(a), augmented with known counts of the number of hosts connected to the Internet (or ARPANET) before 1993.

The figure shows rapid growth at all times since the network's inception. In particular, the nearly straight line during the 1990s is suggestive of exponential growth. However, since the late 1990s the rate of network growth by this measure has slowed somewhat and no longer appears to be well modeled as exponential.

Stability. On shorter timescales, changes in network topology can arise due to system instability. The components making up the network infrastructure are continuously subject to failures, restarts, and reconfigurations. This affects the AS graph and router graph in two ways: first, the structure of the graph can be altered – nodes and edges can disappear and then reappear. However a second, often more noticeable effect is that *routes* through the graph become unstable.

In particular, equipment failures, router misconfiguration and policy changes can

---

[3]We discuss exponential growth of traffic volume in Chapter 6 (Section 6.4.1).

cause instability in the BGP system [MWA02, TSGR04]. This instability takes the form of long sequences of BGP updates – repeated announcements and withdrawals of routes. The frequent changes in routing can cause temporary routing loops, so during this time, there is a possibility for regular data packets to experience increased delay and loss rates.

On the one hand, the nature of the BGP system is such that significant instability can occur. When routing changes take place, the BGP system can require a long time and many message exchanges to converge [LABJ01]. Moreover, although most BGP routes are highly available, there is some evidence of decline in availability over time, and route stability in the inter-domain system has declined over time [GR97].

On the other hand, it appears that BGP routing instability primarily affects a small fraction of Internet traffic. The vast majority of route instability is caused by a few relatively unpopular destinations, and BGP advertisements associated with most of the traffic in the Internet are reasonably stable [RWXZ02]. More discussion of BGP traffic under stress is in Chapter 6 (Section 6.4.4).

At the router level, measurements show that some routes do exhibit significant fluctuation, and that this trend may be increasing slightly. This is consistent with the behavior of AS-level paths, and the fact that router-level paths are partially determined by AS-level paths. Measurements from the mid 1990's showed that time periods over which a particular route remains unchanged can range from seconds to days, with the majority of routes going days or weeks without change [Pax97a]. When a router-level path becomes unavailable the duration can be highly variable, with most path failures lasting less than 5 minutes but some extending much longer [FABK03].

Instability in the router graph itself can arise due to failures of routers or links. While most network equipment is stable and well-engineered, equipment failures still occur at steady rates for a number of reasons. First, changes in link availability occur due to planned maintenance. Among unplanned failures in a backbone network, a minority are due to router failure; most are due to failure of links. In a backbone network, the majority of link failures are concentrated on a small subset of the links [MIB+04]. The majority of link failures are short-lived – less than 10 minutes in duration [ICM+02].

Geographic Location

As already mentioned, the physical location of network infrastructure is of interest for the insight it provides into how infrastructure relates to population, social organization, and economic activity.

Not surprisingly, there is a strong relationship between density of population and density of network infrastructure. However, this relationship is not the same in all parts of the world. Table 5.1 shows data from 2002 for various regions of the world,

Table 5.1 Variation in people/interface density across regions [LBCM03].

	Population (millions)	Interfaces	People per interface	Online (millions)	Online per interface
Africa	837	8,379	100,011	4.15	495
South America	341	10,131	33,752	21.9	2,161
Mexico	154	4,361	35,534	3.42	784
W. Europe	366	95,993	3,817	143	1,489
Japan	136	37,649	3,631	47.1	1,250
Australia	18	18,277	975	10.1	552
USA	299	282,048	1,061	166	588
World	5,653	563,521	10,032	513	910

including both less developed regions and highly developed regions.[4] This data was obtained by mapping a large set of IP addresses using geolocation methods described in Section 5.3.6 as detailed in [LBCM03].

The *Interfaces* column shows the number of IP addresses from the dataset that were mapped into this region. *Population* numbers are from the CIESIN database [Cen], and the number of *Online* users per region is from the repository of survey statistics gathered and maintained by Nua, Inc. [Nua].[5]

Looking at the first three columns of the table, it is clear that penetration of Internet infrastructure varies dramatically across regions; the ratio of people to interfaces varies by a factor of over 100 from less developed to highly developed regions. This makes it clear that studying population vs. interface density over the entire world will be misleading. On the other hand, the last two columns provide a different perspective: the ratio of online people to interfaces shows much less variability – only about a factor of four across the regions studied. This suggests that the number of online users in an area may provide a rough indicator of the amount of network infrastructure present. Additional results on the geographic distribution of network infrastructure are in [YJB02].

5.4.3 Interaction of Traffic and Network

Many important properties of traffic are influenced by network conditions, including packet delay, packet loss, packet reordering, throughput, and jitter. These properties tend to vary widely across different paths and links in the Internet.

---

[4]Regions are delineated by simple latitude/longitude boundaries, and as such are only approximate.

[5]According to Nua, an online user is defined as an adult or child who has accessed the Internet at least once during the last 3 months, although not all of their data is strictly based on this definition.

Packet Delay

Packet delay (in the form of round-trip time, RTT) has been a principal metric of network performance since the earliest days of the Internet [NO74].

It is hard to find a single distribution that is a good model for packet delays along all paths in the Internet. In general, packet delay distributions show high variability, but the nature of the particular distribution varies strongly from path to path in the network [CMZ$^+$04]. As a result it is more useful to divide the various sources of packet delay into two types: *deterministic* delays that affect each packet on a network path equally; and *stochastic* delays that vary from packet to packet on the same path. The first category includes transmission and propagation delays, while the second category includes forwarding (mainly queuing) delays. This breakdown into types makes it easier to characterize the nature of packet delays.

Transmission and Propagation Delays. Transmission delay in the Internet is only significant on slow access links. For example, transmission delay for a 1500 byte packet on a backbone-type OC192 link is only 1.2 microseconds. On the other hand, transmission delay for the same packet on a 56 Kbps dialup link is over 200 milliseconds (Table 2.1 in Chapter 2 lists other link speeds).

Propagation delay in the Internet is largely influenced by geographic distance. In fact for most long-distance links, propagation delay is simply proportional to the physical length of the link itself [FML$^+$03, PV03, LS01]. This helps explain why minRTT over a given path shows only a weak correlation with the path's length in hops [QP01].

Conceptually, minimum RTT (minRTT) and minimum one-way delays are primarily measures of aggregate transmission and propagation delay and hence can be considered *deterministic* delay. A number of studies have looked at the collective properties of minRTT measurements taken between many pairs of nodes on the Internet. Such delays are strongly affected by topology, but can often be approximated as if the measurements were straight-line distances between points in a high-dimensional Euclidean space [NZ02, TC03], as discussed earlier. Typical measurements show that a Euclidean space with dimension anywhere from 7 to 10 can be used to model Internet minRTTs. It is possible that this phenomenon may arise in part due to geometry imposed by physical location of the nodes [TC04].

Forwarding Delays and Congestion Events. The stochastic component of packet delay is due to forwarding and congestion. This component can dominate the deterministic component in many cases. For example, minimum RTT is rarely more than 200 milliseconds, and is often below 50 milliseconds. However, the additional stochastic component can result in RTTs of hundreds of milliseconds, and in some cases tens of seconds or more [SSB$^+$02, AKSJ03].

The most salient characteristic of the stochastic component of packet delays on many paths is the presence of large 'spikes' – short intervals showing highly elevated RTTs [ZDPS01, CMZ+04]. The causes of these spikes are not fully understood, but one factor may be routing changes in the network leading to temporary instability of paths. Another factor may be temporary buildup of queues within routers [PCD03].

The queuing delays at routers show high variability and long-tailed models such as the Weibull or Pareto distribution seem appropriate for characterizing these delays [PMF+02, LR02]. Highly variable queuing delays can be expected due to the self-similarity of network traffic (see Chapter 6, Section 6.4.1). Furthermore, the distribution of RTTs observed within a single TCP connection can show high variability, which has implications for modeling TCP flow control [AKSJ03].

It is not clear *which* links are primarily responsible for congestion events in the network, or whether packets typically pass through more than one congested link along a network path. Some studies have indicated that congested links are largely those that cross inter-AS boundaries [QP01], but other studies suggest that congestion events are not primarily at AS boundaries [ZCBD04] or evenly split between boundary and non-boundary links [ASS03].

Packet Loss

Another important determiner of network performance is packet loss. The most significant cause of packet loss in wired networks is packet discard within routers in the presence of congestion; in paths that include wireless links, packet corruption, radio interference, and multipath fading are the main causes of loss.

Packet loss has been shown to occur in 'bursts,' probably due to persistent congestion events at routers. Measurements in [Bol93] show that for packets with spacing less than 200 ms, a packet was much more likely to be lost if the previous one was also; and [Pax99b] reports a similar pattern for consecutive TCP packets. The authors in [YMKT99] examine packet loss over a range of timescales and find that losses show correlation at timescales up to 1000 msec.

To model the correlation properties of packet losses, one can use hidden Markov models; for example, see [SV01, JS00]. A model that is commonly used is the Gilbert model, which is a two-state Markov model [Gil60]. Evidence shows that models with a small number of states (two or three) are generally sufficient to capture empirically observed loss patterns. Looking more closely at loss patterns, it appears that correlation in losses primarily occurs due to the occurrence of consecutive losses, rather than nearby but non-consecutive losses [ZDPS01]. As a result, the average loss burst length depends on how closely the packets are spaced during transmission [LR02].

Overall, measurements suggest that loss rates on many wired Internet paths are very low, generally less than 0.1%, and declining [Cot05a]. On the other hand, loss rates on paths that include wireless links can be very high – as high as 2% or more [BVR02].

Packet Reordering, Duplication, and Jitter

Packet reordering occurs when the network inverts the order of two packets. This can occur due to parallelism within a router [BPS99], load sharing between multiple paths in the network, or due to route changes [Mog92].

Packet reordering has implications for TCP behavior, so most studies of packet reordering have been done in the context of TCP connections. Note, however, that in a TCP connection, packets can arrive out of sequence for three reasons:

- True packet reordering occurring within the network;
- Packet duplication occurring within the network; and
- Retransmission by the TCP sender, in which case the retransmitted packet will appear to arrive out of order.

Of these three reasons, the vast majority of out-of-sequence arrivals are due to retransmission. However, in practice the majority of TCP connections do not experience any packet reordering [FML+03].

As with other metrics, the rate of out-of-order packet delivery varies widely among paths in the Internet. As many as 1 to 2% of packets in a TCP connection may arrive out of sequence when measuring long-lived flows [Pax99b]. However, measurements of packet reordering in a set of connections of various lengths shows much lower rates of reordering – from 0.03% to 0.72% [LR02, JID+03]. However, many paths show the *potential* for reordering packets at least once over a long period. Measurements consisting of 500 connections to each of 100 Web servers showed reordering occurred at least once on 35% of the paths from the client to the server and at least once on 10% of the paths from the server to the client [LC05].

Packet duplication in the network is even rarer. Packet duplication can appear to occur when the measurement point is inside a routing loop and the same packet is seen more than once; it can also sometimes occur due to the network itself actually duplicating packets. Measurements show packet duplication rates to be negligible [JID+03, Pax99b].

Finally, jitter occurs when inter-packet gaps are made less uniform due to variable queuing delay in the network. Delay variation due to queuing has been found to occur primarily on timescales of hundreds to thousands of milliseconds – i.e., in a range somewhat larger than typical RTTs in the Internet [Pax99b].

Bandwidth and Throughput

Comparatively little data is available on the distribution of bandwidths across paths in the Internet. Link speeds have steadily and rapidly increased and are continuing to increase. Based on observed declining trends in both loss rate and RTT, throughput across the Internet is expected to be increasing; furthermore, empirically measured bulk transfer rates have been increasing over certain paths [Cot05a].

Measurements made in 1997 show that T1 speed (1.544 Mbps) was the most common bottleneck bandwidth observed over a set of more than 1000 paths; however, the paths measured did not include many home users of the network, and the rapid change in link speeds throughout the Internet means that this is probably not the case at present [Pax99b]. For example, more recent measures of *available* bandwidth that include home users show values in the range of 200–900 bps [LP03].

On shorter timescales, throughput of individual paths is a relatively steady metric. In contrast to RTT and loss rates, TCP throughput rates change slowly. Throughput rates can vary by less than a factor of three over the course of an hour [ZDPS01]. This is important for measurement of available bandwidth, and indicates that such measurements are useful at least on the order of hours.

6

Traffic

The Internet's infrastructure, as described in the last chapter, is designed to support the transmission of large collections of packets – i.e., traffic. In this chapter we describe the traffic properties that are important to understand and measure; the challenges encountered in traffic measurement; the tools available for traffic measurement; and the most important results regarding properties of Internet traffic.

Traffic measurement and modeling is important to a wide range of activities. *Performance analysis* requires accurate traffic measurements in order to construct models useful for answering questions related to throughput, packet loss, and packet delay induced by network elements (links and routers). Performance analysis problems are generally concerned with timescales from microseconds to tens of minutes, and so the corresponding traffic measurements are concerned with accuracy over relatively short timescales.

Another set of activities relying on traffic measurement can be broadly called *network engineering*. Network engineering is concerned with network configuration, capacity planning, demand forecasting, traffic engineering – generally, monitoring and improving network operations. The questions that arise in network engineering are usually concerned with timescales from minutes to years (the timescales over which engineers can react to current conditions and change network operation).

Because these two sets of activities are concerned with accuracy over dramatically different timescales, measurement methods and analysis will often differ as well. Measurement at fine timescales can be very dependent on clock accuracy and precision (see Section 4.2), while measurement at long timescales is less demanding. More generally, it is impractical for a single measurement method or model to try to provide accurate traffic measures at both ends of the timescale range (say, microseconds and months). As a result some of the topics discussed in this chapter will mainly apply to only one of these sets of traffic analysis activities.

6.1   Properties

This section examines the properties of Internet traffic that can be important to measure in various settings. Our starting point is the fundamental entity in the IP protocol suite: the packet.

All Internet traffic can be viewed at the IP level as simply a set of packets. Thus the most basic view one may take of traffic on some portion of the Internet is as a collection of packets passing through routers and over links.

6.1.1   The Basics: Packets and Bytes

We start with a single network element (a link or a router), through which passes a collection of packets. At some location (perhaps one end of the link) one can capture or observe the packets. How should one summarize the traffic observed? For this we use the framework of stochastic processes as discussed in Section 3.2.1.

To begin, we can consider only those points in time when a packet arrives at our observation point: $\{A_n, n = 0, 1, ...\}$. This set of points in time can be modeled as an arrival process. One simple summarization of an arrival process consists of a characterization of the distribution and perhaps the higher-order properties of interarrivals – i.e., the distributional properties of the set $\{I_n, n = 1, 2, ...\}$ where $I_n \equiv A_n - A_{n-1}$.

Often, the arrival process view of packet traffic may contain more information than is needed or desired; sometimes the measurement effort required to capture the necessary detail outweighs the benefits. In this case one may use the time series of counts of traffic at some timescale T. For a fixed time interval T, this yields $\{C_n, n = 0, 1, ...\}$ where $C_n \equiv \#\{A_m \mid nT < A_m \leq (n + 1)T\}$. Again, the resulting time series of counts may be approximately summarized via its distribution and higher-order properties.

Although packet arrivals are important, a more commonly used measure of traffic is the number of bytes it contains. This is distinct from the packet view simply because packets come in varying sizes. The time series of counts can be easily used in this case, by counting the number of bytes contained in the packets arriving in each interval: $\{B_n, n = 0, 1, ...\}$ where $B_n \equiv \sum_{nT < A_m \leq (n+1)T} size(A_m)$ and $size(t)$ is the size of the packet arriving at time t. When using this view, we generally define $size()$ to include the bytes in a packet's payload as well as all relevant headers. For example, measurements of byte traffic on an Ethernet would include packet payload, IP and TCP or UDP headers, and Ethernet headers – the entire Ethernet frame size.

These three views of traffic are illustrated in Figure 6.1. The figure shows A_n, C_n, and B_n for a single trace.

The time series of byte counts is the most commonly used measure of the workload represented by traffic, since it captures the amount of bandwidth consumed as

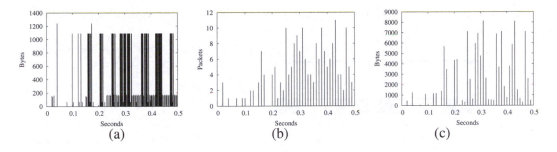

Figure 6.1   Three views of a traffic trace: (a) Arrivals. The points marked along the x axis form the arrival process A_n, and the height of each mark is the size of the arriving packet $size(t)$ at that time. (b) Time series of counts of packets, C_n. Here T is 0.01 sec. (c) Time series of counts of bytes, B_n. Data collected at Bellcore as described in [LW91]; available as trace `BC-pAug89` from the Internet Traffic Archive [DMPS].

packets pass through routers and over links. The time series of packet counts is useful for understanding the workload generated by traffic on a per-packet basis, such as address lookups performed by routers.

Since packets vary in size, another occasionally used view of packet-level traffic is in terms of the distribution of packet sizes encountered, which is useful in informing router design.

Finally, the discussion in this section has focused on measurements taken from a single point in the network. In some cases it may be desirable to collect measurements from multiple network locations. For example, one may collect traffic measurements from all links in a network simultaneously. In this case the time series of counts B_n and C_n become multivariate time series $\vec{B}_n$ and $\vec{C}_n$ with dimension equal to the number of observation points.

6.1.2   Higher-level Structure

While the simplest view of traffic as simply a collection of packets is important to understand, there is considerable *structure* in traffic that matters to Internet engineers and users. This structure is imposed by transport protocols (e.g., TCP, UDP, and RTP) and by the ultimate generators of network traffic – namely, applications. Understanding this structure helps us interpret the observed properties of network traffic; conversely, we can often learn about the higher-level protocols and applications generating network traffic by examining this structure.

We can describe structure in traffic as the result of a collection of ON/OFF processes. An ON/OFF process is one that alternates between an 'on' state in which it generates network activity, and an 'off' state in which it is silent. ON/OFF processes create bursty workloads that can present challenges for system performance and design.

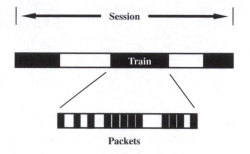

Figure 6.2   Three levels of structure in traffic.

There are three principal levels of ON/OFF activity in network traffic, as shown in Figure 6.2. At the lowest level, packets themselves are an ON/OFF process: network state at the link level alternates between packet transmission and silence.

Above the packet level, one finds that packets form *trains* from source to destination, as first noted in [JR86]. That is, when looking at the subset of packets in a trace corresponding to a single source and destination, a distinct ON/OFF pattern is generally present. These ON periods are referred to as *packet trains*.

Given a trace of packets from a single source to a single destination, one may delineate packet trains by placing a threshold on interarrivals. A train is then taken as a sequence of packets which is preceded and followed by an interarrival greater than the threshold, but within which no interarrival exceeds the threshold. As long as the threshold chosen is considerably larger than a typical interarrival, its precise setting does not usually have a strong effect on the distribution of train delineations [CBP95] (for reasons to be discussed in Section 6.4.3).

Above the packet train level, it is often the case that a collection of trains forms a *session*. A session can be thought of as the set of packet trains corresponding to a single execution of an application. From a measurement standpoint, a considerable fraction of network traffic is human generated: sending email, browsing the Web, or running a chat session. Such applications tend to have well-delineated start and end times, corresponding to some time period during which the person is using the application.

The discussion here has focused on the descriptive view, in which trains and sessions are identified by thresholding interarrivals. From a constructive standpoint, both packet trains and sessions arise out of system structure. Trains arise out of the transfer of data objects that are larger than a single packet. We can observe that the introduction of the IP architecture shifted the fundamental communication primitive from the variable-length 'call' or 'connection' (in telephony terms) to the fixed-length packet. The existence of packet trains reflects the persistence of higher-level 'connection'-like activity among applications [Cla88]. Likewise, as already mentioned, the properties of human activity as translated into demands for network service can be seen to cause session structure. Additional discussion of the structure in network traffic can be found in [Rob04, FP01].

6.1.3 Flows

Without looking at packet contents (and understanding application behavior) it is often impossible to precisely identify application-level data items. Moreover, in many cases it is not as important to identify these data items as it is to simply collect all the packets associated with the exchange of data between two endpoints into a single entity for billing, modeling, and traffic summarization.

The term 'flow' is used to capture this notion. The IP Flow Information Export standard [QZCZ04] defines a flow as a set of packets passing an observation point during a time interval, with all packets having a set of common properties. These common properties may be based on a packet's header field contents, characteristics of the packet itself (such as layer-2 labels), or how the packet is processed (its next hop IP address or output interface).

Note however that the term *flow* has also been used to mean slightly different things in different contexts. In particular it has often been used in the sense of packet train. We will keep the terms distinct, and use flow in its more general sense.

IP Flows. A set of packets distinguished by their source and destination addresses, or any other function of their IP or transport header fields, is called an *IP flow*. Thus, for example, packet train structure exists within IP flows between individual endsystems as defined by their IP addresses.

IP flows may be defined at a variety of aggregation levels. Flows may be aggregated by port, protocol, address, or combinations of these. Address aggregation can be done at varying levels by prefix, in which all IP addresses belonging to a given prefix are assigned to the same flow. Useful sets of prefixes include those which are globally routed via BGP and those corresponding to the autonomous system originating the address.

Network-defined Flows. In the context of a particular network, flows represent natural units of traffic engineering. Thus flows are often defined with respect to a particular network's workload.

For a network in which routing is not changing, an important flow definition is based on ingress and egress. The set of packets entering a network at a given point and exiting at another point is called an origin–destination or ingress–egress flow. This definition takes into account routing; if routing changes, the mapping from IP flows to origin–destination flows changes.

As discussed in Section 3.4.2, given counts of bytes (or packets) in origin–

destination flows $\vec{B}_{(f)}$ and a routing matrix $A = G^T$, the corresponding count on links is given by $\vec{B}_{(l)} = A\vec{B}_{(f)}$. The complete set of origin–destination flows in the network is called the *traffic matrix* [MTS+02] and the mapping of flows to paths in the network is called the *path matrix* [DG01].

Because there may often be multiple routes to a destination prefix, a set of packets destined for a common endpoint may have multiple possible exit points from a network. The set of origin–destination flows at any time are a realization of point to multipoint demands as determined by routing policies [FGL+00].

6.1.4   Semantically Distinct Traffic Types

Another important dimension for traffic measurement is traffic purpose. Most traffic consists of the transport of data between applications running on endsystems. However, the network also carries packets with other purposes, and these can be important to measure.

Control Traffic.   IP networks are controlled via packets that are sent over the same media as regular data packets. These two kinds of packets are referred to as belonging to the *control plane* and the *data plane*. Control plane packets include packets implementing routing protocols (most commonly BGP, OSPF, and IS–IS); measurement packets (SNMP); and general control packets (ICMP). Measuring this traffic may be of interest in order to reproduce it in simulation [MF02] or because it reflects the performance of the routing system [LMJ98, SMD03].

Malicious Traffic.   Network operators are vitally concerned with misuse and abuse of their networks, and so commonly seek to distinguish and measure malicious traffic. Chapter 9 will look at measurement of malicious traffic in detail. Here we simply note that separating malicious from normal traffic is usually a difficult problem.

6.2   Challenges

Effectively measuring the traffic properties described in the last section can be challenging for a number of reasons. The reasons include both practical issues and more fundamental statistical difficulties.

6.2.1 Practical Issues

Unfortunately, even the simple process of obtaining traffic measurements can be hindered by a variety of issues; these issues include the inability to observe, to manage, or to share the measurements of interest.

Observability

The Internet architecture has certain distinct characteristics that tend to interfere with easy measurement of network traffic.

Core Simplicity. As discussed in Section 5.2.1, the emphasis on simplicity of router functions has led to a lack of observability at many points in the network.

With respect to traffic, examples include:

- Flows. Since per-flow state is not required to be maintained in routers, flow measurements are difficult to obtain. Flow measurement capabilities have been added to routers (see Section 6.3.3). However, standards for flow measurement have taken considerable time to emerge and idiosyncrasies in flow measurement have made interpretation of measurements difficult [SF02].
- Packets. The emphasis on network simplicity has meant that packet capture in the network is generally not available. Capturing packets must generally be implemented at endsystems or by additional hardware added to the network.

Distributed Internetworking. The distributed packet-switching architecture of the Internet (Section 2.1.1) exists not just at the level of routers, but at the network level as well.

As described in Chapter 2, before 1995 the Internet had a single backbone, the NSFNET. This network provided a measurement point for the majority of traffic passing through the Internet. However, following the transition of the Internet to private operation in 1995, the largest autonomous systems that make up the Internet have come to interconnect at multiple points. There is no longer a single backbone network and there is no network that provides a convenient measurement point for the majority of Internet traffic.

This fact brings into focus the difficulty of characterizing traffic on 'the' Internet. Any measurement point presents a local view of traffic and network properties which may not be representative of other measurement points. Traffic seen in home networks, enterprise networks, access networks, and backbone networks can all be expected to differ considerably. Even different kinds of backbone networks (commercial and non-commercial) will show different properties (an example is discussed in [BGP04]).

The IP Hourglass.   The IP hourglass, discussed in Sections 2.1.3 and 5.2.2, also affects observability of traffic characteristics. Packet corruption, delay, and loss at the physical layer may be masked by link-level retransmission or forward error correction. These traffic properties are generally not visible when measurements are taken at the IP layer and above.

Data Volume

As discussed above, the most broadly useful form of traffic monitoring is full packet capture. Unfortunately, as link speeds increase, full packet capture becomes increasingly challenging. Packet capture on an OC-48 link with 50% utilization yields 155 megabytes per second of data to be stored. For an OC-192 link, this is 625 megabytes per second.

Such data quantities are challenging to process, to store, and to manage. Algorithms for processing the data must be efficient. Storage needs to be on media local to the link being monitored – usually on a dedicated disk that is part of the network monitor. Finally, if captured data is to be moved to another location for processing, the timing and rate of transfer needs to be carefully chosen.

For these reasons, full packet capture on high-speed links is only appropriate for short timescales (often only a minute or less is collected). With sampling or summarization (Section 6.3.3) it can be feasible to scale up to days, especially if flow summaries are computed.

A number of problems arise indirectly due to data rate and volume. To extend the sampling period, often only packet headers are stored, which can frustrate subsequent analysis that depends on packet contents (e.g., HTTP or SMTP headers). Data collection can be lossy due to buffer overflows. The resulting data set is stored and processed in nonstandard formats (often flat files processed by scripts), which can interfere with the repeatability of analysis. More details are discussed in [Pax01].

Data Sharing

Network measurement data and network traffic contain considerable amounts of information that is sensitive. Full packet capture essentially records the activity of network users. Such traces can be used to extract information such as Web sites visited, passwords, and contents of email messages exchanged.

Furthermore, even when traffic measurements are not detailed enough to provide records of user activity, they can still provide information about the configuration and functioning of the network being monitored. For example, network measurement may uncover the identities or nature of a provider's peers, customers, interconnection points, and traffic routing policies. For many network service providers, such information is competition-sensitive. Since network service providers must cooperate to provide service, and yet are in competition for customers, details of internal network engineering are often treated as highly confidential.

The goals of protecting the privacy of network users and protecting the competitive secrets of network providers are in tension with network measurement. The most common resolution of this tension is for network providers to avoid or prohibit sharing of measurements outside their organizations. However, network measurement is not typically concerned with questions that violate privacy or divulge engineering secrets. Therefore it is sometimes possible to share data that has been processed in such a way that it can be used to answer some, but not all questions.

One simple step in this direction is to capture only packet headers. Without packet payloads, much (though not all) of the personally sensitive information in traffic is discarded. A further step is anonymization of various kinds, which we cover in Chapter 8.

6.2.2 Statistical Difficulties

Beyond the practical challenges inherent in traffic measurement, a number of issues arise when statistically characterizing the results.

Long Tails and High Variability

A number of properties of Internet traffic show high variability, as defined in Section 3.2.2. The presence of high variability complicates statistical analysis in a number of ways.

Instability of Metrics. The most basic problem in working with high variability data is the instability of traditional summary statistics, particularly the sample mean and variance. High variability data exhibits many small observations mixed in with a few large observations. In such datasets, most of the observations are small, but most of the contribution to the sample mean or variance comes from the rare, large observations. This phenomenon is illustrated in Figure 6.3 (an early use of plots like this is [Man97]). On the left of the figure, 1000 samples of a long-tailed distribution are plotted. Note the extreme variability in the values: typical values are small (in the range 1 to 5) and cannot be seen in the plot, while the few large values are all that are visible. The center plot shows the running mean of this dataset. Note how the large values affect the running mean: the mean does not appear to stabilize to any particular value. On the right of the plot, we see that the situation is even worse for the running standard deviation. The net result is that sample means and sample variances of such data are not reliable statistics for summarizing dataset properties.

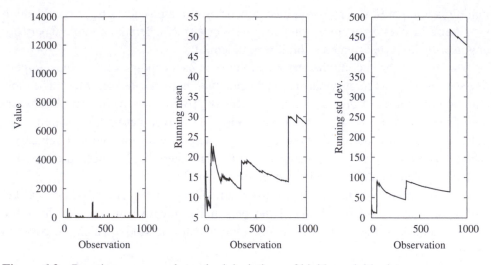

Figure 6.3   Running means and standard deviations of highly variable data.

This is particularly problematic for simulations involving long-tailed models, which may be very slow to reach steady state [CL99].

These problems become more acute when using probability models to describe such data. A heavy-tailed model for such data may appear to be appropriate; however, for such models, even low-order distributional moments can be infinite. For a heavy-tailed model with $\alpha \leq 2$, variance is infinite; when $\alpha \leq 1$, even the mean is infinite. Of course, infinite mean or variance can only be a property of a model; for real data, such properties are exhibited as a failure for sample means and variances to converge (as suggested by Figure 6.3).

The presence of infinite moments in a distributional model means that many traditional system metrics can be undefined. As a simple example, consider the mean queue length in an $M/G/1$ queuing model with infinite buffering, which is proportional to the second moment of service time [Kle76]. When service times are drawn from a heavy-tailed distribution, many properties of this queuing model (mean queue length, mean waiting time) are infinite. Thus, analysts dealing with heavy tails may need to turn their attention away from means and variances and toward understanding the full distribution of relevant metrics. Most early work in this direction has focused on the shape of the tail of such distributions (*e.g.,* [Nor94]). Many questions related to such models must be evaluated numerically rather than analytically, and even then with considerable care (e.g., see [RVR98]).

Because arbitrarily large observations cannot be ruled out, issues of scale should enter into any discussion of heavy-tailed models. No real system can experience arbitrarily large events, and generally one must pay attention to the practical upper limit on event size, whether determined by the timescale of interest, the constraints of storage or transmission capacity, or other system-defined limits. On the brighter side, a useful result is that it is often reasonable to substitute finitely-supported distributions for the idealized heavy-tailed distributions in analytic settings, as long as the approximation is accurate over the range of scales of interest [FW97, GJL99, HBCP98].

Modeling Difficulty.   A related issue is that it can be difficult to choose the best probabilistic model for describing highly variable data. A central point of contention often rests on the choice between a heavy-tailed model (with a strictly power-law tail) and some other subexponential distribution (such as the lognormal). The difficulty arises due to a combination of factors. First, many datasets show a dynamic range of only three or four orders of magnitude. This means that the tail behavior can only be measured over a limited range. Second, the differences between (say) a Pareto distribution and a lognormal distribution can be quite small when attention is restricted to a limited range of values, such as only three or four orders of magnitude. The perceived differences between two such distributions are strongly affected by the parameters of the distributions chosen (see Section 6.3.3 for discussion of distribution functions). In many cases, proper choice of parameters can appear to make a Pareto or a lognormal fit the tail of a dataset equally well.

The result is that different investigators, looking at slightly different datasets, and using slightly different methods, can reach very different conclusions about the presence of power-law shape in the dataset's tail. Because different explanatory mechanisms are associated with different distributional models, the resulting differences can seem to extend more broadly to conclusions about the underlying systems. See for example [Dow01, WAL04].

Confounding Intuition.   More generally, when working with heavy-tailed models it is important to keep in mind certain statistical properties that differ from what is usually expected. Although these properties are counterintuitive, understanding them can improve the design of networks and distributed systems [Cro00].

The first property is related to the fact that heavy-tailed distributions show declining hazard rate, and is most concisely captured in terms of conditional expectation:

$$E[X|X > k] \sim k$$

when X is a heavy tailed random variable and k is large enough to be 'in the tail.' This is called the *expectation paradox* in [Man83]; it says that if we are making observations of heavy-tailed interarrivals, then the longer we have waited for an event, the longer we should expect to wait. (The expectation is undefined when $\alpha \leq 1$, but the general idea still holds.) This should be contrasted with the case when the underlying distribution has exponential tails or has bounded support above (as in the uniform distribution); in these cases, eventually one always gets to the point where the longer one waits for an event, the less time one should expect to continue waiting.

The second counterintuitive property of heavy-tailed distributions is the disparity between the size and count of objects in a sample. In such distributions, the number of objects seen is a poor measure of the total size seen. In other words, the majority of size measure in a set of observations is concentrated in a very small subset of the observations. This can be visualized as a box into which one has put a few boulders, and then filled the rest of the way with sand. There is a significant difference between a typical particle in the box, and the most massive particle in the box.

The disparity between size and count can be so great that for heavy-tailed random variables, the shape of the upper tail of the distribution of a sum of random variables is determined by only the maximum value in the sum. This property can be stated formally as [GK98]:

$$\lim_{x \to \infty} \frac{P[X_1 + ... + X_n > x]}{P[\max(X_1, ..., X_n) > x]} = 1 \text{ for all } n \geq 2$$

which is the case when the X_i are i.i.d. positive random variables drawn from a heavy-tailed distribution. Thus, when considering collections of observations of a heavy-tailed random variable, the aggregated size measure contained in the small observations is negligible compared to the largest observation in determining the likelihood of large values of the sum.

Size–count disparity is commonly expressed as an '80/20' or '90/10' rule. This has been termed a *crossover* statistic in [BHGkc04]; it expresses the fact that a fraction $1 - c$ of the size measure is contained in a fraction c of the largest observations. The size of objects at the crossover threshold is a reasonable separator between mice and elephants. This size–count disparity means that one must be careful in "optimizing the common case" [Lam83]. The typical *observation* is small; the typical *unit of work* is contained in a large observation.

Size–count disparity can be studied by defining the size-weighted distribution function:

$$F_w(x) = \frac{\int_{-\infty}^{x} u \, dF(u)}{\int_{-\infty}^{\infty} v \, dF(v)} \tag{6.1}$$

and comparing $F_w(x)$ with $F(x)$. Varying x over its valid range yields a plot of the fraction of total size measure that is contained in the fraction of observations less than x. An example of this comparison is shown in Figure 6.4. This figure shows $F_w(x)$ vs. $F(x)$ for the case where all observations are equal, for the uniform distribution, for the exponential distribution, and for a particular heavy-tailed distribution. The heavy-tailed distribution is chosen to correspond to empirical measurements of file sizes in the World Wide Web (from [BC98]); it has $\alpha = 1.0$. Since the denominator in (6.1) is infinite for heavy-tailed distributions with $\alpha \leq 1$, the actual distribution used has been truncated to span six orders of magnitude, which is reasonable for file size distributions.

In this figure, the corresponding crossover statistics are marked on each curve. For the case in which all observations are equal, the crossover is 50/50; for the uniform distribution it is the golden ratio, approximately 62/38; for the exponential distribution it is approximately 68/32; and for the heavy-tailed distribution it is 85/15. Note that this statistic can only be applied to heavy-tailed distributions with $\alpha \leq 1$ if an upper size cutoff is used; the particular crossover statistic varies considerably depending on the value of α and the upper size cutoff used [BHGkc04].

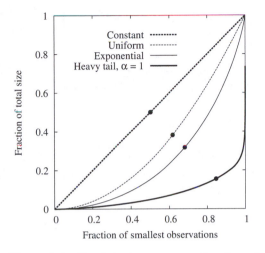

Figure 6.4   Total size measure as a function of smallest observations.

The figure shows that the exponential distribution has disparity and crossover statistic not too different from the uniform distribution, suggesting that the exponential does not strongly incorporate a size–count disparity. On the other hand, for the heavy-tailed distribution, the total size measure is not at all commensurate with the fraction of observations considered; about 60% of the size measure is contained in the upper 1% of the observations.

In referring to traffic flows, size–count disparity is often called the "elephants and mice" phenomenon. This phenomenon will be discussed in Section 6.4.

Size–count disparity has also been extensively studied in economics (e.g., in relation to income levels) where plots like Figure 6.4 are called *Lorenz curves*. A measure of disparity used in that setting is the *Gini coefficient*. If the area between the curve for the constant distribution (the line $y = x$) and the Lorenz curve is A, and the area under the Lorenz curve is B, the Gini coefficient is $A/(A + B)$.

Stationarity and Stability

A central question in studying network traffic is the nature of traffic *stability*. Stability refers to the consistency of traffic properties over time. Stability is distinct from *stationarity*, which is a formal property of a stochastic model. When measurement

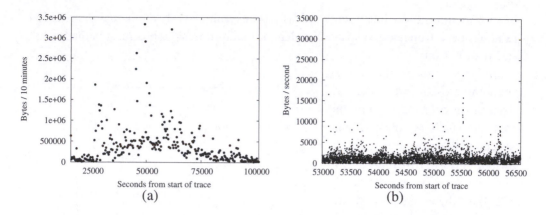

Figure 6.5   Traffic at two timescales: (a) unstable (24 hours) vs. (b) stable (1 hour). Data collected at Bellcore as described in [LW91]; available as trace `BC-Oct89Ext` from the Internet Traffic Archive [DMPS].

properties are stable, it may be appropriate to describe the measurements using a stationary model.

The question of stability (and the appropriateness of using a stationary model) is closely tied to timescale. Many traffic properties may be thought of as unstable at some timescales and stable at other timescales.

An important example is traffic volume (bytes or packets per unit time). In many networks, traffic volume is strongly driven by patterns of human behavior. A typical example is shown in Figure 6.5. This data represent byte counts of traffic between a research laboratory and the rest of the Internet [LW91]. The left-hand plot shows traffic over a 24-hour period; a diurnal pattern peaking around midday is clearly visible. The right-hand plot shows traffic for a single busy hour, corresponding to a period approximately in the center of the left-hand plot. The right-hand plot shows stability in the typical values seen (despite their overall high variability).

Different goals for traffic measurement and modeling are associated with different assumptions about traffic stability. Performance analysis questions are generally concerned with short timescales (an hour or less), and usually assume that traffic is stable over these timescales. This is justified based on observations such as shown in Figure 6.5, and suggests that stationary models are appropriate for describing traffic over such timescales.

Network engineering is generally concerned with longer timescales (hours to years), over which traffic cannot be assumed to be stable. Models describing traffic over these timescales need to incorporate changing means (and perhaps other parameters) and thus are not stationary.

Stability in network traffic is a special case of the general notion of constancy in network measurements. One can distinguish three kinds of constancy: mathematical, operational, and predictive [ZDPS01]. In mathematical constancy, a set of measurements is well described as arising from a stationary stochastic process. Operational constancy refers to stability within ranges that do not affect application performance. Finally, predictively steady measurements are those which are amenable to prediction of future values based on past values.

Operational notions such as constancy are critically tied to particular timescales. For example, the properties of congestion events differ depending on the timescale of measurement. Coarse timescale traffic measurements (e.g., 5 minute SNMP counts) will tend to obscure traffic bursts which are important for performance analysis. Finer timescale traffic measurement may require more difficult techniques such as packet capture but can give insight into questions related to router performance and packet loss [PCD03].

Autocorrelation and Memory in System Behavior

A further complication related to timescale of measurement is the presence of memory in system behavior. Networks and endsystems show memory because they contain buffers and control algorithms that maintain past history in a way that affects current behavior. For example, when a network link is running at high utilization, routers may build up large queues which take a long time to drain. Thus the departure of a packet from the router can be delayed because of events that took place long in the past. This leads to autocorrelation in system behavior – the system's current behavior is very similar to its behavior in the recent past.

The effects of system memory can be good and bad. System memory makes the near future more predictable: one can have increased confidence that if packet delays were high in the recent past, they will still be high at the present time. However they also decrease the amount of information that is obtained in measurement. If one is interested in estimating the value of a system property that shows strong memory, confidence intervals will be larger than had the property been memoryless. Worse yet, if one constructs confidence intervals using statistical formulas that assume independence of observations, the confidence intervals will be misleadingly small, leading to a false sense of precision in the results.

This can be illustrated as follows, based on the exposition in [Ber94] and [Rou05]. Assume we wish to estimate the mean of a process given measurements $\{X_t, t = 0, 1, 2, ..., T\}$. The expected value of the estimator $\hat{X} = 1/T \sum_{t=0}^{T-1} X_t$ is the true mean $E[X]$. However, the *variance* of this estimator depends on the correlation present in the measurements.

The usual Central Limit Theorem concerns independent X_t, and states that:

$$\sqrt{T}(\hat{X} - E[X]) \to \mathcal{N}(0, \sigma^2)$$

where $\mathcal{N}$ refers to the Normal distribution, $\sigma^2 = \text{Var}(X)$ and $\to$ here means 'converges in distribution for large T.' On this basis one can form confidence intervals for $\hat{X}$ which are proportional to $\sigma/\sqrt{T}$. However, when X_t are not independent, the estimator converges to a distribution with higher variance:

$$\sqrt{T}(\hat{X} - E[X]) \to \mathcal{N}(0, s^2)$$

where s^2 is the *asymptotic variance*. The asymptotic variance is larger than σ^2 because of autocorrelation between the X_t. The appropriate confidence intervals are correspondingly larger, proportional to $s/\sqrt{T}$.

One can quantify this inflation in estimator variance using the autocorrelation function $r(k)$ of the underlying (continuous) process being sampled. If the process is being sampled at uniform periodic intervals δt, then:

$$s^2 = \sigma^2 \left[1 + \sum_{k=1}^{\infty} r(k\,\delta t) \right] \tag{6.2}$$

and if the process is sampled at Poisson intervals with rate λ:

$$s^2 = \sigma^2 \left[\frac{1}{\lambda} \int_0^{\infty} r(u)\, du \right].$$

A practical implication of the increase in estimator variance is that confidence intervals for any given estimate are enlarged. Thus, confidence intervals based on an assumption of independence will be incorrectly small and misleading. An example showing the error that can arise in estimating the mean is shown in Figure 6.6. The figure shows a realization of a highly autocorrelated zero-mean process (an EWMA process with $r(k) = 0.9^k$). In addition, the running average is plotted (which is the estimator of the true mean) as well as two sets of 95% confidence intervals. The true confidence intervals are constructed based on the asymptotic variance s^2 while the false confidence intervals are constructed based on an assumption of independence, i.e., σ^2. The figure shows that the true confidence intervals contain the correct mean (zero) while the false confidence intervals generally do not. Furthermore, the figure shows the considerable growth in the sizes of the confidence intervals that can occur when autocorrelation is taken into account.

The memory present in network measurements can arise from a number of sources; an instructive example is queuing delays. For an M/M/1 queue (a FIFO

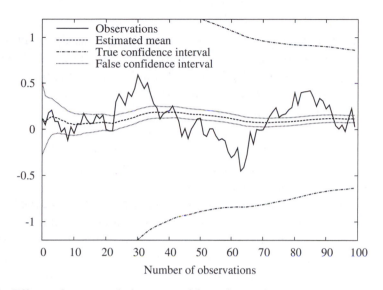

Figure 6.6 Effects of autocorrelation on confidence intervals.

queue with Poisson arrivals and exponentially distributed service times), the resulting asymptotic variance is:

$$s^2 \approx \frac{4\rho^2}{(1-\rho)^4}$$

where ρ is the utilization of the queue (arrival rate times mean service time).

This expression exposes an important principle: autocorrelation, and therefore
asymptotic variance, increases with increasing system load. The relationship to system load is very sensitive, as shown by the fourth power in the denominator. When
load is high, large queues build up, and queuing delays lead to larger autocorrelation
at greater time lags k. As a result, estimates of system mean have higher variance
(perhaps much higher) and are less reliable.

Throughout this discussion we have assumed that the sum of autocorrelations is
finite, i.e., $\sum_{k=1}^{\infty} r(k \, \delta t) < \infty$. For some traffic models this is not the case, leading to the condition called *long-range dependence*, which will be discussed in Sec-
tion 6.4.1.

Last, it is important to note that, as discussed in the previous section, many system
properties may only be stable over limited timescales. Thus the effects of autocorrelation can make it difficult or impossible to estimate a property like system mean
before it changes.

High Dimensionality

Finally, we note that many traffic metrics are naturally expressed as multidimensional (vector) time series. Section 6.1.1 noted that traffic measured from multiple locations in a network can be thought of in this way. A similar case is the time series of byte counts in origin–destination flows in a network

Traffic measurements from a single link can also be cast as multidimensional time series. For example, the set of source IP addresses (or any combination of IP header fields) active in successive time intervals forms a multidimensional time series. Likewise, the set of BGP updates arriving at an observation point organized by relevant prefix forms a multidimensional time series.

A central difficulty in dealing with such time series is the so-called *curse of dimensionality* [Don]. For most such time series, the number of dimensions involved is very high. For example, the time series of active source IP addresses in traffic trace conceptually has 2^{32} dimensions. Even worse, the set of IP flows (defined by the source and destination address and port 4-tuple) occupies a space of dimension $2^{32} \times 2^{32} \times 2^{16} \times 2^{16}$.

High dimensionality tends to prevent easy visualization of data, and complicates data modeling and analysis. Visualization is difficult beyond three dimensions. Moreover, extracting useful summaries of high dimensional data is difficult, because accurate characterization of the relationships between D dimensions can in the general case require a number of measurements exponential in D. A number of approaches to dealing with high dimensionality in traffic data are discussed in Section 6.3.3.

6.3   Tools

In this section we discuss the types of tools and methods that are useful in capturing and analyzing network traffic.

6.3.1   Packet Capture

The most fundamental tool for traffic analysis is packet capture, which is also called *passive* traffic measurement.

Packet Capture on General Purpose Systems.   An end system can typically capture and record all packets that pass through its network interfaces, and is often the most convenient and practical means for doing so [Mog90]. The most common API is `libpcap` which is available on most operating systems.

The `libpcap` library includes entry points for specifying the interfaces to be monitored and the types of packets to be collected. An interface may be placed in *promiscuous* mode, meaning that it will report all packets received, not just those destined for the current host. On broadcast LANs, this allows capture of all LAN traffic. On switched LANs, this allows capture of all traffic if the host is connected to a switch monitoring port.

A key idea is placing packet selection code into the kernel, so that packets need not be copied across into user space unless they are of interest [MRA87, MJ93]. Using `libpcap` one installs *packet filters* which are patterns specifying which packets should be returned to the application. The packet filter also allows one to specify how much of each packet should be captured. It is possible to capture just link-layer and TCP/IP headers, or full packet contents including data.

The `libpcap` library merely delivers raw packet data to the application. Higher-level software is generally needed for parsing packet header fields and interpreting protocols. Public domain tools for this purpose include `tcpdump` [tcp] and `ethereal` [Eth]. Sophisticated protocol analyzers are available as commercial products.

Most Ethernets today are switched, meaning that each host only receives the traffic destined for it. Before the advent of switched Ethernet, a monitor placed anywhere on the LAN could capture all traffic passing over the LAN. In switched Ethernets, one can capture all network traffic via *port mirroring*, which is supported by many Ethernet switches. When port mirroring is turned on, copies of Ethernet frames sent to one port on the switch are also sent to the monitoring port. This allows capturing all the packets sent over one network link (e.g., the external or upstream link of the LAN) via `libpcap` running on a host connected to the monitoring port of the switch.

In general, unrestricted access to the network interface as required by `libpcap` raises security issues, and network administrators are often hesitant to grant such access. In response tools such as `pktd` [GP03] and `scriptroute` [SWA03] have been developed. These tools allow unprivileged users the ability to capture packets from the network, and inject packets into the network, within policy boundaries established by system administrators.

Packet Capture by Special Purpose Systems.   While capturing packets within a LAN is relatively straightforward, capturing packets from other links in the Internet can be considerably more difficult. As one moves to links with higher levels of traffic aggregation, the traffic captured tends to become more representative and diverse. However, there are a number of problems as well: transmission technology tends to be more varied, and line rates can be much higher – placing more stringent performance demands on the packet capture system.

Monitoring core network links (T1 and faster, as shown in Table 2.1) generally requires specialized hardware.

At the lowest level, the link must be tapped to provide physical access and copies of the data on the link. For electrical (copper) links, this can be done with an electrical splitter (or a monitoring port on a switch at one end of the link). For optical links, this can be done via an optical splitter [AkcTW97, CJS03].

Packets must then be captured. At high link speeds, packet capture with standard interface cards can overwhelm the CPU and bandwidth of a typical capture host. OC12 speeds (622 Mbps) are faster than the speed of a standard PCI bus; and usual network processing generates a CPU interrupt for each arriving packet. Hence, specialized network interfaces and interface drivers are generally required [EMG].

A wide variety of special purpose commercial products are available for packet (or packet header) capture. Examples of non-commercial products are the OC3MON and OC12MON systems [Cor, TMW97]. In older versions of these systems, a standard network interface card is used. In later versions, specialized network interfaces are used.

Control Plane Traffic.   In contrast to generic packet capture, it is possible to obtain control packet traffic by directly participating in control plane communication, i.e., the exchange of routing messages.

For example, one can passively obtain a local view of the BGP system in a straightforward manner. The idea is to register to receive BGP updates by establishing a session with a BGP-speaking router. It is not necessary to use an actual router to receive such messages; a standard PC can be configured with software to speak BGP (such as GNU Zebra [gnu] or Quagga [quaa]). Establishing such a connection only involves finding a BGP router – in other words, finding a system administrator of a BGP router who is willing to establish the BGP session. The BGP router then passes messages as if the listening device were another BGP router. The listening device is entirely passive and never generates any BGP updates.

GNU Zebra captures data in the binary format that is used by BGP. The data can then be translated to human readable form using tools from the MRTD toolkit (in particular, the program `route_btoa`) [MRTa]. A large repository of BGP traffic collected in this manner, along with the associated BGP tables inferred from the traffic, is archived and made available by the *Routeviews* project [Rou]. Discussion and caveats on interpreting such data are presented in [MBGR03, WZP$^+$02].

Finally, we note that in principle one can also collect traffic from interior routing protocols in a similar manner. For example, both GNU Zebra and Quagga can also act as OSPF and RIP routers.

6.3.2 Data Management

Full packet capture and storage is quite challenging, and grows more so as link speeds increase. The challenges are created by limited bus bandwidth and memory access speeds on commodity PCs, and limited speeds and capacities of disk arrays. Even when full packet traces can be captured and stored, their immense size can make subsequent analysis and management difficult.

One way to address such data management and analysis challenges is through the construction and use of specialized tools. The common thread among these toolsets is the use of sophisticated algorithms for operating on large streams of data.

Example toolsets include the *smacq* system [FV02], which is a set of modules useful for processing packet capture data. The system is organized into a set of components which can be combined in various ways to accomplish traffic analysis tasks, and incorporates special features for extensibility. Windmill [WMJ04] is a system focused on protocol performance measurement; it is organized around a packet filter for traffic capture, a set of modules incorporating Internet protocols for packet processing, and an extensible experiment engine. A system similar to Windmill, but explicitly incorporating online data reduction to improve scalability, is Nprobe [MHK$^+$03]. The FLAME system [AIM$^+$02] is focused on providing more extensive in-kernel processing through the use of safe kernel extensions. A system organized as a set of tools for reading and processing traffic data in a variety of formats is Coral Reef [KMK$^+$01]. A set of tools that eases analysis of packet header data in a high-level statistical package ('S') is described in [CCS02].

As a database management problem, network data has special characteristics: it consists of very large data sets that arrive incrementally over time, and queries may be continuous or ongoing rather than one-time [BBD$^+$02, Mut03]. Database researchers have begun to address these challenges in the context of *data stream management* systems [GGR05]. One of the first such systems to focus specifically on network data was Tribeca [SH98].

Some notable projects in data stream management include the STREAMS system [ABB$^+$05] and TelegraphCQ [KCC$^+$03, PGB$^+$04]. In these two systems, continuous queries over data streams are written in SQL with the SELECT statement. However, only a subset of the full SQL syntax is supported, and additional clauses may be added to specify a time interval or window for computations (such as aggregations and joins) that implicitly operate on a finite data set.

A large-scale system combining aspects of much of the above is Gigascope. Gigascope is a well-developed data stream management system specialized for network traffic analysis, and used in conjunction with high performance packet capture [CJSS03b, CJSS03a].

Queries in Gigascope are expressed in GSQL which uses SQL-like syntax, but includes both extensions and restrictions compared to standard SQL. It is restricted in requiring blocking operations (aggregations and joins) to operate over a fixed size time window. It is extended in providing support for common networking computations such as longest-prefix matching. It is further extensible with user-definable functions to perform more complex processing, such as protocol simulation.

```
select tb, srcIP, sum(len)
from IPv4
where protocol = 6
group by time/60 as tb, srcIP
having count(*)>5;
```

Figure 6.7 Example query in Gigascope (from [CJS03]).

Stream database queries in GSQL receive one or more tuple streams as input, and generate a single tuple stream as output. A stream field can have an ordering property, which captures the temporal ordering necessary to generate stream outputs. These are the fields which specify how aggregation is to be performed. An example GSQL query is shown in Figure 6.7. This query examines a stream of IPv4 packets and finds all cases in which a single source sends more than five packets in a 60-second window.

A number of optimizations are incorporated in Gigascope. Low-level queries are optimized to perform data reduction as early as possible. Queries are optimized and compiled to C and C++ modules, each of which performs either a filtering, transformation, or aggregation function. The entire system is structured as a set of communicating processes coordinated by a registry.

Gigascope is in regular use and has been applied to a range of network analysis tasks. It has been used for network analysis and network health; protocol analysis and performance analysis; and various research projects.

6.3.3 Data Reduction

Another response to the challenges of high-speed packet collection and management is to reduce the volume of data requiring processing. A wide variety of methods have arisen to perform traffic data reduction. Traffic data reduction can be thought of as methods for lossy compression designed with specific traffic features in mind.

There are many traffic data reduction methods, and different methods can take widely varying approaches. The most common methods are the use of traffic counters as provided by SNMP, and the collection of flow records. More sophisticated methods include sampling-based approaches, sketch-based summarization, and dimensionality reduction. Finally, probabilistic models are also a kind of data reduction. Each of these broad approaches is discussed in this section.

Counters

The most common form of traffic summarization is to use aggregation to form time series of counts of traffic statistics – for example, bytes or packets per unit time. This is supported in all current routers via the MIB-II Management Information Base, accessed via SNMP [MR]. In an Ethernet, corresponding statistics can be obtained from the RMON Management Information Base [Wal00]. These Management Information Bases provide running counts of statistics; time series are constructed by periodic polling. These statistics are often generically called *SNMP counts*.

The MIB-II MIB is the primary source of basic counts within backbone networks. MIB-II is the only MIB that has reached IETF standard status and all SNMP agents are likely to support it. The MIB-II MIB contains a group "Interfaces" which, among other information for each interface, consists of a structure called an `ifEntry`. Fields in the `ifEntry` are shown in Table 6.1.

The number of bytes received and sent on each interface are given by the `ifInOctets` and `ifOutOctets` fields; other counters are available for packets (divided into unicast and non-unicast packets). The MIB counters record totals since the last time the interface was initialized (generally at router reboot). To form a time series of counts one polls the MIB at regular intervals and records the difference since the last poll. Thus a basic view of activity on all links is available by polling the set `ifEntry`s on the MIBs of all the network's interfaces. A common tool for doing this (along with plotting the results) is the *Multi Router Traffic Grapher*, MRTG [MRTb].

SNMP counts have some distinct advantages as a form of traffic summarization [Rou02]. They can be captured easily without much performance impact on routers. Furthermore, SNMP counts are extremely compact compared to traffic traces.

However, there are complications associated with collecting SNMP counts. Since SNMP transport is via UDP, measurement packets can be lost. This leads to missing data points in a time series of counts. In addition, since data is collected via polling, it can be difficult to obtain precisely synchronized time series measurements across multiple interfaces of a network, if poll events occur at slightly different times on each interface. Finally, MIB-II measurements are too coarse-grained for many needs. There have been recent attempts to put finer-grained counters into routers. Cisco routers now offer per-prefix counters, and Juniper's DCU defines 16 traffic classes over which counts can be maintained [VE03].

Table 6.1 Fields in the `ifEntry` of the MIB-II interfaces group (from [MR]).

Field Name	Meaning
`ifIndex`	A unique value for each interface
`ifDescr`	A text string including the name of the manufacturer, the product name and the version of the hardware interface
`ifType`	An indication of the link layer technology of the interface
`ifMtu`	The size of the largest datagram which can be sent/received on the interface
`ifSpeed`	An estimate of the interface's current or nominal bandwidth in bits per second
`ifPhysAddress`	The interface's address at the next lower protocol layer, if such a value exists
`ifAdminStatus`	Desired state: "up," "down," or "testing"
`ifOperStatus`	Operational state: "up," "down," or "testing"
`ifLastChange`	The time the interface entered its current operational state
`ifInOctets`	The total number of octets received on the interface, including framing characters
`ifInUcastPkts`	The number of subnetwork-unicast packets delivered to a higher-layer protocol
`ifInNUcastPkts`	The number of non-unicast (i.e., subnetwork-broadcast or subnetwork-multicast) packets delivered to a higher-layer protocol
`ifInDiscards`	The number of non-corrupted inbound packets which were chosen to be discarded (e.g., for lack of buffer space)
`ifInErrors`	The number of corrupted inbound packets
`ifInUnknownProtos`	The number of packets discarded because of an unknown or unsupported protocol
`ifOutOctets`	The total number of octets transmitted out of the interface, including framing characters
`ifOutUcastPkts`	The total number of packets to be transmitted to a unicast address, including those that were discarded or not sent
`ifOutNUcastPkts`	The total number of packets to be transmitted to a non-unicast (i.e., a subnetwork-broadcast or subnetwork-multicast) address, including those that were discarded or not sent
`ifOutDiscards`	The number of outbound packets that were chosen to be discarded (e.g., for lack of buffer space)
`ifOutErrors`	The number of outbound packets that could not be transmitted because of errors
`ifOutQLen`	The length of the output packet queue (in packets)
`ifSpecific`	MIB definitions specific to the particular media used on the interface

Flow Capture

While counters provide basic information about network activity, almost all traffic semantics are absent. An alternative that preserves more of the information important to ISPs and traffic analysts is to capture and store packet trains or flows.

Packet Trains. The rationale for capturing packet trains was first articulated in [CBP95]. Packet train traces are a broadly useful summary of traffic: they can be used for monitoring basic network activity, monitoring users and applications, network planning, security analysis, and accounting and billing (details are in [Cis]).

Tools for capturing packet trains are present in all major routers. In general, a packet train record consists of the IP header 5-tuple (source IP address, source TCP or UDP port, destination IP address, destination port, and protocol id) along with other header fields; and the start time, end time, number of packets, and number of bytes contained in the packet train. This representation can provide a dramatic decrease in trace size compared to full packet (or even just packet header) capture; Cisco `NetFlow` is typically about 1.5% in volume compared to the actual traffic being summarized [Cis].

A complication arising in packet train capture is defining the end of the packet train. In principle, application-level analysis could be used to determine when a high-level data transfer is completed. However, most implementations avoid this computational demand and use simpler methods to determine packet train completion. The criteria used to choose to end a train can include: a timeout threshold applied to interpacket gaps; a timeout threshold applied to entire flow length; observation of a FIN or RST packet; and the decision to reclaim memory within the router [Cis]. This leads to varying definitions of what constitutes a packet train and can result in an incorrect identification of TCP connections [SF02].

Packet Flows. In some settings, it is not necessary to know packet train start and end times, but only the number of bytes or packets that carry a particular 5-tuple value in a given time interval. This amounts to capturing packet flows, rather than packet trains.

Although most routers and switches can export some sort of flow records, higher-level software is generally needed for processing and interpreting the raw data. `Flowtools` is a set of tools that can collect, send, process and generate reports from Cisco `NetFlow` or Juniper `cflowd` data [Ful]. Commercial products devoted to flow analysis are also available [PPM01].

The IETF is currently developing standards for flow capture, in the context of the IP Flow Information Export effort (IPFIX) [QZCZ04]. The IPFIX framework defines a flow in a very general way: a flow consists of all packets that satisfy all defined flow properties, where flow properties are based on applying a function to:

1. one or more packet header fields (e.g., destination IP address), transport header fields (e.g., destination port number), or application header fields;
2. one or more characteristics of the packet itself; and
3. one or more of fields derived from packet treatment (e.g., next hop IP address, the output interface, etc.).

The complete IPFIX architecture specifies standards for *exporters* (providers of flow data) and *collectors* (consumers of flow data). IPFIX is implemented in the packages `ntop` [Der] and `flowtools` [Ful].

Real Time Flow Metering (RTFM) is an earlier set of standards for flow reporting [Bro99c, Bro99a, BMR99, Bro99b, HSBR99]. The RTFM architecture defines the *meter* MIB that can be accessed via SNMP, *meter readers* that collect flow data, and *managers* that coordinate meters and meter readers and download configuration to them. NeTraMet is a publically available implementation [Nete]; the use of NeTraMet in DNS-related measurements is discussed in Chapter 7 (Section 7.2.3). Other tools for capturing and monitoring flows include Flowscan [Plob]; lists of flow processing tools are available at [Lei, CDA].

A disadvantage of train and flow capture is that individual packet arrival times are lost, complicating fine-timescale traffic analysis. An approach that attempts to preserve packet arrival times is proposed in [IDGM01]. In this scheme, each packet train generates a new identifier, and packet arrivals are recorded using only the identifier. This takes advantage of the packet train structure of traffic to compress trace data.

Sampling

Another approach to dealing with traffic volume is sampling. In a sampling scheme, a subset of packets are chosen for capture. A sampling rate of 1% reduces the traffic trace size by a factor of 100. Packet sampling schemes for routers were first proposed in [AC89, CPB93b].

Two questions arise with respect to sampling: first, how should packets be chosen for sampling? And second, how should one correct or compensate for the sampling process when performing analyses? These two questions are related, because the choice of sampling scheme can make some subsequent analyses easier than others.

Basic Packet Sampling.   In the basic form of packet sampling, the sampling process is performed independently on each link being monitored.

Packet sampling may be done at either constant or variable rate. Constant rate sampling is conceptually simpler and easier to implement, but variable rate sampling allows freedom to achieve a wider range of measurement goals. For constant rate sampling, one may take a number of approaches:

- *Random sampling.* Packets are chosen for sampling with some fixed probability $0 < p < 1$.
- *Deterministic sampling.* Packets are chosen periodically, i.e., every Nth packet is sampled.
- *Stratified sampling.* The sampling process is divided into multiple steps. Packets are first divided into subsets, and then sampling is applied within each subset.

In many cases the difference between random and deterministic sampling may be minor. For example, [DLT03] shows data in which the difference in packet train size distributions between periodic and random sampling is minor. Differences between the two methods will tend to diminish for more highly multiplexed links, in which packets from many flows are intermingled.

When packets are sampled at constant rate one can form a reasonably accurate estimate of the true number of packets or bytes by scaling up the corresponding counts by the sampling rate. However, other statistics are not recovered so readily. For example, longer trains are more likely to show up in the trace than are short trains; so accurate estimates of the total number of trains, and the lengths of each, are not simply obtained by scaling the corresponding statistics.

Two methods have been proposed to attack these problems [DLT03]. To estimate the true number of trains present, one can exploit protocol-level detail reported in flow records. This method takes advantage of the fact that Cisco netflow reports whether it has seen a SYN packet among the samples used to construct the packet train record. As a result one can estimate the original number of trains that contained a SYN packet (i.e., TCP connections). This method can be used for estimating the number of compromised hosts during a worm infection. To estimate the true distribution of train lengths, one can use statistical inference to allocate the unobserved trains among the various possible size bins.

Another approach to estimating packet train lengths as well as other statistics from sampled data is stratified sampling at the packet train level [HV03]. By sampling each packet train with fixed probability, the original distribution of packet train lengths is straightforward to estimate.

Another stratified sampling method called *sample and hold* exploits the size–count disparity of packet trains [EV02]. Packets are sampled with fixed probability. Each packet from a flow not seen before triggers the creation of a new entry. Subsequently, *all* packets from that flow are sampled and for each such packet, the corresponding flow table entry is updated. This results in accurate accounting of number of packets for those flows that are sampled. By the nature of the sampling process, high-volume flows are virtually guaranteed to be sampled, while most low-volume flows will not be sampled. As a result, only a small amount of space is needed for traffic accounting, but most packets are accounted for.

A related approach to estimating the sizes of the largest flows in a network is described in [JPP92]. In that scheme, statistics for the top flows are kept in a list, and when new flows are encountered, one or more of the lowest-rate flows are dropped from accounting. Confidence intervals for the flow sizes estimates obtained under this method can be constructed. With regard to counting the number of flows above a given threshold (heavy hitters), one can also apply Bayes' rule to correct for the packet sampling process [MUK[+]04].

In general, the accuracy of statistics obtained via sampled traffic depends on the sampling rate, and thus the amount of memory and processing resources allocated to sampling. One can examine this tradeoff for constant sampling rates, with the goal of dimensioning measurement infrastructure to meet accuracy goals [DL03].

Variable sampling rates have been developed to address shortcomings in accuracy, performance, and resource consumption. It is possible to obtain improved accuracy by adjusting the sampling rate with particular attention to short-term traffic load [CPZ03]. In this case adaptive sampling can guarantee that variance introduced by variability of packet sizes does not exceed a pre-set limit. One can adjust sampling rate to provably stay within fixed resource consumption limits while using the best possible rate under those constraints [EKMV04]. One can take into account the variance of estimates obtained and use methods that minimize that variance while remaining within resource consumption limits [DLT04]. Adaptive sampling can also be used on other traffic statistics [DC98]. Apart from packet trains and flows, sampling can also affect observed packet size distributions [CPB93b].

Trajectory Sampling.   Basic packet sampling provides useful traffic summaries, but has certain drawbacks compared to full packet capture when performed at multiple points in a network. The drawbacks arise because in basic sampling, packets sampled at each point in the network are likely to be different. This means that one cannot obtain per-packet delays, and cannot track the flow of traffic through the network.

In response a technique called *trajectory sampling* has been developed [DG01]. The basic idea is that if a packet is chosen for sampling at any point in the network, it is chosen at all points in the network. The method is implemented as follows: traffic measurement devices (e.g., routers) calculate a hash function for each packet based on the value of certain header fields. The header fields used are only those that do not change as the packet moves through the network, and are sufficient to identify the packet uniquely. The measurement device selects a packet for reporting if the hash value falls in a specified range. By varying the range size the rate of packet sampling can be varied.

Trajectory sampling allows reconstruction of (sampled) traffic matrices without knowledge of the state of the routing system. Using trajectory sampling it is relatively straightforward to obtain metrics on customer performance (per-customer packet delays, which can be a component of service level agreements), to detect routing loops, and to trace denial of service attacks. It is even possible to craft packets specifically so that they will be sampled, and inject them into the network, allowing a form of combined active/passive probing.

Trajectory sampling can be complicated by the use of unreliable transport (UDP) for the reporting protocol [DG04]. Using UDP allows a much simpler implementation of the reporting device. However, methods are needed to compensate for the loss of reporting packets. One way to compensate is using packetized Bloom filters, which provide a measure of robustness to loss (Bloom filters are discussed in Section 6.3.3).

A technique similar to trajectory sampling based on matching fixed reference patterns has been proposed for sampling ATM cells [CG98]. Hash-based selection of packets for the specific problem of denial of service attack traceback has also been proposed [SPS+01]. A number of statistical issues arise when using this method to estimate the distribution of per-packet delays [Zse02]. One can increase accuracy of per-packet delay estimates via stratified sampling based on packet size, by noting that packet delays are often related to packet size [Zse03].

Both basic packet sampling and trajectory sampling are being standardized in the IETF by the PSAMP working group [PSM]. Standardization topics include sampling and filtering techniques, an SNMP MIB for sampling, and protocols for sampling.

Finally, apart from packet sampling, one might choose to sample flows directly; this can provide accurate usage estimates for billing and accounting [DLT01].

Summarization

Yet another approach to dealing with the large volume of data obtained in Internet traffic measurement is to form compact summaries that are useful for answering particular questions. These include Bloom filters, sketches, and a variety of specialized data structures.

Bloom Filters. A Bloom filter is a summary of a set that supports membership queries. The idea of a Bloom filter is to allow a small false positive probability in exchange for a large reduction in the required storage space (compared to storing the original set) [Blo70]. (For more details on the material in this section see the survey article [BM05].)

The basic operation of a Bloom filter is illustrated in Figure 6.8. Given a set of keys $A = \{a_1, a_2, ..., a_n\}$, a Bloom filter provides a data structure and algorithm allowing one to ask whether key a_n is present in the set A. The data structure is a vector of m bits. The algorithms used are based on a set of k independent hash functions $h_1, h_2, ..., h_k$ each having range $\{1, ..., m\}$. The hash functions are chosen so as to map each item in A to a random number uniform over the range $\{1, ..., m\}$. Initially all bits are set to zero. Then, for each key $a \in A$, the bits $h_i(a)$ are set to 1 for $1 \leq i \leq k$. Setting a bit to 1 multiple times leaves it in the 1 state.

To check if an item b is in A, one checks whether all bits specified by $h_i(b)$ are set to 1. If not, then clearly b is not a member of A. If so, then it is assumed that b is in A, although it is possible that this conclusion is incorrect. As a result, the Bloom filter may yield a *false positive* with some probability that depends on k, m, and n.

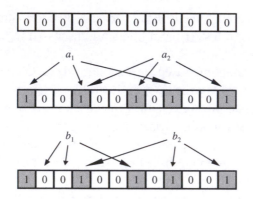

Figure 6.8 An example of a Bloom filter. The bit array initially contains all 0's. Each item in the set a_i is hashed k times, setting corresponding bits to 1. To check if an element b_i is in the set, hash it k times and check the bits. The element b_1 cannot be in the set, since some of its bits are 0. The element b_2 is either in the set or has yielded a false positive [BM05]. Reproduced by permission of AK Peters Ltd.

After all the elements of A are recorded in the Bloom filter, the probability that a randomly chosen bit is still 0 is

$$(1 - 1/m)^{kn}.$$

So the probability that k randomly chosen bits are set to 1 is

$$\left(1 - (1 - 1/m)^{kn}\right)^k.$$

This expression can be interpreted as the probability of a false positive; that is, the probability that a key selected uniformly at random from the set of all keys not in A will in fact be assumed to be in A.

To minimize the above expression for false positive rate given some values of m and n, one seeks a number of hash functions that equalizes the number of 1's and 0's in the bit vector. The optimal number of hash functions is then $k = \ln 2 \cdot (m/n)$. In this case the false positive rate is $(1/2)^k \approx (0.6185)^{(m/n)}$. In practice of course k must be an integer so this performance may not be strictly achievable.

An important characteristic of Bloom filters is that they allow a constant false positive probability while using only a constant number of bits per set element (recognizing that to do so, one must construct different sized Bloom filters for different sized sets A). This allows one to achieve a constant compression ratio regardless of the size of the dataset being represented. For example, imagine one wishes to construct a database of IP source/destination pairs encountered in a traffic trace. Each pair consists of 64 bits. If we employ a Bloom filter with false positive rate of 1%, we should be able to store a set of such address pairs using only about 9.58 bits per element – a compression factor of more than 6.

Bloom filters are not suited to storing sets whose members may depart over time. One cannot simply delete a key from the Bloom filter by setting its corresponding bits to 0, since some of these bits might need to be 1 to record the presence of other, remaining keys. One way to address the problem is by using a *counting Bloom filter* [FCAB00]. In this case, each entry is a small counter rather than a single bit.

Inserting an item increments the counters for the corresponding hashes, and deleting an item decrements the counters.

Bloom filters have been used in a variety of Internet measurement applications, beginning with [MB97]. An early use was in summarizing the contents of Web caches to facilitate sharing cache contents [FCAB00]. Later networking applications have been in the area of peer-to-peer systems [BCMR04], routing [RK02], active queue management [FKSS01], and topology discovery [DFC05]. In the hash-based trace-back scheme described in [SPS$^+$01], Bloom filters hold IP addresses that may be targets for traceback.

While Bloom filters store sets, many traffic measurement applications require the storage of *multisets*, that is, sets in which elements may occur multiple times. For example, in traffic accounting applications each element of the set is a traffic flow and the multiplicity of the element is the number of packets or bytes exchanged [KXLW04].

An approach which generalizes Bloom filters to this task is the multistage filter described in [EV02]. The specific problem addressed is the identification of 'heavy hitter' flows – the largest-volume flows in a traffic stream. The data structure is similar to the counting Bloom filter, but it is used in a different way.

The multistage filter works as follows. In this construction there are k bit vectors of length ℓ, and k hash functions each returning values in the range $\{1, ..., \ell\}$. Each packet's flow ID is hashed k times and the corresponding counters in each vector are incremented by the number of bytes in the packet.

To identify a heavy-hitter flow in this way, note that if a flow containing M bytes has been processed, then all that flow's counters will hold values at least equal to M. Thus, given some suitably chosen volume threshold T, the largest flows are those whose minimum counter value is at least T.

While the multistage filter only attempts to estimate the sizes of the largest flows, the *space-code Bloom filter* [KXLW04] can be used to estimate the sizes of all flows in a trace. A space-code Bloom filter consists of multiple Bloom filters operating in parallel. For each update, one Bloom filter is chosen at random, and only this Bloom filter is modified. To perform a query for flow ID f, one checks how many of the Bloom filters contain ID f. This value can be used to estimate how many times flow ID f was seen in the original trace, within certain bounds. Techniques can be used to overcome the limitations on bounds, and confidence intervals can be constructed on the resulting estimates.

Sketches.   As already mentioned, the multistage filter can be thought of as a generalization of a Bloom filter. Another view of the multistage filter is that it is a set of random projections, in the following sense.

Let x be the histogram of flow counts observed in some trace. Then x_i is number of packets or bytes observed for flow i, with $1 \leq i \leq n$. This is a vector in a high-dimensional space. Now one can form a random lower-dimension projection as follows: for $m \ll n$, construct the $m \times n$ 0–1 matrix P, such that each column of P has a single 1 in a randomly chosen row; all other entries in the column are 0. Forming the product Px is then equivalent to constructing a single counter set of the multistage filter.

In fact, random projections have many useful qualities as traffic summarizations. When used to answer approximate queries over large datasets, dimension-reducing random projections are called *sketches*. An important property of sketches is that they are *linear*, so the arithmetical sum of two sketches is the same as the sketch of the superposition of the two corresponding datasets. The linearity of sketches makes them particularly well suited to processing via wavelets.

Sketches have been proposed as a general tool for addressing a range of problems including traffic compression, traffic similarity detection, and heavy-hitter estimation [GKMS01].

An example is the count-min sketch [CM04]. The count-min sketch uses a data structure like the multistage filter, but incorporates algorithms for answering a wider variety of queries. In particular, algorithms for computing point queries, range queries and quantiles of the original traffic distribution have been developed, along with associated accuracy bounds.

An issue that arises with both sketches and Bloom filters is that the set of keys encoded cannot easily be retrieved directly from the data structure. To address this problem one can employ a hashing scheme that improves the efficiency of searching for keys that map to given counters [SGPC04].

Beyond answering queries on traffic data streams, sketches have been put to other uses. Sketches can be used to detect significant changes in the distribution of addresses in a traffic stream [KSZC03]. The basic idea is to use time series methods to predict the sketch value in the next time interval based on past values. Time series methods used can be simple moving averages, or more sophisticated Holt–Winters or ARIMA methods; the linearity of sketches allows a wide variety of methods to be used. In each case, the difference between the prediction given by the time series model and the actual observed value can be used as a metric for detecting anomalous traffic.

Other Approaches.   A variety of other data structures and algorithms have been proposed to support various specific queries on summarized network traffic streams.

A useful data structure for storing traffic summaries is the trie [ZSS$^+$04]. Tries can be constructed based on address prefixes, so that each node in the trie stores (either explicitly or implicitly) the traffic volume corresponding to all addresses contained in the prefix. This data structure can allow identification of heavy hitters among traffic aggregations of any size (based on prefix).

A number of methods can be used to count the number of distinct values in a traffic trace, with particular attention given to counting distinct flows. A key idea in this context is *probabilistic counting*, by which one can form a rough estimate of the number of distinct items seen without maintaining a record of what items have actually been seen [FM85]. Bitmap algorithms can be used to count distinct values in a traffic trace with better accuracy than probabilistic counting, while taking advantage of traffic properties to improve performance [EVF03].

One of the problems with the approaches described so far are that they are formulated with respect to an infinite stream of traffic. That is, it is assumed that all data ever seen is relevant. In reality, at some point old data should be ignored. The approach usually taken in practice is to use the *landmark window model*, in which the traffic summary is constructed with respect to a fixed window. For example, multistage filters might be constructed for each 5-minute interval of traffic. Thus, as a practical matter, the window and associated traffic summary begins with size zero and grows until the next landmark, at which point it is reset to zero. This is a disadvantage, as the size of the window is constantly varying, and because of edge effects when phenomena span two windows. These drawbacks can be addressed with regard to identifying heavy hitters by using algorithms based on the *sliding window model*, in which the traffic summary is always taken with respect to some fixed window extending back from the present [GDD$^+$03]. A related goal is the ability to handle deletions as well as additions to a traffic summary; algorithms have been developed for handling online deletions to the stream summary [CM05b].

Dimensionality Reduction

As already mentioned, the problem of high dimensionality is an additional difficulty encountered in processing traffic measurements. The features present in traffic (e.g., flow identifiers) occupy a very high-dimensional space which can complicate traffic analysis.

Usually, the fact that traffic features occupy a high-dimensional space is an artifact of traffic representation rather than a fundamental property of the traffic. That is, although the space of possible observations is quite large, certain traffic features tend to co-occur so that the set of data points actually found tends to occupy a (much) lower-dimensional subspace.

This suggests employing a general approach commonly used in dealing with high-dimensional data, which is to find an alternate representation of the data that takes advantage of and exposes the true (low-dimensional) structure in the data. This is termed *dimensionality reduction*. After dimensionality reduction the traffic can be described in terms of a much smaller number of new features, allowing simpler analysis.

As already mentioned, sketches can be viewed as a kind of dimensionality reduction on the traffic feature histogram. However, sketches do not attempt to discover the underlying structure of traffic in order to perform dimensionality reduction, and as such are mainly used in a probabilistic manner. In contrast to sketches, two approaches that do attempt to discover structure to aid in traffic dimensionality reduction are *clustering* and *principal component analysis*.

Clustering.   The idea behind clustering is that it is often the case that data features do not vary independently but instead certain combinations of data features tend to co-occur. For example, in the case of traffic, certain source and destination addresses or address ranges may tend to occur together in a trace. This tendency may be captured using clustering.

Clustering relies on a *similarity metric* defined on the set of traffic features. Within each cluster, traffic features are fairly similar, and between clusters features are dissimilar. Given such a set of cluster definitions, traffic can be summarized based on its clusters rather than its original features. Using cluster definitions as summaries of high-dimensional data is a form of *vector quantization* [GG91].

The challenge in clustering lies in discovering a set of cluster definitions that succinctly describe the traffic; this is essentially a search problem in a high dimensional space. Clustering is a large and active area and there are a wide variety of clustering approaches and algorithms [And02, ELL01].

For example, traffic clusters can be defined in terms of the five header fields generally used for flow analysis (source and destination address, source and destination port, and protocol) [ESV03]. Similarity among addresses is then expressed by the natural hierarchical grouping of addresses into prefixes. For ports and protocols, similarity is more complicated. Two ports may be considered similar if they are identical, or if they are both statically allocated, or both dynamically allocated. Two protocols are similar only if they are identical.

This view of similarity is driven by the needs of traffic analysts and the questions they commonly ask. For example, such an analysis might find high volume of traffic in a cluster of TCP connections between a specific ISP's customers and a particular group of Web servers. Efficient algorithms for clustering these metrics that take advantage of the hierarchical structure imposed by IP addresses are described in [ESV03].

Another goal of clustering can be to expose underlying structure that is hidden by the particular features used to describe traffic. For example, one can use clustering to discover how flows correspond to applications [MHLB04]. The obvious approach of using IP protocol and port may not be effective for a number of reasons: the HTTP protocol may be used to transport a wide variety of different object types (text, multimedia, continuous media); the same object type may be transported over different protocols (FTP, HTTP); and when traffic is encrypted, protocol and port numbers may not be available.

Principal Component Analysis. Clustering is a form of nonlinear dimensionality reduction, in contrast to linear methods like sketches. Among linear methods *principal component analysis* (PCA) can be shown to be optimal, in the sense of capturing maximum variability in the data using a minimum number of dimensions.

PCA is a coordinate transformation method that maps the measured data onto a new set of axes. These axes are called the principal axes or components. Each principal component has the property that it points in the direction of maximum *variation* remaining in the data, given the variation already accounted for in the preceding components. As such, the first principal component captures the total variation of the original data to the maximal degree possible on a single axis. The next principal components then successively capture the maximum variation among the remaining orthogonal directions. Thus the principal axes are ordered by the amount of variation in the data they capture, and by selecting an initial subset of axes one can form a low-dimensional representation of the original data.

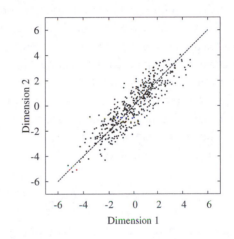

Figure 6.9 Illustration of PCA on a correlated, 2-D dataset.

PCA can be illustrated geometrically, as shown in Figure 6.9 for a two-dimensional dataset. The first principal axis (shown) points in the direction of maximum variation in the data. Mapping each data point to its closest location on the first principal axis provides the best possible one-dimensional approximation to the original data.

PCA is defined in terms of a $t \times p$ *data matrix* X. Each of the t rows of this matrix is a single data sample. For example, each row may be a single traffic measurement. The p columns correspond to different data features found in that measurement – e.g., different measures of traffic volume. To apply PCA, take the rows of X as points in Euclidean space, so that we have a dataset of t points in $\mathbb{R}^p$. After constructing the principal axes, one may be able to find a set of $r \ll p$ axes that capture most of the variability in the data.

To define the PCA algorithm, we shift from the geometric interpretation to a linear algebraic formulation. Calculating the principal components is equivalent to solving the symmetric eigenvalue problem for the matrix X^TX. The matrix X^TX is a measure of the covariance between data features. Each principal component $\vec{v}_i$ is the ith eigenvector computed from the spectral decomposition of X^TX:

$$X^TX\vec{v}_i = \lambda_i\vec{v}_i \quad i = 1, ..., p \tag{6.3}$$

where λ_i is the eigenvalue corresponding to $\vec{v}_i$. Furthermore, because X^TX is symmetric positive definite, its eigenvectors are orthogonal and the corresponding eigenvalues are nonnegative real. By convention, the eigenvectors have unit norm and the eigenvalues are arranged from large to small, so that $\lambda_1 \geq \lambda_2 \geq ... \geq \lambda_p$.

Once we have computed the principal axes, they can be used to inspect the patterns present across multiple dimensions in the data. This is done by mapping the data onto the principal axes (essentially, rotating the data points in space to align the principal axes with the coordinate system). For principal axis i, this mapping is given by $X\vec{v}_i$. This vector can be normalized to unit length by dividing by $\sigma_i = \sqrt{\lambda_i}$. Thus, we have for each principal axis i,

$$\vec{u}_i = \frac{X\vec{v}_i}{\sigma_i} \quad i = 1, ..., p. \tag{6.4}$$

The $\vec{u}_i$ are vectors of size t and orthogonal by construction. Since the principal axes are in order of contribution to the overall variability, $\vec{u}_1$ captures the strongest trend across all traffic features, $\vec{u}_2$ captures the next strongest, and so on.

The elements of $\{\sigma_i, i = 1, ..., p\}$ are called the *singular values*. Each singular value is the square root of the corresponding eigenvalue, which in turn is the variability attributable to the respective principal component:

$$\|X\vec{v}_i\| = \vec{v}_i^TX^TX\vec{v}_i = \lambda_i\vec{v}_i^T\vec{v}_i = \lambda_i \tag{6.5}$$

where the second equality holds from Equation (6.3), and the last equality follows from the fact that v_i has unit norm. Thus, the singular values are useful for gauging the potential for reduced dimensionality in the data, often simply through their visual examination in a *scree plot*. Specifically, finding that only r singular values are nonnegligible implies that X can be approximated as occupying only an r-dimensional subspace of $\mathbb{R}^p$. In that case, we can approximate the original X as:

$$X' \approx \sum_{i=1}^{r} \sigma_i\vec{u}_i\vec{v}_i^T \tag{6.6}$$

where $r < p$ is the effective intrinsic dimension of X.

For any matrix X, PCA can be efficiently performed via the *singular value decomposition* (SVD), which is a standard linear algebraic procedure. SVD decomposes the matrix X as:

$$X = U \cdot W \cdot V^T.$$

The columns of U are the vectors $\vec{u}_i$; the rows of V^T are the vectors $\vec{v}_i$; and W is a diagonal matrix holding the singular values ($W_{ii} = \sigma_i$) [PFTV88].

An example use of PCA in traffic analysis is [LPC+04]. In this PCA was used to characterize the set of all origin–destination (OD) flows observed in two backbone networks: Abilene, the Internet2 backbone having 121 flows; and Sprint-Europe, the European backbone of the Sprint network which has 169 flows. The data matrix X in each case has a row for each 5-minute traffic sample and a column for each OD flow.

Scree plots for four datasets (one week from Abilene and three separate weeks from Sprint-Europe) are shown in Figure 6.10. The figure shows that the vast majority of singular values are small, with less than 10 singular values that are non-negligible. This suggests that although each collection of OD flows is nominally a high-dimensional time series (dimension 121 or 169), each effectively occupies a low-dimensional subspace (dimension less than 10). Thus, the entire collection of > 100 traffic time series X can be approximated as a linear combination of a small number of individual time series $\vec{u}_i, 1 \leq i < 10$. This phenomenon has been used as the basis for anomaly detection schemes in [LCD04b, LCD04a, LCD05].

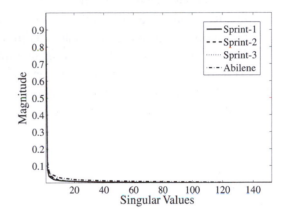

Figure 6.10 Scree plot for origin–destination flows [LPC+04].

Probabilistic Models

Finally, a common approach to dealing with large volumes of traffic measurements is to summarize the results in the form of probabilistic models. A probabilistic model treats observations as if they were generated by a random process. Although this assumption is not strictly true, it often provides a good approximation to reality. The basic tools of probability models were covered in Section 3.2.

Distributional Models.   Features in a traffic trace may be summarized by providing a probability distribution that matches the empirical distribution found. These are sometimes called *analytic* models. For example, one might attempt to fit a distribution to the time series of counts $\{C_n,\ n\ =\ 0, 1, ...\}$ or packet interarrivals $\{I_n,\ n\ =\ 1, 2, ...\}$ in a traffic trace. Some distributions commonly used in traffic modeling are given in Table 3.2 in Chapter 3 (Section 3.2.1).

The benefits of using an analytic model include [Pax94a]:

1. Such models can be manipulated mathematically, leading to improved understanding. For example, given a probabilistic model it is often possible to analytically compute its mean, variance, or other summary statistics.
2. Analytic models are concise and easily communicated. In most cases, only the distribution type and two or three parameters suffice for a complete specification.
3. The particular values of a model's parameters can give insight into the nature of the underlying data. As model parameters vary, the nature of the underlying distribution varies in a predictable way.

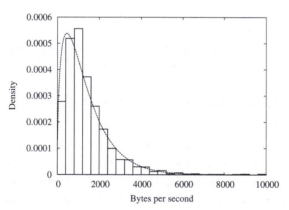

An example of a distribution fit to a dataset is shown in Figure 6.11. The bars are a histogram of counts of bytes per second, for the traffic trace that was previously shown in Figure 6.5(b). The smooth curve is a fitted distribution (in this case, a Gamma distribution) chosen to match the data. The mass of information present in the traffic trace has been reduced to the small set of parameters needed to specify a particular instance of the Gamma distribution.

Figure 6.11   Fitted distribution to traffic data from Figure 6.5(b).

Probabilistic modeling involves two steps: the choice of distribution function, and the estimation of the relevant parameter values. These decisions can be approached separately or they can be combined, since the general goal is to choose a distribution that agrees well with the data. Both choice of distribution and setting of parameter values affect the resulting agreement.

A general approach that is sometimes taken is to choose a collection of distribution functions, estimate appropriate parameter values for each, and then choose the resulting distribution that fits best. One may use goodness-of-fit tests to determine whether a particular distribution fits data well; such techniques are well developed [DS86]. Goodness-of-fit tests used in choosing models for traffic data are discussed in [Pax94a].

Note, however, that the choice of distribution function is also frequently taken to implicitly concern data that *has not* been observed. It is often assumed that a model's validity extends more generally to datasets collected under 'similar conditions.' This *inductive assumption* should always be critically examined, but it is a very useful conclusion. As such, the choice of distribution function often carries with it more import than the fixing of parameter values, because parameters may be more readily expected to vary from one setting to the next.

Another significance accruing to the choice of distribution function concerns the distinction between constructive and descriptive models, as discussed in Chapter 3 (Section 3.6). Various distribution functions are associated with particular generative processes. For example, the Normal distribution arises as the sum of a large number of random variables (independent or weakly correlated, and having finite variance); the lognormal arises when random variables are multiplied (again, independent or weakly correlated, and having finite variance); the exponential arises in settings where many point processes are superimposed (as long as they are independent and properly 'thinned'); and so on. This means that the analyst's insight into the structure of the system being modeled bears on the choice of distribution. As a result, it is difficult to reduce probabilistic modeling to a purely objective process.

In any model fitting situation, visual checks for goodness-of-fit are important. Three useful methods are shown in Figure 6.12. Figure 6.12(a) shows the most basic method: plotting the empirical CDF against the analytic CDF. Note that although goodness-of-fit tests often focus on a histogram, for visual analysis plotting the CDF yields more information. This is because the CDF uses all of the data in forming the figure, while the histogram hides individual data values by placing them into bins. Figure 6.12(b) shows an example of a *quantile–quantile* (QQ) plot. In a QQ plot, one plots the quantiles of the data against the corresponding quantiles of the analytic distribution. A perfect fit will fall along the reference line $y = x$. Deviation at the upper end of the line gives evidence about the fit in the upper tail. Finally, for highly variable data, one may examine the fit in the upper tail using a *log–log complementary distribution* (LLCD) plot. An LLCD is a plot of $\log(1-F(x))$ against $\log x$ for comparing the empirical and analytic CDFs. An example LLCD plot is shown in Figure 6.12(c).

An example of the use of distributional model fitting to describe traffic measurements is [Pax94a]. This study is concerned with constructing analytic models for various properties of TCP connections, as a function of protocol (TELNET, FTP, NNTP, and SMTP). The starting point for the analysis is 15 detailed traces collected from a variety of locations; such a varied sample is essential to lend confidence that

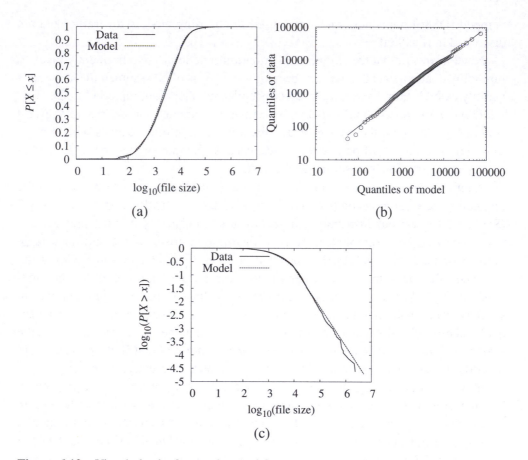

Figure 6.12 Visual checks for goodness-of-fit. (a) analytic and empirical CDFs; (b) Q-Q plot; (c) log–log complementary distribution. Data is collection of file sizes from [BBBC99].

properties seen are likely to apply to other, unobserved data as well (the inductive assumption).

The discussion in [Pax94a] touches on a number of important points for probabilistic modeling of traffic. First, careful attention must be paid to the nature of the goodness-of-fit tests used when the goal is to choose between a number of different candidate distributions. The paper develops and demonstrates methods that address this issue. Second, the paper discusses the presence of high variability and discusses the use of logarithmic transformations in this case. Finally, a crucial point brought out in [Pax94a] is the importance of careful attention to the tails of the distribution.

The tails of the distribution function are of critical importance because they determine the likelihood of large observations. In a setting where data shows high variability, proper agreement in the tails may be the most important property to examine in judging goodness-of-fit. Apparently minor differences in tail shape may have dramatic influence on the performance implications of workloads generated using a probabilistic model.

The distributions shown in the upper part of Table 3.2 are light-tailed, and as such are more useful when applied to data showing a narrow range of variability. Those in the lower part of the table are subexponential distributions and are more appropriate for data showing high variability. Judging between goodness-of-fit for different candidate distributions in the lower part of Table 3.2 can be very difficult using standard tests, or by inspecting histograms or empirical distribution functions. Generally the most sensitive method is to examine the model and data in a log–log complementary distribution.

Finally, a practical alternative to the difficulties of model fitting in some situations is to use empirically-derived distributions directly. For example, one may collect a dataset of measurements and then generate new data by randomly sampling the dataset. This is the approach taken in TCPLIB [DJC$^+$92] for modeling characteristics of TCP connections.

Dependence Structure. Modeling a traffic time series such as $\{C_n, n = 0, 1, ...\}$ solely in terms of its distribution may not capture all of its important properties. As noted previously, many measures of network traffic show dependence among successive values in time, which can have a strong influence on system behavior.

One can assess the degree of dependence present in a time series using the empirical *autocorrelation function* (ACF). Autocorrelation is the correlation of a series with a time-shifted copy of itself. The autocorrelation $r(k)$ of a time series $\{X_n, n = 1, 2, ...\}$ is defined as its normalized autocovariance at lag k:

$$r(k) = \frac{\text{Cov}(X_n, X_{n+k})}{\text{Var}(X)} = \frac{E[X_n X_{n+k}] - E^2[X]}{\text{Var}(X)}$$

and is naturally estimated for a finite sample $\{x_n, n = 1, ..., T\}$ by the empirical ACF:

$$\hat{r}(k) = \frac{\frac{1}{T-k} \sum_{i=1}^{T-k} (x_i - \bar{x})(x_{i+k} - \bar{x})}{\frac{1}{T-1} \sum_{i=1}^{T} (x_i - \bar{x})^2}.$$

Note that, as with many moment-based estimators, the empirical ACF can be unreliable when applied to highly variable data, and that empirical autocorrelation estimates for large k may be based on a small number of samples.

Autocorrelation gives a measure of dependence among random variables as a function of distance (or time) k. Values close to 1 or -1 indicate strong dependence, while independent random variables will have autocorrelation 0. Figure 6.13 illustrates the empirical autocorrelation function for the traffic data previously shown in

Figure 6.5(b). The figure shows that the traffic has non-negligible correlations up to approximately lag 8, i.e., 8 seconds.

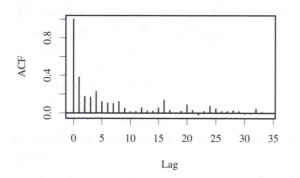

Figure 6.13   Autocorrelation function for traffic data from Figure 6.5(b).

If the autocorrelation function shows significant dependence, data can be modeled by choosing an appropriate stochastic process, e.g., an autoregressive (AR), moving average (MA), or other process, and then estimating the parameters of the process. Estimation techniques, and the relationship between a particular stochastic process and its autocorrelation function, are treated in the field of time series analysis. Time series analysis is a well-developed field; good references are [BD81, BJR94].

6.3.4   Inference

As previously noted, hidden data is a significant challenge in traffic analysis. Just as inference can play a role in filling in missing information about Internet structure (as discussed in Section 5.3.7), it also plays a role in replacing missing data about traffic.

Traffic Matrix Estimation.   Network operators need an accurate view of traffic demands in order to properly engineer their network. In particular, a key summary of a network's workload is its traffic matrix [FGL$^+$00, MTS$^+$02]. Traffic matrices may be needed at varying levels of detail; between points-of-presence, routers, or IP prefixes. In what follows we focus on the case of origin–destination (OD) flows.

Directly measuring a network's traffic matrix can be difficult; on the other hand, SNMP counts of traffic flowing over each link in the network are generally readily available. Thus, one approach to obtaining a traffic matrix is via inference, starting from link counts.

As discussed in Chapter 3 (Section 3.4.2), the set of link counts $\vec{y}$ is related to the routing matrix A and the set of OD flows $\vec{x}$ (the traffic matrix) by $\vec{y} = A\vec{x}$. The traffic matrix estimation problem is then: given a set of link counts $\vec{y}$, infer the set of OD flow counts $\vec{x}$. In a typical network, the dimension of $\vec{y}$ is much less than the dimension of $\vec{x}$. Thus traffic matrix estimation is an *ill-posed linear inverse problem* [O'S86]. In such problems, the constraints are not sufficient to dictate a single solution; in fact, there are infinitely many solutions that are consistent with the observations.

The traffic matrix estimation problem was first defined in [Var96]. That paper called the problem "network tomography," but we will call it traffic matrix estimation to distinguish it from the network structure tomography problems described in Section 5.3.7. Good reviews of the traffic matrix estimation problem are [CHNY02, CCL+03, BR04].

As discussed in [ZRLD03], the key to effectively solving ill-posed problems is to bring additional information or constraints into the problem. The various solutions that have been adopted differ in the kind of additional constraints (*priors*) brought to bear.

In early solutions, additional constraints were incorporated by assuming a Poisson traffic model [Var96, TW98]. Later work [CDWY00] assumed a more flexible Gaussian traffic model in which the mean and variance have a known relationship. This model can be solved to yield a maximum likelihood estimate of $\vec{x}$, but the solution may not exactly agree with $\vec{y} = A\vec{x}$. To address this, one can use a technique called *iterative proportional fitting* to find a set of flow counts close to the maximum likelihood estimate that agrees with the measured link counts. It is also possible to reduce the computational demands of the maximum likelihood step by using a faster algorithm that yields an approximate solution with acceptable accuracy [LY03].

The accuracy of the methods from [TW98], [CDWY00], and [Gol00] has been compared using synthetic traffic data [MTS+02]. All the methods generate significant errors, especially when test traffic does not match the particular priors assumed by a method. In response, choice models have been proposed. A choice model considers the aggregate traffic entering at a particular origin point in the network, and applies a stochastic decision process to apportion that traffic among the various destination points.

A unified framework that encompasses all the preceding approaches can be constructed [ZRLD03]. The framework is based on regularization theory, and casts the problem as one of minimizing

$$\min_{\vec{x}} \|\vec{y} - A\vec{x}\|_2^2 + \lambda J(\vec{x}) \tag{6.7}$$

where $\| \cdot \|_2$ denotes the l_2 norm, $\lambda > 0$ is a regularization parameter, and $J(\vec{x})$ is a penalization function. The particular choice of $J(\cdot)$ captures the nature of the particular prior constraints. In this framework, the most appropriate regularization is to start from the *independent* model (sometimes called the *gravity* model).

The relationship between the volume of traffic in each network flow and the traffic entering and leaving a network can be expressed as follows. In a network with a set of ingress and egress points S, we can denote the total traffic flowing over some fixed time interval from ingress point i to egress j as f_{ij}. Then, as shown in Figure 6.14, the total traffic entering the network at node i is $f_{i*} = \sum_{k \in S} f_{ik}$, and the total traffic leaving the network at node j is $f_{*j} = \sum_{k \in S} f_{kj}$. We use f_{**} to denote all traffic flowing in the network, i.e., $f_{**} = \sum_{i \in S} \sum_{j \in S} f_{ij}$.

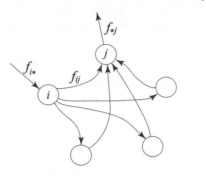

These frequencies can be used to form empirical probability estimates. Consider a packet chosen at random from the entire set of packets flowing through the network during the time interval. The joint probability that the packet entered at origin i and exited at destination j is $p_{O,D}(i, j) = f_{ij}/f_{**}$. The marginal probability of entering at origin i is $p_O(i) = f_{i*}/f_{**}$

Figure 6.14   Flows in a network.

and the probability of exiting at destination j is $p_D(j) = f_{*j}/f_{**}$.

The independent model assumes independence of origin and destination, i.e.:

$$p_{O,D}(i, j) = p_O(i) \cdot p_D(j).$$

That is, the probability that a packet entering at a node i exits at another node j is the same as the probability that any randomly chosen packet exits at node j.

This model is rarely a perfect prediction of actual traffic behavior. That is, it is unlikely that it is ever exactly the case that

$$f_{ij} = \frac{f_{i*} f_{*j}}{f_{**}} \quad \text{for all } i \in S, j \in S.$$

However, it is often a very good first approximation. Adopting this model for traffic flows suggests a particular function $J(\cdot)$ which can be used as the constraining factor in (6.7) [ZRLD03].

A different approach to addressing the under-constrained nature of the problem is to actually change the network's routing over time [SNC+04]. In that case, additional network paths are used. Each additional path in effect adds a row to the matrix A. Eventually the augmented matrix becomes full rank and the problem becomes adequately constrained.

The traffic matrix estimation problem was originally motivated by difficulty in obtaining network flow data. However, as previously noted, flow data is becoming increasingly available. Flow measurement for a limited training period can be used to build models for how *fanout* distributions change with time [PTL04]. The fanout of a given node i is defined as $\{p_{ij}/p_{i*}, \forall j\}$ Once such models have been constructed, it is only necessary to measure the aggregate incoming traffic p_{i*} at each node to infer traffic matrices at points in the future. New methods have been proposed based on partial flow measurement, using either PCA or tracking via Kalman filters; such small amounts of flow measurement can significantly improve accuracy [SLT+05].

The emerging availability of flow data has also made it possible to evaluate traffic matrix estimation methods on empirically measured workloads. Evaluations have shown that regularization methods work well when the regularization parameter λ is chosen appropriately [GJT04]. The methods of [ZRLD03], [SNC+04], and [PTL04] have also been compared on real data; these methods differ noticeably in terms of their bias and variance properties [SLT+05].

Other Traffic Inference Problems. Inference methods have been used for a number of other traffic estimation problems. As already mentioned, sampling tends to disturb the distribution of observed packet train lengths. One can use maximum likelihood estimation to infer the original distribution of packet train lengths from sampled net-flow data [DLT03]. It is also possible to estimate the number of packets in a given flow via an inference procedure based on summarized data in the space-code Bloom filter [KXLW04].

6.4 State of the Art

So far, we've reviewed the features of Internet traffic that are important, and the tools and methods used to learn about those features. We now turn to what is known about the various features of Internet traffic.

As described in Chapter 2 (Section 2.1.1), there is no single point in the Internet that provides a global view of all traffic. As a result, many features of today's Internet traffic can be rather slippery to describe precisely. The difficulty of obtaining comprehensive measurements generally means we must settle for samples from a relatively small set of locations and a limited range of durations. Unfortunately, those samples may not be representative, because of the great heterogeneity of applications and infrastructure across the Internet. And even given representative samples, the rapid pace of change of the Internet (both in terms of its infrastructure and the applications that it supports) means that the results of past characterizations need to be used with care, and frequently re-examined.

In the face of the Internet's size, heterogeneity, and change, a useful strategy is to search for *invariants*. These are properties that appear consistently – both throughout the Internet, and over time. Another useful strategy is to identify *trends* – properties

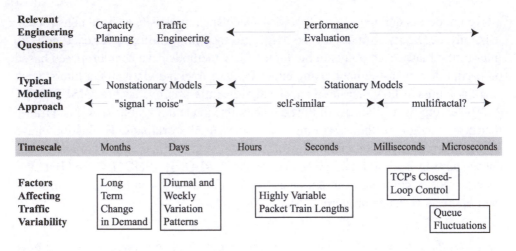

Figure 6.15   Overview of traffic analysis.

changing in apparently predictable ways. In this section we will review the various
traffic properties defined in Section 6.1, focusing on invariants and trends.

6.4.1   Packets and Bytes

Many issues in traffic analysis depend strongly on the particular timescale of interest.
A broad overview of traffic analysis issues is shown in Figure 6.15. This figure shows
that engineering questions, modeling approaches, and important phenomena all vary
depending on the particular timescale at which traffic is measured and analyzed. The
various issues shown in the figure are described in detail in this section.

   The discussion in this section proceeds from left to right in the figure. First, we
review long-timescale issues, which are relevant for network provisioning, engineering, operations, and management. Next, we cover short-timescale issues, which primarily concern performance evaluation. Finally, we touch on what is known about
traffic on very short timescales, then discuss traffic measures other than volume.

Long Timescales: Trends

As already mentioned, at timescales longer than an hour or so, traffic is not well modeled as being stationary. At these timescales, there are strong predictable variations
present in traffic, i.e., trends.

Signal and Noise.   A typical example is shown in Figure 6.16. The figure shows one
week of traffic on two links of the Abilene network, which is the backbone network
of Internet2 [Intb]. The figure shows that daily variation is the dominant component

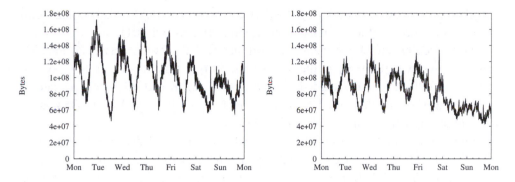

Figure 6.16 One week of traffic on two links of the Abilene network. Data courtesy of Internet2 [Intb].

of overall traffic variability on timescales greater than an hour. The difference between weekday and weekend activity is clearly visible. In addition, superimposed on daily variation is considerable *noise* – random variation. This noise generally shows Gaussian-like variability, except for occasional distinct *spikes* in which traffic briefly departs very far from the mean.

Thus long-timescale network traffic may be thought of as possessing a *predictable* component and a *stochastic* component ('signal and noise') [RGK+03]. The properties of the stochastic component will be discussed in the next section. The predictable component can be modeled as a time-varying mean.

All networks (going as far back as the ARPANET [KN74]) show diurnal variation in mean traffic corresponding to patterns of human activity. Different flows within a network can show different time of day effects, peaking in different hours [FGL+00], and the strength of this effect will vary depending on the degree to which a network's user population is globally distributed; but the phenomenon is universal.

At even longer timescales (weeks to years), networks show increasing levels of traffic [PTZD03]. This increase results from both growth in user population and greater demand per user [Pax94b].

Modeling and separating predictable from stochastic variation in network traffic has been approached via a variety of methods, including time series [PTZD03], wavelet analysis [BKPR02], and principal component analysis [LPC+04].

Growth of Traffic. Throughout its history, claims have been frequently made that Internet traffic growth has been 'exponential.' In fact, measurements show that traffic on the ARPANET grew approximately exponentially for its first two and a half years [KN74].

Continuing throughout the 1980s and 1990s, traffic growth across the Internet showed signs of growing exponentially. NSFNET backbone statistics showed roughly exponential growth during the period 1988–1995 [NSF]. Additional examples of exponential traffic growth are presented in [Pax94b, FP01].

The particular rate of exponential growth has varied considerably over time. The fastest growth was probably in the mid-1990s. At that time, traffic growth rates reported in the popular press tended to be exaggerated. In fact, the best estimate for aggregate traffic growth on the US Internet backbone in the period 1996–2000 is that it was doubling approximately annually [Odl01].

However, exponential growth of course cannot continue indefinitely (witness the US railroad system which experienced exponential growth in terms of miles of track built from 1830 to 1900 [AH88]). For this reason, understanding the growth of traffic on the Internet is an important ongoing question.

Short Timescales: Scaling

At shorter timescales, one can usually use stationary models to describe network traffic. There is no predictable variation and stochastic models are appropriate. However, one finds that the stochastic variation in Internet traffic generally shows some rather unusual characteristics. These surprising properties can be described in terms of *scaling behavior*, meaning the manner in which statistical properties vary as one observes traffic at different timescales.

Given some time series of traffic counts $\{B_n, n = 0, 1, ...\}$ at a particular timescale T, one can form a rescaled view of the traffic $\{B_n^{(m)}, n = 0, 1, ...\}$ by defining

$$B_n^{(m)} = \sum_{i=nm}^{nm+m-1} B_i$$

for some positive integer m. Thus $\{B_n^{(m)}\}$ is just $\{B_n\}$ summed over non-overlapping blocks of size m, and so rescaling a traffic time series by m is equivalent to having observed the original traffic at the timescale Tm. Scaling behavior refers to how the statistical properties of $\{B_n^{(m)}\}$ vary with m. The surprising scaling behavior of network traffic can be described in terms of two interrelated phenomena: long-range dependence and self-similarity.

Long-range Dependence.   The first way of looking at scaling behavior of network traffic is in terms of the timescales over which correlations are present. To understand the importance of correlation, it's useful to start by discussing the alternative: independence.

Consider the case in which we model traffic counts as a stationary stochastic process $\{X_n, n = 0, 1, ...\}$. If the $\{X_n\}$ are independent, then many of the properties of the process are simple to compute and understand. All joint distributions can be expressed in product form; for example:

$$p_{X_0,X_1}(x_0, x_1) = p_{X_0}(x_0) \cdot p_{X_1}(x_1) = p_{X_0}(x_0) \cdot p_{X_0}(x_1).$$

So to describe the distribution of the entire process $\{X_n\}$, it suffices to characterize the single distribution $p_{X_0}(\cdot)$. Independence affects scaling properties as well: if X_0 has mean μ and standard deviation $\sigma < \infty$, then by the Central Limit Theorem any component of the scaled process $(X_0^{(m)} - \mu)/\sqrt{m}$ will converge in distribution to the Normal distribution with mean 0 and standard deviation σ.

Independent models have a long history of successful use in performance analysis, most notably in engineering the telephone system. Telephone traffic analysis, beginning in 1909 with the work of A. K. Erlang, has relied on the Poisson process to model the arrival of calls at links in the phone network, and the use of exponential distributions to model the durations of phone calls. Erlang and others chose these models based on empirical measurements of operating telephone networks; measurements over many subsequent decades have confirmed the validity of these models.

The Poisson process has a number of advantages for performance modeling. It is described by a single parameter λ, the rate of arrivals. The number of arrivals occurring in any two non-overlapping intervals are independent, and the distribution of number of arrivals in an interval of length T follows the Poisson distribution:

$$p_{X_0}(n) = e^{-\lambda T} \frac{(\lambda T)^n}{n!}, \; n \geq 0.$$

The Poisson process often yields tractable analyses for practical problems – for example, Erlang was able to derive expressions for the probabilities of call blocking (busy signals) and waiting time that have been used throughout the telephone industry.

Of course, we have already seen that Internet traffic typically shows correlations and therefore cannot be modeled with convenient, independent models like the Poisson process. However, one might ask whether independent models can still be used as an approximation, especially if the timescale of analysis is long enough. In other words (in terms of a stochastic process) even when independence doesn't hold for $\{X_n\}$, it still might hold in an *approximate* fashion for $\{X_n^{(m)}\}$ if m is large enough.

How could this be the case? Consider a situation in which $p_{X_0,X_n}(x_0, x_n) = p_{X_0}(x_0) \cdot p_{X_n}(x_n)$ whenever n is larger than some threshold θ. From a practical standpoint, this means that traffic observations that are far apart will be independent. This condition will be reflected in the autocorrelation function; it will be zero at long lags, i.e., $r(k) = 0$ when $k > \theta$. Now consider the m-scaled process $\{X_n^{(m)}\}$, where $m \gg \theta$. In this process, the random variables $\{X_n^{(m)}\}$ will be approximately independent. To see this, take $X_0^{(m)}$ and $X_1^{(m)}$. Most of the random variables in the

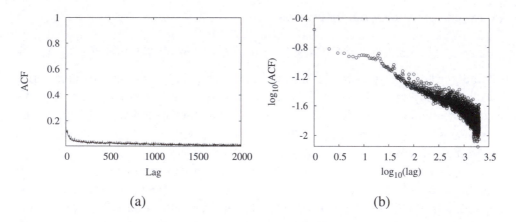

Figure 6.17   Autocorrelation function of byte counts $\{B_n\}$: (a) linear scale (b) logarithmic scale. Data available as trace `dec-pkt-4` from the Internet Traffic Archive [DMPS].

block sum that formed $X_0^{(m)}$ are independent from most of the random variables that formed $X_1^{(m)}$, and so we would expect that the sums $X_0^{(m)}$ and $X_1^{(m)}$ are themselves approximately independent.

This notion can be defined formally as *short-range dependence*. A stationary stochastic process with autocorrelation function $r(k)$ exhibits short-range dependence if and only if:

$$\sum_{i=1}^{\infty} r(k) < \infty.$$

Two important cases of short range dependence are:

- $r(k) = 0$ whenever $k > \theta$, for some $\theta > 0$ and
- $r(k) \sim a^{-k}$ whenever $k > \theta$, for some $\theta > 0$ and $a > 1$.

Short-range dependence allows us to perform some useful analysis based on independent models, by applying such models at timescales long enough for approximate independence to hold.

Given the success of the independent model in telephone traffic analysis, and the fact that the independent model can be adapted to account for correlations through the notion of short-range dependence, we might expect that independent or short-range dependent models would be reasonable ones to use for network traffic as well. In fact, reality doesn't agree with independence assumptions for network traffic.

Correlations in network traffic are not well modeled as short-range dependent. Figure 6.17 shows a typical case, for one hour of TCP traffic captured at the access link between a large organization and the Internet, as described at [DMPS]. The auto-correlation function is computed over the byte counts $\{B_n\}$ having a timescale $T =$

10 ms. Figure 6.17(a) shows that the autocorrelation function does not go to zero, even at large lags, and the shape of the autocorrelation function is not exponential. The log–log plot in Figure 6.17(b) shows that the autocorrelation function behaves more like a power law, i.e.,

$$r(k) \sim k^{-\beta}, \tag{6.8}$$

with a value of β that is less than 1.

An autocorrelation function like (6.8) is characteristic of *long-range* dependence. A stationary stochastic process shows long-range dependence if and only if:

$$\sum_{i=1}^{\infty} r(k) = \infty.$$

In practice this implies that for large values of k, $r(k)$ has approximately power-law shape $k^{-\beta}$ with $0 < \beta < 1$. Long-range dependent processes have very different properties from traditional (i.e., independent or short-range dependent) processes. Intuitively, observations that are arbitrarily far apart in time have non-negligible correlation.

The presence of correlation over many timescales makes network traffic very different from the kinds of traffic encountered in other settings (such as telephone traffic). Long-range dependent traffic shows fluctuations at a wide range of timescales. Thus, there is no timescale at which the independence assumption even approximately holds. Quoting from [FL91]:

> "an intuitive interpretation ... is that traffic 'spikes' ... ride on longer term 'ripples,' that in turn ride on still longer-term 'swells.'"

Self-similarity. The occurrence of traffic fluctuations over a wide range of timescales means that traffic does not appear to be 'smooth' at any timescale. This property is captured by the notion of *self-similarity*. More specifically, the phenomenon of self-similarity is concerned with how fluctuations in $\{X_n^{(m)}\}$ vary with timescale m.

A zero-mean discrete-time stationary process $\{X_n\}$ is called self-similar with *Hurst parameter* H if, for all m, the aggregated process $\{X^{(m)}\}$ has the same distributions as $\{m^H X_n\}$. More precisely,

$$\{m^H X_n\} \stackrel{d}{=} \{X^{(m)}\} \quad m > 0, \ 1/2 \le H < 1 \tag{6.9}$$

where $\stackrel{d}{=}$ means that the processes on each side have the same distributions. That is, the aggregated process statistically 'looks like' the original process scaled by a factor m^H. Thus traffic self-similarity has a connection to the self-similar properties of fractals, but in a statistical, rather than exact sense.

As the timescale m of a stationary self-similar process changes, its standard deviation follows m^H. Of course the process $\{X_n\}$ must have zero mean in order for (6.9) to hold. However for any process $\{X_n\}$ with nonzero mean μ, we can ask whether its mean-centered version $\{X_n - \mu\}$ is self-similar.

If the process $\{X_n\}$ consists of independent random variables with finite variance, then the Central Limit Theorem shows that standard deviation will follow $\sqrt{m}$ (that is, $H = 1/2$). If the process has $\mu \neq 0$, the mean will grow proportional to m, i.e., much faster than the standard deviation. Thus the apparent variability of the process shrinks with increasing m. More precisely, the coefficient of variation σ/μ of an independent process shrinks proportional to $1/\sqrt{m}$, i.e., fairly rapidly with increasing timescale.

However, when the mean-centered version of the process is self-similar with $H > 1/2$, the apparent variability of the aggregated process does not shrink so rapidly with increasing levels of aggregation. The coefficient of variation of the aggregated process follows m^{H-1}. In fact, when $H = 1$, the coefficient of variation of the process does not change at all with increasing aggregation.

This phenomenon is illustrated in Figure 6.18. The figure shows views of three different time series over four different timescales. In the lowest row of plots, timescale of measurement is $T = 10$ ms. Proceeding upward, each view increases the scale m by a factor of 10: $mT = 100$ ms, 1 sec, and 10 sec. Both the x-axis and the y-axis are rescaled by a factor of 10 in each case to make clear how variability changes with timescale.

The plots in Figure 6.18(a) are views of actual network traffic, in particular, the traffic trace previously examined in Figure 6.17. The Hurst parameter for this trace is estimated at approximately 0.83 (we discuss estimation of H later). The plots in Figure 6.18(b) are of synthetic traffic that is constructed to match the mean, variance, and Hurst parameter of the real traffic. And the plots in Figure 6.18(c) are of synthetic traffic with matching mean and variance, but Hurst parameter of 0.5 (corresponding to that of an independent or short-range dependent process).

The figure shows how H relates to the scaling of variability. At the smallest timescales, the sizes of typical traffic fluctuations appear to be similar to those of both synthetic traces. However, as the timescale increases, variability in real traffic does not 'smooth out' rapidly in the manner of an independent process. Rather, the figure shows that considerable traffic fluctuation is present over four orders of magnitude. This property is much better captured by the synthetic trace with $H = 0.83$.

In a nutshell, the importance of self-similarity for traffic modeling lies in the scaling of variability. Self-similar traffic (with $H > 1/2$) contains noticeable bursts or fluctuations at a wide range of timescales. So self-similarity is another way of describing the phenomenon of "spikes riding on ripples riding on swells."

Clearly, self-similarity arises due to correlations in traffic. But what sorts of cor-

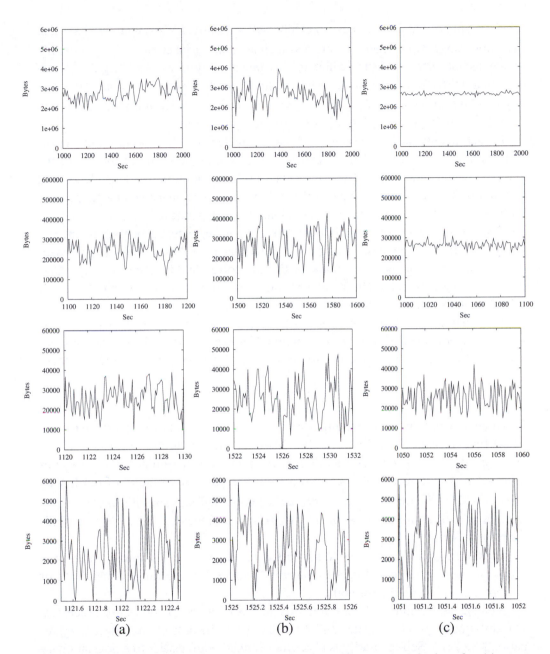

Figure 6.18 Traffic scaling properties; time series of bytes per unit time for (a) trace `dec-pkt-4` from the Internet Traffic Archive [DMPS]; (b) synthetic traffic with $H = 0.83$; (c) synthetic traffic with $H = 0.5$. The timescale varies by row. Top row: $B^{(1000)}$ ($mT = 10$ sec). Second row: $B^{(100)}$ ($mT = 1$ sec). Third row: $B^{(10)}$ ($mT = 100$ msec). Fourth row: $B^{(1)}$ ($mT = 10$ msec).

relations are needed for a process to exhibit self-similarity? We saw in Section 6.2.2 that short-range dependence in a process increases the variance of $\{X_n^{(m)}\}$, but only by a constant factor – a factor which is the same at all timescales m (e.g., as shown by Equation (6.2)). In other words, short-range dependence does not change the way in which the variance of $\{X_n^{(m)}\}$ grows with m. Indeed, self-similarity in $\{X_n\}$ with $H \neq 1/2$ is only possible if $\{X_n\}$ is *long-range dependent*.

In fact, a stationary process with Hurst parameter H will be long-range dependent with $\beta = 2 - 2H$, where β describes the asymptotic shape of the tail of the autocorrelation function in (6.8). Thus the notions of long-range dependence and self-similarity are closely linked; self-similarity of a stationary stochastic process with $H \neq 1/2$ implies that the process is long-range dependent.

The converse is not necessarily true: a long-range dependent process is not necessarily self-similar. The reason can be seen intuitively as follows: long-range dependence is a statement about the shape of the autocorrelation function for large lags, that is, at long timescales. On the other hand, self-similarity as we have defined it is a statement about traffic properties at *all* timescales.

As a result, other definitions of self-similarity are sometimes used. One such definition concerns the autocorrelation function. If we denote the autocorrelation function of $\{X_n^{(m)}\}$ as $r^{(m)}(k)$, then self-similarity can be defined as the condition that

$$r^{(m)}(k) = r(k), \quad k, m > 0,$$

It can be shown that if this condition holds, then $r(k)$ must have a particular functional form in which $r(k) \sim k^{-(2-2H)}$. This definition is useful because it allows us to speak of *asymptotic* self-similarity. Asymptotic self-similarity is the condition that as m increases, $r^{(m)}(k)$ converges to the particular function form having $r(k) \sim k^{-(2-2H)}$; that is, $\{X_n^{(m)}\}$ becomes 'more' self-similar with increasing m. In contrast, self-similarity as defined by (6.9) is *exact*, meaning that $r^{(m)}(k)$ has this form for all m.

In examining real traffic, we do not expect to see exact self-similarity in general. Most analyses of traffic scaling are concerned with either long-range dependence or asymptotic self-similarity (or both).

Finally, the definition of self-similarity in (6.9) applies to *stationary* processes. The self-similar property relates different versions of the process (at different aggregation levels m). Self-similarity is also often defined with respect to a nonstationary continuous time stochastic process $\{Y_t, t \geq 0\}$ with stationary increments as:

$$Y_{at} \stackrel{d}{=} a^H Y_t, \quad a > 0. \tag{6.10}$$

This form of self-similarity relates a single process to itself at different times. The

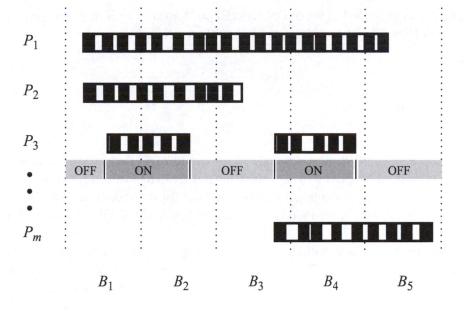

Figure 6.19   Packet trains and autocorrelation.

connection to self-similarity as defined in (6.9) is that if $\{X_n\}$ is an increment process of $\{Y_t\}$ at any timescale $T > 0$, that is,

$$X_n = Y_{(n+1)T} - Y_{nT}, \quad n \geq 0,$$

then $\{X_n\}$ is a stationary process that is self-similar by (6.9), with the same value of H.

Connection to Heavy Tails.   A variety of factors may contribute to the presence of long-range dependence and asymptotic self-similarity in network traffic. However, the principal cause is the influence of packet trains.

Intuitively, packet trains induce correlation in traffic. A packet train spanning many observations contributes packets to each observation, as shown in Figure 6.19. The figure shows a set of m source–destination pairs $P_1, P_2, ..., P_m$. Each pair has a session in progress, and is exchanging data objects that become packet trains. From a descriptive standpoint, each pair has a distinct ON/OFF behavior. When we construct a time series of counts of bytes per unit time $\{B_1, B_2, ...\}$ we find that many packet trains (ON periods) contribute to more than one counting interval. When a packet train contributes to a range of counts $\{B_i, B_{i+1}, ..., B_{i+n}\}$ then values in the range become correlated.

To understand how long-range dependence arises, the key observation is that *packet train lengths are generally heavy-tailed.* If one looks at the durations of packet trains (i.e., the lengths of ON periods) one typically finds that they are heavy-tailed [WTSW97]. That is, if L is the length of an ON period:

$$p_L(t) \sim t^{-\beta} \quad 0 < \beta < 1 \tag{6.11}$$

or, equivalently:

$$P[L > t] \sim t^{-\alpha} \quad 1 < \alpha < 2 \tag{6.12}$$

where $\alpha = \beta + 1$. When packet train lengths follow (6.11), then we might expect that the resulting byte counts $\{B_n\}$ show long-range dependence according to (6.8). In fact, this can be proven mathematically to hold for the specific case of ON/OFF sources with either heavy-tailed ON times or heavy-tailed OFF times [TWS97, Cox84].

Thus, the phenomenon of self-similarity and long-range dependence can be traced to the presence of heavy tails in the durations of packet trains. But why are packet trains heavy-tailed? The best answer seems to be in the distribution of sizes of data objects themselves. The number of bytes contained in long packet trains is often heavy-tailed [PF95].

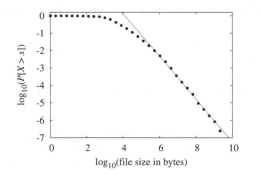

Tracing this phenomenon back to file systems, many researchers have noted that the sizes of data files appearing in general purpose computing environments show long-tailed distributions [DB99, BHK$^+$91, OCH$^+$85, Sat81]. In fact, closer examination suggests that heavy-tailed models may generally provide good fits for file size distributions. A typical example is shown in

Figure 6.20   LLCD of file sizes on Unix systems from [Irl94].

Figure 6.20. This shows the LLCD plot of a collection of over 12 million file sizes obtained by surveying over 1000 separate Unix file systems in 1993. The plot shows that the tail of the distribution shows approximate power-law shape with $\alpha \approx 1.2$.

The particular values of α found for data objects are generally between 1 and 2. Some typical examples include [PF95], which found that the upper tail of the distribution of data bytes in FTP bursts was well fit to a Pareto distribution with α between 0.9 and 1.4, and [CB97], which found that the sizes of objects transferred over the Web are typically heavy-tailed with α in the range 1.1 to 1.3. Assuming these yield packet train distributions with the same tail properties, we would expect such transfers to result in network traffic with H values relatively close to 1, as predicted by the relation $H = (3 - \alpha)/2$, which is derived in [TWS97].

Although file sizes are clearly long-tailed, there is debate whether it is always best to model them with heavy-tailed distributions, as opposed to other subexponential distributions [Dow01, WAL04]. As previously noted, the problem of assessing the shape of the extreme tail of a distribution is difficult. For each type of distribution (heavy-tailed, or other subexponential) there are file size datasets which appear to match that distribution best. However in most cases the use of heavy-tailed models for file size distributions yields good agreement with the data.

Measuring and Modeling Self-similarity. One of the principal advantages of using self-similar models to describe network traffic is that they are parsimonious. A reasonable model of traffic can be formulated using just three parameters: traffic mean rate μ, traffic variance at some timescale σ_0^2, and Hurst parameter H.

A variety of methods can be used to estimate the Hurst parameter [TTW95]. The simplest is the *aggregated variance* method, which derives directly from the definition of self-similarity in (6.9). Given a series of counts B_n, the variance of $\frac{1}{m} B^{(m)}$ is plotted against m on a log–log plot. If the original data is well modeled by a stationary self-similar process, the variance of $\frac{1}{m} B^{(m)}$ will follow m^{2H-2}, so the plot will show a straight line with slope $(-\beta)$ greater than -1. The parameter H can be estimated by $H = 1 - \beta/2$.

While the aggregated variance method is simple, it is quite sensitive to violations of the underlying assumptions of stationarity and exact self-similarity. For example, a change in the true mean of the traffic process can appear in sample statistics as a higher variance at long timescales, yielding a misleading estimate of scaling properties. As a result, a much better method for estimating scaling properties of traffic is the *logscale diagram*.

The details of the logscale diagram method are beyond our scope and can be found in [VΛ99, ΛFTV99]. However the key idea is to analyze traffic using wavelets. The use of wavelets as a traffic summarization tool allows the resulting estimates to be robust in the presence of deterministic trends. The analysis measures *energy* over a range of timescales, which is directly related to variance. Furthermore, the method allows confidence intervals to be constructed for H, rather than just a point estimate.

Thus the logscale diagram is a plot of energy at various timescales. An example is shown in Figure 6.21, for the same traffic trace (dec-pkt-4) used in previous figures. Both axes are plotted in log scale; the x-axis is the timescale, $\log_2(m)$ and the y-axis is the log-energy at that timescale. Linear behavior on this plot is evidence of a scaling relationship between variance and timescale. Linear behavior beginning at some scale θ and extending for all $m > \theta$ is consistent with long-range dependence or asymptotic self-similarity. As shown in the plot, confidence intervals can be placed on the energy estimates at each timescale, allowing the analyst to make a careful decision regarding the presence of linear behavior. In the plot in Figure 6.21, a fitted line beginning at timescale $\log_2(m) = 5$ lies within all subsequent confidence intervals, suggesting that this traffic trace shows long-range dependence.

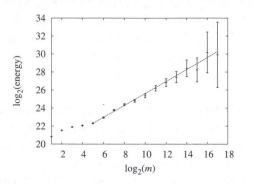

The process of analysis starts with traffic and estimates its parameters. Synthesis is also important: it is often useful to start with particular parameter values and generate synthetic traffic matching those properties. A straightforward method is to begin with a stochastic process (i.e., a model) that incorporates self-similarity or long-range dependence. A variety of models are available for this purpose including *fractional ARIMA* and *fractional Gaussian noise*; for

Figure 6.21   Logscale diagram for traffic data from Figures 6.17 and 6.18(a). Fitted line yields an estimate of $H \approx 0.83$; 95% confidence interval on H is (0.82, 0.84).

more details on these processes, see [Ber94]. The synthetic traffic in Figure 6.18(b) is an example of fractional Gaussian noise generated using the method described in [Pax95].

These methods can easily produce a pre-computed trace of synthetic traffic with given scaling properties. However, synthetic traffic is often used in the context of a network simulation; in that case, a pre-computed traffic trace may not be appropriate. Network traffic reflects the combined effects of user activity, applications, and control protocols. The interaction of traffic with the network (e.g., packet loss and queuing delay) feeds back to users, applications, and protocols causing modification of subsequently arriving traffic. A pre-computed traffic trace will not reflect these closed-loop effects.

A good solution in this case is to generate self-similar traffic in a manner that reflects understanding of how self-similarity actually arises in networks. In particular, a simulation involving many concurrent transfers of data objects ("files") whose sizes are drawn from a heavy-tailed distribution will generate self-similar traffic in a natural way. A simulation using TCP to transfer data objects whose distribution is heavy-tailed with exponent α according to (6.12) will tend to generate self-similar traffic with $H \approx (3 - \alpha)/2$ [PKC96]. This approach allows one to perform closed-loop simulation experiments with realistic network traffic exhibiting a given Hurst parameter. This approach has been used both in simulation [JRF$^+$01] and in live traffic generation [BC98].

Implications of Self-similarity. The primary impact of self-similarity from a performance standpoint lies in its effect on the queuing behavior of traffic. This is important because the interaction of traffic with queues inside routers leads to packet delays and packet loss.

From an analytic standpoint, a number of long-range dependent traffic models have been shown to result in long-tailed queuing behavior. These results are generally asymptotic – they apply only to queues with infinite buffering. However, the results are dramatically different from the case where traffic is short-range dependent, and so they suggest that queuing behavior is likely to be very different even for the realistic case of finite queues.

More precisely, if we denote queue length as Q, typical results show that for certain long-range dependent traffic processes,

$$p_Q(x) \sim \exp(-\kappa x^{(2-2H)})$$

where $\kappa > 0$ is a constant that depends on the particular traffic process [Nor99, BSMV99]. When $H > 0.5$, this is a subexponential distribution (a Weibull distribution; see Table 3.2). This situation is in distinct contrast to the case of short-range dependent (or independent) traffic processes, in which queue length distributions typically decline exponentially.

While these analytic results cannot provide exact expressions for finite queues, experience with simulation bears out the prediction that self-similar traffic will have radically different queuing behavior than short-range dependent traffic. Usually, queue lengths, packet delays, and packet losses will all be larger for traffic showing long-range dependence than for traffic with the same mean and variance, but showing only short-range dependence [ENW96]. Simulations show that as buffer size increases, buffer occupancies grow dramatically when traffic has high Hurst parameter [PKC97]. In fact for traffic with high Hurst parameter, average queuing delay can increase in direct proportion to the amount of buffering provided. This has serious implications for the sizing of buffers in routers, and suggests that adding buffering in order to decrease packet loss (and thus increase throughput) may result in unacceptable delays for self-similar traffic.

These results show that the primary effects of self-similarity on queuing arises as buffer sizes grow. On the other hand, when buffer sizes are kept small, long-range dependence may not have a significant impact on performance. This can be the case for highly delay-sensitive applications such as real-time video transmission [HL99].

More broadly, an important implication of self-similarity for understanding traffic patterns lies in the connection between self-similarity (a traffic property) and heavy tails (a property showing up in diverse aspects of computer systems workloads). Heavy-tailed packet train lengths seem to be a result of heavy-tailed size distributions of files and other data objects – drawing a causal connection between phenomena from the worlds of both networking and file systems. Seen in this light, self-similarity is another facet of the phenomenon of heavy tails that is pervasive throughout computing systems (as well as many other man-made and natural systems).

In summary, the formalism of self-similarity provides a concise way of expressing a key property of network traffic: variability on a wide range of scales. This insight affects the way that network analysts approach many issues in network design and engineering; thus the recognition of this phenomenon represents a fundamental step forward in the way that analysts think about traffic.

Development of Self-similar Modeling.   The first step in development of self-similar traffic modeling was the characterization of traffic as a superposition of packet trains [JR86, Cla88] which challenged the independence assumption. Shortly thereafter the extreme variability of traffic on many timescales was documented in [FL91] based on high time-resolution Ethernet packet capture [LW91].

The introduction of self-similar models to express variability over a range of timescales in terms of a single parameter H was due to [LTWW93, LTWW94]. The self-similar approach was cast in sharp contrast with the Poisson model in [PF94]. The connection between self-similarity and heavy-tailed packet train lengths was made in [WTSW97, TWS97] and relates to earlier results in [Man69, Cox84, TL86].

Since its introduction as a modeling formalism for network traffic in 1993, models incorporating long-range dependence or asymptotic self-similarity have been proposed as appropriate for traffic of many different types and at many different locations in the Internet. Examples include Ethernet traffic [LTWW93], wide area traffic [PF95], ATM cell traffic [JW97], Web traffic [CB97], video traffic [GW94], and GPRS traffic [KI04].

Good reviews of self-similarity and long-range dependence in traffic modeling are [WTE96, PW99]. Statistical issues involved in estimating parameters of self-similar processes are reviewed in [Ber94]. Finally, we note that self-similarity in network traffic has connection to fractals and power-laws in science, engineering, and nature [Man83, Sch91].

Marginal Distribution of Traffic.   Apart from the correlation structure of traffic, it is also important to understand the marginal distribution of traffic. For this we use probabilistic models as described in Section 6.3.3.

The most common distributional model used to describe byte traffic is the Gaussian distribution. The Gaussian distribution is appealing because it is parsimonious (requiring specification only of mean and variance) and because the Central Limit Theorem suggests that when traffic is highly aggregated, its distribution should tend to the Gaussian. Referring to Figure 6.19, the number of bytes in time interval n

(i.e., B_n) is the sum over the contributions of a number of concurrent flows. As the number of flows or the timescale T increases, traffic should tend to Gaussian.

However, the marginal distribution of traffic is only Gaussian at sufficiently high levels of aggregation, in terms of both number of concurrent flows and amount of time [KN02]. In particular, the convergence to Gaussian may not occur in practice if the traffic sources being aggregated show high variability in terms of their sending rates.

In fact, many traffic traces do show high variability in the sending rates of different sources. In many cases a few high-volume and high-rate connections can cause dramatic 'spikes' in traffic, meaning that the distribution of B_n departs significantly from Gaussian. This effect can be seen in the traffic trace in Figure 6.5(b) which shows a small number of unusually large values; and its marginal distribution in Figure 6.11 which shows a long upper tail.

High-rate, high-volume connections have been termed *alpha traffic*, in contrast to *beta traffic* composed of the more common connections that are either low volume or low rate or both [SRB01]. Alpha connections may constitute a very small fraction of all connections (e.g., less than 0.1%), but can have a strong effect on traffic properties. Beta traffic generally shows a Gaussian marginal distribution, while alpha traffic shows highly variable marginals.

Separating traffic into alpha and beta components can be done on a per-connection basis. For example, one can identify alpha connections by looking for times n such that B_n exceeds a threshold and then choosing the highest-rate connection occurring in that time interval. Removing all such connections leaves behind the beta traffic.

Alpha traffic seems to arise in the relatively rare case that a sender has a high traffic volume to transmit over a high-bandwidth network path [SRB01]. Thus the prime cause of high variability in traffic rates is heterogeneity in bottleneck bandwidths. There is evidence that this heterogeneity is influenced by round trip time; network paths with low round trip time are more likely to show high bottleneck bandwidth [WSRB02].

The alpha / beta distinction adds a further dimension to traffic models in addition to the phenomenon of long-range dependence. Long-range dependence in network traffic is understood in terms of the ON/OFF model as arising from heavy-tailed connections whose transfers are spread over time (Figure 6.19). On the other hand, if some connections can proceed at high rate their traffic may *not* be spread much over time. In that case, long-tailed connections result in long-tailed traffic *marginals* rather than long-tailed *autocorrelation*. This yields a more general view of traffic that is the natural result of the interaction of long-tailed demands with network structure.

Very Short Timescales

Evidence shows that long-range dependence is most clearly present in network traffic at timescales from hundreds of milliseconds up to approximately an hour. Beyond the upper limit (about an hour) traffic is not well modeled as stationary. On the other hand, the lower limit (hundreds of milliseconds) is approximately the range of round trip times (RTTs) in many parts of the Internet.

At sub-RTT timescales packet arrival patterns are affected by a number of factors. A significant influence is the dynamics of transport protocols – principally TCP [FGPW99, JD03]. Another factor is the time variation of queue lengths in routers, which affects downstream interpacket spacing. In addition, the particular mixture of high-rate and low-rate flows at any given instant also affects short timescale behavior [ZRMD03, JD04b].

These effects combine to make traffic at fine timescales very bursty, but not in a way that can be described as self-similarity. Rather, fine timescale burstiness has been characterized as *multifractal*. Briefly, a multifractal process shows different scaling behaviors at different instants in time.

To make this more precise, consider a traffic arrival process $\{Y_t, t \geq 0\}$, where Y_t denotes the total amount of traffic that arrives from time 0 to time t. The corresponding time series of counts at a particular timescale Δ is the increment process,

$$X_t^{(\Delta)} = Y_{t+\Delta} - Y_t, \quad t \geq 0.$$

The process $\{Y_t\}$ has *local scaling exponent* (or *local Hölder exponent*) $\alpha(t_0)$ at time $t_0 \geq 0$ if

$$X_{t_0}^{(\Delta)} \sim \Delta^{\alpha(t_0)} \quad \text{as } \Delta \to 0.$$

There are a number of distinctions between local scaling and the scaling properties associated with self-similarity. First, local scaling is concerned with behavior of traffic in the limit of *small* timescales, while asymptotic self-similarity is concerned with traffic in the limit of *long* timescales (i.e., the difference between $\Delta \to 0$ and $\Delta \to \infty$). Second, local scaling allows a process to have *different* scaling behaviors at different points in time. Third, local scaling can apply to a process $\{Y_t\}$ that has nonzero mean (for an exactly self-similar process with stationary increments this can only be true if $H = 1$).

What is the local scaling behavior of an exactly self-similar process? Equation (6.10) shows that an exactly self-similar process has $\alpha(t) = H$ at all t. For this reason, exactly self-similar processes are called *monofractal*.

However, as we have seen, below a certain timescale traffic diverges from exact self-similarity; in these timescales it is better described as multifractal, meaning that $\alpha(t)$ varies as a function of time t. This distinct change in scaling behavior has been termed *biscaling*.

Multifractal scaling captures time-varying burstiness. Loosely, when $\alpha(t_0) > 1$, traffic in the time period near t_0 has a relatively low intensity. When $\alpha(t_0) < 1$, traffic in the time period near t_0 shows a burst. The overall nature of fine-timescale burstiness can be captured using the *multifractal spectrum* which summarizes the statistical distribution of local scaling exponents found in a traffic trace.

A good introduction to the use of multifractals in network traffic modeling is [Gil01]. Multifractal modeling has been shown to be useful in characterizing the fine-timescale behavior of traffic [VR97, RV97, FGW98]. It can be shown to be useful in understanding traffic dynamics [FGPW99] and predicting queuing behavior of traffic [RRCB00]. The multifractal modeling approach leads to methods for generating synthetic network traffic that closely match the statistical properties of traffic, and are strictly positive (unlike, e.g., fractional Gaussian noise) [RCRB99].

Other Traffic Measures

Apart from byte and packet counts, an important metric of traffic is packet size distribution. Packet size distributions are important for router designers; they can give insight into traffic mix; and unusual packet size distributions can signal the presence of anomalous traffic.

Packet size distributions are typically trimodal, clustered around a few particular sizes: 40–44, 552–576, and 1500 bytes. The smallest packets include TCP acknowledgments and control packets and TELNET packets carrying single characters. Packets in the size range 552–576 are the default maximum segment size for nonlocal destinations as specified by IP. Hosts that do not use Path MTU Discovery use these size packets. Finally, packets of size 1500 bytes correspond to Ethernet-connected hosts using Path MTU Discovery. In situations where specific applications predominate there may be other modes in the packet size distribution [FML+03].

Since packet size distributions are strongly concentrated around particular values, average packet size does not reflect typical packet sizes, but does give information on application mix. In fact, average packet size has been observed to vary with a daily pattern [TMW97].

Traffic mix has changed dramatically over time. The applications dominant on the early ARPANET were remote login, file transfer, and email. Web traffic came to dominate circa 1995. Around 2001 peer-to-peer traffic became a large fraction of traffic in many networks.

6.4.2   Higher-level Structure

The structure present within traffic can be characterized in terms of two dimensions: packet trains and flows. The most significant conclusion from a broad study of packet trains and flows is that a surprisingly wide array of properties show high variability, and that high variability seems to be an invariant in these settings.

Packet Trains.   When considering the sequence of packets flowing between two given hosts, packet trains alternate with silent periods, leading to the strictly alternating ON/OFF model shown in Figure 6.19. As already noted, ON times (packet train durations) show heavy-tailed behavior. Evidence for this is widespread, including [Bkc02, TWS97]

Apart from packet train duration, packet train *volume* (the number of bytes or packets contained in the packet train) also shows heavy tails; typical values of α are in the range 1.0 to 1.5 [PF95, CB97, OB01]. This leads to extreme skew in crossover statistics. For example, traffic analyzed in [PF95] showed that 50–80% of the bytes in FTP transfers were due to the largest 2% of all transfers. In another case, [TMW97] found that in MCI's commercial backbone, about 50% of the packets were contained in 20% of the packet trains.

The fact that most packet trains are small, while most bytes are contained in long packet trains, is a classic example of a mass–count disparity. This property of network traffic is often called the 'elephants and mice' phenomenon. Treating traffic as a few 'elephant' packet trains mixed with many 'mice' is a useful approach when thinking about router and server design questions, network measurement algorithms, and traffic engineering.

Beyond packet trains, OFF times (sometimes called 'think times') also typically show heavy-tailed durations, with exponent α often in the range of 1.0 to 1.5 [WTSW97]. Further, OFF times within the set of all packet departures or arrivals from a single workstation also show heavy-tailed distributions with α in a similar range [CB97].

The heavy-tailed nature of OFF times has implications for identifying packet trains. As described earlier, packet trains are generally identified in a descriptive manner by setting a threshold θ for packet interarrivals. Consider a trace with packet interarrival times $\{I_n, n = 1, 2, ...\}$, where I_n is the time between the arrival of packet $n - 1$ and packet n. A packet train is then defined as a sequence of packets $\{i, i + 1, ..., i + m\}$ such that $I_i > \theta$, $I_{i+m+1} > \theta$, and $I_k \leq \theta$ for all $k \in \{i + 1, ..., i + m\}$.

Because OFF times show heavy tails, many results are relatively insensitive to small changes in θ. For example, [WTSW97] shows that the heavy-tailed property of packet train durations is robust with respect to the cutoff threshold. They use a threshold value of 2 seconds, but find that values spanning two orders of magnitude give similar results.

The strict alternation of ON and OFF periods between two hosts means that the arrival process for packet trains has a strong dependence structure. This occurs simply because a new packet train arrival cannot occur while the previous packet train is in progress. As one looks at higher levels of aggregation (e.g., traffic flows defined at the prefix or ingress/egress level) the dependence structure in the packet train arrival process becomes weaker, but is generally not well described as Poisson. In the particular case of TCP connections, interarrival time has been shown to exhibit asymptotic self-similarity [Fel99]. However, self-similar scaling *at the packet level* does not seem to depend to any significant extent on the TCP arrival process [HVA02].

The heavy-tailed nature of OFF times influences the interarrival time distribution of TCP connections. TCP connection interarrivals are highly variable and have been modeled using Weibull distributions [Fel99, OB01]. This burstiness in connection arrivals is important for systems such as Web servers.

Packet Train Rate.   Another important property of packet trains is their rate – the speed at which bytes flow. Transfer rate of an individual packet train is influenced most directly by the transport protocol in use. RTP and UDP impose no particular upper limit on transfer rate, although application-level control can limit rate in many cases.

In the case of TCP, connection rate is controlled by the protocol, which responds to the properties of the network path as well as endsystems. The rate achievable by TCP as a function of these properties has been well studied [MSMO97, PFTK98, CSA00]. In general it has been shown that when packet loss is low (less than 2%) steady-state TCP throughput can be approximated by

$$R = \frac{\text{MSS}}{\text{RTT} \cdot \sqrt{p}}$$

where R is throughput in bytes per second, MSS is maximum segment size of a TCP packet, RTT is the round trip time of the connection, and p is the packet loss rate experienced by the connection. This shows that observed connection rate is dependent on both network conditions (packet loss rate) and network path (RTT).

The net result is that observed connection transfer rates are highly variable [ZBPS02]. Typical results show that within a window of 5 seconds, 1% of the connections can send about 50% of the bytes passing through a router [MFW01]. Another view of this phenomenon is the alpha / beta traffic distinction: a small number of connections have very high rate [SRB01]. This conclusion is supported by application-level measurements: the rates experienced by connections at a Web server can show high variability, and are well modeled by a lognormal distribution [BSSK97].

Packet train rate shows correlation with transfer size, for large transfers [ZBPS02]. This suggests that user behavior may change in response to network performance.

Packet train rate is also dependent on duration. Long duration trains (greater than 15 minutes) tend to carry multimedia or interactive traffic, and so can be either high or low rate. Medium duration trains (between 2 seconds and 15 minutes) tend to be file transfers and proceed at high rate, while short duration streams proceed at varying rates [Bkc02].

Sessions.   Above the level of individual connections are user sessions. There seems to be little evidence of any constraints that impose dependences among user sessions. In fact the arrival process of sessions is generally well described as Poisson [PF95]. Thus, at the very highest level of network traffic structure, an independence assumption seems valid. This property can be useful in designing traffic shapers and admission control algorithms [Rob04].

Within a session, one can ask how many packet trains or connections are observed. Typically, the number of TCP connections in a session shows high variability as well [FGWK98]. This is consistent with results in [BC98] showing that the number of Web pages contained by reference in a typical Web page shows a long-tailed distribution.

6.4.3   Flows

Traffic flows can be defined at various levels of aggregation: IP flows, network flows, or AS-level flows. In each case, one finds further examples of high variability.

The number of bytes transmitted by an IP flow in a time bin has been described as following Zipf's law [WDF$^+$05]; this description has also been applied to AS-level flows in [FP99]. The degree of mass–count disparity in flows seems greatest at the IP level where crossover values are often higher than 80/20 and can be as high as 95/5 [BHGkc04].

Traffic Matrices.   A closely related question concerns how traffic is distributed among the various end-to-end paths in a network.

Given the results so far in this section, it is not surprising that traffic matrices show high variability in the volume passing over various paths. At the level of IP flows, this shows up as a very sparse traffic matrix; for example [WTSW97] found that only 6.8% of host–pairs on a 121-host Ethernet exchanged data in an hour. They also found that 1.6% of all host–pairs were responsible for 98% of the bytes in an hour.

A traffic matrix usually consists of the set of origin–destination flows in a network. In the notation of Section 6.3.4, these are flows f_{ij}, while traffic entering the network is f_{i*} and leaving the network is f_{*j} (as shown in Figure 6.14).

At this level, one finds again that the rates of different flows f_{ij} vary widely. This has been a consistent property since the early ARPANET [KN74]. This property is called "locality" in [JR86]; it has been noted in NSFNET [Hei90] and in modern commercial backbone networks [BDJT01]. The property arises in point to multipoint flows as well [FGL$^+$00]. The imbalance in flow volumes can tend to induce a strong imbalance in link traffic levels across a network as well [BDJT01].

A related property concerns total traffic entering or leaving the network at a point of presence (PoP), i.e., f_{i*} or f_{*j}. In fact, the distribution of traffic flowing into or out of a network at different ingress and egress points shows high variability as well [BDJT01]. High variability in traffic entering or leaving at a PoP may occur for a number of reasons. Different network ingress and egress points serve user populations of varying size. There is some evidence that traffic entering or leaving at a PoP shows a relationship to local population [FCE05]. Further, some ingress and egress points will connect to high-volume traffic sources or sinks such as busy Web servers.

In Section 6.3.4 we discussed the problem of inferring the set of flows f_{ij} given only ingress counts f_{i*} and egress counts f_{*j}. Evidence shows that the independent model is often a reasonable approximation, i.e.,

$$f_{ij} \approx \frac{f_{i*} \cdot f_{*j}}{f_{**}} \quad \text{for all } i \in S, j \in S.$$

This suggests that high variability in origin-destination flows may be strongly influenced by high variability in the traffic entering and leaving at each PoP.

On the other hand, measurements show that the independent model is often violated in consistent ways. One way concerns the influence of distance. Early measurements of the ARPANET showed that short paths tended to carry more traffic than long paths [KN74]. This is consistent with historical observations concerning communication and transportation patterns which show that the interaction between cities drops off as a function of distance [Zip46, Isa60]. Even communication methods in which price is independent of distance (such as postal mail) show a preference for local over distant communication [CO98, Odl00].

In summary, most measures of the structure in network traffic exhibit high variability, with crossover statistics at least as extreme as 80/20. In particular, packet trains and flows show high variability in volume, duration, and rate. Moreover, the distribution of traffic across origins, destinations, and origin–destination flows shows high variability as well.

6.4.4   Control Traffic

Control traffic – the exchange of routing messages – can be measured in two ways. The *volume* of control traffic is important for performance evaluation of routers; and the *content* of control traffic is important for understanding the behavior of the routing system.

Frequent changes in the network reachability or topology information exchanged via routing protocols is called *routing instability*. Routing instability can be caused by human errors in configuring routers, by link or equipment failures, and by bugs in routing software. Routing instability can lead to packet loss, increased variability in performance measures, and additional resource consumption in links and routers.

BGP.   While interior gateway protocols (IGPs) such as OSPF and IS–IS are important within an organization, global routing over the Internet relies on BGP. A general overview of BGP is in Chapter 2 (Section 2.2.3).

Early experience with BGP showed that the failure of a BGP router can cause a 'storm' of instability. A router that is overloaded can fail to respond to BGP Keep-Alive messages. The router's peers will then mark it as unreachable and generate updates reflecting the change in topology, which they will send to their peers. The overloaded router may then begin responding again, requiring it to obtain entire BGP table dumps from each of the peers. This increased load can cause more routers to fail or become temporarily unavailable.

Many changes have been made to BGP and to router software to mitigate effects such as storms. However, measurements still show considerable instability in the Internet. Internet routing can show routing loops, short timescale changes in connectivity, and rapidly oscillating routing, among other pathologies [Pax97a, ZDPS01].

The first detailed measurements of BGP [LMJ98] showed some surprises: the volume of routing updates in BGP was found to be much higher than expected (typically by a factor of 10); and the majority of routing updates exchanged via BGP were redundant or pathological. Subsequent changes to router software have decreased but not eliminated the generation of redundant BGP messages [LMJ99].

The arrival process of BGP routing messages is fairly complex. BGP message arrival is extremely bursty, it shows strong periodicities, and it shows strong auto-correlations [LAJ99]. The main periodicities in BGP arrivals occur with periods of 7 days and 24 hours. Since these periods correspond to timescales of data traffic variation, it is conjectured that one factor in BGP instability is the effect of congestion in the Internet. Another factor that can increase BGP traffic load is delayed convergence, in which routers repeatedly exchange messages with each other in the process of forming a consistent global network view [LABJ01, Obr02].

Instability in BGP shows high variability across prefixes and destinations. That is, most BGP instability comes from a relatively small set of prefixes. However, the prefixes causing the majority of instability correspond to networks with small traffic loads [RWXZ02]. Of course, this is possible because of the already mentioned property of data traffic, in which most traffic flows to a relatively small set of destinations; from a BGP standpoint it appears that routes to this small set of prefixes are relatively stable.

Finally, another source of BGP instability is the interaction between IGPs and BGP. Intradomain protocols such as OSPF and IS–IS choose an egress point for a prefix based on shortest path according to the routing metric. An internal event can cause a change in the egress point for a prefix, resulting in an iBGP update being sent to all BGP speakers within the network [TSGR04, ACBD04].

IGPs. In contrast to BGP, traffic due to IGPs (OSPF and IS–IS) tends to be much more stable. The daily and weekly fluctuations in signaling traffic seen in BGP do not seem to be present in IGPs [LAJ99]. Periodicities in OSPF messages seem to be mainly caused by protocol and implementation issues [SIG$^+$02]. In fact, the principal cause of instability in internal routing appears to be due to external route changes, i.e., BGP [WJL03]. This externally-induced instability can be important in network dynamics, for example, it can be a cause of routing loops [SMD03].

6.4.5 Wireless

Finally, an important emerging category of Internet traffic is wireless – packets that flow for some part of their path over a wireless link. In particular we concentrate on traffic flowing over wireless access points, which is an important class of traffic. This is a new and evolving area, so traffic studies are not yet extensive. However some properties of wireless traffic are starting to become clear.

In general, the basic structure imposed by sessions, flows, and packets is unchanged in the wireless environment. As with wired networks, traffic is bursty and shows daily variation.

User Access Patterns. The most common wireless networks today are access networks. As such, each serves a distinct physical location and user community. Thus (similar to wired networks) specific traffic demands and properties vary from one wireless network to another as a function of location and user set.

Traffic loads on wireless networks tend to follow diurnal variation similar to what is found on wired networks. However, average and peak bandwidths per user are generally lower than in a wired, campus network. This may be a result of the lower performance delivered by wireless networks; as technology improves this difference may diminish.

Just as in wired networks, many measures of user activity show high variability. Among these, most notably: session durations show high variability, as does average transfer rate per user [BVR02, BC03, HKA04]. These results are consistent with the use of long-tailed distributions for wired networks in Sections 6.4.1–6.4.3.

Spatial Distribution.   One way in which wireless traffic differs from wired traffic is in the significance of spatial distribution. The physical location of users affects traffic patterns: e.g., it affects the load seen across a set of access points, and it affects the interaction of traffic due to physical properties of the radio medium.

In general, users tend to have irregular distribution in space. Furthermore, the load on access points tends to be highly uneven. Although users are distributed irregularly, the highly variable rate at which individual users transfer data seems to be the main cause of the uneven demand placed on access points [BVR02, BC03].

Mobility.   Related to the question of location is the nature of user mobility. The most significant aspect of wireless network access for the end user is the ability to change location both during and between accesses to the network. This results in a new aspect of user demand which factors into the demand patterns a network must support.

User mobility varies across different environments. In a conference environment, users can be mobile in bursts (for example, at the end of conference sessions) [BVR02]. In a university campus building, mobility is more limited [TB00]. In general, only a small fraction of users are mobile (active at two or more access points) within a single day. Among mobile users, most do not move much, but a few users are highly mobile. Further, in that environment, users fall into distinct communities based on location, with users in different communities showing different mobility characteristics.

Since wireless is a relatively new access medium, trends are important. Mobility has been shown to increase over time in a campus network [KE05, HKA04].

7

Applications

So far in this ("In Depth") part of the book we have seen two of the three pillars: infrastructure and traffic. These two pillars exist to support the superstructure of applications. Applications are the visible part of the Internet for millions of its users. The infrastructure supports the flow of the traffic originated by the different applications. A primary focus of Internet measurements is to examine the movement of traffic over the existing infrastructure to help improve the end user's perception in interacting with a variety of applications. The measurements done at the application layer can lead to improvements in the applications, the flow of traffic, and the infrastructure.

In order to get a good handle on the numerous applications on the Internet, it is enough to examine a few of them since historically only a handful of applications have been responsible for a significant fraction of traffic on the Internet at any given time. This has been true virtually throughout the existence of the Internet, although the degree to which the top few applications dominate has varied along with the actual mix of the applications. Likewise, the speed with which a new application increases its share from trace amounts to a visible fraction of traffic has varied over time.

In this chapter we will begin by examining this meta-phenomenon: how has the application mix changed over time? Then we will examine in more depth three key applications that have been popular during the last decade. These applications are the DNS, Web, and Peer-to-Peer (P2P). DNS is formally not an application in the same sense as Web or P2P as users do not typically interact with it directly. However, the key role played by DNS in the Internet merits its separate examination. DNS is a request–response protocol that involves a client and potentially multiple DNS servers (including potentially different kinds of servers such as top-level domain name servers, other authoritative servers, and local DNS servers). HTTP typically involves a client and a Web server though intermediaries such as proxies and gate-ways may be present. P2P involves a client that may interact with multiple servers and some intermediate clients that may forward requests and responses.

We will then take a look at the rapidly growing recent application of online net-worked games. This application has had the largest growth in terms of users and some popular games have hundreds of thousands of subscribers paying monthly fees to participate. Networked games have many clients playing against each other, often with a central server mediating their communication.

In the last section we will examine a miscellaneous collection of less popular applications including multimedia streaming. It is possible that one of these applica-tions could become a dominant application in the near future. Our focus is not aimed at stressing the popularity of any particular application but to examine the similarity and differences of measurements across applications.

Each of the individual application sections follow the template used in the two earlier major components (infrastructure and traffic) and are thus viewed along the four axes of properties, challenges, tools, and state of the art. The analysis along the axes will necessarily differ as these are application-dependent.

The idea is to list, for each application, the key measurable properties that can be used to characterize the application and provision infrastructure for the applica-tion. The properties axis presents the properties of interest of the application from a measurement perspective. The challenges in carrying out these measurements and potential inferences from them are discussed next. The tools axis discusses the tools that are available to aid in the measurement, and state of the art gives a current snap-shot of recent measurement results as a way to illustrate the methodology used. The measurements may use the generic tools described or some locally created ad-hoc mechanisms. The measurements carried out relate to the properties mentioned and serve to illustrate some of the challenges described.

It should be noted that the state of the art in this section is likely to have a shorter shelf-life than in the earlier two chapters owing to rapid changes in traffic patterns, evolution of the applications and the manner in which users interact with them. How-ever, both the axes we use and the categories of analysis are likely to apply to new applications that may gain traffic share over the next several years. Also, even when a particular application's traffic pattern changes, the methodologies of measurement are less likely to change at the same speed.

7.1 Application Mix

Although there have been few popular applications at any given time the set of these applications has changed over time. In the early days of the Internet, File Transfer

Protocol traffic dominated followed by modest amounts of electronic mail and Telnet, and several smaller applications. FTP was created specifically to transfer files between any pair of machines on the Internet, and multiple files could be sent or received over a single FTP connection. The anonymous mode of exchange in FTP allowed rendezvous points on the Internet to be set up where a collection of files would be stored. Clients from different spots on the Internet would connect to the FTP site and download files. Clients, however, had to know the location of the servers in order to download the files. Through the early 1980s the primary way to distribute files on the Internet was over FTP. Electronic mail was exchanged between machines using FTP before the introduction of the Simple Mail Transfer Protocol (SMTP).

The first major new application to involve significant number of machines was the Network News application, although the overall traffic due to this application in the mid-1980s was low. Many hundreds and then thousands of machines were involved in exchanging short (and later longer) articles posted to multiple newsgroups. The standardization of the Network News Transport Protocol was done in 1986 [KL86], a year after FTP [PR85]. In 1990 the World Wide Web was yet to be created. Network news allowed for *automatic* distribution of collections of files to any subset of interested client sites. Client sites could choose between the rapidly growing numbers of newsgroups (basically, bulletin boards) and update their local copy of the news items. The NNTP protocol replaced the then-popular UUCP (Unix-to-Unix Copy Protocol) and introduced several new features tailored to network news exchange such as creation of new newsgroups. Likewise, mailing lists that were popular before the advent of NNTP could now rely on NNTP for more efficient transfer of the data rather than SMTP.

It should be noted that although protocols evolved to be increasingly tailored to specific applications, there were a lot of commonalities in their interface, command structure, statefulness, and underlying transport. For example, FTP, SMTP, and NNTP all use TCP. The changes between the applications would be more due to application-specific differences. The manner in which the applications used TCP would show differences depending on how closely the various applications were tied to the transport protocol. This fact became particularly clear at the next stage of evolution to HTTP.

Approximately in a 6-year period after 1992, the traffic due to HTTP, the protocol underlying the World Wide Web, became the majority of traffic.

A large number of measurements have been carried out covering nearly all aspects of this complex application and so the Web is covered in depth in this chapter. The Web has transformed the Internet and is the primary application to have brought tens of millions of users to it. With the dramatic growth in the number of users, the Web became the gateway for many applications. Electronic commerce began to spread rapidly. The improvements in the infrastructure of the Internet had not kept pace with the torrid growth in the number of users. The early days of the Web witnessed what became notorious as the 'World Wide Wait' [Wor] due to the significant delays experienced by users visiting Web sites.

The Web is a rich space for carrying out extensive measurement given the world-wide deployment of Web sites and users. The creation of cybercafes and the advent of wireless has led to location transparency greatly increasing the transformation of the Web as a primary communication medium. The need for measurement first for the cause of delays, then for alternate solutions, and finally for infrastructural alternatives has driven much of the measurement in the Web arena.

Towards the end of the 1990s, well after the Web had become the dominant application on the Internet, a sudden explosion in sharing files came about by the introduction of Napster [Nap]. Napster was the first large-scale P2P protocol. The instant popularity, attractiveness of the content (initially mostly audio files), and the demographics of the population subgroup (students with access to high-speed connectivity on college campuses) all led to the creation of multiple P2P networks with differing protocols. Additional content quickly followed, including large video files (movies). Since the advent of peer-to-peer traffic, Web traffic as an overall fraction has come down to some extent although many of the downloads on the popular P2P protocols are actually carried out via HTTP transfers. The reduction has actually been in the user-initiated downloads of Web traffic from Web sites which has been supplanted largely by the P2P downloads. P2P is a good example of a novel application that arose out of nowhere and came to dominate Internet traffic within a short period of time (about 3 years).

In the early part of the 21st century, several other applications have started to become visible on the Internet. Chief among them are network games, although other applications such as chat have been increasing in traffic volume. Many of the applications are also being accessed using wireless means, introducing another class of measurements.

7.2   DNS

We begin our look at measurement of applications with DNS. Although DNS is considered a base protocol and an Internet infrastructure entity, we discuss it here due to its important role in several applications.

DNS is one of the base protocols providing key infrastructural support for the Internet. In Chapter 2 (Section 2.3.8) we presented a brief introduction to the DNS protocol and the service. The key observation from a measurement perspective is that most of the traffic in DNS is over UDP. There are two reasons for this: first, the most common traffic variant in DNS is a query and a response and typically both can fit

Table 7.1   DNS properties of interest to measure.

Measured property	Why measured	Where measured
Fraction of Internet traffic	Guides other issues	Across the Internet
Availability	Critical to infrastructure	Root servers, ADNS sample
Number of entities	Performance	Remote reverse engineering
Response latency	Performance	Targeted set of servers
TTL assigned/honored	CDN–server selection	At sampled LDNS, clients
Extent of caching	Performance	At multiple sites
Software configuration	Correctness/variance	Locally
Location of DNS server	Mapping	Globally
Characteristics of queries	Correctness	LDNS
Validity of queries	Access control	Locally
Frequency/count of lookups	Application popularity	Locally

in a single datagram. Second, UDP scales much better for the DNS application. The few top-level domain name servers would be overwhelmed if they had to accept TCP connection attempts for all their communication. However, a small fraction of the traffic is over TCP. This is primarily for zone transfers (administrative responsibility for addresses within an organization can be divided into zones with local autonomy and backup servers may take control of a zone when such control is transferred to them). Occasionally due to policies of firewalls disallowing any UDP traffic, the use of TCP is mandated for DNS. However, the issues of interest are characterizing the traffic and exploring information that is generally hidden behind local administrative control. The different implementations of DNS servers and their impact is also of interest.

7.2.1   DNS Measurement Properties

DNS has several measurable properties of interest. They range from broad character-ization and performance issues to narrower protocol-specific issues. We present the motivation for measuring each of the properties before discussing the details of what is measured and how. Table 7.1 lists the properties of interest to measure along with the reason for measuring the property and where it is typically measured.

Fraction of Internet Traffic.   Across the Internet, the fraction of traffic that relates to DNS (queries, responses, forwarding of queries and responses) amid the overall traffic is an interesting metric. Like any other application on the Internet, this metric is important, independent of the role played by DNS. As an overall metric of the impact of different applications, it would be useful to know about the evolution in the fraction of Internet traffic contributed by a particular application. Traffic of applications that comprise a large fraction would often require special attention to better shape, transmit, and handle. However, an application could be a small fraction of the Internet and yet play a critical role. DNS is one such application – currently, it is a relatively small fraction of overall Internet traffic (below 5%).

Availability.   The availability of a DNS server is defined as the probability of a DNS client being able to send a query to it and get back a response. Availability is a key requirement from a user-level application's point of view as DNS is often the first step in a series of application steps (as discussed in Chapter 2 (Section 2.3.8)). Access to the Internet has increasingly become vital to millions of users on a daily basis and is often predicated on a successful DNS lookup of a server. Without being able to translate the name to an IP address, no further steps in the transaction are possible. If the root server or servers that are authoritative for domains of interest are unavailable, numerous classes of applications will be severely affected. If the mapping is cached it would of course be used. Any inaccessibility of the DNS system becomes obvious almost immediately due to the widespread dependence of numerous popular applications. From a measurement perspective the availability of DNS entities has rarely been a significant problem. However, there has been a continuing problem associated with delegations to authoritative servers that do not exist. From a security viewpoint DNS servers are on the front line in the battle against attacks on the Internet. They can also be seen as the weakest link as they are often viewed as easier targets. Thus, the availability, reliability, and redundancy metric of DNS servers is an increasingly interesting property to be measured.

Number of Entities.   The number of entities participating in DNS-related activities is an essential metric required for obtaining a measure of the scale of the application. Knowing the different entities involved in a DNS transaction helps study the variability in behavior and obtain a broad perspective on DNS. A single DNS transaction involves a client and one or more DNS servers which could be a combination of local and authoritative DNS servers. The number and distribution of the different entities involved: clients, local DNS servers, and authoritative DNS servers are some of the basic characterization parameters of the DNS application. The set of root DNS servers is known and largely static as is the set of top-level domain name servers. At a narrower level, knowing the number of clients served by a specific local DNS server can be a potential indication of its importance and expected performance. However, the number of clients *behind* a local DNS server is largely unknowable although some reverse engineering efforts have been carried out.

Response Latency.   The time between the issuance of a DNS request and the receipt of the response is the DNS response latency. The time spent by an application in its DNS portion of the transaction is governed by this response latency which is of interest from a performance viewpoint. DNS response latency depends on the availability of different DNS servers and the impact due to DNS caching. Studies have explored the distributions of delays, with special emphasis on popular servers such as the root servers and authoritative servers of popular domains.

TTL and Extent of Caching.   A Time-To-Live (TTL) value is the validity duration of the mapping returned by authoritative DNS servers to caching DNS servers. Each DNS resource record [Moc87a] has a time-to-live value. Applications, such as Web browsers, do their own caching of DNS mappings to avoid repeated lookups of popular servers. The proper assignation of TTLs and more importantly honoring these TTLs is important for a variety of applications. TTLs represent a tradeoff between speed (to avoid repeated issuance of the same query), control on the part of the authoritative DNS server assigning the TTL, and the overall number of DNS messages that may be exchanged. TTLs have allowed DNS to scale and handle the rapid growth in the Internet. The TTL value has also played an important role in novel applications such as Content Distribution Networks and other forms of dynamic redirection of client traffic between multiple application servers providing the same service.

Software Configuration.   There are a variety of different implementations of DNS and each variant of the server has numerous configuration options. If the software is buggy or the server is misconfigured, wrong mappings could be returned and caches may ignore the returned TTLs. The caches may be deliberately poisoned with long TTL values and/or bad data. Some studies have shown that misconfigurations of DNS servers can lead to significant performance problems. In addition, misconfigurations can lead to internal information leaking, violating the privacy of clients or providing useful information to competitors. The manner and correctness of configuration of DNS servers is thus an interesting property. Measuring this requires correlating with the software implementation variant. Identifying the variant helps fix any configuration problems in all the sites where the variant has been deployed. Spurious traffic to name servers can be detected and stopped once the implementation version has been reverse engineered.

Location of DNS Server.   The physical and topological locations of DNS servers on the Internet can provide a rough map of where the clients are since the clients tend to be close to their local DNS servers. The authoritative DNS servers are far removed from the clients. In order to provision new services, applications need to have a view of the actual physical distribution of DNS servers (local and authoritative) on the

Internet. Attempts have been made to map the DNS servers from network topology to physical locations. The proximity of the DNS servers in the network topology has been used in novel applications such as Content Distribution Networks.

Characteristics of Queries.   The type of DNS queries (QTYPE) and popular destination of query messages is another property of interest to measure at the local DNS server. Clearly the most common query types will be for name to address translation and vice versa. Examining popularity of other query types can give us an idea of the extent to which certain features of DNS are used. Even for the popular query types examining client's name and domain against its query can help characterize unnecessary queries such as ones for its own domain or even a name to address conversion request (QNAME) where the name is already an IPv4 address! Some queries, such as ones with recursion desired bit set and sent to servers that have recursion disabled (such as root name servers), won't yield a reply.

Validity of Queries.   The validity of a DNS query examines if the requesting client has the necessary authorization to receive a response. Although DNS traffic is not significant enough to negatively impact the performance of DNS servers, security issues have led to the DNS administrators enforcing limited access through the use of Access Control Lists (ACLs). This has led to numerous mapping attempts failing when requests are made by clients who are not in the ACLs. An estimate of this fraction would thus be an interesting property. Rate limiting may also be done, although this could lead to incorrectly penalizing legitimate traffic from a busy entity and allowing small amounts of entirely unwanted traffic from malicious entities. A combination of ACLs and rate limiting would be a more equitable approach.

Frequency and Count of Lookups.   The number of lookups of a particular address may be an indication of the popularity of the service provided at that address. The lookup count depends both on the TTL provided by the DNS server as well as the extent of caching at other locations. From a traffic perspective, the amount of traffic that stays within a network as opposed to the fraction that is visible outside indicates the extent of caching.

7.2.2   DNS Measurement Challenges

There are many challenges in carrying out DNS measurements. Although widely used and key to the Internet's proper functioning, the configurations and the setting of the various DNS parameters are left to the individual administrators of networks. The *impact* of these settings on the rest of the applications on the Internet is primarily of interest to us. It should be noted that the degree of control exercised by

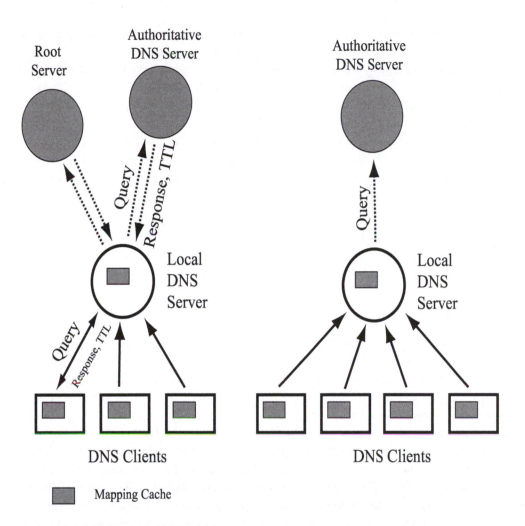

Figure 7.1   DNS entities and transactions.

the local administrators is considerable and beyond traditional protocol compliance, it is hard to expect much cooperation in terms of measuring from outside. For example, access control lists can prevent any DNS-related measurement probes from outside. It has been pointed out that at least one root DNS server may be rate limiting queries [Vix04].

Figure 7.1 is a composite figure showing many of the entities and some of the steps involved in DNS transactions. Since there is no published directory of all the entities involved in DNS, queries are required to identify them. The mappings between names and IP addresses are cached for the durations of time assigned via a TTL value. As the figure shows, numerous entities may be involved in a transaction depending on whether a particular mapping is cached and current. Some queries require communicating with the root server and some do not.

TTL values can be ignored and considerable guesswork may be involved in reverse engineering the values assigned to the local DNS servers. Further, in the key metric of DNS latency, one needs to separate out the latency across the potential hops between the client and the root server.

There is also variance in results of DNS measurements (successful lookup ratio, latencies) depending on where the measurements are done implying that multi-site measurements are warranted. The consequent concern that arises is the representativeness of the sites to draw reasonable and stable inferences.

Hidden Data

There are no published directories of local or authoritative DNS servers although the list of the top-level and root DNS servers is well known. Efforts have been made in the direction of locating local and authoritative DNS servers. There is even less information about the number of clients behind a specific local DNS server – a count that is much harder to glean.

At a local or site-specific level information about the implementation of the DNS server, its configuration parameters, and access control list is typically not available. Some questions may seem to be not of significant import. For example, configuring a set of clients to a local DNS server is an issue of interest only to a local administrator. Outside that administrative domain, few would care about it since their activities are not affected. However, this is not the case when it comes to adherence to the time-to-live since it may inhibit efficient administration of certain applications as we will see later in Section 7.2.5. Some data are of interest simply from a characterization or statistical perspective. Other more important reasons to identify the data behind a DNS server have to do with checking protocol compliance – a non-compliant server may be responsible for errors manifesting themselves in severe performance problems. Section 7.2.3 presents many successful reverse engineering tools that have been created to ferret out some of the hidden data.

At a traffic level there is little information available about intranet-DNS traffic to the outside world. Access control lists often prevent lookups behind a network. Firewalls typically won't allow UDP packets that don't meet the local policy on the DNS port. In fact, some organizations handle internal DNS requests on their own. A DNS proxy can be used to filter internal queries and can check for bad responses.

Hidden Layer

Although most DNS requests go directly to the intended DNS server, there is a slow increase in the deployment of *anycast* at least for root servers. Anycast [PMM93] allows delivery of a datagram to one server in a set of servers on the network, providing a basis for delivering a packet to a nearby (in a network sense) mirror server. While some popular servers (e.g., some root servers and several top-level domain name servers) use anycast, it is hard to measure all nodes from a single location or even a few locations.

Hidden Entities

The entities involved in DNS, as mentioned earlier, are clients, local DNS servers, authoritative DNS servers, top-level domain name servers, and root servers. In a single DNS transaction, say a client lookup, it is theoretically possible that all these entities would be contacted or just one (the local DNS server). The lookup sequence follows an iterative route or a recursive route. In the iterative mode of operation, the client is made aware of the other servers it needs to contact. In the recursive mode the intermediate server follows the chain of communication steps before returning the answer to the requesting client.

7.2.3 DNS Measurement Tools

DNS measurements benefit from the presence of several tools and some techniques tailored for DNS. A majority of the tools available for DNS are related to characterization although some performance measurement tools are available. We will examine tools created for characterizing DNS via online or offline analysis of network data. The traffic characterization of DNS is done primarily to examine the traffic load on DNS entities, the nature of the queries and their relative usefulness. Next we look at tools that aid DNS performance analysis through passive and active measurements. Performance issues concentrate on areas of both local impact and at the more central authoritative and root servers. Subsequently and separately, we will examine the category of DNS tools used for a variety of other (i.e., non-DNS-related) applications.

The most common tool used to query the Domain Name System from a command line, used by virtually all DNS administrators is *dig* (Domain Internet Groper). It is a primary tool for troubleshooting problems associated with DNS. *dig* is used to look up information in the global DNS database and has largely superseded the earlier *nslookup* tool. The flexibility of *dig* ranges from choice of protocols used to communicate with the name server (UDP or TCP), automatically checking the client's authentication to query the server, controlling whether the query should be

Table 7.2   DNS measurement tools.

	Source/Name of tool	Primary function
Passive measurement	Netflow logs	Local characterization of DNS traffic
	DNS update logs	Traffic characterization and authentication
	Graph representation	Classifying DNS entities
	NeTraMet	DNS spectroscopy
Active monitoring	dnsstat	Local DNS statistics
	dnstop	Local DNS statistics, highlighting unusual events
	dsc	Local DNS statistics filtered to aid troubleshooting
Active measurement	fpdns	Identifying DNS implementation
	dnschecker	Identifying nodes in DNS resolution path

tried recursively or iteratively, setting a time out period for the query and the number of times it should be tried, etc. Although *dig* is used for troubleshooting, it is not a measurement tool.

Table 7.2 lists the data sources for DNS characterization (e.g., netflow logs or DNS update logs) and the primary use of these data sources. A small subset of the DNS tools available are enumerated along with applications ranging from identifying the configuration information to obtaining numerous statistical measures.

DNS characterization techniques range from passive offline analysis of DNS-related data to active monitoring of DNS-related traffic, and active DNS measurements that generate and send probes. Traditional tools for characterization and traffic monitoring might suffice although some tailored ones have been created for DNS. These tools range from identifying information related to the DNS server software implementation, the path taken by DNS queries, validating responses, to showing statistics about DNS queries at a local level.

Passive Measurement for Characterization.   Offline analysis of DNS-related data uses DNS logs, traffic records (in the form of Netflow), and packet traces. Logging is relatively rare at local DNS servers and client sites. However, logging is done at many authoritative servers, top-level generic domain servers (such as .com, .org, etc.), and at the 13 root server installations. Simple characterization examining the diversity of clients accessing root servers has shown [CDR] the changes in the sets of clients accessing them and the distribution of access. More than half the clients send just a handful of messages since most of the information can be cached. Outliers that send way too many requests can be easily identified. RFC 2870 [BKKP00], the RFC describing the best current practice of root server operational requirements suggests that logging be done to detect intrusion attempts and other ways to compromise this critical resource. Logging is also useful when the name server synchronizes its clock with Network Time Protocol (NTP [Mil92, ntp]) servers to facilitate fault isolation.

Netflow data is gathered at several places and sites interested in DNS activities can restrict their attention to flow records related to DNS (often just by examining UDP/TCP traffic at port 53). Packet traces can also be gathered to look for DNS traffic at a fine grain level. Obviously gathering data at the few root DNS servers is harder given their importance and difficulty of access. However, even this has been carried out [WF03] by mirroring the DNS port and running *tcpdump* on another host so as not to interfere with the root server. Studies have used packet traces to examine a variety of DNS problems related to repeated queries for non-existent top-level-domains or asking for an address by supplying an address. Simultaneous examination of packet traces of DNS and TCP traffic given their serial use in Web transactions, has shed light on patterns of DNS caching and whether different values of TTL affect hit rates [JSBM01].

Including the dozen or so generic domains like .com and .org there are over 250 top-level domains, with one for each of the countries on the planet which has a presence on the Internet. Each of the generic top-level domains has between thousands and millions of zones underneath them. Each zone can have one or more authoritative servers associated with it responding to queries for DNS names under their control. There are even separate logs maintained for DNS updates. The logs are available for analyzing the amount of traffic at the servers as well as ensuring that the traffic is warranted. Traffic reports are posted at several Web sites on a regular basis. For example, constant updates of a status summary of DNS Query response times from a handful of ASes to the root servers and several of the top-level domain name servers are available [Cym]. In some sense, such sites perform the role of a heartbeat check on the critical DNS infrastructure. Consistent delays or inability to reach top-level domain name servers can trigger administrators to examine the servers. Further, they provide an historical log of reachability and performance.

DNS traces can be manipulated and analyzed in the format obtained using a variety of tools. Another strain of tools transform the gathered data into an alternate representation. The transformation aids in enabling both quicker processing of large amount of data and extraction of semantically interesting insights. For example, the *netflow* data associated with DNS flows could be converted into a graph representation with the entities representing nodes, the connection between the nodes represented by edges, directionality depicting the flow of queries and responses, with edge weights as number of packets or bytes. Alternate representations allow for potentially novel insights to be gleaned from a jumble of data. A detailed example of a large-scale data conversion tool will be presented in Section 7.2.5.

NeTraMet [Nete] (Network Traffic Flow Measurement Tool) implements an IETF-generated traffic flow measurement architecture called Realtime Traffic Flow Measurement (RTFM [BMR99]). In RTFM, a flow is an arbitrary collection of bi-directional packets with a large (over 40) number of attributes such as source and destination addresses, protocol type (IPv4 or v6), packet and byte counts, prefix masks, start and end times, etc. RTFM attributes are similar to *netflow* flow attributes. The IETF working group that generated RTFM focused on consistently applying traffic flow models for measuring different protocols and reducing generation and transmission of flow data. Rules are specified as part of a RTFM meter specification in NeTraMet, where a meter is any mechanism (hardware or software) that has passive access to packets. Attributes of packets seen by the meter are used as parameters in the rules. NeTraMet can be tailored to examine traffic aimed at a narrow set of machines (e.g., the set of 13 root DNS servers) on a uni- or bidirectional basis. NeTraMet is capable of logging time of request/response, the source and destination IP address, the type of DNS query, and optional information such as second-level domain names.

Combined logging of DNS packets in a TCP trace along with certain special TCP packets (e.g., SYN, RST) can help in better identifying the purpose of the DNS lookup. Spectroscopy tools have been created to aid in both DNS update traffic characterization as well as reusing it for BGP updates. A secondary tool of interest is *tcpdpriv* [Min97] that can capture packet traces and/or anonymize traces which are needed in certain data-gathering environments for privacy reasons. *Tcpdpriv* is discussed in more detail in Chapter 8 (Section 8.6.3).

Active Monitoring for Characterization.   At a local area network level there are several tools available to show DNS-related information. CAIDA's *dnsstat* [Dnsf] monitors port 53 and presents statistics on DNS queries aggregated on a source/destination IP basis and other parameters such as query type. Dnsstat has to be able to see all DNS-related traffic to the monitored entity (client or nameserver). Statistics, such as number of queries and type of queries is recorded. Unusual events, such as sudden increase of traffic to a particular server are highlighted. Dnsstat was the tool used to gather characterization information about clients contacting DNS root servers [CDR] (mentioned earlier in this section). Examining query types that come to root servers indicates that nearly three out of four queries are of type A (asking for the IP address for a specified string) and over 8% are for an IP address to be converted to the string equivalent. Examining the client distribution provides a measure of the global connectivity of the root server being studied. Such an application of *dnsstat* was carried out in a study about optimizing the placement of DNS root servers [LHFC03].

Measurement Factory's *dnstop* [Dnsg] tool uses the *libpcap* library on top of *tcpdump* generated traces to display DNS-related information similar to *dnsstat* with some additional information such as the top-level and second-level domains. A *tcp-dump* generated file can be replayed via *dnstop*. The tool has options to anonymize addresses (so they can be shared), and can filter the data so that only suspected erroneous information is presented. For example, bogus queries for top-level domains or queries that attempt to convert an IP address to an IP address due to buggy DNS server implementations can be output.

A extension on *dnstop* is *dsc* [Dnsd] which collects statistics at busy DNS servers into XML format files and displays them graphically after being filtered via an extractor program. For example, *dsc* can generate graphical representations of rate of DNS replies and their length in bytes. With the realization that DNS servers are busy and are performing an important task, *dsc* is capable of gathering the data on an alternate machine to which the DNS server is connected over a switch and using port mirroring. Typical statistics generated include classifying query types on a per-TLD basis or queries on a subnet basis. Such tools are handy for local troubleshooting.

Active Measurement for Characterization.   Beyond the large number of offline analysis and active monitoring tools, there are some tools that actively send out probes to help characterize DNS-related entities and examine the paths taken by queries. As active probing implies an additional load on the DNS infrastructure, such tools must be used prudently.

A simple Perl-script called *fpdns* [AS] is able to create a rough fingerprint of DNS servers; specifically it is capable of identifying the implementation behind a DNS server which can be handy to trace spurious DNS traffic to buggy versions of name servers. *fpdns* operates by testing a variety of hypotheses much like a reverse engineering tool except that it does this remotely by sending a set of queries. Numerous surveys of different domains have been undertaken using *fpdns*. For example, a survey [Moo] examined 38 million domains and attempted to fingerprint over a million unique nameserver names and over half a million unique nameserver IP addresses using *fpdns*. This survey found that 70% of the name servers use BIND. The most common error (over 98%) was the query timing out. *fpdns* was also used to examine [Lot] the distribution by domain server software in which BIND was found in nearly 78% of the surveyed servers. A smaller survey [Koc04] focusing on name servers for Germany (.de) surveyed 55000 servers and found many servers to be multihomed with roughly 87% of servers running BIND variants.

A wide range of smaller tools that can check timestamps on DNS servers, paths taken by DNS queries, the correctness of responses, changes in DNS records, etc. are available. The *dnschecker* [DNSc] tool outputs the list of servers involved in a particular query's resolution. For any record name and type, the *dnschecker* tool traverses the DNS hierarchy starting from the root and explores the different routes the request could travel and the different resolvers involved. Periodic examination of output of *dnschecker* can aid in understanding the reasons for delay. The tool also gives an indication of server load balancing done and the fraction of queries that would be answered by the authoritative servers for a domain.

To avoid repeated checks from multiple client locations, a snapshot of the health-iness of certain zones is provided in a periodically updated database [DNSa]. Begin-ning from verifying whether a zone has at least two nameservers and validating the authoritativeness of authoritative server's responses, to whether both UDP and TCP are handled correctly, a wide variety of checks are carried out. Tracing the name-server hierarchy can help identify *lame* delegations – a persistent problem over the years whereby the server designated as authoritative has long ceased to exist. Er-rors in this regard are only found at the time of a query. A collection of pointers to these and other DNS-related tools can be found in the Measurement Factory Web page [MFA].

Performance Measurement Tools. The primary interests in measuring performance of DNS lie in examining how the query load is spread over the root and top-level domain name servers and how well the queries are handled. The actual impact of DNS on clients, the role played by caching and its effectiveness also necessitate performance examination.

Active and passive techniques have been used to examine a variety of DNS per-formance issues. The metrics of interest are availability of servers, latency, number and rate of queries handled at busy servers (especially the root DNS servers), and extent of caching. Passive techniques largely involve examining DNS-related logs at the application level, focusing on DNS traffic records gathered at the flow level or through packet monitors. Application-level logs may consist of entries resulting from a slightly augmented version of popular software such as BIND. Active mea-surement has been done via tools distributed to different client locations and seeking their cooperation to carry out a stream of requests. The goal of such a technique is to get slightly more representative measurements of perceived latency felt by clients at these sites. Depending on the level of representativeness, uniformity in results could indicate that DNS-related delays are within the resulting band, while wide disparities would necessitate additional measurement. DNS name server and resolver library implementations in most places on the Internet are variants of BIND. However, there are different implementations of the BIND software instantiated with various param-eter settings leading to significant variance in performance.

7.2.4 Use of DNS in Other Applications

Most protocols have specific uses outlined in RFCs and are used in the prescribed manner when deployed in practice. However, many protocols are routinely used in

Table 7.3   Using DNS for other applications.

Technique	Use in application
Content distribution	Locating nearest replica
Load balancing	Server selection
Examining proximity to clients	Estimating latency between nodes
Piggybacking small messages	Reducing latency in Web transaction
Examining lookup frequency	Inferring popularity of applications
Blackhole lists and spam	Spam avoidance
Tunneling non-DNS traffic through firewalls	Attacks

alternate ways or subverted for use in applications not conceived of by the original designers. This has been true for many protocols on the Internet. Piggybacking, whereby additional information is braided with the regular protocol communication, either physically or semantically, is a common practice.

In some cases, a protocol ends up being used in a manner that it was *not* designed for, leading to poor performance of the application and/or overall degradation of the Internet. A good illustration of this was seen in the preliminary version of the HyperText Transfer Protocol (HTTP/1.0). HTTP uses the highly popular TCP for its transport function although TCP was designed for long-lived connections. The multiple TCP connections required to download a Web page with many small embedded images led to poor use of TCP. The problem of poor use of TCP was mitigated to some extent by the introduction of persistent connections in the HTTP/1.1 version of the protocol. Thus, there is no guarantee that using DNS in an application different from the ones it was designed for would be necessarily beneficial.

In other cases, a protocol is used for helping a completely different application. The benign use would be to extract available information from the protocol and apply it to enhance a different application. Such an application would be an example of a low-cost way to extend the use of a deployed system. It is also possible to use a protocol in a manner that shifts cost to that protocol and potentially impacts the original stated goal. The Content Distribution Network application for delivering Web objects on behalf of origin servers replicates such objects among a set of replicas and uses DNS to locate the replica closest to the requesting client.

DNS was designed [Moc87b] as a general purpose hierarchical mechanism to name resources on the Internet. The names could be used by various networks and administrative entities. In practice, DNS is used largely to translate a name to an IP address and vice versa. Given the widespread dependence on and ubiquitous use of

DNS, it is not surprising that it has been used for purposes beyond simply translating names and addresses.

DNS has been used in a variety of other applications that are often not directly related to DNS itself. Many of the alternate applications arise naturally from some of the key properties of the DNS system. The DNS infrastructure is viewed as a stable, reliable collection of hosts spread throughout the Internet. The DNS servers reliably reply to queries from many DNS clients across the Internet, modulo the aforementioned access control list issue. The typical setup of DNS clients and local DNS servers has led to the widespread assumption of the proximity of the local DNS server to its clients. Thus the DNS servers are considered as proxies for the location of clients behind them. This has led to one of the most popular uses of DNS at the application layer since the protocol's inception – Content Distribution Networks (CDN) and their role in selecting servers dynamically. The use of DNS in the CDN context has spawned a variety of related applications ranging from replica selection for mirroring to dynamic server selection based on the current load. Next, since DNS is used ubiquitously by virtually all applications, it is logical that *inferences* are made based on the use of DNS. Since DNS is often the first step in a sequence of transactions in many applications, some of the later stages of the application can take advantage of this fact. For example, unused space in a DNS response packet can be used efficiently by information related to a later stage in the application transaction. The access patterns of DNS can be used to examine popularity of applications. Later, while examining the state of the art, we will see examples of the ways in which DNS has been used in diverse applications. Table 7.3 enumerates several techniques along with the application where DNS is used.

7.2.5   State of the Art

We examine the state of the art of issues related to DNS measurements in four categories: results in characterization, dealing with challenges, use of various tools, and in using DNS for other applications. As mentioned earlier, the goal of the state of the art section is to highlight novel methodologies and their use in the application rather than the actual results, which may not remain useful for long.

Results in DNS Characterization

The characterization concerns discussed in Sections 7.2.1 and 7.2.3 reflect an interest in knowledge of entities participating in DNS, their distribution and location. Some studies present techniques to circumvent the challenges we discussed in Section 7.2.2 while others demonstrate the inherent problem of unreachability of some of the data.

We begin by examining the growth in the number of hosts and the trends in the fraction of Internet traffic that is DNS. DNS was introduced in 1984 and there were barely 1000 hosts then [Dom04]. The earliest measurement of fraction of Internet traffic that is DNS was carried out in 1992 [DOK92]. This study claimed that DNS was nearly 14% of Internet traffic and a significant portion of traffic was erroneous resulting primarily from misconfigurations. However, popular applications were few and the installed base of caching DNS servers was presumably not significant. In fact there were just around a million computers that implemented DNS at that time. The challenges faced then in terms of accessibility of information, if anything, have worsened due to a variety of reasons.

Over the course of the next several years numerous DNS characterization studies have been done and have reported varying fractions. The number of flows related to DNS actually increased although the number of packets had come down due to caching [JSBM01]. By 2003, the number of queries at each of the root servers has exceeded 100 million on a daily basis [CDR, WF03]. Although there are only 13 root server installations, there are physically over 100 root servers [WFBkc04] that handle these queries. The fraction of queries that yield no answers has varied with numbers up to 23% reported in 2001 [JSBM01].

Graph-based Characterization of DNS Entities.   DNS is a service that is provided by a collection of hosts that may change over time. A single host can be both a local DNS server and an authoritative DNS server. While the list of root servers of DNS is available, there is no list of local DNS servers or authoritative DNS servers. Even when one has a list of IP addresses of hosts that participate in DNS traffic, it is not always easy to distinguish between a client sending a request, a local caching DNS server, or an authoritative server. Identifying the entities involved in DNS traffic can help trace the interactions between them.

A study [CGKS01] that attempted to characterize entities involved in DNS trans-actions transformed traffic data in *netflow* form into a graph-based format to facilitate easier and quicker characterization. All IP addresses suspected to be involved in DNS traffic (based on either the source or destination port numbers being 53, the well-known port for DNS, in either UDP or TCP) were extracted from *netflow* records and stored as nodes in a graph. Communication between the pairs of IP addresses involved in the flow represented edges (with head of edge associated with the port 53 IP address) and the number of packets exchanged the weight of the edge. Most DNS requests and responses are in UDP but transactions, such as zone transfers, could be in TCP and thus separate graphs were created for the two protocols.

Figure 7.2 shows the steps in this study used to convert *netflow* data into separate UDP and TCP graphs, and the manner of identifying potential zombies (machines that have been taken over for the purpose of launching attacks). The *netflow* data

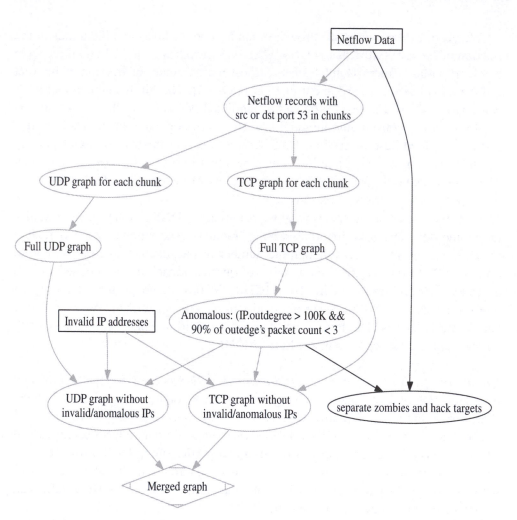

Figure 7.2   Converting *netflow* data into a graph.

over several days is broken into chunks and the daily UDP and TCP graphs are gathered into separate large graphs ('Full UDP' and 'Full TCP' in the figure). Potential zombies are identified via a two-stage process. First a threshold for out-degree of a node (the number of distinct IP addresses with which any node communicates) is set. Next, if a large fraction of such edges have fewer than three packets (i.e., a TCP handshake was never completed), it is an indication of suspicious activity. Processing such predicates is significantly faster once the graph transformation has been done. Along with this set of anomalous IP addresses, invalid IP addresses (those beginning with 0.x.x.x, 10.x.x.x, etc.) are also filtered out of the UDP and TCP graphs to end up with a clean merged graph.

A set of external data sources such as the list of known DNS root servers, NS records of many top-level domains (generic and national), and Web server logs were also gathered to validate and use the characterization. Using knowledge of how DNS entities behave and examining a variety of graph attributes, such as in- and out-degree of the nodes, the nodes were classified into clients, and local/authoritative DNS servers. For example, local DNS servers always contact root servers and authoritative DNS servers do not generate queries. Tail nodes of edges whose heads are root servers, are candidates to be local DNS servers. If the nodes had a zero out-degree they are likely to be authoritative DNS servers.

The study examined a terabyte of netflow data and identified over half a million local DNS servers and 3 million authoritative servers. The study also serendipitously helped identify certain anomalies: attack traffic was observed in examining a node in the TCP graph with a large (more than a million) out-degree. Each of the edges emanating from this node had edge weight less than the minimum required for the three-way handshake of the TCP protocol, indicating that the traffic was anomalous. The generic nature of graph-based analysis enables it to be applied to other protocol data. Studies have been done using P2P data and a similar graph-based approach as we will see later in Section 7.4.4.

Closer Look at DNS Root Servers. A one-day study [WF03] of over 150 million DNS queries was done on one DNS root server in late 2002. The chosen root server was authoritative for several root zones (edu, gov, etc.) at that time. To avoid interfering with the root server, the server's switch was configured to do port mirroring whereby all frames arriving at or leaving from the DNS ports are copied and sent to the monitor. Nearly 400000 unique source IP addresses were seen during the day but some of them generated a significant and abnormal amount of queries. One organization that was responsible for over 15% of traffic had a misconfiguration in their packet filter which blocked responses from the root server. In terms of DNS pollution, 70% of the query traffic involved identical queries (queries with same class, type, etc. parameters) or repeated (identical query but with a different query ID). In fact the study claimed that only 2% of all queries were really legitimate.

Results in DNS Performance

When users attempt to contact any Internet server, DNS is triggered to transparently obtain a mapping although the actual details of the transaction are hidden from the user. As mentioned earlier, steps in a DNS transaction may include contacting a local DNS server, an authoritative DNS server, and a root DNS server. In case of timeouts and failures, multiple servers may be contacted. Performance may be affected by the delays at any of these servers, the time-to-live assigned by them, and any redirections.

A wide-area study [LSZ02] of DNS performance was carried out in 2002. The methodology was to modify BIND (the resolver library) in order to log relevant information of the DNS transaction. The study installed clients in 75 sites in over a score of countries in diverse ISPs using different access: dial-up, DSL, cable modem, etc. The performance characteristics examined included time to complete a lookup, RTT to server, number of retries as a measure of loss rate, average response time to a fixed set of servers, and the specific performance of the top-level domain name servers and the root servers. The results showed that over 96% of the queries completed and around 93% succeeded. While the success of the lookup was largely consistent, the mean response time and the response time to root/TLD servers varied significantly. Between 20 to 30% of time was spent in querying the generic top-level domain name servers and delay due to root servers was negligible. If a nameserver returned a response with type CNAME, then that query was for an alias for a canonical name; a quarter of the names in the study were aliases. TTLs assigned varied but most common TTLs were 1 day, 1 hour, and 2 hours. The study concluded that root servers consistently had very good performance whereas the top-level domain name servers varied in their responsiveness. The ability of root servers to perform well even under server request load is important: it implies that in the presence of a denial of service attack, the root server will be able to handle load. While there can be a bandwidth attack whereby the links to all the root server mirrors can be clogged, there is currently no risk of failure at the root servers themselves due to a large number of requests.

A 2003 study [WFBkc04] of DNS traffic in academic networks used the network flow measurement tool NeTraMet (discussed earlier in Section 7.2.3). The study examined packets from and to the root and the generic top-level domain names for durations ranging from two days to about a week. The study examined response times, the choice of servers that were selected, repeated queries, and query rates. Most of the queries were for name to address translation which is typical of other studies. The distributions of response times had a long tail and were correlated to the geographical distance from the measurement point to the root server. The resolvers in the measurement sites differed in their choice of server selection with some picking root servers without taking latency into account. Caching of responses was inadequate for some of the TLDs; a server sent a query for .net every two minutes! The study showed almost no packet loss.

Results in Using DNS for Other Applications

Here we examine a few novel uses of DNS for applications not related per se to DNS. Later in the Web application section's state of the art discussion we will see the special role played by DNS primarily in server selection.

Using Proximity of DNS Servers to Clients. The suspected co-location of local DNS servers near their clients has spawned interesting applications. If the assumption that clients are close in a network sense to their local DNS servers, and since LDNS are potentially more accessible than the arbitrary number of clients behind them, it is natural to treat the local DNS server as a stand-in for the clients. In other words, measurements done against the LDNS server can be approximated to the clients. The network proximity of local DNS servers to clients was first exploited in a large way in the context of Content Distribution Networks. We will see a more detailed discussion of proximity in the state of the art discussion in the Web applications section (Section 7.3.4).

The proximity assumption of local DNS servers to clients was ably used to compute the network distance between arbitrary pairs of IP addresses on the Internet. The King [GSG02] tool was constructed as a general mechanism for selecting nearby mirrors, wide-area latency measurements involving a large number of hosts on the network, without constructing any new infrastructure. With the stated goal of leveraging the DNS infrastructure and not requiring more than a few DNS queries for each estimate, the tool was designed to be a low-cost mechanism for estimating latency between any two end hosts on the Internet. The tool identifies name servers near each of the two hosts in question and estimates the latency between them as an approximation of the actual latency between the end hosts. Note that such an application has nothing to do with the traditional role played by DNS on the Internet.

The actual distance estimation technique is straightforward and is represented in Figure 7.3. Suppose H1 and H2 are the two hosts whose network distance is in question. The King client first sends a query for a host in H2's domain to be resolved by the name server for H1. H1's name server forwards the request to H2's name server, receives the resolved reply and forwards the reply back to the King client. The latency between the client and the name server for H1 is computed separately via an iterative DNS query to force the name server to reply from its cache without forwarding or via an ICMP ping. This latency is subtracted from the first query resolution time to get an estimate of the latency between H1 and H2.

The King tool makes some reasonable assumptions: name servers must be able to support recursive queries. Their experimental verification at that time indicated that this was true for a large fraction of name servers. Further, since King can measure the latency in either direction between the hosts in question, it was enough if one of the two name servers handled recursive queries. The second assumption is that authoritative name servers for the hosts in question are both geographically and topologically close to the hosts. While this assumption is true in general, large ISPs can be an exception and place their authoritative servers in diverse locations that are not necessarily close to the hosts. The authors use `traceroute` deviation metric as a way of testing their assumption. This metric is defined as the maximum num-

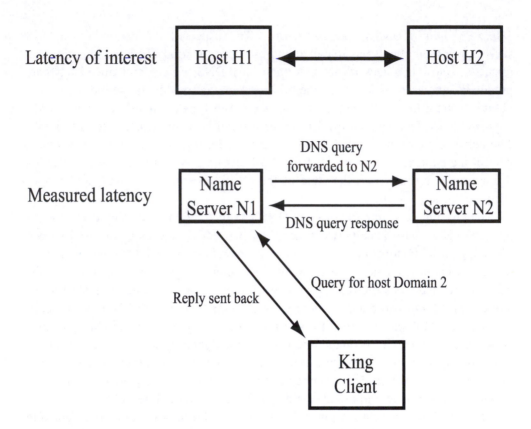

Figure 7.3   King tool operation.

ber of different hops from probing site to the client and its name server. But, as an added measure, they translate deviation hop count into a more meaningful metric: difference in latencies as a result of the deviation. When two `traceroute` paths diverge, around two-thirds of the paths differ in latency by only 10 ms in their experiments. Along the way the work also reported that the application-level latency of DNS queries is negligible.

The King tool is thus an interesting example of a novel use of DNS for an entirely different application. It should be noted that King was hardly the first tool created to estimate distances between arbitrary hosts. It was, however, the first to use the existing DNS infrastructure to do this although there is a small risk in that remote queries may not always be answered.

Piggybacking on DNS.   Piggybacking is a tried and tested technique in networking. From the early days of TCP, piggybacking acknowledgments with data was done to obviate the need for an additional packet and reduce delay. Piggybacking has been proposed in HTTP in different contexts [KW97, KW98]. A standard attempt to improve efficiency in many protocols and applications is the use of piggybacking. We will examine use of piggybacking on DNS here and we will see additional uses in the later sections dealing with other applications.

Most DNS queries fit in a single packet as do most responses. The most common DNS exchange involves a query and a response. The response can be from the local DNS server or a remote DNS server after one or more steps. The typical size of a DNS UDP query packet is around 40 bytes, since the only information in the payload is either the representation of the Internet address in name or four-octet form. The typical DNS response is less than 512 bytes fitting in a single UDP packet. It consists mainly of the translated name or address mapping. The rest of the packet is often empty depending on the number of name server records. There are exceptions in the case of a zone transfer when the packet may not only be full but the response may be split across packets. However, zone transfers comprise only a small fraction of DNS traffic. Also, in a few cases error messages may be returned when access control lists prevent a mapping being returned to an unauthorized client. A disproportionate fraction of DNS responses that are seen on the Internet (i.e., the queries for which the local DNS server in the Intranet could not provide a cached response) are short responses consisting of the requested mapping. A logical question to ask is: can the remaining space in the DNS response packet be used for something?

The DEW (DNS-Enhanced Web [KLR03]) project examined the potential of piggybacking short HTTP responses along with DNS responses. Many HTTP requests are preceded by a DNS lookup of the Web server on which the Web content is present. The authoritative server for the Web server is likely to be near the Web server, as discussed earlier in this section in the context of the King tool. The DNS lookup is followed by a TCP connection between the client and the Web server. In DEW, it is possible to piggyback the HTTP request on the forward DNS query since most HTTP requests are small. If the Web server has a short HTTP response that is going to be sent on this TCP connection, it would be worth considering piggybacking the HTTP response on the DNS response. If such piggybacking were to be feasible, it would obviate the need for the TCP connection between the client and the server to be set up at all. This reduces the overall latency for the response.

Figure 7.4 shows the architecture of the DNS-Enhanced Web. As can be seen in the figure, the local DNS server can cache the DNS results as well as the short HTTP response if it is returned from the remote DNS server. The remote DNS server can maintain a persistent HTTP connection with the Web server to further reduce the overall latency as it does not have to make a separate connection for each potential DEW request.

DNS features allow for such additions. The HTTP request is embedded in the DNS request via the widely-used OPCODE=Query setting in the DNS request header to let the DNS server know that DEW-style piggybacking is being done. The

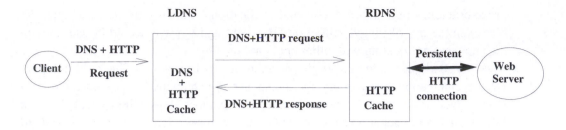

Figure 7.4   DNS-Enhanced Web architecture.

QNAME field in the DNS header would carry the HTTP request allowing non-DEW-compliant DNS servers to ignore this portion of the query. Local DNS servers can specify the size of piggybacked HTTP response they would be willing to accept.

   The DEW work evaluates a variety of scenarios: *strict* piggybacking where the entire HTTP response fully fits into the DNS response packet, or *extended* piggy-backing where a couple more datagrams would be sent with the DNS response. The amount of reduction in latency depends on the client's connectivity and the number of different Web servers that have to be contacted for fulfilling a request. The most logical place for DEW to be deployed would be in Content Distribution Networks (discussed earlier) which use DNS to find replicas close to the clients and often de-liver small static images. The size distributions of these static images are such that most of them will fit well into DNS responses. Through trace-driven simulations it is shown that a quarter of pages at content providers sites can benefit from DEW. The DNS-Enhanced Web is thus another novel example of a technique that makes an alternate use of the existing DNS communication paradigm.

Relative Popularity of DNS.   The relative popularity of applications can be de-termined by examining DNS traffic. This was explored by Wills et al. [WMS03]. Since the local DNS server caches requests for lookups related to numerous appli-cations, querying this cache would provide a rough estimate of popularity of Inter-net applications. Although this is limited to Internet applications that require peri-odic name/address translations, such applications are often the vast majority of non-intranet applications. Examples of applications that may not require lookups would include highly popular applications with either hardwired IP addresses or DNS map-pings with high time-to-live values (such as multicast services). If a particular appli-cation is very popular then periodic examination of the LDNS cache would result in a hit. Applications with low popularity will result in a cache miss during the exami-nation. With this straightforward scheme, at a cost of doing local cache examination it is thus possible to rank the popular applications at a site. Note that this information is necessarily of local value since the examination is only of the local caching DNS server. If the same methodology is used to probe remote DNS servers the experiment would have to contend with the ACL problem and the resulting 50% failure rate in obtaining a response. The examination of the local cache must ensure that the query does not result in actually polluting the cache. This is because the success of a cache hit does not alter conditions in the local cache but the failure might trigger an external query by the cache and thus modify the cache. However, it is possible to issue a non-recursive DNS query that will not pollute the cache.

In order to safely query the local cache, the methodology needs to have a list of servers to examine their relative popularity. Here the approach has been to narrow this space by sub-grouping application domains and effectively looking up relative popularity of a set of known servers involved in that application. For example, to examine the relative popularity of Web servers one could start with published collections of popular Web sites available from many sources such as 100 Hot [Hot], Netratings [Netf], or Alexa Top 500 [Ale]. Likewise the authors of [WMS03] point out that popularity of network games and streaming media sites can also be ranked. Beyond examination of relative popularity of applications, it is possible to zoom in on a particular site's domain (such as www.cnn.com) and examine the popularity of sub-domains on that site (such as weather.cnn.com and money.cnn.com).

There are two possible benefits from such an examination when carried out at larger sites. First, it indicates what applications are popular in different sub-classes at the same time. Second, if this information is made available to the applications, it can provide a measure of adherence to the TTL assigned to the local DNS server.

An early tool that aided in providing a degree of privacy for users of DNS is the *dnscache* [Dnsb] tool. *Dnscache* shields local users from examining each other's DNS queries, it drops non-recursive and inverse queries, and by default allows TTL to be set to 0 in its responses. A different kind of snooping [Gra04] of DNS caches was carried out based on other existing work, chiefly, the *dnscache* tool. The intriguing use of snooping here is to ferret out abuses and leakage of information present in DNS caches. The paper points out the problem of *dig* returning information about negative caching of non-existent domains. Normally this would not be viewed as a bad idea; however a potentially useful inference that is more useful to *domain typosquatters* is the count of misspelled variants of popular domains. Domain squatters are eager to register common misspellings of popular domain names to attract traffic and attempt to redirect them to a site of their choice. Common variants of popular Web sites like http://www.nytimes.com include nyimes.com or nytime.com. An easy way to locate a list of popular misspellings is to query caches to see if they occur often enough. This is an example of a bad use of caching; the no-such domain record – the RFC 1035 response code RCODE of 3 is returned when the domain name referenced in the query does not exist. The error is known as NXDOMAIN in BIND. The no-such domain record is then made available to anyone. A simple fix would be to return equivalent information about all non-existent domains so that no useful information can be reverse engineered. Even when legitimate information is cached, knowing the names of some domains can give an indication beyond popularity. For example, the research paper [Gra04] talks about learning if particular software updates are requested often at a given site. The issue of separating the caching service of DNS and the regular role of a DNS server has been a controversial topic and discussed at length on implementer's mailing lists.

Blackhole Lists and Spam.   The dramatic rise of email spam has led to moves to counter the phenomenon using virtually any means. One suggestion was to simply blackhole the domain of the server alleged to be involved in spamming by asking DNS resolvers not to reply to queries about those domains. The MAPS project [Map] (Mail Abuse Prevention System, formerly known as the RTBH (Real-Time Black Hole)) sought the cooperation of domain name system administrators to help block reverse lookups. By publishing a list of domains that were considered to be abusing email, other administrators could voluntarily agree not to forward queries or help resolve name to address translation. DNS was thus being used as a gatekeeper to bar communication about an entire domain or a sub-domain based on its nefarious use. False positives such as names that may have inadvertently been added to the blackhole lists as well as throwaway domain names that spammers have been using are some of the problems with this approach. Reverse MX record (RMX [RMX]), DomainKeys [Dom], and Sender Policy Framework (SPF [SPF]) are among a variety of spam mitigation schemes that have been proposed. They all use DNS as a primary ingredient in their solution strategy. RMX adds a new resource record to DNS and IP addresses of servers that are authorized to send mail on behalf of a domain are registered in DNS. The receiving SMTP server queries DNS to ensure that the sender's From domain is not forged. One of the RMX records associated with sending servers in the From: address must match the reverse MX record returned. DomainKeys uses public key infrastructure: the originating domain's private key is included in mail header to allow the receiver to compare the public key in DNS listings. SPF also requires domain owners to designate mail servers in DNS.

Tunneling non-DNS Traffic through Firewalls.   One of the key advantages of DNS turns out to be a potential liability. DNS is very widely deployed throughout the Internet. As we have discussed before, virtually all applications contact one or more DNS servers at some point in their Internet transaction. Many hosts act as a DNS client and they along with hundreds of thousands of local and authoritative DNS servers are capable of communicating with each other. As significant fractions of the Internet hosts move behind firewalls, the hierarchical and overlay nature of the DNS network leaves these nodes communicating using a protocol that is not fully secure. Several attempts have been made to use this communication hierarchy for unusual purposes [Kam] ranging from a remotely addressable trojan horse to a covert means to deliver a segmented audio-file. Ways to tunnel DNS traffic through firewalls have been described in popular Web sites [Tac00, Hei] with the basic idea being encapsulating IP packets in DNS requests.

7.3 Web

The World Wide Web remains the single most popular application since the creation of the Internet. The Web experienced a meteoric rise in terms of number of users who joined the Internet in a short time. In the first decade of the existence of the Web, the fraction of HTTP (HyperText Transfer Protocol, the protocol underlying the Web) traffic on the Internet grew from zero to over 75%. Subsequently, the popularity of peer-to-peer applications began to erode the fraction of HTTP traffic.

Yet, the World Wide Web is the single largest application that has been studied in depth from the viewpoint of Internet measurement. By the Web, we mean the millions of Web sites, the billions of Web pages (although only a tiny fraction of them are accessed frequently), the large number of Web applications accessed increasingly by a variety of devices ranging from desktop browsers to mobile devices, and the different hardware appliances and software intermediaries that participate in the transaction. The number of users who have access to the Internet and use the Web is around a billion [Int05b] according to estimates in the summer of 2005. This is a close approximation to the number of users who access the Web since many users use the Web for sending and receiving email and even to download resources from peer-to-peer networks.

The concurrent growth of electronic commerce and the dot-com phenomenon, led to external measurement companies offering monitoring and measurement services for the industry. Research efforts played a key role in introducing novel methods of measurement, validating the measurement methodologies of companies offering such services, and in pushing for industry-wide benchmarks. Several commercial services exist to measure access and latency of Web sites and to compare products in specific areas such as caching. The commercial offerings take into account that customers of a Web site are distributed across the Internet and thus their access is affected by numerous factors beyond just the provisioning of Web servers at the Web site.

Similar to the DNS application, we will examine the key properties that are of interest from a measurement perspective in the Web application, the challenges faced during measuring these properties, and the plethora of tools created and used for Web measurements. We will conclude with an examination of the state of the art in Web measurement from the viewpoint of the best results in this area.

Unlike other applications covered in this chapter, an extensive amount of work has taken place in this application; a fact reflected in the more in-depth coverage of this application.

7.3.1   Web Measurement Properties

Although DNS is occasionally visible at the application level, it is an infrastructure-level protocol. It is often hidden from most users and becomes visible only when there are failures. Unlike DNS, the Web is an application that is at the most-visible level for all users of the application. Even when the delay is due to DNS the blame is often placed on the Web site. Thus, a variety of metrics, such as the availability of a Web site or the user-perceived latency in downloading a Web page, are felt directly by end-users and heavily influence the measurement efforts. Some of the properties are decomposable into components at other layers of the protocol stack. For example, Web latency is a result of the sum of latencies that is experienced by the user at different layers: DNS, TCP, HTTP, as well as delays at the Web server and finally rendering at the Web client. The end user experiences the overall delay without being aware of the individual components or their respective contributions to the delay. Measurements at the Web application layer thus have to identify the distinct components and measure each of them separately while examining the overall delay.

The measurement properties of interest at the Web application can be divided into several largely distinct classes. Table 7.4 presents the classes, the actual properties measured, and the primary reason for measuring the property. The classes range from high-level characterization of Web application as fraction of Internet traffic, location of Web entities and how they are configured, user workload models useful for postulating protocol changes in the absence of data, traffic-related issues such as caching, flow of an actual Web transaction from user click to bytes being returned, ambient network conditions impacting the Web, and finally performance issues such as application-to-application data transfer and latency. Some of the properties intersect: performance issues overlap strongly with manner of configuration and caching, for example. One reason to separate them is to bring certain underlying issues into sharper relief from a measurement perspective.

Now we delve into the details of the different entries in Table 7.4.

We begin with the first property class: high-level characterization. As mentioned in Section 7.2.1, measuring the overall fraction of a particular application helps to identify a sudden increase or decrease in popularity of that application. Significant shifts have implications to both that application as well as to other applications. The way to obtain the measure of the fraction of Web traffic on the Internet is to measure the use of HTTP protocol. One way to view Web traffic is restricting it to those inter-actions where users or programs are fetching bytes from Web servers. However, there

Table 7.4 Web properties of interest to measure.

Class	Measured property	Why measured
High-level characterization	Fraction of traffic Number of entities	Examining overall trends
Location	Presence of Web entities	Handling population distribution and mobility
Configuration	Software/hardware configuration	Load handling ability
User workload models	Access pattern	Modeling Web phenomena, shifting user populations
Traffic properties	Caching, flash crowds	Provisioning for regular and abnormal conditions
Application demands	Impact on network	Protocol improvement
Performance	Web components performance	Maintaining site popularity

is considerable traffic that is over the HTTP protocol but the participating clients and servers are peer-to-peer nodes. In other words, HTTP is simply used as a transport-level protocol in these cases, although it is largely an application protocol. In this section, we only examine Web traffic that involves either browser clients or other Web clients (such as crawlers) communicating with a Web server. In later sections we will examine use of HTTP for non-Web traffic.

Again, similar to DNS, knowledge of the entities involved in Web transactions – clients, proxies and other intermediaries, servers – are of interest. Along with overall Web traffic trends, measuring the count and growth of the different Web entities can provide interesting insights into how the Web has evolved and is being used. For example, the number of clients behind a proxy can provide insights on the extent of caching, an important metric in Web performance.

The next property class is location of the entities involved in the Web transaction. Identifying where clients and proxies are present can help content providers move resources closer to them if necessary, to provide better performance. Demographic and location data can aid businesses tailor content, manner of delivery, and consider alternate architectural improvements in placement of services. The location is primarily in a network sense although there has been interest in geographical, i.e., physical location as well. The situation is a bit murky because of the growth of Web farms and data centers where there is consolidation and co-location of multiple servers belonging to different administrative entities for business efficiency.

The third class deals with the different ways in which the numerous entities involved in Web transactions can be configured. Configuration differences between

Web servers have implications for performance as do the type of server software used. Within an administrative entity, the precise manner in which clients and proxies are configured can significantly alter the user's Web experience. The presence of forward and reverse proxies, redirections of requests and responses, the protocol variants supported, and compliance with the protocol specification all have varying degrees of impact on the overall Web experience. Similarly, if the connectivity of clients is known, it can be used by Web servers to deliver alternate and tailored content to improve their experience. Although there has been a steady increase in the connectivity capability of users accessing the Web, there are still multiple classes of users. Many use dial-up while increasing numbers in a few countries have broadband access.

The fourth property class is concerned with workload models. Within a Web site there is considerable interest in how resources are accessed – this helps in reconfiguring the Web site, modifying the resources if needed, and exploring alternatives for delivery of popular resources. At a broader level, user workload models need to incorporate the temporal, spatial, and object-level characteristics on the Web. A variety of properties ranging from sizes of resources to time between user fetches have a heavy-tailed distribution and thus the self-similarity phenomenon is observed with dramatic variations in traffic across numerous timescales. User workload models play a role in constructing models for 'think-time' of users (the time between the downloading of one Web page and the next click) and in modeling novel phenomena such as flash crowds and attacks on Web sites. Data for the newer phenomena are much harder to obtain. Finally, workload models can also help in dealing with new classes of users who use wireless devices or PDAs or for extensions to the base protocol. The next property of interest involves resource and access-level characterization: what is the pattern of resource accesses at a given Web site, how are resource sizes distributed across the Web, etc. – all key to generating the workload model.

Next, we look at the class of properties dealing with traffic issues such as reduction of redundant transfers and sudden surges in traffic. Significant reductions in bandwidth and user-perceived latency can be obtained by eliminating redundant downloads and shortening the distance traversed by the bits of interest. Historically this has been achieved by caching resources closer to users. Although the effectiveness of caches on the Web has largely peaked due to the increasingly dynamic nature of Web traffic and presence of user-customized entities (such as cookies), there are still significant savings in bandwidth and latency. The next property of interest thus continues to have a significant impact on the Web – the cacheability of resources, the deployment and use of caches, and their performance.

The term *flash crowd* in the Web context refers to a situation where a large number of users simultaneously and unexpectedly try to access a Web site. The term was adopted from a 1971 science fiction short story [Niv71], where thousands of people could go back in time to see specific historical events again. These people found that, not too surprisingly, many others chose the same time in history to visit, thus creating a very large crowd suddenly. Popular Webcasts like that of Victoria's Secret company or special events like Olympics cause flash crowds on the Web. Some events are known *a priori*, while events with no advance warning like the September 2001 terrorist attack in the United States can cause flash crowds on news Web sites, and the load causes many sites to become unavailable. Congestion at the network layer causes requests not to be delivered and the turnaround time for a response can lengthen to minutes causing frustration to the users. The Web server may have to be restarted due to the effects of the flash crowd [Lor]. Given the widespread impact of such flash events we need to have a deeper understanding of traffic patterns under such circumstances and how such conditions may be handled.

The next property class is concerned with application demands on the underlying network. The manner in which Web applications create network demands by invoking transport services aids in better understanding of the interaction between the application and transport-level protocols. Improvements in the protocol, reducing the 'time-to-glass' (the time lag between the user clicking on the browser and data from the Web server actually appearing on the screen), are all impacted by this interaction. The actual flow of a Web transaction from the user click to displaying data is another measurable property of interest.

The final and key property class is that of Web performance – a catch-all class that dominates much of the Web measurement work. The popularity of a Web site is often driven by how quickly responses can be obtained by clients worldwide. Even if the content on a Web site is of much interest, there is more than anecdotal evidence that poor performance significantly detracts from the popularity of a Web site. The increase in the number of users who use newer media, such as wireless, has led to concentration on reducing the delivery time of pages. The final property is in some sense the most crucial one from a user's perspective: Web performance. Various measurements have been carried out to uncover the reasons for delay and ways to reduce them. Performance is often the key in e-commerce and other business applications. The sources of slowdowns in application-to-application data transfer and the role played by critical path analysis is examined here.

7.3.2   Web Measurement Challenges

Similar to DNS, there are numerous challenges in carrying out Web measurements. However, given the application-level nature, the dependence on multiple protocols (at least DNS, TCP, and HTTP), the potentially large sets of entities with varying configurations, and the equally diverse user population, the range and complexity of Web measurements is significantly more challenging. We examine the challenges along similar axes as DNS challenges, that of hidden data, hidden layers, and hidden entities.

The extensive set of Web measurements carried out over the last few years have had to deal with all the challenges outlined here. Some measurements narrow their examination in such a way to bypass certain challenges thus limiting their inferences. Other measurement methodologies have proposed novel and clever techniques to overcome some of the challenges. We will examine the techniques in more detail in the state of the art discussion later in Section 7.3.4.

Hidden Data in Web Measurement

The primary difficulty in Web measurements is the size and scope of the World Wide Web. It is well-nigh impossible to carry out global measurements even if all of the Web entities were accessible. In reality, a significant portion of Web traffic is intranet and thus inaccessible to external measurements. Typical measurements are done at a few dozen client sites (if that) and a few server sites. Access to information about remote servers or old server logs are often unavailable. At the server end, information about key properties of clients often has to be reverse engineered or guessed. These include the client's connectivity information, variety of TCP and HTTP configuration options, and browser options. If measurements can only be done at the client or server end, then the impact of the network component will not be reflected. The network component includes significant contributions to different properties of interest such as the network delay, the intermediaries such as proxies (both forward and reverse proxies), or the presence of overlay network in the guise of content distribution network.

Figure 7.5 shows a Web server complex with multiple Web server mirrors (WS1...WS3) receiving connections from clients that vary widely in terms of their access technologies in connecting to the Internet. Requests from clients 1...4 are routed through a proxy. Although the proxy has a cable modem connection to the Internet, clients 1 and 2 are using dialup links. Client 9 has a DSL connection and client 5 has a higher-speed T-1 connection. Client 10 connects to the Web server complex over a wireless link. The Web server complex has to handle the requests from clients of such diverse access potential. It may seek to distinguish between them if it wants to provide a different level of service for its different client classes.

Earlier in Chapter 4 (Section 4.1), we discussed the problem of ensuring representativeness of entities being measured. This is especially difficult in the Web application where there are millions of Web clients. For example, in Figure 7.5 there is no easy way for the Web server to know that there is a mix of dialup clients and cable modem clients behind the proxy that is communicating directly with the Web server. Wireless users and other mobile clients complicate matters further. Demo-

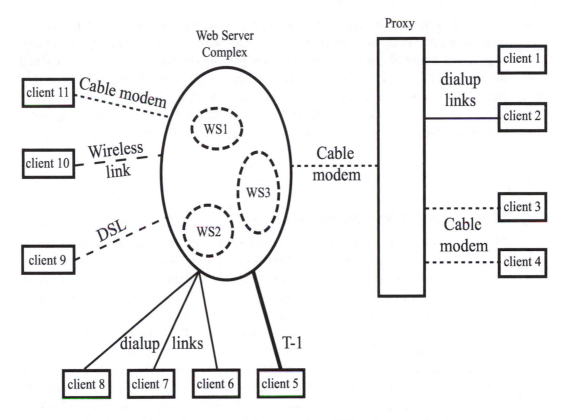

Figure 7.5 Clients with varying connectivity accessing a Web server complex.

graphic information about number of clients using different access technologies has to be constantly updated. Unlike client information, since a small fraction of the Web sites are accessed often and only a few resources on a given site are accessed frequently, it is possible to come up with a cross-section of Web sites and resources.

The rate of change of content on the Web can have implications on measurements for a variety of applications such as searching, caching (especially, staleness of cached information), etc. New pages are constantly added, old ones are modified or removed. The links between pages both on an intra-site basis or inter-site basis may also change regularly. Individual Web sites do not have a digest of changes that may have happened deep within their site. Additionally, the meta-properties of pages such as object sizes and content types themselves might change. Access information of Web pages: their popularity, frequency of access, etc. are not made available. The input to CGI scripts, popular search terms, and other form input data is not visible externally. While there are legitimate privacy and security reasons for such decisions, sample information can be quite helpful in aiding measurement.

At the lower level the specifics of the TCP parameters at the Web site can have significant impact on the performance. While some aspects of the setup can be reverse engineered, most of the TCP configuration parameters are not readily ascertained remotely. Tools like TBIT (TCP Behavior Identification Tool [PF01]) have been created to distinguish between the different variants of TCP which might aid in testing impact on Web performance due to TCP variants like Reno, Tahoe, or Vegas. Chapter 8 of [KR01] goes into details on the interaction between HTTP and TCP.

Hidden Layers in Web Measurement

Measuring in the Web has often ended up measuring server overhead rather than protocol and network overheads. This is both due to the relative ease with which server overhead can be measured remotely and the typical stability of the measurement. The network overhead measurement requires both deep knowledge of the individual network protocol as well as an understanding of the precise interactions between the different protocol layers. A combined examination of TCP options and behavior of packets in flight between an HTTP client and server during conditions of network change is considerably more complicated than directly measuring server overhead in responding to a specific request. The server overhead can be trivially measured locally where all the necessary information is under experimental control. Popular Web servers are fairly well tuned to narrow variance in response time at the server level, given that they have complete control for provisioning computing cycles. However, no one has control over the particular network path taken by the request and response.

A Web server may not know the number of different end-clients it is interacting with since many clients may be behind proxies. Likewise, a client's request may be redirected at different layers of the protocol to different servers in a manner that cannot always be traced. The redirections can happen at DNS, TCP, or HTTP level. Overlay networks complicate even the basic assumption of path stability. Redirection may even be carried out at lower levels of the protocol stack via hardware such as switches. Each redirection, be it at the DNS layer or HTTP layer, introduces another level of measurement variability.

As can be seen in Figure 7.6, a client's request for index.html is satisfied by multiple servers: content distribution network nodes CDN1 and CDN2, advertisement servers (Ad Server1, etc.) with just the text portion of the file being supplied by the Web server. The location of the CDN or advertisement server that delivers the figure *foo1.jpg* or the advertisement *ad1* may be dynamically located based on a DNS lookup and the load in the set of CDN mirrors. A measurement of latency for example has to take into account this hidden layer.

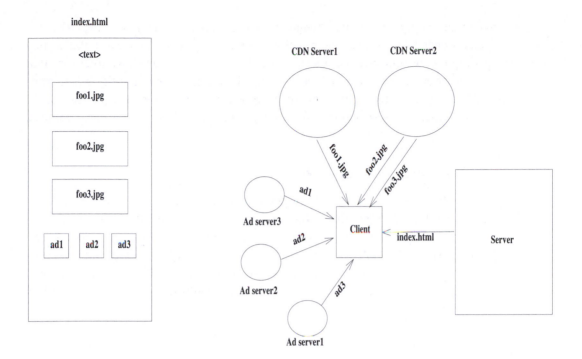

Figure 7.6 Multiple servers and layers involved in fetching a resource.

Hidden Entities in Web Measurement

In the course of examining challenges thus far, we have mentioned several entities that may not be directly visible to the measurement. These include interception devices at different layers of the protocol stack, HTTP or TCP-level redirectors, and intermediaries such as proxies. Each of these hidden entities can present different challenges to measurement. There could be overestimation or underestimation of response times if the response is not being received from the object node being measured. If the traffic to the measured node is redirected to other nodes based on the current network or server load characteristics, then there would be variance in the results as measurements are repeated over time and each time a potentially different actual node is contacted. The hidden entity can be present at the edge of a Web server farm intercepting all packets between the clients and the server. Switches may examine the TCP SYN packet to decide if redirection is warranted. Since the behavior of a switch varies based on the incoming traffic being Web-related or not, measurements performed at non-Web layers may yield a different result than ones done using application-level tools such as *httperf*. Examining the client side, interception proxies placed close to clients may play a role in skewing results. Often interception proxies are transparent to the clients and low-level packet interceptors may redirect traffic towards an interception proxy which may then return results from an associated cache. Responses cached at or near interception proxies may lead clients to believe they are getting the current version of a resource. Measurements thus have to ensure that requests are reaching the intended destination. The lack of predictability due to multiple hidden entities at various layers of the protocol stack and the precise manner in which combinations of such interactions might take place complicates measurement.

7.3.3 Web Measurement Tools

Several Web measurement tools have been created in the years in which the Web was the most dominant fraction of Internet traffic. We examine them along the axes that we divided Web properties of interest. This section is not an exhaustive catalog of Web measurement tools; our intent is to give a flavor of some well-known measurement tools. Later in the state of the art section (Section 7.3.4) we will see how these tools have been used to present snapshots of results of the different properties handled by the tools.

Web Characterization Tools

Web characterization was one of the early areas of research as the Web grew. The Web has been constantly studied since its inception. The Web's contribution to Internet traffic steadily increased from 1992 onwards until the early part of the 21st century when peer-to-peer traffic began taking the lead in terms of number of bytes. In terms of number of active users, the number of requests issued and responses received, the Web still remains the number one application on the Internet. The number of users on the Internet, a vast majority of whom use the Web is fast approaching a billion [Int05a].

Sampling traffic in a few key parts of the Internet can give an estimate of the fraction of the traffic that is related to Web. Simple techniques such as examining traffic to the HTTP port (default 80) in *netflow* records or packet monitors allow an ISP to judge the fraction of incoming and outgoing Web traffic. A secondary way of measuring is examining DNS traces to see what IP addresses are looked up – well-known Web servers are likely to be high on the list. At another extreme, one indication is demand to a particular service that can consume a significant part of bandwidth to an administrative entity. The sudden popularity of a particular Web site can impact other services offered within the same network. The amount of resources provisioned at a site for a service is thus another indication. Continual measurements are carried out along all these lines to obtain estimates of Web traffic.

From a Web site's point of view, it is easy to get an accurate count of the number of requests and thus unique clients that access its resources. Most of this information is routinely logged in Web server logs in widely understood uniform formats (such as Common Log Format, discussed in [KR01], Chapter 9). A variety of Web log analyzers have been built to generate the necessary statistics. Some data is obscured due to the presence of proxies and other intermediaries, as well as due to the impact of caching. Although hundreds of clients may be behind a proxy, the Web site's log may have just a single IP address – that of the proxy, to identify them. However, there have been tools and techniques that can help identify proxies and thus separate them for purposes of analysis. These tools take into account the inter-arrival time of requests from individual IP addresses, the range and diversity of resources requested especially when compared with other clients that are known not to be proxies. Proxies are just one example of an artifact that leads to blurring of data at a Web server. Anonymizers in the path may obscure the client originating the request for privacy reasons. If the client's request is satisfied at a cache near the client's site, then the request would often never make it to the Web server. If the client or the cache uses an `If-Modified-Since` request modifier, and the resource has not changed since the specified time, the Web server would return a `304 Not Modified` but the request would still be logged. Other atypical clients, such as crawlers and spiders, have to be identified as such so as not to overwhelm analysis, since they make a disproportionate number of requests from one of a few IP addresses. Although well-behaved crawlers tend to identify themselves in the `User-Agent` field and obey conventions specified in `robots.txt`, there are clients that do not follow such proper etiquette. Generally speaking, it is easier to identify spiders than proxies given the disproportionately large number of requests made by them and a more regular access pattern.

Estimating the number of Web servers accessible on the Internet has been carried out via surveys (such as Netcraft) and direct measurements. Surveys, probe-based measurements, or measuring via toolbars downloaded onto browsers, all present estimates of popularity. While the total number may just be of overall statistical interest, the number and identity of the small fraction of the millions of Web servers that are actually popular is an important metric. Popularity measures have business, technical, and social implications. From a business point of view, advertising rates are set based on the 'number of eye-balls' that visit a site or unique pageviews in a given time period. From a technical point of view, the fact that there are a few popular Web sites overall, has led to innovations in different areas: improving availability of these sites under heavy load, creation of overlay networks to reduce the load on the busy servers at these sites, new architectures for designing and deploying the Web servers. Additionally, concentrated load at a few sites has led to work in redirecting traffic at various layers of the protocol stack: DNS, TCP, and HTTP. From the social point of view, the few well-known Web sites wield disproportionate influence in different spheres of life: be they search sites, news sites, or e-commerce sites. Such visibility has even led to focused attacks on the sites.

Locating the Web entities is an increasingly difficult problem and the various tools created go only half way in solving the problem. Compared to clients, there is an expectation that Web sites will be in a single location. But the advent of CDNs and the large number of resources maintained on popular Web sites has led to distribution of a site's resources geographically. Separately, sites may be mirrored to increase availability and to be 'closer' to client populations. The inverse is also true: a variety of Web sites are virtually hosted at a single location in Web-farms by a large provider. Tools for locating clients range from traditional `traceroute` to more sophisticated techniques such as network aware clustering [KW00].

As the Web grew exponentially different attempts were made to provide a structural view of the static Web based on the linkage structure. The identification of hubs and authorities in the Web via the HITS algorithm [Kle98] led to a deeper understanding of the nature of connections between different Web pages. A hub is a page that has multiple high-value links about a topic and an authority page is one that has high-quality content on a given topic. The HITS algorithm first samples pages to gather authorities then uses a weight-propagation step to iteratively obtain estimates of scores of hubs and authorities. Most of the links at this stage of the Web were created by human users and were not inserted automatically. Web pages were seen as nodes in a graph with the link between them as edges. Pages that had a significant number of incoming links were viewed as authorities on the topic covered in that page. For example, there may be numerous links to popular Web sites like `http://www.nytimes.com`. The biggest payoff from this kind of analysis was in improving Web searching. The work done later in ranking pages closely followed such analysis.

Graph modeling allowed researchers to come up with a macro-level view of the global collection of Web pages. Three distinct chunks of the Web were identified based on the static links. It is important to note that this analysis examined all links between Web pages regardless of whether the links were ever traversed. The generality and simplicity of the graph model allowed for natural modeling of the Web structure at a high level. The work in modeling went hand in hand with the crawling and search index generation tools. The graph modeling hinted at portions of the Web that changed often as well as portions of the Web that were more popular in terms of link structure.

The impact of caching has been studied due to the considerable potential of reducing the number of redundant bytes sent over the net and to lower the user-perceived latency. Quick examination of the HTTP response code `304 Not Modified` gives a lower bound on the amount of caching as this response code is generated in response to a `GET If-Modified-Since` request by a client which has some version of the resource in its cache.

Web Searching and Crawling

One of the most popular applications on the World Wide Web has been searching. Long before the popularity of AltaVista and the subsequent popularity of search engines like Google, HotBot, Teoma, and Yahoo!, searching was one of the prime applications even during the inception of the Web. Thus it is not surprising that searching has become a key application on the Web and several tools to improve searching and information retrieval in general have been constructed. Web search has three broad components: a *crawler* that traverses the accessible part of the Web to fetch Web pages to be indexed, an *indexer* that constructs a merged reverse index of the crawled pages, and a search tool that accepts queries from users and returns pointers to the pages matching the search terms.

Broadly a complete crawl of the Web can be done by periodically replacing the set of pages each time or via an incremental crawl that updates portions of the collection. The choice is based on the rapidity with which the crawler can complete the traversal of the Web and the rate of change of pages on the crawled sites. Additionally a focused crawl can simply fetch only a limited set of pages without going beyond the chosen set of Web sites.

Given the scale of the Web and the billions of pages to be fetched from tens of millions of Web sites, characterization of the sites and pages seeded much of the crawling work. Architectures for crawling the Web need to be tested on substantial subsets of the Web. Most crawlers begin with a seed collection of pages that have enough links and carry out breadth-first and/or depth-first traversals of the pages. One example of a good seed page is the Yahoo! home page. Popular crawlers use a cluster of workstations, each with multiple threads connecting to as many different Web sites as possible.

Industrial-strength crawlers also require considerable bandwidth and high-speed connectivity. Large-scale search engines such as Teoma, Yahoo!, MSN, Google, etc. use between hundreds to thousands of PCs each equipped with a large RAM and access to a significant amount of shared disk space.

Often crawlers may also limit the number of pages fetched from a Web site or a server, the frequency with which it visits a site, and the amount of time it spends at a site in order not to overload it with requests. Additionally, well-behaved crawlers obey certain rules. These include honoring Do-Not-Follow links on HTML pages indicating that links within that page are not to be fetched. Likewise, `robots.txt` file indicates on a site-wide basis what pages and trees should not be fetched for indexing purposes. Well-behaved crawlers also identify themselves in the `User-Agent` field so that sites can monitor their behavior. Pages can also be directly supplied by individual Web sites to search engines, although this is fairly tedious and error-prone.

Depending on the goal of the crawl, some crawlers only fetch Web pages that are HTML (often based on the content type) and ignore images and other content types. If the crawler is planning to index the pages for searching purposes this might suffice. If the crawler is intended to study the rate at which Web pages change, then it may be necessary to fetch all pages. Currently, HTML pages are less than a quarter of all Web resources. Crawlers may simply choose to obtain Web pages that are accessible over HTTP, ignoring other protocols such as FTP or HTTPS. Resources fetched over HTTPS are generally sensitive, not meant for everyone, and might require passwords not available to crawlers.

The diameter of a crawl is defined as the time it takes a crawler to obtain a complete (or as nearly complete as possible) copy of the accessible portion of the Web. Typically, this requires two weeks of constant fetching. The delay in crawling stems from a variety of factors: connecting to the remote Web site and fetching the HTML page (TCP and HTTP delays), waiting for such connections to be scheduled on the remote site, parsing the page so as to continue the process in a depth- or breadth-first fashion after allowing for good behavior time out between fetches from the same site. The pause between fetches may be based on the delay on a particular site thus respecting the load on the site. The response code from the Web site may cause additional delays: some crawlers prefer not to follow HTTP redirections (3xx level response codes), some will abort a site if they received multiple 4xx or 5xx level error codes. Since there is a certain degree of duplication of Web pages and sites, it may not make sense to fetch the same or nearly-identical content multiple times. Thus, techniques that examine similarity of sites may be used before blindly continuing with the crawl. For example, when a link changes on a page it is often expected that the text surrounding the link may also change. All of these are examples of semantics-driven decision making that govern crawling. Results from crawling, as we will see in the state of the art section, may show interesting dispersions based on the top-level domain of the Web sites or their page sizes.

Web Performance Measurement Tools

The single largest collection of measurement tools in the Web arena has been in the aid of tracking Web performance. Web performance measurements resulted in improvements to the HTTP protocol, development of caching appliances, and later the introduction of Content Distribution Networks. Numerous tools were created by researchers and commercial organizations to measure Web performance. The tools can be broadly categorized into a few areas:

1. Ongoing measurement of a particular Web site's service in terms of availability and latency from diverse user viewpoints. By identifying clients' connectivity classes, a site may be able to create and deliver tailored content or alter the manner of delivering content to the users in the various classes.

2. Local tailored measurements carried out by examining individual latency components with suggestions for improvements. Tools in this category examine TCP stack differences, HTTP protocol differences, and the impact of DNS and Content Distribution Networks.

3. Global measurements to examine protocol compliance and ensure reductions of outage due to sudden surges.

A variety of companies offer Web performance measurement tools. They include Keynote [Keya], Akamai [Aka], eValid Test Suite [Eva], and Gomez [Gom]. Keynote and its affiliated services (such as Internet health report [Intc] and Netmechanic [Netd]) perform various performance measurements using a distributed infrastructure. Several smaller companies offer a narrower set of services. A common technique is to have a distributed set of monitors around the world, and monitoring customer Web sites by sending periodic requests to selected pages within a site to ensure availability and at the same time measuring latency. Often the difficulty is in ensuring that the monitoring sites are able to approximate the locations of the actual clients of the customer's Web site. For example, if a significant fraction of the clients of a Web site are located in Southern Europe, checking latency by monitoring clients located in North America may not be useful. Since the location of the monitoring clients is often known, it is not surprising that some Web sites game the system by providing a different (higher) quality of service to requests from such monitoring clients to be perceived as a better provisioned site. The actual user experience of a site may differ due to responses being cached or routed through intermediaries, such as proxies, etc. Remote probing entities cannot always capture such variations. The newer systems allow peers to join and report on performance such as Gomez [Gom]. There are also standalone systems (e.g., eValid [Eva]) that provide Web site capacity performance analysis.

Companies also have products to check protocol compliance (e.g., Co-Advisor [COA]).

Role of Network-aware Clustering

A common refrain in network measurements is to obtain summary information about a set of IP addresses. If a set of IP addresses are topologically close to each other, it would be useful to refer to them collectively. Network-aware clustering [KW00] has been shown to be an effective technique to group IP addresses that are close topologically and under some common administrative control. Grouping IPv4 addresses that share the same first 24 bits turns out to be ineffective. The technique that has been empirically shown to be effective with a high degree of accuracy uses BGP routing table snapshots and performs longest prefix matching on the IP addresses. Addresses that belong to the same prefix are considered to be in the same cluster. This basic idea has been used in numerous networking applications where IP addresses need to be automatically and quickly grouped. Applications abound in DNS, Web, and P2P contexts. In the Web context this has been used to group client IP addresses found in Web server logs. Proxies and spiders can be more readily recognized, and content access can be better predicted allowing content distribution networks to move appropriate content closer to a set of users.

Figure 7.7 shows how proxies and spiders can be easily distinguished from normal clients by examining the arrival rate of requests. Figure 7.7(c) shows the arrival pattern of requests from a spider which contrasts sharply with that of the request patterns of requests from the overall set of clients shown in Figure 7.7(a). Comparing the access pattern of requests from a proxy shown in Figure 7.7(b) and that of the entire log shows that the spike observed in the proxy access pattern matches the daily spike in the access pattern of the full log. In the state of the art section next, we will see how network-aware clustering has been used in several other Web applications.

Tools for Handling Mobile Clients

The number of mobile Web clients has continued to grow. There is a significant difference in the nature of Web content accessed by mobile clients – often limited to smaller Web pages like stock quotes, database queries for telephone information or online travel sites. The access technologies used include wireless laptops, PDAs that download content and allow users to browse the content offline later, etc. Many users subscribe to notification services that trigger based on registered interest and send requested information via email or through wireless notifications to cell phones and pagers. Partly this is a change in the paradigm of gathering information: being notified instead of periodically polling. However, it is also due to the access delays in wireless networks and the lack of content that can be easily displayed in the smaller screens inherent in such technologies. The latter problem has been increasingly addressed: there is a growing amount of Web content that is tailored for mobile clients. Cell phones are capable of displaying stripped down versions of XHTML and have browsers that can alter media-rich content so that it can be displayed in the small windows of cell phones.

Specialized intermediaries [SP02] have been proposed to customize the stream of flow to mobile clients. Examples of software modules that can be dynamically inserted into the flow range from mechanisms to reduce image sizes or an image filter

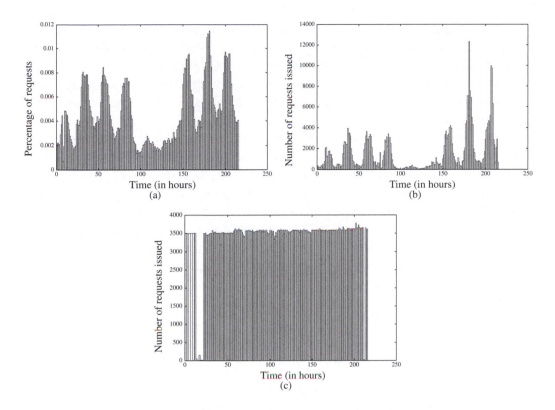

Figure 7.7   Time-series of counts of the requests in a server log: (a) the entire server log; (b) client cluster with a proxy; (c) client cluster with a spider. From [KW00].

that adapts itself to the available wireless bandwidth and aims for a uniform transfer time. Adaptation is done via piggybacking the measured transfer time over a new HTTP header which helps in computing the most recent available bandwidth and ascertains the degree of compression needed. Even a proxy server can be inserted into the path to intercept the request and deliver responses tailored to the wireless device. The proxy can be a single component or a chain of service objects that adapt to changes in the wireless environment. Alternate approaches involve modifying the content. For example, a larger page is converted into a smaller one with a high-level overview and a way to zoom into the sub-pages on demand. Fractal summarization models [YW03] have also been proposed to create a brief skeleton first and a subsequent semantically deeper view created on sections of the page on demand. In a thin-client approach, the browser can run on remote tailored servers that have better (wired) connection to the Internet and send display updates to the mobile client.

The mechanisms used to study mobile clients are similar to that of regular clients. They include examining accesses via server logs of mobile content as well as subscription and notification logs, carrying out lab experiments and wide-area experiments. Lab experiments can include testing against a set of popular Web pages on modified browsers or using a benchmark and network emulators.

Tailored benchmarks, such as the i-Branch benchmark [IBe], have been created with both text and graphics-laden Web pages. Packet losses are induced to study the system under various conditions.

Smaller-scale studies such as all wireless accesses during a technical conference [BVBR02] lasting 3 days, a 3-month long study [TB00] of 74 users, and a medium-scale study [BC03] involving several hundred corporate users have been carried out. The last study used a 5-minute SNMP poling trace over a 29-day period. A wider area experiment (explained in more detail in the state of the art section) involved a campus-wide wireless access network that has been studied in depth for multiple weeks 2 years apart. The study examined several thousand users and required significant equipment set-up at considerable cost.

7.3.4   State of the Art

Although the state of the art in the Web is changing, there is some stability in techniques used for measurement. We examine the state of the art in four parts:

1. Web properties including high-level characterization.
2. Traffic data gathering and analysis, and software tools.
3. Performance issues (CDNs, client connectivity, compliance).
4. Applications (searching, flash crowds, blogs).

Web Properties

Web properties are examined in a few categories: high-level characterization of the entities, the location of entities, how they are configured, creating user workload models, a perspective on Web traffic, and the access dynamics of Web sites.

High-level Characterization.   The number of Web sites is in the tens of millions and the number of Web pages number several hundreds of billions according to different estimates [Deeb]. Popular search engines index billions of Web pages that do not take into account the inaccessible portion of the Web inside organizations not traversable by spiders. Estimates of intra-net Web traffic are not widely available, but general trends indicate that such Web traffic is at least 25% of the traffic in backbones.

There are two broad reasons for reductions in global Web traffic estimates. Due to attacks on the Internet, a significant fraction of corporate administrators have erected firewalls and other administrative barriers such as password-protected sites. Information that used to be in private files accessible to even authenticated users only with the involvement of human administrative intermediaries has steadily become available on *internal* Web sites. Such information is necessarily outside the reach of external search engines' crawlers and spiders. The second, and more important reason is the shift in application traffic away from the Web towards P2P and now slowly towards networked games. In smaller studies, such as those restricted to wireless users on a campus (discussed later in this section), it has been seen that there is a significant fall off in Web traffic as compared to P2P.

Beyond the number of users drawn to P2P, the volume of traffic is much larger thanks to the popularity of large content exchanged on such networks. With the increase in networked games activity (discussed in Section 7.5) there will be a further migration of users. However, newer users who join the Internet in the developing countries and those with limited bandwidth capacity are likely to continue to use the Web. The number of users is in the hundreds of millions. The number of client machines has also grown due to the increase in laptops, PDAs, and other wireless devices used to connect to the Web.

There have not been widespread studies of number of intermediaries such as proxies and gateways, but the task has been complicated by transparent intermediaries and other hardware devices that do not play the traditional role of a proxy and identify themselves as an active and visible participant in Web traffic. Even the definition of a proxy has been stretched due to the role played by Content Distribution Networks which explicitly serve as originators of specific portions of Web content of busy Web sites. While CDNs are not proxies in the traditional sense of being in the path of receiving requests and sending responses back, they act as forward caches for many Web sites and offload traffic from busy Web servers. Tens of thousands of Web sites use the services of CDNs delivering a significant fraction of static objects and in some cases streaming media as well. In traditional proxies, there can be significant differences in terms of the number of clients served by them or the volume of traffic seen emanating from them. Unless there is a way to tailor each user's request with cookies or other personalized information, it is impossible to estimate the precise number of clients behind a proxy.

Monthly surveys by sites like Netcraft [Netb] have shown increases of around a million new Web sites a month. Estimates in fall of 2004 showed around 60 million Web sites on the Internet. However, a vast fraction of them had little or no traffic as compared to the top few hundreds. The surveys have also shown that Apache and Microsoft server implementations together have 90% of the market, with Apache having close to 68%. The percentages have remained fairly constant.

Location of Web Entities. A steadily growing fraction of users are in heavily populated Asian countries such as China and India. The increase is both due to the high population and the increasing improvement in Internet infrastructure and consequent accessibility. With populous African countries on the verge of joining the Web revolution there will be a further shift away from traditionally represented countries in Web traffic. Already the fraction of Web content in English is beginning to fall. The shift in client populations has implications on where servers will be mirrored and the set of languages supported. Multinational bank Web sites for example, already support multiple languages.

The three broad category of users are in homes, educational institutions, and in corporate sites. There is however a small but steadily growing set of mobile users: either accessing over wireless links or through cybercafes and similar setups. The Web's role as a key portal for daily social interactions such as email, instant messaging, and as a source of information, has been responsible for bringing a much broader demographic into the set of Web clients beyond students, scientists, and academics.

Configuration Issues. Popular and busy Web servers use a variety of configuration mechanisms to ensure that their clients are able to access their resources quickly. Content distribution techniques basically involve moving some or all of the resources of a site closer to the users. Within a Web server complex, numerous techniques can be used to reduce the latency experienced by a client. Web server farms have often used reverse proxies and other server accelerator mechanisms that can redirect incoming requests to the least loaded server within the farm. By caching some frequently requested resources at the reverse proxy (closer to the origin server), latency can be reduced. Numerous popular Web sites use such techniques; notable among them are sites carrying popular events such as Olympics and World Cup soccer. For example, the 1998 World Cup soccer Web site `www.france98.com` was hosted [AJ99] on a set of four servers, three in the USA and one in Paris, France, where the World Cup was held. A Cisco product, Distributed Director [Del97], forwarded requests from clients to sites that were topologically closer. Internal load balancing was done on each site among the collection of servers.

User Workload Models. The characteristics of interest of resources that have been studied closely over the years include the content types, size, rate of change, popularity, number of embedded objects in a Web page, and whether a resource is dynamically generated or not. From the viewpoint of connections the characteristics include the duration of HTTP connections, request and response sizes, unique number of IP addresses contacting a given Web site, number of distinct sites accessed by a client population, number and frequency of accesses of individual resources at a given Web site, distribution of request methods and response codes.

Traffic Perspective: Caching. A large number of cache-related appliances and devices have been available for several years. Cache appliances operate at different layers of the protocol stack: from network and transport layer all the way to the application layer. A redirector device, typically located at the edge of the ISP's network, can intercept request traffic and decide if the response can be delivered from a cache. Such a transparent way of providing caching eliminates any need for configuration by the clients. A more comprehensive discussion of different cache hardware can be found in [KR01] (Chapter 11). Layer-3 or layer-4 switches are capable of looking at more detail of the incoming packets (such as port numbers) before deciding on request redirection.

Over the years the hit rates for Web caches have steadily declined [BBBC99] even with large cache sizes, especially when compared to processor memories. The various reasons for this include the first fetch miss, the dramatic increase in uncacheable objects including dynamic resources and presence of user-tailored entities like cookies. Traditional cache companies like Network Appliance [Neta], Foundry Networks [Fou], Cisco, and Nortel (which sells the former Alteon appliance) are still selling a range of products. With the overall reduction in cache hit rates, most companies have moved towards products that bundle caching with other activities. Such activities include blocking unwanted traffic filtering packets, or handling application-specific data, such as databases. The companies that have products in this space include NetScaler [Netg], Redline Networks [Red], and Expand [Exp].

Content/Access Dynamics of Web Sites. In exploring access patterns of Web sites, spatial and temporal locality play a key role. It has been long known that out of the tens of millions of Web sites, a few sites are disproportionately popular and a few resources in a site receive most of the accesses. Zipf's law – probability of a request to the ith most popular page is proportional to $1/i$ – has been found to be true in numerous fields. In the case of Web page access, it has been experimentally verified to follow a Zipf-like distribution [BCF$^+$99]. The relative probability that a Web page would be requested is proportional to its popularity. The kth most popular page will be requested with probability $1/k^x$ for some value of $x < 1$ although it would vary with the site. The access probability has significant impact on design of Web caches and in fact several studies have shown that hit rates do not continue to grow at the same rate as increase in cache size.

Web Traffic Data Gathering and Analysis

In order to examine properties on the Web, measurements on a large scale have to be carried out about numerous Web sites from multiple locations. Such measurements may have to be done repeatedly given the changes in the Web and depending on the property being measured. If temporal characteristics are studied then the experiments have to be repeated at different times of the day without being biased by the geographical location of the entities involved in the study. Software and hardware platforms are needed for gathering data and for subsequent analysis. The role of software is generally not well understood or appreciated by the consumers of results of Internet measurement studies. Later in Chapter 10 we will examine a couple of measurement platforms (NIMI and PlanetLab) that are playing a role in measurement in general.

The sources of Web traffic data are at or near the entities involved in Web transactions. Clients, proxies, servers, and intermediate points in the network are all places where data can be gathered. Each of them poses a different set of challenges: at the client end the experiment can be local and thus under the complete control of the measurer. As one moves away from the client, control reduces and uncertainties increase. With remote clients used for measurements, experiments have to be scheduled and monitored. If the platform is shared among many, interference can be a problem. Scheduled experiments may not complete and may fail in different ways. The resulting analysis should take all this into account.

Critical Path Analysis.   Web transactions involve complex data transfers between client and server. To understand where delays are introduced in Web requests, one can apply *critical path analysis*. By constructing and profiling the critical path, it is possible to determine what fraction of total transfer latency of a Web request is due to packet propagation, network variation (*e.g.,* queuing at routers or route fluctuation), packet losses, and delays at the server and at the client.

The central observation of critical path analysis as applied to distributed systems is that only *some* of the component activities in a distributed application are responsible for the overall response time; many other activities may occur in parallel, so that their executions overlap each other, and as a result do not affect overall response time. In other words, reducing the execution time of any of the activities on the critical path will certainly reduce overall response time, while this is not necessarily true for activities off the critical path.

Properly constructing the critical path depends on the details of the TCP implementation being used. Methods and tools for constructing the critical path for TCP Reno are described in [BC01].

Software Aid for Measurement.   Data can be gathered passively or actively. It can be analyzed offline or online. Most Web measurements have tended to do offline analysis independent of how the data was actually gathered. Online analysis is needed only to test the feasibility of deploying modifications. Passive analysis does not have a serious constraint on volume of data to be analyzed or resources needed to process the data. More importantly the data can be transformed into other formats that lend themselves to more sophisticated analysis.

httperf: httperf [MJ98b] is a widely used tool that functions as much more than a simple Web client. *httperf* can send HTTP requests, monitoring the time spent in different stages, and parse the responses received. The tool has three logical components. The first component is an HTTP engine that accepts a variety of arguments and sends suitably tailored HTTP requests and handles incoming HTTP responses. For example, the options can add a variety of HTTP request headers, specifying requested ranges, etc. The second component is a workload generator that is capable of generating a stream of HTTP requests while the third component gathers statistics on the exchanges. Unlike many other tools, *httperf* has long been able to support the HTTP/1.1 version of the protocol and is thus an indispensable part of experiments involving persistent connections, pipelining, range requests, entity tags, and other new features of HTTP only available in HTTP/1.1. The entire package is available freely in source code allowing additional modifications to suit the needs of a specific project.

Among the other popular tools to fetch Web pages are numerous scripts and short C programs that emulate a HTTP GET request, and often HEAD and POST as well. An interesting addition to this collection is *wget* [Wge] which is capable of fetching a large collection of pages rooted at a particular node. An early proposal in improving HTTP had suggested a `MGET` method to fetch multiple pages on the same TCP connection. The list of pages is specified as a URI list within the MGET request; HTTP request modifiers (such as `If-Modified-Since`, could be associated optionally and separately with each of the specified URIs. Wget goes further by accepting a level as an argument and recursively fetching all pages up to that level. However, no tailoring of the request is possible. Unless used judiciously this can be a severe load on a remote Web site. Wget has been used to fetch sample content of Web page collections in different research projects.

Moving from requesting one or a handful of pages to entire collections of Web sites we examine personalized crawlers. While crawlers have been traditionally used only by search engines, personalized crawlers can be used for obtaining snapshots of small portions of the Web. The Mercator [HN99, NH01] personalized crawler is an example of an incremental crawler; we will discuss large-scale crawlers later in this section. Crawlers take seed pages to start their crawls by doing a depth-first or breadth-first approach; Mercator uses a breadth-first traversal strategy and gives higher weight to pages that have more incoming links. Among the interesting options available in Mercator are its ability to ignore HTTP redirections or to download the pages in the seed set without following any links. In this sense, it acts as `MGET` with a long list of pages to be fetched. The crawler is also able to include a variety of request headers and is even able to track cookie information.

Examining Mobile Users. Until now we have examined traditional clients accessing Web sites but with the increasing number of mobile users and servers designed to handle such users, we next examine the set of issues regarding mobile users.

A detailed study [ABQ02] (with an extended version in [ABQ04]) was carried out over a 12-day period in 2000 from over 33 million requests of over 50000 users who used wireless connections and PDAs. Many had signed up to receive notifications on changes in content: stock value, weather, etc. The top 1% of notification objects were responsible for around 60% of all messages. The most popular notification content categories were weather, news, stock quotes, and email. Not too surprisingly there was geographical locality seen in the interest for notification messages. Wireless users had more interest in weather than those browsing information offline. Like typical Web accesses, notification messages also had a Zipf-like distribution with α between 1.1 and 1.3. However, the popularity of documents was *not* Zipf-like: there was extreme locality of reference with less than 0.5% of URLs requested more than 90% of the time. The set of URLs that were popular was stable, making such documents ideal candidates for caching especially if they do not change often. The most popular pages that transcended geographical locations were the entry pages for popular applications such as the login page of email, and some highly popular stock quotes.

A more recent study [HKA04] of 7000 users over a 17-week period in the Fall of 2003 and Winter 2004 was carried out in Dartmouth College in New Hamphsire. This study was a follow-up to an earlier study [KE02] done 2 years earlier. The studies gathered SNMP data by polling each of the over 550 wireless access points every 5 minutes and recording volume of incoming and outgoing traffic as well as *tcpdump* trace of all packets. Each access point had also been configured to send syslog messages which had a 1-second timestamp resolution, to a central data gathering point. For the later study VOIP call detail records were also gathered.

There was a three-fold increase in the average daily traffic per active wireless card between the two studies. The more recent study showed a significant decline in Web traffic offset by a corresponding increase in P2P and filesystem-related traffic. Web traffic declined by over half while P2P and filesystem traffic (which included NetBIOS, NFS, SMB, etc.) quadrupled. Another manifestation of the traffic shift was seen in the examination of traffic destinations: Web traffic in 2002 dominated indicating that most of the inbound traffic was from remote Web sites. In the later study, the surge in local P2P traffic (almost three quarters of P2P traffic was intra-campus) resulted in a significant drop in incoming Web traffic.

Web Performance

User-perceived latency remains the key measure of Web performance for any given Web site as there is a strong correlation to how long users would stay at a Web site and the frequency with which they return to the site. Reducing the delay between the browser click and the delivery and display of the resource on the user's screen (the so-called 'time to glass') has been the active focus of many research projects and corresponding measurements efforts. Web sites that have a critical need to retain users beyond the first page have a strong motivation to deliver the content quickly to the user.

Studies have been carried out to examine the impact of the underlying network conditions on the user's Web experience. Bandwidth and latency are the key factors examined in one study [KH02] that passively gathered data for a day and used a semantic traffic analyzer to reconstruct HTTP exchanges. The study looked for user cancellations (aborting a download or a reload) as an indicator of dissatisfaction. Beyond a certain delay the rate of cancellations increased significantly. One conclusion of the study was that performance needs to be improved to a certain degree to significantly reduce cancellation rate. In effect, a marginal rate of return in improvement of user experience is computed. The effective bandwidth is equally important: the higher the bit rate of delivery the lower the cancellation rate. The behavior of the server due to impact of lower layers of the protocol stack has also been examined. A tool (TBIT [PF01]) was created to identify the TCP variant on a remote Web server.

CDN: Content Distribution Networks. A key area of growth in the Web application in the late 1990s was that of content distribution networks. The increasing popularity of a small number of Web sites and the large number of small objects repeatedly requested led to the outsourcing to intermediaries of work traditionally done by Web servers. Instead of creating a separate intermediary for each site, CDNs offered a service to offload work from a number of busy Web sites. The managing of largely static content (later, delivery of dynamic resources were also handled) on behalf of the customer Web sites involved creating replicas of these resources in numerous CDN mirror sites, tracking where the clients were, and delivering the resource from a mirror that was 'close' to the client. There are numerous publications, books, and companies that have been formed around the area of CDNs and we will not cover that well-trodden material here.

The key idea is straightforward: busy Web servers outsource delivery of some of their pages – primarily the frequently requested and infrequently changing static images – to a collection of CDN servers. CDN servers use different techniques, including DNS-based redirection (either for the full site or for a part of the site), rewriting the URL to force redirection, and a combination of the two techniques. The goal of using DNS to redirect client requests to mirrors is to ensure redirecting client requests to servers that are 'nearer' to the clients in a network sense. The CDN also does load balancing to ensure that their mirrors don't get too overloaded. Thus CDNs successfully reduce the load on busy Web servers by serving less frequently changing content from their mirrors (hence *content distribution*) and at the same time aim to find a mirror that is near the client to lower the network latency in fetching those bytes. The choice of mirrors and their load balancing is made by pushing some of the work to the DNS layer by reducing the time-to-live value associated with the mapping for the mirror sites. Multiple companies were formed around this idea in the late 1990s and several of them are still in business. Content distribution is no longer the sole focus of these businesses, many of which have branched out to provide streaming and other services.

Although assertions were made that CDNs always reduced latency to end users and often by dramatic factors, they were never experimentally verified. A comparison of performance of different CDNs [KWZ01] surprisingly showed that the low TTL values provided by the DNS servers of the CDNs do not always contribute to overall lowering of latency experienced by end users.

As we saw in Section 7.2.5, the widespread presence of DNS servers makes it a suitable mechanism for use in a variety of applications. DNS has been used to reroute requests by the use of a modified DNS server that can return different DNS records (name, address, or canonical name) depending on different user-defined policies and metrics [BCNS03]. Higher-level applications can use this feature of DNS without having to modify application code. Several load-balancing appliances have been sold relying on DNS-based redirection. The mapping of a name to an IP address can be controlled to a fine degree by the DNS server returning shorter time-to-live period. However, such mechanisms have to rely on the caching server obeying the given TTL. The more basic assumption in DNS-based server selection is that the client sending the application-level request is close to its local DNS server. The network proximity assumption is used by the redirection mechanisms to locate a server or content replica closer to the local DNS server. We had discussed geo-location earlier in Chapter 5 (Section 5.3.6).

Two studies examined the proximity question in detail. The first study [STA01] collected HTTP and DNS traces from a popular Web site complex with multiple Web servers. The study separately probed the clients and name servers to extract their network distance. About 1.5 million Web requests and nearly 300000 DNS requests over a 2-day period were examined in the study. By examining time stamps of DNS requests and HTTP requests the clients were matched with their corresponding name servers. The probe to examine proximity between client and name server consisted of using `traceroute` and looking for the common ancestor in the two paths. Multiple ISP dial-up clients were also used since it was easier to map the client to its name server (this information is available in the PPP configuration step of the dial-up connection). In nearly 80% of the cases it was seen that if a name server was closer to a site then the client was also closer but there was weak correlation between latencies of the client and name server. This was mainly due to the fact that the paths between the client and the Web server and the name server and Web server are disjoint. The problems in measurement included clock skew between the DNS machine and the Web servers, browsers doing their own caching of DNS name resolution, and bugs in BIND (name resolver) code.

The second study [MCD$^+$02] used a significantly different methodology. A small (1x1) transparent GIF image was stored on a few Web pages. Requests to this embedded image caused a HTTP 302 redirection message to another machine whose name had to be resolved before the image could be fetched. Over 20 million hits were recorded on a highly popular Web site with this embedded image in a period of two months. On less popular Web sites studied for three months, the number of hits varied from under 2000 to over 4 million. In all over 3 million unique client IP addresses and over 150000 local DNS server IP addresses were recorded. The test of proximity used network-aware clustering [KW00] – a technique that automatically groups IP addresses into their smallest enclosing BGP prefix, discussed in detail earlier in Section 7.3.3. Proximity test examined if the client and local DNS server are in the same cluster, by clustering autonomous systems to see if client and LDNS are in the same AS, by correlating RTTs, and examining divergence of `traceroute` similar to the previous study. A client and its local DNS server were found to be in the same AS 64% of the time but only 16% were found in the (more fine-grained) network-aware cluster. A DNS-based server selection can safely choose a DNS server in the same AS as the client but if any AS had more than one server to choose from, then the selection would be inaccurate. The study showed that if a client and DNS server were in the same cluster, then latency will not diverge.

One of the key claims of CDN operations was that the latency to the user would be lowered as a result of finding a mirror server closer to the user. The notion of closer is not geographical but one of network latency proximity. In other words, if a client could fetch content from a CDN mirror faster than it could from the origin Web server, then the client is considered closer to the CDN mirror. In any case, the work associated with handling the client's request and sending the response is eliminated from the Web server. The Web server could thus handle requests from more clients without being overloaded. From an individual user's viewpoint the overall latency to fetch a resource is the primary concern.

As discussed earlier in Section 7.2.5 in examining DNS-based server selection, proximity to the client and latency are not always synonymous. Introducing an intermediary entity like a content distribution network involves moving some additional traffic on DNS in order to alleviate load on the origin server. A two-part study [KWZ01] done over four months ending in January 2001 examined the different techniques employed by CDNs to redirect clients' requests, the fraction of requests offloaded from the server, and how the various CDNs differed in their performance from a user-perceived latency viewpoint. The hidden data the study had to deal with included the internal operational details of the different CDNs. The challenges involved examining different CDNs that used a variety of techniques.

The methodology used in the study was to construct a canonical page reflecting the distributions of static images that CDNs typically serve. Almost all the content served by CDNs then were images and their size distribution was approximately lognormal. Information about typical sizes was obtained by examining proxy logs and popular Web sites. The canonical page was then matched against images that are roughly similar in size and actually delivered by each of the CDNs to facilitate a fair comparison between them. Clients from various locations in five countries (although many clients were concentrated in the US east and west coasts) repeatedly fetched the resources from the various origin sites and from the CDNs. The overhead of DNS and HTTP was measured for different connection setups (parallel non-persistent connections, persistent connections, and persistent connections with requests being pipelined). The study showed that CDNs generally provided much shorter overall download times when the DNS overhead was excluded. But as a realistic comparison would involve DNS overhead, a full comparison showed that DNS overhead was a serious performance bottleneck in some CDNs. With HTTP/1.1 and accounting for caching of some images there was no significant difference between fetching from origin sites and CDNs. Most importantly, the study showed that small DNS TTLs generally did not improve download times either in average-case or worst-case. If an older IP address was reused by ignoring the DNS TTL, the user-perceived latency would be lower.

Identifying Client Connectivity to Tailor Response.   Since the Web site has control over its contents it can move them closer to the client via CDNs, as discussed above. However, Web sites cannot do anything about the vagaries of network delays, presence of intermediaries, and the user's network connectivity. Knowing the quality of the connection between the user and the server and thus any inherent limitations, the server could deliver the most suitable (dynamically generated or statically selected) version of the requested content quickly to the user. A server could actively probe the path to the client to learn all the dynamic components of the end-to-end delay, such as the bandwidth of the client or delays in the network. However, such an active approach is impractical given the number of different users accessing a busy Web server. An alternate way would be to use information already available at the server. Such an approach was explored and discussed in two papers [KW02b, KWZV03]. We briefly describe the major findings in the studies.

The level of client's connectivity can be classified in a coarse-grained fashion, such as poor, normal, and rich. Based on the stability of the client classification a variety of different server actions can be taken. By mapping versions of resources in advance to the client categories, the suitable response version can be sent as soon as the client is categorized. Alternately, the server could deliver the same content in a different way. An example of the former is sending just the base document without the embedded images and an example of the latter is sending a compressed version of the request resource. Tailoring the server's policy is another option: the server could keep persistent connections open longer with poorly connected clients to avoid them having to pay the overhead of setting up new HTTP and thus new TCP connections. A feasibility step is required first to ensure that there are enough frequently requested resources that have alternate versions, and there is a diversity of clients that send requests to a site so that classification would be valuable. Network-aware clustering [KW00] can be used to group clients for classification and application of server actions. A passive methodology would examine a heterogeneous collection of Web server logs and an active implementation should be able to react to new client requests based on historical information.

Classification simply requires examination of the inter-arrival time of requests at a site; the heuristic is that well-connected clients would send requests for embedded content shortly after requesting the base page. Poorly connected clients are likely to exhibit longer latency between the time they request the base object and the various embedded objects. The study examined a heterogeneous collection of Web server logs gathered over different durations anywhere from one week to seven months, with the number of unique clients ranging from over 37000 to over 3.3 million. These clients sent between 1 million and over 48 million requests. The set of possible server actions examined included reducing the number of embedded objects, reducing the size via compression, bundling base and embedded objects as a single object so it could be fetched via a single request, redirecting the request to a mirror, and keeping persistent connections open longer. A sequence of requests was identified as requests from the same client for a base object and at least one embedded object with a maximum timeout of 60 seconds after the base object was downloaded. The first study [KW02b] bore out the feasibility of such an approach. A large fraction of clients classified as poor, normal, or rich tended to stay in the same category over the duration of the study. The stability of client classification is an important metric since it obviates the need for frequent reclassification. In fact, by using network-aware clustering, a client that had not been seen before could be assigned to the same class as another client that belonged to the same network-aware cluster and had been seen already in the trace. This helps in the initial classification for a client about which no information is yet available. The study showed that client classification works best for sites that had a variety of clients. If there was considerable delay to retrieve the first embedded object, redirection to a different site was a good server action and compression was reasonable when the resources were more than 40 kilobytes in size. Bundling was warranted when there were more than ten objects in a sequence. While no single server action was the best for all sites, each of the different server actions was applicable to a significant number of sequences of accesses.

The follow-up study [KWZV03] implemented a modified Apache Web server that could dynamically classify the client's connectivity class and evaluated alternate server actions. The implementation also dynamically clustered an incoming client's IP address that was sending its request for the first time, into its corresponding network-aware cluster to give it an initial classification. The implemented Apache server's overhead due to the classification was measured and shown to be negligible. The evaluation was done by sending a workload from multiple clients with different degrees of network connectivity ranging from dial-up modems geographically closer to the instrumented Web server, a client sending request over a dedicated 56 Kbps transatlantic link, to a cable modem. Three different server locations spread across the United States were used in the test to ensure geographical and network location diversity.

The servers were populated with representative content drawn from proxy logs of a large manufacturing company with over 100000 active users. The distributions of the various resource sizes and number of embedded objects were extracted from the logs. The contents were grouped into buckets representing small, medium, and large in terms of number of embedded objects and number of bytes. The *httperf* [MJ98b] client tool was used for all the retrievals. The actual examination retrieved the container object in compressed form and embedded objects (uncompressed) using combinations of parallel HTTP/1.0 connections, serial connections over two persistent HTTP/1.1 connections, pipelined requests over a single persistent HTTP/1.1 connection, and finally as a single bundle of embedded objects.

The client classification results showed three groups: the poorer modem and transatlantic clients with low throughput and variable RTT to all three servers, one with moderate throughput involving the cable client and a well-connected server, and the rest with higher throughput. None of the clients that would be considered poor were classified as rich and none of the clients with high throughput were ever classified as poor – a desirable result. In terms of server action, compression yielded consistently good results for poorer but not well-connected clients. Reducing the quality of objects (substituting poorer quality images, for example) only yielded benefits for a modem client. Bundling was effective when there was good connectivity or poor connectivity with large latency. Persistent connections with serialized requests did not show significant improvement while pipelining was only significant for clients with high throughput or RTT. The study thus showed that it was quite feasible for a

Web server to classify clients in an online fashion, and deliver tailored content to the different client classes to reduce user-perceived latencies with negligible overhead to the Web server. As a policy measure it is possible to turn off classification when the server is overloaded and with a judicious choice of pages and thresholds, tailoring delivery to the client based on connectivity could help improve Web performance.

Protocol Compliance. The IETF RFCs that outline the protocol standards indicate the compliance requirements of implementations to ensure interoperability between them. Any compliant implementation has to meet all the MUST-level requirements; an implementation is considered non-compliant if it does not meet all the MUST-level requirements. An implementation can be considered to be conditionally compliant if it were to meet all the SHOULD-level requirements, while the MAY-level requirements are optional. Protocol standardization requires interoperability testing of components for all the features. Of late there have been tools developed to test compliance in some protocols (such as HTTP/1.1). Checklists have been created so that the different implementors can agree on the various features. As discussed in a previous book ([KR01] Chapter 1), the lack of a reliable, comprehensive, and, mandatory compliance testing mechanism is a weakness of the IETF standardization process.

PRO-COW [KA01], a 16-month longitudinal compliance study of HTTP/1.1, tested servers of many popular Web sites. The testing was done by examining key protocol features and using *httperf* [MJ98b] to fetch appropriate resources from popular Web sites and analyzing their compliance. For example, the absence of a required header would be an indication of non-compliance. The place from which tests are carried out is not relevant as compliance of servers should not change based on location of clients although intermediaries on the path might skew responses. The PRO-COW study tested popular methods like GET and HEAD and noted the absence of required headers (such as `Date`) or different entity headers in responses for GET and HEAD. A significant fraction of the servers did implement persistent connections, a key innovation in HTTP/1.1, although nearly half did not implement `Range` requests, a way to obtain only portions of a resource. More significantly, inability to handle long URIs in a graceful manner (the tested server crashed) foreshadow the potential for attacks. The popular Apache Web server was found to be the most compliant among the servers tested, with Microsoft's IIS next.

Web Applications

Measurements Related to Searching. Although there are many popular search engines, many of the key details of production crawlers have not been widely published. Research crawlers are somewhat limited in the sense that they gather merely a fraction of the Web. However, there have been a few large-scale studies that discuss some of the key issues in measuring the size of the accessible Web.

We first begin with an examination of the static structure of the Web's interconnection. In Section 7.3.3 we discussed the role of graph modeling in constructing a macro-level view of the Web page collection. A key work in this area was the identification of the static structure of the Web in 1999 that examined 200 million pages and 1.5 billion links [BKM+99]. They constructed a directed graph with the static pages as nodes and the hyperlinks between the pages as arcs. A basic property verified in this work was that the probability of a node having in-degree i is proportional to $1/i x$, for some $x > 1$; also known as a power law. In terms of connectivity structure of the Web, the study pointed out that not all pages can be reached by starting anywhere and that there is a four-part separation in the structure of the Web. A central core of the Web exists with two other parts consisting of pages either pointing to it or being pointed to from it. The last part remains disconnected from this core component in either direction. Surprisingly, all the components have roughly an equal number of pages. An important caveat in the study is that it only studies the static hyperlink structure: the fact that there is a link from Web page A to Web page B does not mean that anyone has ever accessed page B through A. The dynamic access pattern on the Web is not covered in this study. It is quite plausible that Web pages that have a lot of pointers to them (i.e., a large in-degree) are likely to be considered somewhat more important (for some definition of importance) and thus a high 'page rank'. Nodes with high in-degrees are called hubs or authorities. The high page rank of a page is used quite frequently in ranking search results by search engines.

The study showed that the in- and out-degree distributions on the Web follow power laws with exponents (x in the definition above) between 2 and 3. Over 90% of the Web pages are reachable from each other, indicating how well the Web is connected. However, the pages in the remaining portion cannot necessarily be reached by starting at a random page. An interesting data point is that the probability of reaching a random page from another is only 0.25. Moreover, in the well-connected component, it is possible to remove nodes with large degrees (hubs), yet leaving the component to be connected.

Another conclusion of the study is that the manner in which crawling is done and the depth of the crawl can severely distort the results. All the pages that are created on the fly will not be included in the study. Avoiding loops and other traps in the crawl leads to parametric constraints such as how deep in a site would the crawl be continued. Given the importance of being ranked highly in search engines, there are a lot of fake linkages, or automated attempts to be added to the search engine's crawler in an attempt to increase the perceived authoritative nature of a page. Since crawlers treat all pages in a content-independent manner and well-behaved crawlers identify themselves via the `User-Agent` field (or their IP address is known), it is impossible to know if the crawled site tricked the crawler by serving a different page than one they provide to non-crawler requests. Many sites also redirect a request to the 'home page' when a sub-page is unavailable.

While it is theoretically possible to fetch all the accessible pages on the Web using dedicated machines and very large bandwidth, there is not much point in repeatedly fetching pages that have not changed nor is there a reason to fetch contents of mirrored sites. Examination of the extent of the change to the various properties of a Web page was the natural first step. Early work on rate of change [DFKM97] of Web pages was done in 1999 which showed that there is a wide variance across different content types. The study examined nearly a million accesses over a fortnight using packet-level traces and used the `Last-Modified` HTTP header as an indicator of change. Image resources changed infrequently and there was periodicity in changes of many text documents. A visible fraction of pages – over 15% in that study – changed each time between accesses. The changes could be the addition of references to other pages or in content. The former had implications on possible additional crawling to be done. Variants of this study have been performed [BC00]. Other studies have tried to model the rate of change of pages as a Poisson process [CGM00]. Some pages had the property of changing back and forth between two versions. Although some sites were true mirrors of others, there were some near-mirrors and thus could not be ignored while crawling. Other studies have examined whether Web sites in certain domains (e.g., `.com`) changed more often than others (e.g., `.gov`) [CGM00, Koe04]. Crawlers incorporate such information into their algorithms to decide the frequency with which they revisit a site or attempt to fetch a page on a site.

A large crawling study [FMNW04] that fetched over 150 million Web pages (6.4 terabytes of data) ten times over ten weeks was conducted in late 2002 using the Mercator [HN99] focused crawler. Just under half the pages were successfully fetched in all ten crawls done in this study. However, only a tiny fraction (0.1%) of the full contents of successfully downloaded pages were saved. Syntactic document similarity metrics were computed similar to the shingling technique [BGMZ97]. Each document is mapped into a set of adjacent words ('shingles') and any two documents that mapped to a similar set of singles were deemed to be identical. The study makes the important distinction that although shingling has been shown to work well for the English language, there is no evidence that it works equally well for Asian languages employing writing systems that do not use inter-word spacing.

A variety of Java-based analyzers were written to process the collected sets of data from the crawls. They included simple examination of HTTP status codes and document lengths. The study also examined the top-level domain names and the number of hosts in each domain, along with the count of unchanged copies of pages across downloads. Over half the pages downloaded were from the `.com` domain. The size of pages in the `.edu` domain were roughly half of overall page size averages. However, pages in .edu remain accessible a lot longer than average pages – overall many URLs become less and less accessible over time. Nearly a third of the pages changed during the multiple crawls although a third of those changes merely involved changes of the HTML markup rather than actual content. Many of the changes are trivial: minor changes in the query portion of the URL (such as those that occur after the '?' character); some of the changes are just advertisements shown with the page. Some of the changes are just to embedded comments in HTML. Examination of top-level domain-related changes confirmed the earlier study [CGM00]. A curious data value was one particular domain that had many pages filled with words generated to fool search engines. A vast fraction of these pages were actually resolved to a single IP address. Examining the set of IP addresses corresponding to all the pages turned out to be a useful way to detect possible attempts at spoofing content. The study also showed that longer documents (such as discussion lists) changed more often than shorter ones. Finally, the study examined changes across weeks to demonstrate that past change was an indicator of future changes with clear implication for incremental crawlers. Overall, crawling can be significantly more efficient if the properties of pages were taken into account and ones with either minor or fake change characteristics are not re-fetched.

Inferences Related to Searching.   Recently there has been an interesting study that showed that ranking of popularity of a page on the Web by popular search engines has a rather significant impact on the ability of new pages to be discovered. The study [CR04] examined if Web pages with many incoming links received even more links over a 7-month period. About 150 Web sites were chosen and all pages inside those sites were fetched once at the beginning and once after 7 months. The incoming links of each of the pages were computed. The set of about 8 million pages common between the two fetches was compared. The general phenomenon of 'rich getting richer' was seen and the pages in the bottom 60% ranking received no additional links during the study period. Thus pages that were not popular to begin with drop further in popularity while the pages ranked as popular in the beginning of the study became even more popular. Search engines need to alter the manner in which pages are ranked, if new high-quality pages need to become visible.

Another study [BYBKT04] examined the measure of dead links on the Web: pages that are either themselves no longer accessible or point to pages that are unavailable. The study examined several subsets of pages: a collection of 1000 randomly chosen Web pages (out of two billion pages crawled), a decade's worth of technical papers presented at a large Web conference, and the leaf nodes of the Yahoo! Web site, etc. The study showed that a significant fraction of the links were unavailable with impact on crawling and page ranking for search engines. In some cases the dead link count was over 50%. By avoiding dead links crawlers can complete the full crawl faster and by proper ranking of live pages, search results would be more useful.

Dealing with Flash Crowds and other Network Events. Ambient network conditions can have a severe impact on the access dynamics and performance of a Web site. Users of popular Web sites may find the site to be sluggish due to significant events occurring in the network. For example, a denial of service attack may cause significant delays at a Web site. However, even when the Web site is not under direct attack there can be situations such as flash crowds (introduced earlier in Section 7.3.1) that could make the site inaccessible to many users. Since many flash events are unpredictable, being able to react quickly is key. Given that both denial of service attacks and flash crowds can result in delays, it is important to distinguish between the two events. Note that the first is an event consisting of generating a large number of unwanted requests that if identified can be safely ignored by the Web site. The latter – a flash crowd – is a large number of legitimate and wanted requests. A good Web site would try to ensure that most of the requests during a flash crowd receive responses.

Although several studies had examined dynamics of busy Web sites such as those hosting World Cup Soccer and Olympics, none had examined flash crowds and distinguished them from DoS attacks. The first study [JKR02] to examine this and to propose solutions for dealing with flash events, analyzed busy Web site logs and used network-aware clustering discussed earlier. The study distinguishes between the two events by examining differences in traffic patterns, client characteristics, and resource access characteristics. One of the busy server logs for the flash events came from a Web site accessed as users watched and played along with the broadcast of a popular TV show; the other was that of the election Web site during the 1999 Chilean presidential elections.

The first key notion in this study was to examine the clients who visit the site during normal circumstances and contrast them against the clients who visit during flash events or DoS attacks. The second notion was to examine the set of documents accessed during normal circumstances and contrast them with the set of documents accessed during an event. First, the nearly 54000 unique IP addresses in the play-along site were clustered to around 14000 BGP clusters and the over 20000 addresses into about 1700 clusters. The average number of requests per client during the flash event remained the same, indicating that the large increase in number of requests was due to the increase in the number of clients. Figure 7.8 shows how the number of distinct clients and client clusters accessing the sites in 10-second intervals change over time. The spikes in request volumes during the flash event aligning well with the spikes in the number of clients accessing the site implies that the number of clients in a flash event is commensurate with the request rate. Examining the number of clusters during the flash event showed no increase, indicating that most of the

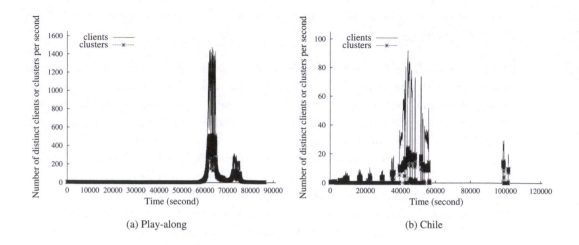

Figure 7.8   Distribution of clients and clusters over time. From [JKR02].

clients disproportionately belong to the existing clusters. In a DoS event, this would be untrue as the attackers have no way of knowing what the typical distribution of client clusters are in a given Web site's access pattern. In terms of resource access, the study showed that between 60% and 82% of the resources in the two sites are accessed only during the flash events. Only a few of these resources (less than 10%) are responses for nearly 90% of the requests during the event; these requests come from a large number of client clusters. These findings suggest that the popular resources should be proactively replicated to the various mirrors of the CDNs helping the Web site.

A different pattern was seen in examining logs of a Web site that included password cracking attempts. Very few resources were ever accessed for the password cracking attempt and there was a dramatic increase in the per-client request rate. Most importantly the set of client clusters of the IP addresses involved in the attack were quite different from the clusters seen hitherto by that site. Similarly, examining numerous Web sites affected by the Code-Red worm [MSkc02], only between 0.5% and 15% of clusters had been seen before. In contrast, the examination of play-along and election Web sites showed that between 43% and 83% of client clusters seen during the flash event were also seen earlier by those sites.

Figure 7.9(a) shows the attack pattern: initially we see a few requests followed by a sudden jump. But as can be seen from Figure 7.9(b), which shows the clusters to which the IP addresses sending requests belong, several new clusters are visible. This implies that the increase in traffic is not just from clusters (and thus IP addresses) that would normally visit the site, but a distinct group of new clients. Now comparing this

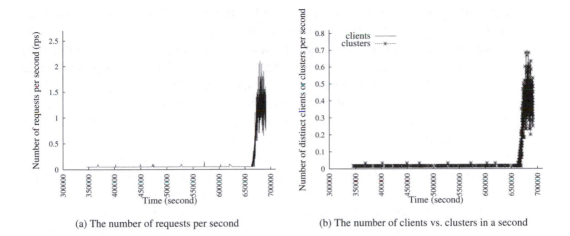

(a) The number of requests per second (b) The number of clients vs. clusters in a second

Figure 7.9 The number of (a) requests per second, (b) number of clients vs. clusters in a second, in an attack victim trace. From [JKR02].

to Figure 7.8, we note that the flash event did not show any sudden increase in the arrivals of new clusters.

Blogs. *Blogs*, short for the neologism 'weblogs', are often a personal journal maintained on the Web. The phenomenon of blogs has grown rapidly as a segment of Web traffic [Blo]. The political blog `talkingpointsmemo.com` claims to have more than 300000 unique readers in a month. Blogs consist of opinions, stories, and random observations about a variety of topics, typically updated on a much more regular basis than homepages. Blogs are similar in spirit to Usenet newsgroups except each newsgroup is a single person's view; a few blogs are shared between multiple authors. A blog is a long Web page, partitioned into archives, with links to other URLs on the Web. Many popular blogs are on content hosting sites that provide space, software to maintain blogs, and generate indices, reverse pointer collections, etc. Additions appear at the top of the page and they are immediately available to anyone accessing the URL of the blog. A typical blog consists of some text paragraphs often with embedded links (either internal links to another section of the same blog or external links), occasionally a few images, pointers to older sections of the same blog, and (in some cases) a set of reverse pointers to the blog itself made in other blogs. While typical Web pages have a single point of entry (the URL), blogs have multiple locations of interest.

Blogs have the potential for providing an early warning of hotspots and flash crowds. The Web site `slashdot.org` is an early example of a blog with significant impact on the future (and often short-lived) popularity of a particular Web site or Web page. The additions of links to a new issue can be an early indicator of its rising popularity. A key distinction achieved by blogs is the original goal of making the Web a two- or multi-way medium rather than the widely prevalent 'write once read many' model. Unlike news sites, popular blogs have the property of a large in-degree especially when one considers that links are not to the top-level URL but to a specific section of the blog. Blogs also offer interesting new collaborative filtering applications. Authors of blogs may be interested in finding out new stories that are related to stories they were previously interested in, blogs that are related to their blog, or ones that have commented on or linked to their blog. The last item is partly expressed through the publication of referrer links – a common blog phenomenon. Blogs that have not changed in a while may no longer be considered active blogs and notice a significant drop in accesses. Different measures for rate of change, amount of change, and last modification time help distinguish blogs and Web pages. Changes in blogs typically occur only at the top and thus it may be enough to fetch the first few hundred bytes via the HTTP/1.1 `Range` request or by using delta mechanisms [MDFK97, MKD$^+$02]).

Several studies [Hen03, KNR03, CK05] have characterized the *blogistan* (the blog world). Here we describe the methodology and some of the findings in one study [CK05] that involved one of the authors of this book. Earlier studies had reported the size of the blogistan to be between 1 and 4 million. This study crawled the blog world by starting out with a collection of seed pages. The seed set itself was extracted from a large list of URLs from the large Web crawling study [FMNW04] discussed earlier in this section. Starting with any URL that included the string 'blog' in its name and removing duplicates, and weighted for representation across many domains, an initial set was constructed. To this several popular blogs were added from collections of popular individual blogs maintained regularly [Sal, Tec, Mos, Use]. A set of about 8700 blog URLs was fetched 171 times, i.e., roughly once every four hours, over a one month period in the autumn of 2003. Meta-information and contents were fetched via `HEAD` and `GET` methods respectively. Links in each of the instances of each of the URLs were used to examine the individual blog page's link structure and how it differed from non-blog Web pages. The crawl data was cleaned using traditional Web crawling techniques: duplicate and near-duplicate pages are eliminated. Duplicate pages are a bigger problem in blogs as compared to traditional Web pages due to the presence of blog archives. Blogs with an abnormal number of new links were also eliminated since it is a sign of programmatic addition rather than human editing.

Static hyperlink analysis depends on in-degrees: the number of pointers to a site. Analysis of single snapshots can work well both for static Web pages and for news sites but not for blogs. The importance of a page depends on the amount and quality of references to it. Newer URLs on blogs will have a lot fewer references than older URLs. The study showed the distribution of 'blog size' in terms of all references and new-URL references the blog contained in the measurement period. The size distribution in terms of all references has the form of a bell curve; for new-URL references, the dependence is monotonically decreasing with more blogs experiencing fewer changes. New-URL references are vastly outnumbered by the sheer number of other references over a collection of pages. The number of new references made to new URLs is considerably smaller than the number of new references made to old URLs. This implies that identifying emerging new URLs requires tracking many pages, over time, and combining the information; as they cannot be distilled from a single snapshot of many pages nor from tracking individual pages. The study also showed that new URL references are much more transient than old-URL references. The traditional Web assertion about objects that had not changed recently being less likely to change appears to hold for references as well.

The crawl of the blogistan could be stopped after a few iterations as a diminishing fraction of the newly fetched pages were identified as blogs. The first iteration from the seed collection of 8700 pages yielded nearly a quarter million blogs, the second yielded over 1.7 million, and the third about 1.5 million. At each step non-blog URLs and duplicates were eliminated. Duplicate removal consisted of case homogenizing the URL strings, removing trailing backslashes, ':80' after the domain names, and trailing #* (referring to different places on the same page). The duplicate-free union of URLs at all the hops of the crawl resulted in roughly 1.24 million distinct blog URL strings. By creating a signature for each page that constitutes the (ordered) 10 keys with minimum hash value, this set was reduced by another 40% to end up with roughly 750000 blogs. Many blogs are hosted in a few blog-hosting sites.

When the nearly quarter million distinct domain names in the study were reverse-mapped using DNS they mapped to fewer than 12000 unique IP addresses. Network-aware clustering of these IP addresses yielded just 3321 BGP clusters. Within the set of clusters, more than 60% contained single address indicating the broad distribution across different prefixes. Among the complete collection of blogs nearly 80% were hosted on Web sites running the popular Apache Web server. The average number of new bytes added between instances is low. A test on a random subset of URLs in that study showed that more than 60% of the URLs changed on average by less than 200 bytes, and 98% of the URLs changed by less than 1000 bytes. In terms of length, nearly two-thirds of the blogs are less than 40 kilobytes. The usefulness of delta mechanisms or `Range` requests is thus obvious. The study unfortunately also pointed out that only around 40% of the sites are able to handle HTTP/1.1 `Range` requests successfully.

The results of the study are that rate of change of blogs is quite different from traditional Web pages and the nature and count of links between blogs and other

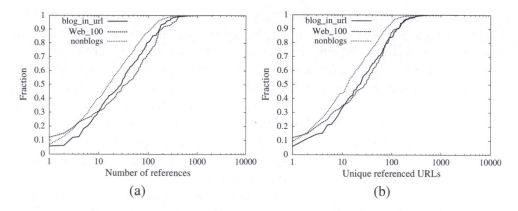

Figure 7.10   The number of (a) links and (b) unique links. From [CK05].

Web pages are quite distinct. As can be seen in Figure 7.10(a) popular Web sites and blogs have considerably more references than unpopular Web sites that are not blogs. Popular Web sites generally have more references than blogs. By examining just the unique references (Figure 7.10(b)) we can see that this difference between popular Web sites and blogs disappears while non-blogs continue to have a lot fewer unique links. Blogs have significantly more self-references than popular Web pages as Figure 7.11(a) shows. Self-references are thus a key indicator of difference between blogs and Web pages, as unpopular Web pages have very few of them. The nature of links emanating from blogs (with a significant fraction going to other blogs) is another key difference. There are implications for separate treatment of blogs from the searching viewpoint: large scope analysis of referenced links and evolution over time are more important.

The aforementioned earlier study [KNR03] also examined the time of the appearance of a reference to detecting groups of blogs that have a burst of inter-references. This is due to the manner of interaction in blogs: a number of people discuss a particular topic fervently which then drops off almost entirely. During the discussion period there is a significant increase in the number of links to each other related to the topic. Communities of interest can thus get formed quickly in blogs but their importance may not be long-lasting. This study examined about 25000 blogs and showed a high average edge-multiplicity of 11, indicating the strong interaction between the community of blogs.

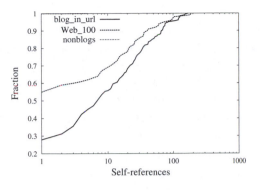

Figure 7.11   The number of self-references. From [CK05].

7.4   P2P

Peer-to-peer traffic rapidly increased as a fraction of overall Internet traffic since the introduction of Napster [Nap] in 1999. In the spring of 2005 it remains the application with the largest share of bytes exchanged on the Internet. A significant fraction of P2P traffic consists of sharing files of dubious ownership between peers that join and leave the network at will. These two factors play an important role in how we cover measurements in this application. A wide variety and growing number of protocols have been implemented and clients implementing them have been distributed within the peer-to-peer community. Table 7.5 lists some of the popular protocols and the years they were introduced.

Research oriented P2P protocols, as opposed to the ones used by a large fraction of users, have been built around the idea of distributed indexing schemes based on hashing to locate the content. These systems (CAN [RFH$^+$01], Chord [SMK$^+$01], Pastry [RD01], Tapestry [ZKJ00]) typically assume a flat content delivery mesh. Each object's location is stored at one or more nodes selected deterministically by a uniform hash function. The queries for the object are routed incrementally to the node. Hash functions can help locate content deterministically but they lack the flexibility of keyword searching – a useful operation to find content without prior knowledge of exact object names. Kademlia [MM02], a P2P network based on Distributed Hash Tables, was used to build a non-hierarchical P2P network called Overnet [Ove]. Overnet remains the most widely used structured P2P system although the number of users is significantly smaller than protocols of unstructured P2P systems.

Unstructured P2P systems do not have any organized structure nor can the objects be forcibly placed in any specific locations. They have been the dominant protocols since the advent of P2P in terms of users, the number of nodes participating in them and the number of bytes exchanged. Centralized protocols obtain information about

Table 7.5   Notable P2P protocols.

Protocol	Significance	Year introduced
Napster	Centralized, earliest, largely extinct	1999
Gnutella	Early popularity, queries flooded	2000
Overnet/Kademlia	Structured, DHT-based	2002
KaZaa	High volume of content exchanged	2001
eDonkey/eMule	First to introduce segmented downloads	2002
BitTorrent	Efficient, highly popular, enforcing high upload/download ratio	2002

files from different nodes and provide responses to keyword queries allowing users to directly download content from nodes with matching content. Decentralized searching protocols flood queries through neighbors and forward responses; they tend not to scale with number of queries. Currently popular protocols in terms of number of users and a large fraction of P2P traffic are KaZaa [Kaz] and BitTorrent [Bit]. Other popular protocols include eDonkey and DirectConnect. A quick introduction to P2P was presented in Chapter 2 (Section 2.3.10).

7.4.1   P2P Measurement Properties

Traffic in P2P is now the majority of bytes exchanged on the Internet. As recently as 6 years ago (2000) this was not the case; in fact the first P2P protocol (Napster) only became known in 1999. By 2002, the traffic in P2P was a significant component of the Internet and for the last 3 years it has been a majority. On some backbone networks, P2P traffic is nearly two-thirds of traffic in terms of bytes. Over 80 million people downloaded music files in 2003 [Dig] and over 4 billion songs were downloaded by P2P users in the USA alone.

   Centralized protocols such as Napster have vanished and the current protocols that hold a disproportionate share of the popularity do not use a central index. The different stages of a typical protocol transaction – issuance of query by the client peer, the propagation of the query through the network, query responses returned to the client, downloading from the chosen suitable peer(s) of the resource – all impose varying degrees of load on the network. Each query may generate multiple query responses and multiple attempts at downloading of the resource may be made. The number of attempts depends on the stability of the peer from which the resource is being downloaded, the connectivity of the client and the congestion on the network. Concentrating entities (such as a DirectConnect hub, Gnutella superpeer, or KaZaa supernode) can help in directing queries. Such hubs typically have higher bandwidth connectivity.

Initially, Napster had 100% of the P2P traffic since it was the only real P2P protocol with pointers to resources of interest. Soon, the next generation of non-centralized index protocols such as Gnutella and DirectConnect were born. Gnutella, originally created inside a division of America Online (AOL) company called NullSoft, was released in March 2000. AOL disavowed the project and an open source version was created and released shortly thereafter. Gnutella spawned a range of variants such as Mutella, Limewire, Bearshare, etc. The popularity of the protocol seemed to be directly correlated with two key aspects: the nature of resources accessible using them (movies and video), and the ability to successfully download a complete resource quickly often in chunks. Once videos and movies began to be available widely on P2P networks, protocols that enabled downloading them immediately gained in popularity. Morpheus, KaZaa and other variants became the dominant protocol in terms of number of users (few millions to tens of millions) and number of bytes (terabytes). The subsequent introduction of eDonkey and BitTorrent enabled fetching of multiple segments in parallel from several peers simultaneously. The reduction in freeriding (downloading much more content than uploading, discussed later in this section) by throttling mechanisms in eMule and BitTorrent has kept their levels of popularity high. The variation in popularity of protocols has also been affected by threats of legal action and legislative attempts to shut down specific networks. Napster has ceased to operate in its original model due to legal action. Most recently Grokster/Sharman Networks lost a lawsuit [Sco05] in the United States Supreme Court on the question of a technology created primarily with the intent to allow infringement of copyright and have agreed to close their business.

Among the characterizations of interest are information about the nodes participating in P2P transactions – their IP addresses, the network prefixes corresponding to them, and the Autonomous Systems to which they belong. P2P clients and servers are spread all over the Internet although demographics play an important role. Examining the nature of resources most frequently downloaded shows abnormally high fractions of content popular with an age demographic correlated to those in educational institutions. College campuses have been bearing the brunt of bandwidth congestion due to a significant number of students downloading and sharing large P2P resources. With the increasing bandwidth capacity due to access technologies like DSL and broadband, P2P traffic to the home has grown steadily. The distribution of P2P clients/servers has closely tracked the access capacity. Peers that are disproportionately servers are more likely to be present in sites with high bandwidth, although the advent of BitTorrent-like protocols have reduced the need for this.

Configuring P2P clients is relatively straightforward: most clients can be simply downloaded and run without any particular tuning. The more recent protocols such as eMule allow for a few tunable parameters, such as maximum number of connections and files, limits on upload and download capacity. If a client is interested in downloading, the primary focus is in locating high-bandwidth peers and trying to connect to them to fetch segments. Clients that upload considerable content may be interested in ensuring that they penalize clients that don't upload as much as they download. Unlike Web and DNS servers which largely deliver legal content, popular P2P peers that deliver content may have to be concerned about becoming too popular. Popularity may raise concerns both in terms of getting too many requests and being discovered. Considering that delivery of P2P content is largely voluntary and without compensation, there is no incentive for servers to explore overlay infrastructure support like Content Distribution Networks.

On the Web, the location of the resource of interest is either known or obtained through an external mechanism. If the user is interested in a popular Web site it is directly accessed. If not, the access of a Web resource is preceded by a search request to a search engine before one of the answers is selected. Even popular resources on P2P networks are present in unknown locations. If the location is known, unlike on the Web, there is no guarantee that the P2P node would be available at the time of request. The search phase thus remains an integral part of each P2P transaction. Requests are often sent over UDP and downloads are done via TCP. Query requests are at most a few hundred bytes across most of the P2P protocols. The initial nodes a request is sent to may have implications on the quality of responses received. The peer selection phase where nodes are chosen to be targets of download requests can play a crucial role.

Since P2P protocols like Gnutella flood the original query request the probability of packet losses does not significantly affect the potential to get back some query responses. There is delay in sifting through the query responses to select suitable nodes that have the resource of interest. From the viewpoint of bytes transferred on the network, downloading of the resource remains the more interesting part of the transaction. Multiple TCP connections may be set up in parallel to fetch segments of the resource. Many of the connection attempts may be queued if the remote peer is busy or enforcing fairness. Also, the connections may be closed by the remote peer at any time even if the peer does not leave the network.

The bigger problem associated with network effects thus occurs during the download phase. Many of the resources downloaded on P2P networks are large. Compared to Web resources where the mean is 6–10K and median is around 8K, in P2P, the mean and median are significantly larger. For example, a recent study [GBG04] reported KaZaa objects to have a median file size of nearly 4 MB. Admittedly, the metrics vary with the type of objects downloaded on the P2P network. A typical song that is a few minutes long encoded in MP3 format (between 128 kbit/s to the near-CD quality of 320 kbit/s) can take up between 3 to 7 megabytes. A two hour MPEG-4 encoded movie (at a typical encoding rate of 500 Kbps) can be 450 megabytes.

A single download may take hours and in some cases days. If a download fails an alternate connection may have to be attempted with no additional guarantee of success. The bandwidth associated with each client or server peer can dictate the possible number of bytes that can be actually exchanged. The traffic volume associated with downloads, the bandwidth used, and the duration of connections between peers are interesting characteristics.

Given that at any given time a few dozen resources are highly popular in a P2P network, caching offers itself as a natural solution to reduce congestion and wasted transfer of the same bytes. Unlike Web and DNS, the nature of the P2P application with contents of questionable ownership, public proxy caches are not highly likely. However, inside large network infrastructures under the control of a single administrative entity, P2P caches are feasible.

Beyond network effects, there are some P2P-specific problems. Although the protocol is named peer-to-peer and technically all P2P clients can be servers and vice versa, in reality, the term is abused. Only in the early phases of the protocol is there a real 'peer-to-peer' nature. Many peers join and leave the network often without serving any content. The phenomenon of downloading content but not uploading (i.e., sharing) with others is called *freeriding*. Freeriding occurs in a widespread manner. Even when clients do share, the fraction of bandwidth dedicated to uploading is much smaller than that of downloading. More content sharers implies more content available to everyone and more overall sharable upload bandwidth. The increased available bandwidth makes it easier for many peers to obtain content of interest. Additionally, such content can be fetched from nearer and lightly loaded links with higher probability. With fewer content sharers, contention increases and all clients are affected. If everyone was a freerider there would be no content to share and consequently no P2P network. While such an extreme is unlikely, freeriding has been a widespread problem. Measurements in this arena have led to the development of new P2P protocols with significant amelioration of the freeriding problem.

Another P2P-specific problem is the lack of authoritative information about the resources the user is seeking. On the Web or in DNS there is a notion of an authoritative owner of every resource and thus valid meta-information about the resource (its size, checksum, owner, last modification date, etc.) is often available. The P2P world largely consists of nodes sharing anonymous content to many users. The same resource may be available in multiple peers under different names. The resource may be downloaded from different server peers in different chunks occasionally in different sized chunks.

The same resource may have to be downloaded more than once to be sure that the complete copy has been received. As one way to reduce the number of resources of questionable ownership being widely downloaded, some content owners have created *decoys* – mangled versions of popular resources. Such practice has been described as a reasonable strategy by the Recording Industry Association of America (RIAA) and supported by record labels. The intent is to frustrate P2P users who spend a long time to download a resource which is not what they really want. In the arms race between content owners and P2P sharers, clearinghouse sites have been created to certify that a P2P resource is actually a valid one and not a decoy. The certification is done with the partial meta-information available from the serving peer: the checksum of the resource or segment to be downloaded. The presence of decoy thus results in an additional step just before a download: the checksum verification. Beyond the network communication necessary for verifying the checksum, decoys may end up adding to the overall number of bytes transferred over P2P networks. This is due to determined P2P clients who even after having downloaded a decoy continue searching for a valid resource and downloading it. Decoys to deter downloads are almost unique to the P2P application; they are quite rare or unheard of in other applications.

The notion of 'think-time' in P2P differs from that of the Web. In the case of a typical Web browsing transaction, a user may pause while reading the page before clicking on an available link on the page or switch to an entirely different URL. Modeling Web transactions required modeling of such think-times. In P2P, the transaction consists of issuing a search string and selecting between the alternatives available to download segments of the resource. Additionally, the user may issue different search strings if they are not satisfied with the initial responses received. The choice of a user in selecting between available nodes to download a segment is driven by network connectivity and extent of sharing by the node. In the Web application, an individual user's think-time can be measured on the server end when interacting with a Web site based on inter-arrival time of requests. In P2P, however, a user may be communicating with multiple nodes, and such a measure is harder to obtain.

Table 7.6 presents the set of properties of interest to measure in P2P networks, along with the reasons and typical locations where they are measured.

7.4.2 P2P Measurement Challenges

P2P measurements face significant challenges as compared to DNS or Web. From the viewpoint of generating significant passive measurements involving P2P server entities, a set of popular resources have to be hosted and distributed. Studying P2P client behavior is significantly easier as queries can be generated and downloads carried out from multiple locations. Use of infrastructures like PlanetLab is also feasible for client-based studies. The choice of protocol to study can raise interesting issues regarding the popularity of a particular protocol as well as access to its source code.

Table 7.6 P2P properties of interest to measure.

Measured property	Why measured	Where measured
Fraction of Internet traffic	Growth patterns	Across Internet
Protocol split	Tracking trends in content exchanged	Across Internet
Location of entities	Grouping/performance	Remote reverse engineering
Manner of access	Improving search and download efficiency	Local/remote
Response latency	Performance	Targeted server set (local/remote)
Freeriding	Solutions to freeriding problem	Local/remote
Node availability	Performance and reach	Across Internet

Hidden Data

Akin to hidden data in the Web application, it is only possible to measure at the peer's end. The path followed by each query request and query response is neither predictable nor recorded. Thus, it is difficult to gather data in the middle of the path of the query. The client originating the query will not know all the nodes that were involved in generating and forwarding the query replies. In the presence of inter-mediaries like supernodes, the origin of the query reply is not known. Even if the measurement is done from a few dozen P2P client nodes, the dynamic nature of the P2P network implies that search results and success of downloads can vary over time due to the potential for random nodes joining and leaving the network.

The fundamental difference in hidden data in P2P measurement as compared to the Web is thus the lack of sustained availability of peers. Both popular and unpopular Web sites tend not to hide their URL. While access may be regulated to authorized users, the location of the site is not hidden. One way to look at this problem is that the significant transfer of bytes occurs only in the direct download phase and thus the unknown path actually traversed by the query is not a serious issue. However, from the viewpoint of optimizing the search phase of the protocol, absence of precise path followed can be problematic. In Section 7.4.4, we will see attempts made to measure in the presence of this difficulty.

On the Web it is the contents of many sites that change frequently. In P2P, the number of new resources that come on line and become popular is a lot less than the churn in the number of nodes that join and leave the network. In a stabler application like the Web where the nodes are stable and the contents change, it is possible to get an idea of rate of change of resources. In P2P, the resources are static files: songs, videos, and movies are rarely, if ever, modified. The resources are write-once-read-many in nature. Thus the resources have a close to zero rate of change but the nodes from which these resources are downloaded constantly shift. With segmented downloads and dynamic uploading while downloading the set of communicating peers change constantly. The number of distinct content types on P2P networks is considerably fewer than the Web. As mentioned in Section 7.4.1, decoys can be considered to be another content type; the checksum of such resources may be added to a list that allows other clients to avoid downloading them.

Given the rate of churn of nodes and the wide-ranging partition of resources into segments, it is nearly impossible to have any predictability in download times. Practically speaking, since most users are sharing content and are not in a position to question the delays involved, this is not a significant issue. However, there is already a significant set of genuinely free resources that are being distributed using P2P networks. A recent example is the complete distribution of Linux Fedora using BitTorrent. Thus, it is worthwhile examining how the random joining and leaving of nodes impact downloads of resource on P2P networks.

One advantage in P2P measurements is that most of the traffic is on the visible part of the Internet as compared to the Web where a considerable fraction is intra-net. Although there are numerous P2P networks, the truly popular ones are few, and thus it is possible to get an idea of overall traffic characteristics by monitoring the highly popular ones. KaZaa has been the popular P2P protocol but the source code, unlike many other P2P clients, is not available. The protocol details are hidden and query requests are encrypted, making a passive study of KaZaa quite difficult. One has to monitor the download attempts of KaZaa resources to get any idea of how resources are exchanged in that network.

Hidden Layers

The various steps in a P2P transaction differ between the variants of the protocols. Some of the steps are hidden from the viewpoint of the client generating the query request. For example, the query may be forwarded only a certain number of steps and silently dropped beyond a certain diameter. Query responses may be forwarded in a similar manner. The first step of the transaction – translating the keywords specified in the query to a set of potential matches – varies with each protocol even if the same resource is sought using the same query string. This is not dissimilar to using different search engines on the Web except that the number of places where the matching of the keywords is done in the P2P context is significantly larger than the single central point in the Web context.

The query replies can potentially come from different subsets for each query.

There is no good algorithm to make a wise choice in selecting among peers that claim to have the resource. The typical ordering is based on bandwidth of the potential server peer but many may deliberately give wrong information either to entice or deter downloading. Backing out of a wrong choice halfway through the download may require the full resource to be downloaded elsewhere. Subjective evaluation of the delay involved at a peer triggering alternate action is hard to model – we will see this dilemma in more detail in the networked games application (Section 7.5).

If the downloading is done in segments via concurrent parallelized downloads from multiple peers, there is still the issue of ensuring all pieces have been correctly downloaded before reassembling the full resource. With the advent of popular protocols like eMule and BitTorrent, it is entirely possible that a considerable fraction of the delay in fetching a resource is due to the queuing of the download request at the peer depending on the upload/download ratio of the client. Clients that have shared an equal amount as they have downloaded may find their download requests moved ahead in the queue but at the time of downloading they have no way of knowing the server peer and the fraction of time they will spend in the queue before obtaining a single byte.

The varying number of segments downloaded, multiple server peers involved in the download transaction, the potential for incomplete download of a segment, potential presence of decoys, being queued for arbitrary lengths of time, are all different strands of hidden layers in the P2P applications.

7.4.3 P2P Measurement Tools

With the increasing popularity of content exchanged over P2P networks, numerous tools were created to study and improve such networks. Many of the ideas were adapted from earlier work in DNS, Web, and other applications. However, unlike DNS and Web, the novel aspects of P2P architecture, manner of node joins and departures, and the resulting traffic flow are idiosyncratic enough to modify existing measurement tools or create completely new ones.

The P2P measurement-related tools can be examined in a few categories:

1. Tools for characterizing P2P traffic at a macro level and within specific P2P networks.
2. Tools for exploring alternate architectures to improve scalability of the protocols or to improve specific phases (such as the initial searching phase, adding query caches, etc.)
3. Tools to address the unique aspects of P2P, such as the rapid rate of nodes joining and leaving the network, tools to help in segmented downloads and improve performance, decoy-avoidance, and reducing occurrences of freeriding.

4. Network-level support for grouping P2P clients and servers or improving transport.

We will look at each of these categories next. In the state of the art section (Section 7.4.4) we will examine how these tools have been used to aid in the broadening of understanding of P2P networks. Not all tools discussed here will have an analogue in the state of the art section as many proposals have never been realized into practical P2P networks with real users exchanging large amounts of content. While partly this is due to the difficulty of creating popular content and waiting for many users to use a new system, there is no getting away from the fact that in P2P contributions from the research community have often been eclipsed by running code that addressed the key problems of freeriding and making efficient use of the capacity of nodes connected to the network at any given point.

P2P Characterization Tools

The set of tools used to characterize P2P traffic passively or actively include the traditional widely used ones in the Web world. P2P crawlers, somewhat similar to Web crawlers, can be used to traverse P2P networks actively. P2P crawlers can be used to map the existing P2P network and also find vulnerable nodes whose removal would cripple the P2P network. Just as every Web crawler is basically a Web client, albeit one that sends many more requests than most clients including proxy clients; a P2P crawler is just another P2P client whose job is to join a P2P network, set up connections with other nodes, and attempt to discover as many of the rest of the nodes in the network. Just as a Web crawler starts with a seed collection of Web sites, a P2P crawler would start with a list of P2P nodes. Unlike the Web application, there is no guarantee that the start list of nodes can be reused in its entirety for the next crawl as many of the nodes may not be active. P2P crawling is how different P2P networks are ranked in popularity.

Like many other applications, low-level (router-level) information can be used to glean characteristics of the P2P network. For example, *netflow* records can be used for passive post-facto characterization by examining records involving all the port numbers related to P2P communication. Another natural tool in understanding P2P traffic characteristics and dynamics is to look at the distribution of number of P2P requests and responses from each of the IP addresses found to be participating in the P2P network. Given that only a few of the resources are popular and these popular resources may be present in only a few nodes, it would not be surprising to see that a few IP addresses are involved in a significant fraction of the traffic volume exchanged. Such nodes are generally called heavy-hitters; a closer examination of such nodes is thus natural. For example, we might want to examine the connectivity of heavy-hitters to see if it is high.

P2P traffic can be examined using a methodology similar to the graph-based examination of DNS traffic, although the patterns of connections are likely to be different. In DNS, individual clients have no reason to communicate with other clients, authoritative DNS servers or any of the root DNS servers. The individual clients only talk to local DNS servers. In P2P, any node could theoretically communicate with any other node, although in practice most nodes only talk to a few others. The same graph methodology can thus be used to examine communication patterns between nodes in terms of how many different nodes any individual node talks to (degree of the node), the volume of bytes exchanged between a pair of nodes (weight of the edge) and thus the total volume. Outliers can also be identified. Comparisons can be done across different protocols as the format of representation – the graph – is the same independent of the protocol.

P2P Architecture Examination Tools

The difficulties of searching on the P2P network due to its architecture as compared to the centralized Web has led to examination of alternate techniques. Early designs did not take into account the heterogeneity among the P2P nodes. A standard technique to address the scalability issue is to introduce a hierarchy. A few central nodes that tend to stay in the P2P network for a longer time could help group nodes that are closer to it in a topological sense and route query responses, using caching where appropriate. Using existing network-aware clustering technology tools is natural for constructing such hierarchies as we will see in the state of the art section.

Recognizing that most of the queries are for well-replicated, i.e., popular content, adding the notion of capacity awareness to clients can help to direct more queries to clients with better capacity [LRS02, CRB+03]. No real hierarchy needs to be constructed; each node can check if its neighbor is overloaded before forwarding a query to it. Nodes can maintain an index of its current neighbors and exchange updates periodically. Simulations showed the potential usefulness of such techniques. Maintaining additional state at the node on either end of communicating links allows for a variety of enhancements. It is possible to cache results [BCG+03] of past searches to reduce future flooding of queries. Nodes can maintain a local index that can be used during the search phase. Similar to the Web, a cache can present answers even if the nodes on which the actual resource is stored is offline. In general the idea is to add semantics to the architectural entities involved in P2P. As another example, edges can be labeled as ones that carry or do not carry forward searches [CGM03].

Tools to Address Issues Unique to P2P

As mentioned earlier, there are numerous issues that are unique to the P2P application. Consequently, new tools were needed to deal with these issues. Foremost among the problems were that peers joined and left the network at will. Many P2P resources are large and thus dependence on a single peer to download the entire resource which could take several hours could be problematic. Many peers did not have adequate bandwidth to support large downloads. This naturally led to the recognition that a resource could be fetched in segments, much like range requests in HTTP. And instead of fetching the full contents of a resource from a single peer, different segments could be fetched from different peers. Since the client had a good idea of its own ability, it could open multiple simultaneous connections with various peers that have the resource and request specific segments from each.

Since many of the resources exchanged on P2P networks are of suspicious ownership, in some cases, the content owners have resorted to deploying decoys as we mentioned earlier in Section 7.4.1. These decoys are of roughly the same size as the actual resource and waste the efforts of downloaders prompting for ways to circumvent them.

In other applications, the notion of a client and a server is clear. A client generates requests (which are small in terms of bits sent upstream) and a server accepts short requests and sends back larger responses. In P2P, a peer was expected to be both client and server, although in reality many peers were in most cases just clients; i.e., (unfairly) only downloading content. In Section 7.4.4 we will present details on how mechanisms were created and enforced in a couple of P2P protocols to address this aforementioned freeriding unfairness issue.

Given the difference between various P2P networks, tailored attempts have been made to measure the rate at which nodes join and leave. In the state of the art section we will see one example of how node availability is measured although it is not a highly popular P2P network.

Network-level Support for P2P

Other tools of interest in carrying out measurements of proximity of P2P nodes include the network-aware clustering [KW00] or some geographic location tools. Picking nodes in the same network-aware cluster allows peers to select closer nodes among the set of query reply choices returned.

Improving the way in which the transport layer was being used by earlier versions of the HTTP protocol helped pave the way for adding persistent connections in HTTP/1.1 [Pad95, KR01]. The insight there was that HTTP was making poor use of the transport-layer protocol. Improving transport-layer support resulted in lowering user-perceived latency for multiple fetches from the same Web site and at the same time reduced the number of unwanted packets on the network. It is not surprising that attempts have been made to add transport-layer support to P2P. In the Web context individual clients maintain persistent connections with just a few Web sites and just for a handful of request–response exchanges. Further, most exchanges are short and the request and response are on the same transport (TCP) connection. In the DNS application, regular queries and responses use UDP while the more important zone transfers are done over reliable TCP. Selection of transport layer and the way in which it can be better used under different circumstances is thus a feature common in multiple applications.

In the downloading phase in P2P networks, peers download from a single peer that has the resource of interest. However, most peers in P2P networks reside on the edge of the network and are not necessarily equipped with enough bandwidth or capacity. Even if the client has enough bandwidth the bottleneck is the serving peer's capacity. Simply selecting higher bandwidth connections at the beginning of the download phase does not make efficient use of the overall capacity in the P2P network [HS04]. The better connected nodes tend to become congested as a result of their popularity. However if the same resource were to be available on multiple peers, a client peer could download segments from the different server peers, often simultaneously. If a client peer wanted to download from multiple peers simultaneously, it has to set up the transport connection first. However, if there is transport layer support for multipoint-to-point communication, this overhead can be avoided [HS02]. An alternative to multipoint communication is exploiting potential redundancy in data and network paths using multiple distribution trees that traverse paths of interested peers. One advantage of such techniques is it lowers the risk of failures during P2P streaming [PS02, PWC03] as nodes leave the network.

7.4.4 State of the Art

P2P High-level Characterization

The first broad characterization study [SGG02] of well-known P2P networks was done in the Spring of 2001. Crawlers for the then popular Napster and Gnutella networks were written in Java and gathered data for four and eight days identifying over a half million and over a million nodes respectively in the two protocols. The two protocols were chosen due to their visibility at that time and subsequent studies have looked at a broader collection of protocols. An even earlier study [AH00] looked at the number of files shared by the peers and had identified the freeriding issue in the Gnutella network. The Spring 2001 study also looked at the distribution of bottleneck bandwidths and the degree of cooperation among the peers. The primary result of this study was the demonstration of heterogeneity in performance characteristics of the peers. The degree of sharing, for example, varied by several orders of magnitude between the peers. One way in which freeriding was being effected was nodes deliberately lying about their bandwidth. Peers that claim to have higher bandwidth naturally received more download requests and the study showed that a fifth of the Napster nodes did not report any information on their bandwidth. It is not practical for every peer participating in a download to actively measure the bandwidth if such information is either not provided or is suspicious. Later we will see how throttling techniques in eMule and BitTorrent addressed this problem.

Both the crawlers in the Spring 2001 study began their crawl similar to Web crawlers: using a seed set of nodes to contact and discovering additional peers through them. Apart from reported bandwidth, the Napster crawler gathered a variety of information about the nodes: its IP address, the number of available files, the number of uploads and downloads in progress, and meta-information about the files (names, sizes). Apart from high-level characterization of node and unique IP address counts, the study reported on latency and lifetime measurements. Active nodes would respond to a TCP SYN with a SYN/ACK packet while inactive nodes would return a RST. The study also measured bottleneck bandwidths of a peer as an approximation of its available bandwidth. The study was originating from a well-connected site and any bottleneck present would be at the last-hop link to the peer. A tailored bottleneck link bandwidth tool was created that detected cross-traffic, and measured both upstream and downstream bottleneck bandwidths. As one measure of freeriding, the study reported that a mere 7% of the Gnutella peers offered more files than the remaining 93% of the peers combined. A significant fraction (30%) of Napster users lied about their available bandwidth.

A study [KWX01] done in the summer of 2001 was based on passive listening but via a modified P2P client. The goal of this study was to move beyond characterization and explore alternate architecture to address the scalability issue inherent in Gnutella-like protocols. An open source Gnutella client was modified to join the network in multiple locations for varying durations of time ranging from a few hours to several days. The client passively listened and logged all messages routed through it. The study proposed creating a network-aware cluster [KW00] of P2P clients that are topologically closer. The clients within a cluster could use a cluster representative – a delegate – which would attempt to handle a query emanating from the cluster first before forwarding it to the rest of the P2P network. The delegate nodes acted as a directory server. Hierarchies have always helped in improving scalability and caching has aided in improving performance. Here the caching was restricted to queries and query responses. The study however showed that nearly half of the queries across clusters are repeated and thus candidates for caching. The study also showed results similar to earlier characterization studies; namely that a few resources are highly popular and clusters that have more files generate more query responses. The simulated portion of the study showed that a much higher fraction of queries would actually result in a successful response in the cluster-based architecture.

Unlike active probing studies or modified clients listening passively, purely passive studies examining flow-level records gathered via *netflow* in a large ISP backbone have been carried out to examine various characteristics of P2P networks. A 2002 study [KW02a] examined router-level data for nearly three weeks from a variety of Internet Gateway Routers and filtered for specific default application ports belonging to a variety of well-known P2P protocols, such as Gnutella (6346/6347), DirectConnect (411/412), and FastTrack (1214, used by KaZaa). Over two terabytes of traffic flow was covered in the study which separated signaling traffic (flow sizes smaller than 4K) from the rest which was classified as data traffic. Several millions of unique IP addresses were identified as participants in the various protocols with FastTrack having already achieved significant numeric superiority over Gnutella. The methodology used to analyze was that of a graph representation of the traffic quite similar to the study discussed in the DNS section (Section 7.2.5).

This study also demonstrated that signaling traffic volume was negligible compared to the data volume. Similar to the previous Spring 2001 study, 0.1% of the IP addresses contributed 30% of the data traffic; the signaling traffic was a bit more evenly distributed: 1% of the IP addresses contributed 25% of the signaling traffic. The inference from the data volume distribution is that popular content is stored at few places on the P2P network. The signaling traffic is more influenced by the application-level topology of the P2P network.

Passive studies have the advantage of examining *all* protocols rather than a restricted focus on popular protocols such as Gnutella or Napster. Examination in a large ISP's backbone can also answer questions regarding spatial distribution of P2P traffic across the Internet and the application-level connectivity of the nodes. In fact the only P2P-specific information used to gather the data was the port number. Since destination port numbers are a field in the *netflow* record, it is easy to filter and separate the various P2P protocols from a collection of *netflow* records. Passive studies inherently do not impose any load on the P2P network and do not interfere with the normal exchange of data. However, passive measurements via *netflow* are limited to where data is gathered. For example, due to routing asymmetry it is entirely possible for some phases of the P2P transaction to be seen but not others. In any large ISP it would be well-nigh impossible to gather data at all routers due to administrative difficulties as well as having to deal with the volume of the traffic. An advantage of passive study is that the duration for which analysis can be done can be significantly longer and a richer set of characteristics can be studied.

Such a broader passive measurement study [SW02] was carried out over four weeks spread out over the last four months of 2001. Several traditional characterization metrics such as host distribution, participating entities, their connection times, and bandwidth usage were studied. Additionally, the study also examined aggregate traffic volume exchanged between nodes at various granularities: IP address-level, prefix-level, and AS-level. In the 800 million flow records analyzed, several million participating IP addresses were observed, with FastTrack being the most popular P2P protocol. Overall traffic volumes approached nearly 2 Terabytes/day. Although Gnutella nodes and FastTrack nodes both on average showed roughly similar daily traffic (around 2 megabytes/day), the number of unique IP addresses involved in Fast-Track grew up to nearly 2 million which was 8 times that of Gnutella's and nearly 270 times that of DirectConnect. However, DirectConnect nodes tended to stay connected longer and exchanged a higher traffic volume daily thanks to the nature of the content being exchanged and better connectivity of the participating nodes. This passive study, like the earlier study, also showed the presence of a few heavy-hitters responsible for a large fraction of the traffic. Primarily due to the use of Supernodes by FastTrack, nearly 90% of the nodes in that network communicated with fewer than 10 other nodes; the top 1% of the nodes communicated with 80 other nodes. In examining dynamics of nodes, the study showed that most nodes remained active for less than half an hour and a significant fraction (20%) of the connections last less than a minute. The latter is presumably reflecting the signaling traffic of queries and responses. Not too surprisingly, nodes that communicated with many other nodes tended to be on the network longer. The study indicated the growing popularity of cable and DSL customers in examining the average downstream bandwidth. In general, the study concluded that the heavy-hitters (top 10%) display a heavy-tailed distribution but not necessarily Zipf-like. Less than 10% of the IP addresses were responsible for over 99% of traffic volume. The top 1% of the FastTrack traffic was responsible for nearly three-quarters of the traffic volume during one 24-hour period. By examining prefix-level traffic dynamics, the study showed that the fraction of P2P traffic contributed by prefixes showed high stability as compared to overall traffic volume, thus providing justification for the cluster-based architecture [KWX01].

Another passive measurement study [KLVW04] examined the query behavior in peer-to-peer systems. This 40-day study of Gnutella was carried out to facilitate construction of synthetic workloads. Among the characteristics studied were time between queries (as a measure of the think-time aspect in P2P), popularity of queries, quiescent sessions, and number of queries in a session. An interesting aspect of this study was contrasting the geographical location of peers with their behavior with respect to diurnal patterns, passive count of peers and duration of sessions. The study reported that a much larger fraction of sessions in Asia were significantly short and issued fewer queries. The pricing model of Internet differs between the regions and is reflected in the relatively shorter interarrival time for queries in Europe compared to North American peers. The study concludes with an algorithm for construction of

P2P workloads with separate steps for modeling active and passive peers, factoring in session length based on time of day, and accounting for geographical location of peers.

Peer Location, Availability, and Selection

In a typical peer-to-peer system a node in the network may not have much choice on selecting peers from which it can download content. If the P2P network has central nodes with high bandwidth to which new nodes connect, the joining node will share the bandwidth of the central node with all other nodes connected to that central node. Given the wide heterogeneity in the set of peers on a network, how can a peer quickly locate better connected peers? In the presence of rapid churn in the set of peers joining and leaving the network, passive past measurements are not likely to be helpful. Many peers also lie about their connectivity. Periodic active probing of the current choice of peers is thus an attractive alternative. With this in mind, several proposals have been made to probe the network to identify the actual bandwidth of peers. Lightweight probes like pings can identify the round trip times. Downloading a certain chunk of content while recording the transfer time and monitoring the transfer itself via tools like nettimer [LB01], can help identify the raw bottleneck bandwidth of the path. One study that combined trace-based and live measurements showed that it is possible to identify near-optimal peers by trying just a handful of candidates [NCR+03]. The problem of selecting peers is similar to selecting Web servers except that the choice in the case of the Web is typically done by the server farm that replicates the content rather than imposing the requirement on the user. However, we can visualize P2P intermediaries whose job it would be to identify the peers with good bandwidth.

Choosing peers requires an examination of node availability. An availability study [BSV03] of the P2P network Overnet done over a week showed that availability depended on both the short and long-term joining and leaving patterns of the nodes in the network. The IDs of nodes in the Overnet network do not change and thus it is easier to track them over a period of time. The node IDs were gathered via a two-week crawl of the Overnet network followed by targeted probes of a subset 72 times a day for a week. This study also pointed out the significant problem of IP address aliasing (only 1 in 4 addresses mapped to a unique host) and the effect of aliasing was seen even within the duration of a single day.

Use of P2P in Other Applications

Measurements on the P2P network have not been just to identify problems with P2P or to improve specific P2P protocols. There have been several other applications proposed to harness the use of P2P paradigm. Among these applications are a P2P-based Web search engine [ZLT04], ways to alleviate flash crowds [SMB02], a hierarchical live media streaming tool [THD03], P2P-support for networked games [KLXH04], and even a spam-prevention mechanism [ZZZ$^+$03]. We briefly discuss some of these applications to give a flavor of the role of measurement in justifying the use of the P2P paradigm for these applications.

Just as searching has been one of the most popular applications in the World Wide Web, the searching phase of P2P protocols is one of the most important. Given the nature of content ownership on P2P networks, it is not surprising that an external search mechanism, such as that of a Web search engine, has not been popular for P2P content. If such a tool existed many, if not all, the search results would point to content of suspect ownership. Napster provided this capability and was shut down due to legal concerns. eDonkey and its variants, as well as KaZaa are among the P2P protocols that provide keyword-based searches. On the Web the popular search engines construct inverted indexes of terms in the Web pages indexed and provide a central searching facility by comparing incoming search queries against the central index. With an array of fast machines and high bandwidth connectivity, popular search engines like Teoma, AltaVista, and Google are able to provide sub-second response to searches. In the case of P2P networks, after Napster's demise, there are no central inverted indices. Instead as the queries are flooded through the P2P network (up to a certain depth), the terms are searched against the local collection of resources or against past cached queries for query responses to be generated. Distributing a global index of all the resources accessible over a given P2P network would require the index to be split and updated if resources are added or deleted. A feasibility study [LLH$^+$03] discusses the challenges in constructing a Web search engine based on the P2P paradigm and is pessimistic about the ability to succeed with existing technology. If the users were willing to compromise on the quality of results there is some potential for such an approach to succeed.

For applications requiring streaming of media that consumes considerable bandwidth, one or more intermediaries might be needed to ensure that all clients who want to receive the streaming content can receive it without facing network delays. Popular videos of news segments or cartoons (such as Jibjab [Jib]) require several megabytes to be streamed to clients. If the content is popular, even in the absence of a flash crowd, the same content has to be streamed to all the clients. If there are caches near the user such content can be prefetched, buffered, and delivered. One possible solution is to use a P2P scheme in conjunction with a multicast tree. It is possible to leverage the bandwidth of intermediate receivers to spread the content to other receivers. A joining node could walk down the tree until it locates a peer that has available bandwidth before attaching itself. Other proposals suggest encoding the media content in multiple ways in different streams. If some peers in the tree were to depart others would be able to make up for the lost signal without the source being burdened with repeated requests.

Characterization of Specific P2P Protocols

There have been several attempts to characterize specific P2P protocols ranging from the early days of Gnutella (which demonstrated the freeriding phenomenon) to the more recent look at popular protocols such as KaZaa, eDonkey, and BitTorrent. Protocol characterization studies by their very nature are likely to have a lower shelf life due to the shifts in popularity of protocols and the shift in the nature of resources exchanged. Napster consisted exclusively of MP3 music files but the portion of network traffic consumed as a result of exchanging movies and videos is much higher now.

We examine two different protocols; both of which are currently popular: eDonkey and BitTorrent. eDonkey is a generic name for a group of P2P protocols that share similar attributes including eDonkey2000 [HB02], eMule [Emu], and mlDonkey [Mld]. Beyond popularity the two P2P protocols chosen have some interesting characteristics that are unique among the dozens of P2P protocols and their variants introduced over the last few years. Note that DirectConnect, which uses a hub (supernode), also requires that each client share a certain number of files with others. The requirement is enforced by the hub to which all DirectConnect clients have to first connect. Each hub is free to decide the number of files that a client connecting to it must share.

eDonkey. Unlike traditional P2P architectures, eDonkey clients participate in exchanging files while eDonkey servers simply return locations of files. eDonkey servers thus act in a manner similar to the centralized Napster server. No files are uploaded to or downloaded from the eDonkey server although, unlike Napster all users are free to operate a eDonkey server. In eDonkey all download requests are queued on the content provider node. Note that the full content is rarely requested; typically it is just a chunk of the full resource. Chunk sizes vary but are often 10 megabytes. It is entirely possible for a download request to be queued and for the requesting eDonkey client not to obtain a single byte of the requested chunk due to several reasons. The reasons could range from the providing eDonkey node being busy, the requesting eDonkey node not having met its required fairness criterion of uploading a number of bytes proportional to what it downloaded, to the providing node leaving the network. At any given time the eDonkey client may be downloading multiple chunks from multiple nodes. All downloads occur over TCP on port 4662 with connections timing out typically when the idle duration exceeds 40 seconds.

A *tcpdump* based study [Tut04] of eDonkey in August 2003 examined nearly

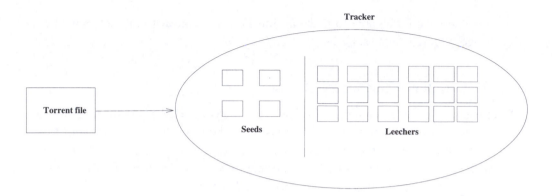

Figure 7.12   BitTorrent seeds, leechers, and torrent file.

3.5 million TCP connections between nearly 2.5 million hosts exchanging nearly 300 gigabytes over a dozen days. Average download stream sizes were around 2.5 megabytes (mainly due to chunking) and follow a lognormal distribution. Download connections on average last less than 15 minutes. Signaling traffic size is around 17 kilobytes on average per flow with a few above 14 Kbytes. The study also showed that eDonkey traffic was more pronounced in Europe than in the rest of the world.

BitTorrent.   BitTorrent introduced another novel feature to P2P: that of simultaneous uploading and downloading, as another attempt to reduce the freeriding problem and to improve the performance of downloads. BitTorrent is used to download newer versions of different variants of the Linux Operating System. While a peer is downloading chunks of a resource, it is requested to upload it simultaneously to other peers interested in the same chunk. A tracker process keeps track of live peers; peers can be *seeds* that donate content or *leeches* that download content. Information about a subset of live peers (called the *peer set*) is passed onto new peers as they contact a tracker process as part of joining the network. A torrent file downloaded from one of several Web sites has information on the tracker processes. Figure 7.12 shows a torrent file that has the IP address of the tracker process that maintains the current list of seeds and leecher.

Figure 7.13 shows how a BitTorrent client peer (a leecher) is downloading chunks of a resource from a set of BitTorrent seeds. A key difference between BitTorrent and other P2P protocols is its focus on speeding up downloads and ignoring the search phase; it thus expands on eDonkey variants in this aspect. Chunks in BitTorrent are typically 256 kilobytes and much smaller than eDonkey. As a chunk is downloaded the peer set is notified about it and any of them can download it. Each peer maintains the upload rate of the peers that sent it data. Similar to eDonkey, the ability of a peer to download from another depends on its upload/download ratio. As can be

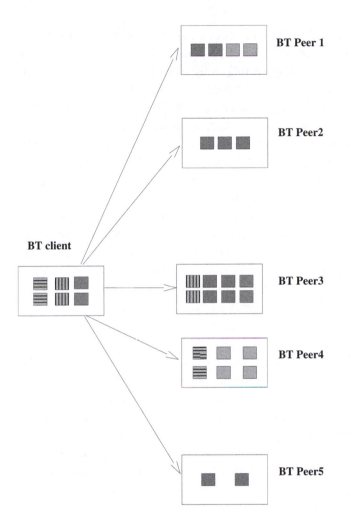

Figure 7.13   BitTorrent client downloading from a peer set.

seen in Figure 7.13, the same chunks may be available on multiple peers and based
on the upload/download ratio and business of the individual seed peers chunks are
made available to the leecher client. BitTorrent peers can optionally *choke* peers that
are considered freeriders. BitTorrent clients can also suspend downloads and resume
them in a later session.

A study [MGW+04] based on analyzing a tracker log over several months was
carried out in 2003 with an overall number of 180000 clients participating. The content being exchanged was a 2 gigabyte distribution of a Linux version. The study had
a period of five days which constituted a flash crowd as several thousands of users
tried to obtain a copy of the Operating System. The first novel inference from the

study was the longevity of BitTorrent clients as compared to other P2P clients: the clients in this study stayed connected for over six hours after joining. One important social reason for this was identified in this study to be the fact that the content downloaded was devoid of any ownership concerns – it was legally free and thus nodes need not be transient. One of the main reasons BitTorrent clients can handle flash crowds is that nodes with more content share more and thus can quickly end up with a full copy of the resource. There are no single choke points and the speed with which other nodes get copies immediately translates into helping with speedier replication of the chunks to other nodes. Another intriguing and beneficial feature of BitTorrent is that a node attempts to copy the least-replicated chunk so that it can more effectively help others. Popular chunks do not end up becoming the dominant copies. The average download rate is significantly higher than other networks; this study showed that the metric was over 500 kb/s. Part of the reason is that clients in BitTorrent are well connected but the other reason is that the protocol scales. A vast fraction of the completed sessions in the study involved the significant portion of overall data volume indicating the efficiency of the protocol. Examination of the geographical distribution showed that the overall spread of BitTorrent clients downloading is more global than eDonkey. An instrumented client was added to interact with the BitTorrent network in the middle of the study and was not present during the flash crowd. The analysis showed that a significant fraction of the time the client was involved in uploading or downloading and it was always able to find chunks from peers and find peers who need the chunks already downloaded. Many peers that had complete copies stayed around long enough to finish delivering its chunks to others. The flexible manner in which peers can choke and unchoke other peers, the good matching aspect, and overall altruism of peers are all responsible for the efficiency of the BitTorrent protocol.

P2P over Wireless Networks

With the growth of mobile clients, it is natural to examine whether there is P2P traffic among mobile clients. There have not been many studies in this regard but Section 7.3.4 earlier discussed the study [HKA04] which examined wireless traffic in a campus involving several thousand users. Between the first study done in 2001 and this study carried out in 2003 there was a 55-fold increase in P2P traffic volume. Although the later study involved more users and increased campus capacity, this is still an impressive increase over wireless networks! In the 2003 study, which showed nearly a fifth of overall wireless traffic was P2P, the DirectConnect protocol was the dominant one with almost three-quarters of the P2P traffic share. While KaZaa, Gnutella, BitTorrent, eDonkey, and Napster were present in the traces, their fraction was much smaller. The campus network also had a packet shaper that enforced bandwidth limits on certain well-known ports associated with P2P traffic. Since Direct-Connect enforces sharing of files at the hub level, the study showed that a significant fraction of clients did share a fair fraction of files. Also, the study showed a large fraction of P2P traffic (over 70%) was *intra-campus* indicating that users shared files with each other locally. The bandwidth limitation thus acts as an interesting traffic redirection mechanism. The other notable observation about P2P traffic in this study was that more than half the traffic involved less than 7% of users. In the beginning of this state of the art section we had discussed the first broad characterization study [SGG02] which had an even higher skew.

7.5 Online Games

One of the fastest growing areas in terms of users, although not yet in terms of traffic, is networked games. Games on the Internet have always been popular and most hosts had single user games from the very early days of computing. Later multi-user games without significant real-time requirements became popular; examples include the older MUDs (Multi-User Dungeons) and turn based strategy games such as the card game bridge. Game participants could be present in random geographical locations and small bits of information would be exchanged between them as each player in turn played their hand. Within the last few years networked games became interactive, enabled non-turn-based playing (simultaneous movements in parallel to other players), and scaled to a large number of players. There are numerous reasons for this including improvement in the network, graphics infrastructure, and CPU. The proliferation of massively multiplayer games with large-scale hosting infrastructures and rapidly growing interest on the part of participants induced by better connectivity from homes with high capacity and low latencies also contributed. Recently introduction of popular games such as EverQuest belonging to Sony Corporation, have drawn in hundreds of thousands of players, willing to pay a monthly charge (or play using prepaid cards, as in Asia) and spend multiple hours a day involved in the game. Large-scale network infrastructure with stringent requirements on avoiding packet loss, link failure, application-level robustness, authorization checks, and fidelity of the user experience have all been mandatory for successful online games. The commercial value of personalities created within the games and certain 'magic' items found in games have increased steadily. The ability to auction these to the highest bidder has led to a steady increase in popularity of the games and the resulting interest in measuring the traffic for a variety of properties. There have been studies of the sales of game elements as part of examination of economies of massively multiplayer online games [Cas03, Cas04]. Many players buy or trade game elements to improve their game playing experience.

Although the networked game arena has only recently become popular there have been several network-related measurements that have been carried out. The nature of measurements is tied to the somewhat unique requirements of this application. We will take a quick look at the application properties and present a flavor of the nature of measurements that have been done. An in-depth examination of networked games measurement is a bit premature at this point as the field is still in its infancy.

7.5.1 Games and Measurement Properties

A key realization in examining gaming applications is that there is a wide variety of networked games. The popular genre of so-called First Person Shooter (FPS) games include Halflife [Hal], Quake [Quab], Counter-Strike [Cou], Battlefield 1942 [Bat], Doom3 [Doo], and Unreal Tournament [Unr]. In FPS games, a virtual character representing a user gathers weapons and tries to destroy other players. As a player 'moves' in the virtual world, the movement is relayed to the game server which then has to broadcast that state change to other players. Meanwhile the other players may also be moving; the lag between the movement and the state update requires players to guess where other players might be and compensate [Ber01] for that. Clients cannot be permitted to simply indicate their coordinates since they could easily cheat and send the wrong information and avoid being hit by other players. Cheating is thus a major concern (both in FPS and in other genres) and a main reason for the central game server to be involved in controlling and directing game movement updates.

Other genres include Massive Multiplayer Online Role Playing Games (MM-PORPG, such as EverQuest), Real Time Strategy (such as Age of Empires [AOE], and Warcraft [War]). Probably the most popular game in terms of sales are the Sims simulation family of games (SIMcity, SIMS2, SIMSonline, etc.) although these are the non-networked single player versions. Separately, there are many games that are tied to a specific hardware platform with proprietary interfaces. Examples include Nintendo [Nin], Sony Playstation [Son], or Microsoft Xbox [Mic]). Each game genre has varying real-time requirements in terms of latency. For example, although the popular GPL Arcade Volleyball (GAV [GAV]) game works fine over wired networks, it is currently impossible [BLME04] to have a version of the game over wireless networks such as General Packet Radio Services (GPRS) or UMTS.

There are significant differences between the various games and thus the set of measurements of interest vary. Table 7.7 enumerates the list of interesting measurement properties that we examine in networked games through the lens of a set of key-related issues. The broader issue of the interactive nature of this application dominates all the measurement properties to some extent. Unpredictability of user behavior can have a significant impact on load on the game server, users' session lengths and other access pattern issues. The type of game could be another broad

Table 7.7   Networked games properties of interest to measure.

Measured property	Why measured	Where measured
Traffic characterization	Growth patterns, popularity	Across Internet
Game system architecture	Difference in architecture	Across Internet
Scalability	Provisioning, performance	Varies with game genre
Real-time requirements	Game viability and latency limitations	Game client
Manner of access	Mobility constraints	Client and server locations
Session duration	State maintenance	Server

axis except that many of the games that are open and thus studied by researchers, fall in the FPS category. Minor variations in game genre do not alter basic measurement concerns.

There is evidence that MMORPG games are even more popular than FPS games [Mmo]. For example, the combined Lineage and Lineage-II game versions have nearly four million players [lin]. This particular game is quite popular in cyber-cafes where access to the games are rented out on an hourly basis. The count of players is obtained by including players who play in cybercafes as opposed to counting actual purchasers or subscribers of the game. There is a general lack of agreement on proper ways to count players. At present, the methodology by which popularity data is gathered depends on news articles, anonymous sources, etc. A clearly articulated measurement methodology for measuring popularity is still a work in progress.

Traffic Characterization

The first property is basic characterization in terms of fraction of Internet traffic and individual popularity of games. Coherent measures of Internet traffic due to games is still in its infancy given the more recent popularity of this application. Most characterization techniques are similar to P2P in the sense of sampling traffic flowing to and from port numbers associated with games. There has also been characterization of individual games. These included both traditional Internet metrics such as size and inter-arrival time of packets (to help in the construction of analytic models for simulation), and network games-specific behavioral differences between clients and server. A sizable fraction of game traffic may stay entirely inside proprietary networks, making it harder to characterize on an Internet-wide basis. Surveys can be used to overcome this difficulty. However, a snapshot of aggregate user population over varying durations of time is available for some Massive Multiplayer Online

Role Playing Games. Such characterization can be obtained via game plugins (e.g., World of Warcraft's census [WoW] tool) or from external aggregators available from GameSpy [Gam] and Steam [Ste].

Game System Architecture

There are three broad architectures of the networked games: centralized, decentralized, and a hybrid of these two. In a centralized architecture, clients send all interaction requests with other clients via a central server that carries out authentication and returns updates of the various client's positions in the virtual world. Not all clients have to know about each move by a client and thus the central game server needs to have an overarching view of what each client needs to know at any given instant. The central server needs to have significant processing capability, must be highly reliable, and the network path between the clients and the central server must have low latency and low packet loss. As mentioned earlier, the primary reason for the centralized architecture is the widespread concern about cheating. The centralized architecture remains the most widely realized version among all the popular networked games.

In a decentralized architecture, such as ones proposed using P2P technologies, clients may be able to interact directly with each other. Examples of proposed decentralized architectures include Mimaze [GD98], Mercury [BRS02], P2P-Support [KLXH04] and Zoned Federations [Iim04]. Partitioning players and associated responsibility into regions is one way to partially decentralize the architecture; an extreme version of this would be to completely decentralize by allowing any peer in a P2P network to carry out the necessary authentication to eliminate cheating and enforce all the rules of the games. Mirrored server architecture is one kind of hybrid distributed architecture with each game having several distributed servers, but clients are partitioned to communicate with just one server each. An example of a game model that uses a hybrid architecture is FreeMMG [CRdOJ$^+$04], which combines a client–server and a peer-to-peer architecture.

Beyond authentication and updating positions there are minor, less intensive functions provided by game servers such as maintaining scores of the players and providing information about different players and teams. In either architecture, the games can be played by each player against all other players or by sets of players (teams) against other teams. The manner in which players join the game can be streamlined or ad-hoc groups may be allowed to form teams dynamically. Managing the forming of teams and maintaining fidelity across teams is part of the responsibility of the server. Beyond forming teams, a combination of real-world and virtual-world phenomena can be used to provide a richer environment for the game participants (e.g., the Human Pacman [CFG$^+$03] or Can You See Me Now? [Can]). In Human Pacman, a game that merges ubiquitous computing and augmented reality, physical location of the players is made available via GPS and players combine physical information with virtual objects such as cookies which can be picked up by the players for interaction.

Scalability

Scalability in networked games primarily deals with the number of players who participate simultaneously. The numbers can vary from a few tens to hundreds or in the extreme cases to over a million users. Examples of such games are EverQuest, Lineage, and Fantasy Westward Journey [Wes] (a massive multi-player online role playing game popular in China). In some games, a single human user can have multiple incarnations (avatars) often simultaneously. With the increased number of players, communication delays between the clients and the centralized server can increase significantly as players randomly join, interact, and leave the game. With feature- and scenario-rich games, considerable information may need to be sent back in updates to the clients at the end of each move of any player. The provisioning of the server's resources in terms of the computational capability and network bandwidth can often dictate the potential for scalability to a large number of players. It is important to note that such highly popular games do split the set of players into a significant number of independent realms that are backed up by individual servers. A single machine may often only support a few thousand players at any given time.

Real-time Requirements

Other applications we have seen thus far including P2P, Web, and even DNS do not have the strict real-time requirements that are often the hallmark of First Person Shooter games. The real-time requirement of a network game varies across game genres – strategy games typically tend to have a less stringent requirement. However, the requirement can often be the limiting factor for the viability of a game – if the game does not meet this requirement the number of players willing to participate may drop dramatically. There are clear implications on allowable latencies (typically less than 100 milliseconds) and packet loss depending on the game genre. The popular console game online Madden NFL football began to show significant variations in user performance when latencies exceeded 500 milliseconds in a study [NC04]. FPS games can add forward error correction to reduce the impact of packet loss but Real Time Strategy games that use TCP (e.g., Warcraft3 [War]) will be impacted. An additional wrinkle is that even within a single networked game the impact of network performance can have varying effects. For example, depending on the choice of weapons in FPS games, delay or loss of packets can render some weapons worthless. High precision weapons such as the Shock Rifle or Lightning Gun in the Unreal Tournament game require timely responses, otherwise the location of the opponent would not be accurately determined [BCL$^+$04]. Low precision weapons in the same game do not require precise location and are thus less prone to any severe impact as a result of lost or delayed packets.

Manner of Access: Wired and Mobile Environments

Networked games may consist solely of wired clients who operate out of fixed network positions or a set of roaming wireless clients that operate under strictly different networking conditions. In a mobile environment locating the client may be part of the game and the increasing popularity of Global Positioning System (GPS) and Bluetooth [Blu] devices harbingers growth in this arena. Active Bat [HHS$^+$99] and Cricket [PCB00] are examples of indoor location systems. Accuracy in locating the client is an important metric in such environments. Earlier we presented the example of GAV (GPL Arcade Volleyball) as a game that while popular in a wired environment may never attain low latency requirement in a wireless environment due to the underlying wireless network's loss characteristics. If the RTT measurements between a client and a server in GPRS networks exceeds one second, it is difficult to play GAV in such environments. In 3G wireless systems such as UMTS networks, the RTT is significantly lower, yet it does not meet the maximum latency permitted, which is often between 100 to 200 ms [BLME04]. The stringent latency demands are not met on many wireless networks. One alternative [FSR02] is an architecture with distinct components for dealing with portions of the traffic. The IP backbone where the game server resides handles authentication and initiation but the actual handling of the busier and latency-critical components of traffic are left to terminals associated with multi-player networks that can handle the stringent latency requirements.

Single-session (Short-term) vs. Multi-session (Long-term) Games

In the early days of networked games, many of the games consisted of a user joining a game, playing a single session, and leaving the game upon its termination. These days many popular games involve players playing for a considerable duration either at a single stretch, or disconnecting and returning to play the game over an extended period of time such as multiple days, weeks or months. Such games indicate a sense of persistence in the virtual world. The value of an online character can grow and ebb over the duration. Even small performance lapses in the network may lead to information about a player (such as obtaining a special object in a game) not being conveyed to other players. In FPS games performance lapses can be catastrophic as a player's character may be killed.

There is no significant interest in measuring properties of games that show non-persistence in the virtual world; we mention them here for historical purposes only.

7.5.2 Networked Games Measurement Challenges

The set of challenges in game measurements are significantly different from those of DNS or Web. The primary reason is that the game application is highly interactive with significantly lower thresholds of tolerance for errors and delays. The network effects have to be studied in isolation from the subjective aspects of a user's interaction with the game. Simulating players via programs is harder in networked games than with the Web. There has been work on source models [Bor99, Bor00] for network game traffic beginning in 1999. Due to the diversity of the possible user actions, work on user workload models does vary across the games, such as Counter-Strike [CF03], HalfLife [LABC03], and Quake [LBA04]. In spite of the challenges, numerous measurements have been carried out in many popular games. We will examine the set of challenges along the axes of hidden data and layers; we ignore entities as there aren't enough measurements of them in this application yet.

Hidden Data

In the various genres of networked games, the players are situated in different segments of the Internet with varying degrees of connectivity to the game server and on personal computers with differing computational ability. In console games, such as Xbox and Sony PS2, there is a general expectation that players have a minimum level of connectivity such as broadband although there may be some minor variations in effective throughput. Non-console games do have a much higher probability of variation in connectivity and computational ability. More importantly, the skill levels of the players, their degree of dexterity and concentration, all vary. During the course of a game there can be considerable variation in these characteristics. The impact of packet loss, latency, etc., will thus not be felt uniformly by all players or even by the same player during the course of a game session [NC04, Arm01]. A player in a weak situation in the game may be doubly hurt by a performance lapse. Unlike a Web session, where users are generally passive and can easily adjust to the ambient network conditions, interactive games generally do not provide ways to overcome even transient troubles. It is thus impossible to measure the perception difficulties across classes of players. Consequently uniform ways of measuring the impact of network problems is hard. Yet, this is one of the key metrics of interest.

The provisioning of the game system's server can have a significant impact on overcoming difficulties perceived by the player. There is a bare-bone minimum threshold above which latency or packet loss on the network path will make the performance unbearable for the client. The information about how well a game system server is provisioned is rarely public and not easy to reverse engineer. Many game servers routinely allow large-scale download of game content or patches to existing software and this traffic can have an impact on the normal game traffic. News feeds provide information on when newer versions or patches become available and the size of the patch can be computed by monitoring the game client. In some cases separate servers are used to deliver the new version or updates so as not to interfere with the regular game servers. If the regular game servers are used, there would be an expected increase in traffic shortly after a new update. Downloads of patches may also be subject to rate limiting. The frequency of such downloads is not often publicly known. Additionally, the algorithms the server uses to arbitrate between the large number of players interacting with the system and the rest of its responsibilities cannot be reverse engineered easily. Typical player-generated traffic is small packets involving update, while servers aggregate such updates over some period of time and may send out larger broadcast packets to all players. Estimating the arrival rate of such broadcast packets may depend on the particular server as well as the player-generated traffic.

Unlike DNS or HTTP, networked games typically do not have intermediaries between the players and the game server for a variety of reasons. The game server is often the centralized entity authenticating the clients and monitoring the different activities. Absence of intermediaries does simplify measurements greatly. One exception is the popular setup involving Half-Life, called HLTV [Hog] that uses proxies to support spectators of the game via a multicast tree.

Hidden Layers

All the popular game genres typically involve authentication, setting up game parameters, the actual playing, and finally departing from the game. In some games one or more of the steps may be avoided by suspending the state and continuing from a previous session. Authentication involves identification of the player, which may be done via a TCP handshake. Game moves are often sent over UDP or TCP; downloads of new versions are often over TCP. Given lack of ordered delivery reliability in UDP, some games, such as Quake, timestamp the packets to restore order and use redundancy to handle packet loss.

Given that a significant fraction of popular games involve clients interacting directly with centralized game servers there are not many hidden layers. Additionally, games rarely involve intermediaries like content redirectors or proxies. Proxies have however been proposed [MW02] apart from the aforementioned HLTV. Finally, long session-oriented applications, such as networked games or FTP, in general are less complex, since a significant fraction of the exchange occurs during the initial authorization step. During the course of the session the measurements can be carried out in a mostly steady state unless many players are joining or leaving the game. Game users tend to leave when they experience lag or delay which may be due to the number of players active as well as the state of the game. In a Web environment, the arrival rate of requests follows a significantly different pattern as most of the interactions are short-lived. Users tend not to back-off from a Web site unless they experience significant delays at a site.

The multiple axes of measurement involving a large number of concurrent players from different segments of the Internet introduces layers of complexity. However, in an interactive game, delays could cause players to react differently. The delays on the server end would have to be factored while measuring delays from the point of view of the player. The 'think time' of the user, pausing between moves, has to be modeled differently between games; although the notion of think time is different in networked games as opposed to Web browsing since the game client may generate updates even if the user is idle. A delay of a few milliseconds in a racing game may not be as critical – a study showed that delays up to 50 ms were not critical [PW02] in a car racing game and up to 500 ms in the online Madden NFL Football game [NC04]. However, in a multiplayer game even a short delay can result in a critical weapon missing its intended target. Even if the network delay is significantly reduced, players who are physically apart by several thousand miles may have to deal with a 10 ms propagation delay across distant continents. Players may be adjusting to delays in unpredictable ways since it is difficult to get accurate measures of how players react during adverse network conditions. Any objective measurement of impact of delays has to take into account players' subjective reactions under normal and abnormal condition as well as checking if they played in a particular way due to external conditions.

Game quality [SERZ02] can be broken into network quality controlled by the transport layer, objective game quality that includes transport, game client and server as well as I/O devices, and finally subjective game quality that includes the human player. Further, it is harder to get objective measures in team-oriented games than individual games as group measurements introduce another level of complexity. Unlike mostly stateless Web transactions, highly stateful game sessions could lead to perceptual difference at more crucial junctures in the game. Path jitter in the early stages of a game may matter a lot less than at later stages of the game where adversaries have more to lose from a bad move induced by network delays. Finally, the effect of adverse conditions is not likely to affect all players equally depending on their location in the Internet. The difference in subjective and objective influences of network conditions is one of the key hidden layers in measurements in games.

Tools

The standard set of network measurement tools are used in the game applications. They include the traditional *ping* for active probing of game servers and *tcpdump* for passive recording of game traffic at the server end. The active probing is aimed at computing networked games-specific metrics like *latency radius*: how many active players are within the bounds of a specified latency threshold. Another application level ping tool created for games is *qstat* [Qst] which displays game server status, player information, and other statistics for a variety of FPS games. The tool was created by reverse engineering the game protocols.

Traditional passive measurements including average bandwidth, packet count and size, packet interarrival time, number of attempted and successful connections, unique clients, etc. are also done at the server end. RTT measurements are typically done at the server end. In FPS games latency is of significant importance and both clients and servers periodically carry out RTT measurements. If the RTT is below the practical threshold required for the game it would make sense for such players to be removed from participation. Some game administrators actually carry out this operation. In certain variants of games like Half-Life, the current latency is displayed in a graph as feedback to the users. Additionally, the impact of latency varies across users [Hen01] in a study of Half-Life as measured via RTT measurements at the game server. Geographic mapping tools used for other Internet applications are used to locate game servers that are close in a network latency sense [CFFS03].

The non-traditional tools needed for this application are tailored to the game under observation: human response time needs to be measured quite differently from network time. For example, it is common in gaming applications that whenever players are presented with a choice of game servers, players tend to pick ones that are close by in the sense of network latency which may not translate to geographic proximity. However, in multi-person games, players tend to congregate around servers that have a certain minimum number of players otherwise the game is not considered to be fun. In fact special applications such as GameSpy [Gam] and Steam [Ste] have been created to inform players of the number of players associated with each game server. Although many games have similar information for the particular game being played within the game browser, Gamespy and Steam provide information across multiple different games, and include geographic mapping tools that helps classify game server locations.

Thus, in order to obtain measurements, several non-network-related issues have to be taken into account. Workload characterization of game traffic is somewhat similar to the Web workload characterization in the sense of capturing aggregate traffic. Each player may play the same game on different game servers requiring aggregation across servers.

7.5.3   State of the Art

We examine the current state of the art in networked games measurement in five broad categories: architectural issues, traffic characterizations of popular games, the impact of network effects, synthetic traffic models generated, and mobile game environments.

Architecture

As mentioned in Section 7.5.1, the centralized architecture model is the most common genre. There have however been proposals to introduce decentralized or hybrid architectures. In fact, most of the newer research proposals have been aimed at addressing the problems with centralized architecture. There is an important distinction to be made between popular commercial networked games with many thousands of players and research proposals that are aimed at examining novel architectures that may not be practical or scalable. This has to be tempered by the view that the cost of setting up and supporting a large-scale game is prohibitively high.

MiMaze [GD97, GD98] is an example of early research on a distributed game architecture on the Internet. MiMaze did not use a central server for players' moves, relying instead on IP Multicast to guarantee consistency in the presence of network delay. Latency was limited to 100 ms and a simple game was chosen to reduce the traffic parameters. A distributed architecture implies that information about moves does not have to be sent to the central server and then resent to the other players. However, the presence of cheating and the lack of a synchronous view of the game by all players have prevented distributed architectures from gaining popularity. An alternate way of improving scalability is the introduction of proxies that would offset some of the work on the part of the central server. Many proposals along these lines have been made; some explicitly postulating a proxy [MW02] while others have suggested a publish–subscribe scheme [BRS02].

Multiple architectures based on peer-to-peer systems have been proposed. Focusing on the nexus between bandwidth requirements of games and its inherent scalability, by moving to a peer-to-peer architecture whereby nodes exchange messages with each other directly allows linear scaling with the number of players. The period of inconsistency between state updates has to be reduced and a centralized arbiter [PD03] communicates with other players only during state inconsistencies. The SimMud proposal [KLXH04] exploits the idea that players in massively multiplayer games are more interested in a narrow area near where the player is situated in the virtual world. Managing accounting information of players and other persistent features, such as the experience points of a character are centralized. Player movement information is distributed in a peer-to-peer fashion via an overlay that can scale with the number of players while maintaining a consistent view. The study did not have actual traces and therefore was not able to carry out trace-driven simulations. Instead they used a generated workload and multicast position updates. Most updates were received within six hops but some took many more hops. The number of players within a region had a bigger impact on the number of update messages generated leading to degradation. Another P2P-based proposal [Iim04] partitioned the game and the network layer by positing a zoning layer between them. Using Distributed Hash Tables (DHT) to construct a P2P network, this proposal, similar to SimMud, also exploited locality in players' accesses to reduce the updates required. However, nodes exchange messages directly avoiding application layer multicast.

Traffic Characterization.   Traffic characterizations of several popular games have been conducted. Characterizations included examination of general game traffic [Joy01] where regular traffic was filtered to look for two games: Quake World and Unreal Tournament. Characteristics such as interarrival time of packets, the size of packets, and differences between client and server behavior were examined. Both the games use UDP for transport and a central game server listening on well-known ports (27500 and 7777 respectively). Data was passively gathered using DAG cards and analyzed using code written to parse the output. The data revealed client packets are smaller but more numerous than the server packets in the Quake case. The data was then used to create traffic models. Specific games have also been characterized: for example, Counter-Strike [FCFW02, Fae02], a common variant of the popular Half-Life game. Here, the authors looked at the resource requirements of the game server of the popular game Counter-Strike with a central server maintaining game state broadcasting periodically to the players (clients). The sources of network traffic examined included player movements sent to the server, state information and special effects like sounds from the server, etc. Half a billion packets were captured in a week from nearly six thousand players. The data characterization showed that updates have to be predictable to compensate for the lag in communicating the state information. The game server had to ensure that players with limited access, such as ones on dial-up modems, were not unfairly treated. Given that many players connect over narrow pipes, the packet sizes from the clients were small and the server sent fewer but larger sized packets as updates. The analysis showed that regular traffic bursts are quite likely and packet sizes vary. The active clients imparted a fairly uniform load on the network as a result of traffic filling the last-mile pipe.

Player behavior was studied [HB01] by polling a few thousand servers running the Half-Life daemon or Quake server to see how many players were present, how long they had been connected, and (in the case of Quake) the IP addresses of the clients. This study posits that time-of-day effects of game traffic might justify a time-of-day pricing and a player's decision to join a game is correlated with the number of players already participating. However, the duration a player continues to play appears to be independent of the number of players still present: the median duration of a player's session is independent of the number of players and is relatively constant. The inter-arrival times of players do not follow a Poisson distribution but is heavy-tailed similar to Web access.

Modeling of session times [CF03] of players was carried out also by studying Counter-Strike. The study gathered traces for a one-week period using the afore-mentioned GameSpy application. Counts of the number of players, sessions, and durations were obtained. Unlike most other Internet traffic models which often have a heavy-tailed distribution, session times were seen to follow a Weibull distribution. Many players played for fairly short durations and only a handful of players played longer than a couple of hours. The failure rate was surprisingly higher when examining shorter sessions. One suggested explanation was that new versions of the game constantly appeared and players were testing the new features. This study points out the difficulty of generalized characterizations of networked games.

Impact of Network Effects

Game players consider network delay to be the principal detractor in their game experience. The quality of games as experienced by end users depends on several factors. Chief among them is the end-to-end delay. Latency is due to multiple reasons: delay in accessing the game server, load on the game server, delays due to load on the network, and finally the subjective delay induced by one player's reaction to other players' moves. The access technologies, which are at least under the control of a user, typically fall into a few broad classes: dial-up, DSL, or broadband. The so-called last mile link (from the user to the ISP) can be a crucial factor for many applications but vital for games requiring split-second reaction. Most players of popular online networked games use DSL or broadband if they are concerned about quick reaction. In fact many console games, such as Xbox Live, require broadband connectivity. Packet loss and jitter – variability in the arrival rate of the packets – may also impact the game experience.

An early study [Arm01] involving a few hundred clients and conducted over several months examined how network latency affected a player's choice of a server in the (then) popular Quake-3 game. The study used two Quake-3 servers – one that was actually in California and the other in London but deliberately misadvertised as being in California to see if it had an impact on users' choice. A player's response time varied with their skill level and the network latency. The study showed that players did select servers that were closer to them – the other server criteria being identical. This study did not include jitter.

Another study [JVC+03] looked at the delay in deployed access networks both in a real and laboratory setting of an ADSL network that had quality of service enabled. In the real network they had to distinguish between game traffic and other traffic.

Similar to other studies described earlier, such as [FCFW02], this study found that the bottleneck was the last mile link and that delays increased with packet size.

The latency study in Quake-3 [Arm01] and user behavior study [HB01] in Half-life and Quake discussed above led to examination of potential for redirection of users to nearby servers [CFFS03] in the popular CounterStrike game. This study used the King tool (discussed earlier in Section 7.2.5) to compare latency between the player and the measurement server and redirected server. The study showed that many clients could benefit from redirection while a few clients did suffer.

A small user study [QML+04] introduced delay and jitter via a piece of software on a router in the path between a game server and the players to study its impact. The players were playing a first person shooter game (Unreal Tournament 2003) on identical client machines. A variety of network conditions were simulated by changing the delay and jitter values. Participants filled out questionnaires about their perception of the quality of the network and how it affected their performance. This was contrasted to the system's rating of the user's skill based on their performance when there was no organized interference. The conclusion of this study, similar to [NC04], was that network delay had both a clear perception impact that varied with the amount of delay introduced. The Unreal Tournament 2003 game was also used in another study [BCL+04] examining effects of latency on user performances, by emulating packet loss and different latencies. The parameters for the emulation were derived by monitoring live game servers. The impact was studied against the different user interactions such as overcoming obstacles or jumping. No appreciable difference in the ability to move was seen due to the inherent compensation for such problems via predictions done at the client side in the game software. The study found that the level of packet loss was quite acceptable and did not impact players' performance. However, even 100 ms latencies caused significant drop in the player's *perceived* performance.

Synthesizing Traffic Model

Unlike other applications described thus far, where there are plenty of traces available, networked games are a relatively new application. Thus, only a few real traces have been gathered and made available for others to use. It is harder to capture traces in subscription-based games where the central server receives the traffic and controls the game. Accordingly, there has been work on synthesizing game traffic and a few of them are examined here.

There has been early work in synthesizing game traffic based on a few games – HalfLife [LABC03] and Quake [LBA04] – with the intention of using the model for future provisioning. A modified version of a Quake-II client was used to create client traffic. Multiple games were based on the engine of Quake-II to be tested against a multi-game service platform [SSR⁺04]. Given the diversity of games and differences in skill levels required for them, each game has to be examined and synthesized separately although there is a potential for reuse if the user accesses and other traffic characteristics are somewhat similar. The difficulties in obtaining data in networked games remain: a representative set of players have to be found and data captured over a period of time. The skill set of the players participating will necessarily determine the representativeness of the data. While FPS game servers can be freely downloaded and studied, it is not feasible to deploy a massive multi-player game server and attract sufficiently many clients at low cost.

The typical information gathered during the synthesizing phase includes the number of packets, packet length and inter-arrival time in both directions, and server response time. Packet tracing tools are used to log information about packet characteristics and inter-arrival times. For some older games, the rate at which a game server communicates with the client has a fairly narrow variance and is thus easy to model. For example, the lognormal distribution was seen as a good fit for packet lengths in traffic originating from the server up to a certain size threshold (400 bytes, which comprised most of the traffic) in the Half-Life game synthesis. The packet lengths of traffic originating from client matches a normal distribution. In the Quake-3 game the packet length of messages originating from the server varied more with additional clients joining the game.

Mobile Environments

In the more recent cases of networked games played over wireless networks, there have been relatively few broad measurements. If we consider the sub-genre of games that meld the physical world and networked world, such as Human Pacman [CFG⁺03] or Can You See Me Now? [Can], there are even fewer measurements. Alternative measurements have been carried out by converting popular wired networked games into mobile equivalents. For example, the GAV game was ported to a PDA and a measurement study was carried out in that environment [BLME04]. The study examined the potential of uniform packet radio service's ability to support the real-time environment of GAV. Standard measurements such as response time of the server, jitter between responses, mean RTT, etc. were done. The study, corroborating other similar studies, concluded that the delays rendered playing GAV over packet radio networks (such as GPRS or UMTS networks) infeasible.

7.6   Other Applications

7.6.1   Streaming Multimedia

A slow but steadily growing part of Internet traffic for the last several years has been multimedia. Multimedia is anything beyond simple text and static images: it includes audio, video, animations, short or long movies, etc. Initially the growth was seen as part of the natural evolution of the Web: pages had short multimedia segments embedded in them. Growing in pace with the access speed of users, multimedia content grew from short audio snippets to full length movies. Audio could be sent alongside video and synchronized. Beyond the Web, as we have seen earlier, P2P became a driving force in exchange of multimedia files.

Although all multimedia resources could just as easily be delivered as standard HTTP or FTP resources, by transferring the complete contents, a key difference is the *manner* of delivery. HTTP is not a suitable protocol: significant control elements of protocol to exchange multimedia are missing. Additionally, more than one stream may be involved simultaneously in a transfer. One of the reasons HTTP is still used is that firewalls avoid blocking Web traffic and tend to allow traffic aimed at default HTTP ports such as 80 or 8080.

The data transfer needs to be augmented with timing properties. An encoder converts digital data into an audio or video format (e.g., MPEG). A decoder on the other end converts the data into a format that can be played back. A stream thus has a sequence of sounds or images spanning a period of time. A multimedia session may have several streams. Associated parameters, such as duration and name of the stream, are part of additional information that needs to be sent.

HTTP is thus often used just to initiate the delivery with a separate process then communicating with the remote media server to transfer the bits. The multimedia resource is often *streamed*; segments of the resource are sent with users 'consuming' the bits by hearing or watching. The received data is processed simultaneously with data being transmitted. Sequencing is crucial in multimedia delivery – audio and video segments may not be comprehensible if they are delivered unsynchronized, at the wrong speed, or out of order. In pure text delivery, it is possible to send chunks of the resource segmented and allowing the browser to render the page properly. Users may skip ahead in text as a page is constructed.

Session Initiation Protocol [SSR99] (SIP) initiates session by inviting users. SIP decides the host to be contacted, checks users' willingness to accept calls, and handles setting up and shutting down of the connection. SIP is used heavily in IP telephony.

Several protocols exist for dealing with different aspects of multimedia transfers. The proprietary Microsoft Media Server (MMS [MMS]) is a popular protocol with a considerable fraction of multimedia traffic. The protocol has commands such as start/stop, and ability to change rates. The MMS player can handle a variety of multimedia encoding formats such as ASF (Advanced Systems Format), MOV (Movie), or AVI (Audio Video Interleave). MMS uses TCP or UDP protocols for transport with the choice of protocol done either transparent to the user or via user configuration.

Real-time Transport Protocol (RTP [SCFJ96]) divides streams into labeled packets before transmission; the associated control protocol RTCP (RTP Control Protocol) is used to obtain information about the transmission quality as well as identity information about participants. The packets themselves can be sent using UDP or TCP. Protocols such as the Synchronized Multimedia Integration Language (SMIL [Smi, Gro98]) were created to synchronize multimedia delivery. SMIL enables control on how the multimedia session is presented to the users.

The open standard with numerous implementation is Real Time Streaming Protocol (RTSP [SRL98]). RTSP, with syntax borrowed heavily from HTTP/1.1, enables users to send multimedia requests via URLs; there are commands (such as play or record) available to interact with the streams. RTSP selects the actual transport mechanism (RTP/RTCP) which delivers the data. RTP uses a UDP port for control and another for data. The telecommunication sector of the International Telecommunication Union has recommended an umbrella standard called H.323 [H32] to define real-time multimedia communications. It is primarily aimed at audio and video conferencing applications and to provide an open standard so that vendors making devices for applications such as Voice over IP (VOIP) could be compatible with each other. Apart from audio and video, H.323 standard covers protocols for system control (call control and framing functions), security (authentication, data integrity, privacy and non-repudiation), and data (collaboration sharing, file transfer, instant messaging, etc.). H.323 uses RTP for data transfer; a tutorial on H.323 is available [H3T].

A client's interactive behavior is one of the harder characteristics to measure in multimedia interactions. In applications such as Web and P2P the user can start and stop downloads; whereas in multimedia streaming interactions, the users can pause, go back, skip ahead, or zoom into a specific location in the stream. User perceptions vary widely when it comes to dealing with audio and video transfers and result in difference in interaction style compared to the Web.

This section briefly examines multimedia measurements. We will look at reference patterns, object size distributions, and how the role of user behavior affects all measurements.

Properties

Multimedia transfers raise interesting questions about characteristics that are different from other applications. As mentioned earlier, the subjective role played by the human user is not just due to latency (as in Web) but a variety of other factors. Similar to networked games where the skill level of the players involved can significantly alter the game experience, multimedia transfers are impacted by network performance as well as non-network (user) issues, such as the reaction to delay or jitter. Packet loss is not a good indicator of multimedia performance [PHH98] due to the built in repair techniques. In terms of protocol use, many multimedia transfers use UDP, since avoiding bursty transfers is a key goal [WCZ01].

As far as video transfers are concerned, the frame rate dominates the smoothness perception by viewers. Full-motion video needs to be around 30 frames/second permitting human eyes to see the video as a continuous stream rather than a collection of still images. Jitter can kill the perception even at higher frame rates. Video quality, a somewhat subjective measure, can also be studied to some extent in an automated fashion. Apart from jitter, delays, and losses, components of quality such as bit-rate, and user's interaction in terms of change of rates can be examined.

Challenges

The perceptive aspects of a multimedia transfer are in general harder to measure. Network characteristics such as jitter have to be experienced to see how the user might react. Aborting a Web transfer is often the only reaction if there are delays on the Web; in multimedia transfers the user may try to skip ahead or rewind, making inferences harder. Measuring quality of Web experience is often dominated by the end to end latency in downloading the page, which rarely takes more than a few seconds. Multimedia transfers can take from minutes to hours and the same stream may be encoded in different ways before being delivered to different users. The bit-rate might depend on the connection at the end host, the user's explicit selection indicating a certain level of connectivity, the length of the resource, etc. On a practical basis certain protocols involved in multimedia transfers (e.g., RTSP) are blocked at firewalls making it harder to study. Just as some static Web content may be delivered via Content Distribution Networks, some streaming content may not originate at the chosen site. Care must be taken to measure the impact of CDNs during measurement.

The quality of a video stream cannot be gleaned by simply examining the transport and network layer information. Higher levels of the protocol stack need to be examined closely. A practical challenge here is that some multimedia protocols are proprietary and their specification has to be reverse engineered. Measuring the effectiveness of the transfers without knowing the protocol details is difficult, For example, the Microsoft Media Server mentioned earlier is proprietary and the details of the protocol have long since been reverse engineered [MMS]. The risk is that the specification could change with a newer version of a player and the reverse engineering would have to be done anew.

Tools

User surveys are a common technique to get an answer to the subjective question of perception-level reaction to a multimedia transfer. Occasionally, comparing the number of times a user moves back and forth in a stream or how they select to skip ahead, may give a crude objective measure. Yet, the subjective nature of reaction to the quality of audio or video often dominates objective measures. Many studies thus involve asking participants to carry out many downloads and record their viewing experiences. Tools for survey-based measurement of performance of streaming have been constructed (e.g., RealTracer [WCZ01]) where users from different parts of the world are asked to download a customized video player and use it to fetch a number of video clips. The tool monitors the performance and the users fill out a questionnaire and the information is compiled centrally.

Several multimedia monitoring tools exist to aid in the capture and processing of multimedia traffic. An early tool in this category was *mmdump* [vdMCCS00], which is capable of parsing packets associated with control protocols (such as RTSP, SIP, and H.323) to identify the dynamically assigned port numbers. Once the port numbers are known, the packet filter is changed to capture the relevant packets on those ports. *mmdump* is implemented as a superset of *tcpdump* with key differences being state maintenance for the duration of a multimedia session which may involve multiple TCP or UDP connections, a protocol-specific parsing engine, and the ability to switch packet filters. The tool has been used on the AT&T network to obtain packet length distributions and other characterization information such as time of day usage. Other tools in the multimedia protocol-specific category include rtpdump [RTP] and rtpmon [BSR]. Rtpmon, for example, is a graphical tool that can display a variety of information about the RTP session such as RTCP statistics, participant information, loss rates, etc. Structured models of Real Audio traffic have been created by monitoring [MH00] popular audio services (such as Broadcast.com) for Real Audio traffic. The monitoring was done via *tcpdump* with the trace host receiving the traffic via a Cisco SPAN port mirroring the traffic on a Ethernet switch. The popular protocol analyzer Ethereal [Eth], which can analyze numerous protocols including P2P protocols (such as eDonkey) and game protocols (e.g., Quake), can handle multimedia protocols (such as RTP, RTSP, SIP) as well.

State of the Art

The RealTracer tool [WCZ01] discussed above was used to test the performance of a video server serving a few hundred Real Video tracks to a small number (63) of users. Jitter–the variability in the arrival rate of the packets – of over 50 ms was deemed as the threshold for non-smooth delivery of video. A frame rate of over 15 frames/second as acceptable. The study (done in 2001) however showed that a tiny fraction of videos attained 30 frames/second and only a quarter attained the acceptable bound of 15 fps. However, even 10 fps was considered acceptable by the users in the study. The split in the use of UDP and TCP for Real Video was roughly half. The large initial buffering done by the RealPlayer was responsible for the relatively low jitter rate which was even lower for higher speed connections. The network configuration at the end-host played a crucial role in frame rate, jitter, as well as the quality perceived by the users. Modem users liked the quality much less than users who had access to cable modems or DSL. Another study of streaming media workload [CWVL01] examined nearly 5000 clients' RTSP sessions over a week in a university setting and compared it to Web workloads. Packets were captured using a passive approach and the control portion of the data indicated the datagrams which carried the streaming data. A small fraction of the sessions dominated the overall byte count downloaded and requests for objects followed a Zipf-like distribution. A few servers were heavily popular as in the case of the Web and thus cache strategies similar to those in the Web would suffice. The temporal locality of access indicates that caching objects for a couple of hours before evicting them would result in high hit rates. A four month long characterization of a commercial streaming service was done [vdMSK02] by examining application level session logs in 2002. The study which also used network aware clustering [KW00] to group IP addresses involved in streaming, examined the different streaming and transport protocols used, bandwidth of the streams, session durations, traffic volume (across different aggregation levels), etc. There were many more high bandwidth streams than low – high bandwidth content was responsible for a rather large fraction of the total traffic. Over a third of sessions used HTTP to transfer the bytes, with TCP accounting for two thirds of all traffic. There were significant differences in peak bandwidth requirement with sharp changes occurring within a short amount of time. Like in other applications, a small number of clips were responsible for a significant fraction of the traffic. A large fraction of the streams lasted for less than two minutes although there were some clips that lasted more than twenty minutes. Most of the downloads occurred from ASes within two hops.

Another early characterization [VAM+02] study examined live streaming media workload of nearly 700000 users over a period of one month. The study showed that user's interactions are different when compared to viewing streaming of stored objects. In live streaming, users know that they will not get an opportunity to view the stream live again and may be more willing to put up with glitches; in a stored stream the users may just prefer to replay the stream when network conditions are better. This distinction leads to more passive behavior on the part of users while interacting with live streams. The duration for which a user is connected to a stream (based on the number of transfers within a session) follows a lognormal distribution while the inactive time follows an exponential distribution. An interesting characteristic studied is the size distribution of individual transfers: the high variability is traced to the client's demonstrating an interest in staying connected to the live stream. The variability is not related to the size of the object transferred.

A longer (seven month) study [LR02] of real-time streaming looked at a contrived dial-up client population's interaction with a video server streaming low bitrate MPEG-4 ten-minute sequences. The key finding of the study was that Internet packet loss rates are fairly low with nearly 40% of the sessions studied suffering no packet loss. Many of the losses involved just a single packet. The study concludes that one-way delay jitter has a more serious impact on the application than other network characteristic similar to [CSMS04] discussed above. The delay variation results in packets arriving past the decoding deadline, indicating a need for a startup delay to avoid late packets. Round-trip delays were found not to coincide with geographical distances; instead the number of end-to-end hops correlated with the average RTT. Packet reordering is an under-studied topic. This study showed that, contrary to expectations, there was a considerable amount of reordering in the traces: in one of the traces nearly a third of the missing packets were reordered.

An examination [CSMS04] of H.323 conferencing performance was carried out to extract acceptable bounds for important network characteristics such as delay, jitter, and loss. Given that user perceptions have to be gauged to decide on the quality of service provided by the conference, subjective quality assessment was done by surveying users. Acceptable bounds for delay are proposed by the International Telecommunication Union (ITU) to be less than 300 ms. The study selected bounds less than 50 ms for jitter (similar to the RealTracer study), and no more than 1.5% packet loss for performance to be termed acceptable. The user sessions were emulated on a LAN for various combinations of good, acceptable, and poor values of delay, jitter, and packet loss. The study showed that user's perceptions are driven more by variations in jitter than other characteristics.

A recent workload characterization [CCB$^+$04] of diverse streaming workload classified them into educational, entertainment video and entertainment audio categories. Anonymized logs were used to analyze the data, which ranges from over a year for the educational content to a few days or weeks for the entertainment data. However, the entertainment content is two orders of magnitude larger in terms of number of sessions and requests. Client behavior was examined in each category: audio sessions had low interactivity while video sessions involved numerous requests with their degree of interactivity increasing along with the size of the resource being streamed. As with most access patterns, a few media files were heavily downloaded; and the time of access is dependent on the nature of the content. Insights are presented towards caching popular files and just the frequently requested segments; for example the early segments of educational content are more popular. A large fraction of files accessed are rarely viewed during the same hour and thus caching them would waste resources. Access frequency of files and the number of sessions are both modeled by concatenating two Zipf-like distributions for all but the video entertainment category; that is modeled by a single Zipf-like distribution. Sessions arrive for the entertainment category in an exponential fashion. Since audio and shorter video content are requested in their entirety, the session ON times for such content follow a Pareto distribution.

A significant examination of the objective aspects of video quality was carried out by examining streaming video sessions in a broadband network [RSdM05a, RSdM05b]. Bi-directional traffic of Windows media ports in TCP and UDP was captured, and participant IP addresses and port numbers were used to capture all packets associated with the streaming sessions. The aspects of quality that were measured include spatial quality: height and width of the image, frame rate, choice of compression algorithm, etc. While more than two thirds of the objects in the study were 320x240, there were numerous other object sizes with the top five resolutions accounting for over 90% of the objects. Nearly two thirds of objects are encoded between 200 and 400 kbps. To overcome jitter, streaming applications tend to buffer some data so that the users can have a smoother experience. If that buffer is emptied for any reason, the experience significantly worsens. Of the small fraction of streams that were live, over a third experienced some form of disturbance during the transfer over the Internet. The live streams had a longer playtime and rate changes or buffer 'starvation' (which increase with playtime) were among the key disturbances noted. Rate changes are attempted for many segments whenever buffer starvation occurred.

Part III

In Perspective

8

Anonymization

Thus far in this book we have seen what kind of Internet measurements are done, the locations in which they are done, and the manner in which they are carried out. Along the way we have examined several challenges to measurement. We have discussed a variety of techniques that enable circumventing some of the challenges.

Although a lot of measurements are done for the purpose of a single organization, it is not uncommon for some measurements to be made available to others. The results obtained from measurements are presented as papers in conferences or on mailing lists. They often include a discussion of the actual measurements in terms of where, how, and what. Details are presented in tables and figures summarizing what led the authors to their key inferences in the research. However, the actual raw measurements themselves are not made available as often as they could be. Additionally, thus far we have not discussed the sensitivity of such measurements as we had not explored sharing of the measurements.

In this chapter we examine the motivations for anonymization and the trade-offs involved in terms of benefits to recipients of data and risks to those sharing it. We start with a set of definitions used in the general field of anonymization and privacy where considerable work has already taken place. Application of several of the notions developed in the field of privacy to network measurements is still a work in progress.

We then explore anonymization along three axes: why traffic data is anonymized, what parts of the data at various protocol layers should be anonymized, and the processes and techniques used to carry out anonymization. We also look at the supporting methodologies and tools for anonymization. Once anonymized, there should be ways of evaluating the success of anonymization. The metrics for success involve identifying a balance between making the data safe to be shared yet not too diluted to render it useless for others. Finally, we look at the practical limits of anonymization and what alternatives are possible to meet the same goals. Along the way we will discuss exemplar measurement studies that have focused on anonymization techniques and their uses.

8.1   Definitions

Before examining how anonymization can help improve sharing of data, we start with some definitions. While there are no globally accepted definitions applicable in all environments for all data elements, there is consensus on some key terms.

There are distinct definitions of *identity* of a person. For example, the European Union's Privacy directive [EU-95] defines an "identifiable person" as "one who can be identified, directly or indirectly, in particular by reference to an identification number or to one or more factors specific to his physical, physiological, mental, economic, cultural or social identity." The World Wide Web Consortium's Platform for Privacy Preferences (P3P [P3P05]) specification allows for the view that most information referring to an individual is "identifiable" in some way. Data that uniquely identifies a person is *identified* data. If the data can be combined with other data to identify a person, then such data is termed *identifiable* data.

Anonymity can be defined as the absence of identity [APE] or as the ability of an individual to prevent others from linking identity to the actions of the individual [GW98]. Since such linkage can be done much later, it is important that anonymization makes it difficult or impossible to create such linkages at any point in the future – this is called forward secrecy.

The anonymized data, provided there is no significant information loss during the anonymization process, can help in validating the results and help other organizations better explore the measured phenomenon. The key difficulty is in balancing the needs of privacy with the ability to draw meaningful inferences from the transformed data. There is not yet a well-defined metric for the *semantic distance* between the anonymized version and the original in the networking community. There is some preliminary work in the simple case of prefix-preservation of IP addresses as we will see later in this chapter.

In this chapter, we extend the definition of anonymization beyond the identity of a single individual or a set of individuals to proprietary information that businesses might want to protect. Data sensitivity is one of the key considerations beyond privacy and identity. The range of proprietary information includes information about assets (number of routers and their locations), specific traffic patterns (frequency of usage or presence of certain applications), and specific performance characteristics (response times, loss rates).

The term *fingerprinting* has been used in the literature to label the technique of trying to de-anonymize an object by matching its attributes against attributes of identified objects. A simple example is examining popular URL strings and matching the size attributes in other Web server logs to de-anonymize the URLs.

Terms such as de-identification (stripping identity information from data before releasing it) and re-identification (ability to relate supposedly anonymous data with actual identities) have also been discussed in privacy literature but with somewhat limited applications in the networking context. Significant work is however expected in this area as concerns for user privacy continues to increase with the increased dependence on the Internet for a wide variety of daily transactions causing access trails to be left in many locations.

8.2 General Motivation for Anonymizing Data

The primary reason behind our examining anonymization is to study the applicability of the anonymized data for a range of applications *without* the data being reverse engineered. Measurements that involve people often have to deal with the key issue of privacy. A significant amount of private information can be revealed by carrying out seemingly innocuous measurements. Beyond individuals, information about organizations or businesses can also be revealed that may prove embarrassing or benefit competitors. Anonymizing measurement data would enable individuals or organizations to share data comfortably with others.

There are many reasons to share data and we believe sharing outweighs the considerable risks and difficulties involved in doing so. First, it is good scientific practice for researchers to share data as it enables other researchers to repeat the experiments and verify the results. In reality, accessibility to measurement data is often limited only to an organization's intranet. Even in the presence of many measurement platforms (such as PlanetLab), the availability of data from *within* other organizations has steadily shrunk. Innocuous data that used to be considered open and widely accessible has now moved behind firewalls. Access is available only if the person sending the query is on an access control list.

Organizations, simply by virtue of sharing their data, might enable others to come up with solutions for problems they face. By anonymizing data in a manner that balances the privacy and security requirements of the data owner, it is possible to share the data to help other researchers or organizations involved in measurements. Apart from altruism, there are selfish reasons to anonymize and share data. The recipients of the data are not the only ones to benefit as a result of data being shared. By sharing data, others could be encouraged to share their measurement data. Often measurements can be expensive to carry out even in a few locations; the lessons learned from others using the data can be useful for those who shared the data. Also, it is not generally possible for an organization to have access to sites of other organizations to carry out measurements on their behalf. Both by anonymizing data and providing other organizations with tools used to carry out anonymization, it is possible to get data back from several locations. By combining the results of individual measurements at various sites, it would be possible to have a broader understanding of the applicability of an idea. The organization that carried out the measurement can thus have their results verified by additional measurements carried out in different locations with possibly different parameters.

Additionally, some sites have a significant amount of interesting data, or particular segments of network demographic such as broadband customers or significant amounts of wireless access traffic. A heterogeneous collection of measurement data is likely to better validate experimental goals since some inherent assumptions may differ across the organizations carrying out the measurements. An in-depth understanding of a particular network phenomena such as a flash crowd can be attained with heterogeneous data from different sites. A collection of measurements obtained via experiments carried out by different organizations is not convincing proof of the correctness of the inferences drawn. However, it is quite likely that inferential errors are more likely to be ferreted out as the number and diversity of measurement sites increase. Researchers who do share data construct elaborate mechanisms to do so. Organizations like CAIDA [CAI] have spent considerable effort in creating repositories of network measurement data and make it available to others. Without traffic traces and logs at various protocol layers, it would have been quite difficult to validate many of the proposed ideas that we have discussed thus far in the book.

8.3   Obstacles and Risks in Sharing Data

The primary difficulty in sharing network measurement data is sensitivity to the privacy of the individuals or the organization where the data was gathered. Some of the risks are well known and widely understood: names of individuals being associated with a particular data record of their access, personal information such as credit card numbers, etc. If such information is released, the organization may be legally liable for violating the privacy of the affected individuals. However, there are many risks that are unknown including the potential of private information being reverse engineered or competitors inferring information useful to them. The fear of unknown risks deters organizations from even considering sharing data.

If the measurements are publicly obtained (for example, RTT measurements to well-known Web sites or HTTP protocol compliance test results) the details could be published. However, in many cases, either the data is gathered from within an administrative entity or under special dispensation. In such cases, the data cannot be made

Table 8.1 Need for anonymization: Attack techniques and targets.

Target	Why targeted	How targeted
Infrastructure	Locating high-value targets/services	Examining traffic patterns
Data stream	Reverse engineering	Seeding data, combining with external datasets
Access patterns	Business data	Sequential inferring

available by default. Obtaining permissions is often a tedious process and difficult to obtain in any case. If a large ISP provides specific services for its customers, it may be reluctant to approach their customers for seeking permission to share data with the outside world.

As we have seen above, not all the problems are technical. There may also be legal considerations in sharing data. Privacy requirements vary significantly between countries. There are significant differences between laws in the United States and many EU nations in this regard. Some EU nations, such as Germany, have strong privacy laws that would constrain unlimited retention of data, let alone sharing it. Germany does not have data retention laws; more importantly there are specific requirements for data *erasure* applicable to telecommunication and Internet providers. A comparison of privacy laws affecting telecommunications between Germany and the United States can be found in [Sch03].

We now examine the potential risks of sharing by examining what might be reverse engineered and the motivations for those who might seek to de-anonymize data. Table 8.1 enumerates some of the targets of attackers, the reasons for their interest in the data, and typical techniques by which attackers try to mine the anonymized data. These concerns have to be addressed by anonymization. The table lists targets at coarse granularity; in Section 8.4 we will see more fine-grained elements, such as IP addresses and user names gathered for purposes of spam, that need to be anonymized.

The first concern is that attackers might want to tailor attacks on weaker links or portions of the infrastructure that lie within a specific range of the chosen attack. Popular services can be identified by examining port numbers or destination IP addresses, for example. Attackers can masquerade better in certain ingress points of the network if they could guess the set of services that lie behind them or use information about the access control lists. The protection provided by anonymization also needs to take into account statistical patterns inherent in traffic access. An example at the TCP layer is the ability to use a list of sequence numbers to identify the operating system or worse yet look for system vulnerabilities [Tal04].

The second concern is that the attackers involved in reverse engineering may use external information in conjunction with released data. Examples of external information include statistical patterns of usage or protocol-mandated counts such as number of typical packets involved in a transaction. Earlier, in Chapter 7 (Section 7.2.5) we showed how the number of packets in a TCP exchange in DNS along with its frequency was used to infer an anomaly in the trace. At the application layer, suppose the URLs accessed at a Web site are anonymized but the actual sizes of Web resources are available in an anonymized Web server log. Such a log can be correlated with other *unanonymized* Web proxy logs to look for popular objects with matching resource sizes.

Beyond explicit matches like this, patterns of access – a series of downloads that are similar between an unanonymized log and an anonymized log can reveal obscured information. As discussed in Chapter 7 (Section 7.2.5) authoritative and local DNS servers can be identified by examining interconnections. Further, authoritative DNS servers have a hierarchical relationship. Similarly, spiders and proxies in Web server logs can often be identified readily by examining request counts and arrival patterns, as discussed in Chapter 7 (Section 7.3.3) and [KW00].

Other overlooked sources of information are ambient collections of either contemporaneous or historical data from other sources. This is an example of the concept of linking [Sam01] discussed in the privacy literature, where data from a voter list and an anonymized medical dataset were jointly examined for a subset of matching fields. In the networking context, archives of past Web pages are available in sites such as Wayback Machine [Way] which stores historical snapshots of Web sites. Even if a set of URLs are anonymized, the sizes of the resources can be compared with those available in such archival sites for linking purposes. Note that external information can actually be inserted into a trace that is being anonymized. For example, by sending a request to a site that is anonymizing request logs, one could reverse engineer the manner in which the fields are anonymized [FT04].

A third concern is the sequential inferencing possibility, whereby one field leads to successive inferences. For example, the header length present in an IP header may be indicative of a particular application which may only run in certain versions of an operating system. Starting from an obscure header length field available in an IP header packet trace it is possible to learn the operating system of the host from which the packet was sent in some cases [FT04].

8.4   What Should be Anonymized: Data Categorization

Each data set, be it the actual measurements gathered or meta-information such as where and when it was gathered, as well as the duration of measurement, has intrinsic value to the person or organization involved in the measurement.

At the lower levels of the network stack, flow data (e.g., from *netflow*) can reveal popularity of certain applications that may be considered questionable, such as P2P or networked games. The information can be seen in terms of number of bytes and packets apart from the set of source or destination IP addresses. From an ISP's competitor's point of view, the list of Autonomous Systems and the volume of data exchanged could have business value. If the *netflow* traffic has information about internal customer prefixes that are normally hidden, that would certainly be of interest to competitors. The list of source and destination prefixes involved in frequent and high volume communication may reveal significant business linkage information. If individual IP addresses are known, they could be aggregated, sampled, and cross-linked with other information to get a better picture of the demographic involved in the traffic. The amount of information leaked varies with the item – aggregate information such as an Autonomous System is less of a serious concern from the viewpoint of a single person's privacy. But a small AS that covers a tiny organization may be more revealing. IP addresses in conjunction with other information may lead to identification of individual users. Even in the presence of Dynamic Host Configuration Protocol (DHCP) IP addresses, whereby a set of addresses is often reused between different hosts connecting to the network, it may be possible to track an individual. This might be done based on the time they were connected to the network and the range of Internet applications accessed. At higher levels, Web server logs reflect the set of URLs that are popular in a Web site. Competitors can use information about the number of requests and the frequency of requests for a particular resource which might indicate its popularity. Such statistics are even more of a concern in E-commerce sites where popularity of a resource may be mapped to that of specific products. Web proxy logs indicate which URLs are popular with the population behind the proxy. Such information may even be gleaned from DNS traces or logs. Cookie information or referrer field, if present in a Web site's server log, can be used to track individual activities. Any time there is content (beyond headers) there is an even higher risk of information leakage.

What we learn from this is that there is a wide range of information that needs to be anonymized before measurement-related data can be safely shared. The nature of the information to be anonymized varies with the protocol and application.

Table 8.2 provides examples of different kinds of data for a subset of protocols and popular applications. The first two axes along which we categorize anonymizable data is identity-related or personal-sensitive data; dealing largely with individual privacy. The difference between the identity-related and the personal-sensitive categories is that the identity-related information can be used to identify a person, based on our earlier definition in Section 8.1. Personal-sensitive information is still important but its use is often limited to a context. If the password used at one Web site is leaked it may cause limited damage as the user may use different passwords at

Table 8.2   Anonymizable data categorization per-protocol/application.

Protocol/ Application	Anonymization categories			
	Identity-related	Personal-sensitive	Organization-specific	Business-sensitive
BGP	N/A	N/A	Prefixes, ASN, community attributes	Routing
DNS	Workstation name	N/A	N/A	Use of specific domains
Web	URLs, cookies, email address	Passwords, search strings	Sites visited, client IDs	Traffic level, commerce
P2P	IP address	Nature of content	Legality	Traffic volume
Games	Name and IP address	Passwords, weapons	Extent of participation	N/A

different sites. Whereas if the identity of the user is revealed, it can be used to associate information about the user in multiple contexts. The third category is examining data at a coarser-level granularity of an organization, where the concerns are about aggregated information that might depict an entire organization. Finally, there is an axis of business-sensitive data: information that can be useful to competitors and thus sensitive from a business perspective. Our goal is to highlight general concerns and thus the entries may not apply equally well for all businesses and organizations. We examine each of the four axes in more detail next.

Identity-related Information.   This category includes IP addresses or hostnames, lower-level domain names, user names, cookies. Although the impact varies with the person and organization, identity-related information is critical when it comes to individual privacy. Information in this category is at the forefront when it comes to organizations refusing to share information on grounds of protecting privacy and often with the widespread support of their customers. Strict anonymization or elimination of values in this field is often required. Fortunately, few scientific reasons exist for having to know the actual values and a one-way mapping that preserves correspondence is often enough to retain usability of the data. As Table 8.2 shows, all protocols and applications considered except BGP are affected by identity-related anonymization unlike the categories in subsequent columns. BGP data by nature is more organization and business-specific. Individuals do not use BGP in a direct manner and route advertisements are done at a coarser level of granularity. Internal BGP updates are not propagated to BGP data aggregation sites like RouteViews [Rou]; additionally such data is organization-specific rather than identity-related.

Personal-sensitive Information. Data that are sensitive to individuals include passwords, credit card numbers or any other information that has financial or other private information. These fall in the category of information associated with an individual user rather than information belonging to the user. Other entities include Web sites visited, search strings issued, or nature of P2P content downloaded. The actual values in this field are often unnecessary for standard network measurement. However they are useful for those involved in nefarious activities (such as gathering passwords and credit card numbers). If search strings and Web sites visited can be separated from the identity of the user, a case can be made for using the information. Knowledge of popular search strings or Web sites can greatly benefit modeling and improving the performance of servers. Thus, the key is separating the association of the individual's identity from those personally sensitive values that have applications in measurement.

In network games that are subscription based, the initial exchange of information for authentication with the central game server includes password exchange but such information will not be shared even in the extreme case of a popular game server sharing their data. Subsequent traffic between the client and the game server consists of game movements, information regarding the set of weapons and treasures possessed by individual players, and the status of each player with respect to the ongoing game. Often the client program downloaded into the user's personal computer or PDA will translate movements into opcodes that are transmitted to the central server. Such data falls into the category of personal information but it is not as sensitive as passwords.

There is no personal-sensitive information at BGP and DNS and risk of non-anonymization is low. For example, BGP tables consist of a set of prefixes and ASes and the originator of advertisements has control over what is advertised, at what granularity (short prefix length encompassing a large address space or much finer granularity prefixes), when such advertisements are made, and to whom. The advertisements themselves include no information that can be viewed as sensitive from a personal viewpoint. As we will see next they do have organizational value. Likewise, in DNS, IP addresses by themselves do not encode any personal information. Although names of machines corresponding to IP address are chosen to reflect the hierarchy, such as organizational set up, they do not necessarily reveal personal information. Many sites also do not allow reverse DNS lookups.

Organization-specific Information. Moving beyond the individual identity, the organization that shares the data may have overall concerns about disclosing even coarse-grained information. Organization-specific information includes address prefixes, autonomous system numbers, domain names, locations of peering points, customer counts, connection patterns with internal or external customers, nature, volume and type of traffic on organization-wide basis, etc. Autonomous system numbers are unique and assigned to specific organizations often for the entire duration of their Internet presence; knowing the ASN can lead to quick identification of the organization. Such persistent identifiers are good candidates for anonymization. At a lower level of granularity, attribute value fields in a BGP announcement [RL95] can also reveal information as they are used to specify tailored policies affecting specific prefixes and AS numbers.

Even at an aggregate level an organization may not be eager to share information about the nature of Web sites visited or content downloaded. However, the values themselves can be further aggregated by mapping them into categories. For example, all sports-related Web sites could be listed as entertainment sites in the modified logs. The number of users in an organization participating in networked games may prove embarrassing to some organizations, especially if the extent of participation is significant.

At the DNS layer, there is little concern about leaking information that is organization-specific. Due to caching of DNS mappings, often only the first instance of a lookup would be available. Repeated lookups, if recorded in DNS logs, could indicate some degree of popularity of certain IP addresses depending on the time-to-live value returned with those mappings. On an organization-specific basis, unless there is significant deviation in the set of resolutions requested with authoritative servers, anonymization is unnecessary.

Business and Security-sensitive.   Beyond primarily privacy-related information and infrastructural entities-related information, businesses and commercial organizations may have other reasons to control sharing of information that is otherwise sensitive. Such information includes internal router configuration (including AS-level neighbors and access control lists), firewall configuration, policy decisions, weights, preferences and capacity associated with routes, etc. This category deals more with the flow of information and how they are controlled rather than just basic entity-related information. Such information about dynamics may be useful to competitors and there may even be concerns of embarrassment about unused resources or faulty configuration. The more pressing reason in revealing information is the fear of making it easier for malicious attacks on a business's infrastructure. Information about the nature of applications typically supported in certain address prefixes and how traffic to them is routed can be used by attackers.

Networked games are typically not played in businesses to the extent that it is a noticeable component of traffic. Even if the data is shared, there is little information in it that is business sensitive. If the business in question is the game company itself, they typically never release such data. If they were to release data, business concerns would relate to number of active players, duration of typical game sessions, etc. which may be useful to their competitors selling other games in the same genre.

8.5 How Data is Anonymized: Process and Techniques

Having seen why data should be anonymized and what key fields in measurement-related data need to be anonymized, we examine the process by which anonymization can be carried out and the various techniques that are currently used. By *process* we refer primarily to *when* anonymization is done: in real time as data is being gathered, or offline at a later time. The *technique* refers to the manner of transformation of data with implications on the achievable degree of anonymization.

Beyond process and techniques, anonymization tools can further the process of sharing. The actual manner by which anonymization is carried out has an impact on potential for sharing data. The use of generic, well-understood anonymization tools might enable organizations to reconsider their reluctance to share data. Anonymization tools have to be generic in order for them to run in different organizations' environments. Once such tools have been developed for distribution, there is still the requirement of crossing the threshold of trust: data owners need to be convinced that the tools actually provide the promised level of anonymity and protection. Automated tools for anonymization clearly have a higher potential for being used, especially after they have been vetted to ensure that it is not possible to reverse engineer the data being anonymized. Another potential incidental benefit of sharing the tool is that the format in which the data is now available from several locations may be uniform if the same anonymization tools are used.

8.5.1 Anonymization Process

Earlier in Section 8.2, we discussed the potential for information leakage in Web logs from knowledge about the sizes of resources. Protection in the form of simply omitting fields or randomly altering the size information can potentially reduce the usefulness of the data. Attempts to use the logs to study data reduction via caching, compressing, or differencing would suffer as the workload will not be representative of the site. Similarly, shuffling the records to defeat pattern-based analysis is not useful if sequential analysis is the goal for using the data. Several applications of measurement data depend on sequential analysis of data. For example, the arrival pattern of subsequent requests from a client at a Web server is often predicated on its past requests. From packet traces it would be impossible to reconstruct an

Table 8.3 Anonymization process.

Process	Advantages	Disadvantages
Online	Real-time	Resource heavy (memory, CPU), may be irreversible
Offline	Tailored to data	Not real-time, storage costs
Parallel	Multiple datasets	Inconsistent mapping of same value

application-level trace if the order of the packets is significantly altered. Many applications expect a sequence of transactions; for example a Web transaction often consists of a DNS lookup, followed by a TCP connection setup, and a subsequent HTTP request–response exchange.

Another anonymization possibility is to merge multiple traces into one to prevent individual analysis. However, temporal information in the form of absolute time or the inter-record difference may be lost even if clock skew between the different origins of the traces is ignored. Note that in general encrypted information is not always private; depending on the choice of encryption there may be ways to recreate and compare against anonymized data. For example, encrypting fields in a *netflow* record by known encryption mechanisms allows for popular values of certain fields to be reverse engineered by encrypting these values and comparing them against the anonymized data. The balance to be achieved is obscuring data elements without destroying the inference potential at a higher level; i.e., at an aggregate level or independent of the particular data value.

Table 8.3 presents the various ways by which the anonymization process can be done. The principal processes are online and offline but a hybrid method where partial processing is carried out on selected fields remains an option. An online process permits real-time anonymization ensuring that private data remains permanently private – the first stored copy is anonymized. Parallel processing of datasets, when done online, may cause the same fields to be mapped to different values.

It is important to note that depending on the actual data being anonymized (e.g., router configuration, packet traces, application-level data, etc.), different processes may be more appropriate. For example, configuration data such as those of routers is generally offline data available in files indicating the absence of consideration of real-time anonymization. While the choice of anonymization process is often based on the coarseness of granularity of the data type, resources such as computation and memory are key issues as well. Offline anonymization allows for experimentations with multiple transformation techniques to explore the space of usefulness of the resultant data while preserving required degree of privacy. Too often the tendency in online anonymization is to forego the possibility of retaining data out of fear of

Table 8.4 Anonymization techniques: transformation.

Technique	Example use	Commonly used application/protocol
Lossless transformation	Two-way hash function	Diverse datasets
Semi-lossy transformation	String portions	Aggregated Web, IP, data
Lossy transformation	Mapping strings to numbers	All

information leakage. Parallel techniques help handle concerns of speed of processing data.

8.5.2 Anonymization Techniques

The techniques used to anonymize data vary along several axes: the nature of the elements of the records in the dataset that need to be anonymized, the volume of the data, whether anonymization is done in real-time or offline, the degree of anonymization needed, etc. We examine the techniques at a coarse granularity level largely along the lines in which data is gathered: at configuration level, router level, packet level, or application level. Techniques at each of the levels may be applicable at others since the constituent elements of what is anonymized tend to overlap. However, the relative importance of the *structure* of the individual anonymized element may vary with the level at which the data is gathered. For example, IP addresses may be grouped into prefixes as a way of aggregating them when they occur in Web server logs. Preserving the prefix structure while anonymizing IP addresses can be important for certain applications. However, within an organization the range of IP addresses is already known and preservation of the structure may not be necessary.

Each technique thus has pros and cons and their applicability varies with the data and the expected use of the transformed data. Once a decision is made on what information should be protected, what information can be shared albeit in a modified form, and what information should not be lost, a suitable technique can be chosen. The choice of a particular technique reflects the balance sought by the provider of the data and its usefulness to the recipient.

Table 8.4 enumerates a set of common transformation techniques on data being anonymized.

Lossless techniques, as the name implies, ensure that the mapping information is not lost as a result of the transformation: it can be reversed if necessary. Such transformation provides a degree of anonymization and often compresses the data. By obscuring but retaining the mapping and being able to regenerate the transformation, lossless techniques can permit regeneration of the original data, if needed. Using random number generation with shared seed is one way to do lossless transformation. Note that compression may often be the by-product of anonymization but anonymization is rarely the by-product of compression.

The semi-lossy transformation category also may not entirely obscure the data. An example of a semi-lossy transformation is random permutation. If the recipient of the data does not know the mapping then they would not be able to reverse the information. Another example of semi-lossy transformation is partially obscuring the information – removing the suffixes of URLs but retaining the server field; or retaining only the first 24 bits of an IP address. Some degree of aggregation is thus still possible with semi-lossy transformation.

The category of lossy transformation destroys the connection between the original and transformed data. A simple example is mapping string fields to integers without preserving the translation – each string is simply replaced by a random number with different strings possibly mapped to the same integer. Lossy transformation is often a safe way to anonymize data as the potential for reverse engineering is low. If true randomization is used during the anonymization phase, even the knowledge of the process of anonymization will not help in regenerating the original data. Lossy transformations obviate the ability to group the transformed data in any semantically meaningful manner. For example, if a set of URLs are mapped to integers, it would not be possible to know that two URLs are from the same site. Likewise, email addresses cannot be grouped to even belonging to the same top-level domain. Obviously lossy transformation is the least costly technique since each field can simply be replaced by a constant value.

Another example of lossy transformation is simply not recording a portion of the data being gathered thus rendering it difficult to be re-created. Later in Section 8.6.4 we will see how the popular commercial product TiVo handles anonymization of users' profiles.

Overlapping with these three techniques, it is possible to have link/structure preserving transformation that is applicable for a wider range of applications. Such a transformation will preserve prefixes, for example, when IP addresses are anonymized. Techniques for anonymizing IP addresses are examined in detail in [SWY]. Other examples of preserving structure include saving partial pathname information in URLs.

In terms of connection between techniques and process: they are largely orthogonal. Most of the processes can be used with any of the techniques. In some cases, the choice of a particular process would be sub-optimal. For example, it is possible to do a lossless transformation using an online, offline, or parallel process. The choice of the technique is dictated more by how the resulting data is going to be used than by the actual data itself. All input data types can be transformed using any of the techniques outlined in Table 8.4.

8.6 Anonymization Examples at Different Layers

In this section we will take a closer look at how data is anonymized at each of four coarse granularity levels mentioned earlier: at configuration level, router level, packet level, and at the application level. We provide examples where warranted and refer to studies that have evaluated techniques using real data.

8.6.1 Configuration Data

Data at this level is less about actual measurements but meta-information about how a site is configured. Absence of such information does not prohibit measurement but availability even in an anonymized format would be useful for several measurement applications. For example, having a real network's topology can help validate some topology-related ideas that have been proposed. The robustness of the design of routing can be tested if the configuration data is available [MZX$^+$04].

The difficulties faced in anonymizing configuration data include the fact that it is specific to a single administrative entity. External information about the entity in the form of Autonomous System numbers and IP address ranges is publicly available. A typical configuration file, such as those of Cisco routers, does not lend itself to simple parsing with a straightforward grammar. AS numbers occur in a position-independent manner. Regular expressions may have to be anonymized by explicitly expanding and anonymizing the member elements. The links between identifiers and policy definitions must be preserved as should specific information about interface types. Simple hashing of all strings, even in comments, might be needed to ensure anonymity of administrative entities.

The Rocketfuel [SMW02] project showed that it was possible to infer the peering structure of various ISPs by remotely examining locations where ISPs exchanged peering or transit traffic. They compared their data obtained by probing using `traceroute`, in conjunction with BGP tables and knowledge of AS degree distribution.

Anonymization techniques for numerous elements in router configuration data have been described [MZX$^+$04]. For example, AS numbers being integers can be safely randomly permuted and AS number ranges can be expanded and individually anonymized. Certain tokens present in configuration files such as keywords used by router companies (e.g., 'interface', 'router') are considered unprivileged and can be left unanonymized. This is similar to frequently used commands in popular software subsystems like FTP as we will see shortly in Section 8.6.3. All other strings are converted into strong hashes protecting information such as route-maps which may yield information about the organization's identity or their routing policies.

8.6.2   Router-level Data

At the router level the first concern is the extraordinarily high volume of the data to be anonymized. Router-level data is not typically aggregated and thus there is a significantly higher potential for information leakage. The most common data at the router level is flow data and the most popular form of it is Cisco's *netflow*. Although there are several versions of *netflow*, most of the flow records include the following key fields: the source and destination IP addresses and port numbers, prefixes, Autonomous Systems, protocol, start and end time, the number of packets and bytes involved in the flow. The Informational RFC 3917 [QZCZ04] outlining requirements for exporting IP flow information suggests support for anonymization of IP addresses and port numbers before they are exported. It is also possible to enable aggregation of flow records based on routers so that only prefix-level information is reported. Since anonymization is not always possible for certain applications such as accounting, the flow collector can apply anonymization later. As of this writing there are no known implementations of such anonymization within *netflow*. Discussions at IETF have converged on the fact that not enough is understood about anonymization as yet to standardize it and implement in routers.

8.6.3   Packet-level Traces

Packet traces have the most detailed information about network traffic. The ability to examine the full packet would reveal *everything*: packet headers have information about connection endpoints, protocol, etc. and the body has potentially even more sensitive information.

A first cut at preserving anonymity might be to just share packet headers. However, packet headers have a considerable amount of information that needs to be anonymized. Ethernet headers and other link-layer headers have MAC addresses that probably should not be leaked. Although MAC addresses may be considered safe in general, the potential of linking all records that have this unique identifier increases the risk of leaking it. In fact, MAC addresses are used as a way to ensure that only specific devices can connect to an intra-net in semi-public corporate locations. In a wireless environment the ability to track the physical location is enhanced with the MAC address. Thus, in the present environment of significant security and privacy risks, it is better to err on the side of not leaking any information that is not absolutely necessary.

Table 8.5 IP header fields to be anonymized.

Header field	Possible inference if not anonymized
Version number	Support for IPv6 in the organization
Header length	May help identify application/OS
TTL field	Distance traversed by packet from source
TOS field	ISP of the trace

A systematic analysis of the fields of an IP packet reveals a variety of information that may be leaked. Table 8.5 documents the fields of concern and inferences that may be drawn if they are not anonymized [FT04]. In the IP header, beyond the source and destination address fields that are obvious candidates for anonymization, the IP options field has to be inspected as well. For example, with loose source record route and strict source record route options the route data may have IP addresses. Relatively key information such as IP addresses may actually be present in upper-layer protocol messages such as ICMP and DNS. Thus, anonymization may need to extend into all protocol headers. Beyond IP and TCP headers, application-level headers such as HTTP headers may have URLs indicating Web sites visited. The sheer volume may also lead to collision if simple hashing techniques are employed for anonymization.

Several solutions have been proposed for anonymizing traces while retaining some internal structure in the anonymized data. An obvious structure to preserve when IP addresses, a common field in most networking traces, are scrambled is its prefix. With prefix-preservation, all IP addresses belonging to a prefix in the unanonymized data also belong to the same prefix in the anonymized version. If there were 20 unique IP addresses in a /24 network in the unanonymized version, they will all belong to a different /24 prefix in the scrambled version. More formally, all IP addresses that share prefix of k-bits will do so in the raw and anonymized versions. Studies that are not interested in the actual IP address but depend on their prefix property could use the anonymized version without any loss of information. Inferences drawn from the anonymized trace will be equally valid if it were to have been drawn from the hard to obtain raw trace. We had discussed one such study [KW00] and its applications in depth in Chapter 7 (Section 7.3). The IP addresses are transformed using a 1–1 mapping and individual IP addresses will not be visible as such in the anonymized trace.

A common anonymization technique preserving prefix and address class (A, B, C, or D) is found in the popular tool *tcpdpriv* [Min97]. *tpcdpriv*, built upon the packet capture library *libpcap*, reads the output of *tcpdump*, removes user-specific data, and scrambles the IP addresses. This table-based technique triggers a longest-prefix match of each new IP address to be anonymized against the existing sets of pairs of raw and anonymized addresses. All information that is not processed, such as the data portion, is deleted. The common anonymization option used with *tcpdpriv* is '-A50', which ensures the *k*-bit sharing between the raw and anonymized versions. The *tcpdpriv* tool also allows for optional anonymization of the port numbers. The technique has been adopted in several summarization and anonymization tools, such as *ipsumdump* [Koh] and *ip2anonip* [Ploa]. Measurement traces with packet headers anonymized using *tcpdpriv* are made available in several locations (e.g., [vdM03]).

Rather than an all or nothing approach, techniques that retain more information inside an administrative entity and share less outside have also been implemented. The Wide project's guidelines for protecting privacy include removing payload with private user information [TWP, CMK00]. The guidelines also call for a notion of varying degrees of privacy. For example, the source and destination addresses in IP headers are scrambled but special addresses, such as broadcast, multicast, and private, are retained since they are safe. Prefix preservation helps retain hierarchical structures. The choice of anonymization method varies with the importance of anonymity and the purpose of the data set. The Wide project also uses *tcpdpriv* but an extended version to support IPv6 and to preserve important TCP options to analyze TCP behaviors.

Various cryptographic encryption techniques have also been proposed for anonymization. Crypto-PAN [XFAM, XFAM01], unlike *tcpdpriv*, uses an algorithm that does not depend on the data to be anonymized. The cryptographic approach uses reasonable sized blocks as a cipher allowing independent anonymizations at each device. This technique has recently been extended with a key generation algorithm where an intermediate key is created from the input data and a second key is extracted by applying the intermediate key to the input data [SWY]. A symmetric encryption [Peu01] based algorithm uses a 128-bit Blowfish [Sch96] key obtained from a secret key and a hash table. The coded IP address consists of 24 bits from the encrypted version and 8 bits from the raw IP address. One advantage of these techniques is that if the same IP address is seen on different traces it will map to the same anonymized IP address as long as the secret key is shared. This allows for comparing measurements obtained from different locations without violating the privacy; although sharing of the secret key may reduce the overall security of the scheme. We will examine the potential risks with prefix-preserving anonymization later in Section 8.8.

The body of packets could have even more sensitive information such as credit card numbers and passwords. Rather than trying to filter out information for anonymizing, it might be easier to specify what information should be included rather than excluded. Such a filter-in idea has been proposed [PP03] and implemented as an extension to the Bro [Pax99a] tool. The goal is for simple policy scripts to be written that specify transformations including anonymizations in a verifiable manner. Verification implies that the anonymization is robust against attacks like fingerprinting and comparing anonymized data with other publicly available information. The flexibility of the filter-in principle becomes clear if we consider the combination of an anonymization technique and the intended use of the anonymized trace. We use the anonymization of FTP trace example presented in [PP03] to illustrate the flexibility. Depending on the intended application and the policy of the site sharing the data, the IP addresses can be simply replaced with a number making it impossible for the original addresses to be recovered. The User IDs on the other hand can leave a few select strings un-anonymized; for example, "guest" and "anonymous" as these strings do not give away too much site-specific information but can be useful to separate out anonymous access from authorized users with a valid user ID and password on the site. Similarly, the path name specified by users can be left un-anonymized for certain well-known files where the common expectation is that there is a need to know about access to such files.

8.6.4 Application-level Data

As we move up from router to packet level to application-level data, it is easier to see what fields need to be anonymized. The semantics of the fields and the risks of them being combined with external data are generally clearer. The records are more often than not in fixed format making it a bit easier to write anonymization code. As data can be often more easily aggregated at higher levels, there is a slightly lower fear of information loss. Data sharing at this level is generally higher although it is not entirely risk-free.

There are several problems with application data, albeit of a different nature. There is plenty of variation between the log formats and a differing subset of fields are logged in each instantiation based on configuration parameters, thus making it a bit difficult to parse. The absence of a self-describing format implies tailored anonymization of the different formats. The switch to XML has helped ameliorate this problem to a certain extent.

One way to anonymize data is not to store any associated information while data is being gathered. Consider the example of the popular broadcast television recording product TiVo. Here, users' preferences in the form of television programs they like or dislike are uploaded to the central server [AvS04]. The purpose of the upload is to combine the profile information with overall popularity of television shows among all TiVo customers and then downloading recommendations to individual customers. The recommendations are combined with the customer's profile locally by the client program running on the TiVo box.

The upload is done on a regular basis suggesting that a delta of the profile might be enough. However, TiVo chose *not* to store (even) an anonymous user identifier between uploads. The time at which the profile is uploaded is masked by setting it to the beginning of Unix epoch (December 31, 1969) rendering traceback and matching of the specific TiVo box and profile impossible. The actual communication between the user's machine and the server is encrypted, and at the time of tearing down the TCP connection between them even the log file name is anonymized to protect the privacy of the user. Information not recorded cannot be easily re-created; thus if the data is safely anonymized at data collection time, there is a lower risk of it being reverse engineered later.

In examining Web data, proxies already play a role in anonymizing some of the key information. Everything from the actual IP address of the client to the user agent being used could be obscured by the proxy. The Web server receiving the request will only have information about the proxy. However, if cookies are required for secondary communication, that will be available to the Web servers. Fortunately, cookies are rarely recorded in logs that are shared; they are not one of the fields in either the Common Log Format or Extended Common Log Format. The filter-in proposal [PP03] (discussed earlier in Section 8.6.3) shows how pathnames can be hashed in FTP traces by including the server's IP address to prevent comparisons across servers. Response codes can be safely ignored during anonymization as they do not reveal private information especially if the file name or URL is anonymized. Anonymizing the `304 Not Modified` HTTP responses would make it impossible for the measurement data to be used in a variety of caching-related research that depend on such responses. When multiple logs from different sites are examined in a study and anonymized using the same anonymizing function it is possible for the results to be compared in a direct manner [WVS+99]. In this study, the IP addresses were first classified as belonging to sub-organizations and then anonymized – another example of structure preserving anonymization.

8.7 Attacks Against Anonymized Data

Beyond what can be learned directly from anonymized data, analysis of the data combined with other datasets may lead to inferences that can help successfully reverse engineer sensitive information. The anonymization process has to keep in mind what additional information may be available to others before settling on a specific anonymization technique. With increasing potential of cross-linkages, such as personal email contents indexed and linked against searches done in popular search engines that offer both services, there is additional concern about releasing raw information. At a business level, searches in external patent information sites for keywords combined with information about the company, can be useful information to competitors. Search strings often reveal information about areas of interest to the searcher and strategic mining of this information can be of use to competitors. Simply anonymizing the user's IP address within the company (say to the nearest /24) is no longer enough to prevent such information leakage.

Consider, for example, an organization that is willing to release information about intrusions on their network. In order to protect their own privacy, they *only* release information about the attackers: the remote source IP address, remote source port, and possibly the specific alarm triggered by the suspected intrusion. However, by examining the range of IP addresses of the suspected attackers and by a reverse DNS lookup, one could guess the organization's identity. Popular source addresses that are nearby may share a DNS server with the organization! Additionally, some internal IP addresses may be included in the 'source' address list. Anonymizing thus requires extra care in removing possible connections to the releasing organization.

The anonymized data must be immune to a variety of other attacks. The *tcpdpriv* tool is vulnerable when used with the '-A50' option [Ylo, CMK00]. The level 50 anonymization option provides the k-bit equal mapping discussed above. The attack combines external information such as popular Web servers and DNS servers with the anonymized traces. Additionally, *tcpdpriv*, when run on two different traces, will map the same IP address to different strings. This is due to its dependence on positional occurrence of address in the trace. An alternative is cryptographically strong techniques such as one-way hash functions that are immune to plaintext attacks. If this is provably secure and is implemented in hardware, online anonymization can be a feasible alternative.

When prefix-preserving anonymization is used it is possible to construct a list of prefixes in an AS and compare it against publicly available BGP tables from sites like RouteViews [Rou] or the RIPE database [RIP]. Attackers can also probe portions of the prefix address space of suspected administrative entities to contrast the allocated portions that respond against the list of prefixes available in the anonymized data. Partitioning inside a network might reduce external identification of this particular vulnerability [MZX$^+$04]. A graph-based reverse engineering technique where the routers are nodes and connections are edges may also aid in identifying them with an elevated probability. Flow lengths can reveal protocol used even if the protocol field is obscured. For example, most DNS flows are short and involve repeated occurrence of local DNS servers and remote authoritative DNS servers. They often precede other transactions such as TCP. An entirely non-payload base identification [KBFC04] of P2P traffic has been carried out involving a combination of flow length analysis and other heuristics such as same source–destination ports appearing in both UDP and TCP.

Earlier we referred to the concept of re-identification, whereby it is possible to combine a collection of anonymous datasets and unanonymized datasets that were released separately, and extract identification information from them. For example, consider two different data sets: one consisting of medical records of patients with just three fields: date of birth, gender, and geographical location information (zip code in the USA). The same information is available in the records of the motor vehicle department, allowing one to combine the two data sets to extract the identity of the patient in the more private medical records. The combination of these few fields are unique for a significant fraction of the population, allowing re-identification.

Recently there has been work on combining identity information by combing through multiple sites where identified and de-identified network-related data are present [Mal05]. This study examines the online usage of a monitored set of users and describes a way to match the trails of accesses by the same user represented, say, by an IP address. Different datasets of their Web access patterns were released with some including IP addresses and sites visited, and others including sites visited, names, and addresses. The study made use of global popularity information with regard to Web site access (that it is Zipf-like) and also examined the reverse popularity ranking of Web sites. As new datasets were added the increase in the number of re-identifications grew steadily. Web sites that were visited less frequently significantly helped in re-identification. The examination of popular Web sites showed that by examining about 25 Web sites virtually all the re-identification could be completed. Distributors of data thus have to be aware of subsets of their data, some with identification and some without, being released and combined later.

8.8   Anonymizing Data: Metrics for Success

A key measure of success of anonymization is how useful the anonymized data is and whether the anonymization ensures that no information is leaked. In the previous section we examined a range of attacks against the anonymized data. Depending on whether the anonymization is done online or offline, performance issues also might be factors in measuring success. Online anonymization helps in ensuring that private information is *never* recorded. As mentioned earlier in the discussion of the TiVo system [AvS04], not recording raw information at the time of gathering data is generally a safer method of providing anonymity.

In the knowledge discovery, data mining and management communities, requirements on degrees of data protection such as *k-anonymity* [Sam01, Swe02] have been introduced. The notion is to introduce a level of obscurity to make it difficult to identify individual data elements based on released data. One way of obscuring an element is to make sure that there are other items that are similar and thus the protected element is not easily distinguished from other similar elements. More formally, units of released data, say a tuple, have to be related to at least k others in order for the anonymization to meet the *k-anonymity* requirement. The notion of being related to *k* implies that a tuple could be matched to *k* different protected elements. Suppose we view the data as a table with rows and columns. Meeting *k-anonymity* would imply that all combinations of values in the transformed (anonymized) table's columns that may be linked with other external tables cannot be matched to fewer than *k* rows [Iye02]. By being related to other elements the identity information of any individual protected data element is diffused. Such degrees of data protection make it harder to map released entries to individual identities.

We can imagine similar metrics for various elements in traces. If all IP addresses are grouped to the level of a higher prefix level such as a /24 at least, then the degree of anonymity would be 1 in 256. However, by judicious active probing it is possible to narrow the set of active addresses to a number smaller than that. If the popular top-level domain name alone is made available (`.com`, `.edu`, etc.), it would be impossible to zoom in much further. Likewise, if just an Autonomous System number is known, depending on the reach of the AS (such as the number of distinct customers), it may not be viewed as a significant enough disclosure.

The speed of anonymization varies with the volume, complexity of the input data, and the nature of anonymization performed. Replacing each field with the same constant takes little time but the anonymized data is not likely to be useful. Prefix-preserving anonymization techniques of IP addresses have pointed out the memory and space constraints under which such systems operate. For example, a trace with 10 million unique IP addresses required approximately 320 MB of main memory space [XFAM01] a few years ago. Even with considerable improvements in anonymization techniques and processor speeds, such an anonymization cannot be implemented in a router.

Traces that are anonymized offline do not face the same performance constraints. Anonymizing 2 GB of daily *netflow* traces even on a laptop was possible offline in under 20 minutes in 2004 [SWY] without risk of missing any data in attempting to keep up with a live flow.

8.9 Alternatives to Anonymization

There are several problems with anonymization. These include the difficulty of convincing organizations to release the anonymized data, the choice of information that is actually included in the released data, and coordinating data from various organizations. Additional problems have been pointed out [Mog]: the anonymizer tool may be buggy and the different datasets need to comprise a general collection. While representativeness of measurement data is a known problem, the skewed nature of the availability of anonymized data aggravates the problem. One alternative is to allow people to share the code used to generate the data rather than the data itself. While this will not increase the nature and number of datasets, a clean, verified, and widely available piece of code could be shipped to various sites and the output can be obtained. It may be easier to validate the source code and it can serve as the unit of information exchange. It avoids the need to worry about anonymizing input data entirely. However, testing of code can be more work and there is a risk of inertia on the part of data owners who may blindly run buggy code or worse yet code with backdoors. However, with the participation of multiple sites errors in code can be isolated and the risk of backdoors lowered. Additionally, the identity of the authors of the code are known which can serve as a deterrent for exploits. An advantage of the same code distributed to many places is that the output format will be similar. As long as there are not too many diverse configuration parameters the output can be compared across sites.

9

Security

One of the key areas where Internet measurement has begun to play an important role is Internet security. Logging of traffic-related information has been carried out for a considerable amount of time. Logs have been maintained at firewalls at egress points in the network, *netflow* data is gathered at router level, and intrusion detection monitors have logged data as well.

While the security field is decades old, the range and complexity of attacks on hosts on the Internet have dramatically increased within the last several years. The terms virus and worm have entered the popular lexicon. The two groups – whitehats (those who work hard to identify weaknesses and ongoing attacks, alert the community, and work to solve the security problems) and blackhats (those who work hard to identify weaknesses, exploit them, and communicate with other like-minded people) have been engaged in an arms race. As new weaknesses are identified and fixed, additional vulnerabilities are often found. The United States Federal Bureau of Investigation has labeled DDoS (distributed denial of service) attacks as the primary threat facing businesses. Given the rate of increase and the automated nature of many attacks, the Computer Emergency Response Team (CERT [CER]) has stopped publishing the number of reported incidents.

Internet security has grown as an important discipline with numerous courses, books, and software. A considerable amount of new research with a strong measurement bias has been done related to Internet security. In this chapter we examine the role that measurement is playing in security. Attacks on the network are aimed at all layers: router level, topology level, and application level. Attacks target specific protocols: IP, TCP, DNS, BGP, HTTP, etc. We examine measurements in aid of security done intranet, at gateways, and across the wide-area Internet. Moving beyond routers, we examine topology-based and application-level measurements that have been carried out to improve network security.

There is a key difference between the various measurement-related discussions thus far in the book and security-related measurement. Until now there were primarily two parties involved: the measurer and the measured entity (or entities). This was true for measurements at all the levels considered heretofore. Ambient problems such as packet loss during measurements or other errors could be tracked and possibly corrected for as part of reifying the measurements.

In security-related measurements, we face the presence of a third party: the adversary. When measurements are carried out to characterize or monitor attacks either passively or actively, detect or deter ongoing intrusions, care must be taken to assume that an active adversary could be involved. The adversary could potentially complicate accuracy or even usefulness of the measurements. Consider the example of a monitor that is watching for attacks and counting packets of specific nature that might be indicators of attacks. It is conceivable that the adversary might be aware of such monitors and vary the volume or frequency of the packets being sent to that destination. The ability of an adversary to actively modify or worse yet tailor their behavior requires an additional level of scrutiny of measurement techniques in the security context. Such scrutiny is required in designing measurement experiments as it would be too late to correct for the presence of adversaries later. Further, inferences drawn have to be filtered through the lens of potential adversarial actions.

9.1   Role of Internet Measurement in Security

There has been a radical increase in the number of users, applications, and hosts on the Internet in the last decade. At the same time, there has been a tremendous increase in the number of attempts to break into networks and compromise the security of machines across the Internet. Zombies – machines that have been taken over for nefarious purposes – have abounded for several years. Estimates for counts of such machines runs into the hundreds of thousands of machines [McL04, CJM05]. Internet measurement is increasingly playing an important role to coordinate information across large networks. Attacks are rarely targeted at a single host but repeated across numerous hosts in various parts of the Internet.

The attacks may be link-flooding high-bandwidth attacks, low-bandwidth ones aimed at particular applications, high-volume attacks from a single source or from a collection of distributed sources. The attacks may be periodic, coordinated, or spaced at uneven intervals to escape easy detection. Attackers often masquerade their identity or usurp others' identity. Beyond simply spoofing the source address, reflector attacks, whereby the source is set to be the attack victim's address, are also used. The use of stepping stone attacks, whereby a compromised machine is used to launch attacks later, has also become common. Man-in-the-middle attacks exploiting trust-based relationships between peers are also possible.

The motivation for attacks may be simply for the juvenile pleasure of displaying the ability to carry out attacks or more economic-based reasons where the attackers work on behalf of spammers and the like. The payback is high for the investment made by the attackers or those on whose behest attacks are carried out. The trust model in the Internet is unsound and exploitation has become natural. Attacks waste resources ranging from computing to human, in terms of productivity loss. If some services become unavailable either partially or entirely, the effects may persist long after the attack has ceased, as many of the affected users may switch to a different service or service provider.

However, many of the attacks are either simple variants of others or attacks that have been obtained on the Internet from other attackers. The widely prevalent denial of service attacks have toolkits that are found on the Internet; many of them have been analyzed [DDO, DLD00]. A *botnet* [Bot] – a set of zombie machines – is rented for the sole purpose of attacking [Bie04] and it is possible to obtain the botnet with the attacks pre-configured on them; the only variable is the set of targets. Given the similarity of attacks, characterizing the attack in one place can be of help at numerous other sites. The set of assets protected at various large sites are often similar; for example a Web server complex or a DNS farm, and network infrastructure components such as links or routers.

Measurements at all layers have been applied in the security domain. Examining basic packet-level characteristics such as inter-arrival times, packet sizes, protocol choices, patterns of interaction between end points (source and destination IP addresses and ports) have all been examined for unusual activity. At higher levels, the ON/OFF patterns of connections, differences in flow-level attributes have also been used in security affiliated applications. Earlier, in Chapter 7 (Section 7.2.5) we discussed the *netflow* record generated graph-based DNS characterization which helped identify possible anomalies emanating from the skewed access patterns of short TCP exchanges. Firewall logs are examined to look for outliers. Router-based Access Control List (ACL) filtering can provide information on false positives: good traffic that may be inadvertently blocked. Other rate-limiting mechanisms, such as Cisco's CAR [Car], may likewise require monitoring to examine if wanted traffic is downgraded leading to poor performance. Anomalies at the inter-domain communication configuration level, either accidental or deliberate, can lead to significant disruptions that may go unnoticed until an attack. Passive monitoring of BGP update messages in conjunction with topology information can help detect presence of such anomalies. At the application layer, everything from contents of protocol headers to payload has been a candidate for possible attack detection. As we saw in Chapter 7 (Section 7.3.4), the lack of protocol compliance by implementations can be exploited to attack servers. Simple tracking of upload versus download ratio of a peer can help identify freeloaders who contribute to the general degrading of a peer-to-peer network. In the case of worms and virus, there has been considerable measurement done to characterize, isolate, and help in earlier detection of such disruptive events. In networked games, the hijacking of a user's identity or a player cheating about their current coordinates are a violation of the system's fidelity; the absence of such fidelity may have a serious impact on the number of participants in the game and thus its overall popularity.

An intrusion is often detected as a deviation from a norm; with the norm defined based on historical access patterns and the policy of the site. An architecture for an intrusion detection system may start by filtering and blocking traffic, gathering additional information about possible attackers, folding in historical statistical information, analyzing across multiple layers of the protocol stack before forwarding the packets to the intended destination. Change detection methods built on statistical measurement techniques monitor traffic levels at different parts of the network to warn of possible attacks. Tools have been created to aid in intrusion detection with basic measurement components built into them. Commercial security products rely on measurements to identify potential threats, to reduce false positives, and aggregate information for forensic purposes.

In the subsequent sections we will examine the role of measurement at various locations: intranet, at network gateways, at the inter-domain level, in the wide area, and finally at the application level.

9.2   Intranet Measurements in Aid of Security

Most administrative entities are only concerned about securing their own network. Depending on the nature of traffic inside their network, the kinds of attacks witnessed, and the importance of the assets being protected, different measurements can be used to characterize security problems. An administrative entity could mine passive measurement information already being carried out, such as SNMP polling data, flow-level information (e.g., *netflow*). Significant deviations in expected traffic may be viewed as potential security violation although some significant deviations may be routine behavior. For example, brief outage of a DNS server may cause an application to be on hold for several seconds, and the subsequent return to normal behavior would confirm the absence of an attack. Similarly, a flash crowd event triggered by sudden interest in a Web site, say, is not an attack [JKR02]. Thus, intranet measurements need to be able to distinguish between different abnormal scenarios.

By its very nature, passive measurements analyzed post-facto are mainly intrusion detection as opposed to active prevention. Firewall logs are routinely gathered on both traffic that was blocked or allowed through. In this section we will examine techniques that have been proposed to use available data at various levels to look for possible security violations. Intranet measurements use SNMP, flow data, and logs at various levels of the stack.

SNMP (Simple Network Management Protocol) data is gathered periodically (typically every five minutes) and consists of a variety of traffic statistics such as packet counters and the number of bytes traversing a link. The polling interval circumscribes the kind of anomalies that might be detected as brief deviations that are less than the interval will not be captured. Flow data is gathered at various routers (access, ingress, etc.) in a raw format. One example of the use of SNMP and flow data to detect denial of service (DoS) attacks, with wavelet-based transformations applied to the data is described in [BKPR02]. Wavelets are used as they take both frequency and time into account in describing time series data. SNMP and flow data gathering are discussed in Chapter 6 (Sections 6.3.3 and Section 6.3.3 respectively).

If the volume of flow data becomes exceedingly large, only sampled data is obtained. The sampling can be simply statistical, such as one in n packets, or somewhat smarter – biased to percentage of traffic in certain applications. The level of detail available in flow data is often sufficient to separate applications, and closely examine source addresses and prefixes of interest. Even if flow data is gathered continuously, due to the nature of flows being exported to the gathering entity, multiple transactions lasting for minutes may transpire before a flow record is written out. Most of the analysis of flow records is thus done post-facto rather than online. Statistical analysis of flow records can quickly identify source addresses that exceed some expected thresholds of packet or byte count on certain applications. However, thresholds are not always the best way to identify attackers. Probe packets sent by attacking IP addresses are always few in number and yet may be a security threat. Since flow records do not have any of the body of the packets they are not capable of identifying content-based attacks. Higher-level application logs often retain headers and in selective cases, deeper levels of packet information; such logs can be mined for additional data. Sampling is discussed in more detail in Chapter 6, Section 6.3.3.

Note that not all intranet measurements related to security issues deal with incoming traffic. As it is possible that attacks could emanate from inside the network, measurements are used to look for outgoing traffic exceeding thresholds. The attacks could originate from a customer's location; it could be unintentional and be triggered by a virus. In general, it is harder to set reasonable thresholds on outgoing traffic as the traffic may indeed be benign. Unlike incoming traffic where capacity constraints and past statistics could help in the creation of meaningful thresholds, it is harder to keep track of statistics regarding external destinations.

9.3   Gateway Measurements in Aid of Security

Firewalls at the perimeter of administrative entities log a variety of network activity. Local measurements have been carried out at the firewall to see if the tools created to withstand flooding attacks can be overwhelmed by increasing the flooding rate. An example of a flooding attack is a sudden flurry of attempted TCP connections resulting in a flood of SYN packets arriving. Beyond enforcing admission control of packets aimed at prefixes behind the network or at certain applications, firewalls often log detailed information about traffic aimed at the installation being protected. These logs are mined to look for a range of interesting information: habitual offending source IP addresses, most commonly probed applications and port numbers, etc.

Most large Internet Service Providers and enterprise networks try to position intrusion detection systems (IDS) at the perimeter of their network in an attempt to keep most of the unwanted traffic from entering their network. Some ISPs additionally position IDS systems in front of certain customer complexes (a set of links and/or prefixes reserved for a particular customer) to provide a more tailored detection service. The basic assumption behind IDS is that legitimate activity inside the network is predictable: it adheres to certain pre-specified patterns. Thus a set of signatures can be specified to watch for traffic that violate the expected patterns of incoming (or outgoing) traffic. The IDSes are configured with access control lists and a range of semantic filters tailored to the expected traffic and the assets that are being protected. The signature sets look for specific patterns of known attack traffic: probes on certain ports using certain protocols that can be unambiguously interpreted as attacks. The information about attackers, the choice of protocol, temporal and packet size distribution, etc. are often pooled in a central database inside the organization. The database can be used to improve prevention of future attacks, reducing the impact of false positives, and to generate system-wide blacklists. Considerable effort has to be expended in tailoring the signature set so the false positives (suspected attacks that turn out to be benign traffic) do not overwhelm the IDS system. Too many false positives will reduce the ability to detect actual attacks. At the same time, we do not want to miss certain infrequently occurring attacks; else the false negative ratio would increase. Specific tools have been created to try and reduce false positives in popular IDS tools [PYD01].

Most firewalls deploy access control lists and can check both for source IP addresses that are not permitted to access the network and destination addresses that are not expecting traffic from outside. For example, an internal DNS server for an internal collection of hosts, would not be expected to handle queries coming from outside. If the volume of unwanted traffic towards a particular prefix, service, or a server complex increases beyond a threshold, additional protection devices may be required; such as a demilitarized zone (DMZ [DMZ]), a portion of the network that is neither on the Internet nor inside the Intranet. Vulnerability testing is carried out by tools such as ISS [Sec] and *nmap* [Yar] that send probe packets to test if the firewall configurations and policies in place are resilient. One way to carry out such tests is to simulate the attacks without causing actual damage. Firewall configurations and access control lists are specified in various formats depending on the manufacturing vendor. For example, Linux *ipchains* [Rus00] and Cisco's IOS [IOS] are quite distinct languages. A generic measurement tool that can process distinct formats is hard although attempts have been made [Woo01].

Numerous tools have become popular over the last few years in the field of intrusion detection. These include Network Flight Recorder (NFR [NFR]), Bro [Pax99a], Snort [Sno], etc. Largely the tools have a notion of signatures that they can match against incoming traffic but in practice they differ in terms of the flexibility they provide. Bro, for example, has a policy script interpreter whereby a site's security policy can be specified in a high-level language. Snort can perform real-time traffic and protocol analysis to help detect various attacks and alert users in real time. Snort also uses a language to specify what traffic should be filtered or allowed to pass through. Beyond IDS, Snort can be simply used as a packet logging mechanism. The various signatures in the Snort database are documented along with the potential for false positives and false negatives, and corrective measures to be taken if a particular alert is raised.

A simple example of a (slightly edited) Snort signature number 119, extracted from the Snort community rules database is:

```
alert tcp $EXTERNAL_NET 80 -> $HOME_NET any
   (msg:"WEB-CLIENT Internet Explorer URLMON.DLL Content-Encoding
     Overflow Attempt";
   flow:to_client,established;
   content:"Content-Encoding|3A|"; nocase;
   pcre:"/Content-Encoding\x3A[^\r\n]{300,}/i";
   classtype:attempted-admin;
   reference:url,www.microsoft.com/technet/security/bulletin/MS03-
015.mspx;
   sid:100000119; rev:1;)
```

This is used to raise an alert when a buffer overflow present in the Internet Explorer browser's urlmon.dll file is attempted. The attack gains the user privileges of the user who is running the browser and is triggered when the `Content-Encoding` header field has a value that is 300 or more bytes long.

Analysis of attacks can be done post-facto; however real-time detection of an attack in progress requires considerable additional measurement. For example, to avoid false positives, packets may have to be inspected at a deeper level, beyond simply a subset of headers. More importantly, possible coordination between multiple IDSes may be needed. Recent research efforts in this direction are discussed later in Section 9.5.

9.4   Inter-domain Measurements Impact on Security

Attacks at the inter-domain level can have large scale and serious consequences. A compromised BGP table may result in blackholing a significant fraction of traffic. Worse yet, traffic going towards a sensitive destination may be hijacked. A large fraction of customers might suddenly find themselves cut off from the Internet. Passive monitoring of BGP messages [KMRV03] combined with a model of AS connectivity can help isolate route advertisements that are inconsistent with the current topology indicating a possible Man-In-The-Middle attack. The technique examines the AS_PATH attribute of BGP update messages and looks for presence of improper sequences. A BGP announcement has a prefix and optional attribute values; AS_PATH is a frequently used `Attribute` value (out of 256 possible ones [Tim02]).

BGP update messages were collected over four separate weeks during the course of a 2-year period, and were examined along with the AS map generated at each of the instances. The first day's data was used as training set to compare against the remaining days of the week to look for anomalies. Most of the violations of claims of incorrect IP ownership were due to misconfigurations; and thus technically not attacks. Another way to look for possible violations is by examining [ZPW+01] prefixes that appear to originate from more than one Autonomous System. However, there may be legitimate reasons for this to occur and false positives need to be filtered out.

When an AS announces either mistakenly or deliberately address space that is not owned by it, it is termed *address space hijacking*. The frequency of such hijacking phenomena along with several other common misconfiguration errors has been measured [MWA02].

Note that measurements related to BGP have several advantages: the potential impact of any detection is high and the various operators and administrators responsible for BGP generally tend to cooperate when attacks or misconfigurations are reported. The volume of traffic to examine is generally lower than large-scale packet monitoring and data needs to be collected at the overall tiny fraction of BGP-speaking access routers. Once measurements indicate presence of problems, filtering policies may be put in place or existing ones modified.

9.5 Wide-area Measurements in Aid of Security

Moving beyond individual hosts and small-scale administrative installations, there has been interest in gathering data across the Internet to measure large-scale phenomena. Considerable amount of measurement work has taken place in the wide area to aid in security and reported in the research literature. Tools have been created to detect and trace back attack traffic. Software has been created to aid in intrusion detection. We do not intend to present a survey of all or even a significant fraction of security tools in this chapter; however we will highlight a few to give a flavor of the role of measurements in these attempts.

Broadly, work in the wide area has ranged from classifying denial of service attacks, detecting and tracing back attackers, handling worms and virus, monitoring and coordination of attack information, issues related to open proxies and spam. This is not exactly an orthogonal classification as some ideas tend to overlap. We will examine measurement's role in each of these below.

Classifying DoS Attacks. Denial of service attacks have been among the most common form of attacks on the Internet. Flooding a link or a particular application (such as a Web server) with numerous simultaneous requests from diverse and dispersed set of sources are typical forms of distributed denial of service attacks. By examining the characteristics of the packets involved in such attacks – their headers, arrival rates, etc. – one could detect occurrences of such attacks.

The backscatter technique [MVS01] discusses ways of monitoring a single egress link of a large enough address space (a /8) as a sampling mechanism to characterize the overall number of denial of service attacks. Since many attackers spoof the alleged source of the attacks by picking them randomly, the receiving entity (victim) will respond to the spoofed addresses. Such responses are likely to be spread across the Internet and by monitoring a large enough space one could characterize DoS attacks. Traditional flow-based classification is used to classify attacks: based on the protocol, checks are made to see if certain fields or headers are present. This is an example of passive monitoring to measure attack rate and to study nature, duration of attacks, domains and autonomous system of victims. Another technique, one that monitors peering links bidirectionally between ISPs to examine how attacks are propagated is described in the Cossack [HHP03a] system. Tools like *tcpdump* are used to capture packet headers to examine if pre-set thresholds are exceeded (e.g., the number of distinct sources that are attempting to communicate with the same host) to identify an attack. Other thresholds include increase in arrival rate of packets and change in volume of attack over time. Frameworks have been developed to classify DoS attacks [HHP03b] using analysis of headers, the speed with which attacks grow, and distinguishing single and multi-source attacks. The goal is to be able to both characterize present attacks and help identify future DoS attacks. The distinction between single and multiple-source attacks is provided by time series analysis.

Tracing Back Attack Traffic and Honeypots.   A honeypot is defined broadly as a *resource whose value lies in its unauthorized use* [Lan, Sha]. Simple honeypot mechanisms involve advertising a set of addresses that are currently not in active use; i.e., there are no active hosts connected to them for the purpose of traditional Internet activity. Such addresses are called *dark addresses*. When traffic arrives at these addresses, the originators of such traffic are considered to be malicious. Many honeypots passively listen to such incoming traffic expending fairly few resources in the process. Some honeypots actively respond to the malicious traffic ranging from sending simple SYN-ACKs to the incoming SYNs, to emulating a login session, and in the extreme emulating a whole kernel. Additional details about the attack traffic can also be gathered: originating AS associated with the prefix to which the (purported) source address is associated with, temporal patterns, protocol of preference, etc. Suspicious IP addresses can be identified by some honeypots [Vin04].

Public domain versions of honeypot code for popular operating systems have been available for different variants of probing attacks [Pro03] along with commercial software [Kfs] indicating the popularity of this technique for identifying probe traffic. The broad notion of honeypots has even been used to locate spam email originators [AS7] although such honeypots need to have more infrastructure in place. *Honeyfarms* [Nic03], have been used to detect worms automatically – they are a centralized collection of honeypots (and related analysis tools) that receive suspicious traffic redirected to them from different detection devices spread around the Internet. *Wormholes* are appliances used to securely transmit the suspicious traffic to the honeyfarm. A set of k honeypots will be able detect a worm when roughly $1/k$ of the vulnerable machines are infected. Honeyfarms use virtual machine images to implement honeypots creating both a 'vulnerability signature' and a possible attack signature. The detection is based on infected honeypots and not traffic from the wormhole. A network *telescope* [Dav02] provides the ability to see victims of certain kinds of denial of service attacks or hosts infected by worms, and misconfigurations from a distance. The telescope work presents global views on DoS attacks using local monitoring. Genii [Gen], the so-called second generation of honeypots, reduced effort to deploy honeypots and are generally harder to detect. Genii relies on a separate, secure network that is used for administration purposes making the gateway difficult to detect due to the absence of associated MAC addresses, or even routing hops or TTL decrements. However, as the authors themselves admit, in the arms race against attackers, security through obscurity has never had a long shelf life of success.

Honeypots gather data at the targets of probes and other unwanted traffic but they are unable to locate the precise entry point of such traffic into the network. Addition-

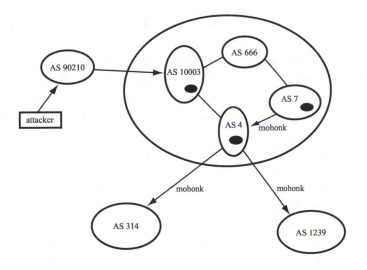

Figure 9.1 Mohonk architecture.

ally some of the source addresses may be spoofed. Traceback to the origination of such traffic is hard due to a variety of reasons including the delay between the time of receipt of the probe and its origin, and the difficulty of maintaining state along the path of such traffic. Most importantly, the ASes in the path towards the destination are not aware that the advertised prefix is dark and that such traffic being carried by them is malicious. Thus, although the ASes in the path carry such traffic, they are unable to benefit from the knowledge that the originators of such traffic are potentially suspect. Even the AS at which such traffic originated cannot learn about the host responsible for originating this traffic or the primary link on which similar such traffic may be injected.

A proposal made to notify the ASes in the path ahead of time about dark destination prefixes posited the creation of *mobile* honeypots. In the Mohonk project [Kri04], there were two aspects to the mobility: the information about the darkness of the prefixes is made available to upstream ASes and the set of such prefixes would change periodically via BGP announcements [RL95] and withdrawals. If the information about the dark prefixes was known to upstream ASes also participating in the scheme, they would know about such traffic and its originators much earlier and could take remedial action. For example, such unwanted traffic could be dropped with just control information passed down about the originators towards the destination. Additionally, by maintaining state about such originators they could add them to a blacklist once the amount of unwanted traffic exceeded an AS-specific threshold. A BGP announcement consists of a prefix and optional attribute values such as next hop, the AS path, or the community attribute. Since the COMMUNITY attribute field has no predefined meaning, it is used as a signaling mechanism to inform upstream ASes that the prefix is dark.

Figure 9.1 shows the Mohonk architecture. Here, the probe traffic enters via AS 90210. The dark circles indicate the dark prefixes. AS 7 is shown sending regular Mohonk tagged advertisements to AS 4. AS 4 passes it on to ASes 314 and 1239, both of which participate in the scheme although they don't advertise their own dark prefixes.

Measurements of ability to detect unwanted originators involve choosing several parameters: prefix lengths that need to be advertised to draw enough such traffic, duration of the life of advertisements, choice of applications to associate with the addresses in the dark prefixes, packet count thresholds that decide if the traffic is unwanted. Measurements based on the honeypot mechanisms have to be resilient against attacks aimed at subverting the setup. Since the blackhat community exchanges information [Jos, Hun] about detection techniques, they might avoid honeypots once they learn about such prefixes. Such a mechanism is called *reverse blacklisting*. Unlike domains set aside to detect email spam [Jen03] and thus probers, the mobile honeypot announcements are transient, random, and varied making it much harder for attackers to use the information. Secondly, the cost for attackers is increased by forcing them to do additional work that has potentially limited value. A measure of the usefulness of such honeypot schemes is the speed with which unwanted traffic originators are discovered and blacklisted across multiple ASes over a period of time compared to the cost to both the whitehats and blackhats.

Virus and Worms.   Among numerous terms used to describe software that has to be executed in order for negative impact, *malware* has recently emerged as a catch-all term. The term malware includes unwanted advertisements, spyware – software inadvertently downloaded onto a machine to monitor certain user activities, backdoor creating software – holes created for later exploitation, virus, and worms. Probably no other topic has been more widely discussed in the popular press with respect to attacks on the Internet as virus and worms. Historically they have caused the most significant damage to the Internet infrastructure and to the productivity of users. They have called into question the very effectiveness of the Internet as a reliable communication mechanism.

Although viruses and worms are technically distinct, the terms have been used interchangeably. A virus requires users participation for the unwanted effect to be carried out, while a worm typically exploits known flaws in an operating system. Viruses requires user actions such as opening an infected piece of email, or a document (such as Microsoft Word or a PDF document) – in effect anything that can automatically trigger code to be executed. The amount of damage caused by a virus differs significantly and in some sense viruses may spread slowly as direct participation by a user is required. Worms enter the internal network through reasonably well-known security holes such as buffer overflow [Gro] problems. If there are no automatic bounds checking done on contiguously allocated chunks of memory, it is possible for a malicious (or even a benign) program to write past such a buffer. A malicious program would overwrite a function's return address and place arbitrary code at that address to be executed next. One of the earliest worms exploited a known buffer overflow problem in the widely used *sendmail* software. Worms can spread quickly or slowly depending on how they are constructed. As recently as 2003, of the top ten so-called viruses, eight depended on user action or presence of vulnerable software [Vir].

Among the measurements of interest with respect to worms are how target lists are chosen, the set of possible entry points, and how quickly they could spread throughout the Internet. Secondarily there is the issue of the extent of economic damage caused by malware either at the time of the attack or as a result of other attacks enabled by opening backdoors. A physical world counterpart of a denial of service attacks that can cause economic damage is automated sending of a large number of fake requests for a catalog.

Some worms use scanning of large portions of the Internet to identify machines that may be victims. Earlier we discussed the ability to characterize DoS attacks via the backscatter technique. Vulnerability of entry points can be detected by applying tools discussed earlier such as ISS and *nmap*. The speed of spreading of a worm varies with the worm and the first worm, known as the Morris worm [Spa88], took just a few hours to spread through a reasonable portion of the Internet.

In 2001, the Code Red [Cod] worm was released in two different forms. The first one used a static seed in the random number generator code for generating IP addresses to attack and thus spread slower than the second one which used a random seed. Code Red took almost 10 hours to spread to nearly 350000 hosts attaining a peak spreading rate of 2000 hosts in a minute. The Slammer [Sla] worm consisting of a single UDP packet (376 bytes) exploited a vulnerability in Microsoft's SQL 2000 code. The Slammer worm had no destructive payload but just set up connections between systems at the UDP/1434 port of the SQL server and simply spread between them. The slammer worm spread nearly 250 times faster than Code Red and affected nearly 100000 hosts in 10 minutes. The propagation strategy was to consume network bandwidth rather than to cause problems within a host by modifying any local files.

Measurements about speed of spreading are crucial in order to evaluate the feasibility of applying dynamic prevention methods once a worm has started to spread. The speed of spreading depends on identifying potential hosts as targets and contacting them by starting with list of hosts known to have good connectivity. Slow scanning can be used as an 'under the radar' mechanism to gather the *hitlist* of such hosts. By repeatedly dividing the hitlist between infected host and handing over half and continuing with the other half, it has been analytically shown that such a theoretical worm can spread across the entire Internet in 15 minutes [SPW02].

A mechanism to create a workload generator for malware is discussed in [SYB04] with the purpose of recreating malicious packet traffic. The idea is to be able to examine both known worms and to explore potential variants that might be created in the future. The performance characteristics of well-known intrusion detection systems can be examined by the generated workloads.

Monitoring and Coordination of Intrusion Detection.   Measurements in combination with statistics have played a key role in improving monitoring and intrusion detection techniques. Several tools have been created in this arena to aid those working in the field of intrusion detection. Among the primary concerns are reducing false positives – if the number of false positives exceeded a threshold, then the overall value of alerts begins to diminish and real threats may be ignored by administrators.

The individual IDS log information can be pooled with other administrative entities to be compiled as a broader information database. For example, organizations participating in the DSHIELD [Dsh] repository, contribute logs which are then used to generate global blacklists and to detect novel vulnerabilities. Attempts [YBU03, Vin04] have been made to build an overlay network that aids collaboration between different intrusion detection systems. This study examine firewall logs over a 4-month period from 1600 networks spanning numerous Autonomous Systems. A few sources were responsible for many of the intrusions. The goal of this work was to develop a quantitative characterization of intrusion activity using firewall logs at various sites across the Internet.

Given that there is attack similarity across the Internet there is an expected benefit by sharing information between intrusion detection systems. Enterprises and large ISPs have been traditionally reluctant to share information about attacks with each other due to privacy reasons and concerns about information about their vulnerabilities becoming public. Neutral organizations like the Computer Emergency Response Team [CER] have played a role in serving as a centre for information exchange. Third-party companies (such as SecurityFocus [Deea]) offer services to both monitor attacks inside companies and to coordinate attacks across the Internet to provide an early warning system. Many of these companies formulate signatures of attacks, compile statistics, create vulnerability databases, and provide possible countermeasures. Since not all intrusions are of equal concern to various cooperating organizations, and since not all organizations can even be trusted to the same degree, the coordinator is left with the task of mediating between the organizations. Among the ideas that have been proposed to handle trust levels are authenticating participants' messages (to ensure malicious entities do not contribute false information) all the way to creating policies and bilateral or multilateral legal agreements.

A key problem in coordinating attack or intrusion information is that depending on the nature of attack (slow-scan as opposed to a rapidly spreading worm) the reaction of both the coordinating agent and the participating organizations have to be different. Since a worm can theoretically spread across the entire Internet in a matter of minutes [SPW02] it may not suffice to exchange attack information periodically.

The Internet Sink project [YBP04] described scalable ways of measuring packet traffic at dark prefix networks. The iSink architecture consists of a set of dark prefixes, a passive monitoring subsystem, and an active responder to the unwanted traffic. Scalability is achieved via the addition of a stateless kernel module to minimize the amount of work that has to be done in responding to the unwanted traffic at the dark prefixes. Responses are generated both at transport and application layers. The study of unwanted traffic at a campus network and an Internet service provider showed that the unwanted traffic was of significantly different volumes in the two different locations with different protocols dominating (TCP and UDP, in that order). The experimental test (in a lab environment) showed that it was possible to respond to unwanted traffic of the order of 20000 connection requests per second with improvements possible via the user of sampling techniques.

The Internet Motion Sensor (IMS [BCJ+05]) provides an architecture that includes a collection of dark prefix networks whose incoming traffic is both passively monitored and an active response generated where warranted, similar to iSink described above. For example, TCP SYN connections generate a SYN-ACK so that the subsequent data payload's MD5 [Riv92] signature can be generated. Since all traffic to the dark prefixes is by definition either unwanted or accidentally generated, the signatures of such unwanted traffic's payload are stored in a database for comparison with other attacks as well as to examine effectiveness of such monitoring techniques.

Recently, a host monitoring component [BCR+05] has been added to the Internet Motion Sensor setup, as a way of extending the architecture to a hybrid model where a significant fraction of traffic going towards a honeypot infrastructure that are not attacks can be filtered, reducing the number of false positives. The insight is to examine the distribution of attack sources and the set of sensors where the attacks are seen, in order to construct filters.

Commercial Products.   A large number of commercial products are available in the attack prevention space. Among them are Cisco's Riverhead [Riv], Arbor Networks' Peakflow [Pea], and MacAfee's Intrushield [Intd]. Peakflow, for example, monitors used and unused services, detects worms by looking for cascading changes in hosts and via intranet traffic analysis, and correlates scans followed by subsequent traffic increases. Riverhead is aimed at distinguishing good and bad flows and preventing bad flows from reaching victims of a denial of service attack. A behavioral anomaly recognition engine is at the heart of this product but dynamic filters enable an on-demand diversion technique with the filters being in-line only for the victim's incoming traffic during an attack.

9.6 Application-level Measurements of Attacks

Individual applications can play a role in mitigating attacks if the lower layers are unable to block the attacks.

The most popular form of attack at the application layer these days that wastes a tremendous amount of resources in the form of user productivity, bandwidth, and storage is spam email. Many large enterprises, and service providers have invested in various filtering techniques aided by application-level measurements to mitigate the considerable impact of spam. In many of these cases the firewalls are the first line of defense and they traditionally scrub the incoming email for viruses but may not be able to do additional application-level checks to filter spam as well.

Large ISPs and enterprise networks have several concerns related to spam. Different kinds of measurements are carried out both to characterize the problem as well as on an ongoing basis. First, they have to ensure that the large mail servers are not overloaded by unwanted mail and tend to partition SMTP senders (technically, the ISPs to which they belong to) into trusted, unknown, and suspicious class. Busier servers are allocated to deal with suspicious SMTP senders who may be responsible for spam. Lightly loaded servers deal with trusted mail senders. Simple statistics about volume of suspected spam can be maintained in order to update such partitioning. At the servers, filtering is done based on a variety of factors related to the incoming email. Based on the results of the filtering techniques, which is often a combination of Bayesian statistical measures and other metrics computed by filtering software (a popular filtering tool is SpamAssassin [Spa]), global information about the remote SMTP sender is maintained. Metering is done based on volume of bytes exchanged in a single message and aggregated over a period of time. Note that such metering can be done bidirectionally to ensure that spammers inside the network are also monitored.

At higher levels, logging is carried out by numerous security-related facilities (such as *syslog*, or *wtmp* in UNIX) which are used by various IDSes. Such facilities log information about users' activities ranging from logging in to use of network resources. Kernel audit information is available in the form of a system call log. Intrusion detection can then be carried out by having the kernel-level data exported to a user-level process. The process which can look for deviations (such as unexpected increases in privilege levels or repeated failures during such attempts) via an analysis engine [CK01].

10

Case Studies

In this chapter we examine several small and large examples of artifacts related to Internet measurement. Artifacts range from packet monitoring tools, software toolsets, combination of hardware devices and software components, and medium and large-scale infrastructures created to aid measurement. It should be noted that, in general, the shelf-life of material in this chapter may be naturally short given the rapid evolution in the area. Wherever feasible we have mentioned the years of development of the artifact and their current status.

We begin with a discussion of a collection of low-level network monitors, then move up to discussing software toolsets that were created due to the lack of flexibility in the individual monitors. The need for generality arose as the data sources that required measuring began to diverge significantly. Ability to query data streams at high speeds without having to store the data has emerged as a new application.

10.1 Low-level Monitoring Tools

As a first representative class of tools we are going to examine the various issues around packet capturing. The set of issues related to this has been discussed in Chapter 6, Section 6.3.1. Increasingly, commercial off-the-shelf hardware is the preferred way to capture high-speed traffic in busy locations before handing the packet collection to software for processing. The set of design issues involve the ability of accepting large volumes of output from the hardware devices (e.g., OC3MON [AkcTW97], DAG [EMG] cards), filtering the traffic selectively based either on pre-specified or a dynamically changing set of rules, transforming the output to enable subsequent processing by a variety of downstream applications, and storing the contents. While it would be an interesting concept to write an entirely generic piece of software that can perform all the roles mentioned, it is significantly harder to do so. It is more common for different pieces of software to be used in conjunction with each other. The advantages are obvious: a more tailored filter and transformation routine can be used for quickly processing certain kinds of data than others resulting in the requirement of changing only a small portion of a toolset rather than a monolithic piece of software.

Passive monitoring of multiple protocols simultaneously at high speeds (over 1 Gbps) requires attention to be paid to a variety of issues including the following:

1. Ability to monitor/capture the traffic and write it to disk. The bandwidth available to the disk and the ability to copy all the bits quickly can be a key bottleneck.
2. Fine-grained time stamping to facilitate subsequent reassembly of the traffic. This requires fine-grained clocks and if data is being captured in multiple locations, synchronization of the clocks.
3. Limiting the amount of CPU resources that can be expended in transforming the captured traffic. For example, the data being captured may have to be compressed or anonymized on the fly. Such on-the-fly compression costs can be higher when the pattern of incoming data is unpredictable, as compared to post-capture compression. Similarly, anonymization done on the fly may cause permanent loss of transformed data. One may have to resort to sampling in order to preserve CPU and disk resources, with the attendant risks of missing data or inability to extrapolate inferences from the sampled data.

At the lower level, the choice of operating system, the number of kernel receive buffers, clock granularity, scheduling priorities all play an important role. Kernel parameters and libraries (designed to work with the monitoring hardware) have to be tailored to the expected volume of traffic and burstiness. Scaling the chosen hardware to meet with traffic arriving at higher speeds is an important concern. Each of the high-level constraints can be addressed using different techniques but some remedies may interact with each other. For example, compressing captured traffic will address the disk bandwidth issue but the amount of CPU available on the capturing device may not suffice to do both capturing and compressing simultaneously. Design considerations including the ones listed above are discussed in [MHK$^+$03].

Active measurements allow for a broader set of data points as measurement infrastructure can be distributed to a few places to capture data from remote locations. Active measurements can be performed interactively or scheduled for periodic executions via a friendly interface. One example of a friendly user interface is ANEMOS [DD03]. Beyond the standard collection of measurements, such as end-to-end performance, ANEMOS allows for the specification of rules such as triggering an alarm if the measured RTT exceeds a threshold. By measuring available bandwidth on different paths, the system allows for inferencing about network conditions. Another example is Pktd [GP03], which allows for control over measurements carried out on external sites by focusing all the rights and privileges in a single deamon. All client requests for measurements are funneled through this daemon which acts as a vehicle for enforcing access rights and controlling the resources. Once significant amount of packet headers have been gathered, tools are needed to process and analyze them. S-Net [CCS02] is an example of such a tool. S-Net stores the packet headers in a database and uses the S statistical language [BCW88] as the mechanism for analysis. S-Net has been used to study long-range dependence of various artifacts related to network traffic: packet arrival times and their counts.

10.2   Individual Toolsets for Network Measurement

There is a wide range of software tools that have been created over the last few years for Internet measurement. We have discussed many of them in earlier chapters; for example we examined bandwidth measurement tools in Chapter 5, tools for capturing and analyzing traffic and flow and sampling tools in Chapter 6, and tools for various individual applications such as DNS, Web, P2P, and networked games in Chapter 7. In Chapters 8 and 9 we discussed a few tools for anonymization and security respectively. In this section we focus on a small but representative set of software tools that have played an important role in network measurement. The main purpose of discussing them here is to present the software side of the story rather than the specific role played by the tool. We are interested in the software architecture, the key requirements, the various ways by which such tools are tested, deployed, and used in the Internet.

Toolsets in the field of Internet measurement are not as widespread as in other areas of computer science. Typically tools have been adapted to the particular measurement application and occasionally a few tools have been combined into a semi-coherent whole. However, there have been a few base tools and combinations that have been assembled for the purpose of processing large amounts of data and tuning it for measurement purposes. Examples of toolsets include modular querying mechanisms [FV02], Windmill [MJ98a], and Click [KMC$^+$00, Koh00].

A set of desiderata for a general purpose platform aimed at processing large amounts of data measurements was presented in [FV02]. Their system is designed as a library that can be merged with applications and has an interface that accepts queries. By ensuring that all data objects are typed, simultaneous access to data is provided to different measurement and data analysis modules. Common analysis modules include ones to count the set of records or filter the records according to a preset criteria (such as requiring certain fields to have occurred enough times). Using a model similar to that of a UNIX command pipeline it is possible to assemble the modules to answer a variety of measurement-related questions such as the distribution of TCP sequence numbers, frequency of accesses to a particular port (to see if there are attempts to scan a network), etc.

In the rest of this section we examine four different toolsets: Windmill and Click (mentioned above), *dss* [FK05], and Gigascope [CJSS03b]. One reason to choose them is the fact that one author of this book has extensive experience with *dss* and Gigascope. More importantly, however, the toolsets represent different points along the software spectra. Windmill is a passive protocol performance measurement tool, while Click has a building block approach lending itself to both passive and active measurements. *Dss* is an example of the traditional UNIX library approach, playing primarily a backend role for processing large amounts of data with minimal effort on the part of the programmer. Finally, Gigascope is a combination of tailored hardware and database software which has been used in passive data capture at high speeds and active processing of specified standing queries and user-specified ones.

10.2.1   Windmill

Windmill [MJ98a, WMJ04] is primarily a passive measurement tool targeted at protocol performance. However, it can be used with external active probing tools without requiring modifications to any substrate. The key construct in Windmill is the separation into three functional components: a protocol filter, abstract protocol modules, and an extensible engine based on a dynamic loader. The protocol filter moves code into the kernel so that complex packet matching can be done efficiently at the lower levels of the machine. The filter constructs an intermediate representation of the packets of interest being monitored and allows simultaneous experiments to access this intermediate representation. The set of protocol modules, one for each of the key Internet protocols (IP, TCP, BGP, HTTP, etc.), are set up in such a way that network events can be mapped easily for reconstruction at higher layers. Additionally the modules are capable of exporting the lower-level events and contents of data structures to multiple experiments simultaneously, reducing redundant work and increasing efficiency. One example of this is that the TCP module will reassemble the packet stream once and make the reassembled stream available to multiple experiments, eliminating expensive redundant work. The third component, viz., the extensible experiment engine uses a dynamic loader which permits modifications *during* an experiment and thinning when portions are no longer required.

A design goal of Windmill was to play one part in a larger Internet measurement setup. The ability to carry out multiple experiments, with some results shipped to remote locations on demand, allows this to meet this goal. Later in Section 10.3.4 we will examine another project (ATMEN) which shares similar design goals. A key observation in Windmill is that with the steady deployment of commercial off-the-shelf protocol implementation software, the ability to reverse engineer actually what is happening during execution of such shrink-wrapped software becomes harder. Thus a passive measurement infrastructure that can communicate with higher-level applications is a step in the right direction.

10.2.2   Click

The Click router allows for assembling complex configurations from simple part pieces that carry out specific router functions such as classifying packets, scheduling, etc. By opening up the functions of a router and mapping modules (called *elements*) to each of the major functions, Click allows for arbitrarily complex router configurations. In philosophy, Click resembles UNIX tools that are combined via pipes. By modifying individual components, new configurations can be tested. A router is assembled by placing the elements as vertices in a directed graph with packets moving along the edges. There are only a handful of elements in Click but they can be extended to implement differentiated services, header compression, etc. Classes of elements include packet sources, sinks, modifiers, and checkers (checking validity of packets). There are also storage elements for storing packets for later use and elements to schedule allowing packets to be chosen from different sources. A declarative language is available for configurations to be specified. Users can create their own libraries of parts of configurations. A variety of related devices such as an IP firewall, transparent proxy, and traffic generators can be easily specified in the Click language. (detailed examples are available in [Koh00]). The functionality of commercial routers is quite difficult for customers to extend primarily due to their proprietary software. Unlike commercial routers, new Click modules can be written to extend the behavior of routers. A toolkit for network address translation has been built [KMP02] in Click that can actually be used for all address and port number rewriting.

Although Click was primarily designed to forward packets, it has been used in Internet measurement [Koh06] and related environments. Given that a significant number of measurements require handling packets and analyzing traces, it is natural to use Click for various packet measurement tasks.

Packet classification using Click is straightforward as a Click element (*Classifier*) is available to process any portion of a packet. However, tailored classifiers are also available, that handle specific packet types (such as IP) or carry out narrow tasks (such as examining validity of headers). Similar to Windmill, Click can help in reassembling packet streams. Modification of packets for applications like anonymization is also possible using Click. For example, the prefix-preserving anonymization of tools like *tcpdpriv* (discussed in Chapter 8, Section 8.6.3) can be carried out. Other features of Click include the ability to aggregate packets as it processes them and subsequently analyze flows to produce a digest.

The active component of the Internet Sink project [YBP04] uses Click. The Internet sink passively monitors traffic capturing header and payload information present in packets sent to an unused address space and actively responds to them to obtain additional information. Click is used to construct a device to poll the interface for new packets and classifying the packets to direct them to appropriate responders (such as ARP responder, ping responder, HTTP requests to Web responder, etc.). The summarization and anonymization tool *ipsumdump* [Koh] uses Click for various activities ranging from reading and writing *tcpdump* files to anonymizing. The presence of Click elements that provided the necessary functionality enabled quick construction of *ipsumpdump*.

10.2.3   dss

Scanning data streams has become increasingly important as the range of datasets has continued to increase in diversity and size. Parsing is a vital part of record oriented data analysis. The schema of the record structure has to be known and made available in a form accessible to a wide variety of analysis tools. Unix tools have long had the ability to mix low and high-level definition details inside the same program. Beyond such simple tools like *awk* and *perl*, one needs programs that can process gigabytes of measurement data in formats that have their own idiosyncratic record descriptions. Relational databases do provide a high-level abstraction for end users; but managing data streams often requires more expertise. For example, it may not make sense to load the entire data unless it is going to be scanned more than a few times.

In Internet measurement, there has been a general tendency to write tailored tools to handle different formats or try to bend the existing set of simple tools to meet the needs of a particular application. The data stream scanning tool *dss* [FK05] provides a data abstraction for reducing parsing differences between various analysis tools, with efficient (in space and time) I/O support *and* a uniform interface for all data. Using the same tool permits data analysts to focus just on analyzing the data and provides a target API for data I/O coders. Additionally, third parties familiar with the data abstraction model become automatically proficient in new data domains.

Consider the basic problem of dealing with various formats of BGP data – *cisco* router table dumps, MRT format data, or ad-hoc flat files. To handle these formats a handful of related but slightly different implementations that had evolved over several years had to be changed. Simply merging the BGP I/O and parsing into a unified API allows instant reuse across datasets, through a single merge interface. Additionally, as a study showed, the *dss* BGP MRT parser is an order of magnitude times faster than the one published by the originators of the format. The same analysts now wanted to process *netflow* data and it was possible to simply extend *dss* to handle various *netflow* version formats.

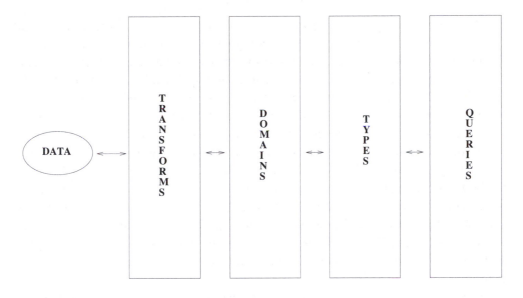

Figure 10.1 *dss* component architecture.

dss partitions data stream access into components that form a uniform model for all data. The model supports independent data methods, each with one or more physical formats. For example, the BGP method supports *cisco* router dump and MRT formats, and the NETFLOW method handles multiple versions of the *cisco* dump format. Each user visible item, whether in the base API or in DLL extensions, is placed in a dictionary. A dictionary entry has a name and descriptive text suitable for inclusion in manual pages.

The essence of *dss* is its data abstraction model; Figure 10.1 illustrates the component relationships in the *dss* model. Some components are part of the default *dss* library, but most are implemented as independent *dss* API dynamically loaded library (DLL). Applications link against the base *dss* library and thus old applications have access to new methods without requiring recompilation.

dss has a few classes of components, such as transform, method, type, and query. Transform class components serve as generic data-independent filters of raw data. Compression transforms are available for numerous compression variants, such as *gzip*, *pzip* [BCC+00], *bzip* and *compress*. A transform can be implemented within the main process or as a separate process. Transforms allow data to be stored in the most efficient or secure manner and only need to be converted when accessed. Given the volumes of available network data, compression along with sampling is essential for archiving.

A method describes the data records for a specific data domain. This includes a dictionary of file storage formats and record field types. The storage format dictionary has an identification function to automatically determine input formats (a format may be a different version (NETFLOW versions 1, 5, 7, and 9) or a completely different structure (BGP MRT files vs. *cisco* router dumps), and record read and write functions. The record field type and name dictionary includes the union of fields available in all supported formats. Extensibility is thus provided: if a new field is introduced in a new version of *netflow* format, then it should simply be added to the NETFLOW method dictionary, and default to empty value in all the other versions.

A type component provides functions to convert data between internal and external data representations. Types are method independent and are often shared between methods. For example, the ipaddr_t type in the *dss* ip_t type library implements an IP address as a 32-bit unsigned integer, and converts between the integer representation and quoted dotted-quad or DNS names as the application requires. Numerous data logs (e.g., Web server and proxy logs) contain a mixture of dotted-quad and DNS IP addresses; both are handled by automatic conversions depending on the context.

The query component, the user visible part of *dss*, is used to select, filter, and summarize data stream records. Interpreted queries are C-style expressions (complete with regular expression matching) on the data fields defined by the current method. For example, ipaddr_t type match function does IP prefix matching: (src_addr =~ "12.34/16") selects all records where src_addr matches the IP prefix 12.34/16. The expression (path =~ "^ 123 [456 789] - 8765$") selects all records where path starts with AS 123 followed by 456 or 789 and ends with 8765.

Dynamic queries provide C-level access to the record stream. The interpreted queries permit experimentation on small sets of data with quick answers to different queries. The user can then switch to a dynamic query for large data sets. Coding the query in a DLL is about 100 lines of C and straightforward; queries can also be composed similar to a UNIX pipeline. A dynamic query is executed within the *dss* process and has four functions: *init* called once before the first record is read, to allocate private data to be used by the other functions, *select* called for each record which on a successful return calls the *act* function and terminates the scan otherwise, and *done* called once after the last record is read to list reports or summaries, and release any private resources allocated by the other functions. This loosely parallels *awk*'s BEGIN, and END functionality.

Several generic dynamic queries are part of dss: *count* to count the number of selected and total records, {stats} computes count, mean, and unbiased standard deviation for the named numeric field arguments, and supports grouping by field value. For example, the *netflow* query

```
{stats --average --group=prot bytes}
```

computes the average number of bytes per packet (the numeric `bytes` field value) grouped by protocol (the `prot` field).

dss removes one of the key bottlenecks for a data analyst: the fear of not being able to test out ideas on significant amounts of data (e.g., a full day's worth of *netflow* dump from a router in a large ISP) in close to real time. The different categories of use of *dss* include parsing data, parsing and processing data into specific formats for different uses later, and finally, parsing and processing data via specific DLL queries with application-specific semantics encoded in the queries without loss of generality. *dss* has been successfully used in numerous research and production projects. Among the various applications are change detection [KSZC03], where large amounts (several billions) of *netflow* data were processed through the addition of 20 lines of C code added to a boiler-plate *netflow* dynamic query. Processing time was of the order of over 220K records/second for most kinds of queries on compressed *netflow* dumps. Another application was the OSPF monitor project [SG01] where Link State Advertisements (LSA) data was collected from the network and LSAs were selected based on user-specified query expressions, for subsequent processing and analysis. OSPF topology changes and OSPF routing table record types emanating from the LSA processing are also parsed by *dss*. A routing emulation tool [FWR04] that performs 'what-if' analysis to predict how changes in BGP routing policies affect the flow of traffic in a large IP backbone used *dss* to process and extract specific attributes from BGP forwarding tables dumped daily from a large number of routers. *dss* was also used to process logs of a tailored variant of *sendmail* in an anti-spam application. Although most fields are of the form *name=value*, the semantics of *name* may depend on the values of other fields. Typical *dss* queries involved extracting `From` and `To` address pair counts, examining error records, correlating mail sizes and suspected addresses, and correlating SMTP error codes and email IDs. Likewise, HTTP server and proxy logs were processed efficiently using *dss* for a wide variety of subsequent applications; with *dss* outperforming tailored tools such as *webalizer* [Web]. The *dss* tool consists of a handful of software components, with the base library and command, methods, types, standard dynamic queries, for a total of about 28K lines of C code. The run times for *all* methods are faster than any comparable *perl* or C code. New networking data domains and formats can be added as the need arises. Related tools, such as Flowscan [Plo00] and flow-tools [Ful] rely on slower *flex* lexer and the filter expression is re-evaluated on a per-flow basis.

10.2.4 Gigascope

Gigascope [JMSS05, CJSS03b] is a data stream management system targeted at monitoring data streams at high speeds. Gigascope is a combination of generic hardware assembled from commercial off-the-shelf components and tailored software, and has been used in a wide variety of applications such as analyzing traffic, intrusion detection, and protocol analysis. Gigascope's architecture is driven by the key realization [CGJ⁺02b] that existing tools have a natural limitation: tools such as *tcpdump* are excellent network monitors but require separate application-level tools to process the output generated. Alternately, high-speed special purpose network monitoring cards ('sniffers') have a rigid set of monitoring tasks associated with them making it harder to augment them later as new needs arise.

Gigascope partitions queries to be handled by a high-level and a low-level component: a data stream emanating from the monitored network interface is sent to the higher-level node. The query language of Gigascope has a syntax that resembles SQL. Input to a Gigascope monitor can be packets of any kind: IP, *netflow*, etc. A library consisting of a variety of functions interprets the stream of packets and a range of queries are available to operate on the input stream. Simple queries include selection based on field values (e.g., protocol==TCP), to more complicated ones that combine source IP address, time, etc. Users can use built-in functions (such as ones to aggregate packet lengths in a duration) as well as define their own. The Gigascope's query language allows for multiple input streams to be merged. The use of Gigascope was discussed earlier in Chapter 6 Section 6.3.2.

10.3 Large-scale Measurement Projects

Having looked at some example toolsets, we now expand our scope and look at large-scale measurement efforts. In this section we review some example measurement projects and measurement platforms.

Our goal in this section is to show how the challenges identified in previous chapters have been addressed in practice, to show how the principles and methods previously described have been realized in practice, and to examine some examples of measurement results that can be obtained. In doing so we will make frequent reference back to the relevant previous sections of this book.

We will look at three organizations: RIPE, the High Energy Physics community, and CAIDA; and we will look at one measurement platform: PlanetLab. These organizations and projects span a range of sizes and goals. These examples were chosen to illustrate the diversity of approaches taken to network measurement: from community-operated infrastructure (PlanetLab) to managed-service operation (RIPE) to centrally operated infrastructure (CAIDA). In addition our examples include those with broad user communities (RIPE and CAIDA) and relatively focused user communities (High Energy Physics).

10.3.1 RIPE

The RIPE Network Coordination Center (RIPE NCC) is a nonprofit organization established in 1992 and supported by membership. RIPE stands for *Réseaux IP Européens*, or *European IP Networks*. The RIPE NCC (hereafter just 'RIPE') provides technical coordination for the Internet in Europe, the Middle East, and parts of Central Asia (the 'RIPE region'). It is first of all the Regional Internet Registry for its region. As such, it allocates IP address space and AS numbers, and maintains the Whois database and other databases for the RIPE region. However, RIPE plays many additional roles beyond that of being a registry. For example, it acts as a coordinator for exchange points and operates `k.root-servers.net`, one of the 13 Internet root DNS servers.

Our focus on RIPE arises because it has a very active measurement agenda. It has taken on the role of coordinating Internet measurements within its region and providing measurement data to its members. As a result, RIPE runs a number of interesting Internet measurement projects that range over many of the topics discussed in previous chapters. We will not look at all of RIPE's measurement projects, but just take a look at three RIPE projects as examples of Internet measurement in actual operation.

RIPE has measurement projects in the following area:

- *Growth and Change of the Internet* (Chapter 5, Section 5.4.2). RIPE's *Hostcount* project is relevant to this question.
- *Interaction of Traffic and Network* (Chapter 5, Section 5.4.3). This is addressed in RIPE's *Test Traffic* project.
- *Passive BGP Measurement* (Chapter 5, Section 5.3.2). These measurements are taken in RIPE's *Routing Information Service* project.

Next we look more closely at each of these projects in turn.

Hostcount. RIPE has been counting the number of hosts registered in the DNS since October 1990. However, RIPE measures only the portion of the DNS containing hosts in the RIPE region (which has changed over time). When the project was started there were only 19 Top Level Domains (TLDs) and 31000 hosts in the RIPE region. The job has grown; currently the RIPE region includes around 100 TLDs. The goal of this project is simply to provide information to the Internet community as a measure of infrastructure growth [Cen05a].

The method used by RIPE starts with each of the TLDs in the RIPE region. First, the zone information inside each TLD is collected. If there are sub-zones within a zone, those are collected as well, until the lowest level is reached. Eventually zone downloads consist of A-records, which are the records within DNS that assign a name to a host. A name may occur in more that one place in the DNS, so only unique names are counted. In addition, multiple names may be assigned to the same host, and these are only counted once. Unfortunately, some zones have begun to block zone transfers, meaning that their hosts are not counted; as a result, absolute numbers are no longer accurate, although trends can be observed.

RIPE performs this process each month and publishes the results. Some summary statistics derived from this project are shown in Figure 5.15 (Chapter 5, Section 5.4.2).

Test Traffic Measurements.   RIPE takes a lead role in coordinating active measurements of traffic conditions throughout its region. The Test Traffic Measurements (TTM) project measures one-way delays between hosts (latency), packet losses, path information ('traceroute'), and delay variation (jitter). The project started in 2000 and is open to any organization worldwide; it currently involves around 100 hosts (including some in North America and the Asia-Pacific region). The goal of the project is to provide participating organizations with measures of quality of connection to the Internet, means for diagnosing performance problems, and measures of long-term trends in network connectivity. The project also makes some data available under an acceptable use agreement [Cen05b].

The project consists of two components:

1. A dedicated measurement system (a TTM system) which is designed and configured by RIPE, sent to a participating institution or network, and connected to the network by the receiver.
2. An operations center at RIPE which provides central storage of all measurements with secure access to participating organizations.

The usual operation of the TTM system is to take periodic measurements to some or all of the other TTM systems. The results are uploaded to the RIPE operations center and made available to users in various formats: graphs, charts, and in raw form.

There are a number of interesting aspects to the RIPE TTM project. First, it measures one-way delays between pairs of TTM systems. As described in Chapter 5, this is challenging due to the need for synchronized clocks on the systems at both endpoints. The solution taken is to use external time sources as described in Chapter 4, Section 4.2. RIPE TTM boxes can be configured with either GPS or CDMA time sources. At the current time the RIPE TTM project is the largest time-synchronized Internet measurement system.

Second, the RIPE TTM systems are designed to take a very wide variety of active measurements: interactions between traffic and network (delay, loss, etc.), topology measurements, and bandwidth measurements. This provides an unusually wide set of data for analysis. The methods used are compliant with the IPPM standards for active network measurement [PAMM98].

Finally, the RIPE TTM system is unusual because it is designed as a fee-based managed service. The user simply connects the system to their network; after that RIPE staff configure the system software and maintain the system on an ongoing basis. This addresses some of the difficult practical issues in operating a large-scale measurement infrastructure, such as support, security, and responding to system failures, attacks, and break-ins.

Routing Information Service.   RIPE also maintains passive measurements of the global routing system. The Routing Information Service (RIS) started as a RIPE project in 1999. The project collects and stores BGP routing information and makes it publicly available for the Internet community. The goal of the RIS project is to help network operators troubleshoot routing problems by providing BGP data collected over time, without being limited to a single BGP view. Archived raw RIS data since September 1999 is also available for research purposes.

The system is implemented by placing 'passive' BGP listeners at peering points and establishing BGP connections to BGP routers present among the networks that peer at that point. Thus, it operates in a manner similar to the `routeviews` project described in Chapter 5 (Section 5.3.2). Currently there are over 450 IPv4 and IPv6 peers at 14 data collection points in Europe, Japan, and North America.

The systems use the Quagga routing suite to capture BGP traffic (as described in Chapter 6, Section 6.3.1). They collect two kinds of data:

1. All BGP packets received: route announcements, withdrawals, and other messages. This voluminous data is stored in 15-minute files.
2. The entire BGP routing table maintained by Zebra. These tables are created every 8 hours.

In addition to providing raw data, the RIS service supports a wide variety of inquiries. It can be queried to determine when an AS number last appeared in the global routing table and when a prefix last appeared in the global routing table. It can provide a list of BGP prefixes that have unusually high activity in the recent past. It also provides an interface to the BGP Beacon system [MBGR03].

10.3.2   High-energy Physics

Since at least 1997, researchers in the high-energy physics (HEP) community have been monitoring various aspects of Internet performance. This initiative arose due to the particular needs of their research, which involves the generation of massive datasets in particle accelerators. For example, HEP researchers routinely move immense datasets around the world; others need to visualize datasets remotely in an interactive manner. Further, HEP computations are increasingly being organized around the notion of Grid Computing–highly distributed, high performance applications [GGF05]. All of these activities place demands on the network to deliver both high throughput and low latency.

The current Internet measurement efforts in the HEP community are organized by the International Committee for Future Accelerators (ICFA), which has a Standing Committee on Interregional Connectivity (SCIC). SCIC is charged with monitoring interregional Internet connectivity, tracking the network service requirements of the HEP community, and making recommendations for improvements to network infrastructure. Its monitoring focus is on both active and passive measurements: measuring the performance of the network (actively) and monitoring the traffic on the network (passively).

In this section we describe the efforts of the Monitoring Working Group within ICFA-SCIC. This Working Group is located at the Stanford Linear Accelerator Center. The mission of the Monitoring Working Group is to "Provide a quantitative/technical view of inter-regional network performance to enable understanding the current situation and making recommendations for improved inter-regional connectivity" [Cot05a]. These efforts are of interest because they represent longitudinal studies of Internet performance, and because they reflect the process taken by a specific user community to understand Internet performance.

PingER.   The PingER project has a very simple methodology: it simply sends `ping` probes from a set of monitors to a variety of sites worldwide and records summary statistics of the results [Cot05b]. Every 30 minutes, PingER probes a set of remote nodes with 11 pings of 100 bytes each. The pings are separated by at least one second, and the default ping timeout of 20 seconds is used.

What is interesting about this project is that it has been in continuous operation since 1995, which makes it unique. Furthermore, the measurement infrastructure is quite large: there are over three dozen monitors and nearly 1000 remote nodes. This yields many thousands of monitor–remote site paths that are being measured. The project makes its raw data freely available to the research community.

One of the project goals is to provide representative values for various regions of the world. To do this, project leaders have emphasized placing multiple nodes in each region, and when possible, in each country of the world. Most of the hosts being monitored are at educational or research institutions.

Although the historical data collected by PingER goes back a relatively long time, it is hard to interpret with precision, since the set of sites monitored has changed considerably over time. However there are clear trends among the subset of measurements that have been taken to consistent sets of remote nodes. These trends show steadily improving performance over various Internet paths. For example, packet loss rates between a specific set of HEP sites has declined from the range of 2–3% in 1995 to approximately 0.01% in 2005. This is consistent with trends observed elsewhere (see Chapter 5, Section 5.4.3).

IEPM-BW. PingER is concerned with tracking latency and loss rates, but HEP researchers also need high throughput for their applications. This has driven the IEPM-BW project.

The IEPM-BW project is concerned with measuring bulk-transfer capacity as defined in Chapter 5, Section 5.3.4. These measurements are most relevant between well-connected sites used by HEP researchers – for example, accelerator sites and major universities.

IEPM-BW uses `iperf`, which opens a TCP connection from a local client to a remote server and attempts to send at maximum possible rate for 10 seconds or more [TCD03]. The method provides a measure of the throughput that is currently possible over the path, as well as information on how to achieve it.

`Iperf` is quite intrusive – it can consume hundreds of megabits per second for a single test. It also requires support from the remote host: a server application must be running on the remote host, and the application consumes disk space and CPU cycles.

Measurements made by the IEPM-BW project indicate that it is regularly possible to obtain throughputs of several hundreds of Mbits/s on production academic and research networks, without using special hardware or software. However, to achieve throughput as high as this requires careful configuration of operating system parameters. In particular, these speeds require large TCP buffers and windows, the use of multiple parallel streams, and sufficiently powerful hardware including a fast enough link (e.g., Gigabit Ethernet speed) to the Internet.

Digital Divide. Another interesting aspect of the ICFA-SCIC monitoring activities is that although it began as an effort to provide support for the HEP community, its focus has shifted largely to quantifying the *digital divide.*

The term 'digital divide' is used to refer to disparity in computing and network infrastructure between developed and less-developed parts of the world; and in some cases even within a single country between communities. The HEP community has placed emphasis on quantifying and addressing the digital divide. This is because it seeks to make scientists from all regions full partners in joint experiments. For this reason significant monitoring effort is now being applied to regional measurements, to comparing Internet performance between regions, and to tracking the different rates of Internet performance improvement across regions.

10.3.3 CAIDA

CAIDA (the *Cooperative Association for Internet Data Analysis*) is an independent nonprofit organization with support and participation from commercial, government, and research sectors. It has undertaken and pursues a wide variety of projects in Internet measurement and Internet data analysis. CAIDA was founded in 1997 at the San Diego Supercomputing Center, which is part of the University of California, San Diego (UCSD).

As described in [CAI05], CAIDA's goals are to investigate both practical and theoretical aspects of the Internet, with particular focus on topics that:

- Are macroscopic in nature and provide enhanced insight into the function of Internet infrastructure worldwide, and
- Provide free access to traffic analysis and visualization tools to facilitate network measurement and management.

CAIDA is of interest because it has actively pursued three distinct thrusts, each of which relates to multiple topics covered in previous chapters. In particular, it has:

1. Built a variety of tools (hardware and software) for Internet measurement.
2. Collected and managed large bodies of Internet measurement data.
3. Performed a range of analyses of Internet measurements in the progress of a number of different investigations.

We focus only on representative CAIDA activities in each of the three thrusts listed. Our goal is to show examples of concepts covered in earlier chapters that are realized in practice.

Tools.   The demands of network measurement have stimulated the development of a wide variety of network measurement tools at CAIDA. Several tools and methods described in previous chapters have been developed or supported by CAIDA. CAIDA was an early developer of tools for collecting and analyzing traffic in terms of flows (as discussed in Chapter 6, Section 6.3.3). Some other examples of tools currently supported by CAIDA are shown in Table 10.1. Besides tool development, CAIDA has sponsored empirical comparisons of the performance of measurement tools [SMH^{+}05] and maintains a taxonomy of Internet measurement tools that have been developed by CAIDA as well as third parties.

Data Collection.   CAIDA has also run a range of data collection projects that embody or illustrate topics discussed in earlier chapters. CAIDA's data collection efforts involve both passive and active network measurement.

First of all, CAIDA has supported the collection of a large body of passively collected traffic traces. CAIDA has been collecting traffic traces since 2002. These

Table 10.1 Example tools developed or supported at CAIDA.

Tool	Function	Related to Discussion in	Reference
Iffinder	Performs alias resolution, mapping IP interfaces to routers	Chapter 5, Sec. 5.3.1	[Keyb]
GTrace	Provides a geographic interface to `traceroute`	Chapter 5, Sec. 5.3.6	[PN99]
NeTraMet	Implements the RTFM standards for flow measurement and accounting	Chapter 6, Sec. 6.3.3 Chapter 7, Sec. 7.2.3	[Nete]
Skitter	Performs large scale topology discovery	Chapter 5, Sec. 5.3.1	[HPMkc02]

span a wide range: from OC-48 links within large ISPs, to regional peering points, to university campus networks. Trace data that are made available are anonymized to protect the privacy of network users, using prefix-preserving anonymization techniques (as described in Chapter 8, Section 8.5.2).

A particularly novel form of passive data collection recently pioneered at CAIDA and UCSD is the so-called *network telescope*. A network telescope refers to a particular set of globally announced IPv4 address space. The address space is not used for standard network connectivity; it contains almost no legitimate hosts. Instead, incoming traffic is collected by routing all addresses in this range to a collection point. The key idea of the network telescope is that, since there are no legitimate hosts in this range, inbound traffic to addresses in this range must be anomalous in some way.

Network telescopes have been found to be very useful in a wide range of security studies. The telescope tends to collect data from any activity that sends packets to addresses that may not be live hosts. This may be due to misconfiguration or other human error. However, the most interesting use is in security analysis. For example, worms regularly scan address space in a mechanical fashion looking for hosts to infect; such scanning traffic tends to arrive at the network telescope. Another example comes from certain kinds of denial-of-service (DoS) attacks that are often mounted against Web servers. In these 'SYN attacks,' attackers flood a Web site with SYN packets in an attempt to overwhelm the server host. The standard behavior of the host is to respond to SYN packets with a SYN-ACK addressed to the source of the SYN packet. However, attackers will try to mask their identity by placing randomly generated addresses in the source address field. As a result, SYN-ACKs arrive at the network telescope. Such 'backscatter' traffic can be used to infer the incidence and severity of DoS attacks throughout the Internet [MVS01].

The UCSD network telescope consists of a range of addresses spanning most of a /8 prefix, i.e., approximately 1/256th of all IPv4 addresses. This makes it one of the largest network telescopes in operation. Thus if an Internet worm were generating addresses randomly and uniformly over the IP address space, roughly one out of every 256 of its scanning packets would arrive at the UCSD network telescope [MSVS04].

Finally, a large-scale active measurement project is the IPv4 Topology project, which we will refer to simply as the *Skitter* project. The Skitter project has been in operation since 1998.

The Skitter project collects topology data using a mechanism similar to `trace-route`. Its purpose is to provide topology data for analyzing paths in the Internet, both from an engineering and a research perspective. The Skitter project operates around two dozen active monitors around the world; these generate traceroutes to hundreds of thousands of target hosts on a roughly daily basis. The resulting datasets can contain millions of paths.

Skitter measures the forward IP path to a destination as well as the current round trip time. It can be used to identify low-frequency routing changes – route changes occurring on the timescale of days.[1] If one resolves interfaces to routers, Skitter data can be used to generate router graphs of the Internet. Furthermore, if one maps routers to ASes, Skitter data can be used to generate AS graphs.

Skitter data has aided numerous research studies. Data from the Skitter project has been used to shed light on many of the topics discussed in Chapter 5, including:

1. Measurement tools that fuse different measurement types (Section 5.3.3).
2. Latency estimation methods (Section 5.3.5).
3. Geolocation methods (Section 5.3.6).
4. Properties of AS graphs (Section 5.4.2).
5. Properties of sampled router graphs (Section 5.4.2).

Example Analyses.   Finally, we will take a look at two examples of the data analysis performed at CAIDA, one based on active measurement and one based on passive measurement.

The first example concerns the placement of the DNS root servers. These servers form a critical component of the DNS system and their performance can impact the response time of the overall DNS system and applications that depend on DNS such as the Web. Nonetheless, the placement of DNS root servers has not been optimized. The locations of most DNS root servers have been chosen primarily for historical

---

[1]Note that higher-frequency repetitive routing changes are harder to detect; these typically result instead in false edges as described in Chapter 5, Section 5.3.1.

reasons; in addition, many organizations are eager to run additional DNS root servers, mainly for reasons of prestige.

To investigate the question of whether DNS monitors were well placed, CAIDA researchers began by installing Skitter monitors at most of the root server locations. The next step was to infer which root server each client would be expected to visit, which allowed a direct measurement of the expected performance that clients would experience if their primary DNS root server were to become unavailable. Results showed that DNS root servers fell into equivalence classes, and that geographic distribution of root servers played the most important role in overall performance. The led to recommendations regarding the value of moving root servers from one geographical region to another [LHFC03].

Most questions involving optimization of the global Internet are hard to answer for lack of relevant measurement data. In this case CAIDA was able to shed light on their question by taking the straightforward approach of actually instrumenting the relevant systems, and measuring the paths of interest.

Our second example involves passive data collection. As described earlier, UCSD operates a large network telescope. This provides a powerful tool for studying the dynamics of Internet worms. In particular, we will look at two Worm outbreaks: the Slammer worm outbreak in January 2003 and the Witty worm outbreak in March 2004.

Starting around 2001, the incidence of new worms being released into the Internet started to rise. The next year researchers predicted that particularly fast-spreading and virulent worms were feasible and should be expected to appear in the Internet [SPW02]. At the same time network telescope technology was being developed, initially to gather data about denial-of-service attacks, and had been used with some success to study the Code Red worm [MSkc02].

The Slammer worm was released in January 2003. Its scanning pattern resulting in significant traffic arriving at the UCSD network telescope. This presented an opportunity to measure the dynamics of the Slammer worm in some detail.

The most startling finding obtained from telescope data concerned the scanning rate of the worm. As predicted the previous year, the Slammer worm used new techniques to reach a very high aggregate scanning rate within three minutes of its release. This was made possible by the architecture of the Slammer worm, which was quite different from earlier worms. While earlier worms had large payloads and used TCP for reliable transfer, Slammer's payload was only 376 bytes and was delivered as a single UDP packet.

Slammer had no malicious payload, though it caused harm by disabling servers and overloading networks. Researchers at CAIDA and elsewhere concluded that the very high rate of scanning made smaller susceptible populations of hosts attractive to future fast-spreading worms, and that malicious fast-spreading worms were likely in the future [MPS$^+$03].

In fact, in March 2004 both predictions were realized in the form of the Witty worm. The Witty worm targeted a relatively small set of hosts: a related set of firewall products all produced by a single company. And the worm was destructive: it overwrote random portions of the system's hard drive until the system was rebooted or became unusable.

Using the network telescope, CAIDA researchers were able to pinpoint new features of the Witty worm. The worm used a relatively large set of 'ground-zero' hosts – hosts that were infected deliberately in order to start the worm in many places simultaneously. In addition, telescope data was able to show that many users were infected via firewalls that were put in place to *protect* them from infection [SM04].

10.3.4 PlanetLab

PlanetLab was begun [PACR02] in 2002 as a global platform for deploying wide area network services for testing new ideas and carrying out various measurements. Although PlanetLab was not the first such platform, it has grown to over 500 nodes present in hundreds of sites and several diverse research projects have used the node collection. There are a few nodes at each site and they are linked over high-speed connections such as gigabit Ethernet. Many of the sites are connected over Internet2 (whose nodes can communicate only with other Internet2 nodes) but several are connected over the public Internet. Such sites' connectivity to the Internet varies depending on the upstream ISP.

PlanetLab was designed to introduce new network services and use the nodes as both clients and servers connected via an overlay network. It is both a vehicle for testing ideas from all or a subset of the nodes and for deploying new services on the nodes. A virtual machine monitoring software runs on each node to schedule resources between the various services and protect the node against intentional or unintentional harm. Members of PlanetLab access PlanetLab resources via *slices*, an abstraction that includes memory, storage, processing and network resources across different PlanetLab nodes. The slice abstraction is the primary mechanism for controlling resources.

PlanetLab is used for a variety of projects, not all of them related to Internet measurement. An annotated bibliography of the use of PlanetLab can be found in [Plaa]. Note that each PlanetLab node runs sensors that make per-node information available so that problems can be quickly detected. Netflow data is gathered, although typically only one-way traffic.

There are problems in treating PlanetLab nodes as a representative collection of Internet measurement sites. Two serial studies that examined the interdomain connectivity of PlanetLab nodes showed that a vast majority (85% in 2004 [BGP04] and 82% in 2005 [ZLPG05]) of the nodes are part of research and educational networks rather than the entire Internet. Several other studies have focused exclusively on the PlanetLab nodes themselves: examining bottleneck capacity between the nodes [LSB+05]. Along the way some of these studies have been helpful to demonstrate the shortcomings of existing tools; for example a wide range of available bandwidth tools were examined and found to be unusable on the range of machines on PlanetLab. Other caveats in the use of PlanetLab for measurement studies include delays arising from increased load when hundreds of slices are simultaneously active. Measurements carried out under such circumstances can result in imprecise inferences. The legitimate attempts to limit each slice owner from access to resources can also skew the extent of measurements carried out.

Distributed monitoring systems, such as Ganglia [MCC04], have been deployed on PlanetLab. These provide information on various resource metrics on the hosts, such as memory, CPU usage, and other aggregated network metrics archived for examination across various time ranges. Distributed query processors (e.g., PIER [HHB+03]) have also been deployed on PlanetLab to distribute relational queries to be answered by the PlanetLab collection of nodes. Another example of a querying mechanism capable of querying across the collection of PlanetLab nodes is IrisLog [GKK+03]. IrisLog combines the node's resource information and application-level logs into an XML database for easy querying.

However, there are various reasons to use PlanetLab nodes for carrying out Internet measurements, including availability, growing and active set of nodes, users, and applications, self-policing mechanisms, and tools. Of the numerous measurement projects that have used the PlanetLab infrastructure, we examine a few related to the focus of this book. The range of relevant measurement projects using PlanetLab range from base measurement tools that use PlanetLab nodes as simply a set of client nodes to gather data, to a basic infrastructure used to compare a variety of measurement-related meta-issues such as stationarity and stability.

Scriptroute [SWA03] was an early tool targeted for Internet measurement that used the PlanetLab deployed collection of nodes. Scriptroute's use for network measurement is enhanced by its ability to use numerous traceroute servers and coordination of measurement across nodes. The measurements are expressed in the form of scripts that run as an ordinary user while a daemon with privileges is used to schedule and manage packet exchanges. Security is a prime concern and users can connect to a server and run measurements in a safe environment guaranteed via a secure raw socket network interface. A large number of popular measurement tools are available to be used as part of Scriptroute, ranging from bandwidth measurement tools such as *pathchar* and *bprobe*, RTT measurement tools like *ping*, to TCP behavior identification tools like *tbit*. By using Scriptroute in the PlanetLab collection of servers it is possible to trigger such measurement tools from any subset of those servers. Primary applications have ranged from validating network positioning tools such as GNP (discussed in Chapter 5 5.3.5) to gathering network routes to a specified target.

In the arena of Content Distribution Networks a few projects have used the PlanetLab infrastructure as a natural staging ground for testing various ideas. Traditional CDNs discussed earlier in Chapter 7 (Section 7.3.4) have manifested themselves as a fairly large infrastructure of servers distributed geographically and serving a large number of Web sites. Popular techniques involve DNS-based redirection of client requests to 'nearest' mirrors of CDN servers. Adopting this model to PlanetLab, the CoDeen [WPP+04] (and related family of projects) system, allows for pushing specified content across the PlanetLab collection of nodes. The primary innovation is breaking large files into smaller ones and using HTTP/1.1 Range requests to obtain partial files and reassembling them along with caching content. Numerous PlanetLab nodes participate in the CoDeeN CDN where the various nodes can be monitored on a regular basis to weed out poorly performing ones. Among the reasons for poor performance are (computationally) busy nodes, packet losses, and poor DNS performance. The delays due to DNS led to work on CoDNS [PPPW04] where DNS lookup failures result in an alternate node being selected for the operation. Such uses of the infrastructure to fix internal problems bear out the usefulness of the PlanetLab testbed.

Given the number of nodes in PlanetLab and their varying paths of interconnection, it is natural to use PlanetLab to monitor failures in Internet paths. Earlier work in this area includes[ICM+02]. PlanetSeer [ZZP+04] monitors TCP connections in CoDeen and triggers diagnosis when anomalies occur. Traffic between several thousand clients that use the CoDeen CDN service exceeding several million requests daily is monitored passively via *tcpdump*. The flow and path-level statistics extracted from the passive monitoring (via RTT and retransmissions) are mined for possible anomalies such as multiple timeouts in a row that may indicate problems in the path. Anomalies trigger active probing, such as *traceroute*, of nodes from the geographically separated nodes of PlanetLab.

Recently there has been analysis of different kinds of stationarity in Internet measurement. Internet measurement is often done from different vantage points (such as numerous nodes in infrastructures like the PlanetLab) and repeated at periodic intervals. The same parameter is often measured by multiple applications, and most measured parameters exhibit varying degrees of stationarity across time and space. Many applications share certain common primitive measurement components and these may be reusable by other applications. It is natural to examine if the number of vantage points needs to be increased or decreased or if the frequency of measurements can be lowered. Stationarity in measurements can lead to reuse of measurements. Reducing measurements can be done by adding more primitives into the network, similar to the techniques proposed for overlay services [NPB03, Jan02] but they do not consider temporal and spatial stationarity or reuse across applications. For example, many performance-oriented applications include DNS measurement which may be reusable across applications within a certain timescale of interest.

The ATMEN [KMS05, KMV05] project examined stationarity across temporal, spatial, and applications. The experiment involved downloading the home page of popular Web sites from several PlanetLab nodes acting as client sites non-stop for two and a half weeks. *httperf* (discussed earlier in Chapter 7 (Section 7.3.4)) was used to track the DNS lookup time, TCP connection setup time, and HTTP transfer time. The study showed that on most PlanetLab nodes, the variability of the TCP setup time and HTTP transfer time even across days is the same as that observed in successive measurements. However, near-perfect stationarity across all PlanetLab nodes is observed only across a couple of hours. However, DNS lookup time did not exhibit similar stability. A bimodal distribution was seen with the two values representing DNS lookup performed with a cache hit and a cache miss. The study also showed that the TCP setup time and HTTP transfer time are highly stable over the period of a couple of hours, and that they are highly correlated for nearby sites, where nearby nodes are defined as being within 20 ms of each other. The experiment is thus another demonstration of PlanetLab's applicability to study general measurement properties on the Internet.

11

Conclusions and Prospects

In this chapter we seek to synthesize many aspects of Internet measurement to understand where the field has come from, and where it is going. To do so, we first examine broad trends and accomplishments that can be seen in past measurement efforts; next, we consider what challenges are most important in measuring the Internet today; and finally we look at how past trends as well as newly emerging trends are likely to shape Internet measurement in the future.

11.1   Trends in Internet Measurement

We've seen that the Internet has been measured in various ways since its inception as the ARPANET in 1969. There have been a number of trends that have affected the way the Internet has been measured over this span of time. Some trends are technological: Internet technology has changed over time, which has made some measurements more difficult and some measurements easier to obtain. Other trends are matters of scaling: the prodigious growth of the Internet has changed what is practical to measure, and has triggered the development of new measurement methods. And some trends are social: the transition of the Internet from government funding to private operation and the economic significance of Internet communication have altered the kinds of measurements needed and the extent to which certain measurements can be made.

The interaction of these trends over time has resulted in some broadly identifiable accomplishments in the nature and focus of Internet measurement. In the rest of this section we will review some of the most salient characteristics of what Internet measurement has accomplished over time.

ARPANET Measurements: 1969–1975.   While the primary thrust behind the initial development of the ARPANET was to connect researchers to distant computers,
an important related question was to explore the feasibility and utility of packet-
switching principles. As a result, the first ARPANET nodes (called *Interface Message Processors* (IMPs)) were designed and built with extensive integrated self-
measurement capabilities as described in [KN74]. These features included the ability
to trace the passage of a single packet through the network, the ability to directly
measure the traffic flowing between any two nodes, and the ability to query routers
for their instantaneous workload statistics. As we have seen in Chapters 5 and 6,
these sorts of features are either lacking or very hard to use in today's Internet.

What happened? As the ARPANET grew, it lost most of its built-in measurement
capabilities. Until 1975 network measurements were coordinated and collected at a
single Network Measurement Center (NMC) at UCLA. After 1975, administrative
control of the ARPANET was taken over by the Defense Communications Agency,
and comprehensive measurement of the ARPANET ceased. At the same time a new
generation of IMPs was deployed, and these may not have contained the same integrated measurement capabilities that the original IMPs possessed.

The evolution of the network away from extensive self-measurement seems to
have developed for a number of reasons. The network was growing in size, and its
function was becoming more focused on providing connectivity rather than supporting packet-switching research. On the other hand, the network was not so large that
extensive measurement for operational purposes was needed. Finally, integrated self-
measurement adds design complexity and economic cost to network devices, which
may have been a factor as well.

Operational Measurements.   By the mid-1980s the network was getting big, and
many independent organizations were purchasing network equipment that they
needed to operate and manage. It was becoming clear that a standard monitoring
capability was needed. A variety of companies were building Internet hardware for
commercial sale, and uniform methods for managing devices purchased from different vendors were needed. In 1987 work on SNMP began, and the definition of SNMP
v1 was finished in 1988. SNMP quickly became the standard method for obtaining
information about the status and operation of network elements.

Furthermore, the need to understand large-scale behavior of the network was becoming an issue. When two hosts were unable to communicate, it was often hard to
determine the location of the problem. In 1988 the first version of `traceroute`
was written. As described in Chapter 5, `traceroute` makes use of ICMP TIME
EXCEEDED messages to discover interfaces on each router along a path. The ICMP
protocol was not explicitly designed to support topology discovery. However the need

for debugging connectivity problems had become so great that `traceroute` was soon widely adopted.

Thus the trends of increasing network scale combined with the emergence of a commercial market for network equipment drove a new kind of network measurement: operationally driven measurements designed to support management and fault diagnosis.

High-speed Traffic Measurement. By the early 1990s the statistical properties of network traffic were emerging as an important question. New networking technologies such as high-speed routers and *Asynchronous Transfer Mode* (ATM) switches were being developed. The statistical properties of network traffic have a strong impact on the design, configuration, and performance evaluation of this type of equipment. In particular, ATM switches were being developed with the goal of supporting both data and voice communication. The statistical properties of voice traffic were well understood as a result of decades of measurement. However, while the basic properties of data network traffic were often assumed to be similar to voice traffic, in fact they were much less well understood.

As a result, systems for high-speed packet capture were developed and deployed in networking laboratories. The subsequent statistical analysis of these massive datasets provided the basis for the emergence of self-similar traffic models, as described in Chapter 6. Self-similar models are very different from the models used to describe voice traffic, and their widespread use represents a fundamental shift in the way that Internet traffic is characterized.

This development represented the beginning of the detailed analysis of very large datasets in connection with Internet measurement. Throughout the book, we have seen that the problems associated with capturing and analyzing massive volumes of data are now an everyday concern in Internet measurement.

The measurement and analysis of high-speed traffic also represented the beginnings of another pervasive trend in Internet measurement: the treatment of the Internet as an object of scientific study. The development of self-similar traffic models treated network traffic as an unknown object that needed to be characterized and understood; and the unusual aspects of self-similarity triggered a large amount of subsequent measurement and analysis. Thus the analysis of high-speed traffic widened the focus in network measurement to include research questions, a focus that had been largely absent since the mid 1970s.

Web and Application Measurements. The explosion of the World Wide Web beginning around 1994 stimulated considerable interest in the properties of Web workloads. Since the Web quickly became the dominant application on the Internet in terms of traffic volume, the properties of Web workloads were important for understanding their effects on Internet traffic. Furthermore, Web measurements were needed to evaluate performance issues and to evaluate proposed design changes to Web servers and protocols.

As discussed in Chapter 7, Web measurement efforts followed a number of different thrusts. A variety of improvements to the HTTP protocol were proposed and measurements were needed to evaluate the costs and benefits of those proposals. The development of Web caching stimulated measurement studies to determine good cache replacement algorithms, cache placement strategies, and cache capacity planning. Finally, the Web quickly became the basis for electronic commerce, and so many companies had an economic interest in measuring and verifying the performance of Web transactions, and ensuring that critical Web servers stayed online, handled requests quickly, and were provisioned to handle surges.

Work in Web measurement uncovered a number of interesting phenomena. These include high variability in Web object sizes; the applicability of Zipf's law in connection with requests to Web pages and Web sites; flash crowd effects; and the interconnection properties of Web pages that impact search engine performance.

The Web was the first example of a 'killer' application that arose quickly and stimulated considerable measurement activity by its very popularity. This pattern has subsequently been repeated, e.g., with peer-to-peer applications and networked gaming.

Network-oriented Traffic Measurement.   As already mentioned, work in traffic measurement in the 1990s focused primarily on questions related to performance evaluation. These efforts focused on short-timescale measurements (milliseconds to hours) and also tended to focus on measurements taken at a single point in the network.

Beginning around 2000, research attention in traffic measurement broadened to include questions relating more directly to network operations and management. As discussed in Chapter 6, these questions concerned traffic at longer timescales (hours to months) and often involved measurements taken at multiple points within a network.

Network-oriented measurement questions tended to focus on topics such as understanding a network's traffic matrix, on characterizing the daily and weekly patterns of traffic variation, and on studying and predicting the way in which a network's traffic grows over time. A related effort beginning around the same time sought to understand the behavior of the global routing system as controlled through BGP. The general properties of BGP traffic, and the specific ways in which BGP events affect individual networks began to be closely studied.

The effort expended on these measurement directions seems to have come in large part from network operators who sought a more principled basis for network operations and management. Large commercial Internet service providers had in many cases been relying on ad-hoc approaches to operations and planning, with each provider developing their own measurement approaches. These operators had been in operation for a number of years (usually since the late 1980s or early 1990s) and some were beginning to look for better tools for managing networks. Hence the trend toward network-oriented traffic measurement that emerged at that time was a natural result of the needs of network operators.

Statistical Inference. As interest in Internet measurement grew in the late 1990s and early 2000s it became clear that many kinds of useful information were difficult or impossible to obtain. Throughout the book we have described the various ways in which information about the network is hidden by administrative boundaries, protocol layers, and lack of measurement capabilities.

This state of affairs stimulated interest in statistical inference as a tool for estimating or replacing missing or unavailable measurement data. Research applying inference to networking problems began around 1996 with methods for traffic matrix estimation [Var96] and was followed in 1999 by work on estimating network-internal properties from end-to-end measurements [CDHT99]. These results stimulated a large amount of subsequent investigation, both into new statistical methods and into application of statistical inference methods to a wide variety of measurement problems.

As described in Chapters 5 and 6, the use of statistical inference in Internet measurement is now widespread. This can be seen as a natural reaction to the lack of observability that is present in many aspects of the Internet architecture.

Interdisciplinary Connections. The rise of interest in statistical methods for analyzing Internet measurements has widened the community of Internet measurement researchers to include many statisticians and mathematicians. Beginning around 2000, the community has further expanded to include physicists working in statistical physics (also called statistical mechanics).

Statistical physics is concerned with the large-scale statistical properties of collections of many interacting components. As the Internet has grown, Internet measurements have become more amenable to the tools of statistical physics. Much of the focus of this work has been in studying and understanding the properties of large graphs derived from Internet measurements (e.g., the router graph and the AS graph). The general field is also referred to as *complex networks* in the physics literature and includes study of large graphs arising in other domains such as biology and engineering.

The trend toward statistical physics approaches has been driven by a desire to understand the global or macroscopic properties of the Internet as a function of local properties, such as business decisions made by individual network operators. This line of research is yet to fully reach this goal, but it has stimulated a wide range of questions and considerable ongoing study. A recent view of Internet measurements from a statistical physics perspective is given in [PSV04].

11.2   Difficulties

The broad trends in Internet measurement just described have been driven by a variety of factors. These trends derive from an interplay of measurement goals and measurement difficulties.

In this section we review the principal difficulties in Internet measurement and how they influence trends in Internet measurement. Each of these topics has been encountered many times in the book in various forms; this section serves to collect and review them all in one place.

Internet measurement issues can be broadly separated into four categories: practical issues, statistical difficulties, architectural issues, and administrative issues.

Practical Issues.   There are a wide range of practical problems that impair our ability to measure the Internet.

First, the sheer volume of data is a considerable challenge. Data volume issues arise in traffic measurements, in application measurements, and in infrastructure measurements. The massive datasets that can be collected present a challenge to store and to process. In cases such as topology measurement, the process of collecting data requires a significant amount of time.

An exacerbating factor is the rate of change of the objects or properties being measured. The system can change during the time period that measurements are taken. For example, in topology measurement, hosts and links can come online and go offline while measurement is taking place. In Web measurement, content can change during the course of a crawl. In P2P measurement, peers can come online and disappear during measurement. During longer measurement periods, average traffic levels will tend to grow over time, and the mix of protocols and applications in use on the network will shift (as has happened with respect to Web and P2P applications).

This constant change makes it difficult to identify 'representative' conditions in many situations. A particular application mix or traffic pattern may only be representative of certain kinds of networks or at certain times. A particular mix of user or client types will tend to change over time as new clients come online around the world with different degrees of connectivity.

These practical issues present challenges that have been dealt with in a variety of ways. Measurements are increasingly performed using sampling to reduce the volume of data that is collected. This had led to interest in and development of methods for inferring the properties of original data from sampled measurements. When data cannot be sampled, systems for collection, storage, and management of large datasets may be employed that make the problem less acute.

Statistical Issues. Throughout the book we have seen that working with Internet data involves unusual statistical difficulties.

The most salient statistical issue in Internet measurement is the phenomenon of high variability. High variability shows up in traffic (flow and connection lengths), infrastructure (node degree in router and AS graphs), and applications (sizes of Web objects). The statistical difficulties of working with highly variable data have been covered in previous chapters; they include the instability of traditional metrics such as empirical mean and variance, the need to focus on distributional tails for characterization purposes, and the shift of focus to unusual (long-tailed) probabilistic models.

A further issue is stability. Measured conditions are subject to unexpected change at any time; equipment failures, flash crowds, and network maintenance all have the potential to drastically affect measurements in a short period. This makes modeling more difficult; stationary models may be inappropriate when large changes in network conditions take place.

We have seen that some measures of Internet properties show strong memory. Most notably, network traffic shows long-range dependence. This makes modeling challenging, requiring the use of more sophisticated models in describing network traffic. Simulation and performance evaluation are also more difficult as a result of the strong memory in network traffic.

Architectural Issues. A number of difficulties in Internet measurement derive from properties of the Internet's architecture.

Core simplicity refers to the idea that network-internal elements (routers and switches) should be relatively simple devices. We have seen that one way such devices can be simplified is to omit sophisticated measurement capabilities. Thus it is generally difficult to obtain information from network elements about queue lengths in routers, or loss and delay of individual packets.

Another aspect of core simplicity is that protocol layers above IP are often not tracked in routers and switches. Thus, for example, it can be difficult to monitor traffic at the flow level or other levels higher than that of packets.

The IP hourglass also creates problems by hiding information about layers below IP. Packets can pass over a range of different physical media with widely varying properties – for example, wireless LANs, optical fiber, copper wire, and satellite links. Some of these media may employ retransmission or forward error correction, masking packet corruption at the physical layer. Measurement at the packet (IP) level does not generally include information about details such as these at lower levels.

Finally, the fact that the Internet has a decentralized organization at many levels means that there is no truly central location in the network for monitoring purposes. For example, there are many top-level autonomous systems in the Internet and a packet may flow through any (or none) of them. Further, top-level autonomous systems generally connect to each other in multiple locations. This mesh-like structure means that measurements made at any single point unavoidably miss a large fraction of network traffic.

Administrative Issues.   As we have seen, the Internet is a network of networks; the component networks are owned and operated by independent entities – Internet Service Providers (ISPs). Many ISPs are for-profit entities in competition with each other.

As a result ISPs are resistant to making important information available outside their own organizations, because this information can be used by their competition. For example, ISPs generally do not publish how much traffic their networks carry, or the size or exact physical configuration of their networks, or the composition of their traffic (such as the application mix or the prevalence of malicious traffic).

This lack of external information about separately operated networks impedes many worthy goals. For example, this secrecy impairs our ability to detect network-wide worm outbreaks, or to understand the rate of growth of network traffic worldwide.

11.3   Future Work

The difficulties listed in the last section provide a backdrop for understanding how future Internet measurement will be constrained and challenged. In this section we take a look at the measurement trends that can be foreseen in the future.

11.3.1   Research Challenges

The effort to increase our understanding of the Internet leads to a number of research challenges. These represent questions regarding how Internet measurement should be conducted in the future.

Measurement Platforms.   In previous sections we have seen that there are many unmet challenges in measuring the Internet; on the other hand, Internet measurement activity has increased dramatically in recent years. These two facts suggest that it seems worthwhile to allocate increased effort to building platforms and infrastructure for Internet measurement.

The projects discussed in Chapter 10 show that a range of architectural options are possible in constructing measurement platforms [EMG]. These options affect the utility and long-term success of the measurement efforts that use these platforms. Some of the considerations are:

- Who should fund measurement infrastructure for the Internet? Both government and commercial approaches are possible.
- Should a measurement infrastructure be controlled by a single organization, or should its control be shared by multiple investigators or groups?
- How should measurement systems be used? How should decisions be made regarding the relative emphasis on different purposes for a measurement platform?
- Should specialized measurement platforms be built, perhaps for specific communities of users, or to answer specific questions? If a platform is to be general-purpose, what form should it take?

The construction of large-scale measurement platforms has the potential to make progress on fundamental open questions regarding the Internet. For example: the global topology of the Internet is poorly known, and could be surveyed more completely; the nature and prevalence of malicious activity on the Internet could be assessed more accurately; and the extent to which traffic is growing and changing on the Internet could be better understood.

Shared Measurement Results. We also note that while obtaining Internet measurements can require significant effort, in many cases measurements are used only for a single study, or only by the organization making the measurements.

This suggests that more work should be done to overcome the barriers to frequent sharing of measurements or related data. These barriers include:

- Organizations may have proprietary interest in some kinds of data that they control, but not in others. There is a need for methods for making measurements available in ways that do not release commercially sensitive information.
- It is often rather difficult to put measurement datasets into a form that others can use. It is important to understand and document how measurements were taken, the quality of the data (including noting which data points are erroneous), the format of the data, and the assumptions underlying the data collection. This effort takes time.
- Storing and distributing large datasets can require significant resources, including disk space and network capacity. These resources are expensive and their use must be justified.

Research in this area is important, because sharing measurements has many benefits. It means that the effort in obtaining measurements is amortized over multiple uses. It allows research results based on analysis of data to be independently verified. And it allows new questions to be asked, questions which may not have been the basis for the original measurement effort.

11.3.2 Emerging Questions

In concluding the book, it is natural to ask: what are the next steps in Internet measurement? Where is the field going and what emerging questions can be foreseen? Of course, it's impossible to fully answer these questions, but in this section we suggest some partial answers. We divide the topics into near-term and longer-term measurement questions.

Near Term.   This book has covered a large range of topics in Internet measurement. The subfields of infrastructure, traffic, and application measurement are each complex in their own right. Furthermore, the related areas of anonymization and security include many additional issues. Nonetheless, there is more to Internet measurement that can be foreseen in the near future. Many of these topics are beginning to receive study, but are not yet developed or mature enough to be covered in this book.

The area of wireless Internet measurements is an important emerging area. On one hand, wireless data transmission has been used in the Internet since its early days as the ARPANET. However, in the early ARPANET experiments wireless links were used for backbone connections to distant locations, usually via satellite. In contrast, the importance of wireless links has grown dramatically more recently with the introduction of wireless LAN technology. The most notable of these are the protocols based on the IEEE 802.11 set of standards (e.g., WiFi).

The nature of wireless measurement is rather different from measurement of the wired Internet. Wireless measurement relies on capture of radio transmissions. This means that accurate wireless measurement and correct interpretation of those measurements involves new issues and constraints. As a result, the field of wireless Internet measurement is still in its formative stages; relatively few definitive studies have been carried out so far.

Another emerging area is sensor networks. These are networks of low-power devices which are expected to form networks without significant infrastructural support. There are significant measurement issues associated with these networks. However the field is even newer than that of wireless networking in general, and work is not yet mature in this area.

Turning to the wired Internet, a topic that is not yet studied in depth are measurements of IPv6 networks and traffic. While the IPv6 protocol has been in use for a number of years, its adoption is not yet widespread. In many ways, the behavior of IPv6 differs from IPv4 in only a few ways with respect to measurements, so we have not focused on IPv6 to a great degree in the book. However as IPv6 becomes more widespread it is likely that new measurement topics will arise.

Additionally, as noted above, the suite of applications in use on the Internet is in constant flux. While we can broadly identify shifts in the dominant application types, e.g., from Web to P2P, there are significant lesser shifts as well. For example, within the P2P application set, early applications such as KaZaa have given way to more recent variants such as BitTorrent. These applications are quite different in many ways, and these shifts from one dominant application to another have a significant effect on the nature of traffic. Looking into the future, networked games have the potential to become a dominant application (at least in terms of users if not in terms of total traffic). We have tried to emphasize the long lasting results in the area of Internet applications. However as new applications emerge there will be a natural shift in the focus of measurement attention.

Finally, we have noted that there is considerable interest in statistical physics models for Internet properties. This is an area of research that often spans additional topics in bioinformatics, social science, and engineering. We have not had the space to cover this broader set of topics. However we have provided an overview of the contributions of statistical physics to date in Internet modeling, and have provided references to that research literature where relevant. Activity in this area will likely continue and grow in the near future.

Longer Term. One of the most open-ended future directions concerns what and how new questions will emerge in Internet measurement. We have seen that the kinds of questions addressed in Internet measurement have evolved over time; in many cases the emergence of new questions has been difficult to foresee.

For example, the explosion of the World Wide Web in the early to mid 1990s stimulated an immense amount of research. On the one hand, this research was largely driven by the popularity of the Web – for example, a number of distributed information systems predated the Web, but they were not subject to significant measurement attention. On the other hand, this research exposed a number of results that can be considered fundamental, such as the presence of high variability in sizes and popularity of Web objects.

This example suggests that some longer-term emerging questions may be driven by new "killer applications" or by new ways of using the Internet. These are by definition hard to anticipate.

Another set of longer-term questions concerns the increasing integration of the Internet into society. As such, new measurement questions will undoubtedly arise in connection with human activity. For example, as the use of the Internet has increased in commerce, there is increasing importance on understanding malicious activity, measuring geographic location, and exploring the relationship between economic development and Internet infrastructure. These questions are beginning to be addressed through work in security, anonymization, and other domains, but there are undoubtedly many important questions yet to emerge.

Bibliography

[ABB+05]   A. Arasu, B. Babcock, S. Babu, J. Cieslewicz, M. Datar, K. Ito, R. Motwani, U. Srivastava, and J. Widom. STREAM: The stanford data stream management system. In M. Garofalakis, J. Gehrke, and R. Rastogi, editors, *Data-Stream Management – Processing High-Speed Data Streams*. Springer-Verlag, New York, 2005.

[ABC+00]   A. Adams, T. Bu, R. Caceres, N.G. Duffield, T. Friedman, J. Horowitz, F. Lo Presti, S.B. Moon, V. Paxson, and D. Towsley. The use of end-to-end multicast measurements for characterizing internal network behavior. *IEEE Communications Magazine*, May 2000.

[ABCdO96] Virgílio Almeida, Azer Bestavros, Mark Crovella, and Adriana de Oliveira. Characterizing reference locality in the WWW. In *Proceedings of 1996 International Conference on Parallel and Distributed Information Systems (PDIS '96)*, pages 92–103, December 1996.

[ABQ02]   Atul Adya, Paramvir Bahl, and Lili Qiu. Characterizing alert and browse services for mobile clients. In *Proceedings of the USENIX Technical Conference*, June 2002.

[ABQ04]   Atul Adya, Paramvir Bahl, and Lili Qiu. Characterizing Web workload for mobile clients. In Sudhir Dixit and Tao Wu, editors, *Content Networking in the Mobile Internet*, chapter 5. John Wiley & sons, New York, NY, August 2004. ISBN: 0-471-46618-2.

[AC89]   Paul Amer and Lillian Cassel. Management of sampled real-time network measurements. In *Proceedings of IEEE Annual Conference on Local Computer Networks*, pages 62–68, 1989.

[ACBD04]   Sharad Agarwal, Chen-Nee Chuah, Supratik Bhattacharyya, and Christophe Diot. The impact of BGP dynamics on intra-domain traffic. In *Proceedings of ACM SIGMETRICS*, 2004.

[ACL00]   William Aiello, Fan Chung, and Linyuan Lu. A random graph model for power law graphs. In *Proceedings of the 32nd Annual Symposium on Theory of Computing*, pages 171–180, 2000.

[AFT98]   Robert J. Adler, Raisa E. Feldman, and Murad S. Taqqu, editors. *A Practical Guide To Heavy Tails*. Chapman and Hall, New York, 1998.

[AFTV99]   P. Abry, P. Flandrin, M. S. Taqqu, and D. Veitch. Wavelets for the analysis, estimation, and synthesis of scaling data. In Kihong Park and Walter Willinger, editors, *Self-Similar Network Traffic and Performance Evaluation*. Wiley / Wiley Interscience, New York, 1999.

[AGR03]   Kostas G. Anagnostakis, Michael Greenwald, and Raphael Ryger. cing: Measuring network-internal delays using only existing infrastructure. In *Proceedings of IEEE INFOCOM Conference*, March 2003.

[AH88]   Jesse H. Ausubel and Robert Herman, editors. *Cities and their Vital Systems: Infrastructure Past, Present and Future*. National Academy Press, 1988.

[AH00]   E. Adar and B. Huberman. Free riding on gnutella. *First Monday*, 5(10), October 2000.

431

[AIM⁺02]   K. Anagnostakis, S. Ioannidis, S. Miltchev, J. Ioannidis, M. Greenwald, and J. Smith. Efficient packet monitoring for network management. In *Proceedings of the 8th IEEE/IFIP Network Operations and Management Symposium (NOMS)*, April 2002.

[AJ99]   Martin Arlitt and Tai Jin. Workload characterization of the 1998 world cup web site. Technical Report HPL-1999-35(R.1), HP Laboratories, September 1999.

[Aka]   Akamai. `http://www.akamai.com`.

[AkcTW97]   J. Apisdorf, k claffy, K. Thompson, and R. Wilder. OC3MON: Flexible, affordable, high-performance statistics collection. In *Proceedings of INET '97*, June 1997.

[AKSJ03]   Jay Aikat, Jasleen Kaur, F. Donelson Smith, and Kevin Jeffay. Variability in TCP round-trip times. In *Proceedings of the ACM SIGCOMM Internet Measurement Conference*, November 2003.

[Ale]   Alexa web search. `http://www.alexa.com`.

[All90]   Arnold O. Allen. *Probability, Statistics, and Queueing Theory with Computer Science Applications*. Computer Science and Scientific Computing. Academic Press, Inc., 2nd edition, 1990.

[All01]   Mark Allman. Measuring end-to-end bulk transfer capacity. In *Proceedings of the ACM SIGCOMM Internet Measurement Workshop*, pages 139–143, New York, NY, USA, 2001. ACM Press.

[All03]   Mark Allman. On the performance of middleboxes. In *Proceedings of the ACM SIGCOMM Internet Measurement Conference*, November 2003.

[AMMP96]   Andrew Adams, Jamshid Mahdavi, Matthew Mathis, and Vern Paxson. Creating a scalable architecture for Internet measurement. In *Proceedings of INET '96*, June 1996.

[And02]   Periklis Andritsos. Data clustering techniques. Technical Report CSRG-443, U. of Toronto, Dept. of Computer Science, March 2002.

[AOE]   The age of empires series. `http://www.microsoft.com/games/age/`.

[APE]   Anonymity and privacy in electronic services. `https://www.cosic.esat.kuleuven.ac.be/apes/`.

[APN]   Apnic: Ipv4 address space distribution. `http://www.apnic.net/docs/policy/add-manage-policy.html`.

[Arm01]   Grenville Armitage. Sensitivity of Quake3 players to network latency and jitter. In *Proceedings of the ACM SIGCOMM Internet Measurement Workshop*, November 2001. Poster.

[AS]   Roy Arends and Jakob Schlyter. Finger printing DNS servers. `http://www.rfc.se/fpdns/`.

[AS7]   Subscription via multihop eBGP4. `http://mail-abuse.org/rbl/usage.html#BGP`.

[ASS03]   Aditya Akella, Srinivasan Seshan, and Anees Shaikh. An empirical evaluation of wide-area Internet bottlenecks. In *Proceedings of ACM SIGMETRICS*, pages 316–317, San Diego, CA, June 2003.

[AvS04]   Kamal Ali and Wijnand van Stam. Tivo: Making show recommendations using a distributed collaborative filtering architecture. In *Proceedings of the 2004 ACM SIGKDD international conference on Knowledge discovery and data mining*, pages 394–401, August 2004.

[BA99]   A.-L. Barabasi and R. Albert. Emergence of scaling in random networks. *Science*, 286(5439):509–512, October 1999.

[Bak]   F. Baker. Requirements for IP version 4 routers. RFC 1812. Available at `http://www.ietf.org`.

[Bak00]   Jeffrey Baker. NAPs, exchange points, and interconnection of Internet service providers: Recent trands. `http://www.ep.net/ep-rpt-sum.html`, 2000.

[Bar64]   Paul Baran. On distributed communcations: I: Introduction to distributed communications networks. Technical Report RM-3420-PR, RAND, 1964.

[Bat]   Battlefield 1942. `http://www.battlefield1942.com`.

[BBBC99]   Paul Barford, Azer Bestavros, Adam Bradley, and Mark Crovella. Changes in Web client access patterns: Characteristics and caching implications. *World Wide Web*, 2:15–28, 1999. Special Issue on Characterization and Performance Evaluation.

[BBBC01]   Paul Barford, Azer Bestavros, John Byers, and Mark Crovella. On the marginal utility of network topology measurements. In *Proceedings of the ACM SIGCOMM Internet Measurement Workshop*, pages 5–17, November 2001.

[BBC+71]   Abhay Bhushan, Bob Braden, Will Crowther, Eric Harslem, John Heafner, Alex McKenzie, John Melvin, Bob Sundberg, Dick Watson, and Jim White. The File Transfer Protocol. RFC 172, IETF, June 1971.

[BBCKM02] Anat Bremler-Barr, Edith Cohen, Haim Kaplan, and Yishay Mansour. Predicting and bypassing end-to-end Internet service degradations. In *Proceedings of the ACM SIGCOMM Internet Measurement Workshop*, pages 307–320, Marseilles, November 2002.

[BBD+02]   B. Babcock, S. Babu, M. Datar, R. Motwani, and J. Widom. Models and issues in data stream systems. In *Proceedings of 21st ACM Symposium on Principles of Database Systems (PODS 2002)*, 2002.

[BBGR03]   Yigal Bejerano, Yuri Breitbart, Minos Garofalakis, and Rajeev Rastogi. Physical topology discovery for large multi-subnet networks. In *Proceedings of IEEE INFOCOM Conference*, March 2003.

[BBH05]   Azer Bestavros, John W. Byers, and Khaled A. Harfoush. Inference and labeling of metric-induced network topologies. *IEEE Trans. Parallel Distrib. Syst.*, 16(11):1053–1065, 2005.

[BC98]   Paul Barford and Mark E. Crovella. Generating representative Web workloads for network and server performance evaluation. In *Proceedings of ACM SIGMETRICS / Performance*, pages 151–160, July 1998.

[BC00]   Brian E. Brewington and George Cybenko. How dynamic is the Web? *Computer Networks (Amsterdam, Netherlands: 1999)*, 33(1–6):257–276, 2000.

[BC01]   Paul Barford and Mark E. Crovella. Critical path analysis of TCP transactions. *IEEE/ACM Transactions on Networking*, 9(3):238–248, June 2001.

[BC03]   Magdalena Balazinska and Paul Castro. Characterizing mobility and network usage in corporate wireless local-area network. In *Proceedings of ACM MOBISYS*, May 2003.

[BCC+00]   A. L. Buchsbaum, D. F. Caldwell, K. W. Church, G. S. Fowler, and S. Muthukrishnan. Engineering the compression of massive tables: An experimental approach. In *Proc. 11th ACM-SIAM Symp. on Discrete Algorithms*, pages 175–84, 2000.

[BCF+99]   Lee Breslau, Pei Cao, Li Fan, Graham Phillips, and Scott Shener. Web caching and Zipf-like distributions: Evidence and implications. In *Proceedings of IEEE INFOCOM Conference*, pages 126–134, 1999.

[BCG+03]   Bobby Bhattacharjee, Sudarshan Chawathe, Vijay Gopalakrishnan, Pete Keleher, and Bujor Silaghi. Efficient peer-to-peer searches using result-caching. In *Proceedings of the International Peer to Peer Symposium*, 2003.

[BCJ+05]   Michael Bailey, Evan Cooke, Farnam Jahanian, Jose Nazario, and David Watson. The Internet motion sensor: A distributed blackhole monitoring system. In *Proceedings of Network and Distributed System Security Symposium (NDSS '05)*, February 2005.

[BCL+04]   T. Beigbader, R. Coughlan, C. Lusher, J. Plunkett, E. Agu, and M. Claypool. The effects of loss and latency on user performances in Unreal tournament 2003. In *Proceedings of the Workshop on Network and System Support for Games*, September 2004.

[BCMR04]   John W. Byers, Jeffrey Considine, Michael Mitzenmacher, and Stanislav Rost. Informed content delivery across adaptive overlay networks. *IEEE/ACM Transactions on Networking*, 12(5):767–780, 2004.

[BCNS03]   A. Barbir, B. Cain, R. Nair, and O. Spatscheck. Known content network (CN) request-routing mechanisms. RFC 3568, IETF, July 2003. Informational RFC.

[BCR⁺05]   Michael Bailey, Evan Cooke, Karl Rosaen, David Watson, and Farnam Jahanian. Data reduction for the scalable automated analysis of distributed darknet traffic. In *Proceedings of the ACM SIGCOMM Internet Measurement Conference*, October 2005.

[BCW88]   R. A. Becker, J. M. Chambers, and A. R. Wilks. *The New S language*. Chapman & Hall, 1988.

[BD81]   Peter J. Brockwell and Richard A. Davis. *Time Series: Theory and Methods*. Springer-Verlag, second edition, 1981.

[BDJT01]   Supratik Bhattacharyya, Christophe Diot, Jorjeta Jetcheva, and Nina Taft. POP-level and access-link-level traffic dynamics in a tier-1 POP. In *Proceedings of the ACM SIGCOMM Internet Measurement Workshop*, 2001.

[BDPT02]   Tian Bu, Nick Duffield, Francesco Lo Presti, and Don Towsley. Network tomography on general topologies. In *Proceedings of ACM SIGMETRICS*, pages 21–30, Marina Del Rey, CA, June 2002.

[Bel92]   Steven M. Bellovin. A best-case network performance model. Available at `http://www.cs.columbia.edu/~smb/papers/netmeas.ps`, February 1992.

[Ber94]   Jan Beran. *Statistics for Long-Memory Processes*. Monographs on Statistics and Applied Probability. Chapman and Hall, New York, NY, 1994.

[Ber01]   Yahn W. Bernier. Latency compensating methods in client/server in-game protocol design and optimization. In *Proceedings of the 15th Games Developers Conference*, March 2001.

[BGMZ97]   Andrei Z. Broder, Steven C. Glassman, Mark S. Manasse, and Geoffrey Zweig. Syntactic clustering of the Web. In *Sixth international conference on World Wide Web*, pages 1157–1166, 1997.

[BGP04]   Suman Banerjee, Timothy G. Griffin, and Marcelo Pias. The interdomain connectivity of PlanetLab nodes. In *Proceedings of the Passive and Active Measurement Workshop*, Juan Les Pins, France, April 2004.

[BHGkc04]   Andre Broido, Young Hyun, Ruomei Gao, and kc claffy. Their share: diversity and disparity in IP traffic. In *Proceedings of the Passive and Active Measurement Workshop*, Juan Les Pins, France, April 2004.

[BHK⁺91]   Mary G. Baker, John H. Hartman, Michael D. Kupfer, Ken W. Shirriff, and John K. Ousterhout. Measurements of a distributed file system. In *Proceedings of the Thirteenth ACM Symposium on Operating System Principles*, pages 198–212, Pacific Grove, CA, October 1991.

[Bie04]   Celeste Biever. How zombie networks fuel cybercrime. *New Scientist*, November 2004.

[BIN]   ISC BIND. `http://www.isc.org/sw/bind/`.

[Bit]   The official BitTorrent home page. `http://bittorrent.com/`.

[BJR94]   George Box, Gwilym M. Jenkins, and Gregory Reinsel. *Time Series Analysis: Forecasting and Control*. Prentice Hall, third edition, 1994.

[Bkc02]   Nevil Brownlee and k claffy. Understanding Internet traffic streams: Dragonflies and tortoises. *IEEE Communications Magazine*, Oct 2002.

[BKKP00]   R. Bush, D. Karrenberg, M. Kosters, and R. Plzak. Root name server operational requirements. RFC 2870, IETF, June 2000. Best Current Practice.

[BKM⁺99]   Andrei Broder, Ravi Kumar, Farzin Maghoul, Prabhakar Raghavan, Sridhar Rajagopalan, Raymie Stata, Andrew Tomkins, and Janet Wiener. Graph structure in the Web. In *World Wide Web Conference*, 1999.

[BKPR02]   Paul Barford, Jeffrey Kline, David Plonka, and Amos Ron. A signal analysis of network traffic anomalies. In *Proceedings of the ACM SIGCOMM Internet Measurement Workshop*, pages 71–82, Marseilles, November 2002.

[BL92]   Tim Berners-Lee. Is there a paper which describes the www protocol. `http://lists.w3.org/Archives/Public/www-talk/1992JanFeb/0000.html`, January 9 1992. WWW-talk mailing list.

[BLFF96]   T. Berners-Lee, R. Fielding, and H. Frystyk. Hypertext Transfer Protocol — HTTP/1.0. RFC 1945, IETF, May 1996. Defines current usage of HTTP/1.0.

[BLFM98]   T. Berners-Lee, R. Fielding, and L. Masinter. Uniform Resource Identifiers (URI): Generic syntax. RFC 2396, IETF, August 1998.

[BLME04]   M. Busse, B. Lamparter, M. Mauve, and W. Effelsberg. Lightweight QoS-support for networked mobile gaming. In *Proceedings of the Workshop on Network and System Support for Games*, September 2004.

[Blo]   Rebecca Blood. weblogs: a history and perspective. `http://www.rebeccablood.net/essays/weblog_history.html`.

[Blo70]   B. Bloom. Space/time trade-offs in hash coding with allowable errors. *Communications of the ACM*, 13(7):422–426, July 1970.

[Blu]   The Bluetooth SIG. `http://www.bluetooth.org`.

[Blu70]   Leonard M. Blumenthal. *Theory and applications of distance geometry*. Chelsea Pub. Co., Bronx, N.Y., second edition, 1970.

[BM92]   I. Bilinskis and A. Mikelsons. *Randomized Signal Processing*. Prentice-Hall, 1992.

[BM01]   F. Begtasevic and P. Van Mieghen. Measurements of the hopcount in Internet. In *Proceedings of the Passive and Active Measurement Workshop*, 2001.

[BM05]   A. Broder and M. Mitzenmacher. Network applications of Bloom filters: A survey. *Internet Mathematics*, 1(4):485–509, 2005.

[BMR99]   N. Brownlee, C. Mills, and G. Ruth. Traffic flow measurement: Architecture. RFC 2722. Available at `http://www.ietf.org`, October 1999.

[Bol77]   Béla Bollobás. *Graph Theory: an Introductory Course*. Springer-Verlag, New York, 1977.

[Bol93]   Jean-Chrysostome Bolot. End-to-end packet delay and loss behavior in the Internet. In *Proceedings of ACM SIGCOMM*, pages 289–298, New York, NY, USA, 1993. ACM Press.

[Bol01]   Béla Bollobás. *Random Graphs*. Cambridge University Press, 2nd edition, 2001.

[Bor99]   Mike Borella. Source models of network game traffic. In *Proceedings of Networld+Interop Engineer's Conference*, May 1999.

[Bor00]   Mike Borella. Source models of network game traffic. *Computer Communications*, 23(4):403–410, February 2000.

[Bot]   Rise of the botnets. `http://www.theregister.co.uk/2004/09/20/rise_of_the_botnets`.

[Bou85]   J. Bourgain. On Lipschitz embedding of finite metric spaces in Hilbert space. *Israel J. Math.*, 52(1–2):46–52, 1985.

[Bou04]   J.-Y. Le Boudec. Understanding the simulation of mobility models with Palm calculus. Technical Report IC/2004/53, EPFL, 2004.

[Box79]   G. E. P. Box. Robustness in the strategy of scientific model building. In R. L. Launer and G. N. Wilkinson, editors, *Robustness in Statistics*. Academic Press, New York, 1979.

[BP00]   Paramvir Bahl and Venkata N. Padmanabhan. RADAR: An in-building RF-based user location and tracking system. In *Proceedings of IEEE INFOCOM Conference*, pages 775–784, 2000.

[BPS99]   Jon C. R. Bennett, Craig Partridge, and Nicholas Shectman. Packet reordering is not pathological network behavior. *IEEE/ACM Transactions on Networking*, 7(6):789–798, 1999.

[BR04]   N. Benameur and J. Roberts. Traffic matrix inference in IP networks. *Networks and Spatial Economics*, 4:7–21, March 2004.

[Bro99a]   N. Brownlee. RTFM: Applicability statement. RFC 2721. Available at `http://www.ietf.org`, October 1999.

[Bro99b]   N. Brownlee. SRL: A language for describing traffic flows and specifying actions for flow groups. RFC 2723. Available at `http://www.ietf.org`, October 1999.

[Bro99c]   N. Brownlee. Traffic flow measurement: Meter MIB. RFC 2720. Available at `http://www.ietf.org`, October 1999.

[BRS02]   Ashwin R. Bharambe, Sanjay Rao, and Srinivasan Seshan. Mercury: A scalable publish-subscribe system for Internet games. In *Proceedings of the Workshop on Network and System Support for Games*, August 2002.

[BS02]   John Bellardo and Stefan Savage. Measuring packet reordering. In *Proceedings of the ACM SIGCOMM Internet Measurement Workshop*, pages 97–105, Marseilles, November 2002.

[BS03]   Stefan Bornholdt and Heinz Georg Schuster, editors. *Handbook of Graphs and Networks: From the Genome to the Internet*. Wiley-VCH, 2003.

[BSMV99]   F. Brichet, A. Simonian, L. Massoulie, and D. Veitch. Heavy load queueing analysis with LRD ON/OFF sources. In Kihong Park and Walter Willinger, editors, *Self-Similar Network Traffic and Performance Evaluation*. Wiley / Wiley Interscience, New York, 1999.

[BSR]   David Bacher, Andrew Swan, and Lawrence A. Rowe. rtpmon: A third-party RTCP monitor. `http://bmrc.berkeley.edu/people/drbacher/projects/mm96-demo/demo1.html`.

[BSSK97]   Hari Balakrishnan, Mark Stemm, Srinivasan Seshan, and Randy H. Katz. Analyzing stability in wide-area network performance. In *Proceedings of ACM SIGMETRICS*, pages 2–12, 1997.

[BSV03]   Ranjita Bhagwan, Stefan Savage, and Geoffrey M. Voelker. Understanding availability. In *Proceedings of the International Peer to Peer Symposium*, 2003.

[BT02]   Tian Bu and Don Towsley. On distinguishing between Internet power law topology generators. In *Proceedings of IEEE INFOCOM Conference*, New York, NY, June 2002.

[BVBR02]   Anand Balachandran, G. Voelker, P. Bahl, and V. Rangan. Characterizing user behavior and network performance in a public wireless LAN. In *Proceedings of ACM SIGMETRICS*, June 2002.

[BVR02]   Anand Balachandran, Goeffrey M. Voelker, and Paramvir Bahland Venkat Rangan. Characterizing user behavior and network performance in a public wireless LAN. In *Proceedings of ACM SIGMETRICS*, pages 195–205, Marina Del Rey, CA, June 2002.

[BYBKT04]   Ziv Bar-Yossef, Andrei Broder, Ravi Kumar, and Andrew Tomkins. Sic transit gloria telae: Toward's an understanding of the Web's decay. In *Proceedings of the World Wide Web Conference*, pages 328–337, May 2004.

[CAI]   Cooperaive analysis of Internet data. `http://www.caida.org`.

[CAI05]   CAIDA. CAIDA 2003-2005 program plan. Available at `http://www.caida.org/funding/progplan/progplan03.xml`, 2005.

[Can]   Can you see me now? `http://www.canyouseemenow.co.uk/cardiff/en/intro.php`.

[Car]   Using CAR during DOS attacks. `http://www.cisco.com/warp/public/63/car_rate_limit_icmp.html`.

[Cas03]   Edward Castronova. Network technology and the growth of synthetic worlds. In *Pro-*

ceedings of the Workshop on Network and System Support for Games, 2003.

[Cas04]   Edward Castronova. The future of cyberspace economies. In *O'Reilly Emerging Technology Conference*, February 2004.

[CB97]   Mark E. Crovella and Azer Bestavros. Self-similarity in World Wide Web traffic: Evidence and possible causes. *IEEE/ACM Transactions on Networking*, 5(6):835–846, December 1997.

[CBC95]   Carlos A. Cunha, Azer Bestavros, and Mark E. Crovella. Characteristics of WWW client-based traces. Technical Report TR-95-010, Boston University Department of Computer Science, April 1995. Revised July 18, 1995.

[CBP95]   Kimberly C. Claffy, Hans-Werner Braun, and George C. Polyzos. A parameterizable methodology for Internet traffic flow profiling. *IEEE Journal of Selected Areas in Communications*, 13(8):1481–1494, 1995.

[CBSK04]   Yan Chen, David Bindel, Hanhee Song, and Randy H. Katz. An algebraic approach to practical and scalable overlay network monitoring. In *Proceedings of ACM SIGCOMM*, pages 55–66, New York, NY, USA, 2004. ACM Press.

[CC96]   Robert L. Carter and Mark E. Crovella. Measuring bottleneck link speed in packet switched networks. *Performance Evaluation*, 27 and 28:297–318, 1996.

[CCB⁺04]   Cristiano Costa, Italo Cunha, Alex Borges, Claudiney Ramos, Marcus Rocha andJussara Almeida, and Berthier Ribeiro-Neto. Analyzing client interactivity in streaming media. In *Proceedings of the World Wide Web Conference*, May 2004.

[CCG⁺02]   Qian Chen, Hyunseok Chang, Ramesh Govindan, Sugih Jamin, Scott Shenker, and Walter Willinger. The origin of power-laws in Internet topologies revisited. In *Proceedings of IEEE INFOCOM Conference*, New York, NY, June 2002.

[CCL⁺03]   R. Castro, M. Coates, G. Liang, R. Nowak, and B. Yu. Network tomography: Recent developments. *Statistical Science*, 2003.

[CCS02]   Jin Cao, William S. Cleveland, and Don X. Sun. S-net: A software system for analyzing packet header databases. In *Proceedings of the Passive and Active Measurement Workshop*, Mar 2002.

[CDA]   CAIDA tool repository and tool taxonomy. Available at `http://www.caida.org/tools/`.

[CDHT99]   R. Caceres, N.G. Duffield, J. Horowitz, and D. Towsley. Multicast-based inference of network-internal loss characteristics. *IEEE Transactions on Information Theory*, 45:2462–2480, 1999.

[CDR]   Clients of DNS root servers. `http://www.caida.org/~kkeys/dns`.

[CDWY00]   J. Cao, D. Davis, S. Vander Wiel, and B. Yu. Time-varying tomography: router link data. *Journal of the American Statistical Association*, 95:1063–1075, 2000.

[Cen]   Center for International Earth Science Information Network (CIESIN), Columbia University. Gridded population of the world. Available at `http://www.ciesin.org`.

[Cen05a]   RIPE Network Coordination Centre. Hostcount. Available at `http://www.ripe.net/hostcount`, 2005.

[Cen05b]   RIPE Network Coordination Centre. Test traffic measurements. Available at `http://www.ripe.net/projects/ttm`, 2005.

[CER]   Computer emergency response team. `http://www.cert.org`.

[CF03]   Francis Chang and Wu-Chang Feng. Modeling player session times of on-line games. In *Proceedings of the Workshop on Network and System Support for Games*, 2003.

[CFFS03]   Chris Chambers, Wu-Chang Feng, Wu-Chi Feng, and Debanjan Saha. A geographic redirection service for on-line games. In *Proc. ACM Multimedia (short paper)*, November 2003.

[CFG⁺03]   A. D. Cheok, S. W. Fong, K. H. Goh, X. Yang, W. Liu, and F. Farbiz. Human Pacman:

a sensing-based mobile entertainment system with ubiquitous computing and tangible interaction. In *Proceedings of the Workshop on Network and System Support for Games*, pages 106–117, May 2003.

[CG98] I. Cozzani and S. Giordano. Traffic sampling methods for end-to-end QoS evaluation in large heterogeneous networks. *Computer Networks and ISDN Systems*, 30(16–18), Sept 1998.

[CGJ+02a] Hyunseok Chang, Ramesh Govindan, Sugih Jamin, Scott J. Shenker, and Walter Willinger. Towards capturing representative AS-level Internet topologies. In *Proceedings of ACM SIGMETRICS*, pages 280–281, Marina Del Rey, CA, June 2002.

[CGJ+02b] Chuck Cranor, Yuan Gao, Theodore Johnson, Vlaidslav Shkapenyuk, and Oliver Spatscheck. Gigascope: High performance network monitoring with an SQL interface. In *ACM SIGMOD conference*, June 2002.

[CGKS01] Charles D. Cranor, Emden Gansner, Balachander Krishnamurthy, and Oliver Spatscheck. Characterizing large DNS traces using graphs. In *Proceedings of the ACM SIGCOMM Internet Measurement Workshop*, pages 55–67, November 2001.

[CGM00] Junghoo Cho and Hector Garcia-Molina. The evolution of the Web and implications for an incremental crawler. In *Proceedings of the International Conference on Very Large Databases*, Sep 2000.

[CGM03] Brian F. Cooper and Hector Garcia-Molina. Studying search networks with SIL. In *Proceedings of the International Peer to Peer Symposium*, 2003.

[CHK+01] D. Callaway, J. Hopcroft, J. Kleinberg, M. Newman, and S. Strogatz. Are randomly grown graphs really random? *Physical Review E*, 64(041902), 2001.

[CHNY02] Mark Coates, Alfred Hero, Robert Nowak, and Bin Yu. Internet tomography. *Signal Processing Magazine*, 19(3):47–65, May 2002.

[Cis] Netflow services solutions guide. Available at `http://www.cisco.com/warp/public/732/Tech/nmp/netflow/v9/`.

[CJM05] Evan Cooke, Farnam Jahanian, and Danny McPherson. The zombie roundup: Understanding, detecting, and disrupting botnets. In *Steps to Reducing Unwanted Traffic on the Internet (SRUTI) workshop*, 2005.

[CJS03] Chuck Cranor, Theodore Johnson, and Oliver Spatscheck. Gigascope: how to monitor network traffic 5Gbit/sec at a time. In *Proceedings of Workshop on Monitoring and Processing of Data Streams (MPDS)*, June 2003.

[CJSS03a] C. Cranor, T. Johnson, O. Spatscheck, and V. Shkapenyuk. The Gigascope stream database. *IEEE Data Engineering Bulletin*, 26(1):27–32, 2003.

[CJSS03b] C. D. Cranor, T. Johnson, O. Spatscheck, and V. Shkapenyuk. Gigascope: a stream database for network applications. In *Proceedings of ACM SIGMOD*, pages 647–651, June 2003.

[CJW01] H. Chang, S. Jamin, and W. Willinger. Inferring AS-level Internet topology from router-level path traces. In *Proceedings of SPIE ITCom 2001*, August 2001.

[CK90] V. Cerf and R. Kahn. Selected ARPANET maps. *Computer Communication Review*, 20:81–110, October 1990.

[CK01] Mark J. Crosbie and Benjamin A. Kuperman. A building block approach to intrusion detection. In *Recent Advances in Intrusion Detection Workshop*, 2001.

[CK05] Edith Cohen and Balachander Krishnamurthy. A short walk in the Blogistan. *Computer Networks*, 50(5), 2005.

[CKC05] David B. Chua, Eric D. Kolaczyk, and Mark Crovella. Efficient monitoring of end-to-end network properties. In *Proceedings of IEEE INFOCOM Conference*, Mar 2005.

[CKL+04] Mark Claypool, Robert Kinicki, Mingzhe Li, James Nichols, and Huahui Wu. Inferring queue sizes in access networks by active measurement. In *Proceedings of the Passive and Active Measurement Workshop*, Juan Les Pins, France, April 2004.

[CL99]   Mark E. Crovella and Lester Lipsky. Simulations with heavy-tailed workloads. In Kihong Park and Walter Willinger, editors, *Self-Similar Network Traffic and Performance Evaluation*. Wiley / Wiley Interscience, New York, 1999.

[Cla88]   David D. Clark. The design philosophy of the DARPA Internet protocols. In *Proceedings of ACM SIGCOMM*, pages 106–114, August 1988.

[CLKO02]   Y. Chen, K. Lim, R. H. Katz, and C. Overton. On the stability of network distance estimation. In *Proceedings of ACM SIGMETRICS Practical Aspects of Performance Analysis Workshop (PAPA 2002), in ACM SIGMETRICS Performance Evaluation Review*, September 2002.

[CM04]   G. Cormode and S. Muthukrishnan. An improved data stream summary: The count-min sketch and its applications. *Journal of Algorithms*, 2004.

[CM05a]   Aaron Clauset and Cristopher Moore. Accuracy and scaling phenomena in Internet mapping. *Physical Review Letters*, 94, 2005.

[CM05b]   G. Cormode and S. Muthukrishnan. What's hot and what's not: Tracking most frequent items dynamically. *ACM Transaction on Database Systems*, March 2005.

[CMK00]   K. Cho, K. Mitsuya, and A. Kato. Traffic data repository at the WIDE project. In *Proceedings of USENIX 2000 Annual Technical Conference FREENIX*, June 2000.

[CMM+04]   J. Cuellar, J. Morris, D. Mulligan, J. Peterson, and J. Polk. Geopriv requirements. RFC 3693. Available at `http://www.ietf.org`, February 2004.

[CMZ+04]   Baek-Young Choi, Sue Moon, Zhi-Li Zhang, Konstantina Papagiannaki, and Christophe Diot. Analysis of point-to-point packet delay in an operational network. In *Proceedings of IEEE INFOCOM Conference*, Hong Kong, March 2004.

[CN00]   M. J. Coates and R. Nowak. Network loss inference using unicast end-to-end measurement. In *Proceedings of ITC Conference on IP Traffic, Modelling and Management*, September 2000.

[CO98]   K. G. Coffman and Andrew Odlyzko. The size and growth rate of the Internet. *First Monday*, 3(10), October 1998.

[COA]   Co-advisor test suite. `http://coad.measurement-factory.com/`.

[Cod]   Inside the Code Red worm. `http://www.caida.org/analysis/security/code-red/`.

[Con05]   Internet Systems Consortium. Internet domain survey. Available at `http://www.isc.org`, 2005.

[Cor]   Coralreef - supported hardware. `http://www.caida.org/tools/measurement/coralreef/hardware.xml`.

[Cot05a]   Les Cottrell. ICFA SCIC network monitoring report. Technical Report Available at `http://www.slac.stanford.edu/xorg/icfa/icfa-net-paper-jan05/`, Stanford Linear Accelerator Center, February 2005.

[Cot05b]   Les Cottrell. PingER. Available at `http://www-iepm.slac.stanford.edu/pinger/`, 2005.

[Cou]   Counterstrike. `http://www.counterstrike.com`.

[Cox84]   D. R. Cox. Long range dependence: A review. In H. A. David and H. T. David, editors, *Statistics: An Appraisal*. Iowa State University Press, Ames, IA, 1984.

[CPB93a]   K. Claffy, G. Polyzos, and H-W. Braun. Measurement considerations for assessing unidirectional latency. *Internetworking: Research and Experience*, 4(3):121–132, Sept 1993.

[CPB93b]   Kimberly C. Claffy, George C. Polyzos, and Hans-Werner Braun. Application of sampling methodologies to network traffic characterizations. In *Proceedings of ACM SIGCOMM*, pages 13–17, September 1993.

[CPZ03]   B.-Y. Choi, J. Park, and Z.-L. Zhang. Adaptive random sampling for total load estima-
            tion. In *Proceedings of the IEEE International Conference on Communications*, pages
            1552–1556, 2003.

[CR04]   Junghoo Cho and Sourashis Roy. Impact of search engines on page popularity. In
            Proceedings of the World Wide Web Conference, May 2004.

[CRB+03]   Yatin Chawathe, Sylvia Ratnasamy, Lee Breslau, Nick Lanham, and Scott Shenker.
            Making Gnutella-like P2P systems scalable. In *Proceedings of ACM Sigcomm*, August
            2003.

[CRdOJ+04] Fabio Reis Cecin, Rodrigo Real, Rafael de Oliveira Jannone, Claudio Fernando Resin
            Geyer, Marcio Garcia Martins, and Jorge Luis Victoria Barbosa. FreeMMG: A scalable
            and cheat-resistant distribution model for Internet games. In *Proceedings of the Eighth
            IEEE International Symposium on Distributed Simulation and Real-Time Applications*,
            pages 83–90, 2004.

[CRN03]   Mark Coates, Michael Rabbat, and Robert Nowak. Merging logical topologies using
            end-to-end measurements. In *Proceedings of the ACM SIGCOMM Internet Measure-
            ment Conference*, November 2003.

[Cro00]   Mark E. Crovella. Performance evaluation with heavy tailed distributions. In *Lecture
            Notes in Computer Science 1786*, pages 1–9, March 2000. Slightly revised version ap-
            peared in Job Scheduling Strategies for Parallel Processing: 7th International Workshop,
            pp. 1-10, June 16, 2001.

[CSA00]   N. Cardwell, S. Savage, and T. Anderson. Modeling TCP latency. In *Proceedings of
            IEEE INFOCOM Conference*, pages 1742–1751, 2000.

[CSMS04]   Prasad Calyam, Mukundan Sridharan, Weiping Mandrawa, and Paul Schopis. Perfor-
            mance measurement and analysis of H.323 traffic. In *Proceedings of the Passive and
            Active Measurement Workshop*, Juan Les Pins, France, April 2004.

[CT91]   T. M. Cover and J. A. Thomas. *Elements of Information Theory*. Wiley Press, 1991.

[CWVL01]   M. Chesire, A. Wolman, G. M. Voelker, and H. M. Levy. Measurement and analysis
            of a streaming media workload. In *Proceedings of the USENIX Symposium on Internet
            Technologies and Systems*, March 2001.

[Cym]   DNS name server status summary. `http://www.cymru.com/DNS/index.`
            `html`.

[Dav02]   David Moore. Network telescopes: Observing small or distant security events.
            `http://www.caida.org/publications/presentations/2002/`
            `usenix_sec/usenix_%sec_2002_files/v3_document.htm`,   August
            2002. Usenix Security Symposium.

[DB99]   John R. Douceur and William J. Bolosky. A large-scale study of file-system contents.
            In *Proceedings of ACM SIGMETRICS*, pages 59–70. ACM Press, 1999.

[DC98]   J. Drobisz and K. Christensen. Adaptive sampling methods to determine network statis-
            tics including the Hurst parameter. In *Proceedings of IEEE Annual Conference on Local
            Computer Networks*, pages 238–247, 1998.

[DCKM04]   Frank Dabek, Russ Cox, Frans Kaashoek, and Robert Morris. Vivaldi: A decentral-
            ized network coordinate system. In *Proceedings of ACM SIGCOMM*, Portland, Oregon,
            August 2004.

[DD03]   Antonios Danalis and Constantinos Dovrolis. ANEMOS: An Autonomous NEtwork
            MOnitoring System. In *Proceedings of the Passive and Active Measurement Workshop*,
            La Jolla, CA, April 2003.

[DDO]   Distributed denial of service (DDoS) attacks/tools. `http://staff.washington.`
            `edu/dittrich/misc/ddos/`.

[Deea]   Deepsight threat management. `http://www.securityfocus.com`.

[Deeb]   The deep Web: Surfacing hidden value. `http://www.press.umich.edu/jep/07-01/bergman.html`.

[Del97]   K. Delgadillo. Cisco distributed director, 1997. Cisco White Paper.

[Der]   Luca Deri. ntop. Available at `http://www.ntop.org`.

[DFC05]   Benoit Donnet, Timur Friedman, and Mark Crovella. Improved algorithms for network topology discovery. In *Proceedings of the Passive and Active Measurement Workshop*, Mar 2005.

[DFKM97]   Fred Douglis, Anja Feldmann, Balachander Krishnamurthy, and Jeffrey Mogul. Rate of change and other metrics: A live study of the World Wide Web. In *Proc. USENIX Symp. on Internet Technologies and Systems*, pages 147–158, December 1997.

[DG01]   N. C. Duffield and M. Grossglauser. Trajectory sampling for direct traffic observation. *IEEE/ACM Transactions on Networking*, June 2001.

[DG04]   N. C. Duffield and M. Grossglauser. Trajectory sampling with unreliable reporting. In *Proceedings of IEEE INFOCOM Conference*, March 2004.

[DHPT02]   N.G. Duffield, J. Horowitz, F. Lo Presti, and D. Towsley. Multicast topology inference from measured end-to-end loss. *IEEE Transactions on Information Theory*, 2002.

[Dig]   Digital piracy - definitive P2P piracy figures for year 2003. `http://www.itic.ca/DIC/News/2004/08/11/P2P_piracy_figures_2003.html`.

[Dir]   Direct connect. `http://en.wikipedia.org/wiki/NeoModus_Direct_Connect`.

[DJC+92]   P. Danzig, S. Jamin, R. Cáceres, D. Mitzel, and D. Estrin. An empirical workload model for driving wide-area TCP/IP network simulations. *Internetworking: Research and Experience*, 3(1):1–26, 1992.

[DL03]   Nick Duffield and Carsten Lund. Predicting resource usage and estimation accuracy in an IP flow measurement collection infrastructure. In *Proceedings of the ACM SIGCOMM Internet Measurement Conference*, November 2003.

[DLD00]   Sven Dietrich, Neil Long, and David Dittrich. Analyzing distributed denial of service tools: The shaft case. In *Proceedings of the Usenix Large Installation System Administration Conference*, 2000.

[DLT01]   Nick Duffield, Carsten Lund, and Mikkel Thorup. Charging from sampled network usage. In *Proceedings of the ACM SIGCOMM Internet Measurement Workshop*, November 2001.

[DLT03]   Nick Duffield, Carsten Lund, and Mikkel Thorup. Estimating flow distributions from sampled flow statistics. In *Proceedings of ACM SIGCOMM*, August 2003.

[DLT04]   Nick Duffield, Carsten Lund, and Mikkel Thorup. Flow sampling under hard resource constraints. In *Proceedings of ACM SIGMETRICS*, 2004.

[DM03]   S. N. Dorogovtsev and J. F. F. Mendes. *Evolution of Networks: From Biological Nets to the Internet and WWW*. Oxford University Press, 2003.

[DMPS]   Peter Danzig, Jeff Mogul, Vern Paxson, and Mike Schwartz. The Internet traffic archive. Available at `http://ita.ee.lbl.gov`.

[DMZ]   Internet firewalls: Frequently asked questions. `http://www.interhack.net/pubs/fwfaq`.

[DNSa]   DNS check database. `http://dnscheck.se/dns-package.pl`.

[Dnsb]   The *dnscache* program. `http://cr.yp.to/djbdns/dnscache.html`.

[DNSc]   DNSchecker – squishywishywoo: Complete DNS traversal checking. `http://www.squish.net/dnscheck`.

[Dnsd]   DSC: A DNS statistics collector. `http://dns.measurement-factory.com/tools/dsc/`.

[DNSe]   Root server technical operations association. `http://www.root-servers.org`.

[Dnsf]   dnsstat. http://www.caida.org/tools/utilities/dnsstat/.

[Dnsg]   DNSTOP: stay on top of your DNS traffic. http://www.caida.org/tools/utilities/dnstop/.

[DOK92]   Peter Danzig, Katia Obraczka, and A. Kumar. An analysis of wide-area name server traffic. In *Proceedings of ACM SIGCOMM*, August 1992.

[Dom]   DomainKeys: Proving and protecting email sender identity. http://antispam.yahoo.com/domainkeys.

[Dom04]   Domain name industry briefs. http://www.verisign.com/Resources/Naming_Services_Resources/Domain_Name%_Industry_Brief/page_002688.html, February 20004. Volume 1 Issue 1.

[Don]   David L. Donoho. High dimensional data analysis: The curses and blessings of dimensionality. AMS Lecture, August 8 2000. Available at http://www-stat.stanford.edu/~donoho/Lectures/AMS2000/AMS2000.html.

[Doo]   Doom3. http://www.idsoftware.com/games/doom/doom3.

[Dow99]   Allen B. Downey. Using pathchar to estimate Internet link characteristics. In *Proceedings of ACM SIGCOMM*, pages 241–250, New York, NY, USA, 1999. ACM Press.

[Dow01]   Allen B. Downey. Evidence for long-tailed distributions in the Internet. In *Proceedings of the ACM SIGCOMM Internet Measurement Workshop*, November 2001.

[DRFC05]   Benoit Donnet, Philippe Raoult, Timur Friedman, and Mark Crovella. Efficient algorithms for large-scale topology discovery. In *Proceedings of ACM SIGMETRICS*, June 2005.

[DRM04]   Constantinos Dovrolis, Parameswaran Ramanathan, and David Moore. Packet dispersion techniques and capacity estimation. *IEEE/ACM Transactions on Networking*, December 2004.

[DS86]   Ralph B. D'Agostino and Michael A. Stephens. *Goodness-of-Fit Techniques*. Marcel Dekker, 1986.

[Dsh]   Dshield: Distributed intrusion detection system. http://www.dshield.org.

[Duf03]   Nick Duffield. Simple network performance tomography. In *Proceedings of the ACM SIGCOMM Internet Measurement Conference*, November 2003.

[DVGD96]   C. Davis, P. Vixie, T. Goodwin, and I. Dickinson. A means for expressing location information in the domain name system. RFC 1876. Available at http://www.ietf.org, January 1996.

[EGE02]   Jeremy Elson, Lewis Girod, and Deborah Estrin. Fine-grained network time synchronization using reference broadcasts. *SIGOPS Oper. Syst. Rev.*, 36(SI):147–163, 2002.

[EKMV04]   C. Estan, K. Keys, D. Moore, and G. Varghese. Building a better netflow. In *Proceedings of ACM SIGCOMM*, Sept 2004.

[ELL01]   Brian S. Everitt, Sabine Landau, and Morven Leese. *Cluster Analysis*. Arnold Publishers, 4th edition, 2001.

[EMG]   Endace DAG network monitoring interface card. http://www.endace.com/.

[Emu]   eMule-project.net - official eMule homepage. http://www.emule-project.net.

[ENW96]   A. Erramilli, O. Narayan, and W. Willinger. Experimental queueing analysis with long-range dependent packet traffic. *IEEE/ACM Transactions on Networking*, 4(2):209–223, April 1996.

[ER59]   Paul Erdös and Alfréd Rényi. On random graphs. *Publicationes Mathematicae*, 6:290–297, 1959.

[ESV03]   Cristian Estan, Stefan Savage, and George Varghese. Automatically inferring patterns of resource consumption in network traffic. In *Proceedings of ACM SIGCOMM*, August 2003.

[Eth]   The ethereal protocol analyzer. `http://www.ethereal.com`.

[EU-95]   European union directive 95/46/EC. `http://www.cdt.org/privacy/eudirective/EU_Directive.html`, November 1995.

[EV02]   Cristian Estan and George Varghese. New directions in traffic measurement and accounting. In *Proceedings of ACM SIGCOMM*, Pittsburgh, PA, August 2002.

[Eva]   evalid WebSite analysis and testing suite. `http://www.soft.com/eValid/`.

[EVF03]   Cristian Estan, George Varghese, and Mike Fisk. Bitmap algorithms for counting active flows on high speed links. In *Proceedings of the ACM SIGCOMM Internet Measurement Conference*, November 2003.

[Exp]   Expand networks. `http://www.expand.com`.

[FABK03]   Nick Feamster, David G. Andersen, Hari Balakrishnan, and M. Frans Kaashoek. Measuring the effects of Internet path faults on reactive routing. In *Proceedings of ACM SIGMETRICS*, pages 126–137, San Diego, CA, June 2003.

[Fae02]   Johannes Faerber. Network game traffic modelling. In *Proceedings of the Workshop on Network and System Support for Games*, 2002.

[FCAB00]   Li Fan, Pei Cao, Jussara Almeida, and Andrei Z. Broder. Summary cache: a scalable wide-area Web cache sharing protocol. *IEEE/ACM Transactions on Networking*, 8(3):281–293, 2000.

[FCE05]   Kensuke Fukuda, Kenjiro Cho, and Hiroshi Esaki. The impact of residential broadband traffic on Japanese ISP backbones. *ACM SIGCOMM Computer Communication Review*, Jan 2005.

[FCFW02]   Wu-Chang Feng, Francis Chang, Wu-Chi Feng, and Jonathan Walpole. Provisioning on-line games: A traffic analysis of a busy Counter-Strike server. In *Proceedings of the ACM SIGCOMM Internet Measurement Workshop*, November 2002.

[Fel99]   A. Feldmann. Characteristics of TCP connection arrivals. In Kihong Park and Walter Willinger, editors, *Self-Similar Network Traffic and Performance Evaluation*. Wiley / Wiley Interscience, New York, 1999.

[FFF99]   Michalis Faloutsos, Petros Faloutsos, and Christos Faloutsos. On power-law relationships of the Internet topology. In *Proceedings of ACM SIGCOMM*, pages 251–262, 1999.

[FGL⁺00]   Anja Feldmann, Albert Greenberg, Carsten Lund, Nick Reingold, Jennifer Rexford, and Fred True. Deriving traffic demands for operational IP networks: Methodology and experience. In *Proceedings of ACM SIGCOMM*, pages 257–270, 2000.

[FGM⁺99]   R. Fielding, J. Gettys, J. C. Mogul, H. Frystyk, L. Masinter, P. Leach, and T. Berners-Lee. Hypertext Transfer Protocol – HTTP/1.1. RFC 2616, IETF, June 1999. Draft Standard of HTTP/1.1.

[FGPW99]   A. Feldmann, A. C. Gilbert, P.Huang, and W. Willinger. Dynamics of IP traffic: A study of the role of variability and the impact of control. In *Proceedings of ACM SIGCOMM*, pages 301–313, 1999.

[FGW98]   A. Feldmann, A. C. Gilbert, and W. Willinger. Data networks as cascades: Investigating the multifractal nature of Internet WAN traffic. In *Proceedings of ACM SIGCOMM*, pages 42–55, October 1998.

[FGWK98]   A. Feldmann, A. Gilbert, W. Willinger, and T. Kurtz. The changing nature of network traffic: Scaling phenomena. *SIGCOMM Computer Communications Review*, 28(2), April 1998.

[FJ93]   S. Floyd and V. Jacobson. Random early detection gateways for congestion avoidance. *IEEE/ACM Transactions on Networking*, 1(4):397–413, August 1993.

[FJP⁺99]   Paul Francis, Sugih Jamin, Vern Paxson, Lixia Zhang, Daniel F. Gryniewicz, and Yixin Jin. An architecture for a global Internet host distance estimation service. In *Proceedings of IEEE INFOCOM Conference*, pages 210–217, New York, NY, March 1999. IEEE.

[FK02]   Sally Floyd and Eddie Kohler. Internet research needs better models. In *Proceedings of the Hot Topics in Networks Workshop*, Oct 2002.

[FK05]   Glenn Fowler and Balachander Krishnamurthy. dss—data stream and scan. Technical report, AT&T Labs–Research, August 2005.

[FKB$^+$03] Marwan Fayed, Paul Krapivsky, John Byers, Mark Crovella, David Finkel, and Sid Redner. On the emergence of highly variable distributions in the autonomous system topology. *Computer Communcation Review*, 33(2):41–49, April 2003.

[FKP02]   Alex Fabrikant, Elias Koutsoupias, and Christos H. Papadimitriou. Heuristically optimized trade-offs: A new paradigm for power laws in the Internet. In *ICALP '02: Proceedings of the 29th International Colloquium on Automata, Languages and Programming*, pages 110–122, London, UK, 2002. Springer-Verlag.

[FKSS01]   Wu-Chang Feng, Dilip D. Kandlur, Debanjan Saha, and Kang G. Shin. Stochastic fair Blue: A queue management algorithm for enforcing fairness. In *Proceedings of IEEE INFOCOM Conference*, pages 1520–1529, 2001.

[FL91]   Henry J. Fowler and Will E. Leland. Local area network traffic characteristics, with implications for broadband network congestion management. *IEEE Journal of Selected Areas in Communications*, 9(7):1139–1149, 1991.

[FM85]   Philippe Flajolet and G. Nigel Martin. Probabilistic counting algorithms for data base applications. *Journal of Computer and System Sciences*, 31(2):182–209, October 1985.

[FML$^+$03] C. Fraleigh, S. Moon, B. Lyles, C. Cotton, M. Khan, D. Moll, R. Rockell, T. Seely, and C. Diot. Packet-level traffic measurements from the Sprint IP backbone. *IEEE Network*, 2003.

[FMNW04]   Dennis Fetterly, Mark Manasse, Marc Najork, and Janet L. Wiener. A large-scale study of the evolution of Web pages. *Software Practice and Experience. Special Issue on Web Technologies.*, 34(2):213–237, February 2004.

[Fou]   Foundry networks. http://www.foundrynet.com.

[FP99]   Wenjia Fang and Larry Peterson. Inter-AS traffic patterns and their implications. In *Proceedings of the 4th Global Internet Symposium*, Rio de Janeiro, Brazil, December 1999.

[FP01]   S. Floyd and V. Paxson. Difficulties in simulating the Internet. *IEEE/ACM Transactions on Networking*, 9(4):392–403, August 2001.

[Fra95]   K. D. Frazer. NSFNET: a partnership for high-speed networking, final report 1987-1995. Technical report, Merit Network, Inc., 1995.

[FSR02]   F. Fitzek, G. Schulte, and M. Reisslein. System architecture for billing of multi-player games in a wireless environment using GSM/UMTS and WLAN services. In *Proceedings of the Workshop on Network and System Support for Games*, August 2002.

[FT04]   Sonia Fahmy and Christine Tan. Balancing privacy and fidelity in packet traces for security evaluation. Technical Report CSD-04-034, Purdue University, December 2004.

[FTD03]   Chuck Fraleigh, Fouad Tobagi, and Christophe Diot. Provisioning IP backbone networks to support latency sensitive traffic. In *Proceedings of IEEE INFOCOM Conference*, 2003.

[Ful]   Mark Fullmer. flowtools. Available at http://www.splintered.net/sw/flow-tools/.

[FV02]   Mike Fisk and George Varghese. Agile and scalable analysis of network events. In *Proceedings of the ACM SIGCOMM Internet Measurement Workshop*, pages 285–290, Marseilles, November 2002.

[FW97]   Anja Feldmann and Ward Whitt. Fitting mixtures of exponentials to long-tail distributions to analyze network performance models. In *Proceedings of IEEE INFOCOM*

Conference, pages 1098–1116, April 1997.

[FWR04] Nick Feamster, Jared Winick, and Jennifer Rexford. A model of BGP routing for network engineering. In *Proceedings of ACM SIGMETRICS*, June 2004.

[Gam] GameSpy: Gaming's home page. `http://www.gamespy.com`.

[Gao00] Lixin Gao. On inferring autonomous system relationships in the Internet. *IEEE/ACM Transactions on Networking*, 9(6):733–745, December 2000.

[GAV] GPL arcade volleyball. `http://www.sourceforge.net`.

[GBG04] Paul Gauthier, Brian Bershad, and Steven D. Gribble. Dealing with cheaters in anonymous peer-to-peer networks. Technical Report 04-01-03, University of Washington, January 2004.

[GCS03] O. Gurewitz, I. Cidon, and M. Sidi. Network time synchronization using clock offset optimization. In *IEEE International Conference on Network Protocols (ICNP)*, November 2003.

[GD97] Laurent Gautier and C. Diot. MiMaze, a multiuser game over the Internet. Technical Report 3248, INRIA Research Report, September 1997.

[GD98] Laurent Gautier and Christophe Diot. Design and evaluation of MiMaze, a multiplayer game on the internet. In *Proceedings of IEEE Multimedia System Conference (ICMSC)*, June 1998.

[GDD+03] Lukasz Golab, David DeHaan, Erik Demaine, Alejandro Lopez-Ortiz, and J. Ian Munro. Identifying frequent items in sliding windows over on-line packet streams. In *Proceedings of the ACM SIGCOMM Internet Measurement Conference*, November 2003.

[Gen] Know your enemy: GenII honeynets. `www.linuxvoodoo.net/resources/security/gen2/`.

[geo] The GeoURL ICBM address server. Available at `http://www.geourl.org/`.

[GG91] A. Gersho and R. M. Gray. *Vector Quantization and Signal Compression*. Springer Verlag, 1991.

[GGF05] Global grid forum. Available at `http://www.gridforum.org/`, 2005.

[GGR02] Mukul Goyal, Roch Guerin, and Raju Rajan. Predicting TCP throughput from non-invasive network sampling. In *Proceedings of IEEE INFOCOM Conference*, New York, NY, June 2002.

[GGR05] M. Garofalakis, J. Gehrke, and R. Rastogi, editors. *Data-Stream Management – Processing High-Speed Data Streams*. Springer-Verlag, New York, 2005.

[Gil60] E. Gilbert. Capacity of a burst-noise channel. *Bell System Technical Journal*, 39(5):1253–1265, September 1960.

[Gil01] A. C. Gilbert. Multiscale analysis and data networks. *Applied and Computational Harmonic Analysis*, 10(3):185–202, May 2001.

[GJL99] Michael Greiner, Manfred Jobmann, and Lester Lipsky. The importance of power-tail distributions for telecommunication traffic models. *Operations Research*, 41, 1999.

[GJT04] Anders Gunnar, Mikael Johansson, and Thomas Telkamp. Traffic matrix estimation on a large IP backbone - a comparison on real data. In *Proceedings of the ACM SIGCOMM Internet Measurement Conference*, October 2004.

[GK98] Charles M. Goldie and Claudia Kluppelberg. Subexponential distributions. In Robert J. Adler, Raisa E. Feldman, and Murad S. Taqqu, editors, *A Practical Guide To Heavy Tails*, pages 435–460. Chapman & Hall, New York, 1998.

[GKK+03] Phillip B. Gibbons, Brad Karp, Yan Ke, Suman Nath, and Srinivasan Seshan. IrisNet: An architecture for a world-wide sensor Web. *IEEE Pervasive Computing*, 2(4), 2003.

[GKMS01] A. Gilbert, Y. Kotidis, S. Muthukrishnan, and M. Strauss. QuickSAND: quick summary and analysis of network data. Technical Report 2001-43, DIMACS, December 2001.

[Gla94] Steven Glassman. A caching relay for the World Wide Web. In *Proceedings of the First*

International World Wide Web Conference, pages 69–76, 1994.

[GMZ03]   Christos Gkantsidis, Milena Mihail, and Ellen Zegura. Spectral analysis of Internet topologies. In *Proceedings of IEEE INFOCOM Conference*, March 2003.

[gnu]   GNU zebra. Available at `http://www.zebra.org`.

[Gol00]   O. Goldschmidt. ISP backbone traffic inference methods to support traffic engineering. In *Proceedings of Internet Statistics and Metrics Analysis (ISMA) Workshop*, Dec 2000.

[Gom]   Gomez Internet performance management. `http://www.gomez.com/`.

[GP02]   Ramesh Govindan and Vern Paxson. Estimating router ICMP generation delays. In *Proceedings of the Passive and Active Measurement Workshop*, Mar 2002.

[GP03]   Jose Maria Gonzalez and Vern Paxson. pktd: A packet capture and injection daemon. In *Proceedings of the Passive and Active Measurement Workshop*, La Jolla, CA, April 2003.

[GR97]   Ramesh Govindan and Anoop Reddy. An analysis of Internet inter-domain topology and route stability. In *Proceedings of IEEE INFOCOM Conference*, pages 850–857, 1997.

[Gra04]   Luis Grangeia. DNS cache snooping or snooping the cache for fun and profit. `http://www.sysvalue.com/papers/DNS-Cache-Snooping/files/DNS_Cache_Snoop%ing_1.1.pdf`, February 2004.

[Gro]   Sandeep Grover. Buffer overflow attacks and their countermeasures. `http://www.linuxjournal.com/article.php?sid=6701`.

[Gro98]   Synchronized Multimedia Working Group. Synchronized multimedia integration language (SMIL) 1.0. Technical Report Recommendation REC-smil-19980615, World Wide Web Consortium, July 1998.

[GS95]   James D. Guyton and Michael F. Schwartz. Locating nearby copies of replicated Internet servers. In *Proceedings of ACM SIGCOMM*, pages 288–298, 1995.

[GSG02]   Krishna P. Gummadi, Stefan Saroiu, and Steven D. Gribble. King: Estimating latency between arbitrary Internet end hosts. In *Proceedings of the ACM SIGCOMM Internet Measurement Workshop*, pages 5–18, Marseilles, November 2002.

[GT00]   Ramesh Govindan and Hongsuda Tangmunarunkit. Heuristics for Internet map discovery. In *Proceedings of IEEE INFOCOM Conference*, pages 1371–1380, Tel Aviv, Israel, March 2000. IEEE.

[GW94]   Mark W. Garrett and Walter Willinger. Analysis, modeling and generation of self-similar VBR video traffic. In *Proceedings of ACM SIGCOMM*, pages 269–280, 1994.

[GW98]   Ian Goldberg and David Wagner. TAZ servers and the rewebber network enabling anonymous publishing on the World Wide Web. *First Monday*, 3(4), 1998.

[GZCF04]   Bamba Gueye, Artur Ziviani, Mark Crovella, and Serge Fdida. Constraint-based geolocation of Internet hosts. In *Proceedings of the ACM SIGCOMM Internet Measurement Conference*, 2004.

[H32]   H.323 forum. `http://www.h323forum.org/`.

[H3T]   Iec h.323 tutorial. `http://www.iec.org/online/tutorials/h323/`.

[Hal]   halflife. `http://www.halflife.com`.

[HB01]   Tristan Henderson and Saleem Bhatti. Modelling user behaviour in networked games. In *Proceedings of ACM Multimedia*, 2001.

[HB02]   Oliver Heckmann and Axel Bock. The eDonkey 2000 protocol, Dec 2002. Technical Report KOM-TR-08-2002, Multimedia Communications Lab, Darmstadt University of Technology.

[HBB00]   K. Harfoush, A. Bestavros, and J. Byers. Robust identification of shared losses using end-to-end unicast probes. In *ICNP '00: Proceedings of the 2000 International Conference on Network Protocols*, page 22, Washington, DC, USA, 2000. IEEE Computer Society.

[HBB02]   Khaled Harfoush, Azer Bestavros, and John Byers. PeriScope: An active measurement API. In *Proceedings of the Passive and Active Measurement Workshop*, Mar 2002.

[HBB03]   Khaled Harfoush, Azer Bestavros, and John Byers. Measuring bottleneck bandwidth of targeted path segments. In *Proceedings of IEEE INFOCOM Conference*, March 2003.

[HBCP98]   M. Harchol-Balter, M. E. Crovella, and S. Park. The case for SRPT scheduling in Web servers. Technical Report MIT-LCS-TR-767, MIT Lab for Computer Science, October 1998.

[HBkC03]   Young Hyun, Andre Broido, and kc Claffy. On third-party addresses in traceroute paths. In *Proceedings of the Passive and Active Measurement Workshop*, La Jolla, CA, April 2003.

[Hei]   Florian Heinz. Nameserver transfer protocol–nstx. `http://nstx.dereference.de/nstx`.

[Hei90]   Steven A. Heimlich. Traffic characterization of the NSFNET national backbone. In *Proceedings of ACM SIGMETRICS*, pages 257–258, 1990.

[Hen01]   Tristan Henderson. Latency and user behaviour on a multiplayer game server. In *Proceedings of the Third International COST264 Workshop (NGC 2001)*, pages 1–13. LNCS 2233,Springer-Verlag, November 2001.

[Hen03]   Jeffrey Henning. The blogging iceberg. `http://www.perseus.com/blogsurvey/`, October 2003.

[HH94]   Andy Harter and Andy Hopper. A distributed location system for the active office. *IEEE Network*, 8(1), 1994.

[HHB+03]   R. Huebsch, J. M. Hellerstein, N. L. Boon, T. Loo, S. Shenker, and I. Stoica. Querying the Internet with PIER. In *Proceedings of the International Conference on Very Large Databases*, September 2003.

[HHP03a]   A. Hussain, J. Heidemann, and C. Papadopoulos. COSSACK: Coordinated suppression of simultaneous attacks. In *Proceedings DISCEX*, 2003.

[HHP03b]   Alefiya Hussain, John Heidemann, and Christos Papadopoulos. A framework for classifying denial of service attack. In *Proceedings of ACM SIGCOMM*, August 2003.

[HHS+99]   Andy Harter, Andy Hopper, Pete Steggles, Andy Ward, and Paul Webster. The anatomy of a context-aware application. In *Mobile Computing and Networking*, pages 59–68, 1999.

[HKA04]   Tristan Henderson, David Kotz, and Ilya Abyzov. The changing usage of a mature campus-wide wireless network. In *Proceedings of the Tenth Annual International Conference on Mobile Computing and Networking (MobiCom)*, pages 187–201. ACM Press, September 2004.

[HL99]   D. P. Heyman and T. V. Lakshman. Long-range dependence and queueing effects for VBR video. In Kihong Park and Walter Willinger, editors, *Self-Similar Network Traffic and Performance Evaluation*. Wiley / Wiley Interscience, New York, 1999.

[HN99]   Allan Heydon and Marc Najork. Mercator: A scalable, extensible Web crawler. *World Wide Web*, 2(4), 1999.

[Hog]   Trevor Hogan. Half-life television. `http://www.planethalflife.com/features/articles/hltv/`.

[Hot]   100hot Web rankings. `http://100hot.com`.

[Hot94]   Steven Michael Hotz. *Routing Information Organization to Support Scalable Interdomain Routing with Heterogeneous Path Requirements*. PhD thesis, University of Southern California, Los Angeles, California,, September 1994.

[HPMkc02]   B. Huffaker, D. Plummer, D. Moore, and k claffy. Topology discovery by active probing. In *Symposium on Applications and the Internet (SAINT)*, 2002.

[HS02]   Hung-Yun Hsieh and Raghupathy Sivakumar. A transport layer approach for achieving aggregate bandwidths on multi-homed mobile hosts. In *Proceedings of ACM MOBI-COM*, Sep 2002.

[HS03]   G. R. Hjaltason and H. Samet. Properties of embedding methods for similarity searching in metric spaces. *IEEE Transactions on Pattern Analysis and Machine Intelligence*, 25(5):530–549, May 2003.

[HS04]   Hung-Yun Hsieh and Raghupathy Sivakumar. On transport layer support for peer-to-peer networks. In *Proceedings of the International Peer to Peer Symposium*, 2004.

[HSBR99]   S. Handelman, S. Stibler, N. Brownlee, and G. Ruth. RTFM: New attributes for traffic flow measurement. RFC 2724. Available at http://www.ietf.org, October 1999.

[Huf]   Bradley Huffaker. AS ranking report. Available at http://www.caida.org/analysis/topology/rank_as/.

[Hui95]   Christian Huitema. *Routing in the Internet*. Prentice Hall, 1995.

[Hun]   Send-Safe Honeypot Hunter. http://www.send-safe.com/honeypot-hunter.php.

[Hus99a]   Geoff Huston. Interconnection, peering, and settlements, part I. *Internet Protocol Journal*, March 1999.

[Hus99b]   Geoff Huston. Interconnection, peering, and settlements, part II. *Internet Protocol Journal*, June 1999.

[Hus05]   Geoff Huston. AS1221 BGP table data. Available at http://bgp.potaroo.net, 2005.

[HV03]   Nicolas Hohn and Darryl Veitch. Inverting sampled traffic. In *Proceedings of the ACM SIGCOMM Internet Measurement Conference*, November 2003.

[HVA02]   Nicolas Hohn, Darryl Veitch, and Patrice Abry. Does fractal scaling at the IP level depend on TCP flow arrival processes? In *Proceedings of the ACM SIGCOMM Internet Measurement Workshop*, pages 63–68, Marseilles, November 2002.

[IBe]   i-bench. http://www.veritest.com/benchmarks/i-bench/.

[ICBD04]   Gianluca Iannaccone, Chen-Nee Chuah, Supratik Bhattacharyya, and Christophe Diot. Feasibility of IP restoration in a tier-1 backbone. *IEEE Networks Magazine, Special Issue on Protection, Restoration and Disaster Recovery*, March 2004.

[ICM$^+$02] Gianluca Iannaccone, Chen-nee Chuah, Richard Mortier, Supratik Bhattacharyya, and Christophe Diot. Analysis of link failures in an IP backbone. In *Proceedings of the ACM SIGCOMM Internet Measurement Workshop*, pages 237–242, Marseilles, November 2002.

[IDGM01]   Gianluca Iannaccone, Christophe Diot, Ian Graham, and Nick McKeown. Monitoring very high speed links. In *Proceedings of the ACM SIGCOMM Internet Measurement Workshop*, November 2001.

[Iim04]   Iimura. Zoned federations. In *Proceedings of the Workshop on Network and System Support for Games*, 2004.

[INI]   InterNIC: The Internet's network information center. http://www.internic.net.

[Inta]   Internet Engineering Task Force. Internet official protocol standards. STD 1. Available at http://www.ietf.org/.

[Intb]   Internet2. http://www.internet2.edu.

[Intc]   Internet health report. http://www.internethealthreport.com/.

[Intd]   Mcafee network protection Intrushield. http://www.mcafeesecurity.com/us/products/mcafee/network_ips/1200.htm.

[Int05a]   Internet world stats. http://www.internetworldstats.com/stats.htm, November 2005.

[Int05b]   Internet world stats news. http://www.internetworldstats.com/pr/

edi007.htm, June 2005.

[InX] Internet exchange point. `http://en.wikipedia.org/wiki/Internet_exchange_point`.

[IOS] Cisco-IOS firewall feature set. `http://www.cisco.com/en/US/products/sw/iosswrel/ps1830/products_feature_guide09186a008008789d.html`.

[Irl94] Gordon Irlam. Unix file size survey - 1993. Available at `http://www.base.com/gordoni/ufs93.html`, September 1994.

[IRR] Overview of the IRR. `http://www.irr.net/docs/overview.html`.

[Isa60] W. Isard. *Methods of Regional Analysis*. MIT Press, 1960.

[Ise97] David S. Isenberg. Rise of the stupid network. *Computer Telephony*, pages 16–26, Aug 1997.

[Iye02] Vijay S. Iyengar. Transforming data to satisfy privacy constraints. In *Proceedings of the eighth ACM SIGKDD international conference on Knowledge discovery and data mining*, pages 279–288, 2002.

[Jac88] V. Jacobson. Congestion avoidance and control. In *Proceedings of ACM SIGCOMM*, pages 314–329, New York, NY, USA, 1988. ACM Press.

[Jac97] Van Jacobson. Pathchar – a tool to infer characteristics of Internet paths. ftp://ftp.ee.lbl.gov/pathchar/msri-talk.pdf, 1997.

[Jan02] J. Jannotti. Network layer support for overlay networks. In *Proc. of IEEE OPENARCH 2002*, 2002.

[JD02] Manish Jain and Constantinos Dovrolis. End-to-end available bandwidth: Measurement methodology, dynamics, and relation with TCP throughput. In *Proceedings of ACM SIGCOMM*, pages 295–308, Pittsburgh, PA, August 2002.

[JD03] Hao Jiang and Constantinos Dovrolis. Source-level IP packet bursts: causes and effects. In *Proceedings of the ACM SIGCOMM Internet Measurement Conference*, November 2003.

[JD04a] Manish Jain and Constantinos Dovrolis. Ten fallacies and pitfalls on end-to-end available bandwidth estimation. In *Proceedings of the ACM SIGCOMM Internet Measurement Conference*, 2004.

[JD04b] Hao Jiang and Constantinos Dovrolis. The effect of flow capacities on the burstiness of aggregated traffic. In *Proceedings of the Passive and Active Measurement Workshop*, Juan Les Pins, France, April 2004.

[JD05] Manish Jain and Constantinos Dovrolis. End-to-end estimation of the available bandwidth variation range. *Proceedings of ACM SIGMETRICS*, 33(1):265–276, 2005.

[Jen03] Jens Knoell. Honeypots: Using specialized honeypots to build up-to-date spam blacklists? `http://seclists.org/lists/honeypots/2003/Jul-Sep/0253.html`, September 2003.

[Jib] Jib Jab. `http://www.jibjab.com`.

[JID⁺03] S. Jaiswal, G. Iannaccone, C. Diot, J. Kurose, and D. Towsley. Measurement and classification of out-of-sequence packets in a tier-1 IP backbone. In *Proceedings of IEEE INFOCOM Conference*, San Francisco, March 2003.

[JKB94a] N. L. Johnson, S. Kotz, and N. Balakrishnan. *Continuous Univariate Distributions*, volume 1. Wiley-Interscience, 2 edition, 1994.

[JKB94b] N. L. Johnson, S. Kotz, and N. Balakrishnan. *Continuous Univariate Distributions*, volume 2. Wiley-Interscience, 1994.

[JKK94] N. L. Johnson, S. Kotz, and A. Kemp. *Univariate Discrete Distributions*. Wiley-Interscience, 1994.

[JKR02] Jayeon Jung, Balachander Krishnamurthy, and Michael Rabinovich. Flash crowds and denial of service attacks: Characterization and implications for CDNs and Web sites. In

Proceedings of the World Wide Web Conference, May 2002.

[JL84]   W. B. Johnson and J. Lindenstrauss. Extensions of Lipschitz mappings into a Hilbert space. In *Conference in modern analysis and probability*, pages 189–206. Amer. Math. Soc., 1984.

[JMSS05]   Theodore Johnson, S. Muthukrishnan, Oliver Spatscheck, and Divesh Srivastava. Streams, security and scalability. In *19th IFIP WG11.3 Working Conference on Data and Application Security*, volume 3654 of *LNCS*, pages 1–15, August 2005.

[Joh05]   Andreas Johnsson. Bandwidth measurements in wired and wireless networks. Technical report, Department of Computer Science and Electronics, Malardalen University, Vasteras, Sweden, April 2005.

[Jos]   Joseph Corey. Local honeypot identification. `http://www.phrack.org/fakes/p62/p62-0x07.txt`.

[Joy01]   Sarah K. Joyce. Traffic on the Internet–a study of Internet games. Technical Report 1, Department of Computer Science, University of Waikato, NZ, April 2001.

[JPP92]   J. Jedwab, P. Phaal, and B. Pinna. Estimation for the largerst sources on a network, using packet sampling with limited storage. Technical Report HPL-92-35, HP Laboratories Bristol, March 1992.

[JR86]   R. Jain and S. A. Routhier. Packet trains – measurements and a new model for computer network traffic. *IEEE Journal on Selected Areas in Communications*, 4:986–994, Sept 1986.

[JRF$^+$01] Y. Joo, V. Ribeiro, A. Feldmann, A. C. Gilbert, and W. Willinger. TCP/IP traffic dynamics and network performance: A lesson in workload modeling, flow control, and trace-driven simulations. *SIGCOMM Computer Communications Review*, 31(2), Apr 2001.

[JS00]   W. Jiang and H. Schulzrinne. Modeling of packet loss and delay and their effect on real-time multimedia service quality. In *Proc. NOSSDAV*, 2000.

[JSBM01]   Jaeyeon Jung, Emil Sit, Hari Balakrishnan, and Robert Morris. DNS performance and the effectiveness of caching. In *Proceedings of the ACM SIGCOMM Internet Measurement Workshop*, November 2001.

[JT03]   Guojun Jin and Brian Tierney. System capability effect on algorithms for network bandwidth measurement. In *Proceedings of the ACM SIGCOMM Internet Measurement Conference*, November 2003.

[JVC$^+$03] T Jehaes, D Vleeschauwer, T Coppens, B Doorselaer, E Deckers, W Naudts, K. Spruyt, and R. Smets. Access network delay in networked games. In *Proceedings of the Workshop on Network and System Support for Games*, August 2003.

[JW97]   J. Jerkins and J.L. Wang. A measurement analysis of ATM cell-level aggregate traffic. In *Proceedings of IEEE GLOBECOM*, pages 1589–1595, November 1997.

[KA01]   Balachander Krishnamurthy and Martin Arlitt. PRO-COW: Protocol compliance on the Web—a longitudinal study. In *Proceedings of the USENIX Symposium on Internet Technologies and Systems*, March 2001.

[Kam]   Dan Kaminsky. Doxpara research. `http://www.doxpara.com`, 29 July 2004.

[Kaz]   Kazaa. `http://en.wikipedia.org/wiki/Kazaa`.

[KBFC04]   Thomas Karagiannis, Andre Broido, Michalis Faloutsos, and K Claffy. Transport layer identification of P2P traffic. In *Proceedings of the ACM SIGCOMM Internet Measurement Conference*, October 2004.

[KCC$^+$03] Sailesh Krishnamurthy, Sirish Chandrasekaran, Owen Cooper, Amol Deshpande, Michael J. Franklin, Joseph M. Hellerstein, Wei Hong, Samuel R. Madden, Vijayshankar Raman, Fred Reiss, and Mehul A. Shah. TelegraphCQ: An architectural status report. *IEEE Data Engineering Bulletin*, 26(1):11–18, 2003.

[KCL+04]   Rohit Kapoor, Ling-Jyh Chen, Li Lao, Mario Gerla, and M. Y. Sanadidi. Capprobe: a simple and accurate capacity estimation technique. *Proceedings of ACM SIGCOMM*, 34(4):67–78, 2004.

[KE02]   David Kotz and Kobby Essien. Analysis of a campus-wide wireless network. In *Proceedings of ACM Mobicom*, pages 107–118, September 2002.

[KE05]   David Kotz and Kobby Essien. Analysis of a campus-wide wireless network. *Wireless Networks*, 11:115–133, 2005.

[Kes91]   Srinivasan Keshav. A control-theoretic approach to flow control. In *Proceedings of ACM SIGCOMM*, pages 3–15, New York, NY, USA, 1991. ACM Press.

[Keya]   Keynote. http://keynote.com.

[Keyb]   Ken Keys. Iffinder software. Available at http://www.caida.org/tools/measurement/iffinder/.

[Kfs]   KFSensor. http://www.keyfocus.net/kfsensor/.

[KH02]   Stas Khirman and Peter Henriksen. Relationship between quality-of-service and quality-of-experience for public Internet service. In *Proceedings of the Passive and Active Measurement Workshop*, Mar 2002.

[KI04]   Roger Kalden and Sami Ibrahim. Searching for self-similarity in GPRS. In *Proceedings of the Passive and Active Measurement Workshop*, Juan Les Pins, France, April 2004.

[KL86]   Brian Kantor and Phil Lapsley. Network News Transfer Protocol. RFC 977, IETF, February 1986.

[Kle76]   Leonard Kleinrock. *Queueing Systems*, volume II. Computer Applications. John Wiley & Sons, 1976.

[Kle98]   Jon Kleinberg. Authoritative sources in a hyperlinked environment. In *Proceedings of 9th ACM-SIAM Symposium on Discrete Algorithms*, 1998.

[KLR03]   Balachander Krishnamurthy, Richard Liston, and Michael Rabinovich. DEW: DNS-enhanced Web for faster content delivery. In *World Wide Web Conference 2003*, May 2003.

[KLVW04]   Alexander Klemm, Christoph Lindemanna, Mary K. Vernon, and Oliver P. Waldhorst. Characterizing the query behavior in peer-to-peer file sharing systems. In *Proceedings of the ACM SIGCOMM Internet Measurement Conference*, October 2004.

[KLXH04]   Bjorn Knutsson, Honghui Lu, Wei Xu, and Bryan Hopkins. Peer-to-peer support for massively multiplayer games. In *Proceedings of IEEE INFOCOM Conference*, Hong Kong, March 2004.

[KMC+00]   Eddie Kohler, Robert Morris, Benjie Chen, John Jannotti, and Frans Kaashoek. The click modular router. *ACM Transactions on Computer Systems*, 18(3):263–297, August 2000.

[KMK+01]   Ken Keys, David Moore, Ryan Koga, Edouard Lagache, Michael Tesch, and k claffy. The architecture of CoralReef: an Internet traffic monitoring software suite. In *Proceedings of the Passive and Active Measurement Workshop*. CAIDA, April 2001. http://www.caida.org/tools/measurement/coralreef/.

[KMP02]   Eddie Kohler, Robert Morris, and Massimiliano Poletto. Modular components for network address translation. In *Proceedings of OPENARCH '02*, June 2002.

[KMRV03]   Christopher Kruegel, Darren Mutz, William Robertson, and Fredrik Valeur. Topology-based detection of anomalous BGP messages. In *Recent Advances in Intrusion Detection (RAID)*, 2003.

[KMS05]   Balachander Krishnamurthy, Harsha Madhyastha, and Oliver Spatscheck. Atmen: A triggered network measurement infrastructure. In *World Wide Web Conference 2005*, May 2005.

[KMV05]   Balachander Krishnamurthy, Harsha Madhyastha, and Suresh Venkatasubramanian. On stationarity in Internet measurements through an information-theoretic lens. In *Network Database Workshop*, April 2005.

[KN74]   L. Kleinrock and W. Naylor. On the measured behavior of the ARPANetwork. In *AFIPS Conference Proceedings, National Computer Conference*, pages 767–780, May 1974.

[KN02]   Jorma Kilpi and Ilkka Norros. Testing the Gaussian approximation of aggregate traffic. In *Proceedings of the ACM SIGCOMM Internet Measurement Workshop*, pages 49–61, Marseilles, November 2002.

[KNR03]   Ravi Kumar, Jasmine Novak, and Prabhakar Raghavan. On the bursty evolution of blogspace. In *Proceedings of the World Wide Web Conference*, 2003.

[Koc04]   Peter Koch. DE DNS software survey. `http://www.ripe.net/ripe/meetings/ripe-48/presentations/ripe48-dns-surv%ey.pdf`, May 2004. RIPE Meetings archives.

[Koe04]   Wallace Koehler. A longitudinal study of Web pages continued: a consideration of document persistence. *Information research: an international electronic journal*, 9(2), January 2004.

[Koh]   Eddie Kohler. ipsumdump. `http://www.cs.ucla.edu/~kohler/ipsumdump/`.

[Koh00]   Eddie Kohler. The click modular router. Technical report, Department of Computer Science, MIT, November 2000.

[Koh06]   Eddie Kohler. Click for measurement. Technical Report TR060010, Department of Computer Science, UCLA, February 2006.

[KR00]   James F. Kurose and Keith W. Ross. *Computer Networking: A Top-Down Approach Featuring the Internet*. Addison-Wesley, July 2000. ISBN 0201477114.

[KR01]   Balachander Krishnamurthy and Jennifer Rexford. *Web Protocols and Practice: HTTP/1.1, Network Protocols, Caching, and Traffic Measurement*. Addison-Wesley, 2001.

[Kri04]   Balachander Krishnamurthy. Mohonk: Mobile honeypots to trace unwanted traffic early. In *ACM SIGCOMM Network Troubleshooting Workshop*, 2004.

[KSZC03]   Balachander Krishnamurthy, Subhabrata Sen, Yin Zhang, and Yan Chen. Sketch-based change detection: Methods, evaluation, and applications. In *Proceedings of the ACM SIGCOMM Internet Measurement Conference*, November 2003.

[KW97]   Balachander Krishnamurthy and Craig Wills. Study of piggyback cache validation for proxy caches in the World Wide Web. In *Proceedings of the USENIX Symposium on Internet Technologies and Systems*, pages 1–12, December 1997.

[KW98]   Balachander Krishnamurthy and Craig E. Wills. Piggyback server invalidation for proxy cache coherency. In *Proceedings of the World Wide Web Conference*, April 1998.

[KW00]   Balachander Krishnamurthy and Jia Wang. On network-aware clustering of Web clients. In *Proceedings of ACM Sigcomm*, August 2000.

[KW02a]   Balachander Krishnamurthy and Jia Wang. Traffic classification for application specific peering. In *Proceedings of the ACM SIGCOMM Internet Measurement Workshop*, November 2002.

[KW02b]   Balachander Krishnamurthy and Craig E. Wills. Improving Web performance by client characterization driven server adaptation. In *Proceedings of the World Wide Web Conference*, May 2002.

[KWX01]   Balachander Krishnamurthy, Jia Wang, and Yinglian Xie. Early measurements of a cluster-based architecture for P2P systems. In *Proceedings of the ACM SIGCOMM Internet Measurement Workshop*, November 2001.

[KWZ01]   Balachander Krishnamurthy, Craig Wills, and Yin Zhang. On the use and performance of content distribution networks. In *Proceedings of the ACM SIGCOMM Internet Mea-*

surement Workshop, San Francisco, November 2001.

[KWZV03] Balachander Krishnamurthy, Craig E. Wills, Yin Zhang, and Kashi Vishwanath. Design, implementation, and evaluation of a client characterization driven Web server. In *Proceedings of the World Wide Web Conference*, May 2003.

[KXLW04] Abishek Kumar, Jim Xu, Li Li, and Jia Wang. Space-code bloom filter for efficient traffic flow measurement. In *Proceedings of IEEE INFOCOM Conference*, March 2004.

[LABC03] Tanja Lang, G. Armitage, P. Branch, and H. Choo. A synthetic traffic model for Half-Life. In *Australian Telecommunications Networks and Applications Conference*, December 2003.

[LABJ01] C. Labovitz, A. Ahuja, A. Bose, and F. Jahanian. Delayed Internet routing convergence. *IEEE/ACM Transactions on Networking*, 9(3):293–306, June 2001.

[LAJ99] Craig Labovitz, Abha Ahuja, and Farnam Jahanian. Experimental study of Internet stability and wide-area network failures. In *Proceedings of IEEE FTCS*, June 1999.

[Lam83] Butler W. Lampson. Hints for computer system design. *Proceedings of the Ninth SOSP, in Operating Systems Review*, 17(5):33–48, October 1983.

[Lan] Lance Spitzner. Honeypots: Definitions and value of honeypots. `http://www.tracking-hackers.com/papers/honeypots.html`.

[LAWD04] Lun Li, David Alderson, Walter Willinger, and John Doyle. A first-principles approach to understanding the Internet's router-level topology. In *Proceedings of ACM SIGCOMM*, pages 3–14, New York, NY, USA, 2004. ACM Press.

[LB00] Kevin Lai and Mary Baker. Measuring link bandwidths using a deterministic model of packet delay. In *Proceedings of ACM SIGCOMM*, pages 283–294, New York, NY, USA, 2000. ACM Press.

[LB01] Kevin Lai and Mary Baker. Nettimer: A tool for measuring bottleneck link bandwidth. In *Proc. USENIX Symp. on Internet Technologies and Systems*, March 2001.

[LBA04] Tanja Lang, P. Branch, and G. Armitage. A synthetic traffic model for Quake3. In *Proceedings of ACM SIGCHI ACE2004 conference*, June 2004.

[LBCM03] Anukool Lakhina, John W. Byers, Mark Crovella, and Ibrahim Matta. On the geographic location of Internet resources. *IEEE Journal on Selected Areas in Communications, Special Issue on Internet and WWW Measurement, Mapping, and Modeling*, 2003.

[LBCX03] Anukool Lakhina, John Byers, Mark Crovella, and Peng Xie. Sampling biases in IP topology measurements. In *Proceedings of IEEE INFOCOM Conference*, March 2003.

[LC01] Jun Liu and Mark E. Crovella. Using loss pairs to discover network properties. In *Proceedings of the ACM SIGCOMM Internet Measurement Workshop*, pages 127–138, Nov 2001.

[LC05] Xiapu Luo and Rocky K.C. Chang. Novel approaches to end-to-end packet reordering measurement. In *Proceedings of the ACM SIGCOMM Internet Measurement Conference*, 2005.

[LCD04a] Anukool Lakhina, Mark Crovella, and Christophe Diot. Characterization of network-wide anomalies in traffic flows. In *Proceedings of the ACM SIGCOMM Internet Measurement Conference*, October 2004.

[LCD04b] Anukool Lakhina, Mark Crovella, and Christophe Diot. Diagnosing network-wide traffic anomalies. In *Proceedings of ACM SIGCOMM*, August 2004.

[LCD05] Anukool Lakhina, Mark Crovella, and Christophe Diot. Mining anomalies using traffic feature distributions. In *Proceedings of ACM SIGCOMM*, August 2005.

[Lei] Simon Leinen. FloMA: Pointers and software. Available at `http://www.switch.ch/tf-tant/floma/software.html`.

[LHC03] Hyuk Lim, Jennifer C. Hou, and Chong-Ho Choi. Constructing Internet coordinate system based on delay measurement. In *Proceedings of the ACM SIGCOMM Internet*

Measurement Conference, 2003.

[LHFC03]   T. Lee, B. Huffaker, M. Fomenkov, and K. Claffy. On the problem of optimization of DNS root servers' placement. In *Proceedings of the Passive and Active Measurement Workshop*, La Jolla, CA, April 2003.

[Lim]   Limewire. http://www.limewire.com.

[lin]   MMOG active subscriptions 18.0, 120,000+. http://www.mmogchart.com/ Chart1.html.

[LLH+03]   Jinyang Li, Boon Thau Loo, Joe Hellerstein, Frans Kaashoek, David R. Karger, and Robert Morris. On the feasibility of peer-to-peer Web indexing and search. In *Proceedings of the International Peer to Peer Symposium*, 2003.

[LLR95]   N. Linial, E. London, and Yu. Rabinovich. The geometry of graphs and some of its algorithmic implications. *Combinatorica*, 15:215–245, 1995.

[LMC99]   Cheng Liao, Margaret Martonosi, and Douglas W. Clark. Experience with an adaptive globally-synchronizing clock algorithm. In *SPAA '99: Proceedings of the eleventh annual ACM symposium on Parallel algorithms and architectures*, pages 106–114, New York, NY, USA, 1999. ACM Press.

[LMJ98]   Craig Labovitz, G. Robert Malan, and Farnam Jahanian. Internet routing instability. *IEEE/ACM Transactions on Networking*, 6(5):515–528, 1998.

[LMJ99]   Craig Labovitz, G. Robert Malan, and Farnam Jahanian. Origins of Internet routing instability. In *Proceedings of IEEE INFOCOM Conference*, 1999.

[Lor]   Scott Lorenz. Is your Web site ready for the flash crowd? http://www. westwindcos.com/pdf/sunserver_11900.pdf.

[Lot]   Mark Lottor. Distribution by domain server software. http://www.isc.org/ index.pl?/ops/ds/reports/2005-07/dist-servsoft.php.

[LP03]   Karthik Lakshminarayanan and Venkata Padmanabhan. Some findings on the network performance of broadband hosts. In *Proceedings of the ACM SIGCOMM Internet Measurement Conference*, November 2003.

[LPC+04]   Anukool Lakhina, Konstantina Papagiannaki, Mark Crovella, Christophe Diot, Eric D. Kolaczyk, and Nina Taft. Structural analysis of network traffic flows. In *Proceedings of ACM SIGMETRICS / Performance*, June 2004.

[LPP04]   Karthik Lakshminarayanan, Venkata Padmanabhan, and Jitendra Padhye. Bandwidth estimation in broadband access networks. In *Proceedings of the ACM SIGCOMM Internet Measurement Conference*, 2004.

[LR02]   Dmitri Loguinov and Hayder Radha. End-to-end Internet video traffic dynamics: Statistical study and analysis. In *Proceedings of IEEE INFOCOM Conference*, New York, NY, June 2002.

[LRL05]   Xiliang Liu, Kaliappa Ravindran, and Dmitri Loguinov. Multi-hop probing asymptotics in available bandwidth estimation: Stochastic analysis. In *Proceedings of the ACM SIGCOMM Internet Measurement Conference*, 2005.

[LRS02]   Qin Lv, Sylvia Ratnasamy, and Scott Shenker. Can heterogeneity make Gnutella scalable? In *Proceedings of the International Peer to Peer Symposium*, 2002.

[LS01]   C. Lee and J. Stepanek. On future Global Grid communication performance. In *Proceedings of the 10th IEEE Heterogeneous Computing Workshop*, May 2001.

[LSB+05]   Sung-Ju Lee, Puneet Sharma, Sujata Banerjee, Sujoy Basu, and Rodrigo Fonseca. Measuring bandwidth between PlanetLab nodes. In *Proceedings of the Passive and Active Measurement Workshop*, April 2005.

[LSZ02]   Richard Liston, Sridhar Srinivasan, and Ellen Zegura. On the diversity in DNS performance measures. In *Proceedings of the ACM SIGCOMM Internet Measurement Workshop*, November 2002.

[LTWW93] W. Leland, M. Taqqu, W. Willinger, and D. Wilson. On the self-similar nature of Ethernet traffic. In *Proceedings of ACM SIGCOMM*, pages 183–193, September 1993.

[LTWW94] W.E. Leland, M.S. Taqqu, W. Willinger, and D.V. Wilson. On the self-similar nature of Ethernet traffic (extended version). *IEEE/ACM Transactions on Networking*, 2:1–15, 1994.

[LW91] W. E. Leland and D. V. Wilson. High time-resolution measurement and analysis of LAN traffic: Implications for LAN interconnection. In *Proceedings of IEEE INFOCOM Conference*, pages 1360–1366, April 1991.

[LY03] G. Liang and B. Yu. Maximum pseudo likelihood estimation in network tomography. In *Proceedings of IEEE INFOCOM Conference*, 2003.

[MA] M. Mathis and M. Allman. A framework for defining empirical bulk transfer capacity metrics. RFC 3148. Available at `http://www.ietf.org`.

[Mal05] Bradley Malin. Betrayed by my shadow: Learning data identify via trail matching. *Journal of Privacy Technology*, June 2005.

[Man69] Benoit B. Mandelbrot. Long-run linearity, locally Gaussian processes, H-spectra and infinite variances. *Intern. Econom. Rev.*, 10:82–113, 1969.

[Man83] Benoit B. Mandelbrot. *The Fractal Geometry of Nature*. W. H. Freedman and Co., New York, 1983.

[Man97] Benoit B. Mandelbrot. *Fractals and Scaling in Finance*. Springer-Verlag, 1997.

[Map] The MAPS realtime blackhole list. `http://mail-abuse.org/rbl/`.

[Mat89] Georges Matheron. *Estimating and Choosing: An Essay on Probability in Practice*. Springer-Verlag, 1989.

[MB97] J. Marais and K. Bharat. Supporting cooperative and personal surfing with a desktop assistant. In *Proceedings of ACM UIST'97*, October 1997.

[MBGR03] Zhuoqing Mao, Randy Bush, Timothy Griffin, and Matthew Roughan. BGP beacons. In *Proceedings of the ACM SIGCOMM Internet Measurement Conference*, November 2003.

[MCC04] Matthew L. Massie, Brent N. Chun, and David E. Culler. The Ganglia distributed monitoring system: Design, implementation, and experience. *Parallel Computing*, 30(7), July 2004.

[MCD$^+$02] Zhuoqing Morley Mao, Charles D. Cranor, Fred Douglis, Michael Rabinovich, Oliver Spatscheck, and Jia Wang. A precise and efficient evaluation of the proximity between web clients and their local DNS servers. In *Proceedings of the USENIX Technical Conference*, Monterey, CA, June 2002.

[McL04] Laurianne McLaughlin. Bot software spreads, causes new worries. *IEEE Distributed Systems Online*, 5(6), June 2004.

[MDFK97] Jeffrey C. Mogul, Fred Douglis, Anja Feldmann, and Balachander Krishnamurthy. Potential benefits of delta encoding and data compression for HTTP. In *Proceedings of ACM SIGCOMM*, pages 181–194, August 1997.

[MF02] Olaf Maennel and Anja Feldmann. Realistic BGP traffic for test labs. In *Proceedings of ACM SIGCOMM*, pages 31–44, Pittsburgh, PA, August 2002.

[MFA] Third-party DNS validation tools. `http://dns.measurement-factory.com/tools/third-party-validation-tools/`.

[MFW01] R. Mahajan, S. Floyd, and D. Wetherall. Controlling high-bandwidth flows at the congested router. In *Proceedings of the ACM 9th International Conference on Network Protocols (ICNP)*, Nov 2001.

[MGW$^+$04] Izal M., Urvoy-Keller G, Biersack E. W., Felber P. A., A. Al Hamra, and L. Garces-Elice. Dissecting BitTorrent: Five months in a torrent's lifetime. In *Proceedings of the Passive and Active Measurement Workshop*, Juan Les Pins, France, April 2004.

[MH00]   Art Mena and John Heidemann. An empirical study of Real Audio traffic. In *Proceedings of IEEE INFOCOM Conference*, pages 101–110, March 2000.

[MHK+03]   Andrew Moore, James Hall, Christian Kreibich, Euan Harris, and Ian Pratt. Architecture of a network monitor. In *Proceedings of the Passive and Active Measurement Workshop*, La Jolla, CA, April 2003.

[MHLB04]   Anthony McGregor, Mark Hall, Perry Lorier, and James Brunskill. Flow clustering using machine learning techniques. In *Proceedings of the Passive and Active Measurement Workshop*, Juan Les Pins, France, April 2004.

[MIB+04]   Athina Markopoulou, Gianluca Iannaccone, Supratik Bhattacharyya, Chen-Nee Chuah, and Christophe Diot. Characterization of failures in an IP backbone. In *Proceedings of IEEE INFOCOM Conference*, Hong Kong, March 2004.

[Mic]   Microsoft xbox. http://www.xbox.com.

[Mic05]   Joerg Micheel. lambdaMON – a passive monitoring facility for DWDM optical networks. In *Proceedings of the Passive and Active Measurement Workshop*, 2005.

[Mil92]   David L. Mills. Network time protocol (version 3). RFC 1305. Available at http://www.ietf.org, March 1992.

[Mil98]   David L. Mills. Adaptive hybrid clock discipline algorithm for the network time protocol. *IEEE/ACM Transactions on Networking*, 6(5):505–514, 1998.

[Min97]   Greg Minshall. Tcpdpriv. http://ita.ee.lbl.gov/html/contrib/tcpdpriv.html, August 1997.

[MJ93]   Steven McCanne and Van Jacobson. The BSD packet filter: A new architecture for user-level packet capture. In *USENIX Winter Conference*, pages 259–270, 1993.

[MJ98a]   G. Robert Malan and Farnam Jahanian. An extensible probe architecture for network protocol performance measurement. In *Proceedings of ACM SIGCOMM*, 1998.

[MJ98b]   D. Mosberger and T. Jin. httperf—a tool for measuring Web server performance. In *Proceedings of Workshop on Internet Server Performance*, pages 59–67, June 1998.

[Mkc00]   S. McCreary and k. claffy. Trends in wide area IP traffic patterns - a view from Ames Internet Exchange. http://www.caida.org/outreach/papers/2000/AIX0005/, September 2000. ITC Specialist Seminar.

[MKD+02]   J. Mogul, B. Krishnamurthy, F. Douglis, A. Feldmann, Y. Goland, A. van Hoff, and D. Hellerstein. Delta encoding in HTTP. RFC 3229, IETF, January 2002. Proposed Standard.

[Mld]   Welcome to the world of MLDonkey. http://mldonkey.org.

[MLMB01]   Alberto Medina, Anukool Lakhina, Ibrahim Matta, and John Byers. BRITE: an approach to universal topology generation. In *Ninth IEEE International Symposium on Modeling, Analysis, and Simulation of Computer and Telecommunications Systems (MASCOTS'01)*, pages 346–356, 2001.

[MM96]   Matt Mathis and Jamshid Mahdavi. Diagnosing Internet congestion with a transport layer performance tool. In *Proceedings of INET'96*, June 1996.

[MM02]   Petar Maymounkov and David Mazieres. Kademlia: A peer-to-peer information system based on the XOR metric. In *Proceedings of the International Peer to Peer Symposium*, 2002.

[Mmo]   Welcome to MMOGCHART.COM. http://www.mmogchart.com.

[MMS]   Streaming download project, MMS streaming protocol.l. http://sdp.ppona.com/zipfiless/MMSprotocol_pdf.zip.

[Moc87a]   P. Mockapetris. Domain names—concepts and facilities. RFC 1034, IETF, November 1987.

[Moc87b]   P. Mockapetris. Domain names—implementation and specification. RFC 1035, IETF, November 1987.

[Mog]   Jeffrey C. Mogul. Trace anonymization misses the point. `http://www2002.org/presentations/mogul-n.pdf`. World Wide Web Conference 2002 Panel on Web Measurements.

[Mog90]   J. Mogul. Efficient use of workstations for passive monitoring of local area networks. In *Proceedings of ACM SIGCOMM*, pages 253–263. ACM Press, 1990.

[Mog92]   J. Mogul. Observing TCP dynamics in real networks. In *Proceedings of ACM SIGCOMM*, pages 305–317, 1992.

[Moo]   Don Moore. DNS server survey. `http://mydns.bboy.net/survey/`.

[Mos]   Most watched blogs. `http://blo.gs/most-watched.php`.

[MPDkc00]   David Moore, Ram Periakaruppan, Jim Donohoe, and k claffy. Where in the world is netgeo.caida.org? In *Proc. of INET'2000*, July 2000.

[MPS+03]   David Moore, Vern Paxson, Stefan Savage, Colleen Shannon, Stuart Staniford, and Nicholas Weaver. Inside the slammer worm. *IEEE Security and Privacy*, 1(4):33–39, 2003.

[MR]   K. McCloghrie and M. Rose. Management information base for network management of TCP/IP-based internets: MIB-II. IETF STD 17, RFC 1213. Available at `http://www.ietf.org`.

[MRA87]   J. Mogul, R. Rashid, and M. Accetta. The packet filter: an efficient mechanism for user-level network code. In *SOSP '87: Proceedings of the Eleventh ACM Symposium on Operating Systems Principles*, pages 39–51. ACM Press, 1987.

[MRTa]   Multi threaded routing toolkit. Available at `http://www.mrtd.net`.

[MRTb]   The multi router traffic grapher, MRTG. Available at `http://www.mrtg.org`.

[MRWK03]   Zhuoqing Morley Mao, Jennifer Rexford, Jia Wang, and R Katz. Towards an accurate AS-level traceroute tool. In *Proceedings of ACM SIGCOMM*, August 2003.

[MSkc02]   David Moore, Colleen Shannon, and k claffy. Code-Red: a case study on the spread and victims of an Internet worm. In *Proceedings of the ACM SIGCOMM Internet Measurement Workshop*, pages 273–284, Marseilles, November 2002.

[MSMO97]   M. Mathis, J. Semke, J. Mahdavi, and T. Ott. The macroscopic behavior of the TCP congestion avoidance algorithm. *SIGCOMM Computer Communications Review*, 27(3), July 1997.

[MST99]   Sue B. Moon, Paul Skelly, and Don Towsley. Estimation and removal of clock skew from network delay measurements. In *Proceedings of IEEE INFOCOM Conference*, March 1999.

[MSVS04]   David Moore, Colleen Shannon, Geoffrey M. Voelker, and Stefan Savage. Network telescopes. Technical Report TR-20040-04, CAIDA, 2004.

[MTS+02]   Alberto Medina, Nina Taft, Kave Salamatian, Supratik Bhattacharyya, and Christophe Diot. Traffic matrix estimation: Existing techniques and new directions. In *Proceedings of ACM SIGCOMM*, pages 161–174, Pittsburgh, PA, August 2002.

[MUK+04]   Tatsuya Mori, Masato Uchida, Ryoichi Kawahara, Jianping Pan, and Shigeki Goto. Identifying elephant flows through periodically sampled packets. In *Proceedings of the ACM SIGCOMM Internet Measurement Conference*, October 2004.

[Mut03]   S. Muthukrishnan. Data streams: Algorithms and applications. In *Proceedings of ACM-SIAM Symposium on Discrete Algorithms*, 2003.

[MVS01]   David Moore, Geoffrey M. Voelker, and Stefan Savage. Inferring Internet denial-of-service activity. In *Proceedings of the USENIX Security Symposium*, 2001.

[MW02]   Martin Mauve and Stefan Fischerand Jrg Widmer. A generic proxy system for networked computer games. In *Proceedings of the Workshop on Network and System Support for Games*, August 2002.

[MWA02]   Ratul Mahajan, David Wetherall, and Tom Anderson. Understanding BGP misconfiguration. In *Proceedings of ACM SIGCOMM*, 2002.

[MZX⁺04]   David Maltz, Jibin Zhan, Geoffrey Xie, Hui Zhang, Gisli Hjalmtysson, Jennifer Rexford, and Albert Greenberg. Structure preserving anonymization of router configuration data. In *Proceedings of the ACM SIGCOMM Internet Measurement Conference*, October 2004.

[Nap]   Napster. http://www.napster.com.

[NC04]   James Nichols and Mark Claypool. The effects of latency on online Madden NFL football. In *NOSSDAV, Proceedings of the 12th international workshop on Network and operating systems support for digital audio and video*, June 2004.

[NCR⁺03]   Eugene Ng, Yang-Hua Chu, Sanjay Rao, Kunwadee Sripanidkulchai, and Hui Zhang. Measurement-based optimization techniques for bandwidth-demanding peer-to-peer systems. In *Proceedings of IEEE INFOCOM Conference*, March 2003.

[Nei]   N. Neigus. Network logical map. RFC 432. Available at http://www.ietf.org.

[Neta]   Network Appliance, Inc. http://www.netapp.com.

[Netb]   Netcraft Web server survey. http://news.netcraft.com/archives/web_server_survey.html.

[Netc]   Introduction to Cisco IOS NetFlow - a technical overview. http://www.cisco.com/en/US/products/ps6601/products_white_paper0900aecd%80406232.shtml.

[Netd]   Site monitoring tool: Reliable service by Netmechanic. http://netmechanics.com/monitor.htm.

[Nete]   Netramet - a network traffic flow measurement tool. http://www.caida.org/tools/measurement/netramet/.

[Netf]   Nielsen Netratings. http://www.nielsen-netratings.com.

[Netg]   Netscaler. http://www.netscaler.com.

[neth]   The net world map project. Available at http://www.networldmap.com/.

[NFR]   Network flight recorder. http://www.nfr.com.

[NH01]   M. Najork and A. Heydon. High-performance Web crawling. Technical Report 173, Compaq Systems Research Center, September 2001.

[NHM⁺98]   Norifumi Nishikawa, Takafumi Hosokawa, Yasuhide Mori, Kenichi Yoshida, and Hiroshi Tsuji. Memory-based architecture for distributed WWW caching proxy. *Computer Networks and ISDN Systems*, 30:205–214, 1998.

[Nic03]   Nick Weaver. Wormholes and honeyfarm. In *WIP session: Usenix Security Symposium*, 2003.

[Nin]   Nintendo. http://www.nintendo.com.

[Niv71]   Larry Niven. Flash crowd. In *The Flight of the Horse*. Ballantine Books, 1971.

[NO74]   W. Naylor and H. Opderbeck. Mean round-trip times in the ARPANET. RFC 619. Available at http://www.ietf.org/, 1974.

[Nor94]   I. Norros. A storage model with self-similar input. *Queueing Systems*, 16:387–396, 1994.

[Nor99]   I. Norros. Queueing behavior under fractional Brownian traffic. In Kihong Park and Walter Willinger, editors, *Self-Similar Network Traffic and Performance Evaluation*. Wiley / Wiley Interscience, New York, 1999.

[NPB03]   A. Nakao, L. Peterson, and A. Bavier. A routing underlay for overlay networks. In *Proceedings of ACM SIGCOMM*, 2003.

[NSF]   Nsfnet statistics. Available at ftp://nic.merit.edu/nsfnet/statistics/.

[NT04]   Hung X. Nguyen and Patrick Thiran. Active measurement for multiple link failures diagnosis in IP networks. In *Proceedings of the Passive and Active Measurement Workshop*, Juan Les Pins, France, April 2004.

[ntp]   NTP: The network time protocol. Available at `http://www.ntp.org`.

[Nua]   How many online? Available at `http://www.nua.com`.

[NZ02]   E. Ng and H. Zhang. Predicting Internet network distance with coordinates-based approaches. In *Proceedings of IEEE INFOCOM Conference*, 2002.

[OB01]   P. Olivier and N. Benameur. Flow level IP traffic characterization. In *Proceedings of the International Teletraffic Congress (ITC-17)*, December 2001.

[Obr02]   Davor Obradovic. Real-time model and convergence time of BGP. In *Proceedings of IEEE INFOCOM Conference*, New York, NY, June 2002.

[OCH$^+$85] John K. Ousterhout, Hervé Da Costa, David Harrison, John a Kunze, Mike Kupfer, and James G. Thompson. A trace-driven analysis of the UNIX 4.2 BSD file system. In *Proceedings of the Tenth ACM Symposium on Operating System Principles*, pages 15–24, Orcas Island, WA, December 1985.

[Odl00]   Andrew Odlyzko. The history of communications and its implications for the Internet. Manuscript, 2000.

[Odl01]   Andrew M. Odlyzko. Internet growth: Myth and reality, use and abuse. *Journal of Computer Resource Management*, 102:23–27, 2001.

[ORe]   O'reilly P2P directory. `http://www.openp2p.com/pub/q/p2p_category`.

[O'S86]   Finbarr O'Sullivan. A statistical perspective on ill-posed inverse problems. *Statistical Science*, 1(4):503–527, 1986.

[Ove]   eDonkey2000 overnet. `http://overnet.com/`.

[Ove02]   Overlay routing neworks (akarouting). `http://www-math.mit.edu/~steng/18.996/lecture9.ps`, April 2002.

[owa]   OWAMP: One way active measurement protocol. Available at `http://e2epi.internet2.edu/owamp/`.

[P3P05]   The Platform for Privacy Preferences 1.1 (P3P1.1) specification. `http://www.w3.org/TR/P3P11`, July 2005.

[PACR02]   Larry Peterson, Tom Anderson, David Culler, and Timothy Roscoe. A blueprint for introducing disruptive technology into the Internet. In *Proceedings of HotNets–I*, October 2002.

[Pad95]   Venkata N. Padmanabhan. Improving World Wide Web latency. Technical Report UCB/CSD-95-875, University of California, Berkeley, May 1995.

[PAMM98]   Vern Paxson, Guy Almes, Jamsheed Mahdavi, and Matt Mathis. Framework for IP performance metrics. RFC 2330. Available at `http://www.ietf.org`, May 1998.

[Pax94a]   Vern Paxson. Empirically-derived analytic models of wide-area TCP connections. *IEEE/ACM Transactions on Networking*, 2(4):316–336, August 1994.

[Pax94b]   Vern Paxson. Growth trends in wide-area TCP connections. *IEEE Network*, 8(4):8–17, 1994.

[Pax95]   Vern Paxson. Fast approximation of self-similar network traffic. Technical Report LBL-36750, Lawrence Berkeley Laboratory, April 1995.

[Pax97a]   Vern Paxson. End-to-end routing behavior in the Internet. *IEEE/ACM Transactions on Networking*, 5(5):601–615, October 1997. Earlier version in Proc. SIGCOMM '96, Stanford, CA, August 1996.

[Pax97b]   Vern Paxson. *Measurements and Analysis of End-to-End Internet Dynamics*. PhD thesis, University of California, Berkeley, April 1997.

[Pax98]   Vern Paxson. On calibrating measurements of packet transit times. In *Proceedings of ACM SIGMETRICS / Performance*, pages 11–21, New York, NY, USA, 1998. ACM Press.

[Pax99a]   Vern Paxson. Bro: A system for detecting network intruders in real-time. *Computer Networks*, 31(23–24):2435–2463, December 1999.

[Pax99b]   Vern Paxson. End-to-end Internet packet dynamics. *IEEE/ACM Transactions on Networking*, 7(3):277–292, June 1999.

[Pax01]   Vern Paxson. Some not so pretty admissions about Internet measurements. Invited Talk, Workshop on Network-Related Data Management, 2001.

[PCB00]   N. B. Priyantha, A. Chakraborty, and H. Balakrishnan. The Cricket location-support system. In *The 6th Conference on Mobile Computing and Networking*, 2000.

[PCD03]   Konstantina Papagiannaki, Rene Cruz, and Christophe Diot. Network performance monitoring at small time scales. In *Proceedings of the ACM SIGCOMM Internet Measurement Conference*, November 2003.

[PCW+03]   Marcelo Pias, Jon Crowcroft, Steve Wilbur, Saleem Bhatti, and Tim Harris. Lighthouses for scalable distributed location. In *Second International Workshop on Peer-to-Peer Systems (IPTPS '03)*, Feb 2003.

[PD03]   Joseph D. Pellegrino and Constantinos Dovrolis. Bandwidth requirement and state consistency in three multiplayer game architectures. In *Proceedings of the Workshop on Network and System Support for Games*, 2003.

[PDM03]   Ravi Prasad, Constantinos Dovrolis, and Bruce Mah. The effect of layer-2 store-and-forward devices on per-hop capacity estimation. In *Proceedings of IEEE INFOCOM Conference*, March 2003.

[Pea]   Arbor networks Peakflow X. http://arbornetworks.com/products_x.php.

[Per99]   Radia Perlman. *Interconnections: Bridges, Routers, Switches, and Internetworking Protocols*. Addison-Wesley, 2nd edition, 1999.

[Peu01]   Markus Peuhkuri. A method to compress and anonymize packet traces. In *Proceedings of the ACM SIGCOMM Internet Measurement Workshop*, November 2001.

[PF94]   Vern Paxson and Sally Floyd. Wide-area traffic: The failure of Poisson modeling. In *Proceedings of ACM SIGCOMM*, 1994.

[PF95]   Vern Paxson and Sally Floyd. Wide-area traffic: The failure of Poisson modeling. *IEEE/ACM Transactions on Networking*, pages 226–244, June 1995.

[PF01]   Jitendra Padhye and Sally Floyd. On inferring TCP behavior. In *Proceedings of ACM SIGCOMM*, August 2001.

[PFTK98]   J. Padhye, V. Firoiu, D. Towsley, and J. Kurose. Modeling TCP throughput: A simple model and its empirical validation. In *Proceedings of ACM SIGCOMM*, pages 303–314, 1998.

[PFTV88]   William H. Press, Brian P. Flannery, Saul A. Teukolsky, and William T. Vetterling. *Numerical Recipes in C: The Art of Scientific Computing*. Cambridge University Press, 1988.

[PG98]   J. Pansiot and D. Grad. On routes and multicast trees in the Internet. *SIGCOMM Computer Communications Review*, 28(1):41–50, Jan 1998.

[PGB+04]   Thomas Plagemann, Vera Goebel, Andrea Bergamini, Giacomo Tolu, Guillaume Urvoy-Keller, and Ernst W. Biersack. Using data stream management systems for traffic analysis – a case study. In *Proceedings of the Passive and Active Measurement Workshop*, pages 215–226, 2004.

[PHH98]   C. Perkins, O. Hodson, and V. Hardman. A survey of packet-loss recovery techniques for streaming audio. *IEEE Network Magazine*, September/October 1998.

[PKC96]   Kihong Park, Gi Tae Kim, and Mark E. Crovella. On the relationship between file sizes, transport protocols, and self-similar network traffic. In *Proceedings of the Fourth International Conference on Network Protocols (ICNP'96)*, pages 171–180, October 1996.

[PKC97]   Kihong Park, Gitae Kim, and Mark E. Crovella. On the effect of traffic self-similarity on network performance. In *Proceedings of SPIE International Conference on Performance and Control of Network Systems*, November 1997.

[Plaa] An annotated bibliography of PlanetLab. `https://wiki.planet-lab.org/bin/view/Planetlab/AnnotatedBibliography`.

[Plab] Planetlab. `http://www.planet-lab.org`.

[Ploa] Dave Plonka. IP anonymization: ip2anonip. `http://dave.plonka.us/ip2anonip`.

[Plob] David Plonka. Flowscan software. Available at `http://dave.plonka.us/FlowScan/`.

[Plo00] D. Plonka. Flowscan: A network traffic flow reporting and visualization tool. In *Proc. USENIX 14th System Administration Conference*, Dec 2000.

[PMDkc03] Ravi Prasad, Margaret Murray, Constantinos Dovrolis, and kc claffy. Bandwidth estimation: metrics, measurement techniques, and tools. *IEEE Network*, November-December 2003.

[PMF⁺02] Konstantina Papagiannaki, Sue Moon, Chuck Fraleigh, Patrick Thiran, Fouad Tobagi, and Christophe Diot. Analysis of measured single-hop delay from an operational backbone network. In *Proceedings of IEEE INFOCOM Conference*, New York, NY, June 2002.

[PMM93] C. Partridge, T. Mendez, and W. Milliken. Host anycasting service. RFC 1546, IETF, November 1993.

[PN99] Ram Periakaruppan and Evi Nemeth. GTrace - a graphical traceroute tool. In *LISA '99: Proceedings of the 13th USENIX conference on System administration*, pages 69–78, Berkeley, CA, USA, 1999. USENIX Association.

[Pos81] J. Postel. Internet protocol. RFC 791. Available at `http://www.ietf.org/`, 1981.

[Pos94] J. Postel. Domain name system structure and delegation. RFC 1591, IETF, March 1994.

[PP03] Ruoming Pang and Vern Paxson. A high-level programming environment for packet trace anonymization and transformation. In *Proceedings of ACM SIGCOMM*, August 2003.

[PPM01] P. Phaal, S. Panchen, and N. McKee. InMon Corporation's sFlow: A method for monitoring traffic in switched and routed networks. RFC 3176. Available at `http://www.ietf.org`, 2001.

[PPPW04] KyoungSoo Park, Vivek S. Pai, Larry Peterson, and Zhe Wang. CoDNS: improving DNS performance and reliability via cooperative lookups. In *Proceedings of the Sixth Symposium on Operating Systems Design and Implementation(OSDI '04)*, 2004.

[PQW03] Venkata Padmanabhan, Lili Qiu, and Helen Wang. Server-based inference of Internet link lossiness. In *Proceedings of IEEE INFOCOM Conference*, March 2003.

[PR85] Jon Postel and Joyce Reynolds. File Transfer Protocol. RFC 959, IETF, October 1985.

[Pro03] Niels Provos. Honeyd – a virtual honeypot daemon. In *Proceeding of the 10th DFN-CERT Workshop*, February 2003.

[PS01] Venkata N. Padmanabhan and Lakshminarayanan Subramanian. An investigation of geographic mapping techniques for Internet hosts. In *Proceedings of ACM SIGCOMM*, August 2001.

[PS02] Venkata N. Padmanabhan and Kay Sripanidkulchai. The case for cooperative networking. In *Proceedings of the International Peer to Peer Symposium*, 2002.

[PSM] Packet sampling IETF working group charter. Internet-Draft. Available at `http://www.ietf.org/html.charters/psamp-charter.html`.

[PSV04] Romualdo Pastor-Satorras and Allesandro Vespignani. *Evolution and Structure of the Internet*. Cambridge University Press, Cambridge, UK, 2004.

[PSVV01] Romualdo Pastor-Satorras, Alexei Vázquez, and Alessandro Vespignani. Dynamical and correlation properties of the Internet. *Physical Review Letters*, 87(258701), 2001.

[PTL04]   Konstantina Papagiannaki, Nina Taft, and Anukool Lakhina. A distributed approach to measure IP traffic matrices. In *Proceedings of the ACM SIGCOMM Internet Measurement Conference*, October 2004.

[PTZD03]   Konstantina Papagiannaki, Nina Taft, Zhi-Li Zhang, and Christophe Diot. Long-term forecasting of Internet backbone traffic: Observations and initial models. In *Proceedings of IEEE INFOCOM Conference*, 2003.

[PV02a]   Attila Pasztor and Darryl Veitch. Active probing using packet quartets. In *Proceedings of the ACM SIGCOMM Internet Measurement Workshop*, pages 293–305, Marseilles, November 2002.

[PV02b]   Attila Pasztor and Darryl Veitch. PC based precision timing without GPS. In *Proceedings of ACM SIGMETRICS*, pages 1–10, Marina Del Rey, CA, June 2002.

[PV03]   Roberto Percacci and Alessandro Vespignani. Scale-free behavior of the Internet global performance. *The European Physical Journal B - Condensed Matter*, 32(4):411–414, April 2003.

[PW99]   Kihong Park and Walter Willinger, editors. *Self-Similar Network Traffic and Performance Evaluation*. Wiley / Wiley Interscience, New York, 1999.

[PW02]   Lothar Pantel and Lars Wolf. On the impact of delay on real-time multiplayer games. In *NOSSDAV, Proceedings of the 12th international workshop on Network and operating systems support for digital audio and video*, May 2002.

[PWC03]   Venkata Padmanabhan, Helen J. Wang, and P. A. Chou. Resilient peer-to-peer streaming. In *Proceedings of the International Conference on Network Protocols*, 2003.

[PYD01]   Sam Patton, Bill Yurcik, and David Doss. An Achilles' Heel in signature-based IDS: Squealing false positives in snort. In *Recent Advances in Intrusion Detection Workshop*, 2001.

[QML+04]   Peter Quax, Patrick Monsieurs, Wim Lamoote, Danny De Vleeschauwer, and Natalie Degrande. Objective and subjective evaluation of the influence of small amounts of delay and jitter on a recent first person shooter game. In *Proceedings of the Workshop on Network and System Support for Games*, September 2004.

[QP01]   L. Qiu and V. N. Padmanabhan. Server-centric view of Internet performance: Analysis and implications. Technical Report MSR-TR-2001-78, Microsoft Research, September 2001.

[Qst]   Real-time game server status. http://www.qstat.org.

[quaa]   The Quagga routing suite. Available at http://www.quagga.net.

[Quab]   Quake. http://www.quake.com.

[QZCZ04]   J. Quittek, T. Zseby, B. Claise, and S. Zander. Requirements for IP flow information export (IPFIX). RFC 3917, IETF, October 2004.

[RAD]   Routing assets database. http://www.radb.net.

[RCR+00]   V. Ribeiro, M. Coates, R. Riedi, S. Sarvotham, B. Hendricks, and R. Baraniuk. Multifractal cross-traffic estimation. In *ITC Conference on IP Traffic, Modeling and Management*, Monterey, CA, September 2000.

[RCRB99]   R. Riedi, M. Crouse, V. Ribeiro, and R. Baraniuk. A multifractal wavelet model with application to TCP network traffic. *IEEE Transactions on Information Theory*, 45(3), April 1999.

[RD01]   Antony Rowstron and Peter Druschel. Pastry: Scalable, decentralized object location, and routing for large-scale peer-to-peer systems. *Lecture Notes in Computer Science*, 2218, 2001.

[Red]   Redline networks. http://www.redlinenetworks.com.

[RFH+01]   Sylvia Ratnasamy, Paul Francis, Mark Handley, Richard Karp, and Scott Shenker. A scalable content-addressable network. In *Proceedings of ACM Sigcomm*, August 2001.

[RFQ] Routing assets database: Frequently asked questions. `http://www.radb.net/faq.html`.

[RGH+04] Jennifer Rexford, Albert Greenberg, Gisli Hjalmtysson, David A. Maltz, Andy Myers, Geoffrey Xie, Jibin Zhan, and Hui Zhang. Networkwide decision making: Toward a waferthin control plane. In *Proceedings of the Hot Topics in Networks Workshop*, 2004.

[RGK+03] Matthew Roughan, Albert Greenberg, Charles Kalmanek, Michael Rumsewicz, Jennifer Yates, and Yin Zhang. Experience in measuring Internet backbone traffic variability: Models, metrics, measurements and meaning. In *Proceedings of International Teletraffic Congress (ITC) 18*, 2003.

[RGM+04] Matthew Roughan, Tim Griffin, Morley Mao, Albert Greenberg, and Brian Freeman. Combining routing and traffic data for detection of IP forwarding anomalies. *SIGMETRICS Performance Evaluation Review*, 32(1):416–417, 2004.

[RHKS02] Sylvia Ratnasamy, Mark Handley, Richard Karp, and Scott Shenker. Topologically-aware overlay construction and server selection. In *Proceedings of IEEE INFOCOM Conference*, New York, NY, June 2002.

[RIP] RIPE database. `http://www.ripe.net`.

[Riv] Cisco threat defense systems. `http://www.cisco.com/en/US/netsol/ns340/ns394/ns171/ns441/net_value_proposition0900aecd8013402e.html`.

[Riv92] Ronald Rivest. *The MD5 Message-Digest Algorithm*, April 1992. RFC 1321.

[RK02] Sean C. Rhea and John Kubiatowicz. Probabilistic location and routing. In *Proceedings of IEEE INFOCOM Conference*, pages 1248–1257, 2002.

[RL95] Y. Rekhter and T. Li. A Border Gateway Protocol 4 (BGP-4). RFC 1771, IETF, March 1995.

[RM90] M. Rose and K. McCloghrie. Structure and identification of management information for TCP/IP-based Internets. RFC 1155. Available at `http://www.ietf.org`, 1990.

[RM99] Sylvia Ratnasamy and Steven McCanne. Inference of multicast routing trees and bottleneck bandwidths using end-to-end measurements. In *Proceedings of IEEE INFOCOM Conference*, pages 353–360, 1999.

[RMX] RMX: Defense against spam and e-mail forgery. `http://www.danisch.de/work/security/antispam.html`.

[Rob04] Jim Roberts. Internet traffic, QoS, and pricing. *Proceedings of the IEEE*, 92(9):1389–1399, Sept 2004.

[Ros02] Sheldon M. Ross. *Introduction to Probability Models*. Academic Press, eighth edition, 2002.

[Rou] Routeviews project. `http://www.routeviews.org`.

[Rou02] Matthew Roughan. SNMP: Simple network measurements please! Talk at invited presentation at the IPAM Workshop on "Large-Scale Communication Networks: Topology, Routing, Traffic, and Control", Institute for Pure and Applied Mathematics (IPAM), UCLA, USA. Available at `http://www.maths.adelaide.edu.au/people/mroughan/Papers/ipam2.pdf`, March 2002.

[Rou05] Matthew Roughan. Fundamental bounds on the accuracy of network performance measurements. In *Proceedings of ACM SIGMETRICS*, June 2005.

[RRB+03] Vinay Ribeiro, Rudolf Riedi, Richard Baraniuk, Jiri Navratil, and Les Cottrell. pathChirp: efficient available bandwidth estimation for network paths. In *Proceedings of the Passive and Active Measurement Workshop*, La Jolla, CA, April 2003.

[RRCB00] Vinay Ribeiro, Rudolf Riedi, Matthew Crouse, and Richard Baraniuk. Multiscale queuing analysis of long-range-dependent network traffic. In *Proceedings of IEEE INFOCOM Conference*, 2000.

[RSdM05a]   Amy Reibman, Shubharata Sen, and Jacobus Van der Merwe. Analyzing the spatial
            quality of Internet streaming video. In *Second International Workshop on Video Pro-
            cessing and Quality Metrics for Consumer Electronics (VPQM)*, January 2005.

[RSdM05b]   Amy Reibman, Shubharata Sen, and Jacobus Van der Merwe. Video quality estimation
            for Internet streaming, May 2005. Poster at World Wide Web Conference, WWW05.

[RTP]   RTP dump. `http://www.cs.columbia.edu/~hgs/rtp/rtpdump.html`.

[Rus00]   R. Russell. Linux IPCHAINS-HOWTO, v1.0.8. `http://www.linuxdoc.org/`
            `HOWTO/IPCHAINS-HOWTO.html`, July 2000.

[RV97]   R. H. Riedi and J. Levy Vehel. Multifractal properties of TCP traffic: a numerical study.
            Technical Report 3129, INRIA, March 1997.

[RVR98]   Matthew Roughan, Darryl Veitch, and Michael Rumsewicz. Computing queue-length
            distributions for power-law queues. In *Proceedings of IEEE INFOCOM Conference*,
            pages 356–363, 1998.

[RWXZ02]   Jennifer Rexford, Jia Wang, Zhen Xiao, and Yin Zhang. BGP routing stability of popular
            destinations. In *Proceedings of the ACM SIGCOMM Internet Measurement Workshop*,
            pages 197–202, Marseilles, November 2002.

[Sal]   Salon radio community server. `http://blogs.salon.com/rankings.html`.

[Sam01]   Pierangela Samarati. Protecting respondents' identities in microdata release. *IEEE
            Transactions on Knowledge Engineering*, 13(6):1010–1027, 2001.

[SARK02]   Lakshminarayanan Subramanian, Sharad Agarwal, Jennifer Rexford, and Randy Katz.
            Characterizing the Internet hierarchy from multiple vantage points. In *Proceedings of
            IEEE INFOCOM Conference*, New York, NY, June 2002.

[Sat81]   M. Satyanarayanan. A study of file sizes and functional lifetimes. In *Proceedings of the
            Eighth ACM Symposium on Operating System Principles*, December 1981.

[Sav99]   Stefan Savage. Sting: a TCP-based network measurement tool. In *Proceedings of the
            USENIX Symposium on Internet Technologies and Systems*, pages 71–79, October 1999.

[SCFJ96]   H. Schulzrinne, S. Casner, R. Frederick, and V. Jacobson. RTP: A transport protocol for
            real-time applications. RFC 1889, IETF, January 1996.

[Sch91]   Manfred Schroeder. *Fractals, Chaos, Power Laws*. W. H. Freeman and Company, 1991.

[Sch96]   Bruce Schneier. Applied cryptography second edition : protocols, algorithms, and source
            code in C, 1996.

[SCH+99]   Stefan Savage, Andy Collins, Eric Hoffman, John Snell, and Thomas E. Anderson. The
            end-to-end effects of Internet path selection. In *Proceedings of ACM SIGCOMM*, pages
            289–299, Boston, MA, August-September 1999.

[Sch03]   Paul M. Schwartz. German and U.S. telecommunications privacy law: Legal regulation
            of domestic law enforcement surveillance. *Hastings Law Journal*, 54:751–800, 2003.

[SCK00]   H. Sanneck, G. Carle, and R. Koodli. A framework model for packet loss metrics based
            on loss runlengths. In *Proceedings SPIE/ACM SIGMM Multimedia Computing and
            Networking Conference*, Jan 2000.

[Sco05]   Metro-Goldwyn-Mayer Studios Inc et. al. v. Grokster Ltd. et. al. `http://www.`
            `supremecourtus.gov/opinions/04pdf/04-480.pdf`, June 2005.

[Sec]   Internet security systems: Internet scanner. `http://documents.iss.net/`
            `literature/InternetScanner/is_ps.pdf`.

[SERZ02]   Christian Schaefer, Thomas Enderes, Hartmut Ritter, and Martina Zitterbart. Subjective
            quality assessment for multiplayer real-time games. In *Proceedings of the Workshop on
            Network and System Support for Games*, August 2002.

[SF02]   Robin Sommer and Anja Feldmann. NetFlow: information loss or win? In *Proceedings
            of the ACM SIGCOMM Internet Measurement Workshop*, pages 173–174, Marseilles,
            November 2002.

[SF03]   Kavé Salamatian and Serge Fdida. A framework for interpreting measurement over Internet. In *Proceedings of the ACM SIGCOMM Workshop on Models, Methods and Tools for Reproducible Network Research*, pages 87–94, August 2003.

[SFFF03]   G. Siganos, M. Faloutsos, P. Faloutsos, and C. Faloutsos. Powerlaws and the AS-level Internet topology. *IEEE/ACM Transactions on Networking*, 11(4):514–524, Aug 2003.

[SG01]   Aman Shaikh and Albert Greenberg. Experience in black-box OSPF measurement. In *Proceedings of the ACM SIGCOMM Internet Measurement Workshop*, Nov 2001.

[SG03]   Clint Smith and Curt Gervelis. *Wireless Network Performance Handbook*. McGraw Hill, May 2003. ISBN 0-0714-0655-7.

[SGG02]   Stefan Saroiu, Krishna Gummadi, and Steve Gribble. A measurement study of peer-to-peer file sharing systems. In *Proceedings of Multimedia Computing and Networking (MMCN)*, January 2002.

[SGPC04]   Robert Schweller, Ashish Gupta, Elliot Parsons, and Yan Chen. Reversible sketches for efficient and accurate change detection over network data streams. In *Proceedings of the ACM SIGCOMM Internet Measurement Conference*, October 2004.

[SH98]   M. Sullivan and A. Heybey. Tribeca: A system for managing large databases of network traffic. In *Proceedings of the USENIX Annual Techical Conference*, 1998.

[Sha]   Shaheem Motlekar. Honeypots: Frequently asked questions. `http://www.tracking-hackers.com/misc/faq.html`.

[SIG+02]   Aman Shaikh, Chris Isett, Albert Greenberg, Matthew Roughan, and Joel Gottlieb. A case study of OSPF behavior in a large enterprise network. In *Proceedings of the ACM SIGCOMM Internet Measurement Workshop*, pages 217–230, Marseilles, November 2002.

[Sim55]   H. A. Simon. On a class of skew distribution functions. *Biometrika*, 42:425–440, 1955.

[SKK03]   Jacob Strauss, Dina Katabi, and Frans Kaashoek. A measurement study of available bandwidth estimation tools. In *Proceedings of the ACM SIGCOMM Internet Measurement Conference*, November 2003.

[Sla]   Slammer worm. `http://vil.nai.com/vil/content/v_99992.htm`.

[SLT+05]   Augustin Soule, Anukool Lakhina, Nina Taft, Konstantina Papagiannaki, Kave Salamatian, Antonio Nucci, Mark Crovella, and Christophe Diot. Traffic matrices: Balancing measurements, inference and modeling. In *Proceedings of ACM SIGMETRICS*, June 2005.

[Sly]   Slyck's database of file sharing programs. `http://slyck.com/programs.php?cat=2`.

[SM04]   C. Shannon and D. Moore. The spread of the Witty worm. *IEEE Security and Privacy*, 2(4):46–50, 2004.

[SMA03]   Neil Spring, Ratul Mahajan, and Tom Anderson. Quantifying the causes of path inflation. In *Proceedings of ACM SIGCOMM*, August 2003.

[SMB02]   T. Stading, P. Maniatis, and M. Baker. Peer-to-peer caching schemes to address flash crowds. In *Proceedings of the International Peer to Peer Symposium*, 2002.

[SMD03]   Ashwin Sridharan, Sue Moon, and Christophe Diot. On the correlation between route dynamics and routing loops. In *Proceedings of the ACM SIGCOMM Internet Measurement Conference*, November 2003.

[SMH+05]   Alok Shriram, Margaret Murray, Young Hyun, Nevil Brownlee, Andre Broido, Marina Fomenkov, and kc claffy. Comparison of public end-to-end bandwidth estimation tools on high-speed links. In *Proceedings of the Passive and Active Measurement Workshop*, volume 3431, pages 306–320, 2005.

[Smi]   World Wide Web consortium, synchronized multimedia. `http://www.w3.org/AudioVideo/`.

[SMK+01]　Ion Stoica, Robert Morris, David Karger, Frans Kaashoek, and Hari Balakrishnan. Chord: A scalable peer-to-peer lookup service for Internet applications. In *Proceedings of ACM Sigcomm*, August 2001.

[SMW02]　Neil Spring, Ratul Mahajan, and David Wetherall. Measuring ISP topologies with Rocketfuel. In *Proceedings of ACM SIGCOMM*, pages 133–145, Pittsburgh, PA, August 2002.

[SNC+04]　Augustin Soule, Antonio Nucci, Rene Cruz, Emilio Leonardi, and Nina Taft. How to identify and estimate the largest traffic matrix elements in a dynamic environment. In *Proceedings of ACM SIGMETRICS*, 2004.

[Sno]　Snort. http://www.snort.org.

[Son]　Sony playstation. http://www.sonyplaystation.com.

[SP02]　Jesse Steinberg and Joseph Pasquale. A Web middleware architecture for dynamic customization of content for wireless clients. In *Proceedings of the World Wide Web Conference*, May 2002.

[Spa]　SpamAssassin. http://spamassassin.taint.org/.

[Spa88]　Eugene H. Spafford. The Internet worm program: An analysis. Technical Report Technical Report CSD-TR-823, Department of Computer Sciences, Purdue University, December 1988.

[SPF]　Sender policy framework. http://spf.pobox.com/.

[SPS+01]　Alex C. Snoeren, Craig Partridge, Luis A. Sanchez, Christine E. Jones, Fabrice Tchakountio, Beverly Schwartz, Stephen T. Kent, and W. Timothy Strayer. Hash-based IP traceback. In *Proceedings of ACM SIGCOMM*, August 2001.

[SPW02]　Stuart Staniford, Vern Paxson, and Nicholas Weaver. How to 0wn the Internet in your spare time. In *Proceedings of the 11th USENIX Security Symposium (Security '02)*, 2002.

[SRB01]　S. Sarvotham, R. Riedi, and R. Baraniuk. Connection-level analysis and modeling of network traffic. In *Proceedings of the ACM SIGCOMM Internet Measurement Workshop*, pages 99–103, 2001.

[SRC84]　Jerome H. Saltzer, David P. Reed, and David D. Clark. End-to-end arguments in system design. *ACM Transactions on Computer Systems*, 2(4):277–288, November 1984.

[SRL98]　H. Schulzrinne, A. Rao, and R. Lanphier. Real time streaming protocol (RTSP). RFC 2326, IETF, April 1998.

[SSB+02]　S. Shakkottai, R. Srikant, N. Brownlee, A. Broido, and k claffy. The RTT distribution of TCP flows on the Internet and its impact on TCP based flow control. Technical Report TR-2004-02, CAIDA, January 2002.

[SSR99]　H. Schulzrinne, E. Schooler, and J. Rosenberg. SIP: Session initiation protocol. RFC 2543, IETF, March 1999.

[SSR+04]　Anees Shaikh, Sambit Sahu, Marcel Rosu, Michael Shea, and Debanjan Saha. Implementation of a service platform for online games. In *Proceedings of the Workshop on Network and System Support for Games*, September 2004.

[SSWY01]　Yuval Shavitt, Xiaodong Sun, Avishai Wool, and Bulent Yener. Computing the unmeasured: An algebraic approach to Internet mapping. In *Proceedings of IEEE INFOCOM Conference*, April 2001.

[Sta99]　William Stallings. *SNMP, SNMPv2, SNMPv3, and RMON 1 and 2*. Addison-Wesley, 1999.

[STA01]　Anees Shaikh, Renu Tewari, and Mukesh Agrawal. On the effectiveness of DNS-based server selection. In *Proceedings of IEEE INFOCOM Conference*, Anchorage, AK, April 2001.

[Ste]　Welcome to Steam. http://www.steampowered.com.

[Ste93]   W. Richard Stevens. *TCP/IP Illustrated Volume 1: The Protocols*. Addison-Wesley, 1993.

[Str88]   Gilbert Strang. *Linear Algebra and Its Applications*. Harcourt, Inc., 1988.

[SV01]   Kavé Salamatian and Sandrine Vaton. Hidden Markov modeling for network communication channels. In *Proceedings of ACM SIGMETRICS*, pages 92–101, New York, NY, USA, 2001. ACM Press.

[SW02]   Subhabrata Sen and Jia Wang. Analyzing peer-to-peer traffic across large networks. In *Proceedings of the ACM SIGCOMM Internet Measurement Workshop*, pages 137–150, Marseilles, November 2002.

[SWA03]   Neil Spring, David Wetherall, and Tom Anderson. Scriptroute: A public Internet measurement facility. In *USENIX Symposium on Internet Technologies and Systems (USITS)*, 2003.

[Swe02]   Latanya Sweeney. k-anonymity: a model for protecting privacy. *International Journal of Uncertain. Fuzziness and Knowledge-Based Systems*, 10(5):557–570, 2002.

[SWY]   Adam Slagell, Jun Wang, and William Yurcik. Network log anonymization: Application of crypto-pan to Cisco netflows. `http://www.slagellware.com/downloads/slagell04c.pdf`. Secure Knowledge Management Workshop, September 2004.

[SYB04]   Joel Sommers, Vinod Yegneswaran, and Paul Barford. A framework for malicious workload generation. In *Proceedings of the ACM SIGCOMM Internet Measurement Conference*, November 2004.

[Tac00]   Commander Taco. IP tunneling through nameservers. `http://slashdot.org/articles/00/09/10/2230242.shtml`, September 2000.

[Tal04]   Greg Taleck. SYNSCAN: Towards complete TCP/IP fingerprinting. `http://synscan.sourceforge.net/`, 2004.

[TB00]   Diane Tang and Mary Baker. Analysis of a local-area wireless network. In *Proceedings of Mobicom*, pages 1–10, August 2000.

[TC03]   Liying Tang and Mark Crovella. Virtual landmarks for the Internet. In *Proceedings of the ACM SIGCOMM Internet Measurement Conference*, November 2003.

[TC04]   Liying Tang and Mark Crovella. Geometric exploration of the landmark selection problem. In *Proceedings of the Passive and Active Measurement Workshop*, Juan Les Pins, France, April 2004.

[TCD03]   Ajay Tirumala, Les Cottrell, and Tom Dunigan. Measuring end-to-end bandwidth with Iperf using Web100. In *Proceedings of the Passive and Active Measurement Workshop*, La Jolla, CA, April 2003.

[TCN01]   Y. Tsang, M. Coates, and R. Nowak. Passive network tomography using EM algorithms. In *Proceedings of IEEE International Conference on Acoustics, Speech and Signal Processing*, May 2001.

[tcp]   The tcpdump project. `http://www.tcpdump.org`.

[TDG+01]   Hongsuda Tangmunarunkit, John Doyle, Ramesh Govindan, Walter Willinger, Sugih Jamin, and Scott Shenker. Does AS size determine degree in AS topology? *ACM SIGCOMM Computer Communication Review*, 31(5):7–8, 2001.

[Tec]   Top 100 Technorati. `http://www.technorati.com/pop/blogs`.

[TGJ+02]   Hongsuda Tangmunarunkit, Ramesh Govindan, Sugih Jamin, Scott Shenker, and Walter Willinger. Network topology generators: Degree-based vs structural. In *Proceedings of ACM SIGCOMM*, pages 147–159, Pittsburgh, PA, August 2002.

[THD03]   Duc A. Tran, Kien A. Hua, and Tai Do. Zigzag: An efficient peer-to-peer scheme for media streaming. In *Proceedings of IEEE INFOCOM Conference*, 2003.

[Tim02]   Timothy G. Griffin. An introduction to Interdomain routing and the Border Gateway

Protocol (BGP). `http://www.cl.cam.ac.uk/users/tgg22/talks/BGP_ TUTORIAL_ICNP_2002.ppt`, November 2002. Tutorial at ICNP 2002.

[TL86]   Murad S. Taqqu and Joshua B. Levy. Using renewal processes to generate long-range dependence and high variability. In Ernst Eberlein and Murad S. Taqqu, editors, *Dependence in Probability and Statistics*, pages 73–90. Birkhauser, 1986.

[TLD]   List of top level domains. `http://data.iana.org/TLD/ tlds-alpha-by-domain.txt`.

[TM69]   J. Travers and S. Milgram. An experimental study of the small world problem. *Sociometry*, 32(425), 1969.

[TMW97]   K. Thompson, G. Miller, and R. Wilder. Wide-area traffic patterns and characteristics. *IEEE Network*, 11(6):10–23, November/December 1997.

[Tor52]   W. S. Torgerson. Multidimensional scaling: I. theory and method. *Psychometrika*, 17:401–419, 1952.

[TS03]   Tomer Tankel and Yuval Shavitt. Big-bang simulation for embedding network distances in Euclidean space. In *Proceedings of IEEE INFOCOM Conference*, April 2003.

[TS05]   Claudia Linnhoff-Popien Thomas Strang, editor. *Proceedings of Location- and Context-Awareness: First International Workshop, Lecture Notes in Computer Science 3479*. Springer-Verlag GmbH, 2005.

[TSGR04]   Renata Teixeira, Aman Shaikh, Tim Griffin, and Jennifer Rexford. Dynamics of hot-potato routing in IP networks. In *Proceedings of ACM SIGMETRICS*, 2004.

[TTW95]   M. S. Taqqu, V. Teverovsky, and W. Willinger. Estimators for long-range dependence: an empirical study. *Fractals*, 3(4):785–798, 1995.

[Tut04]   Kurt Tutschku. A measurement-based traffic profile of the eDonkey filesharing system. In *Proceedings of the Passive and Active Measurement Workshop*, Juan Les Pins, France, April 2004.

[TW98]   C. Tebaldi and M. West. Bayesian inference on network traffic using link count data. *Journal of the American Statistical Association*, 93(443):557–576, 1998.

[TWP]   MAWI Working-Group The WIDE Project. Guidelines for protecting user privacy in WIDE traffic traces. `http://tracer.csl.sony.co.jp/mawi/guideline. txt`.

[TWS97]   Murad S. Taqqu, Walter Willinger, and Robert Sherman. Proof of a fundamental result in self-similar traffic modeling. *ACM SIGCOMM Computer Communication Review*, 27(2):5–23, 1997.

[Unr]   Unreal tournament. `http://www.unrealtournament.com`.

[Use]   Userland site report. `http://stats.userland.com/groups/radio1/ report.html`.

[VA99]   Darryl Veitch and Patrice Abry. A wavelet based joint estimator of the parameters of long-range dependence. *IEEE Transactions on Information Theory*, 45(3):878–897, 1999.

[VAM+02]   Eveline Veloso, Virgilio Almeida, Wagner Meira, Azer Bestavros, and Shudong Jin. A hierarchical characterization of a live streaming media workload. In *Proceedings of the ACM SIGCOMM Internet Measurement Workshop*, 2002.

[Var96]   Y. Vardi. Network tomography: Estimating source-destination traffic intensities from link data. *Journal of the American Statistical Association*, pages 365–377, March 1996.

[VBP04]   Darryl Veitch, Satish Babu, and Attila Pasztor. Robust synchronization of software clocks across the Internet. In *Proceedings of the ACM SIGCOMM Internet Measurement Conference*, pages 219–232, 2004.

[vdM03]   Remco van de Meent. M2C measurement data repository. Technical report, University of Twente, Enschede, The Netherlands, December 2003.

[vdMCCS00] Jacobus van der Merwe, Ramon Caceres, Y-H Chu, and Corman Sreenan. Mmdump - a tool for monitoring Internet multimedia traffic. *ACM Computer Communication Review*, 30(4), October 2000.

[vdMSK02] Jacobus van der Merwe, Subhabrata Sen, and Charles Kalmanek. Streaming video traffic: Characterization and network impact. In *7th International Workshop on Web Content Caching and Distribution (WCW)*, August 2002.

[VE03] George Varghese and Cristian Estan. The measurement manifesto. In *Proceedings of the Hot Topics in Networks Workshop*, Boston, November 2003.

[Vin04] Vinod Yegneswaran and Paul Barford and Somesh Jha. Global intrusion detection in the DOMINO overlay system. In *Proceedings of ISOC 2004*, February 2004.

[Vir] Top 10 virus in 2003. `http://www.sophos.com/virusinfo/topten/200312summary.html`.

[Vix04] Paul Vixie. BCP38 making it work, solving problems. `http://www.merit.edu/mail.archives/nanog/2004-10/msg00199.html`, October 2004.

[VR97] J. Vehel and R. Riedi. Fractional Brownian motion and data traffic modeling: The other end of the spectrum. *Fractals in Engineering*, January 1997.

[Wal00] S. Waldbusser. Remote network monitoring management information base. RFC 2819. Available at `http://www.ietf.org.`, 2000.

[WAL04] Walter Willinger, David Alderson, and Lun Li. A pragmatic approach to dealing with high-variability in network measurements. In *Proceedings of the ACM SIGCOMM Internet Measurement Conference*, 2004.

[War] Warcraft. `http://www.blizzard.com/war3/`.

[Way] Internet archive: Wayback machine. `http://www.archive.org`.

[WCVY03] Daniel G. Waddington, Fangzhe Chang, Ramesh Viswanathan, and Bin Yao. Topology discovery for public IPv6 networks. *SIGCOMM Computer Communications Review*, 33(3):59–68, 2003.

[WCZ01] Yubin Wang, Mark Claypool, and Zheng Zuo. An empirical study of RealVideo performance across the Internet. In *Proceedings of the ACM SIGCOMM Internet Measurement Workshop*, November 2001.

[WDF+05] J. Wallerich, H. Dreger, A. Feldmann, B. Krishnamurthy, and Walter Willinger. A methodology for studying persistency aspects of Internet flows. *SIGCOMM Computer Communications Review*, April 2005.

[Web] The Webalizer. what is your Web server doing today? `http://www.mrunix.net/webalizer/`.

[Wes] Fantasy Westward Journey. `http://corp.163.com/eng/games/fantacy_westward.html`.

[WF03] Duane Wessels and Marina Fomenkov. Wow, that's a lot of packets. In *Proceedings of the Passive and Active Measurement Workshop*, La Jolla, CA, April 2003.

[WFBkc04] Duane Wessels, Marina Fomenkov, Nevil Brownlee, and kc claffy. Measurements and laboratory simulations of the upper DNS hierarchy. In *Proceedings of the Passive and Active Measurement Workshop*, Juan Les Pins, France, April 2004.

[WG03] Feng Wang and Lixin Gao. On inferring and characterizing Internet routing policies. In *Proceedings of the ACM SIGCOMM Internet Measurement Conference*, 2003.

[Wge] wget. `http://www.gnu.org/software/wget/wget.html`.

[WJL03] David Watson, Farnam Jaharnian, and Craig Labovitz. Experiences with monitoring OSPF on a regional service provider network. In *23rd IEEE International Conference on Distributed Computing Systems (ICDCS)*, pages 204–213, May 2003.

[WMJ04] David Watson, G. Robert Malan, and Farnam Jahanian. An extensible probe architecture for network protocol performance measurement. *Software – Practice and Experience*,

34(1):47–67, 2004.

[WMS03]   Craig Wills, Mikhail Mikhailov, and Hao Shang. Inferring relative popularity of Internet applications by actively querying DNS caches. In *Proceedings of the ACM SIGCOMM Internet Measurement Conference*, November 2003.

[Woo01]   Avishai Wool. Architecting the Lumeta firewall analyzer. In *Proceedings of the USENIX Security Symposium*, 2001.

[Wor]   W3C recommendations reduce 'World Wide Wait'. `http://www.w3.org/Protocols/NL-PerfNote.html`.

[WoW]   Wow census. `http://www.wowcensus.com`.

[WPP+04]   Limin Wang, KyoungSoo Park, Ruoming Pang, Vivek S. Pai, and Larry Peterson. Reliability and security in the CoDeeN content distribution network. In *Proceedings of the USENIX 2004 Annual Technical Conference*, June 2004.

[WS98]   D. Watts and S. Strogatz. Collective dynamics of small-world networks. *Nature*, 393:440–442, 4 June 1998.

[WSRB02]   Xin Wang, Shriram Sarvotham, Rudolf H. Riedi, and Richard G. Baraniuk. Network traffic modeling using connection-level information. In *Proceedings SPIE ITCom*, August 2002.

[WTE96]   W. Willinger, M. S. Taqqu, and A. Erramilli. A bibliographical guide to self-similar traffic and performance modeling for modern high-speed networks. In F. P. Kelly, S. Zachary, and I. Ziedins, editors, *Stochastic Networks: Theory and Applications*, pages 339–366. Clarendon Press, Oxford, UK, 1996.

[WTSW97]   Walter Willinger, Murad S. Taqqu, Robert Sherman, and Daniel V. Wilson. Self-similarity through high-variability: Statistical analysis of Ethernet LAN traffic at the source level. *IEEE/ACM Transactions on Networking*, 5(1):71–86, February 1997.

[WVS+99]   A. Wolman, G. Voelker, N. Sharma, N. Cardwell, A. Karlin, and H. Levy. On the scale and performance of cooperative Web proxy caching. In *Symposium on Operating Systems Principles-17*, December 1999.

[WWTK03]   Wei Wei, Bing Wang, Don Towsley, and Jim Kurose. Model-based identification of dominant congested links. In *Proceedings of the ACM SIGCOMM Internet Measurement Conference*, November 2003.

[WZP+02]   Lan Wang, Xiaoliang Zhao, Dan Pei, Randy Bush, Daniel Massey, Allison Mankin, S. Felix Wu, and Lixia Zhang. Observation and analysis of BGP behavior under stress. In *Proceedings of the ACM SIGCOMM Internet Measurement Workshop*, pages 183–195, Marseilles, November 2002.

[XFAM]   Jun Xu, Jinliang Fan, Mostafa Ammar, and Sue Moon. Crypto-pan: Cryptography-based prefix-preserving anonymization. `http://www.cc.gatech.edu/computing/Telecomm/cryptopan/`.

[XFAM01]   Jun Xu, Jinliang Fan, Mostafa Ammar, and Sue B. Moon. On the design and performance of prefix-preserving IP traffic trace anonymization. In *Proceedings of the ACM SIGCOMM Internet Measurement Workshop*, November 2001.

[Xml]   Web characterization repository. `http://www.w3.org/1998/11/05/WC-workshop/Presentations/abrams/abrams/in%dex.htm`.

[Yar]   Fyodor Yarochkin. NMAP - the network mapper. `http://www.insecure.org/nmap/`.

[YBP04]   Vinod Yegneswaran, Paul Barford, and Dave Plonka. The design and use of Internet sinks for network abuse monitoring. In *In Proceedings of Recent Advances in Intrusion Detection*, 2004.

[YBU03]   Vinod Yegneswaran, Paul Barford, and Johannes Ullrich. Internet intrusions: Global characteristics and prevalence. In *Proceedings of ACM SIGMETRICS*, June 2003.

[YH87]   F. W. Young and R. M. Hamer. *Multidimensional Scaling: History, Theory, and Appli-
            cations*. Lawrence Erlbaum Associates, Hilldale, N.J., 1987.

[YJB02]   S.H. Yook, H. Jeong, and A. Barabasi. Modeling the Internet's large-scale topology.
            Proceedings of the National Academy of Sciences, 99:13382–13386, 2002.

[Ylo]   Tatu Ylonen. Thoughts on how to mount an attack on tcpdpriv's -a50 option. `http://
            ita.ee.lbl.gov/html/contrib/attack50/attack50.html`. Web White
            Paper.

[YMKT99]   Maya Yajnik, Sue B. Moon, James F. Kurose, and Donald F. Towsley. Measurement and
            modeling of the temporal dependence in packet loss. In *Proceedings of IEEE INFOCOM
            Conference*, pages 345–352, 1999.

[YW03]   Christopher C. Yang and Fu Lee Wang. Fractal summarization for mobile devices to
            access large documents on the Web. In *Proceedings of the World Wide Web Conference*,
            May 2003.

[ZBPS02]   Yin Zhang, Lee Breslau, Vern Paxson, and Scott Shenker. On the characteristics and
            origins of Internet flow rates. In *Proceedings of ACM SIGCOMM*, pages 309–322, Pitts-
            burgh, PA, August 2002.

[ZCBD04]   Amgad Zeitoun, Chen-Nee Chuah, Supratik Bhattacharyya, and Christophe Diot. An
            AS-level study of Internet path delay characteristics. In *Global Internet and Next Gen-
            eration Network (GINGN) Workshop*, Dallas, TX, November 2004.

[ZDPS01]   Yin Zhang, Nick Duffield, Vern Paxson, and Scott Shenker. On the constancy of In-
            ternet path properties. In *Proceedings of the ACM SIGCOMM Internet Measurement
            Workshop*, November 2001.

[ZFdRD04]   Artur Ziviani, Serge Fdida, Jose de Rezende, and Otto Carlor Duarte. Toward a
            measurement-based geographic location service. In *Proceedings of the Passive and Ac-
            tive Measurement Workshop*, Juan Les Pins, France, April 2004.

[Zip46]   G. K. Zipf. Some determinants of the circulation of information. *American Journal of
            Psychology*, 59:401–421, 1946.

[Zip49]   G. K. Zipf. *Human Behavior and the Principle of Least-Effort*. Addison-Wesley, Cam-
            bridge, MA, 1949.

[ZKJ00]   Y. Zhao, John Kubiatowicz, and Anthony Joseph. Tapestry: An infrastructure for fault-
            tolerant wide-area location and routing. Technical Report UCB//CSD-01-1141, U. C.
            Berkeley, April 2000.

[ZLPG05]   Han Zheng, Eng Keong Lua, Marcelo Pias, and Timothy Griffin. Internet routing policies
            and round-trip-times. In *Proceedings of the Passive and Active Measurement Workshop*,
            April 2005.

[ZLT04]   Jin Zhou, Kai Li, and Li Tang. Towards a fully distributed P2P Web search engine. In
            *10th IEEE International Workshop on Future Trends of Distributed Computing Systems
            (FTDCS'04)*, May 2004.

[ZLX02]   Li Zhang, Zhen Liu, and Cathy Xia. Clock synchronization algorithms for network
            measurements. In *Proceedings of IEEE INFOCOM Conference*, New York, NY, June
            2002.

[ZM03]   Shi Zhou and Raul Mondragon. The missing links in the BGP-based AS connectivity
            maps. In *Proceedings of the Passive and Active Measurement Workshop*, La Jolla, CA,
            April 2003.

[ZPW+01]   X. Zhao, D. Pei, L. Wang, D. Massey, A. Mankin, S. F. Wu, and L. Zhang. An analysis
            of BGP multiple origin AS (MOAS) conflicts. In *Proceedings of the ACM SIGCOMM
            Internet Measurement Workshop*, November 2001.

[ZRLD03]   Yin Zhang, Matthew Roughan, Carsten Lund, and David Donoho. An information-
            theoretic approach to traffic matrix estimation. In *Proceedings of ACM SIGCOMM*,

August 2003.

[ZRMD03]   Z.-L. Zhang, V. Ribeiro, S. Moon, and C. Diot. Small-time scaling behaviors of Internet backbone traffic: An empirical study. In *Proceedings of IEEE INFOCOM Conference*, San Francisco, CA, Mar 2003.

[Zse02]   Tanja Zseby. Deployment of sampling methods for SLA validation with non-intrusive measurements. In *Proceedings of the Passive and Active Measurement Workshop*, Mar 2002.

[Zse03]   Tanja Zseby. Stratification strategies for sampling-based non-intrusive measurements of one-way delay. In *Proceedings of the Passive and Active Measurement Workshop*, La Jolla, CA, April 2003.

[ZSS+04]   Yin Zhang, Sumeet Singh, Subhabrata Sen, Nick Duffield, and Carsten Lund. Online identification of hierarchical heavy hitters: Algorithms, evaluation, and application. In *Proceedings of the ACM SIGCOMM Internet Measurement Conference*, October 2004.

[ZZP+04]   M. Zhang, C. Zhang, V. Pai, L. Peterson, and R. Wang. Planetseer: Internet path failure monitoring and characterization in wide-area services. In *Proceedings of the Sixth Symposium on Operating Systems Design and Implementation(OSDI '04)*, 2004.

[ZZZ+03]   Feng Zhou, Li Zhuang, Ben Y. Zhao, Ling Huang, Anthony D. Joseph, and John Kubiatowicz. Approximate object location and spam filtering on peer-to-peer systems. In *ACM Middleware*, 2003.

Index